Across the Sea to War

*Australian and New Zealand Troop Convoys
from 1865 through Two World Wars to Korea and Vietnam*

Moravian departs Woolloomooloo wharf on 17 January 1900. Note the crowds on the wharf to wish the troops farewell. (*National Library of Australia*)

Across the Sea to War

Australian and New Zealand Troop Convoys from 1865 through Two World Wars to Korea and Vietnam

Peter Plowman

Rosenberg

First published in 2003 by Rosenberg Publishing Pty Ltd
P.O. Box 6125 Dural Delivery Centre NSW 2156 Australia
Phone 02 9654 1502 Fax 02 9654 1338
Email rosenbergpub@smartchat.net.au   Web www.rosenbergpub.com.au

© copyright Peter Plowman 2003

All rights reserved. No part of this publication may be reproduced, stored in a retrieval system, or transmitted in any form or by any means, electronic, mechanical, photocopying, recording or otherwise, without the prior permission of the publisher in writing.

Cover design by Highway 51 Design Works. The main illustration is a painting by Stephen Card showing *Queen Mary* passing through Sydney Heads during World War II (reproduced by kind permission of Stephen Card).
The small photograph shows troops boarding *Orcades* in Sydney on 9 January 1940. (RJ Tompkins collection)

The National Library of Australia Cataloguing-in-Publication data

Plowman, Peter.
Across the sea to war Australian and New Zealand troop convoys from 1865 through two world wars to Vietnam.

Bibliography.
Includes index.
ISBN 1 877058 06 8.

1. Australia. Army - Transport service - History. 2. New Zealand. Army - Transport service - History. 3. Transportation, Military. I. Title.

355.4110994

Set in 11 on 13 point New Baskerville
Printed in China by Everbest Printing Co Limited

Contents

    Acknowledgments   6
    Introduction   8
1 The Sudan Campaign   11
2 The Boer War   18
3 World War I   35
4 Between the Wars   75
5 The First Convoy   82
6 The Second Convoy   102
7 The Third Convoy   114
8 August to December 1940   145
9 From Britain to Egypt   180
10 The 'Monster' Convoys   200
11 Reinforcing Singapore   227
12 The Final Middle East Convoys   239
13 Airmen at Sea   257
14 Darwin and the Pacific Islands   288
15 The Singapore Convoys   312
16 Operation Stepsister and the Fall of Singapore   325
17 Operation Pamphlet   365
18 New Guinea and the Islands   385
19 Coming Home   419
20 The Korean War   442
21 The Vietnam War   450
    Appendix   Major Convoys of World War II   485
    Bibliography   488
    Merchant Ships Index   492
    Naval Ships Index   498
    Military Units Index   501

Acknowledgments

This book had its beginnings about ten years ago, when I decided to write a short article for a local shipping magazine about the convoys that carried Australian troops to the Middle East in World War Two. However, I found there was so much to write about it could not be contained in just one article, and so I began what turned out to be the long haul of putting the facts into a book. At times the research was fascinating, at other times tedious, but in the end I feel it was all well worth the time and effort. I would like to express my warmest appreciation for the encouragement I received from my good friend David Finch to continue working on this project, especially when it seemed to have reached a dead end.

I have used many sources. As can be seen by the extensive bibliography, much of the material came from books published over the years on the wartime exploits of numerous military outfits or individuals, but the sections describing trooping voyages comprised only a small part of each book. This is the first time all these individual stories have been brought together in one book, to provide an extensive overview of the conditions and hardships faced by troops on their way to war, and sometimes coming home too.

During my research I came across several books written in Dutch and published in Holland which included extensive information on some of the larger Dutch flag liners that carried Australian and New Zealand troops during the Second World War. As I have no knowledge of the Dutch language, my attempts to translate the relevant sections using a dictionary were not very successful, but then I was fortunate to find that the father of a close friend of mine was of Dutch origins. When I asked Joseph Hoogendoorn if he could assist me by translating the material I had obtained, he could not have been more helpful. Within a couple of weeks I had all the material available to me in English, and this added greatly to the sections in the book in which they are included, for which I am very grateful.

When it came to gathering pictures, I had already compiled a reasonably extensive selection over a number of years in my own collection, but I knew that more were required. I first went to the obvious sources, only to be faced with extreme disappointment. Although extensive photograph collections are held by various public bodies, the excessive charges they levy for the publication of such material made it impractical to include them. Instead I turned to other sources, and was able eventually to secure a varied and interesting selection of photographs covering all the various war periods.

Taking photographs of merchant or naval ships in Sydney Harbour during the Second World War was officially not allowed, and film was also very difficult to obtain. However, a few individuals did manage to hide their activities well enough to obtain pictures of some of the notable liners that came to Australia to transport troops overseas. One of these was the late Charlie Reddings, who also later obtained an extensive set of pictures taken by the Royal Australian Air Force during the war years. Photographs from the C T Reddings collection form the bulk of the images in this book, for which I am most grateful to Robert J Tompkins, who also allowed me free access to his own very extensive photo library. In addition, I would like to express my thanks to Stephen Card, Ross Gillett, Stuart Braga, the family of Allan Batt, the late Fred Roderick, the late Vic Scrivens, the National Library of Australia and the Wellington Maritime Museum for assisting me with some wonderful pictures.

The period that caused me the most problems in seeking suitable photographs was the Vietnam War. My initial attempts to locate good pictures of HMAS *Sydney* brought no success, but eventually I was fortunate to get in touch with Rodney T Nott in Brisbane, who had already authored a book on the trips made by the Sydney to Vietnam. He could not have been more helpful, and kindly supplied me with most of the photographs I have included in my chapter on the Vietnam War, and gave me permission to quote material from his book.

I would like to extend my thanks to my good friend and noted maritime artist Stephen Card for allowing me to use on the cover of this book his superb painting of the *Queen Mary* .

I have drawn on a number of first hand accounts published in various books over the years. I have made every attempt to contact the the copyright owners for their permission to use this material, but in some instances this proved impossible. I would like to express my sincere thanks to the University of Queensland Press for allowing me to use material from *The War Diaries of Kenneth Slessor*, which added greatly to several chapters on Second World War troop movements. In the chapter on the Vietnam War, I would like to thank Allen & Unwin for permission to use extracts from *In Good Company* by Gary Mckay. Permission to use extracts from *Down a Country Lane to War* by Gary Blinco, *View From a Long Bough* by Barrie Crowley was granted by the authors, while Rodney Nott very kindly allowed me to use a considerable amount of material from *The Vung Tau Ferry*.

Introduction

Australia has been fortunate enough to be spared the full horrors of war being fought on its own soil. There were various skirmishes and minor battles during the early years of European settlement, and of course the dark days of 1942 when Japanese aircraft made numerous bombing raids on Darwin and Broome, but there has never been an invasion of the island continent to be repulsed by our military forces. Despite this, Australia has a proud record of fighting service, but to get to the scenes of battle the Australian troops had to be transported overseas, and this was primarily done by troopship. This book is a general record of these voyages, where possible as remembered by the men and women who travelled.

The first involvement Australians had in fighting a foreign war was in 1863 and 1864, when more than 2,000 men enrolled to join the New Zealand colonial forces. This enrolment was not officially sanctioned by the colonial governments, but was the result of a recruiting drive conducted by the New Zealand government to enlarge their forces then engaged in the Waikato Wars. This was one of a dozen outbreaks of conflict between Maoris and the British during the nineteenth century, and by 1864 a force comprising 22,000 Imperial and Colonial troops had been raised to counter an uprising by the Maori tribes whose territory lay south of Auckland.

In August 1863, New Zealand sent two representatives to Australia to recruit men, and also to purchase arms, ammunition and other war stores. At first only married men were recruited, but when the numbers fell short of requirements, single men were also allowed to sign up. Most were drawn from Sydney and Melbourne, as well as the Victorian goldfield towns such as Ballarat and Bendigo. Eventually eleven ships were chartered to transport these recruits to New Zealand, along with nearly one thousand wives and children. After a brief training period, the recruits joined the four Waikato Regiments that had been formed to combat the uprising, and went into battle. While this was the first time Australians travelled overseas to a conflict, it was not in a body raised and sanctioned by the governments, and therefore is outside the bounds of this book.

The first Australian troops to go overseas as an official body with government backing left Sydney in March 1885, to join British forces fighting an outbreak of hostilities in Sudan. This small contingent was raised in New South Wales and enjoyed a less than glorious period overseas before returning home in June 1886. Australia's first major involvement in a foreign war came right at the end of the nineteenth century, when the colonies raised individual contingents to travel to another African war, this time to assist the British in putting down the Boer uprising in South Africa. By the time the final contingents left for South Africa in May 1902 the conflict was over, and the colonies had joined to form the Commonwealth of Australia.

Australian troops were heading overseas again at the end of 1914 following the outbreak of war in Europe between Great Britain and Germany in August that year. Yet again their destination was Africa, this time Egypt, but that was only a brief stopping point before moving on to fight on European soil, starting with the lasting glory of the ill-fated Gallipoli campaign, and ending the war in the fields of France.

All hope that the Great War, as it was originally known, would truly be 'the war to end all wars' was dashed in September 1939, when Great Britain and Germany again were in conflict. January 1940 saw another contingent of Australians being farewelled by loved ones as they left home shores, yet again bound for the African continent and Egypt. This time the Australian troops would see considerable action in North Africa, writing their names in the history of warfare during the courageous siege of Tobruk, and then at the Battle of El Alamein, which proved to be a crucial turning point in the war.

When Japan entered the war in December 1941, and threatened to engulf Australia from the islands to the north, the troops found themselves on board ships heading to New Guinea to stop what appeared to be the unstoppable, but they succeeded where many thought it impossible.

The end of World War II did not bring with it the hoped for tranquillity of peace. Now there was a new threat to face, that of communism, and its appetite to conquer the world. The outbreak of war in Korea at first seemed far removed from our soil, but all too soon Australian troops were being loaded onto ships yet again, and transported to join a United Nations force in a country about which we knew almost nothing. This time the outcome was less than satisfying, with a negotiated settlement that resolved nothing and still creates problems to this day.

Combating the spread of communism was again the reason when Australian troops found themselves being transported overseas in the 1960s to another Asian hotspot, Vietnam. Unlike previous overseas involvements, which usually enjoyed popular support from those at home, the Vietnam conflict almost tore Australia apart, and many men who fought as bravely as their fathers had in previous conflicts found themselves almost ostracised when they returned. Despite this, the valour of the troops who fought in Vietnam cannot be questioned, nor can their many victories, often against overwhelming odds, be denied.

The end of the Vietnam War brought about the longest period of peace during the twentieth century. While there was some Australian involvement in the 1991 and 2003 actions against Iraq, Operation Desert Storm and Operation Iraqi Freedom do not come within the confines of this book, nor do other military involvements such as those in Afghanistan. It is highly likely that there will never be another mass movement of troops by sea, and the day of the troopship is over.

However, over a period of just under a hundred years, ships played a major role in conflicts by moving troops in large numbers and amazing safety. This is the story of those ships and those men.

1 The Sudan Campaign

The first Australian troops to go overseas left Sydney in March 1885, when, following the murder of General Charles Gordon in Khartoum, the colony of New South Wales raised a small contingent to assist British forces fighting an outbreak of hostilities in Sudan. This first deployment of Australian troops overseas was rapidly arranged, in response to the public outcry over the death of Gordon, who was the most famous British general of his time. Although Gordon was killed on 26 January 1885, news of his death did not reach Australia until 11 February. Two days later, William Dalley, Acting Premier of New South Wales, sent a message to the British government offering the service of a contingent of soldiers from the colony to assist British soldiers already fighting in Sudan. It was decided the New South Wales force would comprise an infantry battalion of 522 men, with 24 horses for officers, and two artillery batteries numbering 212 men and 172 horses, to be dispatched as soon as possible.

Once the decision to raise this force had been taken, there were some doubts that it could be achieved, given the short time available to select and equip the contingent, but so many men volunteered the major difficulty was in choosing the right men for the job. Those selected were immediately sent to Victoria Barracks, in the Sydney suburb of Paddington, for training.

Meanwhile, two passenger vessels then berthed in Sydney, *Iberia* and *Australasian*, were requisitioned to transport the contingent to the Sudan. *Iberia* was the larger and older, having been built in 1874 for the Pacific Steam Navigation Company. Initially used on their service

The P & O liner *Iberia* was requisitioned to carry troops to the Sudan.

from Britain to South America, *Iberia* joined the Australian trade in 1883, and had already been used to transport British troops to Egypt for the Sudanese war. The single-funnelled *Australasian*, owned by the Aberdeen Line, was quite new, having entered service in 1884, and was one of the first steamships in the world fitted with triple expansion machinery, but as with *Iberia*, having a hull built from iron. The black hulls of both ships were quickly repainted white for their trooping duty, and they looked very smart. Also, as befitted their temporary status as troop transports, they were given official numbers, with *Iberia* having 1 NSW painted on its sides, while *Australasian* was 2 NSW.

On Saturday, 28 February, with 50,000 people watching, the entire contingent paraded in an official review in Moore Park, while the following day, special church services were held in honour of the troops, and 2 March saw many of the men making their final farewells.

Tuesday, 3 March 1885, was to become one of the most important days in the history of New South Wales, for, as the *Sydney Mail* stated that day, 'our men have the proud pre-eminence — in the matter of which every good and true man in the other colonies will envy them — of being the first selected to strike a blow for the old country in her hour of need in Africa.' In the morning, the troops gathered in the grounds of Victoria Barracks, where they had a final chance to enjoy the company of family and friends. At midday, a bugle sounded for the troops to fall in, and they prepared to march to Circular Quay, where the *Australasian* and *Iberia* awaited them. A newspaper recorded how, following the bugle call, there were 'hurried squeezes of the hand, a last kiss to sweethearts, wives or sisters, and the men seizing their rifles rush off amidst numerous goodbyes to their position. There occurs a brief interval during which the roll of each company is called. The men amidst loud cheering, waving of handkerchiefs, and the tap of the drum, the movement from New South Wales to Egypt had commenced. The band played one of the liveliest marches and the men trooped out, their bearing, their physique, and the smartness of their dress, at once challenged and won general admiration.'

Along the route from Victoria Barracks to Circular Quay the marching men passed down streets thronged with an estimated 200,000 cheering spectators, about two-thirds of the population of Sydney. On reaching the wharf, all the infantrymen and some members of the artillery boarded the *Iberia*, on which the officers were allocated berths in cabins while the other ranks had to make do with hammocks strung up in the 'tween decks. The majority of the artillerymen went on board the *Australasian*, where the officers were again allowed to use cabins while the other ranks were allocated the accommodation used by emigrants on the voyage from Britain to Australia. Also going on board the *Australasian* were the 218 horses, which were put into specially constructed stalls in the holds.

As the ships prepared for departure, the troops were addressed by Lord Loftus, the Governor of New South Wales, who told them: 'Soldiers of New South Wales, for the first time in the great history of the British Empire, a distant colony is sending, at her own cost, a completely equipped contingent of troops who have volunteered with enthusiasm of which only we who have witnessed it can judge.' As departure time neared, an armada of vessels of all shapes and sizes began to throng the harbour. Despite the seriousness of the occasion, the day assumed more of a festive air, though before it was over there would also be tragedy.

Iberia was the first of the troopships to leave the wharf, shortly after 3 pm, followed minutes later by *Australasian*. As the pair proceeded slowly down harbour, they were surrounded by steamers carrying well-wishers, while every vantage point ashore was packed. As the two ships rounded Bradleys Head, *Australasian* moved ahead of *Iberia*, while bands aboard surrounding boats played merrily such patriotic tunes as 'Rule Britannia.'

One of the larger vessels escorting the troopships that day was the coastal steamer *Nemesis*, owned by Huddart Parker Limited, which was carrying a large number of relatives and friends of departing soldiers. Among them was Elizabeth Sessle, waving farewell to her husband,

Private F. Sessle, who was on board *Iberia*. Elizabeth was carrying their fifteen-month-old child, and with them on the *Nemesis* was a friend and neighbour, Ann Capel. Elizabeth located her husband standing at the railings of *Iberia*, and to get a better view moved forward on the starboard side towards the bow of *Nemesis*, then held her child up for her husband to see.

By now, *Australasian* had passed through Sydney Heads and was heading off down the coast, while *Iberia* was off South Head, still moving very slowly. Suddenly *Iberia* began to surge ahead as power was increased, and in doing so the order was given to turn to starboard. In performing this manoeuvre, the port quarter of *Iberia* smashed into the starboard bow of *Nemesis*, with a crash that could be heard by those on shore. The impact caused minor damage to one of the lifeboats on *Iberia*, but the forward section of *Nemesis* was devastated by the accommodation ladder still hanging down the side of the troopship. In an instant, Ann Capel was killed, while Elizabeth Sessle was severely injured, and the infant she was holding suffered a fractured thigh.

Despite the collision, *Iberia* continued on course and was soon out at sea, joining up with *Australasian*. The two ships were accompanied by some of the vessels that had escorted them down the harbour, until off Bondi the last escort vessel turned around, and the pair of troopships disappeared to the south at the start of their long journey, raising sail on their masts to increase their speed. On board *Iberia*, Private Sessle, who had seen the collision, could only wonder what had happened to his wife and child. Immediately after the collision, *Nemesis* steamed at top speed back to her berth. Elizabeth Sessle was rushed to hospital, but so severely had she been injured, she died the same night.

Such was the nationalistic fervour generated by the departure of the first Australian troops overseas, the next day the *Sydney Mail* trumpeted: 'Tuesday the 3rd March 1885, will be forever a red-letter day on which this colony, not yet a hundred years old, put forth its claims to be recognised as an integral portion of the British Empire ... This day marks an entirely new departure as regards the relations between the Old Country and her colonies. Hitherto the colonies have been regarded by many politicians as a drag upon the home country, and statesmen have been heard to say that the colonies of England were a source of weakness to her, not strength. The fallacy of such statements was demonstrated beyond dispute by the events of yesterday. If ever there was in the history of the world an occasion where everything that had been arranged was performed to the letter, if ever there was a day when a programme literally arranged was carried out satisfactorily it was yesterday, when the chosen troops of New South Wales, the picked men of the colony, embarked for the purpose of assisting the British arms in the Sudan.'

As the troopships headed south from Sydney they ran into bad weather and heavy seas, which resulted in many men succumbing to seasickness. One trooper wrote in his diary how 'the 'tween deck was so crowded and the stench was horrible.' After passing through Bass Strait, the two ships headed west, but *Iberia* took a more northerly course and on the evening of 6 March stopped for two hours off Kangaroo Island, where it was soon surrounded by numerous pleasure craft packed with residents of Adelaide. During the brief stop, troopers were able to send off final letters to loved ones, and Private Sessle left the ship to return to Sydney. A large quantity of fruit was taken on board, while two men and a young boy who came on board *Iberia* tried to stay as stowaways, but were found and sent off in a boat before the *Iberia* continued its voyage. The last sight of Australia for the troops on board was on 10 March, as *Iberia* passed Cape Leeuwin.

More bad weather was encountered as the two ships crossed the Great Australian Bight. This caused the captain of the *Australasian* to order a reduction in speed, primarily to avoid an injury to the horses in their stalls. Instead of slowing to stay with her companion, *Iberia* steamed on ahead at her normal speed.

On board, a daily routine was quickly established. Breakfast was at 8 am, lunch at 1 pm and supper at 5 pm, and on the whole the food supplied was good and in adequate quantity. During the day, fruit was issued at 11 am, and at 1.30 pm there was an issue of beer and lime juice. In between meals, the troops went through exercises and training routines, except on Saturday, when sports contests were held, and Sunday, when religious services were held, led by the Anglican and Roman Catholic chaplains on board.

As the ships steamed across the Indian Ocean towards the Sudan, back in Sydney parliament convened on 17 March to actually give their approval to the dispatch of the troops. So swiftly had the contingent been organised and sent away that parliament had not had an opportunity to meet and debate the matter, but there were only a few dissenting voices when the members did get down to discussions. One notable voice of dissent was Sir Henry Parkes, who was a persistent critic of Dalley and the contingent. As Dalley said, 'We have undoubtedly strained the law ... It is for parliament to determine whether we are to be censured or supported.' In the end the motion to support the dispatch of the contingent was passed without a division on the evening of 19 March.

By then, *Australasian* and *Iberia* were well into the Indian Ocean, following a north-westerly course that soon took them into the tropics, *Iberia* crossing the equator on 22 March. Of course, the ships were totally out of touch with events happening in the Sudan, so as the voyage progressed some of the officers from the contingent pressed the ship's captain to increase speed, as they were fearful the conflict might be over before they arrived. Their first port of call was to be Aden, at the southern end of the Red Sea. As *Iberia* neared Aden, she passed another Orient Line vessel, *Lusitania*, bound for Australia, and the troops lined the rails to wave to the passing ship, whose passengers waved back. The next day, 26 March, *Iberia* dropped anchor off Aden, and those on board finally received news of what was happening in the Sudan. Orders were received that the contingent was to proceed to Suakin, and the troops would be sent to the front right away. This news filled all on board with pride and excitement. Prior to leaving Aden, two men were sent ashore, one with a broken ankle, the other with spinal damage, to be returned to Australia on the first available ship. As *Iberia* steamed up the Red Sea, live ammunition was distributed to all troops, who busily cleaned their rifles and other weapons.

Iberia dropped anchor off Suakin at noon on Sunday, 29 March, and the Australian troops marched ashore to begin an association with Africa that would encompass four wars. *Australasian* arrived the next day and immediately disembarked her troops and horses. Despite the promise of being sent to the front straight away, the New South Wales force saw very little action, their only time under enemy fire being the attack on 3 April 1885 on the rebel stronghold at Tamai, during which three men were slightly wounded. In fact, the soldiers were in far more danger from disease and the first Australian soldier to die overseas, Private Robert Weir, succumbed to dysenteric fever while on board the British hospital ship *Ganges*, berthed in Suakin, while two others died from typhoid fever.

After little more than a year overseas, the troops returned to Australia, with very little fanfare or recognition. On 17 May 1886 they marched back to the harbour at Suakin and boarded the troopship *Arab*. The horses they had taken did not make the return trip, but were handed over to the British troops. *Arab* left Suakin on 18 May 1886, but many of the troops were sick with typhoid and dysentery. *Arab* was smaller than either of the ships that had carried the contingent to the Sudan, but the men were allowed to sleep on deck to ease the crowded conditions below. When the ship stopped at Colombo on 29 May, twelve of the sickest men were taken to hospital ashore, where three of them later died. From Colombo to Albany, at least one in ten of the men reported for the daily sick parade, and on 9 June the veterinary surgeon, Captain Anthony Willows, died, being buried at sea. After a brief stop at Albany to take on coal, during which no-one was allowed ashore, the *Arab* reached Sydney on the night of Friday, 19 June. Instead of going to a berth, the vessel anchored and all the troops were put into the quarantine station at North Head, where one more man died.

On the morning of Tuesday, 23 June, the survivors were released from quarantine and taken back to the *Arab*, which then proceeded up the harbour and berthed at Sydney Cove. The Governor of New South Wales along with the Premier and ministers were waiting to accord the men an official welcome, but the rain was pouring down and the original plan of a march through the city to Moore Park for an official review was cancelled. Instead, the troops marched to Victoria Barracks, where the official speeches of welcome were delivered. A few days later another trooper died, the result of a cold he caught while taking part in the march. As Colonel A.J. Bennett, a member of the contingent, later summed up the Sudan campaign, 'a few skirmishes and many weary marches provided much sweat but little glory.'

Despite the fervour with which they were dispatched to the war zone, the first departure of Australian troops for overseas service is not well remembered today. In fact it is almost forgotten.

Troops arrive at Circular Quay to board *Australasian* and *Iberia*. (*NSW State Library*)

2 The Boer War

Fourteen years after the dispatch of troops to assist the British in the Sudan, Australian troops were again sent to Africa, this time to assist the motherland in South Africa. All the Australian colonies raised forces to be sent from 1899 to 1902 for the Boer War, but while the initial response by the general public was strongly in favour of involvement in the conflict, the appropriateness of this effort did not generate any great nationalistic fervour. It was questioned by some colonists, both for reasons of cost and morality, and general support among the populace for participation in overseas conflicts was minimal.

During 1899, the political situation in South Africa deteriorated. The British had ambitions to develop a direct trade route from their colonies in the south to Egypt by building a railway, but it would have to pass through the two Boer republics, the Orange Free State and the Transvaal. Pushing the British cause was their High Commissioner in South Africa, Sir Alfred Milner, who arranged a conference with the presidents of the republics. The meetings did not go the way the British desired and President Kruger of the Transvaal eventually walked out, declaring, 'What you really want is my country.' The British then issued an ultimatum to the two republics in September, but this was ignored and open conflict began on 11 October 1899.

The probability of civil war breaking out in South Africa had been evident for some time. The question of the Australian colonies sending military forces to assist the British had been raised in each colonial parliament, and an offer of such assistance had been sent to the Colonial Office in London. Their reply, sent on 3 October 1899, accepted the offer of troops but also stipulated that the first contingents must depart Australia 'not later than 31 October.' This left the colonies little time to call for volunteers, equip them and arrange suitable transport, but it was achieved, and the first 1200 men, along with a large number of horses for the cavalry, embarked at various ports around the country between 28 October and 5 November. The ships they travelled on were usually employed in the cargo and passenger trade between Britain and Australia, and were specially chartered.

However, the first Australian troops to arrive in South Africa to join the conflict travelled from Britain. On 3 March 1899, 100 members of the NSW Lancer Squadron and their commanding officer, Captain Cox, embarked on the *Nineveh* to travel to England, at their own expense, for six months training. On arrival in Britain they were transported to Aldershot, which would be their base, but they also travelled around the country taking part in several military events.

Several weeks before the Australian troops were due to return home, Captain Cox volunteered them for service in South Africa, and permission for them to do so was granted by the New South Wales government. While most of the men were keen to fight, some wished to return home as planned, for a variety of reasons. The entire Squadron boarded the liner *Nineveh* once again, this time in London, and voyaged to South Africa. Arriving in Cape Town on 2 November 1899, 72 members of the Squadron disembarked, while 29 remained aboard *Nineveh* for the voyage to Sydney.

The first soldiers to embark in Australia for South Africa were from New South Wales. As had happened for the troops going to the Sudan in 1885, the men paraded through the streets of Sydney from Victoria Barracks to the wharf, the first group, numbering 130 men, boarding the *Kent* on 27 October 1899. That day the rain poured down on Sydney, but an estimated crowd of 300,000 turned out to cheer the troops as they marched off to war. Local politicians were much in evidence, and a special launch carried dignitaries down the harbour as the *Kent* steamed off on its mission, but the weather at sea was so bad the troopship anchored near the Heads overnight, slipping away the next day.

Meanwhile, another group of volunteers was due to board their troopship in Newcastle on 27 October. These 61 men were from the New South Wales Mounted Rifles and the First Australian Horse, who also took their horses with them. Again a huge crowd was on hand to cheer the troops as they marched to the wharf, but here there was anticlimax as the ship they were due to board, *Langton Grange*, was not ready to receive them. Instead, the troops went aboard a small steamer, which left the wharf with great fanfare, only to take them on a trip around the harbour and back to the wharf. Here the troops disembarked and spent the night in a drill hall, boarding the *Langton Grange* the following day, and departing for South Africa. The following Friday, 2 November, the second group of troops to depart Sydney, numbering 204 men, also paraded from Victoria Barracks to the wharf through cheering crowds, then went aboard the *Aberdeen*, which left the same day, again accompanied down the harbour by small craft.

It was also on 27 October that the Victorian contingent marched through the streets of Melbourne and embarked on the *Medic*, which at that time was the largest vessel ever to have come to Australia. Included in this group were volunteers from Tasmania, and they were given a rousing send-off by the local populace. Leading politicians and their families boarded the Union Steam Ship Company liner *Monowai* to follow the *Medic* to Port Phillip Heads. Two days later the South Australian contingent also boarded the *Medic*, in Adelaide, and they were joined a few days later by the soldiers being sent from Western Australia, who boarded the *Medic* in Fremantle. The four troopships, *Medic, Langton Grange, Aberdeen* and *Kent*, joined up to form a convoy at Albany, from where they departed on 3 November. They were carrying 1200 men from New South Wales, Victoria, Tasmania, South Australia and Western Australia. Also on board was a half-unit from the New South Wales Army Medical Corps, comprising six officers, 85 other ranks, and a 50-bed field hospital, but no nurses.

The voyage from Western Australia to South Africa took almost three weeks, and life aboard the ships was both monotonous and arduous for the men. The cavalry troops had to attend to their horses almost constantly, while the infantry engaged in regular parades, drills and lectures, with the occasional diversion of shooting practice, using boxes thrown over the side of the ship into the sea as targets. There were some discipline problems, including the occasional theft of personal equipment, but on the whole an atmosphere of harmony existed on the troopships. The convoy arrived in Cape Town on 26 November. The first Queensland contingent, comprising fourteen officers and 250 men, made their way to South Africa aboard the *Cornwall* independently of the forces from the other colonies, arriving on 13 December.

There were a number of notable opponents to sending Australian

Medic carried the first Victorian contingent to go to South Africa. (*Fred Roderick collection*)

Monowai carried a contingent of New Zealand troops to South Africa.

troops to South Africa, the conflict there being called 'a tinpot struggle' by members of parliament in both New South Wales and Victoria. In a letter published in *The Bulletin*, Henry Lawson stated, 'Some of us are willing — wilfully, blindly, eager, mad! — to cross the sea and shoot men whom we never saw and whose quarrel we do not and cannot understand.' Despite such opposition, a second contingent was soon on its way to South Africa, comprising a further 1500 men, the majority being civilians who had volunteered for duty in Bushmen's Corps. Again, these troops were sent to South Africa by the individual colonies, but they travelled independently on different transports, not in convoys. Three ships were organised to depart Sydney, the largest being *Moravian* (see page 2), carrying 9 officers, 85 other ranks, 52 horses and 12 carts It was accompanied by *Surrey*, carrying the 1st Australian Horse, comprising 4 officers and 100 other ranks, 112 horses, a medical officer and a veterinary officer. The third ship was *Southern Cross*.

On the day of their departure, 17 January 1900, there was a patriotic meeting at Sydney Town Hall, during which pupils from Sydney Girls High School presented bugles to the contingent. The troops then paraded through the streets of Sydney, which were crowded with well-wishers, to Woolloomooloo, where the three vessels were berthed, bedecked with flags. Although admission to the Woolloomooloo wharves had been restricted to ticket holders, every possible vantage point, including the shed roofs, was thronged with people. The waters around the berthed ships were also filled with boats of every size, while more people crowded onto hills that encircled the bay. Once the troops had boarded, the troopships moved slowly away into the harbour, cheered on by the enthusiastic crowds. Still surrounded by small craft, they made their way slowly towards Sydney Heads, and then out to sea.

In addition to the troops and their equipment, *Moravian* also carried another half-unit from the New South Wales Army Medical Corps, five ambulance wagons, and fourteen nurses, the first time Australian nurses went overseas with troops. In previous conflicts, the only nurses in the field had been attached to the British Imperial Nursing Service, and nurses from the colonies had not been able to serve overseas. During the latter part of 1899 the first steps had been taken to establish an Army Nursing Service within the New South Wales Medical Corps, and the nurses who departed on 17 January 1900 were the first to join the new service.

Although the three ships left Sydney together, they did not make the voyage to South Africa in convoy. *Moravian*, being faster than the other two, went on ahead, arriving in Cape Town on 17 February. *Surrey*, which had called at both Adelaide and Fremantle before crossing the Indian Ocean, arrived a few days later, as did *Southern Cross*. It was recorded that on *Surrey* only one horse died during the voyage. Further New South Wales troops, including one officer and 40 men from the NSW Lancers, embarked in Sydney on the *Australasian*. This vessel, which had carried troops to the Sudan campaign fifteen years previously, arrived at Cape Town on 19 March.

Among the other units included in the second contingent were eight officers and 113 men from the South Australian Mounted Rifles, among them Lance Corporal H.H. Morant, regimental Number 37, who landed at Cape Town on 25 February. Later immortalised as 'Breaker' Morant, he served out his one year with the regiment but, deciding to remain in South Africa, he joined a newly formed outfit called the Bush Veldt Carbineers, who engaged in irregular fighting against the Boers. On 27 February 1902 Morant and another Australian, Peter Handcock, were executed by firing squad, having been found guilty by a court martial of killing a missionary. This was one of the most significant events of the war as far as Australia was concerned.

These initial deployments were generally supported by the people of Australia, but already there were some who opposed sending troops to South Africa, and over the next few years this opposition grew stronger. There was even an attempt at sabotage when the *Maori King*, designated to transport soldiers from Queensland, was set on fire in Brisbane. Despite this, the Queensland second contingent left as planned, but in the Indian Ocean there was a second attempt to set the *Maori King* on fire. This time kerosene was poured on hay in the hold, then ignited, but the blaze was soon detected and quelled. As the ship had German crew members, who were known to be sympathetic to the Boers, it was initially thought one of them was responsible for the fire, but eventually it was found to have been caused by a British crew member.

New Zealand had also rushed troops to South Africa, marking the first involvement of that country in a foreign war, though not from lack of trying previously. Early in 1899, the New Zealand government had been keen to send a force of 500 men to Samoa when civil unrest broke out. This offer was declined by the British government and Samoa was subsequently divided between America and Germany. When war broke out in South Africa, New Zealand was ready in an instant, the first troops going into camp at Wellington the day after war was declared. New Zealand organised to send a force of 210 men, who landed in Cape Town on 23 November 1899, making them the first Empire troops to arrive. They were followed by two further contingents, numbering 737 men, who arrived in South Africa during the first months of 1900. A fourth contingent, comprising 239 officers and men and 220 horses, boarded the liner *Monowai*, owned by the Union Steam Ship Company, at Port Chalmers. Departing on 24 March 1900, the troops and horses were taken via Albany and Durban to Beira, where they disembarked. The *Monowai* then returned directly to Hobart and resumed her place on the trans-Tasman trade.

In late February and early in March 1900, the third contingent of Australian colonial troops boarded their ships at various ports around the country. One contingent consisted of 1300 volunteers, the New South Wales Bushmen's Contingent. The first group, comprising 23 officers, 327 other ranks and 396 horses, along with 11 carts or wagons, were embarked on the *Atlantian*, berthed at Woolloomooloo, and left Sydney on 28 February. A further group of Bushmen departed Sydney aboard the *Euryalus* on 10 March. Included in this party were a further nine nurses, but there were more nurses anxious to go to the war zone to look after injured troops. Unable to travel with Australian troops, a party of eleven nurses from Western Australia arranged to travel to South Africa independently, their fares being paid out of the funds from a public appeal.

The group was due to board the *Salamis* in Albany on 10 March 1900, but, as later reported in the *Albany Advertiser*: 'When the nurses first volunteered, it was understood they were to be given first saloon passage to Cape Town. Later on they were informed they would have to sleep in the steerage, but dine in the saloon. Immediately prior to leaving Perth in the train on Saturday afternoon they received the information that they would only be provided with steerage accommodation ... The cabins were found to be ten-berth and the beds were minus sheets and pillow slips ... Among those who knew the situation the nurses had been placed in there was an intense feeling of disgust at the treatment they had received.' When the nurses arrived in South Africa they found themselves in a difficult administrative situation, and the group soon disbanded. Some remained and joined British nursing units, while others returned to Western Australia.

The British government wanted still more Australian and New Zealand troops to be sent and a fourth contingent, known as the Imperial Bushmen, was organised in Australia. Numbering 2000 troops in all, they were dispatched from various colonies, the largest contingent comprising 762 men who departed Sydney on board the *Armenian* on 23 April 1900, arriving at Beira on 17 May.

Among the men to depart Melbourne as part of the fourth contingent was George Witton, who rose to the rank of lieutenant but was tried for the same crimes as Morant and Handcock. Found guilty, he was sentenced to death, but this was commuted to imprisonment for life by General Kitchener. However, Witton was released in August

1905 and returned to Australia where he wrote a book about his involvement in the Boer War and other happenings in South Africa. In 1899, Witton was attached to the Royal Australian Artillery and had tried to be included in the first contingent, but he was not selected for active service until March 1900, then sent to a camp at Langwarrin where he prepared for departure. Witton wrote:

> We left Langwarrin in full marching order about midday on 28th April, and reached Mentone, where we bivouacked. In the morning my horse's nosebag was missing, but I found it some months later on the South African veldt. We arrived in Melbourne about noon on 29th April, and expected to embark the same afternoon on the transport *Victorian*, lying at the Port Melbourne pier. Through some hitch, the boat was not ready to receive us, and we were again quartered at the show-ground at Flemington. On Tuesday, 1st May, we broke up camp. It was a glorious and never-to-be-forgotten day, and our march through the city was signalised by an unparalleled demonstration of popular applause. The streets were packed, and in places the troops could only pass in single file. Handkerchiefs, sweets, and all kinds of good things were pressed upon us as we passed through the crowd.
>
> On arrival at the pier, the work of embarking the horses was at once commenced, and over 700 were shipped and stalled in less than four hours. Getting the troops on board was a more difficult matter, as there was so much leave-taking and so many good-byes to say. The boat was cleared of visitors and put off from the pier, anchoring for the night opposite Williamstown. All on board was confusion and bustle, and many of the crew had been having a jolly time and were incapable of performing their duties. We got nothing that night in the shape of rations; fortunately we had our haversacks to fall back on, which provided sufficient for the day. Later on hammocks were brought out and slung. It was a new experience for me to sleep in one, and I fancy I must have slung mine too slack, for when I got into it my head and my feet almost touched, and I think I must have resembled a mammoth wood-grub in repose. We weighed anchor about 7 am on Wednesday morning, and passed through the heads about 11 am ... Cape Otway was the last glimpse we had of the home land, and owing to the *Victorian* keeping well out to sea, no more land was sighted until we were off the coast of Madagascar.
>
> As this was my first experience of a sea voyage, I fully expected that a bout of sea-sickness would be part of the programme, but such was not the case as far as I was concerned, and when I saw scores of my comrades hanging limply over the side and lying like dead men about the deck, I congratulated myself in the words of the Pharisee, 'Thank God I am not as other men are.' Everything on board was soon got into ship-shape order,

and we lived fairly well. A large quantity of fruit and butter had been sent on board as a gift for the use of the troops, and was greatly appreciated as a welcome addition to the bill of fare. My duties were to assist the regimental quartermaster-sergeant and superintend the distribution of the horse feed. This was stowed in the hold, hoisted up daily, and portioned out to the different squadrons. The horses were a splendid lot, and stood the voyage remarkably well, only one dying during the trip.

On the whole, the voyage to South Africa was not an unpleasant experience for Witton and his fellow troopers, though he did record that, a few days after leaving Melbourne: 'we were paraded before the medical officers and vaccinated; it affected some very badly, and for a time they were quite incapable of doing any duty. After about five days out I was agreeably surprised when I was informed that I had been promoted to the rank of sergeant. I was put in charge of a squad to instil into them the contents of the "Red Book" on Infantry Drill. At times though, when the boat gave a roll, more turnings were gone through than were set down in the drill book.'

As the long voyage continued, Witton wrote that

> it was now drill continuously all day and every day. Sergeant-Major Oakes, of the Victorian Rangers, held a class of instruction for non-commissioned officers every morning, and during the day Lieut-Colonel Kelly would read to us from the bridge extracts from Queen's Regulations and Military Law, specially impressing upon us those parts which referred to the first duty of a soldier, 'obedience to orders.' Every Sunday church parade was held on deck; the services were conducted by the Rev. Major Holden, who accompanied us as far as Beira. Everyone had a good word for the chaplain, who was always moving among the men, providing them with all kinds of books and writing material, and his many kindnesses were greatly appreciated by all. He edited and published a paper on board named 'The A I Register', which was a great success. The demand for copies was so large that the supply of paper ran out, and publication ceased after the first issue.
>
> Occasionally we would have a shooting competition between different squadrons; an empty box or fruit case would be dropped overboard as a target, and when it was about 200 yards away we would fire volleys at it. The results were watched by a party of officers on the bridge, and points were awarded for the best shooting. Almost every evening concerts were held on deck, a very fine piano having been given for the use of the troops by the Acting-Governor of Victoria, Sir John Madden. A phonograph was also much in evidence, and at times a boxing contest would also be indulged in. When we began to steer north-west the weather became very hot, and consequently trying for the troops, being almost unbearable day and night.

Instead of arriving at one of the major South African ports, as might have been expected, the *Victorian* and several other troop transports were directed to Beira, in the Portuguese colony of Mozambique. According to Witton:

> Beira Harbour was reached on the morning of 22nd May 1900. The British gunboat *Partridge* came out and met us. We were all very anxious to know how the war was going, as we had not heard any news since leaving Melbourne. Mafeking had been relieved on the 17th, but there was still plenty to do. Pretoria had not then been occupied. We anchored in the harbour, opposite the town. The *Armenian*, with the New South Wales contingent on board, had arrived a few days before, and we were greeted with ringing cheers when we dropped anchor alongside.
>
> As there was no pier, everything had to be landed in lighters. The horses were taken off in a kind of flat-bottomed barge 20 feet square; a tug boat would take it within a chain or so of the land, and a team of Kaffirs would then wade in and seize hold of a rope and haul it on to the beach. Owing to the harbour being full of shipping, we had rather an exciting time on one of the lighters. In dodging among the other boats, we got foul of an anchor chain, and were cast adrift, starting off with the tide at a great rate. Our tug-boat, while manoeuvring round to pick us up, was run into by another tug. After much gesticulating and vociferating on the part of the Portuguese captains, we were taken in tow again, and eventually landed on the beach.
>
> While we were waiting in the harbour, the *Manhattan* arrived with the South Australian, West Australian and Tasmanian contingents; she afterwards returned to Durban and landed her troops there. The 24th being the Queen's Birthday, there was a great display of bunting in the bay. At night there were fireworks, and a patriotic concert held on board.

Following the departure of the fourth contingent, for almost a year no further troops were sent from Australia. New Zealand sent smaller numbers of troops in two further contingents, followed by a sixth contingent which departed Wellington on 29 January 1901.

Apart from the upheaval in South Africa, there was also a major conflict developing in China, which became known as the Boxer Rebellion. Although not a British possession, a large number of foreigners in China found themselves besieged by the marauding Boxers, and during 1900 an international force was organised to rescue them. Some of the Australian colonies offered to send small forces, with South Australia being prepared to send their entire navy — the small, but heavily armed cruiser *Protector*. Victoria and New South Wales offered to send a naval brigade, and these forces were accepted by the British authorities.

Late in the afternoon of 30 July 1900, the chartered transport *Salamis* departed Melbourne carrying 200 Victorian Naval Brigade Volunteers, who were joined in Sydney a few days later by a further 260 Naval Brigade men from New South Wales, plus 25 soldiers, in a unit called the NSW Marine Light Infantry. On 8 August, the *Salamis* left Sydney for China and arrived in Hong Kong eighteen days later. As had happened in the Sudan campaign, the Australian forces saw very little action, the six men who died succumbing to either illness or injury rather than battle wounds. The force returned home in March 1901.

The China upheaval did not receive the same coverage in Australia as the fighting going on in South Africa. When Australia became involved in the Boer conflict, it was generally considered that the superiority in numbers and equipment of the British and colonial troops would soon win the day, and peace would be restored within a matter of months. As a result, the troops sent to South Africa in the first four contingents were all on one-year drafts, and as 1900 drew to a close they began returning to Australia. Having departed as heroes, the welcome these men received on their return was quite subdued, reflecting a change in the public attitude. Initially seen as a glorious military campaign, it was soon realised that the troops were actually fighting against Boer farmers with no military

Salamis, which carried the first Australian nurses to South Africa, later transported Australian troops to the Boxer Rebellion in China. (*Fred Roderick collection*)

background or training, who nevertheless proved themselves to be such tough and fearsome adversaries that the British forces were less than adequate in trying to suppress them.

One of the first contingents to return to Australia arrived in Sydney on 6 December 1900 aboard the *Harlech Castle*. Others travelled on the *Orient*, which was owned by the Orient Line, and the first ship to be built for them, in 1879. At that time it was the largest vessel operating to Australia, but was soon outclassed by newer tonnage. When the Boer War started, *Orient* was one of the first ships to be requisitioned by the British government and as Transport No. 24 it made numerous voyages between Britain and South Africa. On 8 January 1901, *Orient* arrived in Sydney from Cape Town with returning soldiers, then went to Brisbane, anchoring in Moreton Bay. As the *Brisbane Courier* reported on 11 January: 'The Queenslanders, men and baggage, were soon transferred to the *Otter*, which amidst much cheering from along the banks of the river, transported the troops up to town.' The *Orient* then went on to New Zealand, returning to South Africa in February. On 15 July 1901, *Orient* was back in Sydney with more troops from South Africa, who had boarded the ship at East London.

In August 1901 another vessel requisitioned by the British government for trooping arrived in Sydney with returning soldiers. This was the former White Star liner *Britannic*, which had previously been in Sydney in January 1901, having conveyed the Imperial Contingent to represent Britain at the Federation ceremonies in Sydney. When completed in 1874, *Britannic* had been the largest ship in the world, at 5004 gross tons, but was soon surpassed, and by 1899 was totally outclassed on the Atlantic trade. Taken over for service as Transport No. 62, *Britannic* completed eleven round trips between Britain and South Africa. In July 1901, *Britannic* boarded Australian troops at East London, and after stopping at Albany, Adelaide and Melbourne, arrived in Sydney on 2 August, by which time there were only 90 troops left on board to disembark.

The voyages home for the Australian troops were not always without incident, however, and some turned quite violent. In May 1901, on the troopship *Morayshire*, which was carrying Bushmen from New South Wales and Queensland, ten troopers refused orders to holystone the decks and were sentenced to 42 days confinement. They were soon set free by twenty of their fellow troopers, but the released men immediately reported to their commanding officer, Major W. Tunbridge. Realising the situation could get out of hand, Tunbridge

Some troops returning home from South Africa travelled on the *Orient*.

The White Star liner *Britannic* also brought troops home from South Africa. (*Fred Roderick collection*)

ordered all troops to gather on deck, read them the Mutiny Act, then defied any of them to make a move to harm him. The troops dispersed quietly and the released men returned voluntarily to their confinement.

Another returning group of soldiers was on the troopship *Aurania*, which stopped at Albany on the way to the eastern seaboard in late May 1901. The troops went ashore and proceeded to go on a looting spree which caused uproar in the local press, one report stating their behaviour 'realised the worst of the evils to be locally expected of militarism, that of forcible domination of citizens by swaggering soldiers.' The captain of the transport *Fortunas* said of the troops he brought home, 'I used to hold a very high opinion of Australians, but if these Imperial Bushmen are a fair sample, then I am compelled to very severely change it. They are the roughest crowd I ever had anything to do with.'

In order to fill the gap left in the British force by the returning Australian troops, during March and April of 1901 a fifth and sixth contingent, totalling nearly 5000 men, departed for South Africa. Even though Australia was now a Commonwealth, as of 1 January 1901, and the former colonies were now known as States, the various elements that comprised the fifth contingent were sent individually from each State, not as an Australian force. There were almost 1800 men from the 2nd and 3rd Regiments of the Imperial New South Wales Mounted Rifles, 1000 Queensland Imperial Bushmen and a similar number from Victoria, 450 South Australian Imperial Bushmen, and a further 400 Bushmen from Western Australia, while Tasmania contributed 250 men in the 2nd Tasmanian Imperial Bushmen.

On 15 March 1901 two ships departed Sydney, the *Custodian* with 521 soldiers on board, and the *Maplemore*, which carried 510. Six days later *British Princess* departed with 415 soldiers, and *Ranee* carrying 247. Almost the entire Contingent on these ships was made up of men from the New South Wales Mounted Rifles, as were a further 379 who departed Sydney on 5 April on the *Antillian*. There were also troopships dispatched from other states, but once again, for almost a year after these voyages, no further troops were sent.

The men in the fifth and sixth contingents had also signed up for one year, and as the time came for them to return to Australia, preparations were made to send more troops to South Africa. The call for volunteers was oversubscribed, despite the antipathy towards the conflict being presented in the press and by some politicians. Within a few weeks, some 4000 men had been selected and were formed into the Australian Commonwealth Horse, comprising eight battalions.

On 11 February 1902 the *Manchester Merchant* left Sydney with 105 members of the newly formed Australian Army Medical Corps. Then on 18 February the *Custodian* departed carrying 375 men of the 1st Battalion, Australian Commonwealth Horse, followed on 1 April by 594 men of the 3rd Battalion, Australian Commonwealth Horse, on board the *Manhattan*. The last ship to depart Sydney with troops for South Africa was the *Columbian*, carrying 469 men of the 5th Battalion, Australian Commonwealth Horse, which sailed on 22 May. At the same time, members of the 6th Battalion departed Melbourne, while the 7th Battalion left from Brisbane. The 8th Battalion was composed of 121 officers and men from Tasmania, 241 officers and men from South Australia and a further 120 from Western Australia.

The first of the vessels to arrive in South Africa was *Manchester*

Merchant, which docked in Durban on 13 March, with the other vessels arriving over the next few weeks. However, before the troops they carried could be too heavily involved in the conflict, the Boers were prepared to lay down their arms and a peace treaty was signed on 31 May 1902. At that time the final elements of the Australian Commonwealth Horse were still en route to South Africa, not disembarking until the 21st and 22nd of June. Within weeks of arriving, the Australian Commonwealth Horse was on the way back home.

The tedium of these voyages to South Africa for the soldiers could be intense, a fact depicted in a letter written by one, George Ware, of the 7th Battalion Australian Commonwealth Horse, to his mother shortly before arriving in South Africa. Although Ware did not leave Australia until May 1902, his comments serve as a general indication of the life of the soldiers on board the transports. Ware boarded the *Custodian* at the Pinkenbar Wharf in Brisbane on 19 May, and sailed the same day. Ware wrote that 'most of the Contingent went to bed, or should I say turned into our hammocks, all right the first night at sea, but oh! what a difference in the morning. The first sight to be seen on rising was a fair number of the Contingent leaning over the shipside suffering from seasickness.'

The *Custodian* followed the coast south into Bass Strait, then across the Great Australian Bight. George Ware 'was sea sick one day; that was the first day we entered the Great Australian Bight.' As the ship rounded the southern tip of Western Australia, 'on about the 10th day from Brisbane we saw Cape Leeuwin in the distance. After passing this we had left the Australian shores behind and were in the Indian Ocean.' Ahead of them lay some two weeks of nothing but sea, as the ship was travelling alone, not in convoy. George Ware wrote: 'the routine on board the ship is as follows: We are to rise at 6 am for breakfast; at 8 am fall in for Parade; at 10 drill till 11.30 then feed the horses. Have dinner at 12.30; fall in for Parade at 2 pm and drill till 3.30; feed horses again at 4 pm; have tea at 5.30 and go to bed at 9.15 pm. One day is much the same as another on board and very little out of the ordinary has occurred on this voyage. There was a bit of excitement one morning when we sighted a sailing ship, with a flag of distress and the Union Jack flying. She was tossing about at the mercy of the waves. We signalled her but as we got no answer we took it for granted that she was abandoned and so steamed on without pulling over to her ... We saw one more steamer in the distance, but with these two exceptions, we did not sight a vessel of any kind on the whole voyage.'

Ware went on to relate some of the unfortunate happenings during the voyage:

> ...sad to relate, there have been two deaths ... The first to die was a bugler, named Anderson, a young fellow 19 years old, the cause of death being poisoning brought on by eating tinned fish. The second death ... was that of a man named Dugdale ... He died on the 15th instant. The funeral service for burial at sea was read by the Ship's Captain and was very sad and impressive.
>
> There was also an outbreak of measles on board but not a serious one and most of the patients are now recovered. Two rather serious accidents occurred on the 29th May, both through the same cause — namely, two men, one the Doctor of the Contingent, Dr Webster, and the other a man named Murray fell down the hatchway which was left open. Murray was brought up unconscious and for a long time his life was despaired of but he is now recovering fast and will, I think, soon be alright again. The other, Dr Webster, was not so seriously hurt but he also is still in bed. It is quite probable that a law suit will eventuate from this accident as it was sheer neglect on the part of the ship's crew leaving the hold open without any light nearby.

However, George Ware ended his account of the voyage on a brighter note, recording that 'everyone is always kept fairly busy on board. We had one Holiday granted to us one day last week, and celebrated it by holding Sports in the afternoon and a Concert at night. With this exception it has been all work and no play but, notwithstanding, I think the majority of the Contingent have enjoyed the voyage fairly well. I myself enjoyed it very much, and only hope I have as good a time over in South Africa as I have had on board the *Custodian*.' Fortunately for George Ware and his comrades, their contingent arrived after the signing of the peace treaty, and they were not required to engage in active service.

In all, New Zealand sent ten contingents of troops to South Africa, but the final two arrived too late to take part in any major action. However, two officers included in the ninth contingent achieved the dubious distinction of being the last casualties of the war. The pair was out hunting wild animals on 4 June 1902, four days after the war officially ended, when they encountered a band of Boers who were not aware the conflict was over. In the ensuing shootout, one New Zealander was killed and the other wounded. Total New Zealand casualties for the Boer war comprised 70 killed in action, 25 killed in accidents and 133 who died from disease, as well as 166 wounded.

By the middle of 1902, most of the Australian troops had left South Africa and returned home. Among the ships used to transport them were *Orient* and *Britannic*, which had done similar service the previous year. *Britannic* arrived in Sydney on 10 August 1902, having first called at New Zealand ports. *Orient* embarked her troops at Durban and also went to New Zealand first, calling at Dunedin before arriving in Sydney on 17 August 1902. After their war service ended, *Britannic* was sold to shipbreakers in 1903, but *Orient* returned to the Australian trade until being sold to shipbreakers in 1909.

The last vessel to transport returning troops was *Drayton Grange*, a cargo ship of just 6591 gross tons owned by Houlder Line, which departed Durban on 11 July 1902. Among the 1983 men on board was the Australian Army Medical Corps, who had done such sterling work in South Africa and who had the continuing responsibility of caring for a number of sick and injured men. However, conditions on board the ship were so appalling that seventeen men died, and eventually the returning troops mutinied.

For Australia, the Boer War marked the first time the country had been involved in an overseas conflict in a major way. Over the three years the Boer War lasted, a total of 16,378 Australian troops were involved, of whom 251 were killed and a further 267 died from disease, while 882 were wounded. Most of the soldiers were members of mounted regiments, who not only took their horses with them but needed to be constantly supplied with remounts. Many horses were killed in battles, while others died from malnutrition or disease. Of the 40,000 horses sent from Australia to South Africa, none returned, the survivors having to remain overseas because of the strict quarantine laws applying in Australia.

While some monuments were erected around the country to commemorate those who fought and died in South Africa, for most Australians their involvement in the Boer War was something they preferred to forget. The change in attitude from strong support to open antipathy over the duration of the conflict had spread throughout the country, and over the next decade Australia enjoyed serenity and growth.

3 World War I

On 4 August 1914 Great Britain declared war on Germany when troops of that country invaded Belgium, in breach of an agreement Germany had made with Britain and France in 1839 to respect the neutrality of Belgium. On being advised that Great Britain and Germany were at war, the Australian government, along with all the other countries around the globe that then formed the mighty British Empire, immediately declared war on Germany as well. Although the war may have seemed half a world away, there were some local situations that could be tackled immediately, as Germany had colonised several areas of the Pacific. Some, such as New Guinea and Samoa, were too close to Australia and New Zealand for comfort.

Even before war had been declared, the certainty of it occurring had resulted in some very positive statements by the members of the government of the day. On 31 July, Senator Millen, Minister for Defence, had stated: 'If necessity arises, Australia will recognise that she is not merely a fair-weather partner of the Empire but a component member in all circumstances.' The following day, Prime Minister Joseph Cook said, 'If there is to be a war, you and I shall be in it. We must be in it. If the old country is at war, so are we.' The Federal Treasurer, Sir John Forrest, reiterated these sentiments on the night before war was declared, stating, 'If Britain goes to her Armageddon we will go with her. Our fate and hers, for good or ill, are as woven threads.'

With war seeming certain, on 3 August the Federal government held a Cabinet meeting at which it was decided to offer Britain the assistance of the Royal Australian Navy and an expeditionary force. A message to this effect was sent to the British government, stating 'In the event of war the Government is prepared to place the vessels of the Australian Navy under the control of the British Admiralty when desired. It is further prepared to dispatch an expeditionary force of 20,000 men of any suggested composition to any destination desired by the Home Government, the force to be at the complete disposal of the Home Government.' On 6 August, the Secretary of State for the Colonies responded that 'His Majesty's Government gratefully accept offer of your Ministers to send to this country force of 20,000 men and would be glad if it could be dispatched as soon as possible.'

At that time the Royal Australian Navy was still quite small, yet it did possess some powerful ships, the battle cruiser HMAS *Australia*, two light cruisers, HMAS *Melbourne* and HMAS *Sydney*, with a third, HMAS *Brisbane*, under construction, as well as three destroyers and two submarines. The 20,000 soldiers to form the Australian Imperial Force were to be drawn, as far as possible, from men who had undergone some training, with half currently serving in the citizen Army of Australia, while the other half would be composed of men who had served in the armed forces previously, including the Boer War.

However, the first response by Australia to the commencement of hostilities with Germany was to send an expeditionary force to occupy Rabaul, the capital of German New Guinea, though it was not a particularly well organised effort. The government hastily gathered a special force for this task. It was called the Australian Naval and Military Expeditionary Force, with one battalion being raised in Sydney, to be augmented by naval reservists. There was also a citizen force raised in north Queensland, called the Kennedy Regiment. The coastal liner *Kanowna* was commandeered while at Townsville, and took on board volunteers from the Kennedy Regiment, which became the first contingent of Australian troops to be sent overseas in the conflict.

One of those to join up was B.A. Cripps, who noted in his diary on 4 August, 'Troops mobilised at Townsville. Members of rifle clubs and those who volunteered came in at all times.' On 7 August he wrote, 'Received orders to leave by the SS *Kanowna* for Thursday Island,' and on the following day, 'Busy all morning loading troops ship with stores. Ship left wharf about 12 o'clock midst the most enthusiastic farewell Townsville has ever seen.' *Kanowna* went first to Thursday Island, where more troops were embarked, then proceeded to Port Moresby. On 14 August Cripps wrote, 'The troops were issued with ball cartridges last night ready for an attack which was expected from the Germans.'

Kanowna was taken over at Townsville to carry troops to New Guinea.

In the meantime, a better prepared expeditionary force comprising 500 men in six companies had been formed in Sydney, and embarked on the auxiliary cruiser *Berrima*. This vessel was owned by the P & O Branch Line, and usually operated on the emigrant trade from Britain via South Africa, but had been taken over by the Australian government while in Sydney. It was sent to Cockatoo Island on 12 August and in six days was fitted out to carry 1500 officers and men, accommodation being arranged in the holds, with latrines and wash rooms beneath the poop deck. A hospital was installed on the upper deck, while some cabins were dismantled to make way for guardrooms, cells and baggage rooms. Four 4.7-inch guns were mounted, one pair on the forecastle, the others on the poop deck, while magazines to supply these guns were constructed fore and aft on the lower deck.

There was apparently some confusion regarding their destination for some members of the Sydney battalion. Bill Mair had signed up with the Australian Naval and Military Expeditionary Force in August, being sworn in to serve 'for a period not exceeding six months' on 16 August. Two days later, Mair sent a telegram to a friend stating 'Leaving for England Tuesday.' In a letter he wrote several weeks later, he stated: 'I joined on the Monday and the following Tuesday we were on the boat ready to sail, so you see they lost no time in getting us off. We were given to understand we were on the road to England, and when we were a few days out from Sydney, were told it was Marseilles in France where we were going.'

Berrima departed Sydney on 19 August, the plan being that it should

Berrima was fitted out in Sydney to carry 1500 troops to the islands.

link up with *Kanowna* at Port Moresby. *Berrima* was escorted by HMAS *Sydney* as far as Palm Island, where on 23 August the light cruiser HMAS *Encounter* joined them. The store carrier *Aorangi* arrived on 30 August, along with the destroyers HMAS *Yarra* and HMAS *Warrego*, submarines *AE 1* and *AE 2*, a collier and an oil tanker. On 2 September this convoy left Palm Island for Port Moresby, where they linked up with *Kanowna* and headed for Rabaul. However, soon after leaving Port Moresby there was a mutiny among the firemen on *Kanowna*, who refused to take the ship any further. Volunteers were drawn from the troops on board, and the ships had to return to Port Moresby. On their arrival in Port Moresby, the troops on board *Kanowna* were inspected by Colonel William Holmes, commander of the contingent on *Berrima*, who concluded they were not fit for active service, being poorly trained and equipped. As a result, on 7 September *Kanowna* left Port Moresby and returned the troops to Townsville, then resumed her place on the coastal trade. Meanwhile the rest of the convoy continued their voyage, and on 11 September reached Rabaul, which was captured two days later. On 22 September *Berrima* steamed on to Madang, which was also quickly captured. *Berrima* left New Guinea on 4 October and returned to Sydney.

The Principal Medical officer on board *Berrima* was Lieutenant Colonel Neville Howse, who had won the Victoria Cross during the Boer War. He wrote of the contingent: 'The selection of recruits was on a very high standard of physical and mental fitness. They got a good outfit — the boots supplied were the best I have seen ... The men were trained in the fitting and use of boots. They were told that if they didn't keep their feet good, they would be thrown out of the

Moeraki carried New Zealand troops to capture German Samoa.

force, which was a serious threat … There was little disease on the voyage apart from a few mild colds and flu and one case of pneumonia. There were no others and no infectious disease … Before landing five grams of quinine was given to every man. The second inoculation for typhoid had been carried out. Naval men had to have two inoculations as they had had none on shore. Only one man refused inoculation, and he was easily persuaded.' Howse also prepared notes for the men on treatment for malaria, heat stroke and dysentery.

New Zealand was also quick to organise a force to send to the islands to capture German territories. On 6 August the Secretary of State for the Colonies sent a message to New Zealand, stating that if they 'feel themselves able to seize German wireless station at Samoa, we should feel that this was a great and urgent imperial service.' In just five days, a force of 1413 troops was organised and the government requisitioned two steamers from the Union Steam Ship Company, *Monowai* and *Moeraki*, which were quickly converted to carry troops to German Samoa.

On 12 August, a particularly miserable winter's day, the men marched through the streets of Wellington and boarded the two vessels. However, their escort of warships was not ready, so it was not until 15 August that the ships departed, carrying the first contingent of New Zealand troops to be sent overseas in the war, and escorted by three small cruisers, HMS *Philomel*, HMS *Psyche* and HMS *Pyramus*. The convoy went first to Noumea, being fortunate to escape an encounter with two heavy cruisers of the German Pacific Fleet, *Scharnhorst* and *Gneisenau*, which had passed by Noumea on the night prior to the arrival of the convoy. While entering the harbour at Noumea, *Monowai* went aground but was soon refloated. Here two Australian warships, HMAS *Australia* and HMAS *Sydney*, and the French *Montcalm* joined the escort. The next stop was at Suva on 26 August, then on 30 August the troops were landed at Apia. They met virtually no opposition and quickly secured the island, including the radio station.

Meanwhile, both Australia and New Zealand had started raising their expeditionary forces to be sent overseas to assist Great Britain. In order to provide the ships to transport this force, both the Australian and New Zealand governments began requisitioning any suitable ships that happened to be in their waters. Surprisingly, the Australians did not take over any of their own fleet of coastal liners, but instead secured British liners and cargo ships, all of which were given troopship numbers, starting with *Hymettus*, which became A1. Among the first ships to be requisitioned was *Medic*, of White Star Line, which had previously carried Australian troops to the Boer War, along with her sister vessel, *Afric*. Also taken over were the Orient Line passenger vessels *Orvieto* and *Omrah*, along with *Benalla* and *Geelong* from the P & O Line, *Ascanius* of the Blue Funnel Line, *Argyllshire* and *Clan MacCorquodale* of Clan Line, *Shropshire*, *Wiltshire* and *Suffolk* of the Federal Line, *Hororata* of the New Zealand Shipping Company, which had only been completed in May 1914, and *Miltiades* of Aberdeen Line, along with *Euripides*, which was brand new, having departed London as recently as 1 July on her maiden voyage, only to be requisitioned when in Brisbane at the end of August. All these ships were refitted to carry troops. *Orvieto*, the largest ship to be requisitioned, became troopship A3 and was converted to carry 209 officers and 1425 other ranks. *Omrah*, dating from 1899, was fitted out to carry 55 officers and 1316 other ranks as troopship A5, while *Benalla* (A24) was given accommodation for 50 officers and 1200 other ranks. Some ships were also fitted out with extensive stabling in their holds, while a number of other ships were requisitioned solely to transport horses.

Some of the conversions were carried out in Sydney by Cockatoo Island Dockyard. *Argyllshire*, which became Australian troopship A8, was taken in hand on 22 August and fitted out to carry 845 men and 392 horses, the work being completed on 9 September. Also converted for trooping by Cockatoo Island during the early months of the war were several cargo ships, including *Marere* (A21) to carry 475 horses and 85 men to look after them; *Star of England* (A15), 524 men and 511 horses, *Anglo Egyptian* (A25), 127 men and 552 horses; and *Armadale* (A26), 284 men and 388

Three of the ships taken over to carry Australian troops in the first convoy were *Afric* (A19), *Hororata* (A20) and *Euripides* (A14).

horses. Three ships, *Euripides*, *Hororata* and *Suffolk*, were converted in Brisbane. The Australians altogether requisitioned 28 vessels, though not all were carrying troops, as some cargo ships were also needed. These ships boarded their troops at all major Australian ports.

The ships allocated to board their troops in Sydney did so over a number of days, then departed individually for the assembly point.

Star of England (A15) was converted to carry 524 men and 511 horses. (*Fred Roderick collection*)

Among the vessels that embarked troops in Sydney was *Euripides*, and among those that boarded the vessel was William McKenzie, of the Salvation Army, who had volunteered to serve as a chaplain to the Expeditionary Force. Many of the troops allocated to join the troopships were awaiting their departure at the Rose Hill Racecourse Military Camp, near Parramatta. In his diary William McKenzie recorded: 'We embarked on the *Euripides* on Monday Oct. 19th from 9 to 1 am. The ship being in midstream, we had to go out on ferry boats. There are 2,500 troops aboard and 300 of a crew. It is a well-appointed ship 15,000 tons. Never before have so many troops left Australia in one single ship. We lay all afternoon and night in the Harbour and set out at 6.30 am. The sea was fairly rough outside so many were sick within a short time. I was OK. I was given a cabin to myself a large roomy state-room, with a porthole, so I am very comfortably fixed up and have heaps of room and plenty of quiet.'

Signaller R.J. Kenny, who also boarded *Euripides*, later wrote: 'When we left Sydney nobody knew where we were going. We were trammed from camp to Circular Quay, where lighters were waiting to take us to *Euripides*. How it leaked out that we were going I don't know but soon people came flooding from everywhere. The police cordon could hardly keep back the women bent on giving father or brother a parting kiss. We were reminded before leaving camp that breaking ranks or any breach of discipline would be severely dealt with, and every man stood like a statue. But I shall not forget the tear-dimmed eyes of the women and girls that I saw on the morning I left Sydney.'

The first leg of their voyage was to Albany, about which William McKenzie noted: 'Commenced official prayers at 8.45 am, these to be held each morning in the fore and aft well decks. We have had a remarkably fast passage across the Bight. Everybody in good spirits. A considerable amount of gambling going on — one man won £50 at Banker and got put in the gaol for 96 hours as did also another man for playing with him. There are fifteen cases of venereal disease in the infectious Hospital and others are ripening for it. Two cases of measles.'

When the ships arrived in King George Sound, the troops were not allowed shore leave, though many did get a trip to land to take part in a route march or other organised excursion. William McKenzie was more fortunate, as he wrote: 'I was able to get ashore on Wednesday morning and spent four hours on land in Albany ... made some purchases and caught the 4 pm tug back but had to go right round the fleet. Our ship was the last to be visited. We took 3¾ hours to do the rounds. I had quite an experience in climbing up the rope ladder 38 feet. On getting on to it the tug steamed off and pulled away the rope ladder, and had me swinging in mid-air, clinging to it like a monkey, and when it let go I was bumped against the ship's side and the ladder was on the outside of me. By sheer physical strength I managed to turn it around and then began climbing. It was a big effort, making my heart thump against my ribs and I was clean done when I reached the upper deck. However, it was soon over and a past experience. It was dark too which made it more trying.'

Geelong, which became Australian troopship A2, was converted in Melbourne to carry 62 officers and 1539 other ranks, then went to Hobart to board her troops of the 12th Battalion to be taken to the Middle East. On the voyage from Melbourne, *Geelong* carried a contingent of South Australian troops, who were to join Tasmanian men in training. Although the trip across Bass Strait was quite short, Private Alan Thwaites later recalled: 'we joined the *Geelong* and had a very rough trip across to Tasmania — everybody on the ship was ill. We were in hammocks and, oh we had a dreadful time — ill as could be and very few survived it well. But we eventually arrived in Hobart and went to camp near Norfolk, joined our battalion there and finished off our training.' Tasmanian William Tope remembered, 'we just manoeuvred and drilled and exercised and went down to the wharves to help stow the vessels up, you know physically pulling merchandise aboard. Then we went straight to Albany on the *Geelong*.'

Among the ships requisitioned in New Zealand to carry troops were *Tahiti* (NZ4), berthed behind an escorting cruiser, and *Maunganui* (NZ3) owned by the Union Steam Ship Company.

In New Zealand, similar events were occurring. Among the ships requisitioned were *Arawa* of Shaw Savill Line, which happened to be loading cargo at Lyttelton; two from the New Zealand Shipping Company, *Ruapehu*, and *Orari*; and three vessels owned by the Union Steam Ship Company, the liners *Maunganui* and *Tahiti*, which were converted into troop transports by the Union Line's own staff at Port Chalmers, and the cargo ship *Limerick*. The vessels were all given New Zealand trooping numbers.

The original plan had been that, rather then send one large convoy, those ships delegated to transport horses, which were also the slowest, would depart first, to be followed by the troop transports as and when they and their passengers were ready. However, the British Admiralty sent a message warning against this, as German warships were known to be active in waters through which the ships would have to sail. These were *Gneisenau* and *Scharnhorst*, which were marauding in the Pacific together, and the smaller cruisers *Emden* and *Konigsberg*, known to be in the Indian Ocean, At that time all the Australian and New Zealand naval vessels were engaged in seeking out the enemy ships.

The Shaw Savill liner *Arawa* (NZ10) was also taken over to carry New Zealand troops. (*Auckland Institute and Museum*)

It was therefore arranged that all the ships carrying Australian troops and horses would make their way unescorted around the coast to King George Sound, near Albany, in Western Australia, to arrive there by 3 October. The New Zealand ships would leave together in a convoy on about 20 September, escorted by two old Royal Navy cruisers, *Psyche* and *Philomel*, on the six-day crossing of the Tasman and then along the southern coast of Australia to Albany. Once all the ships had gathered, they would depart as a convoy, being escorted by three cruisers, HMS *Minotaur*, which was the flagship, HMAS *Melbourne* and HMAS *Sydney*, and the Japanese battle cruiser *Ibuki*.

Minotaur, completed in June 1906, was armed with four 9.2-inch and ten 7.5-inch guns, as well as having five torpedo tubes. With a displacement of 14,600 tons, the cruiser carried a crew of 755 officers and men and could attain a maximum speed of 21 knots. Although 40 feet shorter than *Minotaur*, *Ibuki* was even more powerful, having as main armament four 12-inch guns as well as eight 8-inch guns and fourteen 4.7 inch guns. With a crew of 845 officers and men, *Ibuki* also had a displacement of 14,600 tons and could achieve over 20 knots. *Melbourne* and *Sydney* were much smaller, with a displacement of just 5400 tons. Both completed in 1913, being Chatham-class cruisers, they carried eight 6-inch guns as main armament, and a crew of 540 officers and men.

Minotaur and *Ibuki* were dispatched from Singapore to Albany, but at the last minute their orders were changed and they continued on to New Zealand, to be added to the escort. These changes caused a delay of three weeks in the planned departure date of the convoy. This was especially difficult for the troops, some of whom had already boarded their transports and left for Albany. The first New Zealand convoy, comprising ten ships carrying 8444 troops of the New Zealand Expeditionary Force to Egypt, finally left Wellington on 16 October 1914 to link up with the ships carrying the Australian Expeditionary Force in King George Sound. The commander of the New Zealand force, Major General Sir Alexander Godley, travelled on board the *Maunganui*.

Hororata and *Benalla* boarded their troops at Melbourne, departing on 17 October for Albany. *Orvieto*, which was to be the flagship of the convoy, embarked the 5th Battalion in Melbourne, along with the headquarters staff, including the commanding officer of the Australian Imperial Force, General William Throsby Bridges, a contingent of nurses and some engineers. *Orvieto* departed for the assembly point in King George Sound on 21 October, arriving five days later.

Another Orient Line vessel, *Omrah*, embarked 32 officers, 999 other ranks and fifteen horses of the 9th Battalion at the Pinkenba wharf in Brisbane, departing on 24 September, while a further ten men and 44 horses were loaded aboard the smaller *Rangatira*, which also carried the bulk of their equipment. The diary of Lieutenant C.F. Ross briefly recorded the details of the early stages of their trip aboard the *Omrah*:

> 24.9.14   Left Enoggera Camp at 4 am entrained — arrived at Pinkenba and embarked and underway before breakfast — very sick with vaccination.
>
> 28.9.14   Arrived at Port Melbourne — still sick — where we anchor some distance down the harbour.
>
> 29.9.14   Move up to Port Melbourne jetty where we remain 3 weeks — and continue our training.
>
> 17.10.14   Leave Port Melbourne on Monday being preceded by *Hororata* and *Benalla* on Sunday.
>
> 21.10.14   Arrive at Albany — route march.

Sixteen ships, including *Orvieto* and *Benalla*, left Melbourne at various times between 17 and 21 October. Sister Alice Kitchen was among the nurses who boarded *Benalla*, and on 19 October she wrote, 'Came on board 12 noon, leaving all the family on the pier. Moved out 2 pm after luncheon. Learned we were going straight to Albany, without any escort or cruisers. Those parts are evidently considered safe.' A further five vessels departed Adelaide between 20 and 22 October, and one, *Geelong*, left Hobart on 20 October. By the time *Orvieto* arrived in King George Sound on 26 October, eighteen vessels

The commanding officer of the Australian Imperial Force, General Bridges, boarded the *Orvieto* (A3) in Melbourne.

were already there, with the remaining Australian transports arriving during the day. Two days later the ten ships comprising the New Zealand convoy, and their escorts, appeared on the horizon, and soon after had entered the huge harbour, while HMAS *Melbourne* patrolled the entrance.

Thirty-six of the 38 ships to be included in the first convoy to Egypt had now assembled in King George Sound. They came from the fleets of over a dozen different companies, including the P & O, Orient, Shaw Savill, White Star, Blue Funnel, Federal, Clan, Aberdeen, New Zealand Shipping, and Union Steam Ship Company, the largest representation being six vessels owned by the Commonwealth & Dominion Line. While the ships carrying Australian troops were still in their civilian colours, the New Zealand ships had been repainted grey.

The original plan had been for the convoy to voyage by way of Colombo and the Suez Canal to Britain, but on 25 October the British Cabinet decided that the ships should travel by way of South Africa, as the troops might be needed there to overcome an uprising among some of the Boers. However, by 30 October the situation in South Africa had stabilised and the convoy was again ordered to sail through the Suez Canal. However, the danger posed by the *Emden* had resurfaced, as the German cruiser had made a sudden attack on the Malayan port of Penang, sinking a Russian cruiser and French destroyer. Although a huge number of ships were searching for *Emden*, the vessel had escaped into the vast expanse of the Indian Ocean and could be anywhere, posing a potential threat to the convoy. To further complicate matters, on 31 October Turkey came into the war on the German side, and began movements of troops towards Egypt.

On 1 November 1914, the convoy departed King George Sound on the first leg of its voyage, which was still expected to take them to Britain. HMS *Minotaur* was the first to leave harbour, at 0625, followed by the ships that would form the central line of the convoy, known as the first division. Half an hour behind them, the ships to form the port column, or second division, steamed out to sea, followed by the third division. After them came the ten New Zealand ships, which formed up into two columns of their own. In each column the ships were separated by 800 yards, so the whole convoy stretched over seven and a half miles of sea. *Minotaur* took up a position five miles ahead of the convoy, with *Sydney* and *Melbourne* on either beam at a distance of four miles. By 0855, all the ships were in position and the long voyage began.

Chaplain William McKenzie on board *Euripides* recorded, 'We lay at anchor until Sunday morning November 1st when we set sail at 6.45 am. A good crowd of people lined the hills at the mouth of the harbour to see the awe-inspiring sight, as the convoy of cruisers with the transports left the harbour under sealed orders … The morning we left was ideal, the atmosphere clear, the sea calm and the sun fairly warm. What a magnificent sight.' Sister Alice Kitchen, on board *Benalla*, wrote on 1 November, 'At 8 am we began to move out in single file to the sea; it was a fine sight to see the long line of ships going out one by one and forming into three long lines, the cruisers leading.'

Two days after leaving, the convoy was brought up to full strength when *Ascanius* (A11) and *Medic* (A7) joined, having embarked their troops in Fremantle. They were escorted by *Ibuki*. Once the two troopships had taken up their convoy formation, HMS *Minotaur* remained on station five miles ahead, with *Sydney* on the port beam, *Ibuki* on the starboard beam, and *Melbourne* astern.

As the journey commenced, Sister Kitchen wrote: 'We travel about 800 yards behind each other, and a mile between the three rows. It seems a little difficult to get the correct speed and they occasionally have to drop out of line if they get too close, but seem to have all sorts of arrangements made for contingencies … It is an anxious time for all those in charge. We hear the Captain never leaves the bridge at night. If attacked by enemy cruisers we are to go three miles out of our course till the cruisers do their work … If the *Emden* comes amongst us in the dark what a commotion there would be … Our Jap cruiser is like a pillar of cloud opposite my port hole … I often rise in the night and look to see if it is still there and feel safer when I see its huge cloud. It draws in much closer to us in the dark night hours.'

For the journey across the Indian Ocean, the disposition of the transports was:

Wiltshire (A18)	*Orvieto* (A3)	*Euripides* (A14)
Medic (A7)	*Southern* (A27)	*Argyllshire* (A8)
Ascanius (A11)	*Pera* (A4)	*Shropshire* (A9)
Star of England (A15)	*Armadale* (A26)	*Afric* (A19)
Geelong (A2)	*Saldanha* (A12)	*Benalla* (A24)
Port Lincoln (A17)	*Katuna* (A13)	*Rangatira* (A22)
Karroo (A10)	*Hymettus* (A1)	*Star of Victoria* (A16)
Marere (A21)	*Suffolk* (A23)	*Hororata* (A20)
Clan MacCorquodale (A6)	*Anglo-Egyptian* (A25)	*Omrah* (A5)
		Miltiades (A28)

Arawa (NZ10)	*Maunganui* (NZ3)
Athenic (NZ11)	*Hawkes Bay* (NZ9)
Orari (NZ6)	*Star of India* (NZ8)
Ruapehu (NZ5)	*Limerick* (NZ7)
Waimana (NZ12)	*Tahiti* (NZ4)

The first destination was Colombo, but it would be a long journey, as the convoy's speed was limited by the slowest ship. In this case it was a small tramp steamer, *Southern*, owned by Harris & Dixon, which had been requisitioned as a horse transport but could only manage just over 10 knots. During the first few days of the voyage, the troops settled into a routine, combining training with other activities to fill in the long days at sea. On most of the ships the only lights to be seen at night were red and green on either side, and a light at the stern, while the lead ship of each column also showed a masthead light. However, on some of the passenger liners, especially the *Orvieto*, which was carrying the headquarters staff, these restrictions at first were not applied However, after a few nights even these ships had to douse all but the most basic of lighting.

Some of the ships had problems maintaining their correct convoy positions, and distance from the ship ahead. On the night of 4 November the problem was so bad that the next morning *Minotaur* steamed between the lines of ships, broadcasting a message to them which stated, 'During last night the second division straggled to seven miles, whereas their distance should have been three miles. The third division straggled to six miles, whereas their distance should have been three and a half miles ... the *Medic* and *Geelong* were signalling last night with lights visible at least ten miles.'

Included among those aboard *Medic* was the 22-year-old John Simpson, later to be immortalised during the Gallipoli campaign as 'Simpson and his donkey,' who rescued many wounded soldiers until he was killed. He was born John Simpson Kirkpatrick in South Shields, England, in 1892, went to sea at the age of seventeen, and jumped ship in Australia in 1910. He spent the next four years working at numerous jobs around the country before obtaining a position on a coastal steamer. Just after war broke out, his ship arrived in Fremantle and Kirkpatrick again jumped ship, this time to join up with the army, which he hoped would result in his being sent to Britain and allow him a chance to see his family again. However, to cover his past he signed up as John Simpson. He was assigned to the 3rd Field Ambulance as a stretcher-bearer and underwent training at Blackboy Hill Camp, where he stayed until it was time to embark.

On 14 October 1914, Simpson had written to his mother, still living in South Shields: 'Just a line to let you know that we are still in camp. We are expected to leave at any moment for the Old Country. The Transport Ships and the warships are in Fremantle waiting to take us away ... Now Mother I can't tell you exactly when we are going to leave but I don't think that we will be long now. I think that we are going to Aldershot when we get to England so I will be able to come up and see you pretty often before we go to the front.' As with everyone else, Simpson had automatically assumed that the AIF would be going to fight with the British Army in France and Flanders.

Somehow Simpson managed to smuggle his pet possum on board

the *Medic*, and it slept in his hammock while he slept on the deck beneath. However, the possum used to go walkabout and Simpson, who still retained a strong Geordie accent, was often found roaming the decks calling out, 'Where's me bliddy possum?'

Also on board *Medic*, Private J.R.T. Keast noted in his diary on the second day of the voyage that the seas were getting heavy, and '50% sick. Beer is sold once a day, 12 noon at 4d per pint ... There is terrific noise at all meal times and a good deal of quarrelling goes on over the food ... There was quite a commotion last night. The lights went out on the Portside where we sleep and some of the chaps thought it a good time to play tricks. Just as everybody was quiet, they started by tying a long rope on the hammocks and three or four getting hold of the end of it and pulling for their lives and giving everybody a rough time.' On the whole, Keast found his time on the *Medic* very boring, writing, 'a lot of time on our hands.'

In his diary, Lieutenant Ross noted that on 5 November the convoy sighted a ship coming up behind them. This caused some consternation but it turned out to be another vessel of the Orient Line, *Osterley*, on its way from Australia to England, or as Ross put it, 'going homewards,' on a commercial voyage. Two days later, Ross wrote, 'Death of Private on *Euripides* — fleet stops for funeral.' This was the first casualty of the voyage, but only two days later Ross recorded that two more privates had died, also on *Euripides*. Charles Bingham, a private with the Australian Casualty Clearance Station, also travelling on the *Euripides*, later recalled, 'there were one or two deaths on board because we had an outbreak of measles, and the measles developed into pneumonia with several fellows. We had one chap, and everyone was curious to watch a burial at sea, and the fellows were all over the ship, hanging on to the side watching the service. It was sad, but just part of the day, you know, and that was all there was to it.'

The service for a burial at sea was conducted by a chaplain, and William McKenzie on *Euripdes* wrote of one funeral,

> The body was buried at 3.30 pm. It was a solemn procedure. We marched with slow stately tread from the Hospital at the poop deck to the forward well deck, the Dean and I alternately reciting the 90 Psalm. I read the lesson, he the committal and prayer and 30 buglers sounded the last post. It was a solemn undertaking; the ship's captain was greatly moved. The band was paraded to play the national anthem and while the strains of this were floating over the water the immortal spirit of Private Loe of B Company 3rd Battalion was called to the presence of his Maker. Another

victim of pneumonia. He was a fine sweet-spirited young man of 21 years formerly resident in Surrey England.'

Referring to the daily routine at sea, Charles Bingham said:

we had physical jerks on the way, just to keep fit, and lectures — talks by the padre on morality, or immorality ... We had mess decks with big tables right along them, and we all had canvas hammocks, and the problem was that you had to stand on this table to hook these hammocks from two hooks on either side. You'd swing as you tried to get into them and fall over the other side. But they were quite comfortable and swung with the ship ... Some fellows were sick all the time all the way over, and they had great tubs there for that purpose — they were regularly cleared out and hosed out over the side. It was contagious: you'd see a man sick and it'd make you feel ill. Deliberate too, for some, because they'd talk about pork chops and things, and 'would you like some beans?', just to make them sick. I'd say about 60% of the men were sick for a week at least ... But we had a lot of fun too. We had games, boxing contests which were really good because it formed a lot of competition among the fellows.

The food was quite good. We got porridge, a lot of boiled eggs and for breakfast, toast and coffee or tea ... Then we'd have tea again at eleven, and about half past twelve would be luncheon. We'd usually have cold meat and salad, but not many fresh vegetables ... and more tea. Then there'd be tea and cake at about 4 o'clock, always big slabs of fruit cake cooked on the ship. And at night-time roast or boiled dinner, and a lot of hash. And there was always a lot of chocolate.

In addition to the troops being sent overseas as the First Australian Expeditionary Force, a party of 25 nurses also boarded the convoy. They were described in a message sent to the Secretary of State for the Colonies as 'Twenty five Australian Army Nurses, highest qualifications' and they travelled on various ships, four each on *Omrah*, *Benalla* and *Ascanius*, two each on *Geelong* and *Argyllshire*, three on *Shropshire*, and six on *Euripides*, including E.J. Gould, the principal matron of the party. All 25 held the rank of either sister or matron, but as Matron Gould later stated, 'all took part in nursing, irrespective of rank, for influenza and pneumonia accompanied us, as well as occasional cases of ptomaine poisoning. There were a few surgical operations who did very well and waves of inoculations, all requiring some little attention from Sister. The staff took it in turn to do night duty. The Matron did afternoon duty each day while others rested for two or three hours. It was a busy ship and consequently a happy one.'

Many of the troopships were also carrying horses, and on some

The Orient liner *Omrah* (A5) embarked troops in Brisbane. (*Fred Roderick collection*)

vessels the conditions for the animals were a cause of some concern. Those detailed to care for the horses had to exercise them on deck when possible, leading them up wooden ramps covered with coir matting to the open decks, and muck out the stalls. Captain Jack Hindhaugh of 1st Brigade staff, who was travelling on board the *Wiltshire*, wrote in his diary early in the voyage, 'This is a bad boat for horses, no ventilation and not able to hose out the decks. Am afraid we will lose a lot of them, poor beggars. They are on five decks ... the bottom deck is called "Little Hell" and is a terror.' By 6 November, after the ships had crossed the Tropic of Capricorn and were steaming into hotter weather, seven horses had already died aboard the *Wiltshire*, and Captain Hindhaugh was writing, 'At this rate, we won't have many horses left by the time we land in England.' As things turned out, of the 497 horses loaded aboard *Wiltshire*, 484 survived the journey.

Ascanius (A11) joined the convoy from Fremantle.

Benalla (A24) was one of several ships that also carried a number of nurses.

The reason for the convoy having such a strong escort was fear of attack by the German cruisers, in particular the *Konigsberg* and the *Emden*, which had been creating havoc in the Indian Ocean since the war started. *Konigsberg* was known to have been operating off the east coast of Africa, but could easily roam further afield. *Emden* was being hunted by some 70 British and Allied warships, but always managed to elude them.

Despite this threat, on 8 November HMS *Minotaur* was ordered to

Quarters provided for troops on the ships was extremely basic, with hammocks hung from hooks over their mess tables. (*Australian War Memorial*)

HMAS *Sydney* was diverted from escorting the convoy to the Cocos Island, where it destroyed the German cruiser *Emden*. (*Ross Gillett collection*)

leave the convoy escort, and proceed at top speed to Cape Town. This left HMAS *Melbourne* as flagship, under the command of Captain Silver. *Melbourne* then took up the leading position formerly allocated to *Minotaur*, while *Sydney* and *Ibuki* continued to protect the flanks, leaving the stern vulnerable. The course they were following would take the convoy 50 miles to the east of the Cocos Islands at about dawn on 9 November, then in a long arc gradually turning more to the west as they passed by. This was a fortuitous decision, as had the ships been routed 50 miles to the west of the Cocos Islands, on a more direct course to Colombo, they would have stood a good chance of being accidentally intercepted by the *Emden*.

Unaware of the huge convoy then proceeding across the Indian Ocean towards Ceylon, with its depleted escort, Captain Karl von Mueller of the *Emden* decided to launch an attack on the British cable installations on the Cocos Islands, arriving off their western coast on the night of 8 November. Early the next morning, *Emden* approached the signal station on Direction Island. The wireless station demanded to know its identity and when no reply was received, it broadcast a message, 'Unknown warship at harbour entrance.' Despite efforts by *Emden* to jam the signal, it was picked up very faintly by the wireless operator on *Arawa*, who passed it on to the escorting cruisers.

At that moment, the convoy was only 50 miles away, and Captain Silver at first turned *Melbourne* towards the west, heading away from the convoy at high speed. Realising that as convoy flagship he had to stay with his charges, Silver returned to the convoy. He then ordered *Sydney* to proceed to the Cocos Islands, even though the *Ibuki* was the most powerful of the escorting cruisers, and her captain argued strongly that his ship be sent. As *Sydney* departed, *Melbourne* took up her former position ahead of the convoy, with *Ibuki* remaining on the starboard flank, thus leaving the port and stern flanks unprotected.

At 9.15 am on 8 November, *Sydney* sighted *Emden* off the islands, and 25 minutes later the two ships engaged in battle. When *Sydney* reported by wireless to Captain Silver that she had sighted the enemy, the captain of the *Ibuki* immediately raised his battle ensign and asked permission to join the battle too, but Captain Silver refused, deciding that the safety of the convoy was paramount. Silver immediately swung *Melbourne* to cover the port flank of the convoy, which was closest to the Cocos Islands, at the same time ordering *Ibuki* to join him on the port flank, so that both cruisers were between the *Emden* and the convoy, should the German ship survive.

The officers on *Emden* at first thought the approaching cruiser was the smaller HMS *Newcastle*, and they began firing their main armaments at extreme range. *Sydney* was soon moving through a solid barrage of shells, but sustained few hits. It was only after several salvos in reply that *Sydney* began to hit *Emden*, but the Australian cruiser soon had her shells falling on target. After 90 minutes *Emden* was a total wreck and was run aground to prevent it sinking. *Sydney* remained in the area all day, in case another German ship was in the vicinity, but the only arrival was the British armed merchant cruiser *Empress of Asia*, which had been searching for the *Emden*. The survivors from *Emden*, which had suffered 134 dead and 65 wounded, were taken aboard *Empress of Asia* and carried to Colombo. *Sydney*, which had four dead and twelve wounded from the battle, remained in the area of the Cocos Islands for several days before making her way towards Colombo, where she arrived on the night of 15 November.

With the threat posed by *Emden* disposed of, the convoy could continue its voyage in greater safety, and when word was received next day that the *Konigsberg* had been located off the coast of Africa there were no other marauding warships to be wary of. Despite this, the escort was increased when HMS *Hampshire* joined on 11 November and took over as flagship. As the convoy approached Ceylon, the ten New Zealand transports and three carrying Australian troops were sent ahead without escort, arriving in Colombo on 15 November to take on bunkers, water and supplies. The rest of the convoy, along with *Hampshire*, *Melbourne* and *Ibuki*, reached Colombo the following day. It was here that the survivors from the *Emden*, including her captain, were put on board *Orvieto* and two other ships, to be taken to Britain.

Despite this being the first time Australian troops had been moved in a convoy, the results were extremely good. On the transports, four men had died of pneumonia, while 142 horses had died, but this was a considerably smaller attrition rate than had been expected. The enormous success of the *Sydney* in defeating *Emden*, combined with the news that *Konigsberg* had been destroyed in another naval action a few days earlier, meant the Indian Ocean was now swept clean of enemy warships and there was no necessity for the convoy to have a strong escort. As a result, the convoy left Colombo in three divisions, depending on speed. The slowest ships left on 17 November, and as they departed one of them, *Anglo-Egyptian*, touched the breakwater, but suffered minimal damage and continued with the other ships. At intervals the second and third divisions also departed, the two groups forming up into a convoy on 20 November, and the next day they caught up with the first division. They were escorted by *Hampshire* and *Ibuki*, as both *Melbourne* and *Sydney* had been ordered to proceed at top speed to Malta to join the British Mediterranean Fleet. Instead they were sent on into the Atlantic.

Crossing the Arabian Sea there was a collision, when *Ascanius* rammed the stern of *Shropshire*. The ships remained locked together for a short time, but on separating, *Ascanius* managed to strike *Shropshire* a second time. The accident left a large hole in the bow of *Ascanius* and damage to the stern of *Shropshire*, all fortunately above the water line, and both ships continued. The troops on board both ships were sent to their evacuation stations, but there was no panic and lifeboats were not lowered.

When the convoy had left Colombo, their ultimate destination was still Britain, but this was in the process of being changed. The plan

Shropshire (A9) was involved in a collision with *Ascanius* (A11) in the Indian Ocean.

had been for the Australian and New Zealand troops to disembark in England and then be transported to a camp on Salisbury Plain, in the south of the country, but in December a very cold and bleak place. The Australian High Commissioner in London, Sir George Reid, had been advised that a contingent of Canadian troops who had used the camp already had found the conditions terrible. Reid was so concerned for the wellbeing of the Australian troops, en route to the same destination and who would soon be passing through the Suez Canal, he decided not to proceed through normal diplomatic channels, which could take weeks Instead, he picked up the telephone and make direct contact with Lord Kitchener, the Minister of State for War. Fortunately, Reid was one of the few men who could make direct contact with the minister and his proposal that the Australian and New Zealand troops be disembarked in Egypt for training soon met with approval.

The convoy arrived in Aden on 25 November, anchoring in the vast roadstead off the port, which was already thronged with ships of all types and sizes. The following day, the convoy departed Aden. The transit of the Red Sea was made more difficult because the coastlines under Turkish control no longer displayed lights, and it was also reported that the Turks had dropped mines in some of the channels. In a subsequent report, Captain Gordon Smith wrote:

> The absence of lights in the southern part of the Red Sea caused us a little anxiety. There are a lot of rocks and small islands scattered about near the entrance, and the currents are strong and rather irregular. We took a very unusual route on account of the possibility of mines. Fortunately the weather was clear, and the captain of the *Orvieto*, having passed through it regularly six times a year, knew the Red Sea from end to end.
>
> It was a good thing he did. On the first night we sighted ahead the shadowy shapes of a group of islands that ought not to have been there according to our reckoning; the convoy was steering straight for them. The question was, on which side should we go? The captain, fortunately, recognised one of the lumps by its outline, and we just had time to signal an alteration of course, which took us clear of the whole group. It was a bit exciting. We barely cleared them. If we had tried to pass on the other side we should have put the whole convoy on a rocky shoal.

For the troops, the passage up the Red Sea was extremely uncomfortable, due to the extreme heat. Private Keast recorded in his diary, 'Slept on deck last night and found it almost as oppressive as below.'

On 26 November, Reid sent a message to General Bridges which read, 'Unforeseen circumstances decide that the force shall train in Egypt and go to the front from there. The Australians and New Zealanders are to form a corps under General Birdwood. The locality of the camp is near Cairo.' When this change of plan was publicised, *The Times*, reported: 'it was learned that owing to the situation in Egypt, due to the attitude of Turkey and the adhesion of the Khedive to the Turkish side, the Australians were to remain for the time in Egypt itself to complete their training there, strengthen the British garrison on the spot and help defend the Suez Canal against any possible land attacks.'

As a result of the change in destination, *Orvieto* and *Maunganui*, which carried the commanders of the Australian and New Zealand contingents, were sent on ahead of the other ships and arrived in Suez on 30 November. The commanders immediately set to work on plans for disembarking the troops and their horses and having them transported to the designated training area. This posed several problems. At Suez the ships could only offload their troops and horses from outside the port into lighters, while at Port Said only one or two ships at a time could go alongside. However, at Alexandria there was space for up to eight ships at a time and a direct rail link to Cairo. As a result, the convoy moved through the Suez Canal, arriving in Port

Orvieto arriving in Port Said, 2 December 1914. (*Australian War Memorial*)

Said on 2 December, with the ten New Zealand transports and some of the Australian ships arriving in Alexandria the following day, to be joined by the remaining ships as space permitted.

There had been a few deaths on the trip, but nothing exceptional, but the men were still glad to be off the ships and back on dry land. It had been expected that, of the 7843 horses that accompanied the Australian troops, as many as 15 percent would not survive the voyage. Precautions taken before departing to ensure their survival had included a flow of fresh air into all horse decks, and a regimen of regular cleaning and massage during the voyage, with the result that only 224 horses — about 3 percent — failed to arrive in Egypt.

The Australian and New Zealand troops were transported through Cairo to an area south of the city, in the area of Mena, within sight of the pyramids. Here they had to establish their camp in the desert, where they completed their training, and also had the opportunity to take in the local sights when on leave. In late December 1914, Sir George Reid arrived in Egypt to inspect the troops, who no doubt were thankful to him for changing their destination from the cold, muddy plains of England in winter to the warm desert.

Meanwhile, in Australia and New Zealand a second contingent of troops was being gathered together. The second convoy, transporting 10,500 Australians and 2000 New Zealanders, was to have comprised nineteen ships, of which seven were over 10,000 gross tons. Among these were two ships of the P & O Branch Line, which had been converted by Cockatoo Dockyard in Sydney. *Borda* (A30) was fitted out to carry 26 officers, 550 other ranks, and 260 horses, while *Berrima* (A35) could transport 60 officers and 1500 other ranks, with no space for horses. *Berrima* had previously been fitted with guns, and was in addition to serve as the escort to the convoy. In addition, *Berrima* would be towing the submarine *AE 2* all the way to Egypt, from where it would be sent into the Mediterranean.

Ulysses (A38) of Blue Funnel Line and *Themistocles* (A32) of the Aberdeen Line were also requisitioned, along with three large White Star Line vessels, *Suevic* (A29), *Persic* (A34) and *Ceramic* (A40), at that time the largest liner serving Australia, which was converted to carry 2800 troops. There were also five German ships, *Cannstatt, Hobart, Melbourne, Pfalz* and *Sumatra*, that had been seized in Australian ports when war broke out and were now being operated by the Australian government. These ships were renamed *Bakara, Barambah, Boonah, Boorara* and *Barunga*. The other ships to be included in the Australian section of the convoy were *Vestalia*

Two of the larger vessels to carry Australian troops in the second convoy were *Borda* (A30) and *Themistocles* (A32).

(A44), *Ayrshire* (A33), *Ajana* (A31) and *Port Macquarie* (A39). The New Zealand contingent was to be transported in three ships, *Verdala* (NZ13), *Knight of the Garter* (NZ15) and *Willochra* (NZ14) which was actually owned by the Adelaide Steam Ship Co., but on charter to the Union Steam Ship Company of New Zealand.

As with the first convoy, the ships of the second embarked their troops and horses at various ports, then voyaged individually to King George Sound. Among those boarding the *Ulysses* in Melbourne on 22 December was the Rev. Andrew Gillison, a Presbyterian minister from Melbourne, who would be going as chaplain to the 13th Battalion.

Willochra (NZ14) carried New Zealand troops in the second convoy.

On embarkation day farewelled his wife at home, and later wrote, 'Today I said goodbye. I made it as short as I could. The circumstances made it doubly hard to me, but especially to Isobel … Some of the officers wives were foolish enough to come down. It was hard enough for them without adding to the pain by witnessing the actual departure. The band played stirring airs — "Tipperary," "Australia will be there" etc. and patriotic airs. We lay off Williamstown for the night, and started at daybreak. The embarkation was much delayed so that officers and men went without food from breakfast till 8 pm.' Andrew Gillison was one of the few Australian chaplains killed during the war, dying of wounds at Gallipoli on 22 August 1915.

The captured German vessel *Bakara* was left behind when the convoy departed. (*Fred Roderick collection*)

The horse transport *Ayrshire* (A33) was unable to maintain the convoy speed. (*Fred Roderick collection*)

All the ships assigned to the second convoy were assembled in King George Sound by 28 December 1914. However, when the convoy departed on 31 December, two of the ex-German ships, *Bakara* and *Barunga*, which were transporting horses, had to be left behind. *Bakara* had arrived in King George Sound with a fire in her coal bunkers, which was not extinguished until 29 December, following which her coal had to be discharged, while *Barunga* developed engine problems on the day the convoy was due to leave.

On 2 January 1915, the *Ajana* joined the convoy, having embarked her troops in Fremantle. So the second convoy finally comprised seventeen troop and horse transports. By the time they departed, the seas on which they would travel had been swept clean of all enemy shipping, so, instead of the heavy escort provided for the first convoy, the second convoy was only protected by *Berrima*, which was also carrying troops and in addition towing *AE 2*. Once *Ajana* joined, the ships formed up in their convoy positions, in three columns, these being:

	Berrima (A35)	
Ceramic (A40)	*Ulysses* (A38)	*Themistocles* (A32)
Persic (A34)	*Vestalia* (A44)	*Suevic* (A29)
Borda (A30)	*Boonah* (A36)	*Ajana* (A31)
Willochra (NZ14)	*Barambah* (A37)	*Port Macquarie* (A39)
Verdala (NZ13)		*Boorara* (A42)
Knight of the Garter (NZ15)	*Ayrshire* (A33)	

The ships remained in this formation for several days as they crossed the Indian Ocean, bound for Colombo, but it was then discovered that the three White Star liners, *Ceramic*, *Suevic* and *Persic*, were running short of coal and they were diverted to a direct course to Aden. After they detached, *Borda* was moved to the starboard column, astern of *Themistocles*, leaving the three New Zealand transports alone forming the port column. One other ship gradually dropped out of the convoy, as *Ayrshire*, which was transporting horses only, was unable to maintain convoy speed and slowly dropped behind.

The voyage was almost free of incident, the only problems arising when the towline connecting *AE 2* to *Berrima* broke on several occasions and the submarine was forced to proceed under its own power until the line was reconnected. Lance Corporal G.C. Grove recorded that the days were filled with such diversions as knot-tying lessons, rifle cleaning, physical drill, semaphore practice, rifle exercises, tug-of-war practice, bedding inspection and sports. In one period of bad weather a heavy sea crashed through many open portholes, and the men spent a long time cleaning up the mess.

During the call at Colombo, no shore leave was allowed. Grove noted that 'Coolies came aboard selling papers, postcards, beads, coins, cigarettes, and catamarans with bananas, pineapples and coconuts manoeuvred alongside for trade.' An armed guard was posted, but 'men broke leave and sneaked ashore down anchor chains and ropes into boats kept waiting by coolies ... Armed guards sent into Colombo to try to bring back absentees. Roll-call of all troops — about 60 missing.' Apparently the guards had a great deal of trouble rounding up the absentees, but once they were back on board they found themselves serving double-shifts as coal trimmers.

From Colombo, the convoy continued towards Aden, arriving off there on 24 January. Once again, no shore leave was allowed, but the ships were again surrounded by Arabs in boats selling fruit and other items. Waiting to rejoin the convoy at Aden were the three White Star liners that had missed the call at Colombo. The day after leaving Aden, Grove noted, 'eye disease caught by 200 men on board, certain parts of the ship in quarantine. About 50 men suddenly seized with ptomaine poisoning.' On 28 January, after a seven week voyage, the convoy arrived in Suez, being joined the next day by *Bakara*, one of the ex-German ships left behind in King George Sound.

By the time the second convoy arrived at the southern end of the Suez Canal, Turkish forces had advanced to within striking distance of the waterway on the eastern side and some British outposts on the western side of the canal had already come under enemy fire. It was feared that the ships might also come under fire as they transited the canal, but the passage was uneventful, the transports arrived safely in Port Said, and later continued on to Alexandria to disembark their troops on 1 February. After completing four months training in Egypt, these troops, subsequently known as the Australian and New Zealand Army Corps, or ANZAC, were sent on to the Dardanelles in April 1915, taking part in the landing at Gallipoli later that month. The survivors of the Australian force were transferred to France at the end of 1915, and served on the Western Front for the remainder of the war.

Unlike the global conflict that existed in World War II, World War I was fought mainly in Europe, and in parts of the Middle East. For the duration of the conflict, Australian and New Zealand troops were dispatched overseas on a variety of ships, most of which were normally engaged in the trades to Australia and New Zealand, and requisitioned by the Australian government for just one voyage. Subsequently, transports were often dispatched singly, with no naval escort, though some still voyaged in groups. For official purposes, these were generally referred to as convoys, but the departure dates of the ships could be spread over as many as three months.

The third contingent of Australian troops was sent overseas during February 1915, followed by the fourth contingent in April and a fifth in June. In late May and June a variety of ships carried 14,000 Australian troops overseas, and these were referred to as Convoy 6. When the 3rd Division, comprising over 25,000 troops, was sent overseas in June 1916, this was known as Convoy 21.

Among the troops in Convoy 6 was the 13th Australian Light Horse Regiment, the third such regiment to be raised in Victoria since the war started. Formed in March 1915, they were based at Broadmeadows Camp until 28 May 1915, when they paraded through the streets of Melbourne. The parade had one unsettling moment, when the horse carrying Captain Mitchell slipped on the wet road surface and was thrown to the ground, hurting his knee, though he remounted and finished the route to Port Melbourne where the *Persic* (A34), which had taken part in the first convoy, was waiting for them. This time the vessel would be sailing alone. When the regiment reached Port Melbourne, the horses were first given a swim in the bay before being loaded, walking up ramps to the ship's deck. Some horse boxes had been erected on the deck, while other horses were led down into the holds, where they were backed into stalls that had been erected for them, and where they would remain standing throughout the voyage.

Once the men and horses were on board, *Persic* departed. As the ship entered the Great Australian Bight, conditions worsened. Captain Mitchell kept a diary, and wrote on 30 May, when he was still laid up with a sore knee, 'Great number of the lads sick. Sea fairly rough.' Next day he noted, 'Sea very rough especially after midday. Storm coming up ... Major Geyer has been sick ever since leaving Melbourne.' The bad weather continued into 1 June, as 'Rough sea today ... Storm all night. Horse boxes washed away. McLeod & Kerr got hurt.' Next day he noted, 'Storm easing off, still rough. Buried 2nd horse today.' By 3 June the storm had passed, Mitchell writing, 'Nice calm day today. I was up nearly all day. Passed Cape Leeuwin and saw vessel going into Albany.'

As the weather settled down, life on board *Persic* settled into a routine. The horses required constant care, being watered from canvas buckets, and fed from bales of hay which were stacked in the middle of the holds. Stalls were mucked out each day, and the horses' legs were massaged to alleviate the effects of continual standing. When the ship was rolling and pitching in rough weather, these tasks were quite difficult. The movement of the ship also caused sores on the flanks of the horses where they rubbed against the rails dividing their stalls.

As the *Persic* steamed into warmer climes, conditions became uncomfortable for the troops, but in the holds where the horses were stabled they were almost unbearable. To overcome the heat problem, the ship's crew rigged huge canvas windsails to direct fresh air into the holds. When *Persic* crossed the equator on 15 June, Captain Mitchell recorded, 'Neptune and spouse held solemn court in afternoon. All the officers and most of crew initiated. Sports all the afternoon. Rained heavily at night and spoilt concert. Very rough night.'

Apart from some horses dying, men were also coming down with illnesses, including pneumonia. On 16 June, Mitchell noted, 'Went in to see Pte Smith bad with pneumonia. Died at 10.30 am and was buried at 1.45 pm.' *Persic* passed Aden on 21 June, and arrived at Suez on the evening of the 26th. However, the regiment did not disembark until three days later, then were transported to Abbasia by train, a journey lasting seven hours, with twenty men and eight horses per rail truck.

On 14 July the Orient liner *Orsova* left Sydney with a complement of troops bound for the Middle East. Among those on board were Bill Mair, who had previously gone to New Guinea on the *Berrima*, and his nephew, Harold Campbell. On the way from Sydney to Melbourne Harold wrote a short letter to his mother, in which he said, 'We are almost in Melbourne now. The weather is quite calm. I was a little bit sick yesterday morning, but I feel the benefit of it now ... We get splendid tucker here: ham, fish, porridge, soup. All good, fit for anyone. We expect to get a full boat load here.'

A few days later Harold wrote,

> When we got to Melbourne, of course no leave was given, so when night came about 20 climbed overboard and the guard collared them and brought them back. And when the rest saw them they rushed the gangway and about 150 got out.' More troops had joined the ship in Melbourne, bringing the number on board up to 1600. After leaving Melbourne, 'We have had rather a rough time this last two days, crossing the Bight. It hasn't been what you would call real rough weather, but it has been squally and swells with a corkscrew motion, meeting the boat half-side on. About two-thirds of the boys are more or less sick. I've been holding out pretty well — neither one thing or the other. I retch one meal up a day. Sunday it was supper, Monday it was dinner and this morning it was breakfast, but I feel rather good just now ... Last night we had stewed rabbit for tea ... We get a complete change every meal — never get the same thing twice. So we are not too bad off. Everybody is on deck, rolled up in overcoat and blankets, making pillows of one and another ... We are going to try and get a route march at Fremantle to get a bit of a change. Of course, we are never satisfied.

In his next letter home, Harold Campbell noted he expected 'the censor will cross a few things out', which duly happened.

> We have had a splendid trip since [censored, probably Fremantle]. We crossed the line this morning about 4 o'clock. There was hardly a ripple on the sea — it was just like glass. One could hardly credit it. We are learning semaphore signalling now. It is very interesting besides very useful. We all have to go bare-footed on the boat in the hot weather. It is beautiful weather now. I can eat like a bloomin' horse — don't seem to be able to get enough. The tucker is very good and plenty of it.
>
> Somehow we are having an eight day sports competition on board. It runs as follows: Boxing, different weights; pillow fighting on the spar; cockfighting; potato race; tug of war; wheelbarrow race and several others ... The day before yesterday [Australia Day] we had a concert. It was very good ... We will soon be to [censored] now and I won't be sorry when we land. We have no idea where we are going to.'

Towards the end of the letter, Harold wrote,

> The sea is a bit rough today and I'm not feeling the best. I've got a bit of a headache, but that will soon wear off.' However, in his next letter, written from Suez on 16 August, Harold explained, 'As you will see I am in hospital, suffering from pneumonia. I have been ill for seven days now and I'm

only just able to move now. It took me very suddenly.' Harold then went on to explain how he took part in the tug of war on board ship on 9 August and went to bed as usual. When he woke 'about four in the morning I felt cold, then my head started to ache and dull pains started coming around my heart and seemed to be catching my breath, so I sat up for about 20 minutes. It eased for a while but started again, so I walked down to the well deck and sat down. Inside a minute I could hardly breathe and was in severe pain. That was about five o'clock. They carried me into the hospital and injected strychnine into me to keep the heart going. We got to Suez on Thursday and me and some more were removed to this hospital. It is a fine place and we are well looked after.

Harold's uncle, Bill Mair, wrote to one of his nieces about Harold's illness, saying that on the night he became ill, 'we were all sleeping on the deck on account of the fearful heat.' As to the trip, 'We had a splendid voyage across. The old *Orsova* was a splendid boat. There were other boats left Fremantle at the same time as us, some three days before us, but we beat them all to the Canal. We caught and passed everything on the trip. Yes, she was a fine boat and we enjoyed ourselves immensely and plenty of good food.'

As well as troops and horses, the ships also carried regular cargo, mostly foodstuffs that were desperately needed in Britain. After delivering their troops to Egypt, the ships would continue to Britain to unload their cargo, but this was sometimes a protracted business, as ports were very congested. Some ships made more than one voyage with Australian troops, and many were converted by Cockatoo Island Dockyard in Sydney. Work began there on *Clan MacGillivray* (A46) on 29 December 1914, and when completed on 23 January 1915 the vessel was equipped to transport 1107 men. *Clan MacEwan* (A65) had space for 450 horses, and 126 men to look after them, while *Uganda* (A66) could transport 136 men and 180 horses. Several ships that had taken part in the first convoy returned to Australia, and made further trips with troops. Between 19 April and 12 May 1915 *Ascanius* (A11) was refitted to transport 1820 men as well as twelve horses, while *Medic* (A7) was converted during May 1915 to carry 531 men and 500 horses, and *Afric* (A19) was refitted to carry 549 men and 500 horses. As the organisers and workers became more familiar with the requirements of converting ships, the time taken for the work to be completed was reduced. In June 1915, the 11,000 gross ton *Demosthenes* was converted in just 60 hours to carry 1500 troops, while it only took 53 hours to

The Orient liner *Orsova* carried Australian troops overseas, but not in a convoy.

transform the cargo ship *Palermo* to take 360 horses.

From 1915, many Australian liners were also requisitioned for duty as troopships or hospital ships. *Karoola*, owned by McIlwraith, McEacharn Ltd, was requisitioned on 9 May 1915, and after embarking troops at Brisbane, Sydney and Fremantle, left for Egypt on 25 June, accompanied by *Wandilla* of the Adelaide Steam Ship Co., which was also carrying troops. *Kanowna* of the Australasian United Steam Navigation Company, which had briefly been requisitioned in August 1914, was taken over again on 1 June 1915 and converted by Cockatoo Island to carry 1100 troops. This vessel then made one trip to Egypt with troops before proceeding to Britain, where it was converted into a hospital ship, as were *Karoola* and *Wandilla*. The New Zealand government tended to use their own ships on a longer term basis. Two New Zealand liners, *Tahiti* and *Maunganui*, made numerous trips to the Middle East and Britain with troops.

The transportation of horses overseas was also a vital part of World War I. The first six convoys to leave Australia carried 25,000 horses, while from January to April 1916 a further 7000 were sent in four convoys, but in twelve convoys there were no horses carried at all. This was mainly due to the voyage of the *Palermo*, which left Australia in May 1915 with 360 horses, of which half died en route to Egypt.

There were some instances where the troops were treated very badly on board the transports. One example of this occurred in May 1915, on board the transport *Ulysses*, as recorded by Lance Corporal Ivor Birtwistle, of the 22nd Battalion. There were irritating restrictions on movement around the ship, and considerable upset at the prices being charged for purchases from the Soldiers Institute canteen on board, with Birtwistle noting, 'Just forced to pay 1/6 for a tin of ordinary fig jam.' When the ship stopped at Colombo, only officers and sergeants were granted shore leave, while the troops were sent on a route march through the town on a very hot day, and 'Nearly every man was angry and grumbling for we were forbidden to buy any fruit from natives who haunted us.'

Those troops who did sneak ashore, and were caught, were severely punished. The canteen had been replenished in Colombo, and again charged exorbitant prices. On 27 May, a few days after departing Colombo, resentment about the punishment handed out to leave-breakers and the canteen prices overflowed and a situation of near mutiny prevailed. Officers were unable to pacify the troops, who eventually broke into the canteen and looted it, then removed the doors from the punishment cells, releasing all the men inside. Eventually the 22nd Battalion's second in command, Major Smith, was able to reduce the tension, following which the Brigadier promised that the men's grievances would be given attention. As a result, the pricing policy of the canteen was amended, and the punishment meted out to leave-breakers reduced.

In 1916, when travelling on the *Berrima*, F.L. Goldthorpe recorded how 'The cooks kept us short of food but made amends by selling it to us in the form of sandwiches after dusk, and every evening when a normal man gets a bit of a thirst, all the drinking taps were turned off. About half an hour later a man would stroll up out of the cook's galley with two buckets of weak lemonade, which he kindly disbursed at 2d a glass. It was the sort of lemonade which left a dry taste in the throat and calls for another glass to wash it away. What a wonderful thing commerce is!'

On 30 May 1916 the 24th Company of the Army Services Corps boarded the White Star liner *Persic* in Sydney and sailed off to the Middle East. Among those on board was Wallace Campbell, who wrote to his mother as the ship neared Melbourne, 'I have had a good trip. Never got a bit seasick, and I am in good health and spirits. A lot of the boys got very sick. The sea has been pretty rough ... We are having a good time on board. Good hammocks to sleep in and plenty of good tucker. Better than we ever got in camp.'

Arriving in Melbourne on 2 June, Wallace wrote: 'After an uneventful journey we arrived at Port Melbourne about two o'clock

PM and were allowed ashore until Midnight, during which time I enjoyed myself well ... We leave Melbourne about one o'clock tomorrow afternoon. We are taking on board about sixty wagons and a thousand men.' Five days later,

> We are nearly across the Great Australian Bight and the sea has been pretty rough. The poor Victorians have been very sick, but I'm still alright. We get to Albany tomorrow night where we will be joined by more transports and an escort of Japanese cruisers. So Mum, our journey ought to be pretty safe. This old boat is a good sea boat. She rides the sea very well indeed. It's been rough enough to break over the deck, so that's not too calm, is it ... We have 1,600 men aboard now, so there's not much room. Our food is good and we get plenty of fruit from our Comforts Stores on board.

There is no record of other letters Wallace Campbell wrote on the voyage, but on 28 July he sent a letter from Salisbury Camp in England. The *Persic* had arrived on 25 July in Plymouth, where the troops all disembarked. As the ship was bound for England, rather than the Middle East, it had proceeded from Albany to South Africa, then travelled through the Atlantic to reach Plymouth.

About the voyage, Wallace wrote,

> All went well until after we left Albany. We had seventeen hundred troops on board, and my word, I can tell you that we hardly had enough room to change our minds in! But worse than that, spinal meningitis broke out on board. It started among the Victorians first. It was amongst them at Seymour Camp. There were 3 or 4 cases every day, and then it spread to us and the Queenslanders. One of our men and seven Queenslanders were taken ill. It takes a man very suddenly ... Fortunately we had a very clever doctor on board, and only one man died, a young Queenslander. Eighteen years old, poor little chap. He was buried at sea. It was a sad sight to see him buried in the blue waves of the Atlantic Ocean. It spoilt all our sports on board and what promised to be a good trip developed into a nightmare.

Throughout the first three years of the war, there was a continual flow of transports from Australia to Britain, but as the greater part of their voyaging was done in seas that had been swept clean of enemy warships and raiders, there was seldom any danger. However, once these ships reached the waters surrounding Britain, the danger of submarine attack was considerable, and several ships that had carried Australian troops to Britain were sunk, though after their troops had disembarked, and only one transport actually carrying Australian troops was sunk.

Ballarat was the only vessel carrying Australian troops to be sunk in World War I.

This was the *Ballarat*, which left Melbourne on 19 February 1917 on her fourth voyage as a transport, carrying 1600 troops. Stopping at Cape Town, the coal taken on there was of an inferior quality, and once the good Australian coal had been exhausted the ship could barely manage 9 knots, which slowed the convoy she had joined at Sierra Leone. At the entrance to the English Channel the convoy dispersed, *Ballarat* being escorted by the destroyer HMS *Phoenix* as she headed towards Plymouth, but her speed was now down to just 8 knots. On 25 April an Anzac Day service was about to begin on board *Ballarat* when the ship was struck by a torpedo, which soon caused the engines to stop. As attempts were made to tow the stricken vessel into shallow water, all 1752 persons on board were rescued by destroyers, a result due primarily to the discipline of both troops and crew. *Ballarat* eventually sank several miles off the British coast.

There were still convoys being sent away from Australia and New Zealand during 1917. One combined convoy departed in May 1917. New Zealand troops were transported aboard *Pakeha* (FO1), *Tofua* (NZ83) and *Turakina* (NZ48), which was also the flagship. They were escorted to Fremantle by the British cruisers HMS *Doris* and HMS *Psyche*. Meanwhile, a number of other ships had boarded Australian troops in Sydney and Melbourne, then made their way independently to Fremantle. Among these vessels were *Port Sydney* (A15), *Suffolk* (A23), *Benalla* (A24), *Ulysses* (A38), *Marathon* (A74), *Shropshire* (A9), *Ascanius* (A11), *Boorara* (A42) and *Clan MacGillivray*. The combined convoy departed Fremantle on 22 May, escorted only by the cruiser HMS *Encounter*. They crossed the Indian Ocean to Port Louis in Mauritius, leaving there on 5 June with two Japanese cruisers as escort as far as Cape Town. Departing Cape Town on 22 June, they were escorted by the armed merchant cruiser *Orama*, formerly of the Orient Line, to

Freetown, where the escort duty was taken over by another armed merchant cruiser, the former P & O liner *Mantua*, for the final leg to Britain. On 17 July, as the convoy entered the dangerous waters off the French coast, six British destroyers of the L class were added to the escort, and the convoy arrived safely in Plymouth on 19 July.

Four years after the war began there appeared no sign that it was nearing a conclusion, and troops continued to be dispatched from Australia. On 23 September 1918, the Australian liner *Wyreema*, which had been retained on the coastal trade throughout the conflict, was finally requisitioned and converted into a troopship in Sydney. In October, the vessel departed with a full load of troops, as well as a group of nursing sisters, all bound for duty in Europe. However, the Armistices was signed before the ship reached South Africa, and on arriving in Cape Town *Wyreema* was ordered to return to Australia. This trip was to end in tragedy.

During the last year of the war, a major influenza epidemic swept through Europe, killing troops and civilians of all countries. It was hoped that the epidemic would not reach Australia, being so far away from Europe, but some of the troops returning home were already infected. A captured German vessel, *Boonah*, had been carrying a contingent of Australian troops home, having completed their term of service in Europe, and reached Cape Town at the same time as *Wyreema*. *Boonah* departed two days after *Wyreema* on the way to Australia, but the influenza was spreading rapidly through the troops on board. At a later date, Lieutenant Colonel P.M. McFarlane, commanding officer of the troops on board *Wyreema*, was to write:

> The troopship *Boonah* was two days behind us and we picked up her wireless messages nightly, detailing the daily increasing number of men suffering from pneumonia influenza. The West Australian Commandant asked me to land twenty nursing sisters to help nurse the *Boonah* patients at the Quarantine Station. Volunteers were called for and there was not only a ready response but so many offered that it was necessary to place the names in a hat and draw the twenty required. They knew perfectly well the enormous risk they were taking. Yet they were eager to undertake the work and those whose names were not drawn were disappointed.

The *Boonah* arrived at the Quarantine Station at Woodman Point, in an isolated area a short distance from Fremantle, and 300 troops were landed, far more than the facility could adequately handle. One sister recorded that 'There was little that could be done for the cyanosis, the croupy cough, the delirium and the final unconsciousness.' Even

An influenza epidemic swept through the troops aboard *Boonah* when it was returning them to Australia in 1918.

the nursing sisters became infected, and four died, along with most of the stricken troops. So widespread was the influenza epidemic that in the year after the war ended 15 million people died from the outbreak, compared to 8 million deaths in the four years of war.

The *Wyreema* continued her voyage as far as Adelaide, when another change of orders resulted in the vessel departing on 27 December, once again bound for England, this time via the Suez Canal, arriving in Liverpool in February 1919, where she was to board Australian troops being transported home. However, the influenza epidemic caught up with the vessel once again, this time sweeping through the crew, of whom fifteen died. It was not until 13 April 1919 that the *Wyreema* was able to depart, carrying troops and their families back to Australia.

In all, Australia dispatched five infantry divisions, known as the Australian Imperial Force, to the Middle East and Europe during World War I. A total of 331,000 Australians enlisted for overseas service, of whom 63,000 were killed and 152,000 wounded, a particularly high casualty rate which was the result of the callous manner in which Australian troops were used by the British High Command.

4 Between the Wars

For two decades after 1919, World War I, or The Great War as it was then called, was referred to as 'the war to end all wars' and many believed that such a major conflict would never occur again. The victors considered that Germany, having been decimated by the war and the subsequent Treaty of Versailles, was no longer a threat to European peace. With this false sense of security, most nations, including Great Britain and the United States, reduced their armed forces. However, the Japanese, who had fought alongside the British, did not go along with this theory, and began a major development of their armed forces, particularly the navy, which came to be seen as a potential threat to British possessions in the Far East and Pacific, including Australia and New Zealand.

In 1920, Britain maintained a small naval presence in eastern waters, but had no major base in the region. To counter the Japanese threat, the Admiralty proposed the establishment of a naval base in the Far East, and an Eastern Fleet, though it would be composed only of older cruisers and smaller vessels. It was implied that, should a serious situation occur in the region, capital ships could be rushed from Europe. Four sites were considered for the location of the base, with Hong Kong and Trincomalee, in Ceylon, being quickly discarded as too isolated and vulnerable. Consideration was then given to Sydney and Singapore, with the latter finally being selected in June 1921 because of its better strategic position. Explaining his government's reasons for establishing the base, Arthur Balfour explained to the Imperial Conference that, 'We have come to the conclusion that one of the pressing needs for Imperial defence is that Singapore should be made into a place where the British fleet can concentrate for the defence of the Empire ... and for that purpose it is absolutely necessary to undertake works at Singapore.' This was a decision that, two decades later, would have a major impact on Australia and her armed forces.

There was already a small naval base at Singapore, in Keppel Harbour, but it was decided that the new base would be built on the other side of the island, on the Johore Strait. It was further distant from the open sea, reducing the chance of a naval bombardment, and well clear of the commercial shipping lanes and docks of Singapore City. In addition, plans were drawn up to construct a Royal Air Force base at Seletar to handle both land and sea planes.

In November 1921, at the Washington Naval Conference, Britain, France, Italy and Japan met with the United States to establish limits on naval power and expansion. Much to the relief of Britain, Japan agreed to restrict their naval strength to 60 percent of that of both the Royal Navy and the United States Navy. They were also not allowed to build any new bases in territories they had captured in the final stages of the war. At the same time, the British were not to build a base in Hong Kong, nor the Americans in the Philippines, but this did not prevent them from establishing new facilities at Singapore and Hawaii.

Despite the decision made in 1921, construction of the new base was slow to start. In 1924, the Labour Party won government in Britain and decided not to proceed, but Labour were defeated at an early election and the new Conservative government reinstated the plan. However, construction still proceeded very slowly, according to the whims of successive governments and ministers. It was not until 15 February 1938 that the Singapore base was completed, being officially opened by the Governor of the Straits Settlements. Among those in attendance was the Japanese Consul General in Singapore. Centrepiece of the base was the King George VI Graving Dock, capable of handling the largest Royal Navy warships, not to mention the largest merchant ships then afloat. There was also a smaller floating dock. Eighteen vessels were present at the opening, the cruiser HMS *Norfolk* being flagship of the Eastern Fleet, but no battleships or aircraft carriers were present, nor was it planned that any would join the Eastern Fleet.

When the Singapore Naval Base was under construction, some attention was given to the defence of the island. At that time any aggressive attack was thought to be only likely from an enemy fleet, as the jungle of the Malay Peninsula was regarded as being impassable, so the main defences and coastal guns were mounted facing the sea. It was not until 1937 that the General Officer Commanding in Malaya, Major General Dobbie, came to the conclusion that it might be possible for enemy troops to be landed on the east coast of Malaya and subsequently launch an attack on Singapore from the north, or landward side. This view did not receive much support, although a small amount of defensive work was carried out along the coastline.

While the British, and the Australians saw the Singapore base as a vital link in the defence of eastern outposts of the Empire, the Japanese looked upon it as an offensive outpost from which the British could launch attacks against their ships and trade routes. Having made military advances through Manchuria in 1932, and entered China the following year, in 1937 the Japanese had inaugurated savage attacks against Chinese cities, then withdrew from the League of Nations. In 1934, the Japanese had rescinded their agreement to the conditions imposed by the 1921 Washington Naval Conference and begun a program of major fleet expansion and modernisation, as the Germans were to do a few years later. The path to future conflict was being laid, and the opening of the Singapore Naval Base was a further catalyst in this process.

As a result of the Washington Naval Conference, in the years between 1920 and 1939 the Royal Navy took delivery of only two new battleships, HMS *Nelson* and HMS *Rodney*, and one battle cruiser, HMS *Hood*, which in fact was the largest warship afloat. This gave Britain a fleet of fifteen battleships and battle cruisers, but most were out of date, as were most of their six aircraft carriers. The United States Navy had also not modernised or enlarged their naval fleet, while the French fleet consisted of five battleships and one aircraft carrier.

The Japanese, after abandoning their agreement to honour the terms of the 1921 conference, began building a new fleet, while the Germans were also keen to add new capital ships to theirs. In 1936, at a naval conference held in Britain, the London Naval Treaty restricted new capital ships to a weight of 35,000 tons and their guns to a maximum 15-inch calibre. While Britain and the United States both complied with these restrictions, the Germans, who had also signed the treaty, ignored it, and began construction of two 50,000 ton battleships which would become *Bismarck* and *Tirpitz*. The Japanese, who refused to sign, went one step further, building the two giant Yamoto-class battleships, weighing 64,000 tons and fitted with 18-inch guns.

The British began construction of a class of five battleships, whose design was limited by the treaty restrictions. They were fitted with ten 14-inch guns, as well as an impressive battery of secondary armament. To reduce weight, they were not fitted with heavy anti-torpedo armour on their hull, but instead had a system of watertight bulkheads and compartments which, it was claimed, made them unsinkable. The nameship of the new class, *King George V*, was launched on 21 January 1939, followed by *Duke of York* on 3 May and *Prince of Wales* on 24 February 1940. Four days later, *Anson* was launched, followed by the last of the class, *Howe*, on 9 April 1940. Thus, none of these ships was actually ready for service in 1939, but their completion was speeded up to enable them to join the fray as quickly as possible.

Meanwhile, the Germans had recently built, or were building, seven battleships, of which five were actually in service by 1939, with *Bismarck* and *Tirpitz* being well on the way to completion. The Germans were also building an aircraft carrier, to be named *Graf Zeppelin*, but it was never completed. The other potential European enemy, the Italians, had six battleships in service in September 1939. The Japanese Navy could boast a fleet of twelve battleships, most dating from World War I. Pride of the fleet were the *Yamoto* and *Musashi*, both completed in 1940. The Japanese also had eleven aircraft carriers in 1939, with more under construction.

During the 1920s the Australian armed forces, including the Royal Australian Navy, had been allowed to run down in numbers by the various Federal governments. The flagship of the fleet, the battle cruiser HMAS *Australia*, which had only been commissioned in 1913, became a victim of the Washington Naval Conference Treaty, being scuttled off Sydney Heads on 12 April 1924. As well, the three Chatham-class cruisers that had served so nobly in World War I were disposed of, *Melbourne* being scrapped in 1928 and *Sydney* in 1929, while *Brisbane* was paid off in 1929 but kept in reserve until being scrapped in 1934. Construction of HMAS *Adelaide*, a cruiser of the slightly larger Town-class, had commenced in 1915 but was not completed until 1922, and she was joined in 1928 by two County-class heavy cruisers, HMAS *Canberra* and the second HMAS *Australia*.

Going into the 1930s, the world political and economic systems were again in turmoil. In Europe, Germany and Italy came under Fascist governments, communist agitators were active in many other countries, and the Great Depression caused problems world-wide. In 1935 a Leander-class cruiser, the second HMAS *Sydney*, which had been

When completed in 1922, HMAS *Adelaide* had four funnels. (*Ross Gillett collection*)

laid down for the Royal Navy as HMS *Phaeton*, was added to the RAN fleet. As Europe plunged into greater political uncertainty, the Australian government took steps to further strengthen the Royal Australian Navy. An improved Leander-class cruiser, which had commissioned into the Royal Navy in 1936 as HMS *Apollo*, was bought in 1938, being renamed HMAS *Hobart*, while in June 1939 a sister ship, HMS *Amphion*, also completed in 1936, was added to the Australian fleet, being renamed HMAS *Perth* when commissioned in Britain in June 1939. The cruiser left for Australia, but first paid a courtesy call at New York, then headed for the Panama Canal.

In September 1939, the Royal Australian Navy had a fleet of fourteen ships, comprising two heavy cruisers, four light cruisers, five destroyers, two sloops and a boom defence vessel. All these units were in Australian waters except HMAS *Perth*, which was still on its delivery voyage. On the RAN active list were some 430 officers and 5010 other ranks, while the Naval Reserve Force totalled 531 officers and 3869 ratings, many of whom were serving in the merchant marine. In addition, there were 459 ex Royal Navy and Royal Australian Navy officers on the Retired and Emergency lists, and 430 ratings of the Fleet Reserve, all available to be called up in the event of war. Thus the Royal Australian Navy very quickly had at its disposal over 10,000 officers and men ready for immediate service.

From June 1921, vessels were lent by the Royal Navy to New Zealand

HMAS *Perth* arriving in New York in 1939.

to operate as the New Zealand Division of the Royal Navy, with the light cruiser HMS *Chatham* as flagship, being replaced in May 1924 by the larger cruiser HMS *Dunedin*. In January 1926 she was joined by sister ship, HMS *Diomede*. These vessels were still known by their Royal Navy title, HMS, but crewed largely by New Zealanders.

In 1935, *Diomede* was sent to the Mediterranean, being replaced in the New Zealand Division by the modern cruiser, HMS *Achilles*, which arrived in New Zealand in September 1936. A year later, *Dunedin* was also replaced, by HMS *Leander*, nameship of the class of which *Achilles* was also a member. In September 1939, New Zealand Naval personnel numbered eight officers and 716 ratings, plus 74 officers and 541 ratings on loan from the Royal Navy. The only units of the New Zealand Division at the outbreak of war were the cruisers *Leander* and *Achilles*, and the minesweeping trawler *Wakakura*. It was not until 1 October 1941 that the New Zealand Division of the Royal Navy became known as the Royal New Zealand Navy, at which time the ships were prefixed with HMNZS.

At the beginning of 1939, the Royal Australian Air Force comprised 3,489 personnel, with twelve squadrons and 246 aircraft, including trainers. The Australian Army consisted of a mere 2795 regular soldiers, backed up by 42,895 militiamen, who only had eighteen days training each year and were very poorly equipped. However, as the political situation in Europe grew more tense during the year, and war between Great Britain and Germany seemed a greater probability, more men joined the militia. The number had increased to 80,000 when Neville Chamberlain announced on 3 September that Great Britain and Germany were at war. The declaration of war was made in London at

9 am — 11 pm eastern time in Australia — and within a short time, Prime Minister Robert Menzies had gone on national radio to advise the population that Australia, too, was now at war with Germany.

The cruisers HMAS *Canberra* and HMAS *Hobart* had departed Sydney on the morning of 3 September, prior to the declaration of war, to patrol sections of the New South Wales coastline, while HMAS *Sydney* was in Fremantle. As soon as the declaration of war was received, the destroyer HMAS *Vampire* was sent out from Fremantle to seek out the Italian liner *Romolo*, which was known to be in the area, as it was thought Italy would soon join the war on the Axis side. *Romolo* managed to elude the warship, but then arrived in Fremantle on 11 September, on her owner's orders.

Little more than three hours after the declaration of war, Australia's first shot in anger was fired, across the bows of a small coastal steamer from a fort at Port Phillip Heads, when the ship failed to stop for the examination vessel. The captain of the coastal vessel later explained that, having signalled his ship's name to the fort, he thought he could enter port without having to heave to.

On the day war broke out there were 154 ships engaged on the Australian coastal trades, both interstate and intrastate. Many were quite small, and could be converted for patrol and minesweeping duties. However, the coastal fleet also included five large, modern liners, which could be converted into armed merchant cruisers or hospital ships. Even before the official declaration of war, the McIlwraith McEacharn liner *Kanimbla* had been requisitioned on 27 August, for conversion into an armed merchant cruiser. Fitted with seven 6-inch and two 3-inch guns, *Kanimbla* was commissioned into the Royal Australian Navy on 6 October. *Manoora*, of the Adelaide Steamship Company, was requisitioned on 14 October, similarly converted, and commissioned on 12 December. *Duntroon* of the Melbourne Steamship Company was also scheduled for conversion into an armed merchant cruiser, but was rejected, and instead the Huddart Parker liner *Westralia* was requisitioned on 2 November 1939, being commissioned on 17 January 1940. The addition of these three vessels to the RAN enabled them to free cruisers for convoy escort duty. The other modern coastal liner, *Manunda*, was converted into a hospital ship, as was another Australian owned vessel, the trans-Tasman liner *Wanganella*.

In New Zealand, the trans-Tasman liner *Monowai*, owned by the Union Steam Ship Company, was requisitioned on 21 October, and converted into an armed merchant cruiser at the Devonport Dockyard in Auckland, being commissioned on 30 August 1940.

5 The First Convoy

Within two weeks of war breaking out in Europe, the Australian government had reached a decision to raise an infantry division for service either at home or overseas, this being totally dependent upon the attitude of Japan, whose loyalties at that time were not clear. The New Zealand government also decided to send troops overseas, but not in a combined force with the Australians, though they would travel in the same convoys.

On 15 September, Prime Minister Robert Menzies made a national radio broadcast which included this statement: 'We propose to enlist forthwith an Infantry Division with its ancillary units, or a total of approximately 20,000 men. This force will be specially enlisted for service at home or abroad, as circumstances permit or require … . As in the case of the A.I.F., there will be one Brigade raised in New South Wales, one in Victoria, and the remainder will be distributed between the other states.'

Menzies went on to explain why the force would be enlisted for service either at home or overseas, then continued:

> The international position will have to be watched very closely from day to day … .it may be that under some circumstances Australian forces might be used to garrison some of the Pacific Islands, to co-operate with New Zealand, to relieve British troops in Singapore, or at other posts around the Indian Ocean. Under other circumstances, it might be practicable to send Australian forces to Europe. As for the ordinary militia, we propose to call up the whole of this force in two drafts, each to receive a months' continuous camp training.

Recruiting and equipping the new force went ahead at great speed. The first group of newly enlisted men was to be known as the 6th Division, and the entire force would be titled the Second Australian Imperial Force. In November 1939, an Australian government delegation went to London for talks with the British government, who soon made it clear they hoped that two Australian divisions would be made available for overseas service. There was considerable discussion regarding the destination of these troops. Originally, the British suggested that they be sent to Singapore, Burma and India to relieve British troops who could then be sent back to fight in Europe.

This was not acceptable to the Australian government, which stated it would not sanction the dispatch of any troops overseas until assurances were given by Britain regarding their intentions in the event of Japan entering the war on the enemy side. However, this position was somewhat weakened when the New Zealand government announced that they would be sending troops overseas, and were raising a force at that time for this purpose. Eventually it was agreed that the Australian divisions would go to the Middle East, to complete their training and then be included in larger forces.

At a Cabinet meeting in Canberra on 28 November, it was agreed that, 'The 6th Division ... can be permitted to proceed overseas when it has reached a suitable stage in its training, which it is anticipated will be early in the new year.' Menzies made an announcement to this effect in parliament on 29 November. This decision was not met with universal acclaim. The opposition Labor Party loudly opposed the decision, while the government was inundated by letters from individuals and groups throughout the country deploring the decision. However, there were many in the country who were in favour of the dispatch of troops overseas, and the government remained firm in its commitment, at the same time deciding that a second division would also be raised, which eventually became the 7th Division.

It was also proposed by the Australian government that the Australian and New Zealand forces be combined into an ANZAC Corps, as happened in World War I, but New Zealand declined. It was agreed, though, that troops from both countries should be sent overseas in the same convoys. With regard to the Australian troops, the first convoy would carry the 16th Brigade of the 6th Division, comprising the 2/1, 2/2, 2/3 and 2/4 Battalions, which had been raised mainly in New South Wales, to the Middle East. The 17th Brigade, raised in Victoria, would be sent in the second convoy, followed by the 18th Brigade in a third convoy.

In World War I, each division of the Australian Army had consisted of about 16,500 men in three brigades divided into four battalions. Initially it had been planned to follow this procedure in 1939, but then it was reorganised to have each Division comprise three brigades composed of only three battalions, or a total of about 14,500 men. Each battalion would be commanded by a lieutenant colonel, and consist of a headquarters company and four rifle companies. Headquarters company would have four platoons, including all ancillary staff, while each rifle company would be composed of three platoons, the strength of a battalion being about 36 officers and 812 other ranks. Also, as the divisions and battalions would carry the same identification numbers as had been used in the 1914–18 war, it was decided that the prefix 2/ would apply in the present conflict, hence the 2/1st Battalion and the 2/6th Division.

The first Australian and New Zealand brigades to be transported overseas would number 13,500 men, and on 1 December 1939 the Australian government agreed that the troops should depart about 9 January 1940. However, prior to the departure of the main contingent, it would be necessary to send an advance party for both the Second Australian Imperial Force and the Second New Zealand Expeditionary Force. The P & O liner *Strathallan*, which was in Australian waters at the time, was ordered to wait in Sydney until the advance parties were ready. The New Zealand advance guard, comprising 25 officers and 88 other ranks, was brought to Sydney on the *Awatea* and boarded *Strathallan*, which then left for Melbourne, where the Australian party of 47 officers and 58 other ranks embarked on 15 December. *Strathallan*, which was also carrying a large number of civilian passengers, departed Melbourne the same day, escorted by HMAS *Adelaide* and also afforded some air cover when possible.

Leading the Australian advance party was Colonel George Vasey, later promoted to major general, who was farewelled in Melbourne by his wife, and General Blamey. Vasey later wrote to his wife: 'We made a very fast trip down the bay and dropped the pilot shortly after 3.30. It was then time for tea and not until after that did I unpack anything ... All the troops remain as passengers until after Adelaide and as we leave there on Sunday we shall do nothing till Monday ... The blackout business has spoiled the ship at night. Ron and I did walk outside for a while and found it difficult to get in again ... I understand we go direct to Bombay from Adelaide.'

After leaving the Australian coast, the liner sailed on alone across the Indian Ocean, during which Christmas Day was celebrated. Vasey described the day to his wife. 'Had a church parade at 10.45 after which Ron and I organised a hamper party in my cabin. At this three of us opened our comfort hampers and drank the last of Syd Rowell's gin. Then all the officers went aft where we had a drink with the NCOs.' On Boxing Day, he noted: 'Up at 5 am to inspect our guards ... it is rather difficult on this ship to make people realise they are not only tourists. We get to Colombo about 1 pm tomorrow.'

Describing the stopover in Colombo, Vasey wrote, 'We landed at Colombo about 3 pm ... got back to the ship at about 10.30 pm. We were due to sail about midnight, but did not leave until 2.30 am as 14 mutineers from a merchant ship had been booked as tourist passengers and the chief officer refused to have them. They had to be thrown off the ship. They had been collected off their own ship at sea by a warship ... We are approaching Bombay now — we are due in at 5 am tomorrow. We have seen nothing of the coast as we are keeping well out.' After Bombay, and a call at Aden on 4 January, *Strathallan* arrived at Suez on the morning of 7 January 1940, when the Australian and New Zealand advance parties disembarked. *Strathallan* then continued her voyage to Britain.

The Director of Sea Transport, Admiralty, was responsible for requisitioning the necessary passenger ships to form the first convoy to transport the Australian and New Zealand troops overseas, and during December these ships began to arrive at various ports in

Strathallan carried the Australian and New Zealand Advance Parties to Egypt.

Australia and New Zealand. All convoys were given special designations, and it was decided that the convoys from Australia to the Middle East would be given the code letters US, followed by the number of the convoy, so the first convoy would be known as US1.

Initially twelve ships were allocated to the convoy, some of which had to voyage out from England. One of these vessels was the Polish flag liner *Pilsudski*, which had been taken over by the British when Poland was overrun by the Germans. Still with a Polish crew, *Pilsudski* departed Newcastle-on-Tyne on 26 November 1939, but struck a mine off the mouth of the Humber River and sank. This left eleven ships to make up the first convoy.

Seven of the liners designated to take part in the first movement of Australian and New Zealand troops overseas were already well known in both countries. These were the P & O sisters *Strathaird* and *Strathnaver*, two pairs of sisters from the Orient Line, *Otranto* and *Orford*, *Orion* and *Orcades*, and the *Rangitata* of the New Zealand Shipping Company. The other four ships were the Polish flag liner *Sobieski*, which had been taken over by Britain in September 1939, *Dunera* of British India Line, one of four small troopships built in Britain just before the war, and *Empress of Japan* and *Empress of Canada*, which were operated by Canadian Pacific from Canada to Hong Kong, Shanghai and Japan before the war.

Some of these liners had not been converted for their troop carrying role, and this work was completed in Sydney by Cockatoo Docks and Engineering Company. Among the ships refitted for trooping in

Empress of Japan in Shanghai in the late 1930s.

Orford was one of the liners converted for war service in Sydney. (*National Library of Australia*)

Sydney was the *Orion*, which had been allocated to the New Zealand contingent, and also nominated to carry the convoy commodore, Captain M.B.R. Blackwood, DSO. *Orion* arrived in Sydney on 29 November and conversion commenced on 8 December, being completed on 28 December. Two days later she departed for Wellington. Her sister, *Orcades*, left Tilbury on 19 November 1939, voyaging via the Suez Canal and Colombo to Sydney. Work began on *Orcades* on 29 December 1939, two days after her arrival, on *Orford* on 31 December and on *Otranto* on 3 January 1940, all being completed on 8 January.

However, in these early days of the war, it was not thought necessary to totally gut the interior of a liner to prepare it for transporting troops. In a review of the conversion of these ships prepared by the Transport Committee, it was stated that 'the fitting out was done in such a manner as to cause the least possible damage to, and dismantling of, ship's fittings.' As a result, most of the cabins were left untouched, apart from the installation of extra berths where possible. These would be utilised by officers and senior non-commissioned ranks, while hammocks were slung in the 'tween decks for the lower ranks. Panelling was protected by plywood, and most of the public rooms were left virtually untouched. This meant that the first troops to voyage overseas would be travelling in reasonable comfort, with none of the crowding and discomfort that became the norm later in the war.

Strathnaver had been partially refitted in Liverpool prior to voyaging to Australia, but the work was done in such a rush that mistakes were inevitable. When the ship steamed into the Irish Sea, it was discovered that some of the pipes had been wrongly connected, with salt water flowing out of drinking water taps. On arrival in Sydney *Strathnaver* underwent further conversion work by Cockatoo Docks and Engineering Company, commencing on 4 January 1940 and being completed in five days. By then the ship had undergone a considerable transformation. Bulkheads and cabin walls on the lower decks were removed, the resultant open spaces being filled with hammocks and mess tables. In the cabins retained on the upper decks, extra bunks were installed, and even the original dining rooms were turned into sleeping accommodation. The original first-class forward lounge became the officers' dining room, and the verandah cafe a warrant-officers' mess. By the time the work was finished, *Strathnaver* could carry about 3000 troops.

Neither *Empress of Japan* nor *Empress of Canada* had been extensively altered for trooping duties when they arrived in Australia, having been requisitioned for war duty. *Empress of Canada* had departed Vancouver on 4 November 1939 on a regular commercial voyage, was requisitioned while in Hong Kong on 29 November, and sailed from there on 8 December directly to Wellington, where she was to take on New Zealand troops. *Empress of Canada* berthed on the western side of King's Wharf, while a few days later *Strathaird* joined her on the eastern side. Berthed on the western side of the next pier was *Rangitata*, with *Orion* on the eastern side.

Empress of Japan had been in Shanghai when war was declared and was due to return to Japan en route to Vancouver. However, all passengers were landed, and the liner left, reportedly for Hong Kong, but instead went directly to Honolulu, arriving on 14 September. Painted grey all over while docked, the liner then made a quick trip back to Vancouver but was not requisitioned until 26 November. She was moved to the Esquimalt naval dockyard to be partially converted for trooping, though most of her peacetime fittings were retained. From there the liner departed on 2 December on a direct voyage to Sydney, arriving on 22 December. On 4 January 1940, *Empress of Japan* left Sydney for Melbourne, where she docked at Station Pier two days later and completed preparations for loading her complement of 773 troops.

With all the troopships in place, another vital matter to be addressed prior to the departure of the convoy was the provision of a suitable escort. During the early months of the war there had been reports of German raiders being active in the Indian Ocean, one of which was

The veteran battleship HMS *Ramilles* was the major convoy escort. (*National Library of Australia*)

thought to be a pocket battleship. It was known that, prior to the outbreak of the war, the German Navy had dispatched a number of warships to sea, among them several battleships and numerous submarines, along with auxiliary vessels to supply them with fuel and other essentials. Within hours of war being declared, a German submarine had torpedoed and sunk the British liner *Athenia*, causing heavy loss of life, and in the days that followed other British merchant ships had been attacked by surface raiders in the Atlantic and Indian Oceans. For this reason, a strong escort was needed for the first troop convoy from Australia and New Zealand, so the battleship HMS *Ramillies* was allocated as the major protection, to be assisted by two cruisers.

Ramillies was one of the oldest serving battleships in the Royal Navy. Built by the Wm Beardmore shipyard in Glasgow, construction commenced on 12 November 1913 and the vessel was commissioned into service in September 1917. Her main armourment consisted of eight 15-inch guns and twelve 6-inch guns, while she also carried eight 4-inch anti-aircraft guns and four 3-pounders. The Parson turbines installed when she was built could originally produce a maximum speed of 21 knots, but by 1939 were no longer capable of such a speed. *Ramillies* had just completed a two-year refit when war broke out but was still outclassed by the battleships of most other navies.

Meanwhile, the troops who would be included in the first overseas movement were completing training and enjoying a spell of special leave before embarkation. In addition to these men, there was also a contingent from the Australian Army Nursing Service, the first of many that would travel overseas. A call for volunteers to serve as nurses had been made a few weeks after war was declared, and four thousand women had responded. To qualify for overseas duty, the nurses had to be registered, experienced, single and medically fit, the preferable age being between 25 and 35, although matrons over this age would also be accepted.

.In the first few days of 1940, the troops were all moved to holding areas near the ports from which they would be departing, and the troopships were assembled. The 7022 troops comprising the 4th New Zealand Brigade would be the first to embark, then carried across the Tasman Sea, where their ships would rendezvous with the ones carrying the Australian contingent. Designated to embark 4397 troops in Wellington were *Orion*, *Strathaird*, *Rangitata* and *Empress of Canada*, while *Dunera* and *Sobieski* were dispatched to Lyttelton to board 2625 troops. In addition to troops, *Rangitata* also loaded up her extensive refrigerated cargo holds with New Zealand meat and dairy produce, while wool was packed in the other holds, all destined for England.

The ships departed on 6 January 1940, the two from Lyttelton leaving first, then proceeding up the east coast of South Island and into Cook Strait, being escorted by the cruiser HMS *Leander*, from the New Zealand Division of the Royal Navy. The Wellington ships were led out of the harbour by the cruiser HMAS *Canberra*, followed in a single line by *Empress of Canada*, *Orion*, *Strathaird* and *Rangitata*, with the battleship HMS *Ramillies* at the rear.

The two groups joined up in Cook Strait, then proceeded across the Tasman Sea, arriving at a point 30 miles south of Sydney Heads in the early hours of 10 January. *Empress of Canada*, which was carrying the commander of the New Zealand force, Major General Freyburg, who later served as Governor-General of New Zealand from 1946 to 1952, detached, and escorted by *Ramillies* and *Leander* entered Sydney Harbour briefly, departing again at 9.30 am. This time the liner was escorted by *Ramillies* and the cruiser HMAS *Australia*, replacing *Leander*, which returned to New Zealand.

Dunera departs Wellington on 4 January 1940 for Lyttelton, with *Strathaird* berthed at Queen's Wharf. (*Wellington Maritime Museum*)

Empress of Canada alongside Queen's Wharf with *Strathaird* in the background. (*Wellington Maritime Museum*)

The four ships that had been allocated to board troops in Sydney, *Otranto, Orford, Orcades* and *Strathnaver*, were all well known in the port. *Otranto* and *Orford* looked little different from their peacetime appearance, still having black hulls and buff funnels, but the former corn-coloured hull of *Orcades* had been repainted black, though the funnel was still buff. *Strathnaver*, on the other hand, looked very different, her previous all-white hull and superstructure repainted

Orion arrives in Wellington on 5 January 1940 to board troops. (*Wellington Maritime Museum*)

black and light brown, the colours associated with P & O liners of a bygone age, while the three funnels, formerly painted yellow, were now black.

On 4 January 1940, the 16th Brigade, under the command of Brigadier A.S. Allan, marched through the streets of Sydney, which were thronged with thousands of cheering spectators. The *Sydney Morning Herald* reported: 'The long khaki columns thrilled the heart of Sydney as it had not been thrilled for a quarter of a century, since that still spring day in 1914 when the First AIF marched through the same streets on its way to Anzac and imperishable glory. The marching was magnificent.' After the march, it was time for the troops to return to their camps and await the day of their departure.

After reveille at 0330 on 9 January, the 2/2 Battalion of the 16th Brigade marched from their training camp at Ingleburn, on the southern outskirts of Sydney, to the local station, where they boarded trains to take them to Pyrmont, where the four ships were berthed. On arriving at the wharf, the troops detrained in groups of one hundred and climbed the gangway to board *Otranto* and *Orcades*. The embarkation officer, Colonel Hector Clayton, said to Paul Cullen as he led the first troops to board, 'Remember this Paul, you are the first man of the second AIF to embark on a troopship.' By mid-morning all the troops were on board, and the two ships pulled away from the wharf and steamed under the harbour bridge, then dropped anchor off Neutral Bay. During the afternoon a flotilla of craft carrying friends and relatives, as well as sightseers, surrounded both liners.

Meanwhile, back at Ingleburn, the 2/1 Battalion of the 16th Brigade awoke to reveille at 0300 on 10 January, marched to the train station, and were taken to the *Orford*, berthed at 12 Pyrmont. However, all did not go quite to plan, for, as the battalion history records: 'Lt Kennedy, leading his group, which was one of the last to go aboard, saw a "Black Maria" pull up nearby. Several plain clothes and uniformed police began a scuffle with one of his platoon. "You cannot arrest that man" said the lieutenant. "Yes, we can" replied a bulky sergeant of police, stripping off the man's equipment and throwing it on the wharf. "What is his offence?" asked Kennedy. "Murder" was the reply.'

The 2/1 Battalion history records that, as the troops embarked on *Orford*, 'they were met by members of the crew who led them down companionways and along spotless passages to their quarters. The men were overjoyed to find that they were to live in four and six berth cabins. These cabins had been converted from two or four bed cabins simply by adding another double set of bunks. Officers had single berth cabins. The Commanding Officer and the Medical Officer were allotted state rooms, which, because of the well sprung double beds, were better known as bridal suites. Some Quartermaster types scored these also … As soon as the first arrivals had dumped their gear, many returned to the decks where they lined the rails or climbed the rigging to shout and wave to the crowd generally and to such friends and relatives as they could identify.' Also embarking on *Orford* that day were the 2/1 Field Artillery Regiment, and the 2/1 Australian General Hospital.

By noon on 10 January *Orford* and *Strathnaver* had completed embarking their contingent of troops, along with a contingent from the Australian Army Nursing Service, then also left the wharf. Shortly after noon the four ships began their passage down the harbour, *Orcades* leading, followed by *Strathnaver,* then *Otranto* and *Orford* in line astern. Around the harbour foreshores, thousands of people had gathered to farewell the ships, many being family and friends of the departing troops. On board the ships, the rails were lined with khaki clad soldiers, all cheering and waving. It was a very emotional moment, especially as many of the men steaming off to the unknown perils of war would never return.

One of the men on board *Otranto,* Roland Hoffman, wrote: 'Sydney with its bridge, its coves and bays and ferries and its sky-flung buildings had never looked lovelier, more entrancingly beautiful than she looked just now to the troops who swarmed the riggings and lined the rails to linger sentimentally and introspectively over her imposing but disappearing skyline … Thoughts were revealed on rugged sunburned faces as clearly as though they lay on X-ray negatives. This leaving home was not coming easy to anyone and these men, tough, carefree citizens, were realising what it meant to them. For the first time, perhaps, some were realising the sacrifice they had undertaken, and many pairs of eyes became unfamiliarly dim.'

At 2.10 pm the last of the ships cleared Sydney Heads, where they were met by their escort, HMS *Ramillies*. Turning south, the four liners and the battleship built up speed, and shortly after linked up with the six ships that had come from New Zealand, which had been standing off the coast. The ten ships formed up into three columns:

Otranto	Orion	Orcades
Strathaird	Empress of Canada	Rangitata
Sobieski	Strathnaver	Dunera
Orford		

Escorting them were the battleship HMS *Ramillies*, in position ahead of the ships, the cruisers HMAS *Canberra* and HMAS *Australia* on either side, and as far as Jervis Bay, HMAS *Sydney*. While proceeding down the New South Wales and Victorian coastline, air cover was also provided during daylight hours by aircraft from bases at Liverpool, Canberra and Lavington. In addition, the 20th Minesweeping Flotilla, comprising the sloops HMAS *Yarra* and HMAS *Swan* along with the converted merchantmen *Doomba* and *Orara*, had swept the entire route along the coast prior to the passage of the convoy, with *Doomba* and *Orara* making a second sweep off Wilson's Promontory in front of the convoy as it passed.

As the convoy proceeded down the east coast, the official diarist of the 16th Brigade, Corporal Roland Hoffman, put pen to paper, waxing lyrically: 'It was an unforgettable sight to see these ten ships, seven of them luxury liners, flanked by warships of the British and Australian navies. They kept in perfect formation — it seemed as if their engines might be throbbing in unison. Here were approximately 13,000 troops on their way. Here was the spearhead of Australia and New Zealand's challenge to Nazism, or any other "ism," that might menace the Empire and democracy at large. It must have given every man who watched this advance a great surge of satisfaction to be of it, a sense of privilege to be one of the chosen of the Second AIF.'

One of the men on board *Orford*, Private Wilson, recalled, 'I would say we were like young fellows going on a Sunday School picnic, finding our way round the *Orford*. Most had never been to Manly. It was a lot of fun. Our accommodation was down near the engine room but we did not care. Our ship was still furnished — they had not had time to convert to troop transport. We had about 1500 aboard, stewards served our meals, and when the bar opened, draught beer was very cheap.'

The eleventh ship allocated to the convoy, *Empress of Japan*, embarked her passengers, comprising part of the 6th Division Headquarters, some base troops and nurses of the 2/1 Australian General Hospital, in Melbourne on the afternoon of 11 January. In the evening the liner pulling slowly away from Station Pier, which was thronged with relatives and friends of the soldiers on board. *Empress of Japan* anchored in Port Phillip Bay overnight, and early in the morning of 12 January, departed to link up with the other ships. Shortly after noon, as the other ten vessels passed Port Phillip Heads, *Empress of Japan* steamed through the Rip, and into Bass Strait. Away to port on the horizon small specks began to appear, which rapidly took the shape of the convoy of ships, which moved rapidly past *Empress of Japan*, which swung slowly to starboard and took up her appointed station in the centre column, astern of *Strathnaver*.

Convoy US1 was now complete, but its speed had to be governed to the slowest ship, *Dunera*, which could only manage about 13 knots at best. The troops found that many of the peacetime amenities were still available on the ships, including hot baths, with a choice of fresh or sea water. Swimming in the ship's pools was also allowed. For the first few days, there was perfect weather and the troops were quite content. However, after passing through Bass Strait, the convoy's course took them well south of the mainland, where they encountered cold weather, with heavy rain squalls, which became worse as each day passed. As Sam Nathan recorded in his diary, 'Not many at mess parade. Convoy pitching and tossing, can just discern *Ramillies* through the rain.' Church Parade on Sunday, 14 January, was held on wind-swept decks in a rough sea.

As the ships headed across the southern reaches of the Great Australian Bight, they could not be covered by land based aircraft, so were totally reliant on the naval escort until coming within 200 miles of Albany, when air cover could again be provided during daylight. As *Orion*, leading the centre column, carried the convoy commander, all other ships had to conform to her movements, though there was no need to follow a zigzag course. The convoy made a 'wonderful sight,' as one soldier wrote to his parents, 'I can't give details but imagine a body of great liners sailing along in formation rising and falling as they carry a load of Australia's men into a heavy sea.'

HMAS *Adelaide* joined the escort on the morning of 18 January, and that afternoon the convoy rounded Rottnest Island and approached Fremantle. *Ramillies* anchored out in Gage Roads, while *Australia* and *Canberra* patrolled the approaches to the harbour. All eleven troopships entered Fremantle and berthed, to take on water, supplies and bunkers, and shore leave was granted. One soldier wrote home: 'Crowds of people under every street light cheering us as busload after busload of soldiers rode past on their way to Perth. A wonderful reception very much appreciated by us all … Perfect summer night … strolled around Perth for a while. Full of soldiers and sailors, Australian and New Zealand and English and French sailors. Everybody on the best of terms with each other and having the time of their lives.' Another soldier wrote, 'You can quite imagine thousands of laughing, singing troops in a place, their last glimpse of

Aussie and all happy. Perth was one of the noisiest places on the map that night. Our last bit of Australia was certainly a snifter.'

On the morning of 20 January, the eleven troopships departed Fremantle, and proceeded to Gage Roads, where they dropped anchor. At noon, *Ramillies* was followed out to sea by *Strathaird*, *Strathnaver*, *Otranto* and *Sobieski*, which would make up the port column of the convoy for the next leg of their journey. They were followed by *Orion*, *Orford* and *Dunera*, which made up the centre column, and later *Empress of Japan*, *Empress of Canada*, *Orcades* and *Rangitata* joined them as the starboard column, the troopships being formed up as follows:

Strathaird	Orion	Empress of Japan
Strathnaver	Orford	Empress of Canada
Otranto	Dunera	Orcades
Sobieski		Rangitata

By 3.30 pm, Convoy US1 had formed into its new order, and soon after the ships disappeared over the horizon, destination Colombo. For this, the longest and most dangerous leg of the voyage, the escort also changed. *Ramillies* remained, but *Australia* and *Canberra* were replaced by two other cruisers, HMS *Kent* and the French *Suffren*. *Australia* and *Canberra* stayed with the convoy until 6 pm on the first day, then passed between the columns, to rousing cheers from the troops, as they turned back to Fremantle, their job completed.

The three escorting warships changed their disposition by day and

Strathaird departing Wellington on 6 January 1940. (*Wellington Maritime Museum*)

The Polish liner *Sobieski* carried New Zealand troops embarked at Lyttelton. (*C.T. Reddings collection*)

night. During the day, *Ramillies* steamed two miles ahead of *Orion*, with the two cruisers ten miles to port and starboard of the convoy. At night, *Ramillies* and one cruiser would close in to lead each wing column, while the other cruiser took up station a mile astern of the convoy.

The ten-day passage from Fremantle to Colombo passed without major incident, and overall was rather a boring time for the troops. On *Otranto*, the troops were subjected to three and a half hour's drill every morning, and a further one-hour session in the afternoon. Fortunately, most of the ships still retained many of their peacetime amenities and there was none of the crowding that would become such a feature of later convoys. The first day out, a man fell overboard

HMAS *Australia* was included in the convoy escort from Sydney.

from *Dunera* but he was quickly rescued by *Rangitata*. Some days the ships practised emergency procedures, such as turns and zigzags, while the escorts livened things up from time to time with practice shoots. On several occasions *Ramillies* passed down the lines of the columns to remind the troops that they were being well protected.

One problem to cause considerable concern aboard *Otranto* was an epidemic of gastroenteritis, which began within a day of the ship departing Fremantle. As the epidemic spread, Jack Smithers wrote, 'hundreds of soldiers sick last night with vomiting and diarrhoea. Medical officer and assistants kept very busy ... Today men still very sick and lying on beds all around the decks.' Some 50 men became so ill they were given morphia to ease the pain.

Since departing Sydney, the troops had been given almost daily boat drill exercises when, in addition to lifejackets, steel helmets and anti-gas respirators also had to be worn, which many found quite irksome. From 25 January, troops were ordered to wear their respirators at all times and to breathe through them for one hour every day. As the weather was getting hotter, this exercise proved very uncomfortable. However, there were some lighter moments, including hearing over the ship's speakers a speech by the traitor Lord Haw Haw, broadcasting from Berlin, claiming that both *Orford* and *Orcades* had been sunk with all hands.

Entertainment was arranged whenever possible for the troops, including deck sports and competitions, and boxing tournaments. On *Orford*, 27 January was Race Day, complete with a tote and bookies, the 9 'horses' being pulled along the track on ropes. Fortunately the weather was perfect, and the sea calm, making it an enjoyable diversion. Next day, the convoy crossed the equator, and on all ships there were the usual crossing-the-line ceremonies.

Colombo was safely reached on 30 January, enabling all the ships to take on water and bunkers, and shore leave was granted. Local merchants also came to the anchored liners in boats, hawking a wide variety of wares. As Jack Ulrick wrote: 'Almost before we dropped anchor the natives were at us in small boats laden with fruit, nuts and all the knicknacks imaginable. Their method of sale was to heave a small rope up to the decks with a canvas bag attached and then the fun began. These nigs were awful rogues and if you did not argue with them you paid treble the value of anything ... Most of their stuff looked alright in the boats but proved very shoddy on examination. The lads would buy fruit and coconuts then pelt the core and skins back at them. Didn't they leap, prance and yabber when hit.'

Strathnaver proceeds down Sydney Harbour on 10 January 1940, with *Orcades* waiting at anchor off Neutral Bay.

On 1 February, the convoy set sail again, having been increased to an even dozen ships by the addition of a French vessel, *Athos II*, which took up the vacant position astern of *Dunera* in the centre column. *Athos II* was not carrying troops but joined the convoy as a safety measure for its voyage across the Arabian Sea.

Ramillies remained with the convoy, but the escorting cruisers changed, *Kent* and *Suffren* being replaced by HMS *Sussex* and HMAS *Hobart*. However, a major uplift to the morale of the troops was the addition of the aircraft carrier HMS *Eagle* to the escort. *Ramillies*

The French cruiser *Suffren* took over escort duty from Fremantle.

HMAS *Hobart* joined the convoy escort in the Indian Ocean.

continued to lead the convoy, with *Eagle* and *Sussex* on either wing, while *Hobart* protected the stern. During the voyage from Colombo to Aden, *Eagle* put up four aircraft every afternoon to search a huge area of ocean all around the convoy for enemy submarines. Off Socotra, the escort was further strengthened by the addition of the destroyer HMS *Westcott* to provide more anti-submarine protection.

This section of the voyage also passed without major incident, though there was some excitement on 4 February when one of the planes from *Eagle* crashed into the sea, but its three-man crew was rescued by *Sussex*. The weather held fine all the way and on the morning of 8 February the rocky cliffs surrounding Aden hove into view. *Ramillies* and *Eagle* were not to continue with the convoy beyond that point, so during the morning the battleship passed between the columns, with her band playing, saluting each ship, while the troops on board cheered in return.

Entering the Red Sea the convoy separated into two sections, with *Orion*, *Strathnaver*, *Orcades*, *Rangitata* and *Empress of Japan* going into the port of Aden. The rest of the ships, escorted by *Hobart*, continued into the Red Sea, though *Athos II* broke off and proceeded independently to Djibouti. *Hobart* stayed with the other ships until they entered Egyptian waters on 10 February, then turned back to join the second part of the convoy. The six troopships continued on their own, dropping anchor in Suez Bay on the morning of 10 February.

The second group of ships had left Aden on the morning of 9 February, being escorted by *Sussex* and *Westcott* until *Hobart* linked up, at which time *Sussex* turned back to Aden. The speed of the group was restricted to 15 knots by *Rangitata*, but on the morning of 11 February she was left behind with *Westcott*, while the other ships increased speed to 18 knots. *Hobart* stayed with the four troopers until they also entered Egyptian waters on the morning of 12 February, and at 10.30 pm the four ships entered Suez Bay, dropping anchor alongside the first section, with *Rangitata* joining them the next day.

The arrival of the first contingent of Australian and New Zealand troops in Egypt was widely publicised. At Ismailia, at the entrance to the Suez Canal, Anthony Eden, then Secretary for the Dominions, accompanied by the British Ambassador to Egypt, Sir Miles Lampson, General Wavell, the Commander in Chief, Middle East, and a horde of newsreel and press photographers, boarded the *Otranto*, where Eden read a message of welcome to the troops from King George VI. As one soldier wrote home, 'All troops had to parade on D Deck while Eden gave a speech ... He then walked among us for a while talking to various chaps.'

The ships carrying New Zealand troops – *Orion*, *Strathaird*, *Rangitata*, *Empress of Canada*, *Dunera* and *Sobieski* — disembarked them at Suez into barges, in which they were ferried ashore. Meanwhile the five ships carrying Australian troops — *Orford*, *Strathnaver*, *Orcades*, *Otranto* and *Empress of Japan* — went on to El Kantara, where they berthed late at night on 11 January. Next morning the troops went ashore, those from *Otranto* having the honour of being the first to set foot in Egypt, having been shipbound for over a month, and boarded trains which took them into Palestine. So ended the first major movement of Australian and New Zealand troops overseas in World War II.

Empress of Japan alongside Station Pier in Melbourne. (*C.T. Reddings collection*)

6 The Second Convoy

While the vessels comprising convoy US1 were still en route to Egypt, plans were already being prepared by the Naval Staff and Transport Committee for the second convoy of troops to be carried to the Middle East. A major consideration was the provision of ships which could carry larger numbers of troops at higher speed, as there were several aspects of the conduct of the convoy US1 that caused concern, and brought forth numerous critical reports.

Most of the criticism concentrated on the slow speed the convoy had to maintain throughout the voyage. This was restricted to the top speed of the slowest ship, in this case *Dunera*, which although newer than most of the other ships, had a maximum speed of little more than 14 knots, but due to fouling of her bottom had been further reduced to just over

Dunera returned to Australia to take part in convoy US2. (*C.T. Reddings collection*)

13 knots. Yet, of the eleven ships, nine would have been capable of maintaining a speed of 18 knots for the entire voyage, while *Rangitata* could only manage 15 knots. Had the convoy been able to maintain 15 knots, it would have reduced the passage time by five days, and at 18 knots many more days would have been saved. There was also greater safety from submarine attack provided by increased speed, and this matter was to be more carefully considered when future convoys were being organised.

On 16 February 1940, a few days after the first convoy delivered its troops safely to Egypt, the Admiralty advised the Naval Board that they would be allocating two of the largest ships afloat, the Cunard liners *Queen Mary* and *Mauretania*, for use as transports in the second convoy. At that time, both these liners were laid up in New York, as they were considered too vulnerable for service in the Atlantic, where U-boats were sinking British ships at a frightening rate. By sending them to the Southern Hemisphere, they could contribute in a major way to the conduct of the war, yet be relatively secure from the dangers of attack by submarine or surface raider.

The anticipated addition of the fastest liner in the world and her smaller consort to the Australian convoys was welcome, but it also posed some serious problems. The speed of the first convoy had been restricted by the necessity to conform to the slowest ship, and when vessels were being organised for the second convoy this problem again arose. When this matter was considered, it was decided that instead of sending one large convoy, it should be split into two, comprising a slow section, which would depart first as convoy US2 in early April 1940, and a fast section, which would depart later as convoy US3.

Convoy US2 was to be composed of five ships, including *Strathaird* and *Dunera*, which had taken part in the first convoy. *Strathaird* arrived back in Sydney on 7 March, while *Dunera* arrived on the 18th. Both were handed over to the Cockatoo Docks and Engineering Company for further conversion. The work on *Dunera* lasted from 19 March to 9 April, involving the installation of additional accommodation for troops on the promenade, shelter, upper and lower decks. Similar alterations were also made on *Strathaird* from 25 March to 5 April, and it was given additional troop accommodation on seven decks. The rest of the second convoy would comprise *Ettrick*, a sister to *Dunera* but owned by the P & O Line, and two vessels from British India Line, *Neuralia* and *Nevasa*. HMS *Ramillies* also returned to Australia to escort the second convoy. On 14 March 1940, the battleship began a refit at Garden Island in Sydney.

Neuralia and *Nevasa* had been built just before the start of World

Neuralia was one of the ships to embark troops in Melbourne.

War I, in which they served as troop transports and later as hospital ships, then from 1925 were operated under charter to the British government as permanent troopships. However, they had ancient quadruple expansion machinery and could only manage 12 knots at best, so this was the speed at which the convoy would have to travel, ensuring a long, slow trip for the troops.

The second convoy was to transport Australian troops only, primarily the 17th Brigade of the 6th Division, composed of the 2/5th, 2/6th, 2/7th and 2/8th Infantry Battalions, most of which had been raised in Victoria. Consequently four of the liners, *Strathaird*, which would carry the convoy commodore, *Dunera*, *Ettrick* and *Neuralia*, were sent to Melbourne to board their troops, the majority of whom were in the final stages of training at Puckapunyal, while *Nevasa* went to Fremantle.

Nevasa berthed in Fremantle, waiting to join convoy US2 (*C.T. Reddings collection*)

During their training, the 17th Brigade had also had a couple of breaks to go to Melbourne for ceremonial duties. The first of these occurred on 24 January 1940, when they took part in a march past, along with other Victorian-based units, and the Governor-General, Lord Gowrie, took the salute on a dais outside Parliament House. Also present that day were Prime Minister Menzies and the man who held the same position in World War I, Billy Hughes. Then it was back to Puckapunyal, where, at the end of February, pre-embarkation leave began, indicating a move overseas was imminent. However, on 4 March members of the 6th Battalion were selected to go to Melbourne to take part in the funeral procession for Lieutenant General E.K. Squires, who was Chief of the General Staff at the time of his death. With this solemn duty behind them, pre-embarkation leave was completed by the end of March, and final arrangements for departure overseas made.

However, not all those in training ended up going overseas, as the battalion history, *Nothing Over Us*, states that 'before embarkation, when the Battalion lists were carefully reviewed, 68 men were discharged according to Regulations, as being unlikely on various grounds to measure up to the high standards required by the AIF. Of these 21 simply "went missing" and therefore were discharged as illegal absentees … There were plenty of keen recruits to take their places.'

On 11 April the Divisional Commander, General Blamey, visited Puckapunyal, and reviewed the brigade. Two days later, embarkation cards were issued, in preparation for the trip to Melbourne the following day. Reveille that day was at 4.30 am, and the battalion was entrained at Seymour by 9.45 am, en route to Port Melbourne. As Lieutenant Keith Carroll later recalled, 'Although the date of departure was meant to be kept secret, information … had leaked out. Once the train reached the metropolitan area there were numbers of civilians at vantage points along the railway tracks who gave the men quite a send-off.' On the way, the train stopped at Flinders Street station, then as it moved on towards Port Melbourne, Ted Cornell recalls, 'one of our chaps looked out at Melbourne and said, "I wonder if we will ever see that sight again …" Then we all turned around and sang "Goodbye Melbourne Town" … Then down to the *Neuralia*.'

On their arrival at Port Melbourne, the troops filed off the train, and marched down Station Pier to the *Neuralia*, which was berthed there along with the other three transports, all busily embarking troops. The men filed across a gangway in single file, each carrying a sack containing personal items and sleeping gear. Also boarding the *Neuralia* were the nurses of the 2/2 Australian General Hospital and the 2/1 Casualty Clearing Station.

Going on board the *Ettrick* the same day were the men of the 2/5 Infantry battalion, the 2/2 Field Company RAE and the 2/2 Field Ambulance, which included some nurses. Despite being little more than a year old, the quarters on *Ettrick* were much the same as on the older *Neuralia*, with cabins for officers while the troops were accommodated in mess decks with hammocks.

That evening, *Neuralia* departed Station Pier and went to anchorage off Sorrento, waiting for the rest of the convoy to join her next day. The movements of the troopships were meant to be secret, but Keith Carroll recalled, 'Motor boat owners did a brisk business taking boat loads of relatives around the ships as security measures prevented civilians from approaching too close from the shore.' On the afternoon of 15 April, army officers, including General Blamey, were on hand to farewell the troops on the other three ships, while a band played popular tunes. As the vessels departed Melbourne, escorted by *Ramillies* and HMAS *Adelaide*, the band played 'Wish Me Good Luck as You Wave Me Goodbye' and then the haunting strains of the Maori farewell, 'Now Is the Hour.'

As the three transports and their escort neared Port Phillip Heads, the *Neuralia* joined them, and the convoy passed through the Rip at 3.30 pm. Lieutenant Quentin Tilley, on the bridge of *Neuralia*, later recalled: 'It was a terrific sight as we went through the Rip to see all the troops lining the rails to get their last glimpse of the heads as we steamed out. We then ran straight into a south-westerly in Bass Strait, and gradually you saw the figures at the rails disappear below. On the *Neuralia* we reckoned that 80 per cent were confined to their hammocks ... The ship's staff had quite a time trying to arrange reliefs for the sentries who went seasick at their posts.'

Speaking of the rough conditions and consequent seasickness, Corporal John Loes recalled, 'A lot of the troops hadn't been to sea before, and they were sick.' Loes was one of those able to clean up, as 'old Sergeant Major Hilditch and I carted tubs of the stuff up from the bottom deck where HQ Company were. Anyway, we eventually got it cleaned up and it smelt a bit better.' Bob Fox remembered, 'When we left many of us were violently ill ... We lay on the scuppers up on deck and the Lascars, who were the crew, just hosed us down with their two inch water hoses next morning, and we used to slide around on the deck ... we didn't have enough strength to get out of the road.'

After passing through the entrance to Port Phillip Bay, the four troopships formed up into a square and turned west. For the 1204 troops aboard the *Neuralia*, conditions were far from ideal, and there was a considerable disparity between the accommodation provided for officers and the spaces in which the other ranks were quartered. According to John Loes, 'The tale went around the ship that she had been used as a horse boat. It should still have been in that trade!' Major Wood described the accommodation provided as 'a good area for us — bad for the troops.' Another officer who was on board *Neuralia* later wrote of the misery suffered by the troops, travelling on what he described as 'an old regular British Army Transport.' After describing in some detail the poor hygiene in the galleys, which were 'awash with overflow from adjacent latrines,' he then commented on the insufficiencies of the other ranks sleeping accommodation, stating, 'The disparity between the saloon accommodation provided for officers and sergeants, and the troop deck accommodation for the men, is so great as to cause embarrassment to those occupying the better accommodation. I should be much happier myself if I lived on a troop deck and shared the hardships of the men.'

As with the first convoy, air cover was provided during daylight hours while the ships were close to the coast. Some of the troops were given sentry posts on board *Neuralia*, including Bob Fox, who 'was singled out for anti-submarine duty ... I had a board with 64 instructions on it, but the point to be remembered was, as soon as the alarm went you had to close the watertight door ... but being a shrewd Australian I found from a study of the instructions that after I had got all the others out and shut the door I would be on the inside ... Luckily we never had to use it.'

After a couple of days the weather improved. On board *Neuralia*, the battalion diary on 17 April recorded that the men 'were recovering rapidly and beginning to enjoy the meals,' which were described as 'very good.' The menus for 17 April were:

Breakfast	Lunch	High Tea
Oatmeal porridge	Tomato soup	Fresh fried fish
Grilled mutton chops	Compressed beef	Mashed potatoes
Boiled potatoes	Salad	Bread and butter
Bread and butter	Plum pudding	Rock Cakes
Marmalade	Rum sauce	Jam and fruit
Tea		Tea

In the evening a light supper was also provided, with cheese, biscuits and cocoa.

Among the troops on board the *Ettrick* was Warrant Officer Percy Bill, who, at age 37 was older than most of the other men, but he had put his age back a few years in order to be accepted for active service overseas. A single man, he wrote regularly to a widowed friend back in Melbourne, whom he eventually married on his return to Australia. In his first letter, dated 19 April, Percy Bill wrote:

> We are well on our way now and what a trip it has been up to date. When we got on the boat on Monday they kept us below decks till we pulled out and I can tell you we were pretty hostile about it.
>
> We did not leave the Bay till Monday afternoon and did we strike some bad weather then. Monday night was very bad and did the boys go down to it, about three quarters of them went down to it. I am jolly glad that I was not amongst them. I have been doing very well, have not felt the least bit sick so far. The food is very good and I have been having my fair share of it. We have our three main meals and also coffee when we get up and again for supper. If anybody doesn't get enough to eat there is plenty you can buy, you can get anything at all in the way of eats, even ice creams. We also have a beer ration which costs 5d a pint but so far have not had any. Tobacco here is very cheap and stuff that cost 2/- in Melbourne we can get for 1/-, so we will be able to do plenty of smoking now.

As with most troops, Percy Bill found his quarters on the ship crowded, writing, 'The chief trouble here is our lack of space. We are well crowded and eat and sleep in the one place. We have collapsible tables and at night they are let down and we hang our hammocks from the roof and when they are up we are packed like sardines. They are very nice to sleep in though as you don't feel too much of the sway of the boat when in them.'

As regards daily duties: 'I have not done too much work since I came on board but what little I have done has been in the kitchen, am on it every second day ... If anybody asks me to peel a spud or wash a dirty baking dish when I get home they will be looking for trouble. On my day off I have to do a few exercises but they are not too bad. It is rather funny to see us marching round the promenade deck and trying to keep a straight line with the boat swaying. I don't think that there will be any of it today as it is very rough and it would be just about impossible to get round in any sort of formation.'

The same day, 19 April, HMAS *Sydney* joined *Adelaide* and *Ramillies* in the Great Australian Bight and the convoy arrived in Fremantle on 21 April, where the troops were granted a day's shore leave. As usual, the people of Fremantle and Perth were extremely generous in their

HMAS *Sydney* escorted convoy US2 across the Indian Ocean. (*Ross Gillett collection*)

invitations to troops, with more being received than could be accepted. For the troops, it made their last day in Australia enjoyable and memorable. At Fremantle *Nevasa* was waiting, having boarded a contingent of Western Australian troops, bringing the total number on the five ships to 7200, while a further group of nurses from Western Australia joined those already on board *Neuralia*.

Convoy US2, now comprising five ships, *Strathaird, Dunera, Ettrick, Neuralia* and *Nevasa*, departed Fremantle at dawn on 22 April, escorted by *Ramillies* and *Sydney*. It was a slow crossing of the Indian Ocean, the route being four long tacks, as reports had been received about

HMAS *Adelaide* escorted the convoy from Melbourne to Fremantle.

Strathaird was the largest transport in convoy US2. (*C.T. Reddings collection*)

German submarines operating in the area. One of the soldiers on board *Strathaird* was fifteen-year-old Bob Holt, who had claimed he was 21 to get into the army. He wrote later about the voyage: 'We lived the "Life of Riley" aboard *Strathaird*. We were sleeping in two- and four-berth cabins without any duties to speak of. We did physical jerks twice a day. The two-up school was booming on deck, as was the dice game in the ship's canteen of an evening.' Anzac Day was celebrated at sea, the escorting warships steaming through the convoy with all flags flying, and on *Neuralia* the Commanding Officer of the 17th Brigade delivered a special Anzac Day message.

On board *Dunera* was Sidney George Raggett, who later wrote:

> The accommodation on board was long mess tables in rows on each deck with 22 men to each table. At night each man slung a rope and canvas hammock from two hooks in the low ceiling above the mess tables. The whole area between the decks was very crowded and very hot, particularly during the journey through the tropics. It was considered worth the effort to sit on deck after the evening meal to secure a place to sleep there in the warm fresh air. One would protect one's mates spot while he went below to collect his hammock at 8 pm, then he would do likewise. We soon found out that one had to have a particular mate to survive among the 1,600 men aboard ... At daylight each day the Lascar seamen arrived with high pressure hoses to wash down the decks amid cries of 'washy deck.
>
> During the first part of the journey any of the troops who were not seasick received at their table sufficient stew each meal to feed 22 men. A feature of the meals aboard was the freshly baked bread. I managed to wangle a job on the night shift in the ship's bakery from midnight to 4 am and enjoyed plenty of freshly baked bread washed down with buckets of hot tea, plus cool water to drink, as the bakery areas were stifling hot

except when the fans were turned on after each batch of loaves was taken from the oven ... The convoy ploughed on day after day in the tropics with little or no ventilation between decks and the days becoming hotter as we approached the Equator. The convoy travelled about 200 miles per day — the speed being governed by the maximum speed of the slowest ship, the *Neuralia*.

While the seas remained calm, making life more pleasant for the troops, the days were getting hotter. Awnings were spread across open deck areas to provide shade, small canvas swimming tanks were erected, and at night troops were allowed to sleep on the open decks. When the ships crossed the equator, suitable crossing the line ceremonies were held. Those on board *Neuralia* were described in a letter home by Ken Brougham, 'The ceremony, although short, turned out to be quite a comedy. Originally four men were chosen from each company to be initiated ... But unfortunately, after about a dozen had been paraded, tried and sentenced, a couple of the "prisoners" got loose and turned a hose on the crowd. Naturally everything went hurly burly and bedlam reigned, so the rest of the ceremony was cancelled ... Punishment had consisted of squirting with ink and a foul smelling liquid and finally tarring and feathering and a ducking in the pool.' On 30 April a mysterious incident occurred, when a young officer was lost overboard from *Neuralia*, though how this happened is unknown.

By now the initial excitement of departure and being at sea had been exhausted, and the troops found the trip increasingly tiresome. Aboard *Ettrick*, Percy Bill wrote a letter home on 28 April, to be posted at the next port, in which he said: 'It is now two weeks since I left and as far as I am concerned the sooner we get to wherever we are going the better. I used to think I liked it hot but I am not so sure now. The last three days have been terrible and not a breath of wind. It is not too bad on parts of the deck but down below on our mess decks it is like a furnace. We are not allowed to have our portholes open and there are not enough ventilators for the number of men that are crowded in such a small place. I really don't know what we would do if it were not for the fact that we are able to get plenty of showers and also have a bathe in a small canvas pool that is fitted on the deck. It is only about ten feet by five feet by three feet deep but we have a fair bit of fun in it. Quite a lot that do go in do not do so on their own accord. In fact I have been pitched in twice myself.'

On 28 April *Sydney* was relieved as escort by the French cruiser

Suffren. Initially *Sydney* was ordered to return to Australia, but on 1 May the warship received new orders and turned north for Colombo. On 2 May the US2 troops were issued with their identity discs, or 'meat tickets' as they were called. The next day the convoy arrived in Colombo but the docks were so crowded the five troopships had to anchor out in the harbour. It also proved to be the hottest day of the year. Shore leave was granted, but as John Loes recalled, 'When we landed in Colombo we were in winter dress, the old serge khaki. It was like a hothouse. The people there in Ceylon, I rather liked them ... I thought they were a good type of people, very clean and very friendly.' The troops were moved between ships and shore by launches.

The men were all keen to go ashore as soon as possible, but some had to stay behind on guard. Among them was Ron Phillips, who was very unhappy about this, so 'I protested to Captain Rowan, and his remark was 'Phillips, in the army you do as you are told and then complain afterwards.' Well, that didn't suit me because if I did as I was told I wouldn't get any leave. However, I got the leave, and it was quite interesting around Colombo. There were facts of life we hadn't seen before.'

Ken Brougham recalled an unusual incident that occurred during the stopover. On their second day there, he and four others were wending their way back to the ship but decided to stop for one more drink.

> We sat down and were about to order a drink when a Lieutenant from the Royal Navy moved in — a tall, good looking chap. He sat down and said, 'I'd like to buy you Aussies a drink. I'm terribly fond of Australians. I've been out there a couple of times on the *Ramillies* ... The next thing, the Provosts arrive ... They said, 'Come along you fellows, come along with us ... ' The naval officer got to his feet and said, 'The Australians are guests of mine, and I want them to stay with me.' The Provost Captain said, 'Who are you?' The naval officer replied, 'I'm Prince Philip of Greece.' The Provost Captain said, 'That'll be the day. Can you verify that?' So the headwaiter was called over and said, 'You're Prince Philip of Greece.' And the Provost Captain said 'If you're Prince Philip, I'm Jesus Christ.' At this point most of us decided it was time to make a move, but we must have left two behind ... We got back to the ship all right, and we were immediately booked for AWL. We realised that our two mates were still missing. Anyway we slept up on deck and about two o'clock in the morning a barge pulled up alongside the ladder and some sailors carted these two up to the deck and laid them down ... And one of them had a card in his hand reading 'Please excuse these two Australian soldiers for

being late. They have been guests of mine in the wardroom of HMS *Ramillies.*' The card was signed 'Philip of Greece.' When Colonel Godfrey read the note he said 'All right, no charges against these boys.' So they got away with it, but we were clobbered.

As the convoy had been proceeding towards Colombo, there was a growing belief that Italy was about to enter the war on the Axis side. In view of this, the Admiralty considered that it could be unsafe to send further convoys through the Red Sea, and it might be necessary to divert them to Britain. When convoy US2 arrived in Colombo it was still uncertain whether it would be allowed to continue to Egypt, or be diverted, so the ships remained in port until it was decided that they should continue as planned.

Departing Colombo at 4 am on 4 May, the escort was strengthened by the addition of HMS *Kent* and convoy US2 headed west. On board *Neuralia,* the war diary recorded the troops were 'very quiet after leave,' but by 6 May everyone was again in good spirits, and 'Tonight the mess burst into song for the first time since Pucka.' On 12 May the convoy arrived in Aden. *Kent* left the escort there, but for the final passage up the Red Sea to Egypt, *Ramillies* and *Suffren* were joined by the cruiser HMS *Liverpool,* destroyers HMS *Decoy* and HMS *Defender,* and the sloop HMS *Shoreham.* As day was breaking on 17 May, the convoy entered Suez Bay and late on Monday, 18 May, the five ships berthed at El Kantara and prepared to disembark their troops. Generally the men were more than happy to finally be going ashore, but they still had a lengthy train journey to undergo before arriving at their camp in Palestine.

As Percy Bill wrote in a letter a few days later: 'I am not sorry that our trip is over, five weeks is a long while to be cooped up in such a small space. We reached our last port at about ten last Saturday night and had quite a long train journey from there to our camp. We did not start on that till about two in the morning. I was unable to get any sleep in the train but did not mind that much once it got light and it started to do that about four ... When we reached our station we came out to the camp by bus. It is a very pretty spot where we are ... The Arabs hang around the camp nearly all day selling oranges and grapefruit.'

7 The Third Convoy

Back in Australia and New Zealand in April 1940, seven large passenger liners — *Andes, Aquitania, Empress of Britain, Empress of Canada, Empress of Japan, Mauretania* and *Queen Mary* — had been gathered to form convoy US3. Three of these vessels, *Andes, Aquitania* and *Empress of Britain,* had already travelled in a major convoy together when, along with *Empress of Australia, Duchess of Bedford* and *Monarch of Bermuda,* they had comprised convoy TC1 in December 1940. This was the first major movement of Canadian forces to Britain and the six ships had carried 7400 men of the 1st Canadian Division from Halifax to the Clyde, where they arrived on 24 December.

Undoubtedly the most notable of the seven liners was *Queen Mary*, which, when completed in 1936, was at 80,774 gross tons the largest passenger liner in the world, and also the fastest, just topping her great rival, the French liner *Normandie*, for both these titles. *Queen Mary* had been built solely to operate across the Atlantic between Southampton and New York, a five-day passage, and due to her enormous size and depth there were few other ports that she could enter, or go alongside a berth. *Queen Mary* had left Southampton on 30 August 1939 on a regular voyage to New York, arriving on 4 September. The great liner was immediately taken out of service and remained tied up at Pier 89 pending a decision on her use during the conflict. At the Pier 88 lay her rival, *Normandie*, also laid up.

Mauretania, completed in 1939, was much smaller than *Queen Mary*, at 35,738 gross tons, and had only made three trans-Atlantic voyages when war broke out. She had departed Liverpool on her maiden voyage

The three largest liners in the world, *Queen Elizabeth*, *Queen Mary* and *Normandie*, berthed in New York in March 1940. (*Vic Scrivens collection*)

to New York on 17 June 1939, and had also made a couple of cruises from New York. The end of August found *Mauretania* in mid-Atlantic, en route to London, but this was changed, and instead the liner berthed in Southampton on 3 September. Repainted grey and armed with two 3-inch guns and one 6-inch gun, *Mauretania* made one further round trip to New York, then was laid up in Liverpool. With the danger of German air attacks on the city and its docks ever present, it was decided that *Mauretania* should also go to New York, where she arrived on 16 December, being laid up at Pier 90.

At first these giant liners were considered by the British government to be of no worthwhile use in the war, as they were too large to be converted into armed merchant cruisers, and initially considered unsuitable for use as troop transports. At one time there was even a suggestion that they be sold to the United States, along with the other giant Cunard liner, *Queen Elizabeth*, then nearing completion in Scotland, which had been scheduled to enter service in April 1940. In fact, the very presence of such a large liner on the Clyde created a tempting target for German bombers, should they penetrate that far into Britain, and eventually it was decided that she would have to be moved to a place of safety, if possible away from the British Isles.

In order to give *Queen Elizabeth*, then the largest liner ever built, a chance of evading German attacks, an elaborate plan was developed. The only drydock in Great Britain large enough to hold the liner was

Two views of *Queen Mary* at anchor in Sydney Harbour. (*C.T. Reddings collection*)

at Southampton, so it was announced that she would be leaving the Clyde on 26 February to go there for docking. On that day the liner left her builder's yard for the first time, having undergone no trials at all, being eased carefully down the Clyde River to Greenock, where she anchored. Instead of wearing the traditional Cunard colours, the great liner was painted grey all over. Her interior had not been fitted out at all and the launching blocks, which were still attached to her hull under water, could only be removed in a drydock.

On 2 March the new liner left Greenock, but instead of proceeding down the west coast of Britain, headed into the Atlantic at full speed, with no escorts. A huge armada of German ships and planes had been assembled to attack the liner as it passed through the English Channel on the way to Southampton, but they waited in vain. On 7 March 1940, *Queen Elizabeth* arrived unannounced off New York and was shepherded by a fleet of tugs to Pier 90, next to *Queen Mary*, with *Mauretania* having been moved hurriedly to Pier 86. For the next two weeks the three greatest North Atlantic passenger liners ever built, *Queen Elizabeth*,

Mauretania berthed at Circular Quay in Sydney. (*C.T. Reddings collection*)

Queen Mary and *Normandie*, were berthed together, becoming a major sightseeing attraction.

By the time *Queen Elizabeth* arrived in New York, *Queen Mary* had been requisitioned by the Admiralty, on 1 March 1940, and *Mauretania* on 6 March. Over the next few weeks, work proceeded with great haste, and the maximum of secrecy, preparing both liners for sea again and the long journey to Australia. Only a handful of people knew where the ships were going, with the master of *Queen Mary*, Captain Irving, only being informed on 19 March. Cunard sent some of their senior office staff to New York to supervise the removal of furniture and other items from the liners and ensure they were safely stored for the duration of the war.

In order to divert attention from the pending departure of *Queen Mary*, *Mauretania* was moved further down river, to Pier 56, on 13 March, but it was noted that something unusual was happening when another Cunard liner, *Antonia*, arrived in New York on 18 March with 760 seamen, who were transferred to *Mauretania* and *Queen Mary*. On the evening of 20 March *Mauretania* slipped quietly out of New York, making use of a heavy fog and driving rain to hide herself, and headed off into the Atlantic, arriving two days later in Bermuda. In equally great secrecy, *Queen Mary* departed New York on 21 March, her destination known only to a handful of senior officers. Her first stop was at Trinidad, to take on bunkers, then the great liner steamed across the South Atlantic, unescorted and relying on her speed for security, to Cape Town. After refuelling, she continued her passage, arriving off Fremantle on 11 April, but being too large to enter the port, had to anchor out in Gage Roads. Two days later, *Queen Mary* left the Western Australian port, and averaging over 28.5 knots, made a record passage of 3 days 6 hours and 42 minutes to Sydney, arriving on 16 April.

Prior to her dispatch to Australia, examination of all the alternatives showed that *Queen Mary* could find safe anchorage in only two ports, Sydney and Hobart, though was unable to actually berth in either place. In Sydney, a mooring site was selected near Bradleys Head, which would provide sufficient swinging room for the liner to be held by a single anchor. The spot where the anchor was to be dropped had to be located accurately, so a dan buoy was placed to mark the position. On her arrival, *Queen Mary* was shepherded to the selected mooring site, and the anchor was dropped so accurately it actually struck the dan buoy.

With the arrival of *Queen Mary* in Sydney, work could commence on converting her from a luxury liner into a troop transport. The job was allocated to the Cockatoo Docks and Engineering Company and was scheduled to be completed in just fourteen days. Commencing on 17 April, and working in continuous shifts throughout the day and night, hundreds of workers were ferried out to the liner. First, all the remaining luxurious fittings had to be removed and taken to places of storage in the country, then the troop quarters could be installed. The conversion of the liners that constituted the first convoy had been done in a manner that caused the least possible dismantling of the ship's fittings, but that attitude had changed and the interior of the *Queen Mary* was gutted. Wooden multi-tier bunks were fitted into cabins, while hammocks were slung in public rooms. Originally designed to carry 2100 passengers, the liner was altered to transport 5000 troops, and this number would be trebled by the end of the war. For protection, anti-aircraft guns were mounted at various points along the upper decks, while a vintage 6-inch gun was installed at the stern. The work was completed on 3 May.

Meanwhile, *Mauretania* had also arrived in Sydney ahead of *Queen Mary*, on 14 April, having taken a shorter route across the Pacific. After leaving Bermuda, the liner had continued into the Caribbean, passing through the Panama Canal, then crossing the Pacific to Honolulu, to take on bunkers and supplies. From there *Mauretania* voyaged directly to Sydney. As with *Queen Mary*, her conversion to a troopship was done by Cockatoo Docks and Engineering Company, who commenced work soon after the liner arrived. In less than three weeks the interior of the liner was totally transformed, with more than half the original carefully planned cabins being replaced with quarters for 2000 troops, but this work was made easier by the vessel being alongside at Circular Quay.

All eight passenger decks were affected by the work. On the sun deck, cabin-class staterooms S17 to S33 on the starboard side were totally removed, along with bulkheads to the verandah cafe, to provide space for a hospital, with extra lavatories fitted. On the port side, the bulkheads of staterooms S2 to S24 were left intact, though the rooms themselves were stripped of all fittings, including the private showers and toilets, and the spaces filled with standee cots.

Similar work was done on the promenade deck, with the observation lounge forward being filled with standee berths, while toilet facilities were installed in former pantries. The cabin-class smoke room became additional hospital space, while the adjacent gymnasium became a medical inspection room. The cabin-class writing room was converted into a guard and orderly room, as was the cabin-class children's room, and the library became a conference room, while the photographic dark room was transformed into a troop latrine. The only room left relatively unchanged on the whole deck was the grand hall, which remained as a public room, though furnished in a far more mundane style than the original fittings. Right aft, on the open deck, a canvas swimming pool had been provided for cabin-class passengers, and this was altered to serve as a shower area for troops. All cabins on main deck, except some of the suites, were totally gutted, and fitted with standee berths, which were also placed in the former tourist-class cinema and main lounge. The tourist-class children's room became another orderly room, while the shop now served as a regimental office. A use was even found for the Tourist cinema projection room, in which batteries for the gyro compass were stored.

Most of the cabins on A deck were also gutted to provide space for standee cots, which were also installed in the former third-class cinema. In addition, fittings were installed for hammocks, should they be needed. The third-class lounge became a canteen, including lockers for troops, counters for serving meals, and storage shelves, while the tourist-class smoke room was converted into a dry canteen.

Tourist-class and third-class staterooms on B deck were totally gutted, and filled with standee cots, while hammock fittings were also installed, and the former third-class smoke room was converted into a wet canteen for troops, meaning it provided alcoholic beverages. Two of the original restaurants had been located on this deck, with the former cabin-class dining room being allocated for the use of officers, while the tourist dining room became a troop mess hall, as did the former third-class dining room, which was located on C deck. Most of the staterooms on both C and D decks were also gutted for troop accommodation, but some of the former third-class cabins on C deck were retained for use by crew.

One of the features of *Mauretania* when built was a delightful indoor swimming pool low down on E deck, but this too was sacrificed for the war effort, being transformed into a storeroom, with fitted shelves. Another storeroom, as well as an armoury and rifle-racks, were installed in lower hold no. 4. Meanwhile, throughout the entire ship a system of loudspeakers was installed, along with extra latrines and numerous other facilities essential for the carriage of a large number of troops. While the conversion was in progress, a fire broke out in the lower section of no. 5 hold, apparently caused by careless handling of an acetylene torch, but only minor damage was caused, and quickly repaired.

It was also necessary to fit a variety of defensive weaponry along the upper decks, primarily to protect the liner in case of attack from the air. A radar tower and gunnery control tower were constructed on the monkey island, high above the bridge, while four rocket containers and four ammunition containers were also installed there. On the captain's deck and sports deck, a further four rocket launchers were installed, along with twelve guns, for which 36 ammunition boxes were fitted. More guns were installed on the engine room casing top, the aft funnel casing, and the upper level of the aft section of the promenade deck. On the after docking bridge, two PAC rocket stands and one 12 pound gun were installed, with another 12-pound gun placed near the steering engine skylight right aft. Two more 12-pound guns were sited on the forecastle section of the main deck, which, being in a more exposed location, were also given an armour plate shield. Nearby were two Oerlikon guns, with magazines, while two more Oerlikons were mounted aft on the main deck. Finally, on the navigating bridge, the wheelhouse was protected by a steel bulletproof screen, as well as plastic armour both on the inside and outside walls. The conversion work on *Mauretania* was completed on 3 May, the same days as *Queen Mary*.

The third giant Cunard liner to be sent to Australia was *Aquitania*, built in 1914 and the last surviving four-funnelled liner in the world. *Aquitania* was serving in her second war, having been used as a troopship during the Dardanelles campaign in 1915, then being converted into a hospital ship for two years before ending World War I as a troopship again. Requisitioned a second time in November 1939, *Aquitania* was converted into a troopship, with quarters for 7724 soldiers, and began her second war carrying Canadian troops from Halifax to England, before being sent to Australia.

Departing Southampton on 9 March, *Aquitania* went first to Freetown, arriving on 16 March, but ran aground off the port and remained stuck for three days. Once refloated, with no apparent damage, the liner continued her voyage, stopping in Cape Town from 25 to 27 March, then crossing directly to Fremantle, and on to Sydney. Following her arrival in Sydney on 10 April 1940, further alterations were made to the liner by Cockatoo Docks and Engineering Company from 12 to 16 April, involving the fitting of additional troop accommodation on seven decks.

In complete contrast to the veteran *Aquitania* was the brand new Royal Mail liner *Andes*, which had only been launched on 7 March 1939. Built for a service from Southampton to South America, her maiden voyage, scheduled to depart on 26 September 1939, was cancelled and the liner hurriedly converted to carry troops. She had departed on her first voyage on 9 December, going to Halifax to embark Canadian troops and transport them to the Clyde, where they arrived on 24 December. On 31 January 1940, *Andes* departed the Clyde on her way to Colombo, Singapore and Hong Kong, then went to Lyttelton.

In addition there were three liners owned by Canadian Pacific — *Empress of Japan* and *Empress of Canada*, both of which had been in the first convoy — and the huge *Empress of Britain*, which had previously visited

Empress of Japan and *Andes* berthed at Aotea Quay in Wellington on 4 April 1940, before *Andes* went to Lyttelton to embark troops. (*Wellington Maritime Museum*)

Empress of Britain berthed in Wellington. (*Wellington Maritime Museum*)

Australia in 1938 during a world cruise. First to arrive in Australia was *Empress of Japan*, which was taken in hand by Cockatoo Dockyard on 12 March to install further troop accommodation on A, B C and boat decks, the work being completed on 26 March. When *Empress of Canada* arrived back in Sydney on 23 March 1940, further conversion work on her trooping accommodation was also completed by the Cockatoo Docks and Engineering Company between 25 March and 5 April.

Prior to the outbreak of war, *Empress of Britain*, had been operating across the Atlantic between Southampton and Quebec, but on arriving in the Canadian port on 8 September 1939, the huge liner had been laid up and painted grey all over. On 25 November, *Empress of Britain* was requisitioned for war service, leaving Quebec on 10 December for Halifax, where she joined the first convoy carrying Canadian troops to the Clyde. After a further two trips across the Atlantic and back, the liner was sent to New Zealand, passing through the Mediterranean and Suez Canal and arriving in Wellington on 19 April 1940.

As with the first convoy, US3 was to carry both Australian and New Zealand troops, some 18,200 in all, to be embarked at four ports in early May. *Queen Mary* and *Mauretania* would board their troops in Sydney, while *Empress of Canada* went from Sydney to Melbourne, arriving there on 28 April. *Andes*, *Empress of Britain*, *Empress of Japan* and *Aquitania* proceeded to Wellington. When the time to board troops arrived, *Andes* made the short trip to Lyttelton. The two Canadian Pacific liners berthed on either side of King's Wharf in Wellington, while *Aquitania* was at the

Transports in Wellington waiting to embark troops, *Aquitania* at Queen's Wharf, *Empress of Britain* (centre) and *Empress of Japan* on either side of King's Wharf. (*Wellington Maritime Museum*)

adjacent Queen's Wharf. The cruisers *Australia* and *Canberra* also arrived in Wellington, berthing astern of *Leander* on 27 April, and next day *Canberra* left for Lyttleton to escort *Andes* on the first leg of its trip. With the situation regarding Italy still causing concern, the boarding of troops was delayed for a day, but then embarkation was approved on the proviso that the convoy proceed only as far as Fremantle, to await a decision as to its final destination.

On 2 May, the same day convoy US2 arrived in Colombo, the four ships carrying 6000 New Zealand troops left their ports. *Andes*, escorted by *Canberra*, departed Lyttelton early in the morning and voyaged up the east coast of South Island to link up with the other three in Cook Strait. *Empress of Japan* left her wharf in Wellington at 7 am and anchored in the harbour, at which time a boat drill was held for the troops, while a flotilla of small boats circled the liner. Shortly before 11 am *Aquitania* also undocked, followed shortly after by *Empress of Britain*, along with the two escort cruisers *Australia* and *Leander*, which led the way out of the harbour, followed in a single file by *Aquitania*, then *Empress of Japan* and *Empress of Britain*.

By 12.30 pm, the six ships were steaming into Cook Strait, where *Andes* joined them at 1.30 pm as planned. The troopships formed into two lines, *Aquitania* ahead of *Empress of Japan* on the starboard line, while *Empress of Britain* led *Andes* in the port line. *Australia* took up position ahead of *Aquitania*, and *Canberra* ahead of *Empress of Britain*, leaving *Leander* to move to varying positions as required. In this formation they made a high speed dash across the Tasman Sea in calm conditions, to reach a rendezvous point off Sydney on 5 May.

Meanwhile, in Sydney and Melbourne 8000 men from Queensland, Tasmania and Western Australia were being loaded aboard *Queen Mary*, *Mauretania* and *Empress of Canada*. These troops, totalling one-third of the 6th Australian Division, comprised the 2/9, 2/10 and 2/12 Battalions of the 18th Infantry Brigade, 2/3 Field Regiment, 2/1 Anti-Tank Regiment, 2/1 Machine Gun Regiment, the 2/3 Field Ambulance, and two units of engineers, the 2/3 Field Company and the 2/1 Field Park Company.

In Sydney, *Queen Mary* was anchored out in the harbour, and a fleet of ferries was needed to transport the 5000 troops she would be carrying from the wharf at Pyrmont to the giant liner. The first to board the *Queen Mary* that day was the 2/3 Field Regiment, among them Lieutenant Michael Clarke, attached to Regimental Headquarters, whose memories of that day are recorded in his autobiography, *My War*. The regiment had been camped at Ingleburn, south of Sydney, and 'at 0400 baggage was ordered out by carriages ... We breakfasted at 0415 and the baggage went off at 0450, taken to the Ingleburn Station ... At 0500 there was a full Regimental Parade, and RHQ and 2/6 Battery marched off at 0535 ... We entrained in dawn light and proceeded to the quay ... RHQ were the first to board the ferry at Pyrmont, to be taken out to the mighty *Queen Mary*, and we had a great sight of the other huge troopship, the *Mauretania*, and the escort cruisers and destroyers anchored in the harbour. We filed up the gangway and were embarked by 0920 hours, the first troops to board.'

Once on board, 'The ship's officers and men led us to our quarters and we were all staggered by the luxury of our accommodation. The men were quartered in tourist-class cabins, while McNamara, Learmonth and I were in a first-class suite, M16, amidships, with sheets and pillows on the beds and a steward to look after us.' During the day the rest of the 2/3 Field Regiment, and numerous other units, came aboard in a steady stream, but 'The first Mess Parade at 1700 hours led to terrific congestion, due mainly to the non-arrival of the mess orderlies' and Michael Clarke found himself 'sorting out leaderless men from all kinds of units. Everyone was surprisingly good-humoured and obedient, and we managed to get the first sitting fed in the end. We then retired to the Officers' Mess in the old Tourist Lounge, and on to the Officers' Dining Mess in the old Tourist Saloon. We were fed right royally, waited on by ship's stewards in a most civilised manner.'

The final contingent of troops arrived on board *Queen Mary* late in the afternoon of Saturday, 4 May, including Norm McKellar of Queensland, who kept a diary of the voyage from which some of the following information was obtained. By 7 am on 5 May, *Queen Mary* had raised her anchor and steamed out of Sydney Harbour. As Michael

Clarke recalled: 'I was awakened by the steward at 0630 hours on Sunday 5 May and found that the ship was moving. I promptly went on deck to view the scene. It was a damp morning, with fine rain. There were few pleasure craft about and the men were sober and quiet ... The men's breakfast was much delayed, due to the mess orderlies staying on deck to watch the last of Sydney, but again everyone was eventually well fed ... It was a calm, overcast day as we passed through the Heads.' *Queen Mary* steamed some distance off the coast, then circled round until about 9 am, when the four New Zealand ships arrived, and the five liners idled off the coast, which caused 'an occasional instance of seasickness' on board *Queen Mary*.

As the great liner had steamed slowly down the harbour, there were still Cockatoo Dockyard workmen on board frantically trying to complete the fitting of the lone 6-inch gun, of 1902 vintage, which needed to be bolted in place at the stern. The job was completed just before the liner passed through Sydney Heads and the dock workers left the ship on the pilot boat. Detailed to the ship as gunners were three Australian naval ratings, Arthur Tate, Wally Taylor and Ted Flynn, who would remain with *Queen Mary* for the next three years.

Back in Sydney, the last of 2184 men were boarding *Mauretania*, which was berthed at No. 4 Circular Quay, though the troops were also brought to the ship by ferry from Darling Harbour. Also joining the ship was an Official Australian War Correspondent, Kenneth Slessor, who wrote in his diary on 5 May, 'This day embarked, by ferry from Darling Harbour, on transport *Mauretania* (9.00 am) ... A wet weeping Sunday, sky full of smoke and rain, greasy clouds, puffs of steam, and rain blowing in drifts, like a Turner print ... Cordon of soldiers ashore kept crowds distant from *Mauretania* at No. 4 wharf as troops filed on board from ferry loaded with field equipment. On the other side of Sydney Cove, crowds, mostly women, stood in rain, clinging to iron railings, and staring through them ... The men had been embarking from early morning, and had risen at 3.00 am in Ingleburn camp, to take trains to Darling Harbour.'

Once on board, Slessor wrote, 'men were immediately ordered to put on sandshoes and remain in cabins until at sea, but looking down over the side from top deck, the whole side of the ship bristled with men's heads from portholes, shouting ashore and arms waving. Before casting off, visitors to ship included Governor-General and staff.' *Mauretania* pulled away from the wharf shortly after 1 pm, and as the ship moved out into the harbour, 'Continuous cheers, cooees, shrieks,

HMS *Leander* was one of three cruisers escorting convoy US3.

women's cries and songs floated over water from shores each side. Windows of flat buildings ... were lined with figures waving what seemed to be towels or petticoats ... A flotilla of yachts, motor launches, ferryboats, speedboats, even canoes, set off with *Mauretania*, but the transport moved out with such speed that she quickly outdistanced all except a speedboat ... Other ferries and launches kept pace for a while by intercepting on the route, but fell back, crowds waving and yelling, girls in slacks crying "You're going too fast" ... Men climbed on rocks at water's edge, shouting. Garrison in formation at Middle Head Fort gave three cheers. The transport followed a course down the harbour marked by buoys with red flags.'

Mauretania steamed out to sea, linking up with the other ships at 3 pm. The six liners were formed up into two columns, *Empress of Britain* leading *Mauretania* and *Andes* on the port side, while *Queen Mary* headed *Aquitania* and *Empress of Japan* in the starboard column. At 3.30 pm the convoy turned south, escorted by the same three cruisers that had come across the Tasman with the New Zealand ships, *Australia*, *Canberra* and *Leander*.

Kenneth Slessor recorded: 'For their first day on board, the men were allowed to roam freely all over the ship. They had been noisy or exuberant on the ferry from Darling Harbour, but straggling through the shining halls of the liner, they became almost awestricken at the sudden magnificence.' Of his own accommodation he wrote, 'My cabin is No. 2 on main deck, facing immediately forward, and has two berths, which I share with Mr McIlveen, a Salvation Army officer, but seems an unassertive genial fellow, not obviously eager to save me.'

On their first day at sea, 6 May, the troops awoke to a smooth sea and bright sunlight. During the day the decks of the ships were filled with men doing rifle drill, physical exercises and other activities. That

Transports and escort of convoy US3 berthed in Fremantle on 11 May 1940. From left, HMAS *Canberra, Empress of Canada, Empress of Britain, Empress of Japan.* (*Department of Defence*)

same day, *Empress of Canada* completed loading her troops in Melbourne, leaving the port early in the afternoon. As the rest of the convoy passed Port Phillip Heads about 4 pm, *Empress of Canada* took up her station as the fourth ship in the starboard column, behind *Empress of Japan*, the speed of the convoy being set at 19 knots as it crossed the Great Australian Bight. The convoy commodore, Captain J.W.A. Waller, RN, was stationed on board *Empress of Britain*.

Despite the work done converting passenger accommodation into troop quarters, the interior of some of these ships still contained some outstanding features, as one writer extolled when describing his unnamed 'real luxury boat' in a letter home, which was intercepted by the censor. 'Our messing hall for instance has marble slab pillars and marble slab walls. Row on row of concealed lights, several big paintings, we have several lifts on board, a grand lounge with deep big chairs, a big foyer which we use for Reg. Orderly rooms, wonderful wooden pannelling [*sic*] in the corridors, some good carvings in wood, plenty of showers etc … '

On board *Queen Mary*, the initial excitement of being on board the most famous liner in the world soon dulled. Men became lost in the endless maze of corridors below decks, while open decks soon became heavily congested. Although the liner was now engaged in military service, there were still reminders of her civilian background. Troops were ordered to wear sandshoes rather then boots, to protect floor coverings and decks. They were also asked not to carve their initials in the woodwork, particularly the handrails in corridors and on stairs, not to use the elevators, and above all, that a hideous fate awaited anyone caught souveniring. While most of these instructions were obeyed, there were always numerous ashtrays, coathangers, pieces of cutlery and other items, all carrying the insignia of *Queen Mary* or the Cunard White Star Line, found in hiding places during kit inspections.

Three meals a day were served, in three sittings, each of which lasted only twenty minutes. However, some troops became lost trying to find their mess area and missed out on meals. According to Michael Clarke, 'The officers were feeding like princes in the old Tourist Saloon and beer cost five pence a pint. The men's food was also excellent and they were settling down happily.' On board *Mauretania*, 'The food on this ship is a ceaseless source of wonder and delight to the soldiers,' wrote Kenneth Slessor. 'The young officers around me at mess are like schoolboys at a dream tuckshop. They wolf icecream with unabashed glee. The meals really are amazingly good and varied — of a kind which would have seemed incredible possibly to the soldiers who filled the troopships of 1914–18 ... Several of the more hopeful lieutenants have expressed the theory that the menus aboard should prove a stimulus and inspiration to the army cooks, most of whom are assisting the ship's chefs for periods each day, as a kind of post-graduate training.'

As the ships crossed the Great Australian Bight the weather stayed fine and the sea remained calm, with the occasional slight swell, but even this was enough to make some on board seasick. After sunset, a strict blackout was applied on all ships. Kenneth Slessor wrote that dark was 'the word for the decks after sunset — not even a cigarette-tip allowed, shaded blue lights behind screen at doors ... other transports reporting instantly if flicker of light is detected on any other ship in convoy.'

During this part of the voyage many of the troops were allocated jobs around the ship. Michael Clarke found himself rostered for duty in command of an anti-aircraft gun atop the superstructure above the bridge. He was instructed: 'Your job is to give the order to open fire on attacking aircraft after identifying them as hostile. You will also give the gun crew orders to abandon ship when necessary, that is, when the water reaches this level and you can shove these rafts over the rail into the sea. See that you do it quick smart, although I don't fancy your chances ... Just remember that the lives of several thousand men will be in your hands, so don't bloody well get seasick up here. After we leave Perth this post will be manned from dawn to dusk, but when we enter enemy waters it will be operative twenty-four hours a day.' A final instruction was, 'This post is out of bounds to all personnel not on duty here, so don't bloody well bring any of those bush nurses up here for sunbathing or other such damn nonsense.'

Convoy US3 arrived off Fremantle early in the morning of Friday, 10 May. At 11 am, *Queen Mary* dropped anchor in Gage Roads, as did

Aquitania taking part in convoy US3. (*C.T. Reddings collection*)

Aquitania and the three Empresses, while *Andes*, *Mauretania* and the escorting cruisers were able to enter the port and berth. The troops on the two transports were granted shore leave, and soon were headed for Perth in packed trains. Kenneth Slessor also went ashore, and returned to his ship 'soon after midnight. Troops were returning surprisingly sober (comparatively) and well-behaved on the whole. In fact, during the whole day ashore I saw practically none of the wildness attributed to the first contingent passing through Perth ... New Zealanders and Australians mixed well ... I saw no brawling.' While in Fremantle, a further 162 men, Western Australians of the 2/11 Battalion, joined *Mauretania*.

Early on the morning of 11 May, *Mauretania* and *Andes* left the wharf at Fremantle and moved out to Gage Roads, which enabled the three Empresses and *Aquitania* to enter the port and berth. Fremantle had never seen such a gathering of great ships, made even more impressive when the three-funnelled trio of Empress liners berthed in a row, along with the three-funnelled cruiser *Canberra*. The troops on board the ships berthed in Fremantle were granted shore leave while their ships were alongside, but no shore leave was granted to the troops on board the anchored *Queen Mary*. Norm McKellar recorded that there was a near riot on board *Queen Mary* when the troops heard this. Another soldier on board *Queen Mary* wrote in a letter home that failed to get by the censor, 'Freemantle [*sic*] was our only Australian port of call, but as the Queen was too big to get anywhere near the shore we had no leave.'

Another letter from a soldier that was intercepted by the censor was even more detailed, stating 'On our way round from Sydney to Freemantle (sic) we picked up the rest of the convoy and when we were all together there were the *Queen Mary, Mauretania, Aquitania, Empress of Britain, Empress of Canada, Empress of Japan, Andes*. Seven of the largest vessels in the British fleet, and they were truly a magnificent sight.' Referring to his quarters aboard *Queen Mary*, the writer continued, 'My steward told me it was the suite Mrs Simpson, or should I say the Duchess of Windsor, used when travelling to England. This was my home for the next 44 days.'

The same day convoy US3 arrived in Fremantle, Germany launched its invasion of Holland and Belgium, both of which were soon overrun, while British forces were effecting a strategic withdrawal from Norway. However, there was still no definite indication that Italy would enter the war, so a decision was made that the convoy would continue its voyage to the Middle East as planned. On the morning of 12 May the ships berthed in Fremantle left port, while *Queen Mary* raised her anchor at 12.30 pm and began moving out to sea, soon followed by *Mauretania* and *Andes*, then the four ships coming out of Fremantle, steaming in single file. Once in open waters, the ships formed into the same two columns as before, and, still escorted by the cruisers *Canberra*, *Australia* and *Leander*, the convoy headed off across the Indian Ocean, bound for Ceylon, with *Queen Mary* due to call at Trincomalee while the other ships would go to Colombo.

Monday, 13 May, Michael Clarke noted, 'brought a rainy morning with the other ships dim shapes partly concealed in a sea mist. The emergency alarm sounded at 1030 hours and we remained at emergency stations until mid-day, being instructed in lifeboat procedure and survival at sea in the boats.' The same day, Norm McKellar noted that a man was lost after falling overboard from *Aquitania*. The next day another man was lost overboard. Kenneth Slessor was being shown around the engineroom of *Mauretania* when 'about 5 pm, bells rang, and power was slackened. After leaving, had a drink with Chief Engineer, and he explained that sudden slackening was due to man going overboard from one of the Empress boats at the rear of the convoy. The convoy immediately slackened to half-speed and the two Empress boats stopped, and cruiser *Leander* raced back to them. At approximately 5.20 pm, convoy resumed normal speed again and Empress boats followed, but much farther astern' Slessor later found out that 'man overboard was a stoker who had fallen from *Empress of Japan*. Ships had been unable to find him, so poor devil had to be left to his fate.'

Two days later Slessor noted, 'We are now evidently well in the tropics. Night was sticky hot, despite ventilator in port of cabin, electric fan going continuously and pressure air-supply at side of berth. Hot overcast day, with occasional blazes of sun ... Late afternoon, there was a stir and everyone rushed to the sides of deck to see cruiser *Leander*, which had stopped its course in front of convoy, and seemed to be going astern. *Leander* lay in middle of two lines of ships as convoy passed it. A few seconds later, *Andes* changed course at rear of convoy, and turned right round in circle. The news came that another man had gone overboard, this time a *Leander* sailor. As *Leander* and *Andes* fell back, cruiser and flagship *Canberra* came racing back and passed us at full speed, a splendid sight. Before reaching *Leander*, *Canberra* turned back, and passed again, back to van of convoy, a sign that the man had been recovered, by a boat launched from *Andes* according to report.'

During the same afternoon, 'shipboard reports that Holland had capitulated unconditionally, and that Italy had joined Germany, caused anxiety, and there was much speculation as to whether convoy would be risked in vicinity of Ceylon or Suez. The night turned hotter and moister, and going up to the sun deck about 11.30 pm, I was surprised to see by the position of the Southern Cross and the setting moon that we had changed our course to southwest — this apparently means we are now heading in the direction of South Africa, and not Colombo.' Norm McKellar also noted in his diary that on 15 May the troops were officially informed that their next destination was Ceylon, but the same day a decision was taken by the War Cabinet that the convoy should be diverted. Michael Clarke was called to a hastily convened officers conference on *Queen Mary*, at which the Commanding Officer informed them, 'Due to the international situation the convoy commander has received orders to alter course and proceed to Cape Town. God knows what will happen after that.' With a rising sea making life unpleasant for the men on all the ships, the change of course had been effected, and an announcement was made to the troops on 16 May regarding the change of destination.

Changes were also made to the escort, *Leander* being ordered to detach from the convoy and continue to Colombo. The cruiser HMS *Shropshire* was diverted from her regular patrol area in the South Atlantic to steam into the Indian Ocean and meet up with the convoy, which she did on 20 May, at which time *Canberra* also detached, and turned back to Australia.

Sickness and accidents were beginning to take a toll of those on board the ships. On 16 May, Kenneth Slessor recorded, 'Flags were flying at half mast on *Queen Mary* this morning, and it was reported that a man had died on board, and had been buried at sea. All these

HMS *Shropshire* joined the convoy escort in the Indian Ocean.

incidents are scarcely a happy beginning for the enterprise. Another reported sea burial from one of the Empress boats makes three deaths and a man overboard since the start eleven days ago.'

As usual on troopships rumours abounded, with much speculation among the troops and ship's crew as to their ultimate destination. Slessor wrote on 16 May he had been told that 'it had been decided to split the convoy into two — *Queen Mary*, *Empress of Britain* and *Mauretania* to proceed to Cape Town, the other Empress boats, *Aquitania* and *Andes* to East Africa, probably Mombasa. *Queen Mary*, *Empress of Britain* and *Mauretania*, being crack liners, are to be put into safety at Cape, and the only conclusion I can draw is that the troops aboard will either be transferred to other transports, or else go on to England, since there is no other destination I can think of as likely after Cape Town.'

The next day came another rumour, when 'Steward today said that *Aquitania* was running short of water, and he believed we would make a brief call at Madagascar tomorrow. This may be only his guess, but it certainly appears that we are still in the Tropic of Capricorn, and have not gone far enough south to suggest we are making for the Cape direct. Isaacs says he believes there is a British fleet of seven warships scouting about fifty miles ahead of us.'

Despite the rumours, the convoy kept together, and on the evening

Queen Mary and *Aquitania* at anchor off Simonstown Naval Base. (*South African Defence Force*)

of 18 May ran into some wild weather, as Slessor wrote, 'sea became turbulent, and ship bucked and rolled more than I have felt it do to date. Next day, 'Sea still rough, and was rattled from side to side, and up and down, in my berth last night. Morning broke dull and sulky, with sleet over sea, and heavy roll ... Pitch and roll of ship continued all day. Walking along deck, lift and dive of boat make you feel like reflections in distorting-mirrors, one moment elongated and scarcely touching floor with your toes, next minute squat and punched down.'

There was also much humour on board the ships, and Slessor quoted one story doing the rounds, regarding 'one of the junior officers, who had persuaded a nurse to take a stroll with him on the sun-deck a few nights ago. Pausing in the darkness and windy silence, he swept his arm at the silver-topped sea beneath, "Wonderful, isn't it," he exclaimed romantically. "Just the sea and the moonlight, and you and I." "What about me, sir?" interrupted a sentry. They hadn't seen him standing at his post in the dark.'

On 20 May, the soldiers on the transports watched as HMS *Shropshire* arrived, and *Canberra* left the convoy. As Kenneth Slessor recorded, the sea was 'calm this morning. A full foggy day. At almost 4.00 in the afternoon, one of the cruisers left the convoy, her place having been taken by an English warship. At about 3.45, she could be seen turning in from the port side. The sea was black and stony, with a white mist blotting out sky and sight just beyond ships in front ... The cruiser came racing out of this like a ghost, and steamed right down the centre-lane between the lines of transports. At 4.00 she passed us ... As the cruiser approached, the troops broke into cheering ... Naval men stood in groups on the cruiser, waving, signal flags streamed from her masts ... In a few minutes she had vanished in the mists behind us ... The lines of huge ships, crammed with soldiers, and the single warship, sea-grey and with guns bristling, sliding down their centre, made a stirring sight.' However, later that evening the weather changed. 'As I write, *Mauretania* is rolling heavily again, and things are sliding to and fro on the desk. The white of the mist curdled into ashen grey, and it is raining.'

Keeping the troops active, or entertained, was a full time occupation for the officers. Apart from daily physical training sessions, and numerous lectures on a wide variety of subjects, a group on board *Queen Mary* put together a stage show called 'Smiling Thru,' which was performed for the first time on 20 May and proved so successful it was repeated several times. On 22 May a sports meeting commenced, covering all manner of events, from boxing to draughts and chess. It was also on 22 May that the emergency stations siren went off, resulting in a mad dash to gun emplacements. It was reported that a submarine had been sighted briefly on the surface, then dived, but after some time it was decided that the offender had probably been a whale.

Despite the change of course, the troops had been given no other information than that their first destination was Cape Town, so rumours continued to fly. Slessor recorded on 22 May, 'Many of the officers still believe we shall finish in Palestine, either by rail from Cape or via Mediterranean; others say East Africa; others the South of France, landing from the Bay of Biscay; and others again seem positive we are going direct to England. For my part, I half-expect that a temporary training camp will be established at the Cape until the situation is cleared up.' Away from the rumour mongering, Slessor 'inspected the troops' mess-rooms with lieutenant in charge, also ship's kitchens. The men eat to clockwork schedule, and the first sitting (of a thousand) is fed by 12.20, starting from about 12.05. As I watched, they were eating barley broth (which looked somewhat grey and dull), followed by lamb pot stew, with pastry and vegetables and baked jacket potatoes, then tapioca pudding. Some brought private bottles of Worcester sauce in tunics, to add flavour. A glance at the kitchens makes you realise tremendous job of cooking for two thousand at a meal.'

A number of men on board *Mauretania* had been hospitalised with a variety of ailments. On the night of 23 May a private from the 9th Battalion died from pneumonia, and preparations were completed for a burial at sea. Slessor wrote of it on 25 May, a 'bleak, leaden morning, with heavy roll on sea. Soon after breakfast, troops lined decks in silence, facing sides, for burial of 2/9 man who died from pneumonia. Captain Helmore read burial service, and body was lowered into sea from stern while bugler sounded "Last Post." It sank smoothly and noiselessly, without even a bubble; an impressive but rather awful ceremony, since I think, even if I were a corpse, I would be appalled by the lonely vastness of empty sea for miles around.'

Approaching the coast of South Africa, the convoy began zigzagging, and on the morning of 26 May the ships arrived off Cape Town. The escorting cruisers left the convoy and went to the Simonstown Naval Base, while *Queen Mary*, *Aquitania* and *Empress of Canada* had to anchor outside the breakwater of Cape Town harbour. The other four liners berthed in the port, eventually being joined by *Empress of Canada*. At Cape Town shore leave was granted to all troops, commencing the day after arrival. For those aboard *Queen Mary*, this entailed being transported to land on two flat-bottomed punts towed by a tug, but only about two hundred men at a time could be carried. This meant that some troops waited hours to get ashore, so it was not surprising that when the periods of leave expired, most of the troops were found to be AWOL. This was also partly due to the weather, as during the afternoon the wind and seas rose, and the tugs had a terrible time trying to nurse the barges loaded with troops back to the giant liner. Eventually the operation had to be stopped, at which time only about 400 of the 2500 men due back had in fact returned to the ship. After taking on bunkers, *Queen Mary* and *Aquitania* moved on 28 May to anchor off the Simonstown Naval Base, about 80 miles from Cape Town, and gradually the missing troops filtered back to the liner, the last not turning up until 30 May.

The weather was to cause several problems for the ships and the troops during their stay at Cape Town, with heavy clouds, some rain, and strong winds. As Kenneth Slessor wrote on the day they arrived, 'Table Mountain was covered all afternoon with sliding reefs of cloud, blowing in long grey streams over summit,' while on 28 May he noted, 'Table Mountain obscured by mist and clouds most of day.' That night the winds got up, and on 29 May, Slessor recorded, 'Weather still bleak; sky and sea gunmetal-colour; clouds, mist and smoke floating heavily over Cape Town ... Soon after 11.00, *Mauretania* moved out from wharf ... Reason for ship moving from wharf is said to be that heavy swell caused her to break two cables during night, and two tugs had to stand by, to keep her moored ... *Mauretania* anchored again outside breakwater ... some miles from city, and next to cruiser *Australia*.' He then continued, 'Worried this afternoon by new rumour that it has now been decided that we go to Suez after all ... Hear that out of convoy's troops ashore there have so far been thirty casualties — rumoured that two men have been drowned through accidents while returning to *Queen Mary*,' this latter story being untrue.

On 30 May, 'In evening, about 5.00, *Empress of Britain* shifted from wharf to midstream, and *Mauretania* moved in to her place at wharf. Sentries were immediately posted at gangway, and no one, except for a few officers, allowed to go ashore. Pipes for taking in oil-fuel attached, and stores loaded.' Although most of the troops on *Mauretania* had returned to the ship, some had overstayed their leave time, and Slessor recorded, 'During evening, AWLs started drifting back ... AWL men so far have been fined £1 per hour absent, with a maximum of £5; others sentenced to confinement to barracks when voyage ends.' He also said he had been told that 'altogether about twenty-seven men are still missing from *Mauretania* rollcall, and that eighteen Australian or New Zealand soldiers have been killed ashore from knife-wounds received in District 6, the local native and underworld zone ... The news about the fatalities and fracas ashore has been hushed up as much as possible. Tonight there was also a minor disturbance aboard *Mauretania* — about three hundred of the troops tried to force their way off the ship, but after blows had been struck, the leaders were arrested, and the remainder sent back to their cabin to be punished tomorrow ... Betting at mess tonight was that we are bound for Suez.'

An unexpected problem arose during the layover at Cape Town, when the Chinese crew members aboard *Empress of Japan* and *Empress of Canada* refused to travel any further. There had been problems with the Chinese stewards on these ships for some time, as they were convinced that soldiering was the lowest type of employment and they would lose face serving mere troops. Also, officers had batmen to serve them morning tea, usually at 7 am, but the Chinese were determined they should perform this task. The first day at sea, the Chinese bedroom boys had served the officers morning tea five minutes earlier than the batmen were due, so the next day the batmen served morning tea five minutes earlier. This farcical situation continued until some officers were being woken at 5.30 am for their morning tea. By then, the convoy had diverted and was heading for South Africa, and possibly on to Britain, but the Chinese crew members objected to sailing into a war zone, demanding double pay. The situation was resolved by removing *Empress of Japan* from the convoy, with her troops being dispersed among the remaining ships, while some of her officers were transferred to *Empress of Canada*. Once these changes had been made, *Empress of Japan*, with all the Chinese crew members of both ships on board, left Cape Town on 31 May and headed back into the Indian Ocean, eventually arriving at Hong Kong on 23 June.

Early in the morning of 31 May, the troopships in Cape Town left their berths and linked up with *Queen Mary* and *Aquitania* off Simonstown to begin the next leg of their long journey to Freetown. Slessor wrote about the departure, 'Ship cast off from wharf at 8.30 this morning ... taken through breakwater (with its defensive boom) by tugs, and at 9.15 dropped anchor again off shore in Table Bay, close to *Empress of Britain* and *Empress of Japan*, which had moved out previously ... Table Bay crowded with shipping — I counted more than twenty craft lying round us ... Lectures proceeding aboard as usual. At 10.40 am, left Table Bay. *Empress of Britain* went first, then *Mauretania*, next *Andes*. Weather still bleak, ashen sky, chill wind — Table Mountain still lost in fog and cloud. This afternoon, the convoy was back in its old formation, six in all, with cruisers ahead. The course, judging by the sun, was approximately southwest by west ... Talked with Brigadier Morshead after luncheon. Morshead said he himself was still ignorant of destination.'

To assist the depleted crew aboard *Empress of Canada*, it was arranged that some of the Australian soldiers on board be used as deck hands and stewards, while a group of New Zealand naval ratings would serve as sailors and firemen. Later the chief engineer aboard *Empress of Canada*, David Smith, noted 'these men had never done a thing like it before, but we got by and not only that, we were able to go at 20 knots. This was no mean accomplishment, and it speaks highly of the *Empress of Canada*'s engineers.' The ship was also short of experienced personnel on the bridge, with wheel watches being taken by young men who had previously never steered anything larger than a small yacht. The admiral in charge of the convoy placed *Empress of Canada* at the end of a column, so that she would have plenty of room in which to manoeuvre.

Still travelling at 19 knots, the convoy was escorted by *Shropshire* and another cruiser, HMS *Cumberland*. Norm McKellar recorded that about 2500 men aboard *Queen Mary* had been placed under open arrest for going AWOL, and during the seven-day trip from Simonstown to Freetown there were continual courts martial being conducted. All warrant and non-commissioned officers were reduced in rank, ordinary soldiers were fined, but officers could not be sentenced, as there was no general on board the ship to confirm the court's decision. When a general finally did board the ship at Freetown, he ordered that all disciplinary action against those who went AWOL be cancelled, a very popular move.

On the first day at sea again, 1 June, Kenneth Slessor wrote in his diary: 'Weather sunny, and distinctly warmer, and course now appears to be west of north, having been changed during night. Orders today make it compulsory for everybody aboard to carry a lifebelt constantly, the ship having moved into "more dangerous waters." Submarine and anti-aircraft lookouts have been increased greatly ... If our present course continues, it seems almost certain that we are making for Europe — some say Glasgow.'

On 3 June, Slessor was writing, 'Temperature is now rising perceptibly every day, and we must be nearing equatorial zone — however, though this afternoon was smouldering hot in sun, Atlantic heat is much less intense that Indian Ocean heat, sticky and stifling ... Numbers of the troops were given permission to sleep on deck ... If the heat continues, the lower cabins, packed with men, will become intolerable, so the men will welcome the chance to sleep in the air; furthermore, it is thought that this will help to check the spread of mumps and bronchitis, two minor epidemics which are circulating, incubated probably in the crowded troops' sleeping quarters.' That night, taking a walk on the deck after dinner, 'I forgot men were sleeping there, and trod heavily on a soft stomach — fortunately I was able to retreat before the owner sat up cursing.'

As the ships continued their passage north, the heat grew more intense each day. At 6.30 in the evening of Wednesday, 5 June, the convoy crossed the equator. That day Slessor had a chat with two New Zealand nurses, who told him there were 'now 150 in the ship's hospital, mostly mumps and influenza.' He also recorded, 'Night outside quite cool for tropics, but blackout makes decks below like an oven. Announced that we are expected to reach Freetown, Sierra Leone, by dawn Friday.'

On the next day, 'Great excitement at about 5.15, when *Aquitania* suddenly changed her course, turned at right angles into middle of convoy line, and cut across bows of *Empress of Canada* behind her. Movement was so smooth that, watching it at time, I thought it merely an action-rehearsal manoeuvre. However, almost immediately two black balls were hoisted by *Aquitania*, a signal meaning "Ship not under control." At same time, *Andes* (behind *Mauretania*) swung out rapidly to port, and *Mauretania* also made a slight turn. *Aquitania* went straight through at right angle, then turned in circle, *Andes* also coming back with caution. By 5.30, *Aquitania* was coming up at rear of convoy, with *Andes* closer, on her port. Evidently something must have gone wrong with *Aquitania*'s steering gear, and if *Andes* had not been alert, she would certainly have rammed her. Naturally, there was a lot of indignant blinking of signal-lights to and fro in convoy for some time after.'

Arriving in Freetown early in the morning of 7 June, *Queen Mary* again went to an anchorage, as did *Aquitania*, *Mauretania* and *Empress of Britain*, while the other two ships were able to berth, but no shore leave was granted. Kenneth Slessor noted, 'The port is jammed with shipping — I counted fifty-six other vessels surrounding the convoy, mostly tankers and freighters, some Belgian and Greek, also Finnish and French. One hospital ship, white with red cross; an aircraft carrier (*Hermes*); several unknown British warships; the aircraft-mother-ship *Albatross*, formerly part of Australian fleet, and built, I believe, at Cockatoo.' This was correct, as this unusual vessel had been built at the Cockatoo Island Dockyard in Sydney Harbour in 1929 as a seaplane carrier for the Royal Australian Navy. It was not a success, being decommissioned in 1933, then transferred to the Royal Navy in 1938 as part payment for the cruiser HMAS *Perth*.

The stopover in Freetown was not to be a comfortable one for the troops. Slessor wrote that the heat was 'heavy and moist all day, and orders issued that all ports and doors would be closed at night, and

Originally in the Royal Australian Navy, HMS *Albatross* was at Freetown when convoy US3 arrived.

sleeping on deck forbidden, on account of the risk of infection from malarial mosquitoes ... To bed in a cabin which felt like a pool of warm glue, despite fan full on.' Next morning he awoke 'feeling glued to the sheet, after a night of acute discomfort. But at breakfast was delighted to find that the air-conditioning plant has at last been used ... The saloon was deliciously cool — these are the conditions in which one really appreciates what air-conditioning means.' It must be remembered that, in the 1940s, air-conditioning was still relatively new, and only a few public rooms on *Mauretania* and some of the other liners were fitted out with it.

Slessor summed up his opinion of Freetown, 'I don't like this place — not only because of its heat, hanging like a heavy breath over it, nor because there has been no shore leave. It seems to have some kind of curse on it ... you can feel something sinister in the air — and I am not unduly sensitive to this kind of thing.' So there was little regret when, on the afternoon of 8 June, the convoy got under way again, the ships all having topped up their tanks with fuel, and by 5.30 pm they had reformed, and headed west, the escort having been augmented by the addition of the aircraft carrier HMS *Hermes*, which detached on 10 June.'

The same evening, the master of *Mauretania*, Captain Edkin, 'addressed all troops on the ship, by means of the loudspeaker system,' wrote Slessor. 'He pointed out that we were now in an active war zone, and that our precautions would have to be increased. All portholes on decks below A deck are to be closed tight at night, and ventilator-shutters are forbidden. Submarine and aeroplane guards have been tripled, and men are to be stationed continuously at Vickers guns on sports-deck.'

The convoy maintained a westerly course for several hours, until it was well clear of land, then turned north. The fact that they were getting closer to the war zone was reinforced when the ships began following a zigzag course. Next day the weather was already appreciably cooler, and on 10 June Slessor wrote, 'A violent change in weather and temperature during night, caused mostly by a blustering cold gale. The ship is now gradually starting to cool inside — the interior has been stovelike for the past week. Before lunch, changed into woollens and sweater, a notion which would have seemed fantastic yesterday.' The same day, Italy came into the war, though Captain Edkin announced after dinner, 'Gentlemen, we are not at war with Italy until one minute past midnight ... .Film screened at night "Dangerous

The battle cruiser HMS Hood *joined the escort of convoy US3 on 14 June.*

Waters," a title which caused a ripple of amusement.'

On 12 June another cruiser, HMS *Dorsetshire*, joined the escort for two days, being replaced by the huge battle cruiser HMS *Hood*, the largest ship in the Royal Navy, along with the aircraft carrier HMS *Argus* and eight destroyers. Kenneth Slessor noted on 14 June, 'The convoy is now an extraordinary sight — the six troopships in the middle, and then at least a dozen warships circling round it as far as the eye can see.' Taking a wide sweep around the Bay of Biscay and Ireland, the convoy was further protected by Sunderland flying boats during daylight as it passed through the U-boat infested waters of the North Atlantic.

By 14 June, the great voyage was almost over, although the troops had still not been advised of their final destination. That evening, Captain Edkin made another address, in which he 'thanked the troops for their co-operation in safety measures, and good behaviour — it had been arranged to charge all ranks sixpence each, to defray damage to ship, but a survey showed that there was only wear and tear in the ordinary way, so no deduction will be made,' wrote Slessor. Captain Edkin also 'Stated that we are expected to berth in Great Britain tomorrow or Sunday, but where, nobody seems to be certain.'

With the long voyage almost over, Kenneth Slessor put the finishing touches to the first story he would file for the papers in Australia, concerning the trip to Britain, one section of which, regarding the *Mauretania* troops, is worth repeating here:

> In more than one sense, this has been one of the most remarkable troopships ever bestowed on fighting men. Hundreds of the troops have slept and eaten in quarters at one time consecrated to fastidious tourists with fat cheque books. In their cabins they have had electric fans and private bathrooms. Through the smouldering moisture of tropic heat, the lounges and dining saloons were air-conditioned, a state of affairs

which would have stunned even a major general with surprise in the last war. For several weeks, two splendid swimming pools were available for daily splashing. Almost every night talking-picture shows were projected with professional excellence. And the food! The food has been a ceaseless wonder and delight to every soldier aboard ... Dinner was never less than seven courses, perfectly cooked and amazingly varied.

However, this is a war after all, and the staggering consolations of luxury-liner life have been matched by the discomforts of those precautions which are essential to the safety of a warlike convoy. A pitch dark black-out every night, meticulously imposed, made the interior of the ship like an oven during the tropical blaze, and in port men were not allowed to sleep on decks, on account of the danger of infection by malarial mosquitoes. Constant boat station and action station drills and continuous 24 hour lookouts for submarines and aircraft kept everyone awake to the knowledge that, at any moment, the bottom might literally fall out of the little floating world.

Today ... the men are fighting fit. Not for one minute has life at sea been allowed to make them flabby. Thanks to regular daily exercises and games, ingeniously contrived to overcome the lack of space, they are as lean and packed with muscle as they were the morning they marched out of Ingleburn. Particular care has been taken with their feet, as vital to an infantryman as his rifle. Seawater and sandshoes can make a soldiers feet dangerously soft, so each day the men were made to parade the decks for a set period in army boots.

Saturday, 15 June, dawned 'overcast and somewhat bleak,' wrote Slessor in his diary, 'but ship's crew seem to regard it as normal weather of a piping English summer ... Another inspection of the amazing Naval escort shows that there are nine destroyers, two heavy cruisers, a battleship and an aircraft carrier, also a couple of flying-boats patrolling in wide circles. The convoy has huddled very close together, which seems to indicate that danger is expected.' An indication of that danger was soon to appear, as 'about 11.00 in morning, we passed through a trail of wreckage, said to be from British ship torpedoed nearby only yesterday. Then, at about 12.30 we came across a ship blazing with fire about twenty miles away, on our port side. The great red flames and the spouts of smoke could be clearly seen, and she appeared to be standing bows up almost vertically in the sea. A fascinating but awful sight ... The escort sailed past without pause ... Ship's story is that she is an American tanker, torpedoed by same submarine which sank the other ship ... News of the submarine's presence in the neighbourhood made everyone jumpy.'

On board the *Queen Mary*, 'action stations' was sounded and the three Australian gunners closed up on the vintage 6-inch gun at the stern. Arthur Tate was the gunlayer, Wally Taylor the trainer and Ted Flynn the breech-worker. Everyone was extremely tense, lookouts scanning the sea for any sign of a periscope, when Tate felt a tap on his shoulder. It was the second officer of the *Queen Mary*, who exclaimed, 'Guns, Guns! For God's sake don't hit the *Mauretania*, will you!' Many years later, recalling the incident, Arthur Tate said his reply to the ship's officer was unprintable.

After a nervous night, the morning of 16 June greeted the six liners with a 'raw, bitter grey day, with a biting wind ... Even at this stage no one seemed sure which port we would enter. The troops were lined on decks by seven, in full marching kit, with rifles, bags and gear stacked at their sides.' Shortly after dawn, the liners formed into a single file, *Empress of Britain* leading, followed in order by *Mauretania, Andes, Queen Mary, Aquitania* and *Empress of Canada*, and finally entered the estuary of the River Clyde, anchoring off Gourock the same afternoon.

On board *Mauretania*, 'All through the afternoon, the troops remained standing at their stations on deck. No one disembarked, and behind us all the other ships of the convoy anchored in a semi-circle ... So we stared at Gourock from the decks until 4.30, when the General Officer Commanding Scotland paid a visit — bearing a message of welcome from the King, which he read to the troops ... the troops cheered. They were obviously elated by their safe arrival after the long and difficult voyage.' None of the troops went ashore that day, having to spend yet another night on board their ships.

The Australian troops aboard *Queen Mary* presented Captain Irving with a polished wooden plaque on a silver mounting to commemorate the 43-day voyage, this memento being given a place of honour aboard the liner for the rest of her career. The next morning, as Michael Clarke recorded, 'Reveille was predictable at 0400 hours ... Breakfast was at 0500 hours and parade at 0530 hours. It was pretty damn cold when we moved into the lighter at 0645 hours for the short trip to the wharf ... Thus, on Monday 17 June 1940 Colonel Hobbs led us ashore at Gourock, the 2/3 Field Regiment being the first Australian unit to land in Britain this war.'

Throughout that day the troops on board *Queen Mary* and *Empress of Britain* were ferried ashore. However, on board *Mauretania* and the other ships it was 'A long and exasperating day for everyone,' wrote Slessor, 'since we had to remain aboard, marooned in midstream, so near land and yet so far away, no one being allowed ashore ... Time went slowly without sign of any attempt to move us ... At last, at 6.00 in the evening, amidst derisive cheers from the men, a neat little riverboat (ambitiously named *Queen Mary II*) came alongside, and half of the troops boarded her, the other half having to wait until tomorrow.'

Kenneth Slessor was among those fortunate enough to get ashore that day, recording that 'The tender did not leave until 7.45, but it was still bright sunlight at that hour. A short trip took us to a wharf next to the Gourock railway station.' The men were loaded onto a train and began a long journey that took them first to Glasgow, then on to Edinburgh, where they arrived at midnight, and 'each man was given a steaming pint-cup of tea and a packet of food, fruit and chocolates.' Soon the train was moving again, this time south, passing through Sunderland, then York, Sheffield, Nottingham and Leicester, where more refreshments were provided. Then it was on further south, through Banbury, Oxford and Basingstoke, until, at 4.30 in the afternoon of 18 June, the train reached its destination, Salisbury.

On reaching Scotland safely, Captain A.T. Brown commented on the fact that the convoy had been forced to travel at 19 knots. He went on to state, 'It might be worthwhile considering the formation of a 22 or 23 knot convoy in order to get the benefit of the faster type of ship. Such a convoy would cut down the long journey from Australia by almost 100 miles per day, and in doing so would decrease the risk of damage from submarine attack.'

By the time convoy US3 reached Britain, Holland and Belgium were under German control, and France was on the brink of falling. Britain now faced the future with great apprehension, so the arrival of the large contingent of Commonwealth troops was a great boost to morale. However, the disembarkation of the troops from *Empress of Canada* created something of a problem, as this left the ship with only about 25 Canadians on board as crew. Eventually about a hundred men were picked up in Glasgow to take the ship down the coast to Liverpool, where it went into drydock.

8 August to December 1940

The disruption to the arrangements for sending Australian and New Zealand troops to the Middle East caused by the diversion of convoy US3 to Britain brought about the temporary cessation of the convoys. Through June and July of 1940 there were no departures, and it was not until the middle of August that ships began arriving in Australia and New Zealand to resume the movement of troops overseas.

Queen Mary and *Mauretania*, which had been intended to transport Australian and New Zealand troops to the Middle East, rather than be involved in the dangers of the Atlantic, had found themselves in the very situation they had been trying to avoid. *Queen Mary* remained at anchor off Greenock until 29 June 1940, when, having boarded 5000 British troops, she joined a convoy heading for Cape Town, with a stop at Freetown. The troops disembarked at Cape Town and transferred to other vessels to complete their trip to the Middle East. From South Africa, *Queen Mary* voyaged to Ceylon, anchoring off Trincomalee on 29 July, leaving three days later for Singapore, arriving there on 4 August. The drydock in Singapore was one of only three in the world large enough to take a ship the size of *Queen Mary*, and on 5 August she entered the drydock for overhaul, remaining there until 16 September.

Meanwhile, *Mauretania*, after disembarking her troops from convoy US3 in Scotland, proceeded to Liverpool, where she arrived on 22 June. From there she made her way back to the Antipodes, as did one other ship involved in convoy US3, *Aquitania*, which left Glasgow on 29 June, voyaging by way of Cape Town, Colombo and Fremantle to Sydney, where she arrived on 15 August.

Aquitania berthed at Woolloomooloo. (*C.T. Reddings collection*)

Also returning to Australia to take part in the next troop convoy was *Empress of Japan*, which had been part of US3 as far as Cape Town but then was sent back to Hong Kong. From there the liner had made two trips with European women and children being evacuated to Manila because of the war involving the Japanese on the Chinese mainland. The liner had then been further refitted for trooping in Hong Kong before departing on 3 August to voyage back to Sydney, berthing in Sydney Cove on 16 August. *Empress of Japan*, *Mauretania* and *Aquitania*, along with *Orcades*, which had taken part in the first convoy, would comprised convoy US4, which was sent to the Middle East as originally planned. It would be predominantly composed of New Zealand troops, to be carried on *Mauretania*, *Empress of Japan* and *Orcades*, while *Aquitania* would embark Australian troops in Sydney.

Prior to her arrival in New Zealand, *Orcades* stopped in Sydney, where the Cockatoo Dockyard workmen were employed over five days, 12 to 17 August, in re-erecting the fittings for troops in some of the hold spaces. This had been removed so that the liner could carry some cargo on her previous trip, mainly foodstuffs bound for England. *Aquitania* also spent two weeks, from 15 August to 30 August, undergoing extensive machinery, boiler, electrical and plumbing repairs by the Cockatoo work force.

Mauretania pulls away from her berth in Wellington Harbour, while *Empress of Japan* prepares to depart as well. The vessel in the foreground is the inter-island ferry *Maori*. (*Wellington Maritime Museum*)

The departure of convoy US4 was thrown into disarray by the sudden appearance of a German commerce raider in the Tasman Sea. The first indication that a raider might be in the area came when a French steamer, the *Notou*, departed Newcastle, NSW, on 17 August, bound for Noumea, but failed to arrive. Then, on the evening of 20 August, the New Zealand Shipping Company cargo ship *Turakina*, on a voyage from Sydney to Wellington, sent a radio message that it was being shelled by a raider some 260 miles off the coast of New Zealand, followed by silence. The cruiser HMS *Achilles*, which was in Wellington preparing to escort the ships of US4 across the Tasman, was dispatched to search for the raider, while HMAS *Perth* was sent from Sydney on a similar mission. In the meantime, sailings across the Tasman were suspended, but several days of searching by the two cruisers, assisted by air searches, failed to find any trace of the missing ships or the raider. It was later verified that the raider was the *Orion*, which attacked both *Notou* and *Turakina* and sank them. The 73 survivors from the New Zealand ship were taken on board *Orion*, which quickly left the scene, and eight months later arrived in Bordeaux.

Trans-Tasman sailings were resumed on 22 August, and six days later the three New Zealand ships of convoy US4 left Wellington, escorted by *Achilles*, bound for Sydney, where *Aquitania* was preparing to load her troops. Previously the ships had always embarked their troops in daylight, but for the first time a night embarkation was organised. The troops were taken by ferries from Darling Harbour to *Aquitania*, which was berthed at Woolloomooloo, and the liner left before daylight on 31 August. Off Sydney, *Aquitania* linked up with *Mauretania*, *Empress of Japan* and *Orcades* and the four ships then headed around the coast to Fremantle, escorted by HMAS *Canberra*. As before, the convoy was also covered by aircraft when close to the coast, but not while crossing the Great Australian Bight.

On 3 September, as the ships approached the western Bight, aircraft from Albany were sent out to scour the route ahead of the convoy, and one sighted an unidentified steamer 130 miles south of Albany. The plane circled the ship twice but could not make a positive identification due to poor visibility, then had to return to base. As no known ship was in the area, it was assumed, correctly as it later transpired, that the mystery ship was a German raider, in fact *Orion* once again. Further aircraft were sent out but failed to locate the ship, which had made off at top speed to the west. Convoy US4 remained on course and arrived on schedule in Fremantle. From there the ships went on to Colombo, still escorted by *Canberra*, then continued their voyage to Egypt, where the troops were disembarked at Suez.

With the departure of convoy US4, the frequency of troop movements from Australia and New Zealand to the Middle East became a more regular operation. However, the next two groups to leave travelled on smaller Dutch flag ships. Following the German invasion of Holland on 10 May 1940, all Dutch shipping that was not in home waters was ordered to proceed to a safe port, in either a neutral country or under French or British control.

The liner *Indrapoera*, owned by Rotterdam Lloyd, was in the Italian port of Genoa on a voyage back to Holland from the Dutch East Indies. As Italy, though nominally neutral, was known to be supporting the Germans, orders were sent to *Indrapoera* to proceed immediately to Marseilles. After staying a few days there, the liner went on to Casablanca, then in early July left on a voyage back to the Dutch East Indies, via Cape Town. In early July, *Indrapoera* arrived in the harbour of Batavia, and was temporarily laid up there, then moved to Surabaya.

Several other liners owned by Rotterdam Lloyd were also sent back to the Dutch East Indies for safety. *Sibajak*, which had also been homeward bound, turned around and was laid up at Surabaya, while *Slamat* went to anchor at Tandjong Priok. Here they were joined by several ships owned by the rival Nederland Line, including *Christiaan Huygens* and *Johan de Witt*. During July and August 1940, the British government came to an agreement with the Dutch government in exile in London that these ships, along with many others, would be handed over to the Allies. Most of the liners were converted into troop transports, while others became hospital ships.

There were also growing fears in Asian countries that Japan could enter the war at any time, and this caused a steady flow of British refugees from China and Hong Kong seeking safety in Australia and other British Empire countries. In July 1940, four of the Dutch liners

The Dutch liner *Slamat* berthed in Sydney. (*C.T. Reddings collection*)

taken over by the Allies, *Christiaan Huygens, Indrapoera, Johan de Witt* and *Slamat*, were ordered to voyage to Manila to board a large number of British refugees who had fled from Hong Kong to the Philippines, and convey them to Australia. The vessels travelled independently to Manila, *Indrapoera* departing Surabaya on 26 July and arrived in Manila five days later, having spent one day stopped at Balikpapan. Departing Manila on 1 August, *Indrapoera* voyaged by way of Thursday Island to Brisbane, arriving on 11 August, then continuing to Sydney, where she arrived two days later. The vessel then went to Melbourne to disembark the refugees, returning on 18 August to Sydney, where it was to be converted into a troop transport.

Christiaan Huygens was the first of the Dutch liners to arrive in Sydney, on 12 August, while *Johan de Witt* and *Slamat* both arrived from Manila on 20 August. *Johan de Witt* also went on to Melbourne, then returned to Sydney on 26 August.

On their arrival, the four liners were still in their pre-war condition, so had to be altered to carry about 1000 troops each. *Indrapoera* was taken in hand by the Cockatoo Dockyard work force on 19 August and extensively refitted. The work, which lasted until 14 September, included the enclosing of the weather deck, fitting additional galley and bakery equipment and four mess decks, providing protection for the bridge, and installing paravane gear, as protection against mines.

Nieuw Zeeland at anchor in Sydney Harbour. (*C.T. Reddings collection*)

A lesser amount of work was done by Cockatoo Dockyard on *Johan de Witt* between 20 and 26 September. *Christiaan Huygens, Indrapoera, Johan de Witt* and *Slamat* were then held in readiness to transport Australian troops to the Middle East.

Two more Dutch ships, *Nieuw Zeeland* and *Nieuw Holland*, were also allocated to the convoy then being assembled. This pair was already well known in Australia, having spent the previous ten years operating a regular service from Malaya, Singapore and the Dutch East Indies to Brisbane, Sydney and Melbourne. Following the invasion of Holland, they had also been placed at the disposal of the British government. *Nieuw Holland* arrived in Sydney on 9 August 1940 and was converted into a troop transport there by Cockatoo Docks and Engineering Company. The work commenced on 12 August, with space for 1000 men being fitted, along with a new galley and bakery, four mess decks, paravane gear and bridge protection, the work being completed on 7 September. *Nieuw Zeeland* was taken over by the British in Singapore on 15 August and was then dispatched to Sydney, where it received a similar refit to *Nieuw Holland* between 4 and 26 September. These six ships all retained their Dutch crews, but were managed on behalf of the British government by various major shipping companies, including P & O and the Orient Line

It had been planned that the six Dutch ships would be dispatched as one convoy to the Middle East, but eventually it was split into two sections. Convoy US5A was composed of *Christiaan Huygens, Indrapoera, Nieuw Holland* and *Slamat*, and departed Sydney on 14 September. The only armour that had been added to *Indrapoera*, which carried the convoy commodore, was an old 4-inch naval gun, which was mounted at the stern, supposedly to fight off submarines. During the first few days of the voyage, selected Dutch crewmen were given instruction in the operation of the gun.

The four ships and their escorts arrived in Fremantle on 21 September, leaving the next day for Colombo, which was reached on 1 October. After another overnight stay, the voyage continued, reaching Suez on 12 October, and the next day continued through the canal to El Kantara, where the troops all disembarked and were taken by train to camps in Palestine. Subsequently, the four ships proceeded Port Said and then to Haifa, where they discharged their cargo and the equipment they had transported for the troops. *Christiaan Huygens*, *Indrapoera* and *Slamat* then went back through the Suez Canal, and after embarking German prisoners of war at Suez, voyaged to Bombay, from where they commenced a shuttle service to Egypt, mostly carrying Australian troops who had left home in later convoys on the larger troopships.

Meanwhile, *Johan de Witt* had departed Sydney on 30 September bound for Melbourne, while *Nieuw Zeeland* arrived in Melbourne from Sydney on 1 October. Among the troops to board the *Nieuw Zeeland* were the 2/14 Battalion. These two ships comprised convoy US5B, which also went to Egypt.

The situation regarding the provision of suitable escorts for the convoys had been resolved, with the cruisers *Perth* and *Canberra* being allocated to this role. *Perth* would escort the ships from Sydney and Melbourne as far as Fremantle, and sometimes beyond to a point near the Cocos Islands, then hand over to *Canberra*, which would cover them to Colombo or Bombay. From there on, the ships would be escorted by elements of the East Indies Station.

During the period that convoys US4 and US5 were being organised, *Queen Mary* had been in drydock in Singapore, undergoing a much needed overhaul. Refloated on 16 September, the giant liner left Singapore two days later, travelling alone and steaming non-stop to Sydney in 6 days 21 hours and 40 minutes, at an average speed of 27.75 knots. On her arrival, *Queen Mary* again went to anchor off Bradleys Head, and was prepared for another trooping trip to the Middle East. For almost a month, *Queen Mary* lay in Sydney Harbour, awaiting the return from convoy US4 of *Mauretania* and *Aquitania*. These three liners, the cream of the Cunard fleet, comprised convoy US6, *Queen Mary* and *Aquitania* embarking their troops in Sydney, while *Mauretania* went to Melbourne. However, although the troops were destined for the Middle East, it was decided that the three liners would only go as far as Bombay, where the troops would be transferred to smaller vessels for the final leg of their journey.

Convoy US6 would transport two-thirds of the 7th Division, the 20th Brigade, comprising 2/13 and 2/17 Battalions, and the 21st Brigade, being 2/14 and 2/27 Battalions, along with the 2/5 Australian General Hospital and the 2/2 Casualty Clearing Station. One member of the 2/13 Australian Infantry Battalion, which had just completed training at Bathurst, in country New South Wales, was Private Les Clothier, who managed to maintain a diary throughout the war, even though soldiers on active service were officially forbidden to keep such personal records. Fortunately, he was never detected, and the daily record of his army life is an invaluable historical document.

On 12 October, Les noted 'more embarkation practice,' while two days later all members of the battalion were given their second tetanus inoculations, and 'everyone is fed up with waiting. Rumours are rife.' On 15 October, 'still there are rumours; the latest is that we won't go at all, but our Advance Party is still on the ship. Mr Powell says we are definitely going shortly.'

'The whole unit was rigged out in full marching order,' Les Clothier wrote on 18 October, 'and we carried two kitbags all around the place. Train embarkation practice they called it.' The regiment had been provided with details of the train that would be transporting them to Sydney, so a simulated station had been outlined in white tape, along with indicators of where the doors would be on the carriages. The companies were divided into groups, and lined up on the 'platform' opposite the doors of the 'ghost train.' When a whistle was blown, the troops were required to file into the 'train,' some enlivening the proceedings by baaing like sheep. The exercise was repeated several times until the officers were satisfied.

At last, on 19 October, the unit marched to Kelso station, just outside Bathurst, to board the train. The troops took up their allotted positions, and the train steamed into the station, stopping at the precise point indicated by the entrainment officer. He then blew his whistle, but none of the troops moved. More whistles and bellowed orders from officers eventually got the troops moving, but in a chaotic mass as they scrambled through any door they could find. The reason for the chaos soon became apparent. The train had been composed exactly as planned, but the carriages were coupled in reverse order, and none of the doors was where it should have been.

'The trip down was uneventful,' Les wrote. 'The train pulled up right opposite a ferry and in no time we were aboard heading for the Cunard White Star liner *Queen Mary*. Colossal is the only word with which to describe it. There are eight in our stateroom, all in bunks arranged in tiers of two. We sleep between a sheet and a white woollen blanket. What a luxury!'

In the battalion history, it is recorded: 'The *Queen Mary* was a very large ship: it was her size which impressed us most even though, lying off Taronga Park where first we saw her, she somehow disappointed. Our minds were on Cunard posters and their exaggerated perspective. It did not take long to change our minds. From the first time we took the wrong door out of the canteen and spent the next half hour trying vainly to find our way back to our respective cabins ....we were constantly reminded of the fact that she was the second largest ship afloat.'

Also heading for Sydney to join the convoy was the 2/14 Battalion, which had been undergoing training at the Puckapunyal camp, in Victoria. Surprisingly, instead of being sent the shorter distance to Melbourne to join *Mauretania*, on 18 October they were taken by truck to the station at Seymour and boarded a train headed north to Albury. There the whole battalion had to change to another train that carried them on to Sydney, where they arrived late the following morning. The men were then transported directly to the Woolloomooloo wharf where the *Aquitania* was berthed, awaiting them. They were able to board the liner directly from the wharf, and soon found their allotted berths which would be their home for the next few weeks. Although *Aquitania* was older and smaller than *Queen Mary*, her striking presence excited the men as they boarded her.

Aquitania arriving in Sydney Harbour, passing the *Sydney Showboat*. (*National Library of Australia*)

Queen Mary at anchor in Sydney Harbour. (*C.T. Reddings collection*)

On 20 October, the day of departure, Les Clothier on board *Queen Mary* wrote:

> Reveille at 6 am. Breakfast at 7 am in the 1st class restaurant. Marble pillars and a wall map of the world showing the ship's position. Relics of former, more peaceful cruises. The kitchen is a cook's delight. I was a mess orderly and had eggs and bacon, porridge, bread, butter and jam. The food is very good, much better than we got in camp. After breakfast we were given our action boat stations and at 9.30 am two tugs steamed alongside. Excitement was rife as everyone realised the time to sail had come. There were hundreds of small craft around the ship, with women crying when they saw their loved ones; others crying when they didn't. The men were waving and laughing at everyone they saw. It was an unforgettable scene. The *Aquitania* started to move first. She had been tied up at Woolloomooloo berth and when she moved out into line astern behind us, we started to move. Police and naval craft kept the smaller craft away and as we moved past Bradleys Head, the tugs cast off and we were moving under our own power. Everyone along the foreshores was waving and the crowd aboard the *Showboat* sang "Freeza" (For He's a Jolly Good Fellow) and gave us three cheers. Major Turner chased me away from a lifeboat and I went forward and secured a good position as we moved out of the Heads. It was blowing a bit and at 11.30 am we lost sight of land.

The two liners swept majestically out of Sydney Heads, *Queen Mary* in the lead followed by *Aquitania*. Escorted by HMAS *Perth*, the convoy headed south at 19.5 knots. Next day as *Queen Mary* and *Aquitania* passed through Bass Strait, they were joined by *Mauretania*, which had on board 7th Division Headquarters, the 2/27 Battalion from South Australia, the 21st Australian Infantry Brigade, 2/5 Field Ambulance, and twelve nursing sisters of the 2/5 Australian General Hospital. Among those on board *Mauretania* was Lloyd Tann, attached to the 2/5 Field Ambulance. Waiting for his departure time to come, he recalled, 'We were almost overexcited. Camp-crazy. We were all frightened the war's over — you know, we might miss out. Little did we know ... At last we're on our way. Vividly I remember we went up to Dysart Siding, outside Seymour. By train to Station Pier at Port Melbourne. We weren't singing so much as waving out the windows to people lining the railway line. Due to secrecy provisions, there was no boat-name, but everyone knew it was the *Mauretania* ... We sailed on the 21st of October'

The convoy crossed the Great Australian Bight in heavy weather, but maintained its high speed. Lloyd Tann recalled, 'I was never terribly sick. She was a 38,000 ton ship, the *Mauretania*. The *Queen Mary* was an 83,000 tonner, and I saw every inch of the keel, because I was alongside of her. Gee, did it roll! The bow'd dip and the stern'd come up!' However, on board *Mauretania*, 'The fumes from the engine-room were slightly nauseating. The smell from the kitchen tucker, quite good. The boat was still first class. Mint condition. Beautiful bed — an original inner-spring, with a light over the bed so I could have a read. Fairly quickly settled into shipboard life.' When asked about his duties on board the ship, Lloyd Tann replied, 'Looking after anyone who was sick. All our officers were doctors, and they were fairly approachable — gave us training on the medical side.'

The voyage round to Fremantle from Sydney was completed in 4 days 22 hours and 12 minutes. On 24 October, Les Clothier noted 'we must be nearing land. Two bombers came out over the convoy several times today. This morning I started training for the boxing tournament.' Arriving off Fremantle on 25 October, *Queen Mary* and *Aquitania* anchored out in Gage Roads while *Mauretania* entered the port, along with the *Perth*. No shore leave was granted, so the troops had to find their own amusements on board the ships. On 25 October, Les Clothier wrote, 'anchored about two miles off Fremantle. Won my bout in the boxing tournament.' The same day 2/16 Battalion, raised in Western Australia, was ferried out on board an old tanker, the *Karumba*, to *Aquitania* while she was anchored off Fremantle. Next day, 26 October, the voyage of the convoy continued, the three liners averaging just under 21 knots as they steamed across the Indian Ocean, still escorted by *Perth*.

The departure was a brief break in the monotony of shipboard life

HMAS *Canberra* escorted convoy US6 in the Indian Ocean

for the troops. Aboard *Queen Mary* that day, Les Clothier recorded that he 'fought again this morning and stopped the other joker in two rounds. In the afternoon I beat another B Company man, O'Sullivan, and won the lightweight championship of the 2/13th Battalion. We celebrated tonight and the officer of the picquet shut the bar ten minutes early. One thing led to another and the mob got nasty. So did the picquet. They pulled their bayonets and George went down. I rushed in and pulled him out and Cpl Neilson and I carried him down to his cabin. The mob roughed the picquet and four officers and tried to throw the sergeant of the picquet through the porthole, but he wouldn't fit. The CO went in and tried to stop it and was knocked over, but he got up and stopped the brawl.

On Sunday 27 October Les Clothier recorded as 'a day of rest. We attended church parade and f.a. all day.' Next day he wrote 'another hot day. Word is the HMAS *Canberra* will relieve the *Perth* — and it's right! We lined the decks and cheered the *Perth* as she went past on her way back. There was an answering cheer as the cruiser flashed past.'

The battalion history noted:

> In daytime we maimed each other with a medicine ball and after dark visited the forward canteen to hear those colourful phrases that denote the National Game: 'a Pony in the guts! a Spin to see him perform! Set on the sides! Come in, Spinner!' This performance would be followed by a reluctant picquet breaking up the game. It happened every night, but was not — we think fortunately — the sole entertainment we enjoyed.

There was the wet canteen in the stern of the ship. A highly commendable regulation was instituted at this canteen and carried out to the letter with typical British doggedness. No person was allowed to be served with more than one 'container' of beer at a time. We quickly appreciated this particular rule had very definite possibilities. Thereafter, the variety of 'containers' produced would have astounded any publican — there were tin dixie halves (generally after a bad night at Swy); glasses (when we were very poor); and all shapes and sizes and breeds of tins from jam tins to seven pound prune tins. The picture show was another very popular retreat, but the gathering, possibly because we were not yet acclimatised to army theatres, lacked the never-ending and animated criticism which was to become so much a part of the pictures, good or bad, that we were to see in later months. However, there were compensating features. How many of us were in the theatre the night Lord Haw Haw announced that the *Queen Mary* had been sunk!

This voyage was the first that had taken *Queen Mary* into the warmest areas in the world with a full load of troops, and a number of problems soon became evident. Under the relentless Indian Ocean sun, temperatures on board soared over the century mark. *Queen Mary* had been designed to operate across the North Atlantic, so had no air-conditioning, only a ventilation system that could not cope with such heat. Apart from trying to find a cool place on deck, there was little relief from the heat for the troops. Many collapsed, several died of heat stroke, and at times the unbearable conditions came close to causing mutinies. At last after eight sweltering days the convoy arrived in Bombay on 4 November. As with so many other ports, *Queen Mary* was unable to go alongside, so had to anchor some distance out. That day, Les Clothier wrote, 'we sighted land at 6.30 am. It is Bombay, India. The 'Mauri' and 'Aqui' are berthed at wharves but we're out in the roadsteads, about eight miles off.'

For the three large troopships, this was the end of the voyage, but the troops on board still had further to go. However, having arrived in Bombay, the troops could not all be disembarked immediately. Among the first to go ashore were those aboard *Mauretania*, including the 21st Australian Infantry Brigade, who boarded a train and were taken to Deolali camp, where they stayed for five days.

On their last night aboard *Queen Mary*, many of the troops went to see the picture show, but, as the battalion history records: 'the show did not go on. Stacked around the walls of the theatre were hundreds upon hundreds of pillows, placed there by troops who had already disembarked. Everyone of us took one to sit on and, when an announcement was made to the effect that there would be no films that night, each and every one of us must have had the same idea, viz., to hurl the pillow at somebody, before leaving. Somebody got up to leave, threw a pillow at someone else who retaliated by shouting: 'it's on!' and throwing his pillow. Within five seconds the air was full of flying pillows. Barricades of forms had been flung up, snipers were shooting from behind pillars, attacks and counter-attacks were launched, succeeded or were repulsed, airbursts, in the form of feathers, were coming down ... Half an hour later the troops nearest the stage had fought their way to the exit and the battle was over. Whoever cleaned up the mess we do not know but we had sufficient heart to feel sorry for them.'

After three days aboard *Queen Mary* anchored off Bombay, Les Clothier and his colleagues finally were able to disembark. The vessel used to transport them ashore was the *Rhona*, a cargo and passenger liner owned by British India Line, which in peacetime had operated coastal services around India. On 7 November, Les recorded, 'went ashore today on the *Rhona*, a vessel of about 7,000 tons. The Battalion was paraded in a square opposite the wharf and given a cup of tea by the natives who were employed by the Army. We were then marched onto the troop train. We were started off by a steam locomotive that looked as if it had come out of the Ark. After about 10 miles an electric engine, the first one I've seen, was hooked on and it took us about another 70 miles. We finished the trip with a decent sort of steam engine hooked on. When we detrained we were supplied with a plate of stew, which was very good. The huts in our camp, at Deolali, are big but very rough — dirt floors, bush timber, bamboo matting for sides and a tile roof, which was the best thing about them.'

The troops had to spend several days in this and other camps, until their turn came to be sent back to Bombay to board one of the smaller vessels that had been gathered there to transport them on to Egypt. On 11 November, Les Clothier wrote, 'after an all-night journey by train, we arrived in Bombay and went aboard the *Christiaan Huygens*, a Dutch packet of about 18,000 tons.' Actually, *Christiaan Huygens* was a 15,700 gross ton liner, built in 1928, which had previously carried Australian troops to the Middle East in convoy US5A.

After five days at the Deolali camp, the 21st Australian Infantry Brigade boarded a train to be taken back to Bombay, where they embarked on an old British troopship, the *Lancashire*, which had been

Some troops boarded the *Lancashire* at Bombay to complete their voyage to Egypt.

built in 1917 and was only a third the size of *Mauretania*. As the Brigade Medical Officer, H.D. Steward, later wrote, 'Conditions were a let down after the luxury of the *Mauretania*. At their first breakfast, still in harbour, the troops made an official complaint that the ship was dirty, cockroaches crawling everywhere, the meat measly and the bread full of weevils. After an inspection, I agreed with them.'

Also going ashore in Bombay from *Mauretania* was Lloyd Tann, who recalled, 'On the 9th of November we boarded the *Dilwara* from Bombay, a 10,000-tonner. It'd been a permanent British India troopship.' *Dilwara* was a sister ship of *Dunera* and *Ettrick*, which had carried troops in the first two convoys. Among the other vessels included in the convoy was *Rhona*, which had ferried some of the troops ashore in Bombay, and a number of ships not carrying troops but joining the convoy for safety. The convoy left Bombay on 9 November, with a heavy escort, comprising the cruiser HMS *Shropshire*, anti-aircraft cruiser HMS *Carlisle* and the destroyer HMAS *Parramatta*. On 12 November, Les Clothier wrote, 'we left Bombay at 11 am. There are 14 or so ships in the convoy and they are zig-zagging all over the place.'

On board *Dilwara*, Lloyd Tann said, 'I was running the RAP — Regimental Aid Post. Some were crook from seasickness. No mishaps. A few scares of enemy action ... On one occasion, we had submarine alarms. A siren. Dog-leg course. Evasive action. Didn't see a sub, but heard depth charges — a dull whoomph, and then a slight shudder of the shock-waves would travel through the boat. Hammocks on the boat. Playing cards — poker, five hundred. Certain amount of two-up. Bored? To an extent.'

After an otherwise uneventful passage across the Indian Ocean, on 18 November 'three more merchant ships and three destroyers joined us today,' wrote Les Clothier. 'We sighted land at 9 am. We passed into the Red Sea at 7 pm seeing Italian controlled territory off to the port quarter. I expected at least one air raid but have been disappointed.' Lloyd Tann recalled seeing Italian planes, 'very high, observing. Just a speck in the distance.' The convoy steamed on unmolested on a glassy smooth sea, frequently passing southbound ships, until, on 23 November, Les Clothier wrote, 'we entered the port of Suez this morning and saw the entrance to the canal. We could see ships steaming up and it looked as if they were moving across the desert.' Some of the ships discharged their troops at Almajdal, but four, *Christiaan Huygens*, *Lancashire*, *Dilwara* and *Rhona*, entered the Suez Canal on 25 November, passed through the Bitter Lakes and finally reached El Kantara, where the troops disembarked, on 26 November.

The arrival in El Kantara marked the end of the long journey for the troops, who had spent just over a month in transit on two ships, with a short spell ashore in India in the middle. Although the trip had been without major incident, those aboard *Christiaan Huygens* left the ship 'without any regret. To us she would have been a nice ship in peacetime.' Now the troops had to come to grips with the reality of conditions in a war zone. As Les Clothier recorded, on 26 November they 'left El Kantara, on the canal, by train — in goods cars, 25 men to a car. We arrived at camp, about three miles past Gaza and were in bed by 11 pm, with three blankets and a hard, board bed.'

Lloyd Tann recalled he too disembarked at El Kantara, 'a port midway down the Suez. A rail-head on the Egyptian side. Almost an anticlimax in a way ... Very much a sleepy little Arab town. Didn't see very much of it. Moved straight on to a train. A steam train, sort of hissing when we got there. Camels were the previous passengers. Straw and dung — stinking hot across the Sinai desert. We were just told we were heading for Palestine ... Reach Gaza 7.30. Eight hour trip.'

Meanwhile, back in Bombay, once the troops had disembarked the three giant liners that had carried them from Australia took on bunkers and supplies, then made the journey back to Australia independently. *Aquitania* steamed to Singapore, remaining there several days before continuing back to Sydney, where she arrived on 25 November. *Queen Mary* departed Bombay on 9 November, alone, at an average speed of

28.58 knots, to reach Fremantle in twelve minutes over six days. The liner remained at anchor in Gage Roads for six days, then made another fast passage to Sydney, travelling at 25.95 knots to arrive on 21 November.

As *Queen Mary* steamed towards Sydney, convoy US7 was on its way to the Middle East. This was composed of four ships: *Orion*, which had participated in the first convoy, the P & O sisters *Stratheden* and *Strathmore*, both very well known in Australian waters before the war, and a Polish liner, *Batory*. It was a sister to *Pilsudski*, which should have been in the first convoy but was sunk en route to Australia.

Both these Polish liners had been placed at the disposal of the British government by the Polish government in exile. *Batory* had been refitted as a troop transport in Glasgow and retained many of her Polish officers and crew. Along with *Stratheden*, *Batory* had taken eleven weeks to voyage from Britain to Sydney to join this convoy, but such a long trip was not unusual during the war years. However, what was unusual was that, in addition to 500 British troops being transported to Singapore, *Batory* had carried 477 British children being evacuated to Australia for safety, along with their adult escorts.

Departing Liverpool on 5 August 1940, *Batory* linked up in the Irish Sea with convoy WS2, which consisted of seventeen merchant ships carrying over 30,000 troops and escorted by two cruisers, HMS *Cornwall* and HMS *Shropshire*. The merchant ships were arranged in a diamond formation, with *Batory* in the safest spot in the middle. As the convoy followed a zigzag course into the Atlantic, one of the older boys on board *Batory* recalled, 'We had the *Stratheden*, a very big liner, dead ahead of us. We all wanted to see her from the side, but for weeks we followed her so we could never decide what she looked like. Off the starboard bow was the *Andes* ... and astern were the *Empress of Canada* ... the *Empress of Britain* and the *Monarch of Bermuda*.'

Conditions for the children on board *Batory* were the same as those for the troops. One boy recalled, 'We always had to carry our lifejackets with us and pity help you if you were caught without it. They went to the dining room with you, and they went onto your bed at night. You sat on them or lay on them on deck — you even took them to the bathroom.' The first four days of the voyage were the most dangerous, but when the convoy reached the middle of the North Atlantic it split into two sections, one bound for the Middle East, the other the Far East. This left *Batory* with six other liners, including *Stratheden*, being escorted by a lone cruiser. They arrived at their first port of call,

The Polish liner *Batory* was taken over by the British when the war started.

Freetown, on 15 August, leaving the next day for Cape Town.

It was during this section of the voyage that one of the children's escorts decided to start singing groups among the children to help them fill in the long hours. Soon all the children were involved and, as one boy recalled, 'the singing never stopped.' This continued for several weeks, with the children entertaining the troops, crew and other passengers on board the ship. As a result, *Batory* became known as 'The Singing Ship.'

Arriving in Cape Town on 25 August, the children on board were allowed ashore for the first time since boarding the ship in Liverpool three weeks earlier. At one time it was planned that the 477 children on board *Batory* would be transferred to *Stratheden* at Cape Town, but they had grown fond of their ship and its Polish crew and did not want to go, so they remained aboard. The vessel departed Cape Town on 31 August in a five-ship convoy, which included *Stratheden*, that hugged the African east coast until they were past Madagascar, then headed straight across the Indian Ocean to Bombay, where they arrived on 15 September. The children were again allowed to go ashore during the two days *Batory* remained alongside, but then the ship had to go to an anchorage off the port, where it remained a further four days.

On 21 September, *Batory* raised anchor and headed off once again, still accompanied by *Stratheden* and now joined by *Orcades*, their escort being the armed merchant cruiser HMAS *Westralia*. After three days the ships arrived in Colombo, where the children had a day ashore, then it was off to sea again, with *Stratheden* still in company. The voyage had already lasted seven weeks, and still they were not heading for Australia, but Singapore, where they arrived on 1 October and the 700 British troops left the ship. Next day the voyage continued, but

Stratheden embarked troops in Adelaide. (*National Library of Australia*)

for the children the ship seemed quite strange, now the troops had gone. Still accompanied by *Stratheden*, *Batory* was headed for Fremantle, which was reached on 9 October, when 56 of the children disembarked. *Batory* and *Stratheden* then continued on to Melbourne, where a further 188 children left *Batory*, and finally the Polish vessel arrived in Sydney on 16 October. The outward voyage had covered over 20,000 miles and included three crossings of the equator. Once the remaining children disembarked, *Batory* was drydocked in preparation for the return trip in convoy US7. *Stratheden* reached Sydney on 17 October. Convoy US7 was to be the first to board troops at Port Adelaide, where elements of the 9th Australian Division AIF embarked on two liners, *Stratheden* and *Strathmore*, which departed Sydney on 7 November and 9 November, respectively.

Among the units allocated to join convoy US7 in Sydney was the 2/7 Field Company, who underwent their training at the Redbank Camp, near Brisbane, from May to October 1940, then were sent on pre-embarkation leave. On 13 November the unit entrained in Brisbane for Sydney, where they embarked on the *Orion*, which was berthed at Darling Harbour, having arrived on 7 November. *Batory* also embarked troops in Sydney. *Orion* and *Batory* left Sydney together on 14 November escorted by HMAS *Perth*.

Included in the units embarking in Adelaide was the 2/23 Battalion, and the 2/12 Field Regiment, which had been training at Puckapunyal, in Victoria. On 16 November the 2/12 Field Regiment, comprising 731 men, boarded a train that carried them west overnight to Port Adelaide, where they immediately went aboard *Stratheden*. They found they were among 2800 troops on board the ship, which had only been partly converted for trooping. The cabins on the upper decks were still intact, while H deck had been stripped bare and hammocks installed. As on other converted liners, the men were ordered to wear sandshoes to prevent damage to the floor coverings. Most of the public rooms were also still intact, with their comfortable furniture.

Also boarding the *Stratheden* in Adelaide was the 2/9 Battalion, which had been formed in South Australia. Prior to leaving for overseas, they were quartered at the Cheltenham Racecourse until, on 18 November, they entrained at Cheltenham railway station and were taken to the Outer Harbour at Port Adelaide, where they embarked on *Stratheden*. As Bill Spencer, who wrote the history of the 2/9 Battalion, recalled: 'We sailed that evening for the Middle East, on our way to the biggest adventure of our lives.' In his diary on 18 November he wrote, 'Slept in hammock in hold, bloody uncomfortable. Stood at rail for a long time watching South Australia disappear. Weather fine.' However, next day, which was also his birthday, he recorded, 'Sea rough. Pommy beer cheap and warm.'

Orion and *Batory* linked up with *Stratheden* and *Strathmore* in the Great Australian Bight on the afternoon of 19 November 1940. Having taken up their convoy positions, the ships then headed west towards Fremantle. For the men of the 2/12 Field Regiment, shipboard conditions were surprisingly good. As the unit's official history records: 'Most of the troops had never seen such grand dining rooms and lounges. The peace-time ship's crew was returning to England so cabin stewards were still in attendance and the ship's dance band played every evening. Army life was never like this again! Even the lowest rankers made their choice from elaborate menus — take breakfast — choice of tea, coffee or cocoa, stewed fruit, rolled oats, fish cakes, calf's liver, grilled bacon, eggs (fried, boiled or poached), potato puree, bologna sausage, ox tongue, scones, toast, bread, jam, marmalade, honey or golden syrup. Believe it or not, that was for the other ranks — not the officers. Sailing along on a calm sea inclined the men to forget that they were at last on the way to war … All were pleased by the conveniences on board and agreeably surprised by the price of cigarettes and drinks.'

Among the troops of the 2/23 Battalion that also embarked in Adelaide was Corporal John Johnson, who, despite being the father of seven young children, six sons and a baby daughter, had enlisted at Albury in June 1940 along with two close friends, Alan Kelly and Pat Joy. Now all three were on their way to the Middle East. John Johnson sent regular letters to his wife and family, though he was not able to identify the ship on which he was travelling.

Early in the voyage, John Johnson wrote: 'I am writing this somewhere at sea, the continual roar and the sway and rock of the ship are nothing to me now. The first day or so I didn't like the trip at all. In fact I was sea sick; but nothing serious, just run to the rail a couple of times. Nearly everybody had a run. We left camp Saturday about three am per bus to station eight miles. Arrived port at ten am, had dinner on the boat and while we were at dinner she left the pier. She anchored for the night after a few hours sail to wait for the other troopships which both joined us Sunday morning after the pilot left us. We passed a minesweeper and were met by a destroyer which led us on our journey till it was relieved by another Monday night. The ship ploughs along at about twenty miles per hour day and night I am told but the water seems to pass about a hundred to me … We have had cloudy weather since we left port and it has been quite chilly. We put our clocks back half an hour yesterday and half today.'

Of course, all letters written by troops and posted on board the ships were first read by censors before being mailed, but some tried to circumvent this. John Johnson wrote, 'My letters are censored but yours to me are not. I could write and tell you everything and post at next port like some mugs intend doing but it is those things which may be signing the death warrant of thousands of others.'

Returning to conditions on board, 'I just put my cig down beside me and it has rolled away about ten feet. That is the side roll which made me sick, the back and forward one didn't worry me at all. Most of the crew are from Bombay and "no savvie" much. Most of us are in hammocks of a night but some got cabins. The hammocks are good to sleep in. We have two blankets. The chap near me last night climbed in one side and fell out the other, blankets and all. He came a cropper too. The vibration of the engines cause a sort of short sharp buck to the ship, also the hammock sways and bucks but are very comfortable to sleep in. We have excellent food here and I am eating ravenously today. We had soup, then beef and spuds and turnip then plum duff for dinner today. We had spud and sausages and gravy for breakfast. Sunday we had bacon and fried eggs and spud.'

As the ships were crossing the Great Australian Bight, reports were received of a series of attacks on British ships in the Indian Ocean by a German raider. In Fremantle, HMAS *Canberra* was waiting in preparation for escorting convoy US7 to Colombo, along with HMAS *Hobart*. On 20 November, *Canberra* was ordered to sea to search for the German raider, whose latest victim, the Shaw Savill cargo vessel

Maimoa, had been attacked only some 800 miles west of Fremantle. The next day another cargo vessel, *Port Brisbane*, was also sunk.

Convoy US7 arrived in Fremantle on the afternoon of Thursday, 21 November, Bill Spencer recording in his diary, '1130 hrs sighted Rottnest Is. Minesweepers about and aircraft above all day. Docked Fremantle 1800 hrs. Leave.' The convoy was scheduled to depart the next day, but instead, the four ships were kept in port while *Hobart* was sent out to support *Canberra* in searching for the raider, later identified as the *Pinguin*, another of the German armed commerce raiders. On 24 November the two cruisers abandoned their search and returned to Fremantle on the 27th. During these six days in port, the troops were allowed generous shore leave, while on 26 November the 2/12 Field Regiment went on a ten-mile route march.

As the 2/12 Regiment history records it: 'On Wednesday, November 27, at 1430 hours, *Stratheden* left the wharf to anchor out in the "Roads." It is hard to describe the feelings of those men who were leaving Australia to return when God willeth. Standing on the deck that night, they realised how lucky Australia was. The war seemed so far from the lights of Fremantle, all burning so brightly and carelessly. It was an emotional night that only the sea, with the stars overhead, could conjure up ... At 0700 next morning, the ship lifted anchor and, escorted by the cruisers *Perth* and *Canberra* sailed north. The days were occupied with lectures, sport, PT and generally taking it easy. On the 29th, the swimming pool was filled for the first time and the swimming and sports decks were allocated to units for different periods. At night the gunners played cards, housey housey and a spot of illegal Crown and Anchor, two-up or "Swy."'

The 13th Battery of the 2/7 Battalion, comprising sixteen officers and 352 other ranks from South Australia, had embarked on *Stratheden* in Adelaide and they were joined on board at Fremantle by the 14th Battery, which had been raised in Western Australia. The artillery regiment was commanded by Lieutenant Colonel John O'Brien, who wrote about the early part of the voyage:

> In those early days of the war, shipboard accommodation for many of the more senior officers was almost on a luxury basis. Except for building two-level bunks for Sergeants in the four-berth cabins and wooden bunks in the cargo holds, many of the other cabins and the public rooms were untouched. Either the ship owners or the Admiralty charterers must have reckoned on the war soon being over and they were not going to have their ships pulled to pieces for a temporary emergency. We had to wear

sandshoes to guard against damage to the decks, companionways and the like.

This peacetime mentality was applied to the passengers. I found myself with Major Jim Irwin, the Battery Commander of the 13th South Australian Battery in a two-berth cabin with all mod cons including a bedside telephone which enabled us to talk to our wives, free of charge while we waited in Perth until a submarine scare was cleared up. The other ranks in the regiment were quartered in the lower deck of a hold right over the propellers and it was certainly a change for many of the 'elite of Adelaide' who had travelled in suites on the same ship in peacetime. But the peacetime mentality of the ship was best exemplified in the arrangements for 'abandoning ship.' All the officers were in the two big power lifeboats; and the rest were in the usual lifeboats and on rafts. This was not good enough for Irwin and myself and we made a fuss on behalf of the men. So it was decided by the Staff Captain of the ship that the peacetime notices of lifeboat allocation which were displayed in the cabins would be replaced and that officers would be spread throughout the life-saving gear with their men.

As the ships headed into the tropics, John Johnson was again writing a letter home. 'I have had a glorious trip since leaving our first port of call and have experienced all kinds of seas from dead calm to darned rough. I am in charge of the machine-gun crew now. Each crew works eight hours. I am at present from four to twelve pm. The gun is mounted about eight feet above the bridge in a steel box that holds three men and gun comfortably. It is for anti-aircraft. There are several such guns on board ... I have a cabin bunk now instead of a hammock and it is much more comfortable and private. All the gun crews have been put in so they can have their sleep at any time ... A fairly strong breeze is blowing but there is no movement in the ship. You will all have to have a sea voyage some day to appreciate all that I am telling you.'

During the voyage, the ships in the convoy practised changing formations, as did the escorting cruisers, but shortly after crossing the equator, *Canberra* departed to return to Fremantle. The four troopships were in line astern formation, and *Canberra* passed down the port side, all personnel on every ship lining the rails to wave and cheer. Colombo was reached on the afternoon of 5 December, the troopships going to anchor in the harbour. Next day, the men of the 2/12 Field Regiment clambered into lighters and were taken ashore for a short period of leave, regrouping at 3.30 pm to return to their ship. However, as the official history tells it, 'Three NCO's, feeling the worse for wear, missed the barges back to the ship. Undaunted they managed to hire a native craft which delivered them to *Strathmore* (not *Stratheden*) and all three went down to their cabin (so they thought) to find it occupied by strangers from another unit. They took a lot of convincing before they accepted the fact that they were on another ship.'

Bill Spencer had a very enjoyable time in Colombo, as he 'made contact with a Mr Wiggins, who was the agent for Lloyd's of London. He was a generous host, and left no stone unturned to make our short stay in Colombo a memorable one. We were chauffeured everywhere, going to a fair in the night at the racecourse and overstaying our leave. But we managed to get a ride out to the *Stratheden* on a native boat. We waited until a sling full of cargo was leaving the loading barge, then grabbed the net and made our journey up in the air and down in the hold. We were lucky — lucky to get aboard, and lucky that my cousin was duty officer in the hold.'

Convoy US7 departed Colombo on 7 December, still escorted by HMAS *Perth*. A few days after leaving Colombo, John Johnson began writing another letter home, starting: 'I am having a good trip and have not had any sea sickness since leaving the last port from which I last wrote. The ship is rocking a good deal at present but I am in a position which catches the sway. I have just done my washing and have it out on a line on the top deck so here I am keeping an eye on it ... There are two large swimming pools on board but they are always crowded. Each are about thirty feet by twenty feet by five feet deep and nice and warm.'

There was not much to break the monotony of daily routine and John Johnson wrote that 'The boats are just changing their positions in the convoy and it's getting quite exciting, all the swimmers are rushing to the rails to see what is happening and the sirens are blowing. It appears to me to be an alteration of formation. We had church parade this morning but it was too crowded with the whole battalion in the tennis courts up on A deck.'

The weather and sea conditions were always a popular topic in letters home, especially for men who had never been on a ship before. Later in the same letter, Johnson wrote: 'The boat is rocking like a cradle now and I am about the middle of the deck and see water and sky alternately on either side and being so high up here you can imagine the rock she must have on. It is surprising you don't notice these things after being used to the thing. It is hard to write this at all as my knees go over one way and then the other so I sit in the life jacket leaning against the canteen wall. I have only had shorts on since the last port as that is our service dress now ... This ship must be quite a luxury liner when not a T-ship as we have all mod cons but too many to take advantage of them. We have blackouts on all decks outside the lounges, cabins etc. every night. The easiest place to lose your bearings I find is a blackout ship as you can go for miles without getting places.'

The convoy entered the Red Sea on Friday, 13 December, at which time the escort was strengthened to three cruisers and three destroyers. During the next two days there were numerous air raid alarms, all of which proved false. On the evening of 15 December the four ships of Convoy US7 anchored off Suez, and the next morning they entered the Suez Canal, *Stratheden* anchoring in the Bitter Lakes at 2.30 pm. Here the ship remained overnight, then the following day continued on to El Kantara, where the troops disembarked. As Bill Spencer recalled, 'Our voyage up the Red Sea and into the Suez Canal was slow and hot. El Kantara was reached at 12 noon on 17 December 1940. The troops disembarked and moved to an area where we had lunch. The heat was stupefying, as was the sandwich we had for lunch.'

After the comforts they had enjoyed aboard *Stratheden*, it was quite a shock for the men of the 2/12 Field Regiment to be loaded into cattle trucks to be transported to Gaza, where they arrived after a very uncomfortable journey at 3 am on the Wednesday. HMAS *Perth* also went through the Suez Canal and into the Mediterranean, to replace HMAS *Sydney* in the 7th Cruiser Squadron. *Orion* also went through the Suez Canal and continued to Haifa, in Northern Palestine, where her troops disembarked on 18 December. As usual, the troops were all relieved to have reached their destination. John Johnson wrote home, 'Feeling really well and I am pleased to be off the boat as we were on it a little too long under T-ship conditions. It would be a very nice trip to make in peace time.'

In an earlier letter home, John Johnson had written, 'We should get some months of training before going into action. In fact I don't expect any action for anything up to eight to nine months. Anyhow the war could be over now for all we hear of it so far.' Not only was the war not over when he arrived in Palestine, John Johnson found himself in action in the Western desert within three months, and by May 1941 was in Tobruk. Tragically, John Johnson and his two good friends, Alan Kelly and Pat Joy, who all enlisted on the same day, were all killed on the same day, 17 May 1941.

The dispatch of Australian and New Zealand troops to the Middle East continued without let up as 1940 came to a close, and at the end

Dominion Monarch carried New Zealand troops in convoy US8.

of December convoy US8 departed. Apart from the three giants, *Queen Mary*, *Mauretania* and *Aquitania*, this convoy included two other ships, *Dominion Monarch* and *Awatea*, both well known in local waters and making their first voyages to the Middle East. They were designated to carry New Zealand troops, while *Queen Mary* and *Aquitania* would board Australian troops in Sydney and *Mauretania* embark her troops in Melbourne.

Less than two years old, *Dominion Monarch* had been built for Shaw Savill Line to carry 500 passengers and a huge amount of cargo, mostly frozen, between New Zealand and England via Australia. Due to her enormous refrigerated capacity, *Dominion Monarch* had been left on her regular service for a year, but in August 1940 was requisitioned and sent to Liverpool for conversion into a troop transport. Accommodation was installed for 142 officers and 1400 other ranks, but the cargo spaces were not altered. On her first trooping voyage, *Dominion Monarch* was sent from Britain around South Africa to Egypt, where her troops were disembarked, then continued to New Zealand, where a full cargo of perishable foodstuffs was loaded. Once this was completed, 1550 New Zealand troops were embarked, and the liner crossed the Tasman to join convoy US8.

Awatea, completed in 1936 for the Union Steam Ship Company, was well known in Sydney. Referred to as the 'Queen of the Tasman,' this magnificent liner had broken all records on the Tasman when operating a regular service from Auckland and Wellington to Sydney. When the *Niagara* was sunk by a mine off the New Zealand coast on 19 June 1940, *Awatea* was called upon to replace her on the important route across the Pacific. First, however, *Awatea* was sent to Manila to

The 'Queen of the Tasman,' *Awatea*, was included in convoy US8, still in full Union Line colours.

embark a party of evacuees from Hong Kong who were taken to Sydney. Having completed two round trips on the Vancouver service, *Awatea* was requisitioned to carry 700 New Zealand troops to the Middle East with convoy US8. However, her luxurious accommodation was not converted in any way, so the troops she carried had probably the most comfortable voyage of any transported to the Middle East. Departing Wellington on 20 December, *Awatea* crossed the Tasman in company with *Dominion Monarch*, entering Sydney Harbour on 23 December and berthing at Pyrmont.

Meanwhile in Sydney, *Queen Mary* and *Aquitania* were boarding their troops, mostly men from 2/15 Battalion and two battalions of the 24th Brigade, 2/28 and 2/43. Among the smaller units on board *Queen Mary* was the 2/4 Field Park Company, which had only been formed in August 1940 and underwent training at Ingleburn. As related in the book, *The Sappers' War*, 'Most of December was devoted to packing and crating equipment including folding boats. On December 27 the company embarked on 'HMTQX' (*Queen Mary*). Quarters seemed cramped and deck space limited … On this trip cabins had 4–8 bunks each.'

On 28 December, *Dominion Monarch* and *Awatea* departed Pyrmont, and as they passed under the Harbour Bridge *Queen Mary* raised her anchor and led them out of the harbour, where they joined *Aquitania*, which had left first. Once they had taken up their convoy positions, the four transports, escorted by HMAS *Canberra*, headed south, maintaining an average speed of over 18 knots.

Meanwhile, on 29 December *Mauretania* completed embarking her troops in Port Melbourne. Among the units boarding the liner was the 2/43 Battalion, which was raised in South Australia in July 1940 and had completed training at Woodside in the Adelaide Hills. On the night of 28 December 2/43 Battalion boarded trains at Oakbank, the first group. Next day they arrived in Melbourne and were taken directly to the wharf to embark. As one member later wrote: 'Within a few minutes of detraining, our feet touched Australia for the last time for who knows how long, and we were finally embarked. We were conducted to our respective sleeping quarters; ours are in hammocks slung in positions on the main deck ... Our departure could hardly be described as a well-kept military secret, but a naval patrol kept pleasure boats overladen with wellwishers at a short distance. At about 5 o'clock, with the assistance of four tugs, the great ship moved slowly out into the bay to the accompaniment of cheers from flag-waving men and women on the distant dock and on crowded pleasure craft near at hand. The big day had come; we were on overseas service.'

Also on board *Mauretania* was the 2/3 Australian Light Anti-Aircraft Regiment. One of their members noted in his diary that they were up at 0100, had breakfast at 0300, then entrained at 0600 at Werribee Racecourse Station, arriving at 0645 at Spencer Street Station in Melbourne, where he had two pies and tea. They then went on by train to Port Melbourne where, 'we boarded the ship at about 0800 and went to our quarters, bunks in the forward cinema, but some men were in cabins holding eight men. Some cabins still had luxurious fittings, tapestry covered walls, electric fan, hot and cold water, marble bath and toilet. We had to remain on the uppermost deck all day until we left Port Melbourne at 1700 and anchored off Dromana for the night. All portholes blacked out.'

Next morning the diary noted, 'Left anchor 0730, through Heads 0830.' As the four liners and their escort from Sydney passed through Bass Strait on 30 December they were joined by *Mauretania* off Port Phillip Heads and the complete convoy continued across the Great Australian Bight. This part of the voyage was most uncomfortable for the troops, as related in *The Sappers' War*. 'The crossing of the Great Australian Bight was very rough and the huge waves frequently covered the portholes on A Deck, 80 feet above the waterline, as spray flew over the top of the ship's bridge. When the next wave lifted the bow, the curve under to the keel was visible, before it was again buried in the huge rollers. Under these conditions many failed to attend meal parades.' One of the men aboard *Mauretania* was Len Hodges, of the 13th Light Horse Battalion, who recalled, 'Got outside the Heads ... Sailed to Perth. In a cabin, we all were. The *Mauretania* was rocking. Rocking! Never been seasick in me life. Pork chops before we left, but I was OK ... Going across the Bight was a bit rough.'

The bulk of the men in 2/43 Battalion were accommodated in hammocks on the main and promenade decks of *Mauretania*. As one member recalled, 'I was a bit dubious, in common with others, as to the comfort of a hammock, but two nights therein have convinced me of their cosiness.' As the 2/43 Battalion history notes, 'Despite the overcrowding, the ship's complement, aided by fatigue parties from the units, succeeded in providing excellent meals in three sittings for the rest of the voyage. As was to be expected on board ship, areas were too restricted to allow for very extensive training. Nevertheless a reasonable amount of weapon training, PT and lectures helped to relieve some of the boredom from the voyage, interspersed with picquet duties and galley fatigues for spud peeling.'

The convoy arrived in Fremantle on 3 January 1941, *Queen Mary* anchoring out as usual while the other vessels entered the port. One diary noted that *Mauritania* berthed in Fremantle at 0930, with all troops being off the ship by 1230 on leave till midnight. However, next day no leave was granted, and the troops remained on board all day, with the liner not leaving the wharf until 1700, then going to anchor in Gage Roads. At 7 am the next day, 5 January, the five ships were on their way again, maintaining a speed of just under 19 knots across the Indian Ocean, still escorted by *Canberra*.

A strict censorship had been imposed on any information being sent through the mails concerning the movements of these convoys, but there were always some troops who tried to get around this restriction. One letter, intercepted by censors in Perth, was written by a soldier aboard *Mauretania*, who hoped to circumvent the system. He wrote: 'Between 5 and 6 pm on the Monday, we picked up with our convoy which consisted of the *Queen Mary*, *Aquatania* [sic], *Awatea* and *Dominion Monarch* escorted by the Australian cruiser *Canberra* ... I shall post this in Perth under a plain envelope so keeping it from the eyes of the censor who scans everything written aboard. I have no scruples in sending this information to you as the "secret" sailing of the *Mauretania* was witnessed by hundreds of Sunday visitors to the beaches who were taken on pleasure cruises about our ship.'

Not all the men being transported overseas were keen to go, as one soldier on *Queen Mary* wrote in another intercepted letter, 'There is things I would like to write but can't ... If I had my chance to leave the Army I would get killed in the rush. There is about 8,000 of us on board this boat not counting what's on the other four. We heard that we only get two pounds till we reach the other side. We sleep in hammocks here.' No doubt there would have been some on every ship who saw Australia's shores slip below the horizon with great reluctance, but whether there would be a rush to leave the army, as suggested by this writer, is highly doubtful.

During the voyage the troops were kept active with physical training each day, as well as exercises involving rifles, machine-guns and explosives, and also lectures on various subjects. Len Hodges on *Mauretania* remembered, 'I had good health, excellent. You had Phys. Ed. as physical education was called. Or else it was called PT. Marched around the deck to keep fit. No laying round on the deck. No getting fat and lazy. I was cocky, young and full of beans. Filled with patriotic zeal. It never entered my head at any stage that I'd never get back.'

There was also a beer ration, for which, as George Bell recalled: 'Troops were issued beer tickets coloured white, yellow or pink. The first issue was for white tickets. The following night's issue was for yellow tickets. Some clever sappers obtained tickets from non drinkers and dyed the white tickets yellow by immersing them into empty food tins containing water and cigarette bumpers. This gave them two nights in a row. For the pink tickets a condies [*sic*] crystals mixture proved effective, thus giving them beer each night. In addition to this device some men obtained large empty bottles from their kitchen picquet duties and presented these for filling. The orders announcing the beer issue did say "one container per person" and the duty Officer's objections were overridden when this was presented as this person's container. Shortly afterwards two sappers presented a wooden pail, normally used for swabbing down the decks. Using the argument that the large bottle had been filled previously and this container was for two men, the Officer reluctantly gave in. The two men took their pail of beer, bugs and bacteria to a quiet corner, and drank it from their pannikins.'

As the convoy steamed north the days became hotter. The 2/43 Battalion history records: 'By the 9th of the month the convoy was just north of the Tropic of Capricorn; the heat during the day was very intense, conditions 'tween decks at night, owing to the need for blackout precautions, were intolerable; many of the troops took their hammocks to the top decks to sleep in the open. Hoses were provided for the troops on the foredeck for ablutions after stand down from training. The wet canteen predictably did a roaring business.'

On the afternoon of 11 January the convoy arrived off Trincomalee in Ceylon, where *Queen Mary* anchored. However, *Mauretania*,

Aquitania, Dominion Monarch and *Awatea* went on to Colombo, reaching there on the following morning. The harbour was full, and as no berths were available the four troopships had to anchor out, bow to stern. The 2/43 history records that 'Almost as soon as the hawsers were fastened to the buoys, tugs and flat-bottomed water lighters came alongside and we began to take in water. On the lighters were numerous coolies, in gay costumes, whose antics delighted the troops: pennies, cigarettes and sticks of chocolate began to rain down upon them, and as each article hit the decking, they fought desperately to secure it — and then stood about and solemnly shared it, with absolute fairness and precision.'

All the troops were to disembark in Ceylon, and be transferred to smaller ships to continue their trip to the Middle East. *Dominion Monarch* then continued to Britain, via South Africa, with her valuable cargo of foodstuffs, while *Awatea* returned to Australia on her own and the other three liners did so together.

After disembarking from *Queen Mary*, the 2/4 Field Park Company, along with some other units, was immediately transferred to the smaller troopship *Dilwara*, which carried them first to Colombo, where the troops were granted shore leave. Other troops from *Queen Mary* went aboard the Dutch vessel *Indrapoera*, which had been operating a shuttle service between Bombay and Egypt since taking part in convoy US5. *Indrapoera* arrived in Trincomalee from Bombay on 10 January 1941 and boarded her troops two days later. The vessel left for Colombo on 13 January, there to await the departure of the convoy for Egypt.

The troops who had transferred from *Queen Mary* to *Dilwara* found,

Some troops from *Queen Mary* transferred to the Dutch liner *Indrapoera* for the final stage of their voyage. (*C.T. Reddings collection*)

'The conditions aboard were very crude compared to the *Queen Mary*. ORs were in hammocks over the mess tables and very cramped. Officers and senior NCOs had much better conditions than the ORs, including good accommodation and table service for meals.' As George Bell recalled about that voyage, 'Toilets were troughs up near the bow which were flushed over the side by pumped up sea water. There was always a queue waiting for seats. On one occasion a loudmouth waiting swore he would fix things when he got in. He managed to get cubicle No. 1, where the sea water was pumped in. Shortly afterwards there were screams and yells from within. Doors flew open and bodies tumbled out with pants around their ankles, cursing the bloke who sent a fireball of burning toilet paper under their backsides. Their places were quickly taken by those waiting.'

Meanwhile, the troops of the 2/3 Australian Light Anti-Aircraft Regiment were transferred from *Mauretania* to a sister ship of *Dilwara*, *Devonshire*, where they also found conditions less than comfortable, with 1600 men on board. They were also allocated hammocks hanging over mess tables, and many men chose to sleep on the open deck. Len Hodges had travelled on *Mauretania* as far as Colombo, where he 'Went aboard a British troop carrier, the *Lancashire*. Terrible. Crewed by Lascars with sacred goats running round everywhere. Very unhygienic. On the nose a bit, to say the least.'

The men of 2/43 Battalion were also less than impressed by their vessel. As the battalion history tells it: 'The battalion was originally intended to tranship into one of the Free French boats which would have been very comfortable; but she had been quarantined for smallpox and another ship *Nevasa* had been hastily substituted. She didn't reach Colombo from Bombay until the afternoon and after waiting impatiently all day the troops began to tranship at 1700 hours. The sea was rough and the troops heavy-laden with all their gear, the decks of the lighters and tugs slippery with spray; it was fortunate there were no accidents. All the ports had been shut during the day and below decks was an inferno. Ventilation was poor, because the ship was lying still in the harbour on a breathless night.'

The convoy that left Colombo on 16 January comprised thirteen vessels, including *Dominion Monarch* from US8, plus *Devonshire*, *Lancashire*, *Dilwara*, *Rhona*, *Christiaan Huygens*, *Nevasa*, *Nieuw Zeeland*, *Indrapoera* all carrying Australian troops, the former Blue Funnel liner *Antenor* which had been converted into an armed merchant cruiser, and three smaller ships. They were escorted by the cruiser HMS *Capetown* and the destroyers HMS *Kelly*, HMS *Kimberly* and HMS

Kashmir, further strengthened by three more destroyers on 22 January. *Nevasa* had carried Australian troops in convoy US2, and had proved less than popular with them. As the 2/43 history describes it:

> The *Nevasa* ... was something like thirty years old, the only coal burner in the convoy and the slowest, and well overdue for paying off ... Conditions were so cramped that the only training possible was PT and lectures for those who were not otherwise occupied on the numerous ship's duties ... Unavoidably (but unfortunately) there was a marked contrast between the excellent accommodation available for officers, WO's and sergeants and the sub-standard lower deck quarters provided for the men. Here, cockroaches abounded; men's hammocks were suspended over their mess tables; the ventilation was poor; and the food was anything but appetising, one lot of rancid meat having to be thrown overboard.

> The ship was only able to keep up with the convoy by sailing a direct course, while the others zigzagged. The other ships, numbering 12, were arranged in five rows ... and they changed their direction every 7½ minutes, the time considered to be the minimum in which a submarine could sight and fire a torpedo. *Nevasa* came along unconcernedly behind, never varying; even so, she received messages requesting her to keep up please, and when the effort was made, she belched forth so much black smoke that another curt order was issued kindly to cease making so much smoke. The Chief Engineer was especially infuriated because he claimed if it weren't for her barnacle encrusted bottom, *Nevasa* would be half a knot faster than at least two other ships in the convoy!

There was one event to provide some light-hearted moments for the troops on board *Nevasa*, as the 2/43 Battalion history relates. 'Belated Christmas cheer of a different kind became available for some when one dark night a raid was made on the grog hatch and a number of cases of beer disappeared. There was heigh ho and hell to pay the next morning when crew members reported to First Officer Dennis Welch, who in turn reported to the Captain, who in turn called in the CO and blew the socks off him. Then it was the CO's turn to blast the company commanders who in turn took it out on the platoon commanders, who of course passed the buck, and the wrath of the CO, down to the lowliest private. The upshot of the incident was that a number of troops had bellies full of beer which every member of the battalion had then to subsidise to the extent of ½d a day until the cost of the grog had been made good!'

Nearing Aden several ships, including *Dominion Monarch*, split from the convoy and headed for South Africa, while the rest continued towards the Red Sea. The escort was strengthened by the cruisers HMS

Carlisle and HMS *Coventry*, as this was the most dangerous part of the voyage and it was possible the ships could be attacked by Italian aircraft based at Massawa, which would have been less than 60 miles away on 24 January. As the 2/43 history notes: 'In view of this likelihood all ranks carried life belts, water bottles, field dressings, steel helmets, respirators and haversacks filled with necessities and personal valuables. Precautions taken by the ship were to ensure that watertight doors were kept shut, hoses were unrolled on the decks, and buckets of sand and long-handled shovels were appropriately sited for disposal of incendiary bombs.' Fortunately no planes came close to the convoy, which later that day passed the Twelve Apostles, described as 'a queer jumble of rocky islets standing out of the sea to some hundreds of feet, bare and staring, in many varied shapes.'

On 25 January *Carlisle*, *Coventry* and two destroyers left the convoy escort. The ships continued on their way north through the Red Sea, and on the evening of 27 January entered the Gulf of Suez. Proceeding at 8 knots, they arrived off Port Tewfik just after daybreak and anchored in the bay. The troops on *Nevasa* were keen to get ashore because 'from the ship the town had a most inviting appearance, an impression which, it seems, was completely reversed by a visit to the shore; it was a case of distance lends enchantment.'

In the early afternoon of 29 January some of the ships entered the Suez Canal However, German aircraft operating from an airfield near Benghazi began dropping magnetic mines in the Canal at that time. Several ships were sunk, and parts of the canal had to be closed while minesweeping was completed.

On board *Lancashire*, Len Hodges was carried as far as El Kantara, where the troops disembarked. 'Transferred to a troop train. Square-wheel train. Rough box-car ride into Palestine to our camp.' *Dilwara* and *Devonshire* also entered the Suez Canal, but stopped in the Bitter Lakes for the night, which was very cold, then continued on to Port Said, where a stop was made to take on water. The voyage resumed, *Dilwara* and *Devonshire* now travelling alone, and encountering particularly rough conditions during the night before arriving in Haifa about 1 pm on 31 January. The troops disembarking from *Dilwara* boarded a train that carried them to Majdal, then it was onto trucks for the final short journey to a camp at El Khassa. The troops on *Devonshire* remained on the ship overnight before also disembarking, and travelling by train to their destination.

Meanwhile, *Nevasa* had remained at Port Tewfik, where a problem of a different kind arose. As the 2/43 Battalion history tells it, 'The *Nevasa* had been recommissioned in haste and victualled for an 11-day voyage; it was now the 16th day and every skerrick of food on the ship had been eaten; the meals for the men had been getting very light and this, combined with wearisome inaction, had made them very outspoken. The troops would certainly be relieved to put the *Nevasa* behind them.' Eventually, 'the *Nevasa* pulled in to the quayside on 2nd February and disembarked the army personnel to enable them to continue the journey to Palestine by train.' It was the first stage of a journey that would eventually take them to the Battle of El Alamein and the defeat of Axis forces in North Africa.

Three of the ships on which the troops had left Australia, *Queen Mary*, *Mauretania* and *Aquitania*, left Ceylon on 14 January, and travelling together at a healthy 26 knots, reached Fremantle in five days and sixteen minutes. Next day *Queen Mary* and *Mauretania* resumed their voyage, reaching Sydney in just under four days at an average speed of over 27 knots. The two ships were back in Sydney Harbour on 24 January, having been away less than four weeks, while *Aquitania* joined them in Sydney five days later.

Awatea arrived back in Sydney on 30 January 1941, then, after one return trip to New Zealand, resumed her regular service across the Pacific to Vancouver, though a large proportion of her accommodation was reserved for military personnel.

Between August and December 1940, six convoys had been dispatched, carrying almost 50,000 Australian and New Zealand troops on 22 ships. Of the troops, 39,800 were Australian, including 500 representatives from the Royal Australian Navy and 50 from the RAAF, while 10,000 were from New Zealand.

Queen Mary back in Sydney Harbour after another trooping voyage. (*C.T. Reddings collection*)

9 From Britain to Egypt

Instead of finding themselves in the warm deserts of Egypt, the Australian troops sent overseas in convoy US3 had arrived in Scotland in June 1940, then been loaded onto trains and sent south to Salisbury Plain in Wiltshire, where they went into camp. The evacuation of British troops from Dunkirk had already been completed and the Battle of Britain was being fought overhead. England expected the Germans to launch their anticipated invasion across the Channel at any time, so the Australian forces were soon engaged in intensive training to prepare them to aid in the defence of Britain. A few months later, with the Royal Air Force victorious in the Battle of Britain, the threat of invasion had receded and the Australian forces in England prepared themselves for another move which would finally take them to the Middle East.

It had always been the intention of the Australian government that their forces sent overseas should operate together, but the diversion of US3 to Britain had prevented this. For some time, Prime Minister Menzies had pressed for the dispatch of the Australian troops in Britain to join their comrades in the Middle East, but this was not approved by Winston Churchill, who wanted the Australians to stay in Britain. During this period, the Australian units in England were reorganised into two brigades, the 18th and the 25th. It was not until the Chief of General Staff recommended to the War Cabinet on 23 September 1940 that the Australian troops in Britain be sent to the Middle East that such a move was given serious consideration, and eventually approved. On 29 September the 18th and 25th Brigades became the nucleus of the 9th Division.

The transfer from Britain to Egypt was effected over a period of time involving various ships and convoys. In June 1940, when the Mediterranean had become too dangerous for convoys to traverse, a new route had been devised to both Egypt and India, going via South Africa with a stop at Freetown. These convoys were given the designator WS, which allegedly stood for 'Winston's Specials.' They departed roughly once a month, and comprised up to twenty troopships each. Convoys WS5A and WS5B, which departed in December 1940, carried 55,000 troops, of whom 43,000 went to Egypt and 12,000 to India.

The first Australian elements to leave Britain for the Middle East were from the 18th Brigade. One of the units that had been carried to Britain, the 2/1 Field Park Company, had been given a new identity when the 18th Brigade was formed, becoming the 2/13 Field Company. On 13 November 1940, the company arrived in Liverpool by train and embarked on the troopship *Reina del Pacifico*, of the Pacific Steam Navigation Company, which before the war had operated on a service from Liverpool to Chile. The troops who had travelled to Britain on the *Mauretania* found conditions on board crowded and uncomfortable. Also embarking on 13 November, but in Glasgow, was the 2/3 Field Company and headquarters for Australforce Engineers, who boarded *Otranto*, of the Orient Line.

Meanwhile, heading north to join a transport for the journey to Egypt was the 2/3 Field Regiment, who had moved in mid-October from Salisbury Plain to Colchester Barracks, in Essex. They had only been there a week when orders were received to prepare for a move overseas, with the unit's guns and transport to be sent first. They duly left Colchester on 22 October, with a small advance party being loaded onto a cargo ship in Liverpool, which joined a convoy and carried the

Reina del Pacifico carried Australian troops from Britain to Egypt.

Empress of Canada was one of the ships that carried Australian troops to Britain in convoy US3, and would now take them to Egypt. (*C.T. Reddings collection*)

materials to Egypt. The rest of the regiment stayed in Colchester until 14 November, when they marched to the local station, boarded a train, and headed north. The journey lasted all day and night, arriving at Gourock at 0635 on Friday, 15 November.

As Michael Clarke recalled, 'We detrained into a bitterly cold dawn. Weighed down with gear, we froze on the platform until it was time to load onto the ferry, in the grey and misty light ... We learned that we were destined for HMT *Empress of Canada*. We were shaken by our first sight of her. Her battered, grey plates were rusty and badly in need of paint. There was a long delay after we came alongside, but the regiment was eventually shunted aboard, myself bringing up the rear. After dumping their gear the men were well fed. Their accommodation was very inferior; hammocks up forward and far too little space. The 2/12 Battalion were with us again, plus 600 RAF, some bound for Crete and Malta, some for Cape Town. The general idea seemed to be Cape Town first stop, with forty-eight hours leave, and then on to Cairo. I was assigned a four-berth inside cabin ... It was pretty cramped after the luxury of a first class outside cabin in the *Queen Mary*.'

As the ship remained at anchor off Gourock, the troops had time to settle in to their new home, while, as Michael Clarke wrote, 'more men were arriving on board and the ship was becoming increasingly overcrowded ... The latest arrivals were 105 civilians, who were reported to be dock labourers and labelled as second class passengers ... On Sunday we lay all day in the Clyde, amongst a vast array of ships. I had time to explore our new home. The men were still very crowded forward. Some had hammocks, while others had mattresses on the floor. However, we were better off than the RAF and RN details, who were sleeping all over the place.'

Empress of Canada finally weighed anchor at 0130 on 18 November and headed down the Clyde Estuary. By the time most of the troops on board woke up, the ship was at sea, accompanied by numerous other vessels, including some carrying troops, and during the day they linked up with ships from other ports. Among the troop transports in the convoy, apart from *Empress of Canada*, were *Otranto*, *Orcades*, *Strathmore*, *Strathnaver* and *Andes*, all of which had previously transported Australian troops to the Middle East, along with *Reina del Pacifico* and *Viceroy of India*, some of which had Australian troops on board, while others were carrying British troops.

As the ships emerged from the protection of Ireland into the Atlantic, they encountered a moderate sea, but it was enough to cause seasickness among many of the troops. As the evening closed in, the wind grew stronger, causing the sea to rise further and create an unpleasant pitching and rolling motion on the ships that further aggravated those already in the throes of mal de mer. The next day the wind was blowing almost at gale force and the sea was rougher, making conditions almost unbearable on board the cruisers and destroyers escorting the convoy.

Captain Bill Laybourne Smith wrote in a letter home that 'a soldier's life is a fair cow. One day settling down reasonably happily in quite comfortable billets; the next dragged out at 0430 in the morning, banged into a troop train and dragged all over the British Isles for twenty-one hours. Then on the third day slung into a troop ship and told to shut up and like it. So here we are, forty hours out from our home and tossing about like a cork ... If I were a man of courage and iron constitution, I would go below and have a look at the others writhing in their beds of agony, but I simply cannot face it ... We are surrounded by a ring of destroyers and they, poor devils, are having a wonderful time. Every second wave goes clean over their bridges, and their decks are constantly awash ... We do not know where we are, such things are not for us, but we do know that dawn broke at 1010 hours this morning and that the sun is now setting at a quarter-to-four. It is intensely cold.'

As the convoy headed south, these were very dangerous waters, and as recently as three weeks previously the huge troop transport *Empress of Britain* had been torpedoed and sunk off the Irish coast with the loss of 49 lives. The troops on all ships were ordered to carry lifebelts at all times, and to sleep partially dressed. There was also the danger of enemy bombers and the decks bristled with anti-aircraft guns, with a constant watch of the skies being maintained. Under such conditions, the bad weather encountered was actually beneficial, as it made life far more difficult for enemy submarines and aircraft.

By 20 November the convoy was well out into the Atlantic, but the seas remained rough. However, most of the troops had found their sea legs and cases of seasickness were greatly reduced. In the crowded conditions on board the ships, there was little room for exercise or training, so the troops were kept occupied with lectures on a wide variety of subjects. However, conditions on board *Empress of Canada* were still a source of complaint. Bill Laybourne Smith wrote: 'Since we started this voyage there has been no hot water, as the steam pipe has a hole in it. The showers of course do not work, so we have iced sea-water plunge baths. Fresh water is scarce, so no water in the basins. Today they turned off the salt water also. Why, God only knows. Outside there are millions of tons of the stuff, and yet we go dirty and stink something awful.'

As the days grew warmer, the convoy continued on its southerly course, and on 29 November arrived off Freetown, the second time the Australian troops had stopped there. As before, the troopships anchored out and were soon surrounded by local merchants in bumboats selling all kinds of wares. No leave was granted and the men sweltered in the hot and humid conditions as the ships swung at anchor for two days, and were mightily relieved when the convoy headed out to sea again. But the days at sea remained intensely dull. 'Life on board is generally boring,' Bill Laybourne Smith wrote. 'There is very little room for training in this little tramp. We have lectures, and work on the miniature range, and sleep and eat ... We have about six hours lectures etc. a day, and how the other eighteen are employed nobody knows. Mainly in gazing over the side, looking at the other ships or the flying fish.'

One amusement to be arranged on *Empress of Canada* was a crossing-the-line ceremony when the ship crossed the equator on 3 December. However, the Australians had all been through the initiation ceremonies on their voyages to Britain. The next day, Bill Laybourne Smith wrote, 'It is still as hot as hell and we all sweat like Christmas brides. The dotards had their fun and games yesterday, and threw a number of poor suffering fools into the swimming pool after first lathering them with Irish batter, or some such filth, amidst roars of laughter from themselves.' At least the weather was better now, as he wrote on 8 December, 'Yesterday the sky was blue, the sea was blue with a lovely, lazy groundswell and the sun shone just the correct amount of heat to be perfect.'

The troops had expected their next port of call would be Cape Town, and there was considerable irritation when it was announced that the convoy would not be calling there, but instead going to Durban, where the ships might stay as long as five days. On 12 December, the South African coast came into view and the convoy entered the port of Durban, where they berthed. Those aboard *Empress of Canada* were not impressed when their ship ended up alongside a refuelling wharf fifteen miles from the town. However, shore leave was granted and special trains took the troops into the centre of Durban. The ships only stayed three days, departing for Egypt on the evening 15 December.

The days continued to drag slowly by, but the weather remained good and the seas were calm. This time the crossing of the equator created no interest at all On 24 December the convoy entered the Gulf of Aden, and dawn on Christmas Day found the ships off Djibouti. After a church parade at 9.30 am the officers attended cocktail parties while the troops had a quiet time until lunch. The mess, formerly the first-class dining room, had been decorated with coloured lights, streamers and flags, and as Gunner George Tyler recorded, 'On the tables was a bottle of beer per man, a present from the Government. The meal was a credit to the cooks. Tomato soup, roast turkey and roast duck with vegetables and seasoning, plum pudding with rum sauce, ice cream, fruit (fresh oranges and apples). For over 1,000 men — a jolly good effort.'

Late in the afternoon the ships formed into a single file to pass through the narrow Straits of Bab el Mandeb, which separates Asia from Africa, then the convoy reformed into its previous formation, five ships abreast followed by four ships abreast, as they entered the Red Sea. As a safety precaution paravanes were streamed to cut the lines of submerged mines. The escort consisted of a cruiser and three destroyers, and there were occasional visits overhead from Allied aircraft.

Boxing Day morning found many troops nursing hangovers and it was reported that only 40 percent of them fronted for breakfast. It was to be another quiet morning, but things livened up in the afternoon when a sports meeting was held on the decks. Next day was to be the last at sea, as on 28 December the convoy finally arrived in Suez. Michael Clarke recorded that, as *Empress of Canada* neared the port, they passed an outbound convoy of five ships, including two familiar to Australian soldiers, *Orion* and *Stratheden*. It was then learnt that the convoy would not be stopping at Suez. The nine ships remained all day at anchor off Suez and at dawn on 29 December they entered the canal, arriving in Port Said the same evening, where they again anchored, staying there all day. The ships were again surrounded by traders in bumboats, who did a roaring trade with the soldiers.

On the evening of 30 December the convoy was on its way again, and the next day *Empress of Canada* steamed into the harbour at Alexandria. Although the sun was shining brightly it was bitterly cold and a greatcoat was needed if one ventured out on deck. Lying at anchor were numerous battleships, aircraft carriers and smaller warships of all types as the troop transports were moved to their respective berths around the harbour. The same afternoon the troops all disembarked and boarded trains which took them to camps outside the city.

Going into 1941, more Australian troops were on the move from Britain to the Middle East. Official war correspondent Kenneth Slessor had arrived in Britain with convoy US3, and stayed there, reporting on the activities of the Australian troops, but now he too was keen to move to the Middle East. Having failed to secure himself a passage on an aircraft, he was offered the alternative of travelling by ship with a contingent of troops, which he reluctantly accepted. Slessor kept a diary throughout this period, but unfortunately the pages covering the first three weeks of January 1941 were badly damaged. Slessor had been staying at Colchester, where most of the Australian troops were based, and he left there by troop train on 2 January, arriving back in Glasgow, and the port of Gourock, where he had disembarked from *Mauretania* seven months earlier, in the middle of summer. Now it was the depths of winter, with short, cold days and snow on the ground. Along with about 2700 Australian troops and some British units, he embarked on the Cunard liner *Franconia* on 4 January for the long journey around South Africa to Egypt. *Franconia* was smaller and older than *Mauretania*, and the quarters provided for the troops were cramped, as usual, but Slessor was allocated a berth in a cabin. After all the rush north to join the ship, it was very frustrating for the troops on board when, due to a persistent heavy fog, they remained at anchor

The Cunard liner *Franconia*.

in the Clyde for a week, during which no shore leave was granted, before finally departing.

It was not until 11 January 1941 that *Franconia* and several other ships departed the Clyde estuary. In the Irish Sea they joined up with a group of vessels from Liverpool, forming a single convoy numbering 21 ships which was designated WS5B. Among the other liners in the convoy were *Empress of Japan*, which had also been involved in convoy US3, another Canadian Pacific liner, *Empress of Australia*, the Union-Castle liners *Arundel Castle* and *Windsor Castle*, *Cameronia* of the Anchor Line, the Furness liner *Monarch of Bermuda*, *Ormonde*, owned by the

Monarch of Bermuda was among the transports making up convoy WS5B. (*Stephen Card collection*)

Orient Line which was en route to Australia, and a Dutch liner, *Pennland*. Escorting the convoy was the battleship HMS *Ramillies*, the cruiser HMAS *Australia*, and two anti-aircraft cruisers, HMS *Phoebe* and HMS *Naiad*. Their route took the ships far out into the middle of the North Atlantic, away from land-based German aircraft flying from bases in occupied France, but the threat of attack by submarines was ever present, so a strong escort was provided. North-west of the Azores, *Ramillies* departed, leaving Captain Stewart of *Australia* as the Senior Officer of the escort.

On 21 January, Slessor wrote, 'Blackout is now lifted at 7.00 in morning, and the air so warm today that changed into shorts and open necked shirt. Strange to think that a little over two weeks before, was shivering in snow. All troops now in shorts ... and many of them scarlet from first contact with sun. Officers wear shorts day, and change to drill tunics and trousers evening. Delightful day, slightly cold wind but plenty of sunshine, sea blue and smooth ... In afternoon late, listened to interesting lecture, crudely phrased but widely informative ... on the political background of Palestine and the Middle East ... Was asked to give a lecture myself on my job as War Correspondent, and think will agree, as it would help clear away misunderstandings as to my job.'

On 22 January, which Slessor described as 'Overcast, but heat still increasing,' he wrote: 'Notice in Orders for the Day today said "We are now approaching Southern danger area. Two, and perhaps three, enemy submarines have been reported in the vicinity of Freetown, Sierra Leone. The convoy's escort has been joined by an anti-submarine escort of two destroyers and two corvettes. In view of this restricted escort, extra precautions must be impressed on the troops against showing lights, smoking on deck, flashing torches, striking matches and opening windows or doors before blackout has ended."'

Next day it was 'Dull and overcast still, but sullen hot. Course in morning east of south. Not expected to reach Freetown now till Saturday, so must either be going very slowly or making an extremely wide detour. At breakfast, issued with quinine tablets all round, which swallowed. This is part of anti-malarial precautions, and will be issued daily. Also there is issue of anti-malarial cream while at Freetown, evidently for use against mosquito or insect bites.' As usual, rumours and wild stories were regularly making the rounds. Slessor wrote that 'Sykes said that chief officer told him that the ships of the convoy had almost piled up just before dawn, owing to error in signalling by officer of the watch aboard a ship ahead, and that *Empress of Japan* just missed colliding with us at right angles. Rumour now is that we are not expected to reach Freetown until early hours of Saturday morning.'

The further south the ships travelled, the hotter it became. Unlike *Mauretania, Franconia* did not have any air-conditioned public rooms and the cabins only had basic ventilation. 'Sweating, steaming hot night in cabin,' Slessor wrote on 24 January. 'Sky white and overcast in morning, sea sluggish, scarcely rippling, horizon heavy with dull white clouds. Thermometer in cabin to my surprise read only 84 degrees, but evidently humidity is high. At about 10.00, ship stopped for a while as convoy manoeuvred into new formation of columns, and one story was that we are almost off mouth of Freetown River, but are not to enter until after dark. *Franconia* to come eighth in the procession. Counted two cruisers, three destroyers and a corvette visible in escort this morning.'

After an uncomfortably hot, long day, darkness brought little relief, as that night, 'heat grew clammy and stickier. Played cards till 12.00, then went to cabin, but air stifling. Went out on deck and watched phosphorus glare in wash of ship like drowned neon sign. Then at about 2.45, couldn't sleep, so put on shorts and shirt and slept in chair on promenade deck — there much cooler, in fact had to get dressing gown during night — woken at 6.30 with cramp and found ships forming into single file.'

At 9.30 the ships of the convoy began passing through the boom at the entrance to Freetown Harbour, but fifteen minutes later alarm bells rang and all troops were ordered off the decks and into their quarters. A plane came flying over but did not drop any bombs, though some intensive anti-aircraft fire was directed at it. Slessor wrote: 'All clear at 10.00. Said to have been a French plane, probably from Dakar. Dropped no bombs. Anchored off naval oil-tanks at 10.45. Freetown seems just as decayed as ever, though not quite as hot as last visit. Harbour packed with shipping — counted sixty-two ships in sight from deck in afternoon, mostly big ones, over ten thousand tons. Everyone expected a raid at night, following visit of reconnaissance plane, but nothing happened ... Did not sleep on deck but stifled in cabin.'

Australia Day, 26 January, found the ships of the convoy taking on fuel, water and supplies as fast as possible. After noting the weather as 'Heat intense, and no wind at all,' Slessor wrote. 'For the last two days ship has had a big list to port, probably due to loading of oil and water tanks. This produces a curious lopsided feeling, as if one was always walking up hill, or as if the ship were in a rough sea, and is most irritating.' As had happened when convoy US3 stopped in Freetown, native boats clustered around the ships in droves, mostly selling bananas, but the troops were forbidden to deal with them, though some managed to, and fire hoses were used to get the boats away from the ships. 'In evening Australian officers entertained British officers and messes at cocktail party, in honour of Australia Day, though none of Australians seemed quite certain what day was anniversary of — some obstinately clung to theory that it commemorated Captain Cook's discoveries!'

For the next two days, the ships of the convoy remained at anchor in Freetown Harbour, much to the discomfort of the troops, who were not allowed ashore, though officers were given leave. On 28 January Slessor wrote, 'This morning, I think, was the hottest and clammiest we have so far had, and everyone is hoping that we can leave tomorrow, as the latest rumour has it.' That evening was 'again choking and frying hot — played bridge with sweat running in continuous streams over face and body. Slept in chair on deck again, and found it much cooler, and an almost cold wind towards morning. But in my cabin, the air still stagnant and oven like.'

On the morning of 29 January, 'Woken by noise of men at work raising the ship's gangway at 5.30 or so. Soon after the *Arundel Castle* went past on her way to sea, and everybody felt immensely glad at this evidence that we could at last say goodbye to Freetown, a truly abominable port for people aboard ships. At about 6.00 our own anchor weighed, and we steamed off, tenth in line of ships. Passed the cruiser *Australia* before breakfast, her decks lined with sailors cooeeing, to the surprise of the Australians aboard transport, who had not realised she was Australian.' *Australia* was one of the two cruisers, the other being HMS *Emerald*, to escort the convoy on the next leg of its long journey. 'Conditions became much cooler as soon as we got into the open sea, with a fresh wind blowing ... Paused at sea in morning while convoy took up formation. Now twenty ships in it, having been joined by *Duchess of Bedford*; steaming five abreast and we are last on the port side ... Sweating, clammy hot again in afternoon, and evening, with overcast sky. Again slept in chair on deck.'

As the convoy steamed steadily south, the weather became more pleasant. At about 4 pm on 31 January the convoy crossed the equator, but there was no special ceremony on board *Franconia*, even though many of the British troops on board had not crossed the line before.

Duchess of Bedford joined the convoy at Freetown.

Slessor wrote, 'Crossed Equator in afternoon, sea calm, sky overcast and wind cool. However, interior of ship still like a stove, and slept on deck again.' Next day the rumour mill was at work again, following an announcement that 'next pay will not be until February 10 ... Thus it appears that we are likely to reach port on February 11, Tuesday, and the general report now is that we shall go directly to Durban ... Weather perceptibly cooler, though we are now directly under the sun, which is approximately in Latitude 22 ... So much cooler that decided to sleep in cabin at night — though air still close and superheated.'

The weather and interior heat of the ship remained a major topic for Kenneth Slessor over the next few days, and recorded on 2 February, 'Another overcast dull day, with a huge slow roll on sea, and much cooler on deck generally ... Owing to the vast stagnant pockets of hot air in the ship, kept there by lack of ventilation owing to blackout, it is still a comparative sweat bath below deck.' Two days later things had cooled down even more so that, 'at night, so much cooler that, for the first time in almost fortnight, slept in both halves of my pyjamas, and under a sheet.' His entry for 6 February stated, 'Cool and delightful weather now ... Boxing competitions held this afternoon on sun-deck, and caused the usual excitement and enthusiasm. A missing word competition at lunch won by Collins ... who sits next to me at the table.'

By now the convoy was approaching the southern tip of Africa, and the Cape of Good Hope. On 7 February, 'Between 10.00 and 11.00, convoy split into two sections — seven ships going to Cape Town moved into columns on port side, eleven ships for Durban starboard. We therefore moved across to the other side of convoy. Information is that we should pass the Cape early tomorrow. One cruiser will go with us, the other with the contingent of ships for Cape Town.'

Empress of Australia was one of the transports to divert to Cape Town.

Early the next morning the two sections of the convoy went their separate ways, the vessels diverting to Cape Town including *Empress of Japan, Empress of Australia, Monarch of Bermuda* and *Duchess of Bedford*, escorted by *Emerald*. The eleven ships continuing on to Durban, escorted by *Australia*, formed into three columns and aboard *Franconia*, 'in afternoon, we had turned course to east, past Cape Agulhas. Ship started to roll a lot, more than I have noticed so far on voyage. Weather now so cool that I changed into woollen singlet under shirt. In evening, while in card room, ship's loudspeakers announced that rough seas and gales were expected at about 10.00 pm and everyone was warned to secure loose objects such as watches, clocks etc. from rolling. We are now, it appears, in notoriously rough area known as the Bay of Storms. However, apart from the same roll, there was no sign of a storm at 10.00, and going on deck at about midnight, I found a blazing full moon, so bright that the whole convoy was lit up as in daylight. The sea frothing with white — but no sign of storm still. And none all night.'

Next morning there was still no sign of the storm though the 'sea heaving with white foam, but sky clear, sun out, and air sparkling.' The ships were now on a more northerly course, following the coastline of South Africa, and once again the days began to get warmer. As dawn broke on 11 February, the ships formed into a single column, *Franconia* being tenth of the eleven merchant ships, and began to close on the entrance to the port of Durban, although it was early afternoon before they entered the harbour. As there were insufficient free berths for all

HMAS *Australia* was repainted in camouflage colours in Durban. (*Ross Gillett collection*)

the ships, *Franconia* had to tie up outside the *Cameronia*, which was alongside the wharf. 'Weather hot and moist, much hotter than Cape Town,' Slessor wrote. 'So hot, that sat on deck gently perspiring until 6.00, when changed into drill, and went ashore.' The troops on board *Franconia* were also given shore leave, though they first had to cross a gangway and the deck of the *Cameronia*. Despite this being their first time ashore in over a month, Slessor wrote, 'Troops in town on whole seemed very well behaved.'

The convoy remained in Durban four days, during which all the troops were able to enjoy a good break ashore. The sailors aboard HMAS *Australia* were also given shore leave, and on 12 February Slessor noted, '*Australia* is to be completely camouflaged here, so looks as if we shall remain in port till end of week.' Next day he mentioned meeting three junior officers from *Australia* at a hotel, and invited them to a party being held ashore that night. After the party, he caught a taxi back to the ship, but 'found *Franconia* moved further down wharves to a separate berth … Spent an amusing hour between 12.30 and 1.30 on deck over brightly lit gangplank watching drunks and picquet-loads stagger up plank, some pushing one another in trolleys, others carried over shoulders of mate. Speaking to steward, he said local trades-people had told him that behaviour of convoy troops so far was best they'd known of all convoys so far visited here.'

After a final day ashore on 14 February, all leave was stopped and the final latecomers, most of whom had overstayed their leave and been posted AWL, staggered back to their ships, which were preparing to depart. The departure of the convoy was supposed to be secret, but as usual word had got around. As Kenneth Slessor wrote: 'At about 10.30, crowds of local people, mostly women, and many of them very pretty girls in slacks and shorts, began to gather on wharf and jetty nearby, waving to men on boats ... The women showed extraordinary patience, as the first ship of the convoy did not move out till about 1.00 — from then on there was a long procession of troopships, bristling to the masts with khaki, slipping out through the narrow harbour channel. As each ship went by she blew three whistle blasts, answered by launches and tugs in harbour, and railway engines on wharf.'

Franconia was one of the last ships to depart, as 'At about 4.00 our gangplank was hoisted up, and soon after we swung out backwards, the men singing "Maori Farewell," and girls on wharf cheering and waving. Two new ships joined the convoy, packed with South African troops. Weather much cooler, with a fresh breeze at sea ... At about 7.00, we were scarcely moving, hove to in the roll of the sea, with about twelve other ships, evidently waiting for a rendezvous.' That night at dinner, a sweep was organised in the officers mess, at 5s. a ticket, on the next port, Slessor drawing 'Ismailia and Calcutta, and some said the first was possible, though I think Suez myself.'

The section of the convoy that had berthed in Cape Town left there on 12 February, and the two sections joined up off Durban. Next morning, Slessor 'counted nineteen vessels in the convoy' and also noted he was told at breakfast, 'that altogether about forty-five Australians are absent from this ship — also four naval ratings and no British soldiers.' The eventual destination of the convoy remained a major topic of conversation, the 'theory most discussed now is that we may probably go to Mombasa. Escort now is two cruisers (*Australia* and *Emerald*), destroyers and corvettes evidently having dropped off. Risk of submarine or plane attack now considered small, and only danger seems to be from surface raider.'

The convoy was now heading in a north easterly direction, and on 17 February Slessor wrote that 'I expect we are now passing through Mozambique Channel, and as we have to go through Red Sea after that, will have to expect heat for some time. Slept on deck once again at night, forced out of cabin by stifling airless heat — above deck, a fairly strong wind blowing, so that had to sleep under a sheet.' That night there was also a culinary surprise for the officers' mess, when 'Caviar served for dinner tonight! A relic of trans-Atlantic days found in larder which they evidently decided to get rid of.'

Unfortunately, the food on board was not always the best. On 20 February Slessor observed: 'Every second person ill today with an epidemic of diarrhoea, caused according to conjecture by either crayfish or ice at dinner last night — in which case I am very lucky, as I ate a quantity of each, but feel no effects ... At 12.26 today, the sun was directly overhead, and hence saw the phenomenon of no shadows being cast. I judge we are now off the coast of Zanzibar ... Still hot, and getting hotter, so that at night when I went out to sleep on deck, found place littered with a crowd of sleepers already there, and had some trouble in finding a space, where I slept on a blanket on the deck itself.'

On 21 February, some ships left the convoy, bound for other destinations. 'At about 9.45,' wrote Slessor, '*Empress of Japan, Empress of Australia, Windsor Castle* and *Ormonde* swung to inside of convoy, ready to leave us for Mombasa, where they are to call before going on to Bombay and (in *Ormonde*'s case) to Australia. At noon they grew further apart, and at 4.00 left us entirely, with cruiser *Emerald. Australia* remained with us, and we were joined soon after by a strange-looking cruiser — more like a battlecruiser, since she has very heavy and big turrets. Some say she is HMS *Renown*, others HMS *Hawkins* or a Norwegian warship.' In fact it was HMS *Hawkins*.

During this part of the voyage, troops were kept active with sport competitions on deck, lectures and training sessions. Everyone on board found the heat inside the ship oppressive, and more of them were opting to sleep on the open decks at night, including the contingent of nurses on board. As a result, 'At night, port side of promenade deck was reserved for nurses only (with picquets posted), so there was great congestion on the starboard side, and I found it impossible to discover enough space to stretch out on deck, so slept till 5.00 in two chairs again. A glorious moonlight night.'

Next day the ship crossed the equator, this being the fifth time the

HMS *Hawkins* joined the escort as the convoy passed Mombasa.

Australian troops had crossed the line in eight months. As a result, there were no ceremonies and the usual round of activities continued. Once again many of those on board slept on the open deck, despite it being so crowded, but the following night the weather had grown cooler and Slessor noted he could once again sleep in his own cabin.

During this part of the trip the card room on the *Franconia* was turned into a court, and those troops who had overstayed their leave in Durban were court-martialled, as well as troops who had committed other offences during the voyage. Slessor referred to one of these, in which 'the sergeant who fired the Bren gun which wounded three men early in voyage was exonerated by the court of inquiry, and the three men are now said to be almost recovered.' Court martial cases continued day after day, and 'Sentences range from thirty days and ninety days detention to one year six months imprisonment,' while another diary entry recorded that one warrant officer had been reduced to the ranks.

Anything was welcome to break the endless monotony of the voyage, and on 27 February, when the convoy was off Aden, a small warship approached the convoy during the morning and closed with *Athlone Castle*, which was carrying the convoy commodore. Slessor noted, 'As it got within range of my field glasses, I noticed to my great surprise that it bears the name *Parramatta*, and is evidently the Australian sloop built at Cockatoo last year ... All the Australians on our boat crowded to side to wave to crew of the *Parramatta*.' The speed of the convoy had been reduced until the ships were almost stationary, then, 'at 1.30 ... we approached four new troopships, in another convoy, evidently waiting to join us ... All speculated whether they were from Australia, via Bombay, Colombo or Aden direct ... The two convoys approached and the four newcomers swung into line behind us ... This made a total of twenty ships now in the convoy, all large passenger boats, none under twelve thousand tons, I should say.'

That night the convoy approached the Straits of Bab El Mandeb. Captain Taunton, master of *Franconia*, told Slessor 'that very strict precautions being taken all this night, sentries and guards specially reinforced and kept on alert, blackout tightened etc., as the skipper of the ship considers that for two hours going through the Straits we are at most dangerous stage of our voyage since leaving Britain, as the Straits are only seventeen miles apart, and no room is allowed for the ships to manoeuvre or escape in the event of a German bombing-plane raid ... Hell's Gate passed through at 8.30 I learned, *Franconia* leading the other nineteen vessels … Somewhat hotter and growing still hotter at night, but slept in cabin in evening.'

The next day the convoy entered the Red Sea. 'Ship lurching in morning when woke, and found the Red Sea, which we're now in, rough and choppy,' Slessor observed. 'Though Red Sea was feared for heat, quite fresh, with cool wind, outside.' Over the next three days the convoy continued its passage up the Red Sea, and on the afternoon of 2 March, 'convoy formed into two long columns of ten ships each, stretching back as far as eye could see — we were third in starboard column … Slept under sheet and quilt in cabin for first time in weeks.'

Next day, Wednesday 3 March, many of the troops were up early seeking their first sight of Egypt and the end of their long journey. Slessor was also 'on deck before breakfast, almost cold in chill wind blowing. We now seem to be in the narrows — land each side about fifteen miles, I should say, apart … Sailed all day between these two coasts … At 3.45 came to a halt about six or seven miles from Port Suez and opposite Port Tewfik — a low sandy shore, clustered with shipping at anchor in front of it. Then moved on again in about twenty minutes, further upstream, to an anchorage in a swarm of vessels near town … Anchor dropped at 4.40. Soon after, a launch came alongside with a crowd of Australian officers, liaison officers etc. … The present contingent is to go to Palestine via Port Said, and the ship will make a trip there, through the Canal, almost immediately.' As a result, no troops were allowed ashore, but faced several more days on the ship.

Franconia remained anchored off Port Tewfik overnight, but any thoughts of an early departure for the passage through the Suez Canal, and disembarkation at Alexandria, were soon put to one side, since, as Slessor recorded, 'the port was so congested already with troops that no one could be allowed to leave *Franconia* until Friday next. Also reported that the Canal was bombed and mined a few nights ago, and the transport cannot go on to Port Said as intended.' Slessor was keen to get off the ship as soon as possible and report to the Australian Corps Headquarters, but initially he found that none of the visiting 'liaison officers' seemed to have the foggiest idea where it was located. Eventually he was informed that headquarters were at Gaza, but in the process of being moved to Haifa. 'As the ship was said to be headed for Haifa, and the troops, Australians, are to camp at Gaza, I decided that if this was the case, I might as well stay with the rest.'

The prospect of spending yet another week on board did not appeal to the troops at all. Slessor wrote, 'Everyone is irritated by the prospect of another tedious wait aboard, particularly after two months of travel, and the week spent in the ship before sailing ... In fact, the general state of uncertainty and lack of organisation in the plans for dealing with the convoy's arrival are sad to see.'

As events panned out, Kenneth Slessor did not stay aboard *Franconia* for the trip through the Suez Canal, as on the afternoon of 5 March an officer from Corps Headquarters arrived on board looking for him. Corps Headquarters was in fact at Ikingi Maryut, about twelve miles from Alexandria, and AIF Headquarters was in Alexandria itself. As a result, Slessor left *Franconia* at Port Tewfik.

Once the Suez Canal had been cleared of mines dropped by German aircraft, *Franconia* and the other ships carrying Australian troops proceeded north to Port Said, and on to Alexandria, where their passengers finally disembarked and went to camps to prepare for their introduction into battles being waged in the Western Desert.

Just what conditions were like on these troopships was graphically described by John Colville, who had been Private Secretary to Winston Churchill, but in October 1941 joined the RAF as an aircraftsman second class. After basic flying training in England he was sent to South Africa to finish his training. In his autobiography, *The Fringes of Power*, he wrote of his wartime experiences, including the trip to South Africa.

> On January 10 1942 a band led a contingent from Padgate, including me, to the railway station where we entrained for Liverpool ... That band was the last cheerful thing I saw or heard for nearly six weeks. At Liverpool the Orient liner *Otranto*, painted grey and converted into a troop-ship, awaited us. Our quarters in the mess decks were daunting. There were long narrow tables to each of which eighteen of us were allocated. They would have been just large enough for twelve. Over them we were supposed to swing our hammocks; but there were only enough hammocks for half of us and there were nightly fights to secure one. The unsuccessful slept, fully dressed, and using a life-belt as a pillow, either on the tables or on the filthy floor.
>
> On board were three hundred aircrew under training, over two thousand soldiers bound for Singapore and a number of unruly merchant seamen bound for Durban to pick up crewless merchantmen. There was a fearsome body of marines charged to keep order and several attractive nurses and WAAFs who shared the comforts of A and B decks with the officers. The rest of us, some three thousand in all, were herded like cattle into the totally inadequate space of C, D and E decks. The water

was turned on for an hour twice in twenty four hours, so that scrimmages rather then queues were the order of the day, and as we were not allowed to undress, in case the ship should be torpedoed, unhygienic is too mild a word to describe what we became, at least until we were ordered, as we approached the Equator, to change into the tropical dress of khaki shirt and shorts, black tie, woollen khaki stockings and a topi.

The convoy in which we sailed contained over fifty ships, guarded by a battleship and six destroyers. We had not been at sea long when a German Focke-Wulff Condor flew over us and was missed by several hundred anti-aircraft guns. Knowing that it would signal our position to the U-boat packs, the Commodore of the convoy changed course to due west, so that before stopping for a day or two in the steaming heat of Freetown, we had sailed almost to the coast of Brazil. We were not allowed ashore at Freetown, and it was over five weeks before, with shattered morale and fed on such delicacies as canned tripe, we finally anchored off Durban. Meanwhile one young airman had died of meningitis and we had all been ordered to parade at 5 am for the macabre ceremony of committing his body to the deep. After that we had to sleep as best we could on the crowded, hard, teak decks in case the infection should spread in the stuffy atmosphere below.

In a letter written to Mrs Churchill after the voyage Colville explained that, while the overcrowding on the lower decks was so intense that it was only sometimes possible to lie flat on deck, or avoid bodily contact with others, the officers and nurses had the two spacious top decks to themselves. 'In the evenings, as we stood or sat disconsolately below, we watched the dancing on A deck and listened to the music from a string orchestra. The menus of the five-course dinners for the commissioned ranks were handed round on the mess decks while we fed on our unsavoury rations. At our cramped meals, the orderly officer would appear and say with monotonous regularity, "Any complaints, other than the food?" It is not surprising that strong and bitter political feeling was rampant on the lower decks long before we reached Durban.'

As he knew would happen, Mrs Churchill showed the letter to the Prime Minister, who insisted that conditions in troopships be examined urgently. However, as John Colville ruefully recorded, 'This had a rapid effect; but I was hoist on my own petard, for when I returned to England twelve months later on another Orient liner, *Orion*, as a sergeant-pilot, we all shared the same food and even officers were six to a cabin.'

10
The 'Monster' Convoys

In the first eighteen months of the war a large number of British and Empire passenger liners were requisitioned for duty as armed merchant cruisers or troop transports. As the demands of the war intensified, it was decided that merchant ships were not really suited to a military role, so many armed merchant cruisers were converted into troop transports. However, the serious situation facing the Allied armies in North Africa led to demands for increasing numbers of Commonwealth troops to be provided.

The Allied trooping fleet had been strengthened by liners from countries overrun by the Germans, including Poland, Holland and France, and during 1941 the largest liner in the world, *Queen Elizabeth*, was also requisitioned for duty as a troop transport. Already three of the largest liners in the world, *Queen Mary*, *Mauretania* and *Aquitania* were engaged in transporting Australian and New Zealand troops to the Middle East, and they were now to be joined by *Queen Elizabeth*, along with the Dutch flagship *Nieuw Amsterdam* and the French liner *Ile de France*, the six liners becoming generally known as the 'Monsters.'

Queen Elizabeth had been laid up in New York since March 1940, being moved to Pier 89, next to *Normandie*, after *Queen Mary* left. As America was still nominally neutral, no major work could be carried out on the liner, though some interior fitting out had been done, with lighting, heating, ventilation and other services being installed. In September 1940, the British government decided that *Queen Elizabeth* should be utilised in a similar fashion to *Queen Mary*. Preparations for the long voyage took some time, and it was not until 13 November

1940 that the giant liner slipped out of New York Harbour. As with *Queen Mary*, elaborate efforts were made to disguise her route and destination. Her first port of call was Trinidad to take on 6000 tons of fuel and 4000 tons of fresh water, then the liner headed out into the South Atlantic, arriving in Cape Town on 27 November. After a lay over of several days to take on more fuel, *Queen Elizabeth* headed for Singapore, where she arrived on 13 December, and shortly after entered drydock for the first time. At last the launching blocks could be removed and the underwater sections of the hull scraped clean. Some internal fittings for troops were installed, along with a 6-inch gun at the stern, as well as numerous anti-aircraft guns along the upper decks, while her hull was repainted black.

While *Queen Elizabeth* was in drydock in Singapore, the overseas movement of Australian and New Zealand troops continued. The first convoy to be dispatched in 1941, US9, consisted of four giant liners, *Queen Mary*, *Mauretania* and *Aquitania* being joined by *Nieuw Amsterdam*. The flagship of the Dutch merchant fleet, she had entered service in May 1938 for Holland-America Line, but was laid up in New York when war broke out. Subsequently reactivated for a series of cruises to Bermuda and the West Indies, *Nieuw Amsterdam* was placed at the disposal of the Allies by the Dutch government in exile following the German invasion of Holland in May 1940, but not taken over by the Allies until September. Managed for the British government by Cunard Line, *Nieuw Amsterdam* was allocated to transport Australian and New Zealand troops, but first was sent from New York on 12 September 1940 to Halifax, where some conversion work was completed.

On 11 October *Nieuw Amsterdam* departed Halifax on a long voyage to Singapore, arriving in Cape Town on 25 October, departing the next day, and berthing in Singapore on 8 November. Over the next six weeks the liner was transformed into a troop transport, with some time spent in the huge Singapore drydock. Troop accommodation was installed in any available area, including 190 wooden bunks in the former grand hall. The whole of C deck and after end of B deck were dismantled to make room for hammocks, the bunks removed being added to tourist-class cabins on other decks, while timber bunks were installed in many first-class cabins. One luxury cabin was retained for the commanding officer of troops, but other officers were accommodated in six-berth cabins. In all, 1933 bunks were fitted along with spaces for 2159 hammocks, a total of 4092 berths. The former smoke room and library were converted into a hospital, with beds for

123 patients, and additional toilets and bathrooms were constructed throughout the ship.

On Tuesday, 24 December 1940, *Nieuw Amsterdam* departed Singapore, with no passengers on board, en route via Torres Strait to Sydney, where she arrived on 3 January 1941. An Australian military officer came on board to inspect the ship, as a result of which further alterations were made. The ship had 22 lifeboats, which could accommodate 1946 persons, but an additional 178 liferafts were installed, each capable of carrying 22 men, for a total of 3916. Meanwhile, all the furnishings from public rooms and cabins, which had been placed in a hold in Singapore, were removed and sent ashore for storage.

The opportunity was also taken to complete loading stores for the upcoming voyage, with much of this being done by guesswork, though the provision of a copy of the storing requisitions for *Mauretania* helped a great deal. It was some of the smaller items that caused the biggest problems. For example, how many toilet rolls would be needed? It was calculated that over 20,000 rolls would be used over a three-month period, and that would mean no. 1 hold would be entirely filled with toilet paper!

For convoy US9, *Nieuw Amsterdam* was allocated to transport New Zealand troops, so the vessel, escorted by HMAS *Hobart*, departed Sydney on 23 January for Wellington, where she docked on 26 January. Here a few cosmetic alterations were completed. In Singapore the funnels had been painted black, while the superstructure was painted

Nieuw Amsterdam berthed in Wellington. (*Wellington Maritime Museum*)

Sydney Harbour excursion vessel *Sydney Showboat* steams past *Mauretania* berthed at Circular Quay. (*C.T. Reddings collection*)

a dull buff colour, and this colour was now applied to the funnels too.

A week after arriving in Wellington, 3675 New Zealand troops came aboard, along with 150 nurses, and on 1 February *Nieuw Amsterdam* departed Wellington, again escorted by *Hobart*, towards Sydney, where she would link up with the other ships making up convoy US9. *Nieuw Amsterdam* arrived off Sydney Heads on 4 February and, according to the official records, 'troopship entered under naval orders, anchored in stream.'

Mauretania, which had been berthed in Sydney awaiting the departure of the convoy, was sent to Melbourne to embark her troops, while *Queen Mary* and *Aquitania* took aboard their troops in Sydney. However, for the first time not all these troops would be going to the Middle East, as *Queen Mary* was being sent to Singapore.

Early in December 1940, the Australian government had expressed concern about the defence of the Malay Peninsula and advised the British government that they would be willing to send, as a temporary expedient, a brigade group to Singapore to complete their training. This offer was accepted by the British government, so the 8th Division Headquarters Group and the 22nd Brigade, which comprised 2/18, 2/19 and 2/20 Battalions, altogether numbering 5,718 men and designated Elbow Force, boarded *Queen Mary* in Sydney bound for Singapore. However, as they joined the huge liner at anchor off Bradleys Head, none of the troops were aware of their destination, having trained in the belief they would be joining the fighting in North

A striking view of *Queen Mary* at anchor in Sydney Harbour. (*C.T. Reddings collection*)

Africa or the Middle East. The men of the 22nd Brigade were also the first troops to embark for overseas wearing shorts. The officer designated to command Australian forces in Singapore, Lieutenant General Gordon Bennett, did not travel with his men, but instead was flown to Singapore in early February.

About 1 pm on 4 February 1941, *Queen Mary* and *Aquitania* departed Sydney, linking up with *Nieuw Amsterdam* outside the Heads. Among those who had boarded *Queen Mary* in Sydney, attached to 8th Division Headquarters, was Captain Adrian Curlewis, later Sir Adrian, whose daughter, Philippa, recalled of that day. 'On that hot February afternoon my mother and I watched as the *Queen Mary* faded into the indistinct haze where sea and sky met. When one has just turned eight, there is still a whole lifetime ahead, and several months with my father away didn't seem to depress me too greatly. We walked home and I set to work to finish off a picture that I had drawn ... Then a sound disturbed me more than anything I could ever remember. My mother was upstairs and she was crying! I didn't know then that mothers ever cried! Certainly children did when they were hurt or when they were angry ... But this was different, for the first time I realised that this

HMAS *Hobart* escorted convoy US9.

parting meant a good deal more than I had previously understood. Perhaps my father wouldn't be away for only a few months; perhaps it might even be a whole year. Could it be that he mightn't return?'

Escorted by HMAS *Hobart*, *Queen Mary*, *Aquitania* and *Nieuw Amsterdam* headed south, where *Mauretania* joined them in Bass Strait on 6 February. The same day, Adrian Curlewis began writing a letter to his family:

> Cheering crowds and waving flags all the way down the Harbour are all very well but I decided, when three miles out, to go below and write my impressions ... I decided my cabin was the best place and as batman and steward were both missing I had to drag a luxurious chair across a heavy carpet without help. Exhausted after this effort I staggered up through Piccadilly Circus to afternoon tea in the lounge and sank into a bottomless armchair of velvet and sponge rubber. With the aid of field glasses I could just see the far end of the lounge and smoothly moving waiters dispensing tea. Then followed a lecture on discipline and duties.
>
> Thoughts are confused and impossible to adjust in these surroundings ... last night I lay in an armchair, coffee and liqueurs beside me, and watched pictures in the most luxurious lounge in the world — white-hooded, red-caped nurses lending colour — and yet almost on the spot we were passing over, ships have been lost in the last three months. To clear my mind I walked the wet decks till midnight and watched moonlight. Still very cold on board and from where I sit I hear the orders of a dozen sergeants drilling men, the rattle of rifles being inspected on a deck where dukes, duchesses and Yankee millionaires have fought for social supremacy.

Among those who had embarked on *Mauretania* in Melbourne were members of the 2/9 Australian General Hospital. A group of nursing sisters from Queensland had travelled by train to Sydney, where they arrived on 4 February and were joined by New South Wales members of the unit. Continuing their journey by train, the sisters arrived in Melbourne on 5 February and, along with a group from Tasmania, immediately boarded *Mauretania* at Station Pier. Next day, the troops embarked, and Sister J.F. Crameri wrote in a letter home, 'To stand on deck and see that unending stream of fine handsome men marching aboard in an orderly fashion — well, I cannot say how sad it was wondering who would come back with us. But they were happy, and I don't think a finer, better-looking crowd of men could be seen.'

Travelling across the Great Australian Bight at just under 20 knots, the convoy now comprised *Queen Mary, Aquitania, Nieuw Amsterdam* and *Mauretania*, escorted by HMAS *Hobart*. As Sister Crameri noted, 'portholes must, of course, be kept closed, and the decks are in darkness. Last night was moonlight, and it was glorious out on deck. It certainly gives one a feeling of safety to see another huge shape not far away.' The members of the 2/9 AGH were rostered for duties on board along with the troops, including rosters in the kitchens where, as Private D.A. Christison wrote, 'Scullery duties were an experience not to be missed. There were three sittings for meals, approximately 1,000 men to each meal, so it seemed as if there was nothing but plates after plates. Fourteen orderlies were on duty in the scullery, and 106 did other duties on the ship ... The *Mauretania* being built for the Atlantic run, was not pleasant in tropical weather, especially below decks in cabins and mess rooms. Everyone perspired most freely, hence most were stripped to the waist.'

Convoy US9 arrived off Fremantle on 9 February, *Queen Mary* anchoring out while the others docked, and the troops were granted shore leave. Adrian Curlewis jotted down more thoughts about the trip so far. 'Still very cold this morning, men moving about the decks in great coats and mufflers — shorts, shirt and exercise keep me warm, not to mention a feeling of well being. The first two days I could not adjust my mind to war, or passage thereto, in these surroundings. Gradually I have become acclimatised and philosophical, and with thoughts of the discomforts ahead, am quite satisfied to take things as they come. The test will be to take the discomforts in the same manner.'

Instead of the usual one day stopover in Fremantle, the ships remained there for three days, departing on 12 February, escorted by HMAS *Canberra*. Once out to sea, the convoy adopted a diamond formation, with *Queen Mary* at the head, *Aquitania* on the port point and *Mauretania* on the starboard point, while *Nieuw Amsterdam* brought up the tail.

With Fremantle behind them, the troops on board *Queen Mary* still expected their next stop would be in Ceylon, but they were now advised their destination was Singapore, where they would join the garrison to defend Malaya. This news was met with anything but approval by the men, who felt themselves cheated. Sir Adrian Curlewis later stated, 'We had enlisted for active service and we had thought until we sailed that we were going to the Middle East. It was such a disappointment. We felt that if people asked us, "What did you do in the great war, Daddy?" then we'd feel a bit ashamed that we were only garrison troops in Malaya.' What no-one could even guess at that time was that, little more than a year later, most of the men on board *Queen Mary* would either be dead or beginning many harsh years as prisoners of war of the Japanese.

Also on board *Queen Mary* were members of the Australian Army Nursing Service, with Matron O.D. Paschke in charge. She issued strict instructions that the nurses must return to their quarters at a respectable hour each evening, but they were allowed to dance with the officers in the officers' lounge, where formal uniform was the order of the day, the nurses wearing their capes and caps. As with the troops on the liner, the nurses had all assumed they were being sent to the Middle East and their response to the information that their destination would be Singapore was similar to that of the troops. As one nurse, Sylvia Muir, later remarked, 'It was all hush-hush in those days; you sailed for a destination unknown. It was most exciting. Then we arrived in Malaya. I was sure no action would ever happen there. We were so far from the Middle East.'

Queen Mary remained with the convoy for the first four days after departure from Fremantle, until a point 200 miles south of Sunda Strait was reached on 16 February. In the distance a British cruiser was sighted approaching the convoy. This turned out to be HMS *Durban*, which had come from Singapore, and *Queen Mary* then detached from convoy US9. *Queen Mary* put on a burst of speed and pulled ahead of the other three liners, then began a long turn to port. Sweeping down the port side of *Aquitania*, the huge liner passed astern of *Nieuw Amsterdam*, then came up the starboard side of *Mauretania*. On each liner all the troops were on deck, and as *Queen Mary* swept past *Mauretania*, appearing to be only a matter of feet away, the troops on both ships cheered each other.

Sister Crameri wrote: 'I have just seen a marvellous sight I will never forget. The *Queen Mary* has just left the convoy. After 2.30 pm word went around that we had sighted another convoy. Well, it was a cruiser to escort the *Mary*. Suddenly, the *Mary* turned right round, almost in her own length, and made off behind us. A message was then broadcast for all our troops to assemble on one side of our ship and cheer her as she went by. She turned again, and passed right up close to each ship. Imagine her six thousand troops in every porthole, lifeboat and deck, and our own four thousand, cheering each other as that beautiful ship passed by. She passed the *Aquitania* and had the same reception, and then she and her escort made off to the north-east.' Escorted by *Durban*, *Queen Mary* proceeded to Singapore, while the rest of the convoy maintained their course for Ceylon.

On board *Queen Mary* there were many men dissatisfied with conditions and their changed destination. Adrian Curlewis wrote that, 'Just as I went to dinner some trouble started in one of the men's Canteens. Hundreds of bodies stripped to the waist, slimy and wet with sweat, confined under a low ceiling, all ports closed, a grievance in all their hearts, beer lukewarm in pannikins. I asked the ship's Staff Captain permission to address them and it was granted. Up on a mess table and in five minutes I had them under control. I was soaked through from inside and soaked outside by contact with bodies. Don't regard this as anything against the men — they have had a terrible time and are herded in foul temperatures.'

The heat grew ever more intense as *Queen Mary* neared Singapore, where she arrived on the morning of 18 February. Adrian Curlewis wrote of his final hours aboard *Queen Mary*, 'Islands have appeared to port since early morning ... I had my last swim in the glorious pool this morning. I am staggered at the amount of water that can come from the pores of the skin and that any substance remains. I woke this morning with my pyjamas saturated. However I am fit as a fiddle and ready for anything.' As *Queen Mary* docked, on the wharf waiting to greet the troops was the Governor of Singapore, Sir Thomas Shenton, and numerous senior army, navy and air force officers. No doubt they were relieved to see the liner arrive, since German propaganda claimed the ship had been sunk. As Adrian Curlewis wrote on 20 February, 'We were considerably worried by a rumour that Lord Haw Haw had broadcast that we had been torpedoed two days outside our last port.' On 21 February *Queen Mary* went into the drydock at Singapore, recently vacated by *Queen Elizabeth*.

There is a story, which many say is true, that there was an extra passenger on board *Queen Mary*, a young kangaroo. It is said to have been captured in the bush by a young soldier from the Riverina and became the unit mascot. When the unit arrived in Sydney to board *Queen Mary*, among their effects was a large wooden box, with holes bored in the sides. In it was Joey, the kangaroo. The box was taken on board the ferry at Pyrmont and smuggled on to the *Queen Mary*. The only person who guessed what was in the box was the unit medical officer, and he did not say anything. Once the ship was out to sea after leaving Fremantle, the kangaroo was let out of the box and became a favourite with the troops. Joey was smuggled ashore in Singapore in his box and seemed to settle in well, but one day some children chased him, and he broke a leg while escaping. This was set in a plaster cast, but the poor kangaroo never recovered and eventually had to be put down. As one soldier wrote, 'Somewhere in Malaya there is a grave and above it a headstone inscribed simply "Joey, the Kangaroo, AIF, 1941."'

Aquitania, *Mauretania* and *Nieuw Amsterdam* continued on their way to Bombay, with *Canberra* handing over escort duty to HMS *Leander* in the middle of the Indian Ocean. This was also an occasion recorded by Sister Crameri, who wrote that, 'the ships in the convoy said "goodbye and thank you" to the HMAS *Canberra* by lining up and flying their flags. The *Canberra* sailed down the line of ships, and everyone on deck cheered her on her way as she sailed out of sight.'

The three troopships arrived in Bombay on 22 February, where the Australian troops disembarked and most transferred to five smaller ships, *Nevasa*, *Khedive Ismail*, *Westernland*, *Slamat* and *Cap St Jacques*. The New Zealand troops aboard *Nieuw Amsterdam* were transferred to the former British India liner *Talma*. These six ships formed a new convoy that departed Bombay on 26 February for the last leg of their voyage to Suez, where the troops disembarked on 13 March, then went by

Westernland carried some of the Australian troops from Bombay to Egypt. (*C.T. Reddings collection*)

train to Kantara, where they arrived two days later. One of the ships that escorted this convoy up the Red Sea was HMAS *Parramatta*.

Among those who remained in Bombay was the 2/9 Australian General Hospital, apart from a group of eight sisters who were posted to join the *Westernland*. As one of them, Sister Welch, recalled, 'Word came through that eight Western Australian sisters were to leave on 26 February after a short three-day stay. We were to sail on the SS *Westernland* which was returning to the Middle East after bringing Italian prisoners of war to India. They requested eight Army sisters to staff the sick bay. I was disappointed to be separated from my unit and friends, but had to accept that the exigencies of the service must come first, and not my personal pleasure.'

It was anything but a pleasant journey for the sisters and troops aboard *Westernland*. According to Sister Welch:

> The ship was dirty, and the food was very poor. I believe the soldiers threw most of the meat overboard as it was rotten, and put their own cooks in the galley. We had to cover our noses with our handkerchiefs when we passed the galley to get to the sick bay, as the odours were so foul. We were always hungry, and were fortunate on occasions to get some sandwiches and apples from an English steward.
>
> The sick bay was low down in the ship. It had panniers of instruments thick with grease, and very little other equipment. We had one case of smallpox and one of chickenpox, both needing isolation. This meant two sisters had to vacate their cabins and 'double up.' Other patients had mostly gastro-enteritis, or 'gyppo' tummy.
>
> We were sailing in convoy, and one of the ships had engine trouble, so we were slowed down by a zig-zag course. Because of the danger of enemy action, boat drill was carried out frequently. Each sister was number one in a different lifeboat, so we would have been separated if anything happened. We always carried emergency rations and lifebelts.
>
> Fresh food had almost run out when Suez was sighted on 13 March. There was an air-raid warning at 10 pm, but nothing happened. Everyone was pleased to disembark as it had not been a happy trip. Overcrowding of the men, lack of water (on for half an hour a day most of the time) did not improve morale.

The sisters joined troops on a train trip to Kantara, where they crossed the Suez Canal by boat, then continued on another train to Gaza, where they remained until they were able to rejoin their unit.

The remainder of the 2/9 AGH, along with some of the troops, remained in Bombay for two weeks, but on 11 March they were taken back to the docks. The 2/9 AGH found themselves on board the Dutch ship *Indrapoera*, which had previously carried Australian troops in convoy US5. The next day, *Indrapoera* joined other ships in a convoy departing Bombay. In contrast to the experience of those on the *Westernland*, the trip on *Indrapoera* was quite pleasant, even though everyone had to carry their lifebelt, waterbottle and a bag containing emergency provisions at all times. The ship was not crowded, the sea smooth, morale high, and the food excellent. 'The meals could not be better,' Sister Crameri wrote. 'They are like home cooking. I think the cooks on the ships could be classed some of the best in the world. We had "Heart of Palm Tree" as a course the other night. It was lovely — I cannot think what it tasted like. I watch the clock for meals.'

For the first part of the voyage escort was provided by a lone corvette, but as the convoy approached Aden on 18 March the escort was increased to three cruisers, two of which departed on 20 March when the convoy was in the Red Sea. *Indrapoera* and the other ships anchored in Suez Harbour on 23 March, and those on board disembarked, being taken by train to Kantara. On 2 April the eight sisters who had endured the discomfort of *Westernland* arrived in Kantara to rejoin their unit.

Of the ships that had carried the troops and others to Bombay, *Aquitania* did not return to Australia for several months, but went to Singapore for a much needed drydocking and refit. *Mauretania* and *Nieuw Amsterdam*, once their troops had disembarked, prepared for the voyage back to Sydney. After calling at Colombo on 1 March, the two liners, unescorted and travelling at top speed, kept company across the Indian Ocean. Following a brief stop at Fremantle, they headed across the Great Australian Bight, then turned north towards Sydney, where they docked on 24 March, and prepared for the next convoy.

On 11 February 1941, *Queen Elizabeth* had left Singapore, escorted by HMS *Durban*, arriving off Fremantle on 15 February and anchoring in Gage Roads. Departing Fremantle two days later, the liner proceeded unescorted at 25 knots across the Great Australian Bight and south of Tasmania, arriving in Sydney for the first time on 21 February. The arrival of the largest liner in the world was supposed to be a secret, yet word had spread and as she came through Sydney Heads and proceeded down the harbour, the shoreline was crowded with thousands of Sydneysiders. Ferries were also running special excursions, and even the footpath of the Sydney Harbour Bridge was packed. *Queen Elizabeth* dropped her anchor in the same spot off Bradleys Head that had been allocated to *Queen Mary*, and dominated the harbour.

Queen Elizabeth arrives in Sydney for the first time on 21 February 1941. (*National Library of Australia*)

Commencing on 25 February, workmen from the Cockatoo Docks and Engineering Co. were ferried out to the liner in 24-hour rotating shifts to transform her interior into accommodation quarters for 5500 troops by installing wooden bunks and hammocks in every cabin. Most of the internal work done in Singapore was also removed and replaced. The first-class dining room became the troops' mess, while the tourist-class dining room became the officers' mess. The dance salon was converted into the main hospital ward, with other wards in the smoke room and garden lounge, while the X-ray equipment was set up in the Turkish bath. Additional freshwater tanks were installed, and the cold storage rooms enlarged, while another storage room was converted into a stockade with several barred cells. As a final touch, hundreds of large life rings and 2000 flotation rings were fitted at numerous points around the ship. The theatre and indoor swimming pool were retained. Work was completed on 31 March.

Sydney Harbour is one of the largest and finest harbours in the world, but it was decided there was insufficient room for both of the Queens to anchor there at the same time and not block the vital waterway. Faced with the situation of both these liners being in Australian waters within a few weeks, it was agreed that, when one was in Sydney, the other would go to Hobart, the only other port large enough to provide them safe anchorage.

Queen Mary remained in drydock in Singapore until 1 March, then underwent further overhaul alongside a wharf before leaving on the

22nd. Four days later she arrived in Fremantle, then continued her voyage to Sydney. On the morning of 30 March, *Queen Elizabeth* raised anchor and departed Sydney, making a fast passage to Hobart where she arrived on 1 April, anchoring in the River Derwent, quite close to the city. *Queen Mary* arrived back in Sydney on 1 April and preparations continued for the next convoy of troops. US10 would be the most notable of all the troop convoys to leave Australia during the war, comprising five of the largest liners in the world. *Queen Mary, Mauretania* and *Nieuw Amsterdam*, all returned from US9, would be joined by two liners making their first trips, *Queen Elizabeth* and *Ile de France*.

Much older than her consorts, having been built in 1927, *Ile de France* was the largest vessel under the French flag until surpassed by *Normandie* in 1935. *Ile de France* had been in New York when war broke out and was ordered to stay there, being laid up at Staten Island. In March 1940 the liner had been lent to the British by the French and was loaded with 12,000 tons of war supplies, and such varied other cargo as submarine oil, copper ingots, brass bars, shells and three uncrated bombers stowed on the open deck aft. With her three funnels repainted black, and the upperworks a dull grey, *Ile de France* left New York on 1 May, bound for Britain, and was then used to carry Free French troops to Indo-China.

When France capitulated to the advancing Germans in June 1940, *Ile de France* was still in the Far East and arrived at Singapore on 30 June still under the French flag, but on 6 July the liner was taken over by the Royal Navy. Subsequently most of the French crew were repatriated, but it was not until November 1940 that a decision was taken regarding the future use of the vessel, which was to be converted into a troop transport, the work being undertaken at Singapore. Quarters for 4300 troops were installed, along with the necessary amenities, while two vintage 6-inch guns were fitted on either side at the stern, along with anti-aircraft guns on the upper decks.

Now under the British flag, being managed on behalf of the government by P & O Line, the ship was placed under the control of British officers, with Captain W.L. Pocock, who had spent 46 years at sea, in command. The chief engineer was G.C. Boulter, who had survived three times when ships he was in were torpedoed and sunk. *Ile de France* left Singapore for Sydney on 21 March 1941, arriving on 3 April. The next day, workmen from Cockatoo Docks and Engineering Company began work on completing the conversion of the liner, including alterations to the mess areas and galleys.

Queen Elizabeth at anchor off Hobart in the River Derwent. (*Stephen Card collection*)

Over the next week, Sydney shops were hard pressed to supply all the equipment required by *Ile de France* to bring the ship up to an acceptable standard to carry Australian troops. Almost every pot and pan in the city was purchased, creating a shortage for housewives that lasted many months. Many tons of meat were also bought and loaded on board, as were eighty tons of potatoes which were placed in a locker hastily constructed on the after deck between the two 6-inch guns. Unfortunately, when the guns were fired later in practice, the locker collapsed, covering the deck in potatoes.

All was now ready for the departure of convoy US10. *Mauretania* and *Nieuw Amsterdam* were both sent across the Tasman Sea to take on board New Zealand troops in Wellington, berthing at King's Wharf, *Mauretania* on the western side, *Nieuw Amsterdam* on the eastern side. Four thousand four hundred troops boarded *Mauretania*, while 2590 went on board *Nieuw Amsterdam*, and the two ships departed Wellington on 7 April, being escorted by the cruisers HMAS *Achilles*, HMAS *Australia* and HMAS *Hobart*.

Meanwhile, the Australian troops for the other three ships were brought to Sydney and prepared for embarkation. Such arrangements had to be very carefully organised, this being the first time both Queens would operate together. *Queen Mary* was already in Sydney, and on 8 April boarded 6000 troops as she lay at anchor off Bradleys Head. For this voyage, Captain Irving was replaced by Captain Fall.

Next morning, *Queen Mary* raised anchor and departed, and as she passed through Sydney Heads, *Queen Elizabeth* came up from the south, having left Hobart on 7 April. *Queen Elizabeth* took a wide sweep as she

Ile de France, shown here berthed in New York early in 1940. (*Stephen Card collection*)

lined up to enter Sydney Heads, allowing *Queen Mary* ample room for her departure, and the two great liners passed at sea for the first time. *Queen Mary*, escorted by HMAS *Sydney*, went the short distance down the New South Wales coast to Jervis Bay, where she anchored. *Queen Elizabeth* entered Sydney Harbour and anchored off Bradleys Head to begin boarding her first contingent of troops, 5333 in all, who were brought to the liner on ferries from Circular Quay. On 10 April *Queen Elizabeth* completed loading her troops.

Inbound *Queen Elizabeth* passes outbound Queen Mary on 9 April 1941 off Sydney Heads, the first time the two liners met up at sea. (*National Library of Australia*)

Nieuw Amsterdam (left) and *Mauretania* berthed at King's Wharf, Wellington. (*Wellington Maritime Museum*)

At the same time, *Ile de France* took on board 3271 troops, some of whom had had quite a long journey just to join the liner. The 2/3 Australian Machine Gun Battalion, which was commanded by Lieutenant Colonel A.S. Blackman, VC, had been training prior to embarkation near Adelaide, and was composed of men primarily drawn from South Australia, Tasmania and Western Australia. As the appointed time for their departure overseas drew near, D Company, which was entirely made up of men from Western Australia, was dispatched by train to their home state for pre-embarkation leave. Then, on 8 April, the remaining four companies of the battalion boarded two trains at Oakbank station for the long trip to Sydney. The first of these trains did not arrive until the early morning of 10 April, pulling up on the wharf at Pyrmont, from where the occupants were ferried out to board *Ile de France*. Seven hours later, the second train arrived at Pyrmont, and the troops also boarded *Ile de France*.

As the men came on board they were met by members of the advance party, who had arrived in Sydney several days earlier and familiarised themselves with the ship. They guided the boarding soldiers to their quarters. As the battalion history described the scene, 'With packs, haversacks, water bottles, rifles, tin hats and kitbags, more familiarly known as "sausage bags," winding along passages and up and down staircases until they reached their allotted dungeons was an experience anyone who ever embarked on a troop ship would always remember.' During the afternoon of 10 April, the Governor-General, Lord Gowrie, VC, paid a visit to the troops on board the ship, wishing them farewell. The same day, *Mauretania* and *Nieuw Amsterdam* arrived in Sydney from New Zealand, and berthed. As *Nieuw Amsterdam* was not full to capacity, she took on board 1213 Australian troops, bringing her total complement up to 3803 men.

At 0700 on the morning of 11 April, *Queen Elizabeth* raised anchor and departed on her first trooping voyage, being followed down the harbour by *Ile de France*, *Mauretania* and *Nieuw Amsterdam*. Although the departure time was supposed to have been a closely guarded secret, hundreds of small craft were on the harbour to wish the ships goodbye, some carrying banners with messages such as, 'God Bless 6th Div. Cav' and 'Good Luck 2/3 M G Bn.' Off Jervis Bay the four troopships met up with *Queen Mary* and the five giant liners, escorted by HMAS *Australia*, assumed their convoy formation, *Queen Mary* on the starboard side, *Queen Elizabeth* in the middle and *Mauretania* on her port side, with *Ile de France* following *Queen Mary*, and *Nieuw Amsterdam* behind *Mauretania*. The columns kept station 1000 yards apart, the two liners in the second row maintaining a gap of 800 yards from the leading ships.

Proceeding at just under 19 knots, the convoy headed across the Great Australian Bight and on to Fremantle. Apart from the four companies of the 2/3 Machine Gun Battalion, the ship was also carrying the 6th Division Cavalry Regiment, several groups of Western Command reinforcements, a number of army nursing sisters, representatives of both the Red Cross and Salvation Army, and the 2/11 Field Regiment, whose commanding officer, Lieutenant Colonel L.R. Stillman, MC, was the senior officer on board and therefore officer commanding troops. However, all was not going well on board *Ile de France*, and there was much discontent among some of the troops.

While officers and sergeants of the 2/3 Machine Gun Battalion had been given berths in cabins, the quarters allotted to the other ranks were hammocks in '99 berth cabins,' as they called them, deep down in the ship at the aft end of D Deck. As one member of C Company, Adye Rockliff, later wrote: 'We were in an area where the cabin partitions had been removed and the whole space hung with hammocks. It was just over the propellers. The normal ventilation system had been sealed off so the air quickly became foetid. When in the hammocks each man found his head wedged between two other people's feet. To sleep under these conditions was a complete impossibility, so very quickly there was an exodus of men and bedding to other parts of the ship, particularly the upper open decks.'

There were major problems with the ship's sewerage system, which was continually blocking up and spilling sewage over the floors. As well, some of the pipes had been wrongly connected, and when one particular tap was turned on, out came oil instead of the expected sea water.

There was also a major problem with the food being prepared by the Asian staff working in the kitchens. As one soldier on board wrote: 'During that first week of our voyage the most notable thing was our meals. They consisted almost entirely of boiled potatoes. The ship's staff responsible for preparing our meals was not familiar with the type of diet we required. Their own staple food consisted mainly of rice laced with large quantities of chillies, so rather than offend us by supplying this type of food they decided that potatoes would be a satisfactory substitute. So that is what we were served — boiled potatoes. Needless to say, after a week of these rations we were almost on the verge of mutiny, so the cooks were hastily replaced by our own army cooks and the meals were much more palatable thereafter.'

While the men of the 2/3 Machine Gun Battalion had been able to sort out most of their problems in the first week at sea aboard *Ile de France*, there were still murmurings of general discontent from other quarters about the shipboard arrangements.

One day, a written order was received by all the army officers that they were to stand by their cabins at a specific time. The signature of the commanding officer had been forged on the document, but the officers complied, at which time a group of soldiers sealed off the companionways leading to the officers' quarters. These soldiers then ordered their commanding officer to appear before them in the main lounge, and when he arrived, they complained about the poor quality of their accommodation and food, the terrible ventilation, disgusting sanitary arrangements, and numerous other things. Then the leaders of the dissidents demanded that *Ile de France* leave the convoy and return to Sydney, where the troops would be disembarked while the ship was refitted to transport them in more comfort. A message was also sent to the ship's officers on the bridge demanding that they turn back, and the ship's officers were fearful that the troops were capable of taking over the ship.

The commanding officer, Lieutenant Colonel Stillman tried to reason with the men but with no success. Then Lieutenant Colonel Blackman, a World War I veteran who had won the Victoria Cross, was able to make his way to the lounge. He poured contempt on the troops, cowing them so effectively that they fell silent, and then gradually began to leave the room. He was assisted in no small measure by Jim Mounsey, who declared that he would knock the head off anyone who laid a finger on Colonel Blackman. As Mounsey had a reputation as a fighter of some standing, the protesters took notice of the remark. The mutiny was averted, but the discontent among some troops remained throughout the rest of the voyage, though no further attempts were made to subvert the course of the ship.

The convoy arrived in Fremantle on 16 April. Both *Queen Mary* and *Queen Elizabeth* had to anchor out in Gage Roads, while the other three liners entered the port and berthed. The ships stayed in Fremantle three days, during which time no shore leave was granted to the troops on board. *Ile de France* was scheduled to take on board a further 778 troops, including D Company of the 2/3 Machine Gun Battalion, but heavy rain delayed their embarkation. The troops already on board *Ile de France* were less than impressed by the new arrivals, which brought the total of troops on board to 4049 and made the ship even more crowded and uncomfortable.

Convoy US10, now carrying over 22,000 troops, departed Fremantle on 19 April, escorted by three Australian cruisers, *Australia*, *Canberra* and *Sydney*. Once clear of the coast, the five liners took up their convoy positions in three columns, steaming at over 20 knots, making an impressive sight as they crossed the Indian Ocean.

Aboard *Queen Elizabeth*, heading north into the heat of the tropics, the initial enthusiasm felt by the troops of being on the largest liner in the world soon dissipated and was replaced by a rather sombre acceptance. As had happened with *Queen Mary*, the sheer size of the vessel caused major problems, men constantly losing their way in the maze of corridors. Mealtimes consisted of three sittings, each twenty minutes in duration, while the newly installed ventilation system was incapable of coping with the demands of so many men in such confined spaces. As the liner crossed the Indian Ocean the heat below decks became almost intolerable.

On board *Ile de France*, personnel from the 2/3 Machine Gun Battalion were designated to man the eight Vickers anti-aircraft guns the ship mounted. This duty was actually very popular, as it enabled the troops to be out in the fresh air at night instead of confined below decks in the heat of black-out conditions.

However, less popular was an order issued by Colonel Stillman in routine orders on 18 April, while the ship was in Fremantle, that 'in addition to the game of two-up the following games are forbidden: Crown and Anchor, dice, heads and tails. Officers, NCOs and sentries, picquets and patrols are to suppress any attempt to play these games. Any offenders disobeying these orders are to be dealt with by COs of units.' To forbid gambling, especially two-up, among troops, was almost impossible, and shortly after the ship left Fremantle wiser council prevailed and the order was rescinded. Instead, arrangements were set up in the aft lounge to enable all the previously banned games, as well as bingo, twenty-one and roulette to be played when the troops were on relaxation periods. There was also entertainment arranged in the main lounge, provided by bands and various musical groups.

To fill in the days there was physical training and games, such as volleyball. On 23 April, the 2/3 Machine Gun Battalion held a boxing competition, with trophies being presented to the winners in each division. There were also lectures on a wide variety of subjects. Several soldiers managed to produce a ship's newspaper, *About Ship*, of which three issues were published. They gave accounts of shipboard events as well as reports on personalities on board and proved very popular.

By now the troops were becoming adjusted to the daily shipboard routine. Lifejackets and full water bottles were compulsory dress at all times, and emergency drills were practised constantly. As the ships entered the tropics, orders were issued that hats must be worn at all times on deck. Sunburn was defined as a self-inflicted wound and would be punished as such. Sitting on the rails was strictly forbidden, and it was made clear that, if anyone did fall overboard, the ship could not stop to retrieve them.

On 22 April, three days after leaving Fremantle, the convoy was reduced to four ships when *Nieuw Amsterdam* changed course and headed off alone towards Singapore, arriving there safely on 24 April. The Australian troops on board all disembarked, to reinforce the local garrison, while the New Zealand contingent was transferred to another troopship, *Aquitania*, which had been in drydock and was now ready to resume service. *Aquitania* departed for Colombo, to join up with convoy US10, while *Nieuw Amsterdam* remained in Singapore until 9 May, then left on a voyage to Mombasa and Durban, having made her last voyage carrying New Zealand troops.

As the four troopships remaining in convoy US10 approached Ceylon, they were met by HMS *Durban* and a flotilla of destroyers to strengthen the escort for the final days. Nearing their destination, the convoy split into two sections. US10A, comprising *Queen Elizabeth* and *Queen Mary*, separated from the others, and escorted by *Canberra* headed for Trincomalee, while *Mauretania*, *Ile de France* and their escorts went to Colombo, both sections arriving at their destinations on 26 April.

On previous convoys it had been considered too dangerous to send large troopships further than Ceylon or India, but with the defeat of the Italians in Eritrea, the situation along the Red Sea had greatly improved and it was now deemed to be safe to send the liners all the way to Egypt. The arrival of the two Queens together at Trincomalee caused some problems for the port officials, as both ships could not be anchored close in for service at the same time. *Queen Elizabeth* went in first, and in half a day took on fuel and stores, then departed for Suez, escorted by HMAS *Canberra*. Once they were clear, *Queen Mary* entered the port, took on her fuel and supplies as quickly as possible, then set off at top speed, unescorted, catching up with *Queen Elizabeth* and *Canberra* the next day.

On 28 April a distress call was picked up from the freighter *Clan Buchanan*, which was being attacked by the German raider *Pinguin* 330 miles south of the two huge troopships. Unable to offer assistance, the two liners continued on their way, while *Clan Buchanan* was sunk. *Canberra* remained as escort for the two liners until they passed Perim Island, at the entrance to the Red Sea, at which point the cruiser diverted to Aden. Now unescorted, the two giant liners were able to increase speed, reaching 27 knots as they raced down the Red Sea. There had been reports of mines being sighted in these waters, so both vessels streamed paravanes for protection. Their destination was Port Tewfik, a short distance from the southern end of the Suez Canal.

As was the case with many other ports, Port Tewfik could not accommodate both Queens at one time, and the harbour was already thronged with ships anyway. Also, the arrival of these two giant ships coincided with the arrival from Britain of the largest convoy yet dispatched to the Middle East from Britain, WS7D43, which had originally comprised 23 vessels. It was decided that *Queen Mary* would press on at top speed to Port Tewfik, while *Queen Elizabeth* slowed down to a crawl. In the unbearable heat, which permeated to every part of the ship, conditions on board were almost intolerable, and tempers frayed. Distribution of beer was stopped and the troops were ordered to wear lifebelts at all times, making them even more uncomfortable. *Queen Mary* arrived in Port Tewfik on 3 May, berthing at the Adabeiah Mole to off-load her troops. This could only be done during daylight hours, as the port was being attacked by German aircraft at night, so the liner went out to sea for the hours of darkness, returning at dawn.

Once all the troops were ashore from *Queen Mary*, German and Italian prisoners of war with their escorts were taken on board and *Queen Mary* left Port Tewfik, enabling *Queen Elizabeth* to enter the port and finally disembark her troops. Leaving Port Tewfik on 6 May, *Queen Elizabeth* linked up again with *Queen Mary*, which had been proceeding at slow speed down the Red Sea, and the two liners travelled together at top speed back to Trincomalee, where they arrived on 14 May. From there, *Queen Elizabeth* went to Singapore for drydocking. *Queen Mary* headed back to Australia, stopping briefly off Fremantle on 21 May and dropping anchor in Sydney Harbour again four days later.

Meanwhile, *Ile de France* and *Mauretania* remained at anchor for ten long days off Colombo, being joined there by *Aquitania*. For most of the troops, this was their first sight of a foreign land, and shore leave was granted, with half the complement aboard each ship allowed ashore at a time, being transported in a fleet of small ferries. Prior to their arrival in Colombo, the *Ile de France* shipboard newspaper, *About Ship*, had published an article under the headline, 'How Australian Money Talks in India and Ceylon,' with the subtitle 'Avoid all native money changers.' Pay was issued to all the troops, officers receiving 50 rupees, while warrant officers and sergeants received half that, and other ranks were given ten rupees each. At that time a rupee was worth slightly less than two shillings, so it was not a lot of money.

Once ashore, the troops found they could obtain a good meal at the Galle Face Hotel for two rupees, while at the Fleet Club a bottle of Australian beer cost less than one. A canteen run by a group of European ladies in York Street served free tea, while cakes and sandwiches could be bought cheaply. Special free buses were laid on to take the men to places of local interest, such as the zoo, museum and Mount Lavinia. For the men of the 2/3 Machine Gun Battalion, there was a route march through the city one day, while a cricket match was also organised against a local team, which the battalion team won. The troops behaved themselves very well and there was little trouble to be dealt with by the picquets or the local police.

On the morning of 6 May, *Mauretania*, *Aquitania* and *Ile de France* raised their anchors and departed Colombo, bound for Egypt. For the next two days the liners ploughed their way through quite rough seas, which caused many men to suffer bouts of seasickness, but the worst enemy was still the heat. At meal times, there were three sittings in quick succession, and the men in the final sitting sat on seats covered in the sweat of those who had eaten before. As Adye Rockliff on board

Ile de France later wrote, 'The ship was a proverbial sweat tank, and for the time we were in the tropics the ever increasing reek of stale sweat was inescapable as it permeated our entire existence.'

As the three ships neared Aden, *Mauretania* and *Aquitania* increased speed, leaving *Ile de France* behind as they approached Port Tewfik, where they arrived on 11 May and the troops were transported ashore, having been cooped up on the ships for five long weeks. *Ile de France* arrived off Port Tewfik on 12 May but had to anchor out for two days until the time came for the troops on board to be taken ashore, which was effected in lighters. As the men prepared to go ashore they had to spend several hours in corridors below decks, cluttered with all their gear, until it was time for them to disembark.

Summing up the voyage, Roy Gordon of the 2/3 Machine Gun Battalion recalled: 'Approaching midday we said farewell to our 'hell' ship and to an experience we hoped might never be repeated. The *Ile de France* was, to say the best, a terribly uncomfortable ship … During our voyage every man who could turn a bolt was employed on repair of the ship. It was amazing what could go wrong, everything did at some stage … We disembarked full of anticipation and excitement that always accompanies one when first setting foot on a foreign land.'

The men of the battalion had understood they would be sent to the Western Desert to fight, but as Roy Gordon later stated, 'instead we were diverted to Palestine. No-one knew why, as happens so very, very often. At that time the position of the British troops in Egypt was very grim indeed. The equipment situation was deplorable. Equipment simply was not there and the little that units had was switched from one unit to another as they went in and out of action.'

The arrival of *Ile de France* at Port Tewfik brought the solution to a puzzle that had mystified the officers throughout the trip. The troops on board were given a daily allocation of beer, though this was limited to one bottle per day, yet throughout the voyage empty beer bottles were being found all over the ship. At first it was thought the troops were drinking beer they had brought on board with them, but after several weeks the number of bottles still being found indicated that every soldier must have carried a case of beer under each arm when they boarded. The ship did have a large storeroom, in which there were supplies of beer and liquor being taken to NAAFI installations ashore in the Middle East, but this was securely locked and the seals on the door remained unbroken.

On arrival in Egypt, all the troops went ashore, but some time afterwards, a strange sobbing sound was heard coming from the storeroom. The door was broken open and a small, young soldier was found in the room, in a very poor state. It turned out that on the second day at sea he had been pushed into the storeroom through a narrow ventilator by his mates, and had stayed there for the next five weeks. In exchange for passing endless bottles of beer out through the ventilator, his mates had thrown him scraps of food from time to time. The room was constantly pitch black, and also stifling hot, so by the time he was released the young soldier was almost blind and feeling very miserable that his mates should have abandoned him when the ship reached port.

No-one was more pleased to see the Australian troops go ashore than the officers and crew of *Ile de France*. As one officer was heard to remark, 'I shouldn't like to be old Rommel, you know ... these chaps are quite bad enough when they're with you.'

As soon as her troops had disembarked, *Aquitania* headed back to Australia to take part in the next convoy bound for Egypt. *Ile de France* and *Mauretania* did not return to Australia, but went on to other areas for further trooping duties, spending some time on the 'Suez Shuttle,' carrying troops to Port Tewfik from Durban, with some trips also to Bombay and Colombo, on which they were later joined by *Nieuw Amsterdam*. US10 was the last Australian convoy in which *Mauretania* was involved, but both *Ile de France* and *Nieuw Amsterdam* were needed in the future to carry Australian troops, though in the opposite direction.

Back in Australia in June 1941, preparations were nearing completion for the dispatch of the next convoy, which it was planned would comprise six ships, including *Queen Elizabeth*, *Queen Mary* and *Aquitania*. The other three liners would be Dutch, the sisters *Johan van Oldenbarnevelt* and *Marnix van St Aldegonde*, along with the *Sibajak*, all making their first trips with Australian troops. Initially all six ships were to carry their troops to the Middle East, but the Australian government was becoming increasingly concerned that Japan might enter the war and attack the Malay Peninsula, including Singapore. With this in mind, it was decided that the troops to be carried by the three Dutch liners would be sent to Singapore as a separate convoy, while the Queens and *Aquitania* would go to the Middle East as planned, being designated Convoy US11A.

After drydocking in Singapore, during which her hull was repainted naval grey, *Queen Elizabeth* was on her way back to Sydney, so on 13

Aquitania arrives back in Sydney, passing the anchored *Queen Mary*. (*C.T. Reddings collection*)

June *Queen Mary*, with Captain Irving back in command, raised anchor and headed south to Hobart for the first time, arriving there next day and anchoring in the spot previously used by *Queen Elizabeth*. On 14 June, *Queen Elizabeth* steamed into Sydney Harbour and was prepared for the next convoy at the anchorage off Bradleys Head.

Having boarded her troops on 26 June, *Queen Elizabeth* left Sydney the next morning, going to Jervis Bay, while *Queen Mary* arrived back in Sydney on 28 June, making the trip in just over 26 hours. *Queen Mary* and *Aquitania* completed embarking their troops and left Sydney on 29 June, and during the afternoon *Queen Elizabeth* joined them from Jervis Bay. Travelling at just over 19 knots, the three liners, escorted by HMAS *Australia*, reached Fremantle on 4 July, the two Queens anchoring out as usual while *Aquitania* was able to berth in the port. The ships remained in Fremantle five days, which was quite difficult for the troops on board as no shore leave was granted, then on 9 July the three liners departed, going first to Ceylon. Weather conditions in the Indian Ocean were perfect, the calm seas allowing the ships to maintain top speed. It was while they were at sea on this leg of the journey that Berlin radio announced, not for the first time, that the *Queen Elizabeth* had been sunk.

When the convoy reached Ceylon, the two Queens went to Trincomalee, while *Aquitania* berthed in Colombo, and again no shore leave was permitted. The refuelling arrangements at Trincomalee were the same as before, then the three liners continued their voyage to Suez, their speed restricted by *Aquitania* to just under 21 knots. The ships also ran into a severe storm as they crossed the Arabian Sea, with most of the troops becoming quite seasick. The troops were disembarked at Port Tewfik on 25 July, and the next day the three liners departed.

Queen Mary and *Queen Elizabeth* travelled together back to

Queen Elizabeth at anchor in Sydney Harbour after her hull was painted grey.

Trincomalee, arriving on 2 August, leaving two days later for Fremantle, where they anchored in Gage Roads on 9 August. Next day they departed, with *Queen Elizabeth* going directly to Hobart, arriving on 14 August, while *Queen Mary* continued to Sydney, anchoring in the harbour on 15 August. *Aquitania* travelled independently back to Australia, and joined her larger consort in Sydney, preparing for the next convoy departure.

11
Reinforcing Singapore

While *Queen Elizabeth*, *Queen Mary* and *Aquitania*, which had comprised convoy US11A, were on their way back to Australia from the Middle East, the three Dutch liners, *Johan van Oldenbarnevelt*, *Marnix van St Aldegonde* and *Sibajak*, which comprised convoy US11B, were just leaving on their way to Singapore. This was not the first major movement of Australian troops to Singapore. *Queen Mary* had already carried over 5700 men there in February 1941, as part of convoy US9, and more were transported by *Nieuw Amsterdam* in convoy US10.

As mentioned previously, early in December 1940 the Australian government expressed concern about the defence of the Malay Peninsula and advised the British government that they would be willing to send, as a temporary expedient, a brigade group to Singapore to complete their training. This offer was accepted, so the 22nd Infantry Brigade, numbering 5718 men, boarded *Queen Mary* in Sydney. This 'temporary expedient' was in fact the first move in sending the Australian 8th Division to Malaya over subsequent months. *Queen Mary* had travelled with the other ships of US9 to a position four days out of Fremantle, at which time she had detached, and arrived in Singapore on 18 February.

It had then been planned that the coastal liner *Katoomba* would undertake a voyage to Singapore in May 1941. However, the vessel had previously been sent on a voyage to Darwin, where unloading delays resulted in *Katoomba* remaining in port for a month, and it was not until 16 May that the vessel departed, carrying 180 evacuees. As a result another coastal liner, *Zealandia*, which had been operating troop

Zealandia made a trooping voyage to Singapore in May 1941

trips to Papua New Guinea, was designated to make the voyage to Singapore instead of *Katoomba*, which arrived back in Sydney on 29 May and was handed back to her owners.

Zealandia, which was owned by Huddart Parker Limited, had been built in 1910 for the trans-Tasman trade, but spent most of her early career on the Australian coastal service from east coast ports to Fremantle. Following a brief stint at the end of World War I as a troopship, *Zealandia* had resumed her place on the coastal trade, but from 1929 had operated between Sydney and Hobart. Requisitioned for war duties in June 1940, *Zealandia* was quickly converted into a troopship by Cockatoo Dockyard workers in Sydney, being fitted out to carry about a thousand troops. Apart from extra bunks being added, No. 2 and No. 4 holds were fitted out as mess decks, while the open section of the promenade deck was enclosed to give additional mess space, and extra galley equipment was installed.

Zealandia departed Sydney on her first trooping voyage on 30 June, carrying 890 troops and their supplies on the first of several trips to Darwin. Then during 1941 *Zealandia* was used to transport troops to Papua New Guinea, until being designated for the voyage to Singapore. The vessel embarked 754 troops of the 8th Division, and 1819 tons of stores, then departed Sydney on 19 May 1941, going south and across the Great Australian Bight to Fremantle. From there to Sunda Strait, *Zealandia* was escorted by HMAS *Sydney*, which handed her over to HMS *Danae* for the final leg to Singapore. *Zealandia* returned to Sydney, and resumed her voyages to Papua New Guinea.

The next major movement of troops of the 8th Division to Singapore was organised to depart at the end of July 1941 in convoy

Johan van Oldenbarnevelt shown here with neutrality markings on her hull.

11B, the men of the 27th Brigade being carried on three Dutch liners, *Sibajak*, *Johan van Oldenbarnevelt* and *Marnix van St Aldegonde*. These three ships had all been built for the trade from Holland to the Dutch East Indies, and were well suited to carrying large numbers of troops in tropical areas.

The oldest member of the trio was *Sibajak*, which had been built in 1927 in Holland for Rotterdam Lloyd, the last and largest of a trio of liners delivered to that company in the 1920s, the others being *Slamat* and *Indrapoera*. *Sibajak* operated on a regular trade between Rotterdam and Batavia, carrying a maximum of 527 passengers in three classes. When war broke out, Holland remained neutral and *Sibajak* continued her regular trade. The German invasion of Holland in 1940 changed that, with the vessel being handed over to the British government and converted into a troop transport, under the management of P & O Line.

The sisters *Johan van Oldenbarnevelt* and *Marnix van St Aldegonde* were both delivered to the Nederland Line during 1930. Despite their rather cumbersome names and boxy profiles, they soon became popular on the service from Amsterdam to the Dutch East Indies, with accommodation for 770 passengers in four classes. When war broke out these ships were initially laid up in the Dutch East Indies, but a few weeks later began operating an abbreviated service, terminating their trips in Genoa, from where passengers were sent overland to Holland. This came to an abrupt end when German forces invaded Holland and both liners then began operating a new service, from New York through the Panama Canal to Batavia, with a call at Cairns en route. However, in early 1941 both liners were handed over to the British government and converted into troop transports.

The work on *Johan van Oldenbarnevelt* was done by Harland & Wolff at Belfast, and on completion she was given the designation Troopship No. 32. On her first trip as a troopship, in February 1941, *Johan van Oldenbarnevelt* carried Canadian troops from Halifax to Glasgow. On 24 March, the vessel departed Glasgow in convoy WS7D43, comprising 22 ships, which stopped first at Freetown, then continued to Durban. There the convoy divided, most ships continuing to Egypt, while others, including *Johan van Oldenbarnevelt*, went to Bombay and Singapore, where the vessel arrived on 20 May.

Meanwhile, *Marnix van St Aldegonde* had arrived in Singapore from Surabaya on 13 May and was undergoing conversion into a troopship when *Johan Van Oldenbarnevelt* arrived there. Further conversion work was undertaken on *Johan Van Oldenbarnevelt* while the vessel was in Singapore, but then it was arranged that the two Dutch sisters, along with *Sibajak*, would be sent to Australia to assist in transporting Australian and New Zealand troops to the Middle East. In the log of *Johan Van Oldenbarnevelt* it had been mentioned that they had passed *Sibajak* on 4 May, outbound from Bombay, and *Sibajak* was in Singapore when *Johan Van Oldenbarnevelt* arrived there, departing on 22 May for Australia.

Johan Van Oldenbarnevelt remained in Singapore until 4 July 1941, when the liner departed without any troops on board, and unescorted, bound for Australia. Passing Thursday Island on 11 July, two local pilots were taken on board to guide the ship safely through the Great Barrier Reef and on to Sydney, where she arrived before dawn on 16 July. During the day, 1500 troops were embarked, and next day *Johan Van Oldenbarnevelt* departed Sydney as Commodore Ship of convoy VBR6, escorted by HMAS *Adelaide*. Battling through a heavy storm in the Tasman Sea, the vessels arrived in Auckland on 21 July, when the troops all disembarked. At 7 pm the next day, still escorted by *Adelaide*, *Johan Van Oldenbarnevelt* departed Auckland, this time without troops, on her voyage back to Sydney, where she arrived on 25 July and prepared for the longer voyage to Singapore.

Sister ship *Marnix van St Aldegonde* completed her conversion into a troopship at Singapore on 9 July 1941, leaving that day for Tanjong Priok, then proceeding to Fremantle, and on to Melbourne, where she arrived on the 23rd, being prepared to join convoy US11B when it departed. The third ship to be involved in this convoy, *Sibajak*, was dispatched to Fremantle, where her troops would embark.

As *Johan Van Oldenbarnevelt* could not carry all the troops designated

Katoomba was called upon to carry troops from Sydney to Fremantle in convoy US11B.

to travel in the convoy from Sydney, *Katoomba* was needed for the first part of the journey. *Katoomba*, which was berthed at Darling Harbour, was to transport most of the 2/15 Field Regiment, which had been based at the Holsworthy Army Camp near Liverpool, outside Sydney, from where they were transported by train directly to the wharf on 29 July, and boarded *Katoomba*. Also on 29 July, *Johan Van Oldenbarnevelt* completed embarkation of 2400 troops in Sydney, along with 77 military vehicles and other supplies. In addition, four nurses joined the ship for the trip to Singapore.

Early in the afternoon, *Katoomba* passed under the Sydney Harbour Bridge and proceeded slowly down the harbour, escorted by several small craft carrying wives and friends of the troops on board. At 3.15 pm, *Johan Van Oldenbarnevelt* departed Sydney Harbour, linked up with *Katoomba*, and the pair turned south, escorted by HMAS *Sydney*, but the log of *Johan Van Oldenbarnevelt* noted that 'cargo boat *Katoomba* can barely maintain 13 mph.' Another note in the *Johan Van Oldenbarnevelt*'s log stated that the ship was travelling 'blacked out' and the Australian troops on board were upset that 'everything is out of bounds.'

Some of the troops on board *Katoomba* had travelled on the vessel prior to the war, and they were surprised to discover that conditions on board were the same as before. They were given berths in regular cabins, and at meal times sat in the restaurants at tables with linen cloths, being able to order from a menu supplied by stewards. The only thing that caused them to protest was the price of beer, 1s. 9d. a bottle. To keep them occupied, the troops were given numerous lectures, and also physical exercise sessions.

In Melbourne, 2500 troops had boarded *Marnix van St Aldegonde* on 30 July and next day the liner departed, escorted by HMAS *Canberra*. Outside Port Philip Heads, the two vessels linked up with the three coming from Sydney, but this manoeuvre nearly ended in disaster, as a sudden compass failure on *Marnix van St Aldegonde* almost resulted in a collision with her sister. Eventually the ships were able to form up, and headed west through Bass Strait. *Marnix van St Aldegonde* was commodore ship, with Commander Hobaert in charge of the convoy, but the log of the vessel also contained complaints about the slow speed of *Katoomba*, which meant the convoy could only proceed at about 10 knots. Once through Bass Strait, *Sydney* left the convoy, leaving *Canberra* as the sole escort. Apart from the slow speed, the ships now ran into bad weather, making things unpleasant for the troops in their crowded quarters.

Life on board the ships tended to develop a monotonous sameness, so on 4 August the military band being carried on *Marnix van St Aldegonde* assembled on the open deck and gave a concert, which could also be heard on the *Johan van Oldenbarnevelt*. Although the intention was praiseworthy, the result was not as uplifting as had been anticipated, as the log of the *Johan van Oldenbarnevelt* notes that most of the troops on board were too seasick to care about the music. The log also reported that during the day a Lockheed bomber patrolled overhead, providing additional cover for the ships and their precious cargo.

As if bad weather and seasickness were not enough to contend with, on 5 August an outbreak of mumps among the troops on *Johan van Oldenbarnevelt* was diagnosed, those affected being described as very sick. Not to be outdone, an outbreak of mumps and meningitis was also reported aboard *Marnix van St Aldegonde*. Fortunately, next day, the three liners and their escort arrived in Fremantle, and berthed. All the troops who were well enough were allowed shore leave and taken into Perth. Waiting in the port was *Sibajak*, preparing to take on board her contingent of troops.

The troops of the 2/15 Field Regiment transported on *Katoomba*

Sibajak joined the convoy at Fremantle (*C.T. Reddings collection*).

all had to disembark in Fremantle, being transferred to *Sibajak*, along with all their equipment, which included 3-inch mortars. Already on board the ship was the advance party that had been sent from Sydney by train. Also joining *Sibajak* in Fremantle was a brigade of troops who had made the long rail journey there from Bathurst, in New South Wales. Among them was Bill Toon, who recalled how he

> took the train from Bathurst to Perth. First time a brigade of troops had gone by train — all in dog-boxes. Got sandwiches at the country stations — someone made them up and they'd be there for you. The women at Young and Cootamundra were up all hours of the night. They were marvellous, the CWA women.
>
> Stopped every so many miles on the Nullarbor to get water. Took us a long time to get across, about a week ... It was very hot going across by train. We wore serge tunics. Take your jackets off. Boots on. Feet got hot, yeah. Our trucks were on the train. You could get out in the cool of night to look after your truck. The soot was the biggest problem — it'd get in your eyes when you wasn't in your truck. First time we changed trains was at Albury, then Port Augusta. Then Kalgoorlie, then Northam — that was the name of our WA camp, 90 kilometres from Perth. Had one month at Northam. It was a football ground. Tents. Rumours. Gossip. We decided to shave our heads because we thought we were going to the Middle East, but we went up to Malaya and Singapore instead.

The troops had still not been told their final destination, but knew it must be either the Middle East or Singapore. However, as one trooper said, 'They're loading vehicles painted yellow for the desert. That's a sure sign we're going to Malaya.' The log of *Johan van Oldenbarnevelt* noted that the catapult aircraft from the cruiser HMAS *Perth*, which was also in port at the time, carried out patrols over the harbour and surrounding area during the day.

Convoy US11B, now comprising *Sibajak, Johan van Oldenbarnevelt* and *Marnix van St Aldegonde*, and the escorting cruiser HMAS *Canberra*, departed Fremantle at noon on 8 August. As the ships steamed past the breakwater, a woman's voice was heard by the troops, singing 'Now is the hour when we must say goodbye.' For many of the troops, this was to be their last sight and sound of Australia. Apart from the 2/15 Field Regiment, the convoy also carried 27 Brigade Headquarters, 2/12 Field Company, 2/6 Field Park Company, 2/26, 2/29 and 2/30 Battalions and the 2/10 Field Ambulance, as well as numerous RAAF reinforcements.

Once out to sea, the four ships turned north, and the troops settled in for another spell of sea time. Those men who had travelled to Fremantle aboard *Katoomba* found their circumstances aboard *Sibajak* quite different. Gone were the berths in cabins, and linen tablecloths, replaced by hammocks slung above mess tables. In fact the hammocks were so close together that, should a man get up during the night, he had great difficulty locating his hammock again, as the gap it occupied would have been filled. It was also very hot below decks, as the portholes were all shut and blacked out at night. To overcome the heat, lightbulbs were removed and portholes opened, but many troops chose to sleep on deck.

There was a large recreation area below decks, which was constantly swathed in a cigarette smoke haze, where men stripped to the waist would try and pass the time talking to each other or playing various games, including two-up, crown and anchor, and roulette. All the time, though, there was the fear of a submarine attack at the back of their minds. The weather did not help, as the seas became very rough, the waves being so high at times that the other ships in the convoy could not be seen.

Bill Toon was also less than impressed by *Sibajak*. 'Greasy food — Dutch East Indies tucker. Bit of rice. Eggs and Bacon. Everybody was sick bar me. They'd give you a bottle of water to wash your backside. There's a spray — you push the bottom of it, and it sprays your backside. Very steamy on the ship. Tried to keep fit by walking around. Halfway out on the *Sibajak* ... an officer said "We're going to Singapore.' It was very disappointing. Some of the kids took it hard. Actually, we had a pretty good idea when we knew we were on a Dutch ship.'

The day after leaving Fremantle, *Johan van Oldenbarnevelt* came to a brief stop to allow the burial at sea of one of the troops who had died overnight. As the convoy continued north towards their destination in heavy seas, attempts were made to lift the spirits of the troops. Aboard *Johan van Oldenbarnevelt* a military band gave a concert, and there was also a divine service, but this was rather upset by the sounds of shooting coming from both *Marnix van St Aldegonde* and *Sibajak*, where contests were organised to keep the troops in training. The next day a similar exercise was held aboard *Johan van Oldenbarnevelt*, using balloons as targets.

As the distance from their destination lessened, tensions aboard all the ships increased. Approaching the waters of the Dutch East Indies, which all three liners were familiar with, orders were given on 12 August for the convoy to assume a zigzag course. This nearly ended in disaster, as a mistake in changing course by *Marnix van St Aldegonde* almost brought the ship into collision with *Sibajak*, which narrowly averted being cut in two. Next day the ship's log noted they had passed Krakatoa, at the entrance to the Sunda Strait. There was also a report on deck sports held on *Johan van Oldenbarnevelt* that day, with particular reference to some hilarity among the troops at the sight of a corpulent priest taking part in the deck quoits competition.

On 14 August the convoy entered the narrowest part of the Sunda Strait, which had been heavily mined by Allied naval forces. In order to pass through the minefield, the three ships formed up in line astern, with *Marnix van St Aldegonde* leading, followed by *Johan van Oldenbarnevelt* and then *Sibajak*. The trip was now almost over, and at 7 am on the following day the troopships entered the harbour at Singapore. Among the cosmopolitan collection of shipping of all shapes and sizes crowding the anchorage outside the port was a Japanese tanker, flying the Rising Sun flag, which no doubt reported the arrival of the convoy back to Tokyo. Once the ships docked, a group of senior army officers boarded them to welcome the troops, and there was also a heavy shower of rain, an occurrence they would soon accept as a fact of daily life in Malaya. The log of *Johan van Oldenbarnevelt* recorded that the decks were covered by kitbags as the troops gathered their belongings, and the same afternoon they disembarked.

Compared to the often uncomfortable, and at times downright abominable conditions that troops had to suffer when travelling on some of the larger liners being used to transport Australian troops overseas, these Dutch liners were far better, having been designed for service in tropical waters. At a later stage in the war, a British officer who travelled on *Johan van Oldenbarnevelt*, or Ship 32 as it was known, wrote a piece about his experience that is worth repeating:

> In nearly forty years of experience of travel in more than thirty troopships, I find that this No. 32 compares more than favourably with most.

In my first trooper we slept above mess tables just as the majority do on this ship, but not in light airy decks with ports that can be opened other than at 'black out' in any but very rough weather. No, we were in the bottom of holds with three decks of horses above us, and our only ventilation was through wind sail shoots.

We have heard of cabins for troops and the resultant comfort, but for tidiness and cleanliness of quarters, give me the open sleeping decks either with hammocks or bunks. The light, airiness and lay-out of the decks on this ship lend themselves to orderliness and cleanliness, so that with a suitable ship under present conditions I favour the sleeping deck and dormitory. Could the sleeping and messing decks be separated, the conditions would be ideal. We are lucky here, too, with the fresh water, which is never turned off during the whole 24 hours of the day.

On embarkation, we looked with apprehension at the hammocks above the mess tables and wondered what would happen when men could reasonably be expected to be seasick. Last night it blew a fair-sized gale with a resultant heavy sea. The men have been a week at sea, and this fact, together with the stability of the ship, allayed our fears. This morning, expecting to find the worst, I went below to the sleeping and messing decks shortly after 'The Rouse,' and found the occupants just as usual. They were getting out of bed, stowing their blankets and hammocks away, and the mess orderlies getting ready for breakfast. Even in 'R' deck mess away aft, only two men failed to breast the breakfast table.

If one leaves our own troop quarters, and goes to the places for which the ship's staff is responsible — galleys, butcher's shop, bakehouse, pantries and so on — one would find it hard to see more efficiently run, and cleaner places.

We British do fancy ourselves, and though our best is not worse than this ship, it certainly is not better. It is true that one nation can learn from another, and we can all learn something about this ship to our advantage.

Where have troops been fed better? Bacon and eggs with boiled potatoes following porridge for breakfast one morning; the next morning smoked terikei and potatoes, and then another morning mince and lashings of stewed tomatoes, and yet another day grilled chops and potatoes. The usual lunch is soup, roast meat, potatoes, one other vegetable and pudding, followed by fruit of some kind. For the evening meal, only once in a week is there cold meat, on other days the fare is curry and rice, stew, and always a variety. Always there is plenty of bread, butter, jam, and the best factory-made tomato sauce.

Have we ever asked for anything in reason from the ship that the personnel have not graciously agreed to? May we go on as we have started, and may we, the passengers, appreciate to the end of the voyage as we are appreciating at present, the interest and kindliness bestowed on us by the captain and all his staff.

The three Dutch liners that had comprised convoy US11B remained in Singapore for about a week, then all departed for Australia or New Zealand, where they were required to take part in the next major movement of troops overseas, convoy US12. *Marnix van St Aldegonde* left Singapore on 22 August, voyaging back to Fremantle, where she arrived on 28 August, then continuing to Melbourne, berthing there on 3 September.

Johan van Oldenbarnevelt departed Singapore at 0600 on 23 August, travelling unescorted. Reaching Thursday Island on 30 August, a pilot was taken on board for the passage through Torres Strait and down the Great Barrier Reef. The ship's log referred to the weather as being quite cool, with officers wearing their winter blue uniforms. On 2 September, *Johan van Oldenbarnevelt* arrived off Rockhampton, where the pilot was dropped, then the ship headed straight out to sea, alone and blacked out, bound for Wellington, where she arrived on 7 September.

With so many Australian troops now stationed in Singapore, it was necessary to provide them with sufficient medical support, so the 2/13 Australian General Hospital unit was sent there on *Wanganella*. This liner, owned by Huddart Parker Limited, had operated across the Tasman Sea, but on 19 May 1941 had been taken over by the Australian government for conversion into a hospital ship. The work was done at Port Melbourne, with the interior being transformed into a floating hospital, complete with wards, operating theatres, X-Ray rooms, and facilities for dental and other specialist services. The hull was painted white with a wide green band interspersed with large red crosses which could be illuminated at night.

The conversion work was completed in late July 1941, following which the vessel moved to Sydney for final touches. At the end of August the 2/13 AGH embarked, and on 30 August *Wanganella* left Sydney, arriving in Melbourne two days later. The following day, having embarked further hospital personnel, *Wanganella* voyaged across the Great Australian Bight to Fremantle, arriving on 8 September, and departing the next day for Singapore, where she arrived on 15 September. Here the 2/13 AGH disembarked. Within six months almost all of them would be incarcerated in Japanese prison camps, where they spent the rest of the war years.

The trans-Tasman liner *Wanganella* was converted into a hospital ship.

Although the war had not yet come to Singapore, there were already Australian troops succumbing to tropical diseases and other sicknesses. *Wanganella* took on board 142 medical patients to be repatriated back to Australia, along with 216 passengers, mostly civilians. *Wanganella* left Singapore on 17 September, calling at Fremantle on the 23rd, then continuing to Melbourne and on to Sydney, where the voyage ended on 2 October.

12 The Final Middle East Convoys

There was still a demand from the British government to send more Australian troops to the Middle East, but the Australian government was more concerned about strengthening the garrison in Singapore. As a result, it was decided that while five of the vessels allocated to convoy US12, *Queen Elizabeth, Queen Mary, Aquitania, Johan van Oldenbarnevelt* and *Marnix van St Aldegonde*, would carry their troops to Egypt, the third Dutch liner from convoy US11B, *Sibajak*, which had also returned to Australian waters, would go to Singapore. However, convoy US12 would also be split into two sections again, this time just *Queen Elizabeth* and *Queen Mary* forming convoy US12A, while *Aquitania* would join *Sibajak, Johan van Oldenbarnevelt* and *Marnix van St Aldegonde* in convoy US12B.

After returning to Sydney from convoy US11A, *Queen Mary* only remained in Sydney for six days, as on 21 August she left for Hobart,

Queen Elizabeth at anchor in Sydney Harbour.

Queen Mary at anchor off Bradleys Head in Sydney Harbour. (*C.T. Reddings collection*)

allowing *Queen Elizabeth* to come to Sydney. Once she had been prepared for her next trip, the troops were boarded, and on 1 September she departed for Jervis Bay, enabling *Queen Mary* to return to Sydney the next day.

Sandy Hirst was a member of a Victorian medical contingent that travelled by train to Sydney to join *Queen Mary*. 'We never went up a gangplank like you see in the newsreels. Went out in barges to board it. We loaded up all right. No-one lost their balance. You had to go down steep into the barge with your kitbag — big haversack thing. Chuck your kit in and go in after the first bloke. You done as he done. In the daytime, this was, early morning. No chance to go to Manly and have a schooner. There were thousands of you. All different types — medical, infantry, artillery. A big operation. We were actually reinforcements.'

Also joining *Queen Mary* was a small contingent of RAAF trainees, among them Harvey Besley, who boarded the liner on the night of 2 September. Leaving his training camp at Bradfield Park, he later wrote, 'by nine o'clock we were on the transport which was to take us down to Sydney's Darling Harbour. From there we went by ferry to board the troopship, *Queen Mary*. Considerable confusion arose as large numbers of troops from both services were embarking until around midnight. There wasn't much organisation. We were eventually shown to a very nice cabin on the port side of the main deck. Unfortunately, we were only left there for one night, and the next morning we were taken to a much smaller cabin on the same deck but about mid-ship. It wasn't too bad really though a bit small with no porthole, which was a disadvantage. There were four of us in the tiny cabin and we were the same four who had been together during the early stages of our training at Bradfield Park.'

Having taken on board about 6000 men, about 4 pm on 3 September *Queen Mary* weighed anchor and departed Sydney, heading south. As Harvey Besley recalled, 'Most of us slept well that first night after the late hour of the night before, and the previous hectic day, not to mention the tension which had built up once we knew we were really departing Australia. The sea was calm and it was hard to credit that we were moving at all.' *Queen Elizabeth* joined them off Jervis Bay and the two liners proceeded south together at just over 20 knots. They were joined in Bass Strait by HMAS *Sydney*, which escorted them part way across the Great Australian Bight, then handed over to HMAS *Canberra*.

For Harvey Besley and some of his companions there was an interesting diversion to daily life on board. 'The Senior Engineer offered to show some of us over the engine rooms, so after lunch on the second day we sought him out. He detailed one of his staff to give us a conducted tour of all the engines, boilers and the whole complicated workings of the ship. It was all very interesting but far too immense and complicated for our lay minds to comprehend in one short tour. We did get a general idea of how the whole thing was laid out. Everything was duplicated and split into three or four sections with double steel partitions to separate each compartment. This was in case any area was holed. It could then be isolated, without any great power loss to the ship. The temperature in the engine room was well over 100 degrees Fahrenheit and it was extremely humid. To counteract the intense heat and to make conditions better for those who worked there, the air pressure was increased.'

Once on board *Queen Mary*, there were several shocks in store for Sandy Hirst:

> We slept on the hammocks down in the holds. You could hear the engines slightly, but you got used to that ... The people who saw the *Queen Mary* never saw the holds, which is where we were. Close? It was bloody close all right. All that BO. Thousands of pairs of rotten socks. No air-conditioning, then ... Hot and steaming in the holds. The sewerage got blocked. It was a hell ship. You didn't have much of a chance to wash your clothes. If the showers weren't blocked you'd hop in under the shower and wash them with the rest of you. Dermatitis, a lot got. You've got to dry them, the toes, straight away. You get used to it, but. You have to. You virtually had no say in it.
>
> Even on the deck at night they had it all blacked out, all shuttered up. During the day you could walk round the deck. Sort of shops there were

up top — hairdressing ones, everything — and lifts up the top for the rich people. I could walk all over the ship, because I had a Red Cross armband round my right arm so I could help out — canteen stuff, cigarettes and stuff.

Crossing the Great Australian Bight the seas, as usual, were quite rough. 'People were crook. Seasick. The *Queen Mary* was that big it rolled. It never bucked, just this roll all the way over, like a camber ... It was that bad sometimes we used to go up on deck and have a cool-off. You couldn't sleep up the top because the seamen would come in and hose the deck down. We felt like underdogs. Only allowed up to certain parts of the ship. There were guards with sidearms. It was pretty restricted, all right. I never got seasickness or nothing. I was spared that. It was a pretty good crossing.'

Harvey Besley wrote of the crossing: 'The fourth day saw us in the Great Australian Bight. The sea was getting very rough with big waves crashing against the ship's sides. The huge boat travelling parallel to the swell which was coming up from the Antarctic, would roll so far off perpendicular, that at times we wondered if it would ever right itself again. We soon got used to the rolling and pitching. Perhaps I should say that I became used to it but many didn't. Sea sickness was very prevalent among the men, especially on the lower deck. The heavy rolling of the ship was not making matters any better for the sufferers.'

As to life on board, 'Even after these few days, life had become very boring on board,' wrote Harvey Besley. 'There was little to do but eat and sleep and play cards. The sea sickness sufferers didn't feel like any of these activities and were content to lie on their bunks.' At night the heavy seas 'sent us tossing and rolling and we had very little sleep. However, sleep was not of any great importance as we had nothing to do during the days except to catch up on the sleep we missed out on the nights before, and we were not expending very much energy.'

After the rough crossing of the Bight most of the troops were no doubt very relieved when the convoy arrived in Fremantle on 7 September. As usual the two liners had to anchor out in Gage Roads, and no shore leave was allowed. More troops were also boarded, with some fifteen hundred joining *Queen Mary*.

The two liners left Fremantle on 9 September, escorted by HMAS *Canberra*, travelling at top speed across the Indian Ocean, bound for Trincomalee. 'There were some sixteen thousand men aboard the two ships,' Harvey Besley noted, 'so naturally security was very tight. A complete black-out at night; not even a match could be struck in the open. As there was a big risk of someone doing just that, no-one was allowed on deck after sundown.'

For the troops, their days were filled with physical exercise and lectures. 'You just put up with the lectures,' recalled Sandy Hirst. 'Lectures about war. You more or less dozed off. It was that hot! Lectures also about morale, discipline. It's going in one ear and out the other. Did we joke about it? You did, but you had to watch it. The punishment for that? Laughing in a lecture? They'd give you what was called bugle call. You had to run to the bugle, no matter what time it sounded, or you got CB — confined to barracks.'

There were also unorganised diversions. Harry Besley recalled, 'The game of two-up was well established. Of course it was banned by the authorities, but still flourished. A section on the main deck in the bow about as big as a tennis court became the main ring. There were no limits and at times the stakes got very high. This was when I pulled out. No-one cared much about money. Easy come, easy go was the motto ... The ring was played directly under the bridge and from time to time the duty officer with a number of sergeants would come along and stop the game, but this was rather futile as it would start again just as quickly as it had stopped. Obviously, the authorities thought it was a pretty harmless passtime and made no real effort to stop it. After all the game kept the men occupied and was mostly friendly. Occasionally it broke into quite a heated argument, but the situation never really got out of hand.'

The two liners arrived off Trincomalee on 15 September, but it was not a welcome stop. 'The heat was oppressive and we were drenched in our own sweat from sunrise to sunset and most of the night as well,' wrote Harvey Besley. 'It must have been hell for the men on the lower decks. The beer we were allowed in the evenings was hot and some of the men drank it out of even hotter mess tins. No wonder many of them were sick.'

Departing the next day for Suez, they arrived off the Egyptian port on 22 September, but again entered separately to disembark their troops, *Queen Mary* going in first, with *Queen Elizabeth* not entering the port until three days later. As Harvey Besley recalled:

> On the Monday afternoon we were told to be ready to leave ship at 5 am on Tuesday, 22nd September. Next morning saw us all out early with our gear packed and ready to leave. We had a makeshift breakfast and were hoping to be among the first off at the appointed time.
>
> One thing we had learnt in service life was that things seldom work out according to plan and this was no exception. After many false orders

to be ready to move off, we finally left the *Queen Mary* and crowded onto a small ferry about 1.30 pm. We were given a most welcome packet of sandwiches as we went onto the ferry. It had been a long time since our meagre breakfast. The *Queen Mary* had dropped anchor some fifteen miles away from Tewfik wharf and we were to be transported across to the wharf in a very hot and dirty Gypo ferry. We crowded in all hot and sweaty and made our way to Tewfik. As soon as we landed we were hustled into Air Force trucks and then taken north along the edge of the Suez Canal to a transit camp on the edge of the Great Bitter Lake.

Meanwhile, the four ships that would comprise convoy US12B were still in Australian waters, travelling at a much slower speed. *Johan van Oldenbarnevelt* had been designated to transport New Zealand troops this time, as had *Aquitania*, which arrived in Wellington on 8 September, berthing at Pipitea Wharf. Both ships spent several days being prepared for the upcoming voyage, then on 13 September the troops began embarking, 7000 on *Aquitania*. This process was slowed by some very bad weather and the departure of the two ships was delayed from 14 September to the following day.

At 0900 on 15 September, *Johan van Oldenbarnevelt* moved away from the quay in Wellington, soon followed by *Aquitania*, while a military band played on the wharf. Escorted by the cruiser HMS *Achilles*, the

HMS *Achilles* escorted *Aquitania* and *Johan van Oldenbarnevelt* across the Tasman Sea.

liners passed through Wellington Heads and into Cook Strait. The log of *Johan van Oldenbarnevelt* made particular note of the *Aquitania* blowing a large plume of black smoke from her four funnels. The two liners crossed the Tasman Sea at speed, and on 18 September were joined by *Sibajak*, which had boarded troops in Sydney, and then

Marnix van Sint Aldegonde embarked troops at Melbourne.

proceeded down the New South Wales coast escorted by HMAS *Adelaide*.

Meanwhile, in Melbourne troops had been embarked on *Marnix van St Aldegonde* on 17 September, and late the next day she departed, escorted by two cruisers, HMS *Glasgow* and HMAS *Sydney*. During the early hours of 19 September, in Bass Strait, *Marnix van St Aldegonde* joined up with *Johan van Oldenbarnevelt, Aquitania* and *Sibajak*. Again the convoy commodore, this time Commander Livesay, was on *Marnix van St Aldegonde*, while *Adelaide* departed, leaving the escort duty to *Glasgow* and *Sydney*.

The vessels were all blacked out at night, and the weather was particularly bad, making station keeping extremely difficult. Signals between the ships were passed by flags, but the log of *Johan van Oldenbarnevelt* noted that the flags on *Marnix van St Aldegonde* were blown away during a violent windstorm. The seas were so rough, speed had to be reduced, eventually to just 10 knots, but even then *Sydney* suffered damage to her armaments and hull plating. There was also a comment in the log questioning why the ship's captain was not allowed to have a revolver, as in the bad weather conditions some of the troops on board may be subject to 'emotional outbreaks.' Despite these fears, the voyage across proceeded smoothly enough and the convoy docked in Fremantle on 26 September.

The troops were allowed shore leave during the stopover, though on 27 September *Johan van Oldenbarnevelt* had to leave her berth and anchor out. During the stopover in Fremantle, a further 500 troops embarked on *Marnix van St Aldegonde*. On 28 September the convoy departed Fremantle, still escorted by *Glasgow* and *Sydney*, heading north towards the Dutch East Indies. The log of *Johan van Oldenbarnevelt* recorded a small outbreak of measles on board, but otherwise things seemed to be going smoothly. For the next three days the four liners and their escorts stayed together, and some of the New Zealand troops aboard *Johan van Oldenbarnevelt* decided to produce a weekly satirical newspaper which they named *Troopship Tattoo*. The first issue, which came out on 28 September, included an interview with the master of *Johan van Oldenbarnevelt*, Captain K.J. Vanderlaan, in which he was quoted as saying: 'This is the first time we have sailed as a troopship carrying New Zealand troops, and I must say that I am very pleased with the way they behave, act, and keep their quarters clean. We became a troopship last year when we carried Canadian troops to England, and since then we have carried British and Australian troops to other parts of the world. Of all these soldiers, I think the men we have on board now are the best as far as keeping the ship clean and tidy is concerned. I hope this will continue until we reach our destination.'

As the convoy approached Sumatra, *Sibajak*, escorted by HMAS *Sydney*, split from the rest of the ships and headed towards Sunda Strait, and then to Singapore. *Sydney* remained with *Sibajak* until they entered Sunda Strait, where the escort duty was taken over by HMS *Danae*, and *Sydney* headed back to Fremantle. Meanwhile *Aquitania*, *Johan van Oldenbarnevelt* and *Marnix van St Aldegonde*, now escorted only by HMS *Glasgow*, turned west, setting their course for Colombo in good weather and at top speed.

The days crossing the Indian Ocean were livened up for the troops by shooting practice each day, while the band aboard HMS *Glasgow* gave a concert on deck on 5 October. Next day the cruiser provided the troops with a display of its fire power, conducting an air defence practice exercise, shooting three mini-rockets at a target in the sky, scoring two direct hits.

On 8 October the ships of convoy US12B arrived in Colombo, and during the two days spent there replenishing fuel and supplies, the convoy commodore transferred from *Marnix van St Aldegonde* to *Aquitania*. Departing Colombo on 10 October, the three liners, still escorted by *Glasgow*, proceeded across the dangerous waters of the northern Indian Ocean towards the Gulf of Aden. The vagaries of the war were brought home to all those on board as they travelled through the night totally blacked out, when an American freighter was passed with all its lights blazing.

The voyage continued in routine fashion, though on 12 October the log of *Johan van Oldenbarnevelt* noted the receipt of six coded telegrams, each of 96 words, for which, to the anger of the captain, the ship did not possess the necessary decoding book. It was not until next day that a copy of the required book was obtained from *Glasgow*. Trying to keep the troops entertained was a constant source of concern. Aboard *Johan van Oldenbarnevelt* on 14 October, it was recorded that Captain Britton gave some troops a lesson in machine-gun assembly, while others were employed in an anti-aircraft exercise. The log also noted that during the day the convoy was asked to slow down while an operation was performed in the hospital aboard *Marnix van St Aldegonde*.

15 October was noted as a very wet day, but the convoy was now entering the Gulf of Aden. At 4 pm *Aquitania* separated from the two Dutch liners, making off at over 20 knots towards Suez. Shortly after, HMS *Glasgow* also left the convoy, heading to Aden. Next day, the troops manning the anti-aircraft defences on the bridge of *Johan van Oldenbarnevelt* were given a practice exercise, but that evening came a touch of farce when *Aquitania* was sighted once again, still steaming at top speed, but headed back towards Aden. The huge liner had been sent a message by the coast guard station at Aden to proceed there, and then a similar message was received on both *Johan van Oldenbarnevelt* and *Marnix van St Aldegonde*, ordering them to turn around and proceed to Aden. As the log of *Johan van Oldenbarnevelt* states, only after two precious hours was the blunder with the *Aquitania* corrected, the situation clarified, and then the bows of all three ships turned around, and once again they proceeded together in the direction of Suez.

Now in the lower end of the Red Sea, the three ships maintained a steady speed, travelling in single file in extreme heat. The troops on board *Johan van Oldenbarnevelt* and *Marnix van St Aldegonde* were far more comfortable than those on *Aquitania*, which was totally unsuited to these conditions. There is also a strange entry in the log of *Johan van Oldenbarnevelt* for the night of 16 October stating that 'on the horizon we could just see the silhouette of the great troopship *Queen Elizabeth*, coming down from the Red Sea.' Just which ship was sighted that day is uncertain, but it definitely was not *Queen Elizabeth*, which on 16 October was lying quietly at anchor in Sydney Harbour, having just returned from convoy US12A. Most likely it was *Mauretania*, which during the war was frequently mistaken for her larger fleet-mate, and was in the Red Sea area at that time.

On 20 October the three remaining ships of convoy US12B reached Port Tewfik. The vessels went alongside in daytime to disembark their troops, but at night were forced to anchor out for safety, as the port was being attacked regularly by German bombers, the log of *Johan van Oldenbarnevelt* noting the ship found a spot behind the wreck of a ship that had succumbed to an earlier attack. The log also made a comment that nearby was the *Georgic*, which had suffered severe damage on 23 April and was anchored out, with a heavy list. Additional notes covered the fact that many ships were flying barrage balloons, while German torpedo-carrying aircraft were sighted flying around the anchorage, just out of gun range. Despite all this, the troops on board, destined for the 8th Army, then operating in North Africa under the command of General Auchinleck, were all safely disembarked.

This convoy ended the association of *Johan van Oldenbarnevelt* and *Marnix van St Aldegonde* with Australian and New Zealand troops for the war. Once all their troops had disembarked, the Dutch liners each took on board about 1000 Italian prisoners of war, and their escort, on *Johan van Oldenbarnevelt* this being 150 South African troops. The log of the ship also recorded that *Mauretania* was in Port Tewfik as well, also loading prisoners of war.

On the evening of 22 October, *Johan van Oldenbarnevelt* and *Marnix van St Aldegonde* departed Port Tewfik, arriving together at Bereba on the morning of the 26th. The same evening, the sister ships went their separate ways, *Johan van Oldenbarnevelt* heading south for Mombasa and Durban, where her prisoners of war would disembark, while *Marnix van St Aldegonde* turned east, arriving in Bombay on 31 October and discharging her prisoners of war. On 3 November, *Marnix van St Aldegonde* left Bombay, bound for Singapore, where she arrived on the 11th, being scheduled to go into drydock there.

The third member of convoy US12B to go to Egypt, *Aquitania*, had also headed back to Singapore from Egypt, stopping first at Colombo, departing there on 6 November and proceeding unescorted. Arriving in Singapore on 11 November, *Aquitania* entered the drydock the following day to undergo general maintenance work. Refloated a week later, *Aquitania* left Singapore on 19 November to return to Sydney. *Marnix van St Aldegonde* was still in drydock when Japan came into the war, and did not leave Singapore until 31 December, going first to Tanjong Priok, then back across the Indian Ocean to Durban, and on to serve in the European theatre of the war.

Meanwhile, having completed their task of transporting Australian troops to Egypt in convoy US12A, *Queen Elizabeth* and *Queen Mary* returned to Australia independently. As *Queen Mary* approached Fremantle, a suspicious ship was sighted off Rottnest Island on the night of 5 October and local authorities feared it might have been laying mines. HMAS *Sydney* was sent out to intercept the liner and prevent her entering the channel to Gage Roads until it had been swept for mines. None were found, and on the morning of 7 October *Queen Mary* followed *Sydney* to her regular anchoring spot. *Queen Elizabeth* was due to arrive in Fremantle the same evening, but it was decided not to send *Sydney* out to escort her in. *Queen Mary* departed Fremantle on 8 October, arriving back in Sydney on 13 October. Two days later she left for Hobart once again, to allow *Queen Elizabeth* to anchor in Sydney Harbour.

These two giant liners would comprise convoy US13, due to depart at the end of October 1941 for the Middle East. On 23 October, *Queen Elizabeth* left Sydney for Hobart, allowing *Queen Mary*, to return to Sydney and be prepared for the next departure. While in Sydney, Captain Irving handed over command of to Captain Townley. Having boarded her troops on 31 October, the liner left the following day for Jervis Bay, at which time *Queen Elizabeth* entered Sydney to load her 4500 troops. Leaving on 2 November, the liners met up off Jervis Bay and headed south as convoy US13, escorted by HMAS *Canberra*.

Among those on board *Queen Elizabeth* was Ron McCathie, a member of an Air Force contingent, who recalled later: 'We sailed from Sydney in convoy with the *Queen Mary* ... During the day the Queens sailed abreast with the escort leading. At night the configuration changed to line astern, always with our escort up front. Crossing the Great Australian Bight we ran into a storm with the wind from the south-west and waves up to 35 feet. Our speed was 26 knots ... and the sight of the *Queen Mary* ploughing into the seaway only half a mile away was spectacular ... every now and then she would take a green sea over the bow that would race back to the bridge and explode ... Of course the *Queen Elizabeth* was doing the same thing but, surprisingly, the motion aboard was really moderate.'

However, Ron also had pity for the crew of the escorting cruiser, which, 'with her low freeboard, was practically under water all the time and having difficulty maintaining station ... Six of us had been detailed for blackout duty at sundown, and each day, after rounds, reported to Captain Lasenby in the Main Lounge — he bought the drinks. One of us asked why we did not slow down and "give the *Canberra* a fair go?"

Lasenby intimated that these two ships never stopped or slowed down, no matter what the circumstances. If you fell overboard the best you could expect was an entry in the ship's log "Man overboard 2000 hours Lat ... Long ... Presumed drowned."' As usual under such conditions, most of those on board both liners were seasick, and longing for the first port of call, Fremantle where they arrived on 6 November, anchoring in Gage Roads.

In addition to troops, the *Queen Mary* was also carrying 200 nurses comprising the first, and only, Voluntary Aid Detachment to be sent to the Middle East. Drawn from all parts of Australia, 175 VAD's had joined the ship in Sydney, with the remaining 25 to be taken on board in Gage Roads. These nurses were brought out to *Queen Mary* on a small ferry boat, the *Zephyr*, but it was rolling so heavily when it tried to come alongside the troopship it proved impossible to embark the nurses, despite the advice shouted down to the ferry captain from troops lining the rails of *Queen Mary*. Next morning the nurses made a second trip out to *Queen Mary*, this time on a more substantial vessel, and were able to embark.

The convoy left Fremantle on 8 November, bound for Trincomalee, still escorted by *Canberra*. Several days out of Fremantle, HMS *Cornwall*, which had come from Colombo, met up with the convoy to take over escort duty. *Queen Elizabeth* and *Queen Mary* came to a stop in mid-ocean, while a pinnacle from *Canberra* collected mail from both liners, which was taken back to Fremantle, where *Canberra* arrived on 15 November.

Ron McCathie recalled, 'The food was excellent and the bars opened three times each day. Pink gin or a scotch cost fivepence. The only universal complaint was the atmosphere once we were battened down for the night. The air-conditioning systems were never designed to cope with so many people. The odours and heat came from the turbines at full speed, cooking (which must have gone on for most of the time), together with the body odours from all of us. Add on a fart or two from the 5000 troops below and, by morning, you could almost cut the air with a knife. It became worse as we moved into the tropics. We had an epidemic of what the medics called "blackout fever."'

The VAD's were allocated duties on *Queen Mary*, mostly in the sick bay. There was an outbreak of a respiratory infection among the troops, and the overcrowded sick bay had to be extended out on to the surrounding deck, where the patients had only mattresses to lie on.

After a quick stop in Trincomalee, the two liners continued to Suez, arriving on 22 November. *Queen Mary* went alongside first, but disembarkation was disrupted by an air raid alarm, during which everyone was required to go below decks until the 'all clear' sounded. Once her troops had disembarked, *Queen Elizabeth* was able to disembark her troops, then took on board a large number of German and Italian prisoners of war to be transported back to Australia. Departing Suez on 23 November, the two Queens voyaged together across the Indian Ocean to Trincomalee, arriving there on 30 November. Here it was planned that they would go their separate ways, with *Queen Mary* to proceed to Singapore for drydocking, while *Queen Elizabeth* returned to Australia.

From late August to early October 1941 there had also been some highly significant political changes in the Australian government. On 29 August, Robert Menzies had resigned as Prime Minister, being replaced by Arthur Fadden, who was the leader of the Country Party. However, on 7 October Fadden also resigned, and John Curtin, leader of the Labor Party, became Prime Minister, a post he would hold until his death in July 1945.

Meanwhile, *Zealandia* had been designated for a second trooping voyage to Singapore. *Zealandia* had arrived back in Sydney on 13 October from Port Moresby, when she had been part of convoy ZK4, but her planned departure date from Sydney was delayed by over a week due to an industrial dispute involving the engineers. This turn of events would have fatal consequences, as it was not until 29 October that *Zealandia* departed Sydney, escorted by HMAS *Adelaide* as far as the Great Australian Bight, where HMAS *Sydney* took over the escort duty off Albany on 5 November. *Zealandia* was not an easy ship to escort, as her speed was unreliable, varying between 7 and 13 knots. In addition, her master, Captain Kerr, reported he was having trouble with some members of the crew.

On 11 November, *Zealandia* left Fremantle, still escorted by *Sydney*. It was the usual practice for cruisers to use the ships they were escorting to train their crews in various procedures, such as dawn encounter, gunnery, shadowing and emergency drills, and *Sydney*'s crew used the time at sea in this way. *Sydney* stayed with *Zealandia* as far as Sunda Strait, where she handed the escort duties over to HMS *Durban* at noon on 17 November. *Sydney* turned around and headed back to Fremantle, as *Zealandia* and *Durban* continued their way north, but little did those on the two ships realise as they watched *Sydney* disappear over the southern horizon that just two days later she would be sunk in almost unbelievable circumstances.

HMAS *Sydney* escorted *Zealandia* to Sunda Strait, then turned back to Australia.

Just prior to leaving Fremantle, *Sydney* had sent a signal stating her anticipated arrival time back in Fremantle, 20 November. When the cruiser did not arrive it caused little concern at first, as information had been received that *Zealandia* and *Durban* had been late arriving in Singapore, so it was anticipated *Sydney* would also be late. When *Sydney* had not returned by 23 November, urgent messages were sent instructing her to report immediately, and when these went unanswered a search was commenced.

As later became known, on 19 November HMAS *Sydney* was sunk with the loss of her entire crew, 42 officers and 603 ratings, in a fight with the German commerce raider *Kormoran*, which was also sunk in the battle with the loss of 78 of her 393 crew and prisoners from captured ships. The fate of the cruiser was not established until survivors from the German ship were picked up and interrogated several days later. One of the ships to pick up survivors was *Aquitania*, returning alone to Sydney from Singapore, which picked up 24 German sailors from a raft on 24 November and carried them to Sydney, where she arrived four days later.

By the time the two Queens reached Trincomalee, the fate of HMAS *Sydney* was known, and the probability of Japan coming into the war was becoming more certain every day. The continuing movement of troops to the Middle East was now a matter of grave concern to the Australian government. The original plan of future troop movements had called for the two Queens to depart Australia again early in 1942 for the Middle East. It was decided to allow *Queen Elizabeth* to continue her voyage to Australia, but *Queen Mary* was detained at Trincomalee. *Queen Elizabeth* was in the middle of the Indian Ocean, en route to Fremantle, when, on 8 December, the Japanese attacked Pearl Harbor and launched a series of landings on the Malay Peninsula. The liner reached Fremantle safely, then continued to Sydney, dropping anchor in the harbour on 16 December.

With the Japanese entry into the war, the plans to send *Queen Mary* to Singapore for drydocking were scrapped. Instead the liner remained in Trincomalee while a decision was made on her future. On 19 December, *Queen Mary* left Ceylon, bound for Cape Town, where she arrived on 28 December. Next day she left for the dangerous crossing of the South Atlantic to Trinidad, then continued to New York, berthing there on 12 January 1942. Two weeks later the liner made the short trip up the coast to Boston, to enter drydock for a major overhaul.

During 1941, seven US convoys departed Australia, comprising 23 vessels carrying 92,000 troops, of which more than 50,000 were transported by the two 'Queens.' Of the troops carried overseas, 70,000 were Australian, including 3800 RAN and RAAF personnel, while the remaining 22,000 came from New Zealand. However, the US convoys to the Middle East now ceased, and attention was focused closer to home.

Of all the major Australian troop movements of the war, those involving the US convoys were by far the most extensive. In total, the 13 US convoys transported 129,200 Australian troops and 46,200 from New Zealand to the Middle East or Britain, while a further 14,000 Australian troops were carried to Singapore. In many cases, the troops had to travel in conditions that were extremely uncomfortable, and often just about intolerable. No doubt many men who travelled overseas would agree wholeheartedly with the soldier who, disembarking from *Ile de France* in Suez, was heard to remark, 'War may be 'ell, mates, but gettin' there is worse.'

With Japan now in the war, and Malaya under serious threat, the further use of large liners for transporting troops from Australian ports was considered too dangerous, and it was also apparent that, with the entry of the United States into the war, such ships could be better utilised elsewhere. In addition, the Australian government was no longer prepared to send troops to the Middle East, but was more concerned with protecting its own shores. Facing an uncertain future, *Queen Elizabeth* lay quietly in Sydney Harbour, along with *Aquitania*, as

1942 began. On 6 February 1942, *Queen Elizabeth* left Sydney, calling at Auckland on 8 February and leaving two days later for Esquimalt, on the west coast of Canada, where she arrived on 23 February and entered drydock. *Aquitania* left Sydney on 10 February, bound for Honolulu, then made her way to San Francisco and on to New York.

Meanwhile, *Queen Mary* had entered the drydock in Boston on 27 January 1942 to undergo a major overhaul. Refloated on 8 February, the liner spent a further ten days in Boston for the work to be completed, then on 18 February departed for Key West, arriving on 22 February. It was here that Captain Townley handed over command to Captain Bissett. Over the next two days the liner boarded 8398 American troops, then departed Key West on 24 February, once again bound for Sydney. First stop on the journey was to be at Rio de Janeiro for refuelling, but while proceeding down the South Atlantic off the coast of Brazil, the radio officer on *Queen Mary* received a most alarming signal, which he rushed immediately to Captain Bissett. German radio had just announced the sinking of *Queen Mary* in the South Atlantic, with the loss of all 10,000 persons on board. Noted for his sense of humour, Captain Bisset told the radio officer to keep it secret, otherwise it might upset the troops on board.

From Rio de Janeiro, *Queen Mary* crossed to Cape Town, arriving there on 14 March to refuel. Prior to departing the next day, the liner also took on board an extra passenger, General Sir Thomas Blamey, who had been in command of Australian troops in the Middle East until being ordered to return home. *Queen Mary* then proceeded to Fremantle, dropping anchor in Gage Roads on 23 March. Here Blamey disembarked, and two days later proceeded by air to Melbourne. Meanwhile *Queen Mary* left Gage Roads on 24 March on the final leg of the voyage to Sydney, where she dropped anchor once more off Bradleys Head on 28 March. The American troops were disembarked and taken to a holding camp set up on Randwick Racecourse, from where they were dispersed to various outposts in the north of Australia and around the Pacific Islands. *Queen Mary* departed Sydney on 6 April with only 58 passengers on board, returning to New York via Fremantle, Cape Town and Rio de Janeiro.

As *Queen Mary* left Sydney, just outside Sydney Heads she passed *Queen Elizabeth* inbound with more American troops. While *Queen Elizabeth* was in drydock in Canada, extra bunks were installed, increasing her capacity to 8000 troops. On 10 March, *Queen Elizabeth* left Esquimalt for San Francisco, berthing there three days later. On

A stern view of *Queen Elizabeth* anchored in Sydney Harbour.

19 March, the liner departed San Francisco with 8000 American troops on board, bound for Australia. Accompanying her were two American ships, *Mariposa* and *President Coolidge*, both carrying troops to New Zealand, escorted by the cruiser USS *Chester*. On 27 March the convoy arrived off Comptroller Bay in Nuku Hiva, one of the Marquesa Islands, part of French Polynesia. Here *Mariposa* and *President Coolidge* entered the bay first to refuel from a tanker, then departed on their voyage, enabling *Queen Elizabeth* and *Chester* to also refuel. These two ships then chased at high speed after *Mariposa* and *President Coolidge*, but after catching up to them, *Queen Elizabeth* continued her voyage alone at 28 knots.

On 3 April, *Queen Elizabeth* met up with an old American four-stack destroyer of World War I vintage, USS *Alden*, which was supposed to escort the liner. However, the old warship could not maintain sufficient speed, even when told to maintain a straight course while *Queen Elizabeth* followed a broad zigzag pattern. This almost produced tragedy, as just before midnight the helm on *Alden* became jammed and the warship began to drift helplessly in the moderate seas. Just at that moment, *Queen Elizabeth* was converging on the destroyer as part of her zigzag course and was headed directly for the stern of *Alden*. Just when a collision seemed inevitable, the lights aboard *Alden* were turned on and the huge liner made a sharp turn, missing the warship by 75 yards.

Queen Elizabeth arrived in Sydney on 6 April, passing the outward-bound *Queen Mary* off Sydney Heads, then going to her usual

Queen Elizabeth arriving in Sydney on 6 April 1942 carrying American troops (*Vic Scrivens collection*)

anchorage off Bradleys Head. The huge liner remained in Sydney almost two weeks, departing for the last time on 19 April on a voyage to Fremantle, Simonstown, Rio de Janeiro and New York, where she arrived on 24 May. Little more than a week later the *Queen Elizabeth* was again carrying troops, this time some 10,000 Americans at a time, on their way to Europe.

13 Airmen at Sea

Prior to 1939, the British government had approached Commonwealth countries, including Australia, New Zealand, Canada and South Africa, with regard to the training of airmen for service in the Royal Air Force in the event of war breaking out in Europe. At the 1937 Imperial Conference, Australia agreed to send 50 air force officers to Britain each year for training, while Canada agreed to train British aircrew in Canada.

A few weeks after war did break out, Prime Minister Menzies offered Britain Australian aircrew for six squadrons, provided Britain supplied the operational aircraft, though they would be operated under Australian command. However, the British decided that they would prefer it if Australia were to assist in a scheme to provide the RAF with 50,000 aircrew a year from the Empire in general. At a meeting held at Ottawa in November 1939, the British proposal was accepted by Australia and New Zealand, and this was developed as the Empire Air Training Scheme. Under this plan, Australian and New Zealand air force recruits would receive their initial flying training in their home countries, then go to Canada for final training proceeding going to Britain to join operational squadrons. Australia would provide about 11,000 trainees per year, who would eventually fly with the RAF under British command, of whom about 200 would leave every month for advanced training in Canada. This was quite an undertaking, as at the outbreak of war the Royal Australian Air Force comprised a total of three and a half thousand men in all, and they were short of training facilities and aircraft.

Some of the men already serving in the RAAF found themselves being sent to the Middle East, though they did not always travel on troopships in convoys. In Melbourne on 18 July 1940, two officers and 183 men, including ground crews, of No. 3 Squadron, Royal Australian Air Force, boarded the *Orontes*, owned by the Orient Line, their destination being Egypt. *Orontes*, sailing alone, went first to Fremantle, departing there on 27 November for the voyage to Bombay. There the men of No. 3 Squadron transferred to the smaller troopship *Dilwara*, a sister of *Dunera*, which had been included in the first and second convoy. *Dilwara* transported them to Port Tewfik, where they arrived on 23 August. After disembarking, the squadron went to Ismailia to complete their training for combat.

The first contingent of RAAF trainees under the Empire Air Training Scheme departed Sydney for Canada on 5 September 1940, arriving in Vancouver on 27 September. A second and third contingent were dispatched during October, and a fourth contingent followed in November. Andy Emmerson was one of the first Australian airmen to go overseas, travelling across the Pacific on the American liner *Mariposa*,

The American liner *Mariposa* carried Australian trainee airmen to San Francisco.

which, with her sister *Monterey*, was still in commercial service from the west coast of America to Australia, operating monthly departures. Although America was still neutral, these ships regularly carried Australian servicemen to San Francisco.

As Andy Emmerson recalled, 'When we went aboard we were given hammocks down in the lower decks. They wanted people with orderly experience to help, so a mate and I volunteered. It got us out of kitchen duties and other fatigues — although we had to take our turn up on the gun mountings. One day we found an empty cabin. We managed to get the window open and got in. It was sheer luxury. Even the toilets had electric heaters in them. No-one found out about it until we got to Hawaii. Then they seemed to admire our initiative and left us there.'

In all, some 10,000 Australians completed their air training in Canada, and then were sent on to Britain, where they joined their operational squadrons. Drafts of trainees, usually 40 in number, were also regularly sent away under the Empire Air Scheme to Rhodesia, the first of these departing on 4 November 1940 on board the *Nestor*, a cargo/passenger liner owned by the Blue Funnel Line. Built in 1913, *Nestor* had a very tall funnel, and tended to roll heavily, even in moderate seas. As a result, all the trainees suffered seasickness, especially when, after leaving Fremantle, the ship followed a route far south of the normal shipping lanes before arriving in Durban on 23 December. Here the trainees disembarked, and travelled by train to Rhodesia. Unfortunately, the trainee who suffered worst from seasickness all the way to Durban, was the only one of the 40 to fail the flying course, or be 'scrubbed' as it was known, because of airsickness! The other 39 were all sent to join squadrons in the Middle East.

The second draft departed Sydney on 10 December 1940 on board *Largs Bay*, which was still in civilian service, though this was its final trip before being requisitioned for military duty. Also on board was the first group of pilots to have completed their training in Australia, who were on their way to England. This was a much more pleasant trip for the airmen, as they were able to enjoy the pleasures of a full meal service, and other passenger ship comforts. The trainees bound for Rhodesia disembarked at Durban on 5 January 1941.

Conditions were rather different for the third draft, which embarked in Sydney on 17 February 1941 on the *Ulysses*, a sister to the *Nestor* that carried the first draft, and subject to the same propensity to roll. The trip was made uncomfortable by bad weather, but the trainees were also not allowed to eat with the civilian passengers, and no doubt were relieved to arrive in Durban on 22 March. Another Blue Funnel Line vessel, *Calchas*, carried the fourth draft, which joined the ship in Adelaide on 7 March. *Calchas* was a 10,304 gross ton cargo ship, built in 1921, and the trainees were accommodated in bunks fitted in the holds. They arrived in Durban on 27 March, and while the trainees went by train to Rhodesia, *Calchas* continued her voyage to Britain, but was torpedoed and sunk off the Canary Islands on 21 April with the loss of 31 lives.

The Blue Funnel liner *Ulysses* carried the third draft of trainee airmen sent to Rhodesia.

Conditions for the fifth draft were very much better, as they travelled on board the liner *Ceramic*, which was also still in civilian service. Departing Sydney on 27 March 1941, the ship called at Adelaide and Fremantle before following the southerly route to South Africa. Built in 1913 for the White Star Line, but now owned by Shaw Savill & Albion, *Ceramic* had been the largest ship operating to Australia when new, with accommodation for 600 passengers. Despite the comfortable accommodation provided for the trainees, the trip had its bad moments. Deep in the Southern Ocean the ship ran into a severe storm, being forced to reduce speed to almost a standstill for four days, while huge waves smashed all the railings in the forward section, and also damaged most of the lifeboats. At one time sections of the

The Shaw Savill liner *Ceramic* also carried trainee airmen to South Africa.

The Blue Funnel vessel *Diomed*, on which Len Williams voyaged to South Africa, at Fremantle. (*C.T. Reddings collection*)

passenger accommodation were flooded to a depth of almost a foot, and most of the passengers were so seasick they could not eat for the entire four days. When *Ceramic* finally arrived off Durban it had to anchor out for a week before entering the harbour and berthing on 24 April, when the trainees disembarked.

Included in the sixth draft that went to Rhodesia was Len Williams, who recorded his wartime experiences in a series of letters to his family back in Sydney. Len was accepted by the RAAF Reserve in July 1940, at the age of nineteen, and commenced his flight training in January 1941. Three months later he was sent to Pearce Air Force Base in Western Australia, where he spent a short time until boarding a ship bound for South Africa, from where he would be sent overland to Southern Rhodesia to complete his training. In Fremantle on Thursday, 17 April 1941, he boarded the *Diomed*, though he never mentioned the name of the ship in his letters. *Diomed* was another Blue Funnel Line ship, 10,453 gross tons, built in 1922, primarily as a cargo ship, but with limited passenger accommodation. It departed Fremantle on 19 April, the same day as convoy US10 left the port bound for the Middle East. In a long letter home that was eventually posted from Bulawayo in Southern Rhodesia, Len began recording the voyage from Fremantle to South Africa, including the following extracts:

'We left Pearce soon after lunch on the Thursday and were taken to Fremantle by tender. After loitering around the wharf for a while we came on board this ship, thinking it an old tub (which it is), dirty (also true) ... The ship which is just more than 10,000 ton displacement carries a cargo of wheat, loose and bagged, some scrap iron and 40 airmen with their officer escort. We are much better off than had we been on a large ship acting as a troop carrier, for here we are passengers. We sailed at 0830 this morning, just as we were finishing breakfast having spent yesterday on leave in Perth as the boat was loading all day. We had a swim this morning just outside Fremantle Harbour. The beach was not the best but the water was wonderful. Just out from us in the roads were the many ships of a large convoy which followed us for a while when we left harbour.' This was US10.

On Wednesday, 23 April, Len recorded:

> This is our fifth day at sea and after leaving the convoy we have not sighted another ship because we are several hundred miles south of the usual course which is a great circle bearing towards the south; by now we must be down in the latitude 40 degrees, and it feels so sometimes with the temperature quite low ... most of the chaps are wearing two sweaters. It is not as though the weather is bad — we have had very good days so far, some quite rough, some of the time fairly calm.
>
> Together with the other six chaps who were originally with me in 10 Flight and a few more chaps I am in the biggest cabin on the boat, a ten-berth cabin aft (deck cabin) which was formerly the seamen's mess so all fittings are new ... the other cabins are all the usual ones amidships, mostly four-berth, but are not as airy and cool as ours especially now with the blackout, as they are all below decks ... Majority of the chaps have been sick but all are over it by now ... I have had a very easy time, for about half an hour before dinner on our first day out I did not feel at all well but after getting rid of my lunch I dressed for dinner and was fine — I haven't missed a meal ... Our meals are very good and as the dining room only seats 28 people there are two sittings for each meal, with our cabin in the first sitting.

On 27 April, the day after the ships of US10 arrived in Ceylon, Len again put pen to paper:

> Today we passed the half way mark of the crossing and it is now evening, so after neglecting this letter for half a week I'll continue. Some of the chaps are a little tired of the trip which is fairly natural as there is not too much to do on a boat of this size. Personally I still find enough to do without the days becoming too monotonous. We have Physical Training and a roll call parade at 0715 each morning, breakfast 0800, lunch 1200, dinner 1730 and lights out 2200 hrs. Usually the rest of the time is our own.
>
> To pass the time we read quite a lot either lying about the deck or in the smoke room or cabins, play deck quoits or deck tennis, darts or cards. As we go to bed somewhere between 2000 and 2100 hrs the days do not

seem too long. There is a deck quoits contest starting tomorrow ... Some of the chaps have visited the engine room, bridge and wireless room but as yet I have not had a chance to do so.

One of the reasons we go to bed so early is the enforced blackout on the ship while at sea — to get from amidships to our cabin back aft is a great undertaking in the dark on these moonless nights. Theoretically we are only allowed to have certain portholes open at night — those that are covered on the outside with boxes, but to get our cabin as airy as possible we take the globes from their fittings so no-one can switch the lights on accidentally, then open everything wide. I had a bath today — on board I have only had a bath every two or three days — reasons being mainly that the bath water is salt — straight from the sea — which even when hot is not entirely a success. One has to use special sea water soap to obtain any lather at all then pour a can of cold fresh water over oneself in an endeavour to wash off the salt — it is disastrous to try to wash your hair in salt water so one has again to use a basin of fresh water.

On 5 May *Diomed* and Len Williams arrived safely in Durban. The final section of his letter to his family was not written until after Len had reached his final destination, Bulawayo in Southern Rhodesia. On 10 May he wrote:

So here I am at last, five weeks after leaving you. I have a lot to tell you but I think I had better continue on from where I left off on board ship. The latter half of the journey was much the same as the first. We mainly ate and slept — in fact so much I am now 10 stone 10 pounds ... We chaps down aft soon tired of trudging forward for a bath or shower till one day we discovered a large salt water tap above the deck just near our cabin so from then on we just stood on the deck under this stream of salt water when we wanted a shower. Well there is not much more I can say without the censor jumping on it, as he may have done with the beginning of this letter so I'll get to the end of the trip.

At 0400 on Sunday 4th May, I looked out the porthole and saw lights on the horizon — they were the lights of Durban where we were to disembark. We dressed quite early that morning in our blues, only to be told a little later that we were to wear drabs and waited around all day for something to happen but all day the boat lay outside the harbour and we had to look longingly at the shore — so near and yet so far. However about 1000 on the Monday morning our ship took aboard its pilot and we sailed into harbour. We had lunch, our last meal aboard and came ashore about 1400 hours.

So ended the voyage from Australia for Len Williams and his companions. They had only a brief time in Durban before commencing the long train journey to Bulawayo in Southern Rhodesia. After completing their flying training in Africa, they were sent to England, travelling by ship from South Africa. Sadly, Len Williams was destined never to return to Australia, as on 6 August 1942 his aircraft failed to return from an anti-submarine patrol over the North Sea.

The seventh draft to be sent to Rhodesia left Sydney aboard yet another Blue Funnel Line vessel, *Sarpedon*, on 26 April, and following a longer than usual voyage along the familiar southern route from Fremantle to Durban, arrived on 1 July. This was the final group to be sent directly to Durban, as when the eighth draft was organised, the 40 men were brought to Sydney, where they boarded *Queen Elizabeth*, along with some 5000 troops. *Queen Elizabeth* departed Sydney on 26 June, waited two days in Jervis Bay, then linked up with *Queen Mary* and *Aquitania* to form convoy US11A, whose voyage to the Middle East is recorded elsewhere. The 40 airmen disembarked with the troops at Port Tewfik, where three of the trainees succumbed to mumps, and had to be hospitalised. The remaining 37 left Port Tewfik on 18 August aboard the *Dilwara*, which carried them to Durban, where they disembarked on 5 September, then went overland to Rhodesia.

The ninth draft of trainee pilots to be sent to Rhodesia was also larger, 120 men, of whom all but two were taken by train from Melbourne to Sydney, where they boarded *Queen Elizabeth* on 1 September. Leaving Sydney the next day, they waited in Jervis Bay until joining *Queen Mary* to form convoy US12A. During the time the two liners were anchored off Fremantle, the final two trainee pilots joined the main group, and they arrived in Port Tewfik on 25 September. On 21 October the airmen boarded *Mauretania*, which was then operating a shuttle service between Port Tewfik and Durban, bringing British troops from South Africa northbound, returning with Italian prisoners of war. They were confined to the lower decks during the voyage, while the airmen had the comfort of cabins, arriving in Durban on 31 October.

The tenth, and largest draft, 127 men, was also to be the last sent to Rhodesia. They also travelled to Egypt aboard *Queen Elizabeth*, which left Sydney on 2 November 1941 along with *Queen Mary* as convoy US13, the final Middle East convoy, which arrived at Port Tewfik on 24 November. On 14 December the trainees embarked on *Dilwarra* for the next leg of their journey, with several stops, the first being at Massawa. Christmas Day was spent anchored off Aden, where they were not allowed ashore, while New Years Day 1942 found them in Mombasa, where they did get shore leave. *Dilwara* arrived in Durban on 6 January 1942. By then Japan had entered the war and the whole airmen training program underwent a major change, with no more groups being sent to Rhodesia.

Not all the men who volunteered to join the Royal Australian Air Force were sent overseas for training. Instead they completed their training in Australia, then were sent to an overseas posting, sometimes travelling in pre-war comfort. Jack Woodward enlisted in the RAAF on 3 January 1941 and completed his training as a navigator in August that year, then was told to be prepared to leave for an unspecified overseas destination. Woodward then spent four weeks in Brisbane at the Sandgate Embarkation Depot, along with numerous other men who had completed their training. He later wrote, 'On Wednesday, 1st October, a group of thirty-five or so ... were handed a green band to put round their kit bags, and they left that morning for Sydney. We found out later that they boarded the *Queen Elizabeth* which left a few days later. As soon as they had gone, my group of fifteen were told that we could go on leave from 1215 until 1515 the next day, and the following night would be a closed camp.' This gave Jack Woodward one last night to spend with his wife, Vera, and his parents.

On 3 October, Jack Woodward recorded in his diary:

> And so this day we thought we knew where we were heading. After leaving Vera the previous night, we all assembled in the Sergeants Mess, and with the others who had not been posted, had a farewell party. We left the Station just after 1 pm being handed presents and parcels from the Comforts Fund and also the RSSILA, and were addressed by the CO and the padre, wishing us all the best.
>
> We were taken to Newstead Wharf, and boarded the SS *Marella*. We were allotted first-class cabins, some three berth and some two berth ... We found out that we were travelling as passengers to Singapore, and not in convoy. We then asked the purser whom we should report to, and he was nonplussed. On enquiring when we would be leaving, he was not certain, but was sure that it would not be before 10 pm. When asked could we go ashore, he just replied, 'please yourself.' And so there was an immediate rush to go ashore.

Jack Woodward managed to snatch a few more precious hours with his wife, but was back on board the *Marella* by 10 pm. However, he wrote later, he 'did not sleep at all well that night, and I am sure that Vera didn't either.'

Marella was, at 7474 gross tons, the largest vessel owned by the

Australian shipping firm, Burns Philp & Co. Ltd, and operated between the east coast of Australia and Singapore. Under construction in Germany when World War I started, the vessel was completed in 1917, only to be seized the following year by the victorious allies. In 1920 the liner, then named *Wahehe*, was bought by Burns Philp, renamed *Marella* and fitted out to carry 100 first-class and 50 second-class passengers. The vessel remained on the Singapore trade after war broke out in Europe in 1939.

On 4 October 1941, Jack Woodward wrote:

> The Marella cast away from the Newstead Wharf at 6 am, and when I woke and looked through the porthole, we were just clearing the mouth of the Brisbane River and entering Moreton Bay. On going down to breakfast, we were waited on by stewards in grand style. This was not hard to take. It was certainly not like the troop ships that most of our fellows going overseas experienced, and was indeed very comfortable.
>
> Sitting down to breakfast, we were all allotted the same table. It was with relief we checked that all fifteen were present, nobody being carried away in some form or another and missing the boat. We were not sure how long the journey would last, but it was estimated that it could possibly be three weeks. Besides ourselves, other passengers on board the ship were about thirty or so navy men, bound for Singapore to man the destroyer HMAS *Vampire* being refitted there ... Also on board were civilians returning to Singapore after holidaying in Sydney. They comprised more than half the complement of passengers on board ship.
>
> The day we left was the running of the Epsom Handicap in Sydney, and the passengers decided to run two sweeps. This put us in mind to run a sweep among ourselves to be called the 'Chunder Derby,' each one of us putting up a pound and drawing someone else from our group as their horse. The first person to become seasick had to acknowledge the fact, and the person drawing him would take out the whole of the prize, which would be worth fifteen pounds. We had a very smooth voyage all the way, and nobody took ill. The whole of the proceeds were added to our bank for the party we provided for the navy and civilians, on the night prior to arriving in Singapore.

Although *Marella* was still in commercial service, wartime restrictions applied. 'We were blacked out on board, and no lights were visible. All out portholes were blacked out, and if we wanted to look out at night or get some fresh air we had to make sure that the lights were out in our cabin. The main lounge on the top deck was also blacked out (lights being on inside), but to enter, one had to go through a door which closed on entering, through a short passage which had a very subdued light, and then through another door into the lounge and bar.'

So the voyage north commenced. 'Late on Sunday night, we passed and observed the light on Flat Top Island ... the anchorage for the town of Mackay. The following day we journeyed through Whitsunday Passage, passing close to Daydream Island. People holidaying on the island came down to the beach and waved to the ship, the *Marella* replying with a long blast on its siren. We arrived outside Townsville during the night and anchored, entering the port early in the morning.'

The airmen were allowed shore leave in Townsville, and

> by 10.30 am the following day we left Townsville to continue our journey. The scenery passing the islands northward was really picturesque, and by midnight we passed outside Cairns. Travelling inside the reef northward to Thursday Island provided a different type of scenery, abounding with coral reefs and islands. We passed several ships; one was a Dutch ship which was quite large ... Another very large ship was the *Stirling Castle* ... The chaps on board remarked they would like to travel on her, with which I agreed, little realising that six months later I would be wending my way back home to Australia on the same ship.
>
> Two days after leaving Townsville, we passed Cape York in the distance, and then pulled into Thursday Island, discharging cargo (mainly cartons of Fosters Lager) and also some passengers. We arrived in Darwin on Monday the 13th October, and spent two days there ... On the day of our arrival in Darwin the wharfies were on strike, so the discharge of our cargo took twenty-four hours longer than the captain would have liked.

As a result, it was not until the afternoon of 15 October that *Marella* pulled away from the wharf at Darwin and headed off to Surabaya.

> Soon after, we had our last glimpse of Australia, some of us for six months, but for quite a number who became POWs the last for four years. All wondered just what the future would hold. We arrived in Surabaya the following Sunday, the 19th October, passing close to many of the islands, including Bali. The harbour was heavily mined, and it was necessary to have a pilot guide the ship through the minefield into the harbour. We berthed at 2.30 pm ... We had the day and night ashore, which was a real education to us, visiting night clubs, and seeing the canals of the Far East.
>
> The following day we left for Semarang. The *Marella* anchored offshore, and we went ashore on the tender ... We had thought that Surabaya

was beautiful, but this place was a complete gem — lovely homes and magnificent gardens ... Our time ashore was three hours, and at 1 pm the ship got under way and on to Batavia, now known as Jakarta. As on the day before, we were met and taken out to a hotel with beautiful gardens and grounds, and were well entertained. Mid afternoon, we boarded buses to take us back to the ship, and they deviated to show us the rich Chinese and Japanese quarters. They had really magnificent homes, and it was easy to tell the difference in the architecture ... The Japanese buildings were all unoccupied, their owners having returned to Japan.

And so we left Batavia, on our last leg to Singapore. We followed the coastline of Sumatra on our port side, and passing tropical islands on the other side made a very picturesque end to our voyage. Singapore Harbour was an eye-opener — being so vast and with much shipping about. We were really impressed. We disembarked at the wharf at 4 pm on Friday the 24th October, 1941, after bidding farewell to our navy and civilian friends with whom we had such a pleasant journey.

On their arrival in Singapore the group was split up, nine men being posted in Singapore, the other six being sent to other areas. Just over six weeks later the Japanese invasion of the Malay Peninsula began. Of the fifteen men who enjoyed their pleasant voyage to Singapore, one was killed through enemy action, five became prisoners of war, and the other nine managed to escape and return to Australia, including Jack Woodward. Four of these men subsequently lost their lives in flying accidents during the war.

At 31, Charlie Williams was older than most recruits when he joined the eleventh intake for the Empire Air Training Scheme in February 1941. Born and raised in north Queensland, he had been to Brisbane only once in his life before reporting to the recruitment centre there, from where he was sent to Sydney to join No. 2 Initial Training School at Bradfield Park. Later training was conducted at Parkes, and completed after six months at Evans Head, with Charlie being commissioned as a pilot officer.

Having completed his training, it was now time for Charlie to go to war, and he prepared for the long journey that lay ahead of him. He travelled by train from Sydney to Townsville, which took three days, in order to spend a few days with his mother, then returned to Sydney and reported to the Bradfield Park Embarkation Depot. In October 1941, Charlie and his fellow fliers were taken to the wharf at Woolloomooloo to board *Mariposa* for the voyage to America.

Once they had boarded the liner, the airmen kept apart from civilian passengers, and after being shown to their cabins stood in a cluster on deck as the liner steamed down Sydney Harbour and out through the Heads. For many, including Charlie Williams, this was to be their last sight of Australia, as they would never return. On the voyage across the Tasman to Auckland, *Mariposa* was escorted by the cruiser HMAS *Sydney*. It was quite a comfortable journey for Charlie, who had been allocated a berth in a first-class cabin. After Auckland, *Mariposa* called at Suva, then went on to Pago Pago and Honolulu. The airmen were able to go ashore for the day spent in each of these ports, where they received generous hospitality from local representatives of the American Red Cross.

On their arrival in San Francisco the airmen boarded a train for Vancouver, then changed to another train which took them across the vast expanse of Canada in five days, during which Charlie saw snow for the first time. This journey ended in Halifax, and within a few days the airmen found themselves on another ship, but this time instead of a comfortable large liner, they were on an ancient, dirty, uncomfortable troop transport, which joined a convoy and carried them safely to Gourock. From there it was another long train journey, south to Bournemouth, where the reception centre for personnel involved in the Empire Air Training Scheme had been established. Charlie Williams later joined the famous 'Dam Busters' bomber squadron, and was killed in action on 16 May 1943.

During the first three years of the war, trainee airmen were being transported regularly on *Awatea* across the Pacific to Canada for training. In all, *Awatea* carried 3600 Australian and New Zealand airmen

Awatea, still in commercial service, carried many trainee airmen across the Pacific.

to Canada for training. When the vessel departed Sydney on 22 February 1941, among the trainee airmen on board was Rawdon Middleton, who would ultimately pay the supreme sacrifice, and be posthumously awarded the Victoria Cross, one of only three awarded to Australian airmen in the war. *Awatea* was escorted by HMAS *Hobart* across the Tasman Sea to Auckland, where they arrived on 25 February. A draft of New Zealand trainee airmen joined the ship, which stopped two days in Auckland, then continued its voyage, now escorted by the armed merchant cruiser HMNZS *Monowai*, a former trans-Tasman liner herself. Arriving in Suva on 2 March, *Awatea* departed next day, now escorted by another armed merchant cruiser, HMCS *Prince Rupert*, all the way to Victoria, on Vancouver Island, where the airmen disembarked on 16 March. They marched through the streets to the ferry terminal, to be taken to Vancouver, and the same evening left on a train for their training camps.

When their training ended, the group was taken by train to Halifax, but Rawdon Middleton became ill and could not travel with the others on the next leg of their journey. Perhaps this was a blessing in disguise, as on 15 June 1941 the others embarked on a Cunard liner, *Ausonia*, which joined up in a convoy of 93 ships. As Len Reid recalled the trip, 'The *Ausonia*, which was the flagship of the convoy, was an armed merchant cruiser, having been modified to carry a couple of 6-inch guns — one at the front the other at the back — not much armament really but enough to outgun a submarine. We used to sleep on the Promenade Deck.' The convoy was attacked by German submarines, and after several ships were sunk it was diverted to Iceland, with *Ausonia* arriving in Reykjavik, where the airmen were put ashore and stayed three weeks. On 23 July they boarded the Dutch liner *Volendam* for the trip to Greenock. As Len Reid recalled, 'The *Volendam*, a dirty ship, was full of troops and we were squashed into a small area in the holds where we slept in hammocks. It was like the black hole of Calcutta — we couldn't see a thing.'

Rawdon Middleton finally left Halifax on 21 August as a passenger on the armed merchant cruiser *Worcestershire*, the primary escort for convoy HX146, comprising 55 merchant ships. A total of 130 airmen were on the ship, 35 of them Australians, of whom all but three were pilots, along with 56 New Zealanders, all pilots, and men from the Royal Air Force and Royal Canadian Air Force, all of whom had completed their training in Canada. On 22 August, convoy HX146 linked up with thirteen ships from Sydney, Nova Scotia, in convoy

SHX146, and they followed a northerly course across the Atlantic. As they neared Iceland, *Worcestershire* left the convoy and docked in Reykjavik while the rest of the ships carried on to Britain. The airmen remained on the ship several days before being transferred to a former Belgian liner, *Leopoldville*, which was already full of troops, that carried them to Greenock, a three-day voyage. From there Middleton and the others went by train to Bournemouth, and subsequently to their squadrons.

Among the young fliers to travel on *Awatea* to Canada in August 1941 was Frederick Keck, one of seven brothers, six of whom served in the war, the seventh being too young to enlist. When the Empire Air Training Scheme was organised in October 1939, many young men rushed to join, including Kingwell Keck, the oldest of the brothers, who began his pilot training in Australia. He then went to Canada for advanced training, on completion of which he was sent to Britain where he joined No. 455 Squadron, Royal Air Force. Frederick also wanted to be a pilot, but he did not pass the initial testing and instead became a navigator. Despite his disappointment at not being a pilot, Frederick continued with the scheme, being trained at Evans Head, in New South Wales. As he wrote home on 30 June 1941, 'At my passing out parade at Evans Head I was presented with my wing which has been very hard-earned but seems to represent the worthwhile part of it all.'

In August 1941, Frederick Keck joined *Awatea* in Sydney for the voyage to Canada, though in his case he was to continue on across the country by train, then join another ship for the voyage to Britain, where he would undergo pre-operational training. Escorted by HMAS *Sydney*, *Awatea* departed Sydney on 8 August. Two days later, crossing the Tasman Sea, Frederick wrote, in a letter home, 'The trip across has so far indicated that that part of the sea we are in deserves its bad reputation, and that I am a good sailor although at times I realise that I could without much persuasion become a bad one ... We are being treated very well on board. I have a first-class cabin with two others and we eat with the first-class passengers so there are no complaints.'

After stopping in Auckland for three days, during which Frederick was able to do some sightseeing and catch up with relatives of his mother, the voyage continued, and he wrote: 'We are still having very rough weather and I am still feeling uncertain of my ability to hold everything. This boat is noted for its tendency to upset the hardiest of sailors and as we are travelling at full speed there are many casualties to Neptune. I am trying to fit this in between my duties as Orderly

Officer today and night, and two lectures which I have to give daily as well as an hour's wireless duty ... We are forced to keep our own studies up to date to be able to lecture to the trainees and together with deck-sports, the work is keeping us out of mischief. I am perfectly fit and doing my best.'

During this part of the voyage, *Awatea* was still being escorted by HMAS *Sydney*, and on 23 August, Frederick was writing, 'We reached Suva three days after leaving Auckland and spent a day ashore. It was terribly hot and although a most interesting place I have no desire to go there again, much less ever to have to live there or anywhere else so hot. Thank goodness I am headed elsewhere than the tropics ... The two weeks since leaving Sydney have seemed much longer than an ordinary fortnight and taking into regard the fact that we average five hundred miles a day, it is no wonder that home appears very far away. One of the highlights of the voyage was when the *Sydney* left us. The entire ship's companies lined the side of their respective vessels and gave each other three cheers, and up on the bridge we flashed messages of good luck to each other. The Navy looked most impressive in their tropical white uniforms and the *Sydney* made us proud of her as she cut through the water full speed ahead with the flags flying.'

As usual, Frederick was not able to be too specific in his letters, but wrote, 'Somewhere at sea is at the moment just north of the equator and well over to the east of Honolulu. Actually we are almost in American patrolled waters so should be quite safe although our escort left us a few days ago. In any case this ship has plenty of pace and if she can't fight very well, she can run pretty fast ... We should reach Vancouver in another six days and on arrival we go straight to the train for our long journey across Canada. It is possible we will have to wait for a convoy then and may not reach England for a month or so after arrival in Montreal. On the other hand, we may get away immediately, in which case I will be there by the time you receive this. One of our escorting officers is returning to Sydney and I am giving him this letter to post there for me. Our trip so far has been absent of anything unusual and there have not even been any rumours ... Appetites are very light these days and my diet consists mostly of fruit, salads, ice cream and lime juice. The ship has an excellent refrigeration plant and summer food is available and fresh.'

Two days later, Frederick wrote in another letter, 'We are now only a few days from our destination and the weather is treating us more kindly. I think that by tomorrow we will be wearing blue uniforms once more and there will be very few who will not be pleased to get into blue again ... It seems a long time already since I had news of home but I must wait until I arrive in England and believe me, that is the only reason I am anxious to get there as quickly as possible.'

On arrival in Vancouver, Frederick and his fellow flying officers bound for Britain boarded a train which took them across the country in five days to a Canadian Air Force base in Halifax, Nova Scotia, from where Frederick wrote, 'I have no idea how long I will be staying at Halifax and even if I had the knowledge, I could not pass it on. However, we will be here for a few days at least because of the fact that we are quarantined for mumps and measles. I hope that I have had mumps before, because it seems to be very infectious and not too pleasant. Our trip across Canada was most interesting, although five and a half days is too long a train journey for my liking. The contrast between the Rockies and prairies broke up the journey somewhat and our frequent stops for an hour's walkabout relieved the monotony. During the trip I must have read every Canadian and US magazine from the *Reader's Digest* to the *Saturday Evening Post.*'

It was not until early September that Frederick received news about his trip across the Atlantic to Britain, writing on 7 September, 'Our party is being broken up for the Atlantic crossing so once again I am being separated from my friends ... In contrast to our trip so far the meals at this station are the worst ever and the boys just can't eat them ... An RAF officer stationed here advised me to take over as much tea, sugar, razor-blades and cigarettes as possible so I am packing my trunk with same. Fortunately I was able to purchase cigarettes in bulk on the *Awatea* and I already have two thousand in my kit.'

A few days later, Frederick Keck was on the last stage of his long trip to Britain. In a long letter home he wrote:

> Well, here I am at sea again and on the last stage of my journey. I am travelling in a much different style from that of the previous sea voyage. This time it is a merchant vessel, which is part of a large and very slow convoy. There are only six Air Force officers on board. Three Australians, one Canadian and two new Zealanders and a crew of less than fifty men make up a very much smaller community than in the other ship which was a passenger vessel of more than twice the size of this. We are very cramped for room, having only very small cabins for two men each and a dining room about the size of yours at home, to live in. The decks are of steel and very low. As the weather is continuously rough we are unable to even walk the short deck for exercise.

The tucker is plain but very wholesome and there is plenty of it. The ship's officers and crew are all English and good blokes. The numerous accents with which they speak is amazing, there are hardly two alike. The only entertainment on board is playing cards and reading. I have been playing bridge with the Captain most nights and have enjoyed the game very much. There are not many books on board ... We are all letting our beards grow while travelling. As well as being a protection from the cold, the lack of hot water is enough to dishearten the most soft-bearded amongst us ... Hot water is obtainable every few days to have a bath. There is no shower and our method of bathing is as follows: Obtain one bucket of hot water from the steward, if you can find him and he is willing to get it for you. Then stand in the bath and try and sponge yourself with one hand while hanging on to a rail with the other. The ship has not stopped rolling since we left port and our antics in the bath are worthy of Charlie Chaplin at his best ... My journey is taking much longer to complete than I expected ... The desire to travel is pretty strong in most people of my age I suppose but after this taste of it I will be quite content to remain put for as long as I am allowed.

At last the voyage was nearing an end when Frederick wrote, 'I am finishing this on the last evening at sea. So far the trip has been uneventful and we can thank our rough weather for that. Not once have we seen blue sky in the daytime or stars at night as the sky has been overcast all the time. This will be posted in England,' but before it was posted he added a final note, 'Am here at last. Bournemouth, a beautiful town.'

Having finally reached England, Frederick was keen to meet up with his older brother Kingwell, but he arrived at his new station just a day after his brother had left for the Middle East. Sadly the two brothers would never meet again, nor would they return home. Kingwell was killed on 31 March 1942, and just ten days later, on 10 April, Frederick also lost his life. Fortunately for their parents, their four brothers who also served in the war all returned safely to Australia.

Another American liner to carry Australian airmen overseas was the *Mount Vernon*, built in 1933 as the *Washington* for United States Line. She had remained in passenger service until June 1941, when she was converted into a troop transport, and renamed. Among those to board her in Sydney in December 1941 was Peter Balderston, who recalled, 'The Japs were in the war when we sailed. We embarked in a ship called the *Mount Vernon* — an American boat — to Wellington, then straight to San Francisco. There were four to a cabin —

comparatively comfortable. The food was good. Before we left Sydney Harbour they opened an ice-cream bar and you could buy a container of ice cream — about a litre — for five cents US — all flavours. I remember I bought one and couldn't finish it so I chucked it overboard.'

On arrival in San Francisco, the airmen were immediately put on a train that took them across America to New York, where they were billeted at Fort Hamilton, in Brooklyn, until it was time to join a ship to Britain. As Peter remembered, 'We went to England on the *Mataroa*. It was a cargo ship of about 8,000 tons. We were in cabins but down in the hold there were British Guianeans who were Negroes. It was a refrigerated ship and all they had done was put planks over the oranges or whatever else they were carrying. The black people were a Forestry unit going to Northern Ireland. They slept in hammocks over the oranges. We played five hundred in our cabin from morning to night, and I've never played a game of five hundred since.'

As usual, the *Mataroa* joined a convoy for the dangerous trip across the North Atlantic, Peter stating, 'There must have been fifty ships in our convoy and we lost thirteen on the way over. It took us seventeen days to cross the Atlantic. The route went right up practically to Iceland and Greenland and it was mid-winter — December. We had PT up on deck every morning. We were so cold we wore just about all our clothes. I had so much on I couldn't do up my double-breasted overcoat — I had to tie it up with string. We were given icepicks and used to go round chipping ice off the superstructure. We were also drafted as lookouts for aeroplanes but our aircraft knowledge was primitive and we wouldn't have known a hostile aircraft if we had seen one.'

Meanwhile, back in Sydney, on 13 December 1941 another contingent of Empire airmen had been scheduled to board the *Mariposa* for the journey to San Francisco, and on to Canada and Britain. The group had completed their training, taken their departure leave, and gathered at the Bradfield Park Embarkation Depot, from where they were taken by bus to the wharf in the morning. After boarding the ship they were shown to their cabins, had lunch, and waited for the three o'clock departure. Half an hour before that time, the airmen were ordered to muster on deck with their complete kit, and once they were gathered they were marched down the gangplank and stood on the wharf, from where they watched *Mariposa* depart without them.

They had not been given any explanation for this sudden turn of events, and all were bewildered, and very disappointed. However, since the entry of Japan into the war a week before, the idea of continuing to send Australian military personnel overseas had been revised, and the airmen instead found themselves dispersed to airfields around Australia. However, the transfer of Australian airmen overseas subsequently resumed.

In June 1942 Alby Silverstone found himself on the way from Brisbane to America, and on to Britain, aboard the *Tasker H. Bliss*. This vessel had carried some 5000 American troops to Brisbane, and which he described as 'said to be of 1921 vintage and was fairly aged as passenger ships go. It was now considerably changed to meet troopship conditions.' *Tasker H. Bliss* was one of a class of sixteen identical vessels built for the United States Shipping Board between 1919 and 1922, then allocated to various America shipping lines. Completed in 1921 and originally named *Golden State*, then renamed *President Cleveland* in 1922, this vessel had been operated by the Dollar Line, which was renamed American President Line in 1938. As built, the vessel carried 260 first-class and 300 third-class passengers, but after being taken over by the United States government in June 1941, and renamed *Tasker H. Bliss*, she was refitted as a troop transport.

'There were no longer cabins available for Australian airmen,' Alby Silverstone recalled, 'only troop arrangements. Despite the fact that our 200 airmen and a handful of US troops (mostly wounded) were the only servicemen on board the ship, the cabins were left empty. Initially we were deposited in four-tiered bunks situated in the forward hold and accessed by twenty-foot steel ladders. Later, as we went through the tropics, the heat of the holds became unbearable and we were allowed to move to deck areas. After leaving Sandgate on 16 June we sailed out into Moreton Bay and were escorted into the Pacific for the first 200 miles by a destroyer.' This was due to the presence of Japanese submarines in Australian waters at that time. 'After that we were on our own. The first few days went smoothly except for the cramped sleeping conditions. But, as the bunks were only for sleeping, the conditions were somewhat tempered by the fact that we had the complete run of the ship — particularly as there were less than 300 troops on board compared with some 5000 on the outward trip.'

About a week into the voyage, Alby Silverstone fell ill, being hospitalised with a slight fever for five days. During this period, 'the ship ran into a violent Pacific storm. It raged for about three days during which the ship tossed and pitched rather badly. On the last day of the storm the nursing sister decided I should have a dose of Epsom salts. It went down and came straight back up again and that started my stomach on a bout of seasickness. I was discharged from Sick Bay that same afternoon and then went through the worst week of my life. The storm slowly subsided and we ran into calmer waters but my seasickness continued. It was pure agony and for days I just laid in a heap. I didn't care if the ship floated or sank. I couldn't eat and even the smell of food sent me hurrying to the ship's rail. For five days I existed on dry biscuits from the ship's PX store [canteen] and after a week of nice calm weather was at last able to look at food.'

By now, the weather was getting warmer as the ship travelled further north, and 'we were moved from the hold to bunks on the promenade deck.' When the ship crossed the equator, 'a special ceremony was laid on for "crossing the line" complete with King Neptune and his retainers. I even received a certificate to commemorate this, per medium of the ship's Gestetner. Church was held each Sunday, conducted by the ship's chaplain, and many of the ship's officers gave talks on topical subjects ... We even had a concert or two organised by our own people who had formed an entertainment group.'

It was a slow crossing of the Pacific, as 'we were into our fourth week before we saw sign of land ... Firstly we came to the twin cities of Balboa and Panama City and then passed through the Canal and into Cristobal Harbour. There we docked for several days while the ship awaited further orders.' However, there was one hitch, as when the OIC Troops on the ship requested further orders from Washington for landing his contingent of Australian airmen, the reply was, 'What Australian airmen?'

Eventually the ship left Cristobal, and moved into the Caribbean, 'as part of a huge six-knot convoy with escort from destroyers and Catalina flying boats. It took a further three weeks to reach our port of disembarkation after calling at Guatemala, Cuba, Key West and finally Norfolk, Virginia. The journey was not without incident and several submarine attacks were turned away by our escorts although not without the loss of two small freighters. In all, our journey from Brisbane to Norfolk had taken almost eight weeks. At Norfolk we boarded a train which transported us north to Lachine, Montreal.'

Another airman to undergo the horrors of seasickness for a lengthy period on his journey overseas, this time directly to Britain, was Ross Pearson. 'We sailed from Port Adelaide — much to our surprise. We had entrained in Sydney, spent three days in Melbourne and then

The cargo liner *Denbighshire* carried some trainee airmen to Britain.

travelled on to Adelaide. We presumed we were bound for Darwin. Our surprise was heightened by the nature and type of ship. She was a small vessel with limited passenger accommodation, and could barely be seen above the wharf at Port Adelaide.' Actually this was something of an exaggeration, as the vessel he was joining, *Denbighshire*, was a 9000 gross ton cargo ship, built in 1939 for the Glen Line.

'The *Denbighshire* ... had carried a load of meat in the hold which was now to accommodate a cargo of airmen. The hold smelt heavily of the former cargo. It was heavily blacked-out — which prevented air getting to those travelling below. We sailed out from Port Adelaide and headed south. I was to create an unenviable record. From Australia to the United Kingdom I was continually seasick. While others prayed for Deliverance, I prayed for the ship to sink to put me out of my suffering. Each day I took my place at the rail and each day I dutifully delivered what little I had eaten to the deep. I am sure that all that kept me alive was the oranges provided by my friends who gave their ration to me.'

Some of the airmen, after crossing the Pacific by ship to either San Francisco or Vancouver, and then train to New York, found themselves crossing the Atlantic in some of the same huge ships that had previously transported Australian troops to the Middle East, Britain and Singapore. Gerry Judd recalled, 'We were supposed to go to New York and on to the *Queen Mary* ... We were stationed in a little American camp just outside Worcester in Massachusetts, which is a really pretty place. Everyone wined and dined us. Then we boarded the *Queen Mary*.

There were about 14,000 American soldiers on board and about 250 airmen. They gave you tickets for your meals and you had to be there dead on time. If you didn't get there you missed out. It was a shuttle service which began at 6 am and didn't finish until nine o'clock at night. You had to have a blue, red or yellow ticket and be in the queue at the nominated time. A friend of mine, Harry Taylor, found out there was a dumb waiter going from one deck down into the dining room which used to be the first-class dining area. The dumb waiter was just big enough to take one person if he folded himself up ... So we'd go along any old time, Harry would press the button, the dumb waiter would come up and I'd get in and go down and Harry would do likewise. We did this the whole way and avoided the queues. We travelled across to Greenock in Scotland.'

Meals were also a major topic of interest for Harry Brabin, who travelled across the Atlantic on the *Queen Elizabeth*. 'It was jampacked with troops so no exercise on deck was possible. Crap, crown and anchor, poker and other gambling games were being played everywhere. We had only two meals each day. The food was placed at the head of the tables and those closest served themselves and passed the dishes on, so that those sitting near the bulkheads were sometimes left hungry. "Chow hounds" was the name given to soldiers who used extra plates and pannikins.' With regard to the accommodation, 'four of us slept in four-decker bunks in a storeroom below the waterline. There was nowhere to put kitbags except at the foot of each bunk. For the first time in my life I was glad to be short as the tall men really had great difficulty sleeping.'

Once the Australian airmen reached Britain, they were sent to various squadrons of the Royal Air Force, some flying fighters but most being included in Bomber Command. However, some found themselves setting off by ship again for bases in foreign lands, including Egypt and Malta. Walter Mould was one of the Australian airmen sent to Malta, who recalled he 'left Gourock on the Clyde in June 1941 on board the Irish Sea mail steamer *Leinster* — chock-a-block with RAF and Army personnel. We proceeded in convoy out into the Atlantic, it seemed half way to Canada, then south, then east to Gibraltar. I cannot remember how long it took, probably five or six days ... I remember the unfinished *Pasteur* was, by far, the largest ship in the convoy ... This journey was without incident — but incidents came very soon after leaving Gibraltar.'

The convoy to Malta in which *Leinster* was included, but not the

Pasteur, was escorted by an aircraft carrier, the battleship *Nelson*, several cruisers and destroyers. They set off from Algeciras Bay and

> I, as did many, slept in a reception area with lifebelt close by. It was hot below deck but we were not there for long. I was awakened by the ship coming to a sudden stop. I thought we had either hit a mine or been torpedoed. It soon became apparent that neither had happened ... The ship was jammed fast on rocks ... we were in Spanish territory. In the late afternoon or early evening of the day before, the ship's officers had held a birthday party for the navigator resulting in him getting us about 40 degrees off course. We were told to collect essentials and take up boat stations ... We could see, in the half-light of dawn, the cliffs a little way off ... To seaward, a British destroyer was heading towards us with its guns trained on the cliffs. It came right into Spanish territorial waters. We could see Gibraltar on the other side of the bay ... By chance I was allocated to the powerful lifeboat on the starboard side ... Our boat was to tow other boats across the bay — aided by their rowing ... We arrived at Gib, were put aboard the *Pasteur*, and were given some breakfast. The *Leinster* was towed off by two destroyers.
>
> We stayed in *Pasteur* for a few days and had a look around Gib ... Then we were off to Malta, this time in the cruiser *Hermione*. In the meantime the convoy had been severely mauled. At least one merchantman had been sunk together with one cruiser and one destroyer. The *Nelson* had been torpedoed ... We may have been very lucky. On the journey to Malta we had three cruisers in line astern and were flanked by a Lightning-class destroyer on one side and the Dutch destroyer *Von Tromp* on the other. The voyage lasted two nights and a day ... During our short voyage we slept where we could. If a hammock was empty we took it. When the sailor came off watch we were tipped out. During the single day of the trip we walked around the deck and gazed at the North African coast around Algiers. We even walked on the quarter deck, which was normally only for officers. We ate well — better than on a troopship or generally in the RN. Hurricanes escorted us from some way out of Malta. An attack by E-boats or Ju 88s had been expected but none turned up so we serenely sailed unmolested into Grand Harbour
>
> We arrived off Malta early on the second day — about 10 am. At dawn that morning the captain's voice had come over the intercom: 'Stand by for ... ' Next moment the cruiser seemed to stop in its tracks — a jarring impact. It had rammed a submarine which had apparently been caught on the surface ... Some of us rushed up on deck at the impact but could only see the coming dawn. The captain explained briefly what had happened ... I don't know whether the sub survived.

For those airmen sent to Rhodesia to complete their training, there was the hazardous journey to be undertaken from Cape Town to Britain, through waters infested with German and Italian submarines as well as German surface raiders, all keen to attack any Allied shipping they could find. A particularly popular hunting area was the route between Cape Town and Freetown, where ships were sunk with alarming regularity.

Geoff Coombes was in a draft of airmen transported from Australia to Egypt on the *Queen Elizabeth* in convoy US13, then put on another vessel that took them to Durban, from where they were taken by train to Bulawayo in Rhodesia, for pilot training. 'As only pilots were trained in Rhodesia,' recalled Coombes, 'everyone was keen to succeed, as, if anyone was scrubbed, he was returned to Australia for remustering.' Geoff Coombes was awarded his wings, and with others who passed the training, was sent at the end of September 1942 to Cape Town, where they embarked on the former Orient liner *Oronsay*, which departed on 2 October.

As Geoff recalls it, 'Being a fast ship we were not in convoy. When sailing due north from Cape Town the weather was very hot so some of us went on deck to sleep, and, as it happened, this probably saved our lives. After seven days out the ship was torpedoed at dawn. We were slammed by two torpedoes which put an end to our little cruise. They couldn't get the lifeboats down on one side. Luckily for me it wasn't where my boat station was and we finally evacuated the ship ... It didn't go down very quickly but the two torpedoes put the whole explosion into the engine rooms. She listed badly. Not long after we got our lifeboat down they slammed two more torpedoes into her and that made her go down fast. I didn't see the submarine. Some of the other fellows did in other boats. They said she asked what ship it was.' The assailant was the Italian submarine *Archimede*, and the sinking cost the lives of five men, but all others managed to get away in lifeboats. The sinking occurred about 600 miles off the Africa coast, just south of the equator.

Having survived the sinking, the survivors were still in serious trouble, waiting for rescue. 'We had two groups, each of six lifeboats,' recalled Geoff, 'and each group towed by a motor launch. The weather was beautiful. At that stage there was hardly a ripple ... Our launch started off for the African coast. The other had a bit of trouble starting and we were a couple of miles away when our launch broke down. Then the survivors on the other launch started their engine and their group passed us and disappeared over the horizon. They got picked up after a couple of days but their group had split up and some didn't get picked up until the eighth, tenth and twelfth days.'

As for his own group, 'We kept together till the morning of the eighth day and we decided we were hindering one another so we split up to make it on our own. Our lifeboats had some crew members in them and some survivors from other torpedoed boats ... There were not many RAAF fellows. There were nineteen in our boat ... Morale was good — we reckoned we could make it. We reckoned we'd rationed the water out well and we were moving in the right direction. On the eighth day we had covered about 320 miles. Happily, we were then spotted by a Sunderland who sent a message that a destroyer would pick us up in four or five hours. They were a long five hours. The destroyer was the *Brilliant*. The first indicator that the destroyer was coming up was the light on the horizon ... We had hand-held red flares going ... Suddenly a searchlight came on behind us. The destroyer had come round behind us. They said, "Come on up the scramble nets." We were the first boat there. We went into Freetown and arrived there in the evening. They took us in a landing craft straight on to a ship to England. It was the *Nea Hellas* — a bloody awful old ship — survivors of fifteen ships on board.'

The *Nea Hellas* was then under the Greek flag, but had been built in 1922 for the Anchor Line as *Tuscania*, operating a service between Glasgow and New York, providing accommodation for 240 first-class, 377 second-class and 1818 third-class passengers. During the 1930s the liner spent some time laid up, and was also used for occasional cruises, then sold in April 1939 to the Greek Line. Now operating under Allied control, she had been refitted for service as a troop transport in 1941. Among those on board the *Nea Hellas* when Geoff Coombes boarded was another draft of Australian airmen who had also completed their pilot training in Rhodesia, and were on their way to England.

One of these pilots was John May, who kept a diary while on the *Nea Hellas*, which departed Cape Town a few days after *Oronsay*. On 9 October 1942, John May wrote, 'Today has been a day of great panic. Last night, over the radio, they heard that five boats had been sunk, one only seventy miles ahead of us, including the *Oronsay* which was next to us at Cape Town with 6,000 troops aboard ... The Captain spoke over the wireless to all. "We're in very dangerous waters ... all to sleep fully clothed ... have a 'panic' bag packed ... carry lifebelt ... keep sharp lookout." The Germans are using Dakar, 200 miles away,

The Orient liner *Oronsay* was sunk when carrying Australian airmen to Britain.

as a base and are watching Freetown like terriers ... crew all frightened ... stokers up inspecting smoke ... Between eight and nine tonight we're supposed to be looking out for survivors from *Oronsay*.' However, the danger they were in was graphically brought home to them. 'Three torpedoes fired at us. One went past stern and blew up some distance off — two more were time torpedoes and blew up too soon. Close enough to shake the ship! We were lucky!'

Two days later, John May noted, 'We're the only ship out of nine from Cape Town to reach Freetown.' Next day: 'Survivors keep coming aboard in those invasion barges — women and kids, some toddlers — and people from Argentina coming to join us in the cabins. A diver has discovered dents in the hull.' On 17 October, John May recorded he 'Saw barge pull alongside with survivors ... five more boatloads still adrift — eight days in open boat.' Among those in that barge was Geoff Coombes, who remembered about the rest of his journey, 'We had an escort of destroyers all the way to England.' Regarding the *Nea Hellas* he wrote, 'The British Admiralty had, I think, condemned it and sold it to the Greeks who had made a sort of cruise liner out of it. Just a boat. Got to England on it anyway.' Despite these caustic comments, *Nea Hellas* not only survived the war, she returned to the North Atlantic trade, was renamed *New York* in 1955, and lasted until 1961, when she went to the breakers' yard. Sadly, John May did not survive the war, being killed in action in December 1943.

The number of Australian airmen being sent to Europe decreased after the entry of Japan into the war, as fliers were desperately needed to assist the Allied ground forces in the islands north of Australia. However, some pilots still went to Britain, among them David Scholes, who departed

Sydney on board *Mount Vernon* on 26 May 1943. He kept a diary from that day, the first note being, 'We leave Sydney Harbour — more than that we leave Australia! The bridge looks greater and more magnificent than ever before. We have an Australian destroyer with us. What for? Don't we all know. A few of us stand at the stern of the ship. I take in everything I see. We pass out through the Heads, the destroyer out ahead. We all seem very silent now, except for an odd wisecrack. I suppose everyone is thinking more or less the same as I am. There is that faint haunting feeling now ... We are still silent, and Australia slowly grows smaller, rapidly becomes more dear to me. It disappears below the green watery horizon. "There she goes fellas"!'

Mount Vernon went first to Auckland, where Scholes managed to get ashore, but, 'Unfortunately it is Sunday and we cannot buy anything.' Departing the next day, the vessel headed north, but the weather was causing an uncomfortable sea. On 3 June, David Scholes wrote, 'Can now almost propel myself in the desired direction in nearly a straight line, perhaps I am gaining my "sea legs"! I do not eat much, in any case the "chow" as the Yanks, who run this apology for a ship, call it is not exactly like Australian food. When it comes to putting jam on bacon and syrup on meats etc, things are a little strange in my opinion. I live by stealing sufficient grapefruit, oranges, apples, biscuits and dry food, and buying at the ship's canteen drinks such as Coca Cola and Pepsi Cola. Have no idea where we are ... however we're still floating.'

The morning of 6 June they crossed the equator, 'and it is extremely hot, although out on deck it is nice and cool with the breeze. We flop about the deck sunbathing and sleeping. The officers go through the 'Neptune' ceremony, a tradition of the Navy, in the form of an initiation.' So the voyage continued, but 'as we find our quarters a bit warm for sleeping we carry all our junk up on deck and camp the night there. I find it wonderful to go to sleep under the stars, until (usually about 2.30 am) rain becomes evident.'

On Friday, 11 June, *Mount Vernon* entered San Francisco Bay. 'It is quite foggy and we cannot see the Golden Gate of San Francisco until we are almost under it. Sure is a noble lump of engineering, but I am not as struck as I thought I would be — most amusing the Golden Gate being painted a dirty red ... At length we dock and we are greatly disappointed because we cannot leave the ship — seeing land again after some time at sea is really something to me now. We gaze at 'Frisco' until it is dark and turn in — what a hell of a long way I am from home!'

Next day the airmen disembarked, only to find that 'part of our baggage that was put in the hold has been ripped open and anything of value at all, especially cameras, new shoes and clothes etc., has been taken. It is too late to do anything about it.' Once ashore, the Australians were put on to a train, and began the long journey to the east coast. It is not until the evening of 16 June that the group arrives in New York, but the train goes on, eventually arriving soon after midnight at an army siding near Taunton, in Massachusetts. 'We are all a bit weary,' Scholes wrote, 'and are not too proud to go straight to bed in very decent quarters.'

Next day the men find out where they are. 'This is Camp Miles Standish. It is an embarkation depot for American forces, and there are thousands of them about — I can see we shall be happy. Providence and Boston are not far away.' Over the next two weeks, the airmen are able to tour the area, and spend several days in New York, but then, on 30 June, 'our train for New York leaves the siding at about 5 pm and most of the trip is in darkness. We have a slap up tea on the train. About midnight we get off the train and are ferried round to *Queen Elizabeth*, on which I had a fair idea we would sail, for I had seen her in dock with *Queen Mary*, *Aquitania* and others, whilst in New York … Just before we board, American Red Cross women come amongst us with doughnuts, lemon drink and chocolates. They are greatly appreciated — I shall never forget them, smiling, cheery and greyclad laughing and talking — it is about 2.15 am. Once aboard and settled in, I go to bed and die!'

With the coming of daylight, it was time to go on deck, where David Scholes discovered, 'We have left New York Harbour some time in the early hours of the morning and are out at sea … She is an immense ship and goes like hell … I am sure that I shall lose myself before long — the most beautiful ship I've ever seen … Feel fine, there is hardly a move out of Lizzie and the Atlantic is very calm although the weather is crook. We steer a zig-zag course.' The days at sea pass quickly but it is not until the fourth day out that Scholes records he has 'Just found out that beer is available on board, but I cannot for the life of me navigate myself to where it is, no matter how good the instructions may be.'

Next day, Monday 5 July, 'Met at sea by two long-range Spitfires (from a carrier no doubt), a Liberator and a Sunderland. Some time during the night it is known we successfully avoided several U-boats. Some of the chaps who were awake felt acute turns and course alterations, also the increased speed, and "action stations" alert. The anti-sub apparatus they have, I am told, is amazing. They can pick up even a wooden floating box on the surface at unbelievable range.' On

6 July, 'we sight the northern coast of Ireland and I believe parts of Scotland. There is great excitement ... In the Firth of Clyde I see the aircraft carrier *Illustrious* which has seen so much action in the Mediterranean theatre ... At length we drop anchor some hundred yards from shore off Gourock. We are told where each of us is going ... I am Brighton bound, on the south coast somewhere.' However, it is not until 8 pm the following day that David Scholes disembarks, lands in Scotland, and is immediately put on board a train that will carry him to his destination. He joins Bomber Command, and is one of the fortunate ones to survive his rotation of operational flights and eventually return safely to Australia.

Fifty-five years after the war ended, the remains of one of the airmen who went from New Zealand to fight in Europe and did not return were finally laid to rest, far away from his native land. Arthur Round was just 23 when he left Wellington by ship in late 1939, bound for Canada to complete his training prior to joining the RAF. On his arrival in Britain he joined 98 Squadron, which flew outdated Fairey Battle bombers. In 1940, the squadron was sent to France, but in August 1940, as France was about to capitulate to the Germans, the squadron was recalled to Britain.

28 Squadron was then sent to Iceland to provide anti-invasion cover, arriving on 27 August at their new home base, Kaldadarnes, near Reykjavik. Arthur Round was a good pilot, and entertained the local inhabitants with displays of acrobatics from time to time, between patrols. In May 1941, Arthur Round and a British officer were detailed to fly to the north coast of Iceland, and collect two other fliers, who had been involved in a road accident and were recuperating in a hospital ship anchored off Akureyri. Round collected the two men, and took off on the return trip to Kaldadarnes. The plane soon ran into heavy cloud, and crashed into a glacier in a remote mountain region. A week later a rescue party, accompanied by an Anglican and a Roman Catholic priest, climbed to the crash site, found the four bodies, and held a brief service. However, they were unable to retrieve the bodies, being forced to leave the area by deteriorating weather.

The wreck site was soon covered by snow and ice, and after the British forces departed Iceland, the exact location of the wreck was lost. In 1980, an Icelandic historian heard stories about the crash, and decided to locate the wreck, but despite many trips to the area, was unsuccessful. By chance, a friend doing research in the Public Record Office in London came across the search party report, which included an accurate location. In 1999, Iceland enjoyed its warmest summer for 30 years, which uncovered the wreck of the crashed aircraft. A group found the site, and the remains of the four airmen, but they were unable to retrieve the bodies at that time.

In the summer of 2000, the RAF mounted an expedition to recover the remains and remove them to Reykjavik, which was done in early August. The RAF also was able to contact relatives of the four men, who were invited to attend a military funeral held at the British war cemetery at Reykjavik on 27 August 2000, 60 years to the day since 28 Squadron arrived in Iceland. Arthur Round was only 26 when he was killed. His two younger brothers also went through the Empire Air Scheme and joined the RAF. One brother, Heathcote, was killed in 1944, at the age of 25, when his bomber was shot down. As a result, the third brother, Ron, was taken off active duty with the RAF.

The following chart indicates the number of Australians and New Zealanders trained to join the Royal Air Force under the Empire Air Training Scheme.

	Pilots	*Navigators*	*Air Gunners*	*Others*
Total Australians	15,465	9,861	13,534	
No. Trained in Canada	4,069	2,399	3,100	
No. Trained in Rhodesia	514	51		
Total New Zealand	2,200	1,553	443	2,754

14 Darwin and the Pacific Islands

The concern of the Australian government regarding the protection of the vulnerable northern regions of the country, and areas to the north, particularly Papua and the mandated Territory of New Guinea, had been expressed in the early days of the war, and had not diminished over succeeding months.

Even prior to the war, the vulnerability of Darwin had been a matter of concern, and late in 1938 the Australian government had given approval for an army contingent to be formed and sent there. The unit, to be known as the Darwin Mobile Force, consisted of 245 men, most of them volunteers from the militia, who came together at Liverpool Camp, south of Sydney, early in 1939 for training. On 9 March 1939 the unit paraded through the streets of Sydney, following which an advance party of nineteen men embarked on the Burns Philp liner *Marella*. On 15 March, the main body of the Darwin Mobile Force boarded another Burns Philp vessel, *Montoro*, which arrived on 28 March. The Darwin Mobile Force became the garrison in Darwin, and remained so after the outbreak of war in Europe in September 1939.

As recorded earlier, the Australian government had initially not sanctioned the dispatch of troops overseas until assurances were received from the British government regarding their intentions in the event of Japan entering the war. Even when troops were sent to the Middle East and Europe, the Australian government was gravely concerned about the safety of the northern areas of Australia, and the regions immediately to the north of them, should Japan come into the war. In the latter half of 1940 it was decided that forces should be

Zealandia was requisitioned for war service in June 1940.

built up in three areas — Darwin, Thursday Island and Papua New Guinea — which would necessitate the transfer of about 1400 military personnel and their equipment. In line with this decision, on 1 August 1940 Papua and the Mandated Territory of New Guinea was designated a new Australian military district.

In order to provide transport for these troop movements, the Department of the Navy decided that it would be necessary to requisition one vessel on a permanent basis, to be joined by other ships on a temporary basis when required. The vessel selected to be requisitioned permanently was *Zealandia*, built in 1910 for Huddart Parker Limited, which had also served as a troopship in the North Atlantic during the latter part of World War I. *Zealandia* was operating on the Australian coastal trade between Sydney and Hobart when taken over by the Department of the Navy on 21 June 1940, being designated a hired transport, number KZ6. The vessel was refitted to transport 900 troops by the Cockatoo Docks and Engineering Company in Sydney between 21 and 30 June. Apart from troop quarters being installed in the original accommodation areas, nos 2 and 4 holds were converted into mess decks, a section of the promenade deck enclosed, additional galley equipment fitted, as well as paravanes for mine protection, and a 4-inch gun.

For its first voyage as a troop transport, *Zealandia* was scheduled to carry a contingent from Sydney to Darwin. At the same time the AUSN coastal liner *Orungal* was also requisitioned in Sydney on 25 June on a temporary basis, to carry troops to New Guinea. Early on the afternoon of 29 June, four officers and 149 other ranks of 54 Anti-Aircraft Search Light Company arrived in Sydney by train from Melbourne, and were immediately transported to Darling Harbour, where they boarded *Orungal*. Meanwhile, 1 Anti-Aircraft Regiment had boarded *Zealandia*,

The AUSN coastal liner *Orungal*.

and at 4 pm on Saturday, 29 June, the two ships departed Sydney together.

During the first two days at sea, the troops were kept busy with physical exercise sessions and some rifle drill. On *Orungal* they were also given lectures, including one on the morning of 1 July by the medical officer, Lieutenant Colonel Cooper, on venereal diseases. Later the same day, the two ships docked at the Pinkenba Wharf, near the mouth of the Brisbane River. Here, *Zealandia* took on board the 2/15 Infantry Battalion, which was destined for Darwin, while *Orungal* boarded infantry reinforcements for Port Moresby. After a stay of just a few hours, the ships continued their voyage, *Zealandia* carrying 890 troops and 728 tons of stores, while *Orungal* carried 500 troops and their equipment.

Passing up the Queensland coast the two ships stayed together, but as they neared the tip of Cape York, *Zealandia* turned west for Darwin while *Orungal* headed for Port Moresby. Among those on board *Orungal* was Sergeant Jack Elton, who recalled that the ship 'was making its first voyage after being converted to a troopship. As I remember only the dining room had been converted to a mess, the cabins had bunks installed, I think six to a cabin. We enjoyed a leisurely trip via Port Moresby to Darwin.' However, Frank Pearson also recalled that, among the troops, 'a large percentage had Rubella. The RAP Corporal did a magnificent job with the sick.'

Orungal arrived in Port Moresby on 7 July, where the infantry reinforcements disembarked, and the same afternoon the ship departed. With a brief stop at Thursday Island en route, *Orungal* arrived in Darwin on 11 July. *Zealandia* had arrived in Darwin the previous day, and her troops went ashore to be entrained in cattle trucks which took them to the camp at 11 Mile. Both ships then returned to Sydney, and *Orungal* went back to commercial service after this one trip. *Zealandia* continued operating between Sydney and Darwin, her next voyage departing Sydney on 3 September. *Zealandia* took on board two companies of the 2/15 Battalion in Darwin, leaving there on 20 September, and bringing them to Sydney. The next voyage by *Zealandia* departed on 10 October, and on both these trips north road-making equipment and construction workers were carried in addition to troops and military stores.

On 22 November 1940, 72 men of the 1st Anti-Aircraft Searchlight Cadre arrived in Sydney by train from Melbourne, and were taken in trucks to Darling Harbour, where they embarked on *Zealandia*. Already on board were 183 men of the recently formed Australian Tropical Force, and the 14th Heavy Anti-Aircraft Battery, among them Jack Mulholland. As he later wrote, 'Sleeping quarters were allotted and I was assigned a bunk in a cabin with three other chaps. The cabin was hot, airless and I suppose could be described as sterile. Originally it would have provided rather cramped accommodation for two steerage fares. With all our gear there wasn't much elbow room and four of us trying to get dressed or clean our rifles and gear at the same time was a problem.'

On the afternoon of 22 November *Zealandia* departed Sydney, passing the anchored *Queen Mary* as she steamed out of the harbour. Once through the Heads, *Zealandia*, escorted by the cruiser HMAS *Adelaide*, turned south, keeping to a passage that had been cleared by minesweepers. Once the pair had disappeared over the horizon, they turned north, commencing what would be a lively voyage.

Jack Mulholland recalled, 'Boat drill was carried out at odd times for the first few days to establish a pattern where everyone knew their stations and what would be required of them in case of emergency. On the second day out, the Battery except those hanging in a limp green condition over the deck rail, paraded on deck wearing life jackets. It was not long before some wag in the back row decided to slyly tie together the tapes of the two life jackets in front of him. Others in the back row followed suit. On the order to dismiss, the parade made a right hand turn with the result that the middle rank collapsed in a heap.'

Over the next few days, *Zealandia* headed north, out of sight of land. This gave Jack Mulholland a chance to get to know other members of his unit as well as those from other outfits on board, and he wrote, 'At least ninety per cent of the other ranks were under the age of twenty years, and I think compared to the youth of today we were generally pretty naïve, ingenuous and little travelled. However what we may have lacked in sophistication we made up for with energy and enthusiasm. Our standard of army experience extended from semi-trained to completely untrained. The NCOs were in their early twenties or younger and as with the officers had a lot to learn. That was understandable as their training until then had only been in a part-time capacity.'

After two days at sea, *Zealandia* arrived in Brisbane, and the troops were given leave ashore. The stay in Brisbane was quite short, then the vessel headed north again. As the temperature and humidity increased, so did the discomfort for the troops on board the vessel. A shortage of fresh water meant they had to purchase bottles of soft drink, which usually cost threepence, but they were charged a shilling a bottle.

Many of the troops were allocated shipboard tasks, and Jack Mulholland was most unhappy with his. 'The job I had been chosen for was Mess Orderly. I would perform in the Gunners' Mess which was located in what was formerly the forward cattle hold ... The position of Mess Orderly entailed eight to ten hours a day serving slops, eating slops and mopping up slops. The aptly named Mess was below the waterline so there were no portholes and only a modicum of fresh air. After a while I developed a little sympathy for the cattle that had previously occupied the hold ... The officers were more fortunate in that they had their meals served in one of the ship's dining rooms and were catered for in a more civilised manner.'

However, that was not the only discomfort faced by Jack Mulholland. 'It was great to finish work for the day, have a shower and step out on the deck for a lung full of fresh air and a view of the world. Having a shower at times could be hazardous. The showers were served by sea water which required a special soap to provide any sort of lather. Whatever was added to the soap burnt the tender parts of the body if the soap was not removed quickly. Sometimes the water was cut off without warning, bringing forth cries of anguish from the showering facilities.'

Jack Mulholland recounted one incident that tickled his fancy. 'The sergeants were issued a bottle of beer per man but it was served warm. In one cabin, three sergeants wet a haversack in salt water and hung it out the porthole with their three bottles therein. When it was considered that the beer had cooled sufficiently they pulled in the haversack — sans bottles! Unbeknown to the sergeants, two RAAF chappies had held one of their jockey sized mates over the side of the ship by his ankles while he lifted the sergeants' beer issue.'

By the time the ship arrived at Thursday Island on 2 December, having been at sea for a week, the troops were in a bad mood, complaining about the lack of water and the poor quality of the meals they had been served. All the troops were taken ashore at Thursday Island and it was planned that they would undertake a route march, but some of the men refused to go. They were later fined for this.

Escorted on the final stage of the journey by HMAS *Adelaide*, *Zealandia* departed Thursday Island on 5 December. They arrived in Darwin three days later, anchoring in the harbour at 12.30 pm, and not docking until the next morning. The first troops disembarked that day, but the last were not ashore until 13 December, including Jack Mulholland. He wrote, 'Disembarkation was delayed several days because the 14th Battery had drawn the short straw and won the right to Clean Ship. I don't know what sort of a contract the Army had with the shipping company but it was a bit tough being required to clean the darned ship after having worked my passage, and put up with pretty miserable conditions.' To add insult to injury, Jack Mulholland also noted, 'all those who had travelled on her had their pay books debited one shilling and threepence to pay for damage caused during our voyage. One would have thought such matters would have been included in the fare. It was not our favourite ship and to have to pay three-fifths of a day's pay did not cause joy.'

Meanwhile, soldiers who were due to return to Sydney joined the ship, including 2 Battery of the 1st Anti-Aircraft Regiment, which would later be sent to the Middle East. *Zealandia* departed Darwin at 8 am on 19 December for the voyage back to Sydney, where the ship was drydocked during early January. *Zealandia* then went to Hobart to transport the 2/40 Battalion to Melbourne. From there the vessel returned to Sydney to again board troops, who were taken to Thursday Island and Darwin.

Another area of concern was the Islands of Fiji, and these were to be protected by New Zealand forces. The inter-island ferry *Rangatira*, operated by the Union Steam Ship Company on the prime overnight service between Wellington and Lyttleton, was selected to transport New Zealand troops to Fiji, but was not repainted or altered in any way for these trips. *Rangatira* departed Wellington on 28 October 1940

The New Zealand inter-island ferry *Rangatira* made several trips to Fiji. with a full complement of troops, who were conveyed to Suva. On returning to New Zealand, *Rangatira* went to Auckland, her first visit to that city, to embark more troops to be transported to Fiji. Following this voyage, *Rangatira* returned to Wellington, resuming her ferry operations on 26 November.

During the latter part of 1940, a new force had been raised in Sydney and Brisbane, known as the Darwin Infantry Battalion, and on 6 December 1940 the Sydney contingent marched through the streets of the city and were preparing to move north, but their departure date was constantly delayed. Eventually it was announced the unit would leave Sydney on 20 January 1941 aboard *Zealandia*, but that was postponed due to a strike by the firemen on the ship. As Alex Rigby wrote in his diary, 'On the afternoon of 23 January 1941 at approximately 1500 hours officers were summoned to the Battalion Headquarters and were informed by the CO that there was a big probability of sailing tomorrow afternoon 24 January. Shortly thereafter the phone rang and we were advised by the embarkation officer that definitely the time had been fixed for sailing — tomorrow night — 24 January 1941.'

During that afternoon the troops were taken in buses from their holding area at the Sydney Showground to No. 3 Darling Harbour, and by 5 pm 526 officers and other ranks were on board *Zealandia*, but this also included some 69 troops bound for Thursday Island. Soon *Zealandia* had left the wharf and proceeded down the harbour, again first heading south after leaving the Heads, and not turning north until she was out of sight of the coast. The seas were very rough, and *Zealandia* was pitching and rolling in a most uncomfortable way, which caused most of the troops on board to become seasick. During the voyage north, the troopship was escorted by the armed merchant cruiser *Westralia*, which was owned by the same company as *Zealandia*, Huddart Parker Ltd.

On the afternoon of 25 January, a problem in the engine room forced *Zealandia* to reduce speed to just 7 knots, which in the heavy seas made conditions even worse for the troops on board. Even when the problem was fixed, the ship continued to pitch and roll heavily, and this continued into the next day. Much to the relief of all on board, on the morning of 27 January *Zealandia* entered Moreton Bay, then moved up the Brisbane River to berth at the Hamilton Wharf. The troops on board were granted shore leave, which was greatly appreciated.

Meanwhile, the Queensland contingent of the Darwin Infantry Battalion, who had been billeted in the Exhibition Grounds in Brisbane, were brought to the Hamilton wharf by train during the afternoon, but did not complete embarkation until 0200 on 28 January. Later that morning *Zealandia*, still escorted by *Westralia*, departed Brisbane, now having over 850 troops on board, of whom 804 were from the Darwin Infantry Battalion. This was the first time the full battalion had been together, and on the morning of 29 January, all officers of both contingents were brought together by the commanding officer, but according to Alex Rigby, they were 'very standoffish and quiet. The feeling between the Brisbane and Sydney groups seems to be reserved, you would think we were two separate units.' However, training and sports were organised to fill in the days during the voyage.

As the two ships headed further north, they ran into heavy rain, which lasted through 29 and 30 January, when they passed through the Whitsunday Passage, and into 31 January, as they passed Cairns. That night the ships were advised they were on the edge of a cyclone that had formed further south, and by 2000 hours visibility had been reduced so much it was necessary to anchor in the channel, which weaved through heavily reefed waters. Next morning it was possible to resume the voyage, as the weather seemed to ease a bit during the day, though it was still raining heavily, but there were a few sunny breaks. However, by late afternoon the wind had come up again and *Zealandia* once more was being tossed around in a heavy sea, much to the discomfort of the troops.

On 2 February, *Zealandia* arrived off Thursday Island, but the sea was still quite rough, so, instead of offloading her troops bound for the island into a launch as planned, the ship had to enter the harbour and berth. As soon as possible, *Zealandia* dropped her lines, got away from the wharf and continued her voyage, now heading westward. Once again the weather turned cyclonic, with heavy rain and strong winds blowing straight into the bows of the ship. Over one ten-hour period the ship only managed to steam a distance of 28 miles, into a wind blowing at 75 miles an hour. At times *Zealandia* seemed to be unable to make any headway at all, as the bows would go right under the onrushing waves, shipping tons of water over the foredeck. Even the larger *Westralia* was taking a fearful beating. The heavy seas meant that the arrival time in Darwin would be delayed by at least 36 hours. Below decks, conditions were atrocious, with almost all the troops, and many of the crew, constantly seasick, and no-one able to take a shower or perform even the most rudimentary hygienic functions.

On 3 February, the weather conditions showed some sign of improvement, but the next day there was another tropical storm, in which the rain beat down in solid sheets. It was a very relieved crew and passengers who saw the coast of Arnhem Land rise on the port side on the morning of 5 February, and that afternoon *Zealandia* glided into Darwin Harbour, but as *Westralia* was to refuel first, the troopship had to anchor out overnight. Finally, on the morning of 6 February, after *Westralia* had vacated the berth, *Zealandia* was able to come alongside, and her long-suffering passengers trooped gratefully ashore.

The Darwin Infantry Battalion took over guard duty from the 2/25 Battalion, who were based at Vestey's Meat Works. On 15 February, the 2/25 Battalion embarked on *Zealandia* and were taken back to Brisbane, where they arrived on 24 February, and three days later *Zealandia* was back in Sydney.

Towards the end of 1940, German commerce raiders became active in the Tasman Sea. These converted merchantmen achieved some remarkable successes, both in sinking ships by their own guns and from minefields they laid along the southern coast of Australia. As a result of these events, trans-Tasman convoys were instituted, the first of which, designated Convoy VK1, departed Sydney on 30 December 1940, bound for Auckland. This convoy was composed of only four ships, the passenger liners *Empress of Canada* and *Maunganui* along with the large cargo liners *Empire Star* and *Port Chalmers*, escorted by the cruiser HMS *Achilles*. These convoys comprised ships still engaged in normal commercial trades, and did not involve any troop transports. Trans-Tasman convoys departed at twenty-day intervals, and continued for the rest of the war.

The same German commerce raiders that had threatened shipping in the Tasman Sea also posed a threat to vessels operating out of ports along the eastern seaboard of Australia to Darwin and Papua New

Katoomba was taken over to transport troops to the islands.

Guinea. Early in 1941 it was decided to inaugurate a system of convoys for this route as well, to be designated ZK. *Zealandia* was to be included in the first convoy, along with another coastal liner, *Katoomba*. Built in 1913 for McIlwraith McEacharn Ltd, *Katoomba* had seen active service in World War I, and was requisitioned in Sydney on 8 March 1941 as a hired transport on a temporary basis.

Unlike *Zealandia*, *Katoomba* was not refitted at all for her transport role, the 443 troops she took on board in Sydney being accommodated in cabins as in peacetime. *Katoomba* then went north to Brisbane, where a further 253 troops were taken on board, being accommodated in hammocks or mattresses set up in public rooms, bringing the total number of troops on board to 696. *Zealandia* left Sydney on 8 March and embarked 800 troops in Brisbane, from where the two ships departed on 15 March as convoy ZK1. They were escorted by another converted coastal liner, the armed merchant cruiser *Manoora*, built in 1935 for the Adelaide Steamship Company. The three ships went first to Thursday Island, then on to Port Moresby, returning to Sydney on 3 April.

The same two ships and escort also made up convoy ZK2, which departed Sydney on 12 April. *Katoomba* had on board 687 troops, as well as the 119 Australian General Hospital, and 3500 tons of cargo for Darwin, while *Zealandia* carried 739 troops of Lark Force, bound for Rabaul. The three ships voyaged together to Cairns, where they arrived on 18 April, then the convoy split into two. HMAS *Adelaide* was

The armed merchant cruiser *Manoora* escorted the ZK convoys.

brought in to escort *Zealandia* to Rabaul, where they arrived on 26 April, and the troops disembarked. From Rabaul *Zealandia* and *Adelaide* went to Noumea, where 578 members of the Free French Expeditionary Force were embarked and transported to Sydney, arriving on 9 May.

Meanwhile, *Katoomba*, still escorted by *Manoora*, had continued on to Darwin, where they arrived on the morning of 21 April and immediately berthed, but none of those on board went ashore until the next day. However, the medical staff of the 119 Australian General Hospital was in for a nasty surprise, for, as Sister Meg Stewart recalled, 'Happens we weren't expected, no accommodation was available. The 500 bed hospital we were supposed to go to wasn't built — the land hadn't even been cleared. We were taken to the Quarantine Station some fifteen miles from Darwin. By the time we reached there, we were covered in red dust and, oh, so homesick.'

It had been planned that when *Katoomba* returned to Sydney, it would undertake a voyage to Singapore. However, unloading delays in Darwin resulted in *Katoomba* remaining in port for almost a month, and it was not until 16 May that the vessel departed, carrying 180 evacuees. By that time, *Zealandia* had returned from Noumea, and was then designated to make the voyage to Singapore instead of *Katoomba*, which arrived back in Sydney on 29 May and was handed back to her owners. Meanwhile, *Zealandia* departed Sydney on 19 May

The Burns Philp vessel *Montoro* carried troops to New Guinea and Darwin (*C.T. Reddings collection*)

for Singapore, and after returning to Sydney on 25 June, resumed her voyages to Papua New Guinea.

During July 1941, the Burns Philp vessel *Montoro* was requisitioned on a temporary basis by the Department of the Navy to accompany *Zealandia* on two trips to Port Moresby and Rabaul, and on to Darwin. *Montoro* had been built in 1911 and was due to have been sold for scrap in 1939, only to be reprieved when war broke out. Initially trading from Sydney to Singapore, since 1926 *Montoro* had been used on the service to Papua New Guinea, and since the outbreak of war had also operated to Darwin. She was sent to Brisbane to collect her troops.

Among the troops designated to join *Zealandia* in Sydney were the six officers and 114 other ranks of 'M' Battery Special Force, who were based at Fort Queenscliff in Victoria, and 145 men comprising the 1st Independent Company AIF. On the morning of 11 July, they left Melbourne by train, arriving in Sydney early the next morning. The 1st Independent Company, which had undergone training at Wilsons Promontory, was transported from Central Station to the wharf in double-deck buses. At the time they boarded *Zealandia*, the men understood their destination to be Rabaul. They were joined by various other units, including 7 MD Survey Company, making a total of about 850 men on board *Zealandia*, which left Sydney on 12 July.

Among the officers with the 1st Independent Company was Lex Fraser, who later wrote, 'We then boarded the *Zealandia*, a coal-burner, and that evening passed down the harbour. On board were a party of Civil Construction Corps (CCC) workers destined for Darwin, and some Gunners bound for the battery at Rabaul. The CCC workers were in cabins, but our troops were in the hold in makeshift bunks, and such was the restriction of space, they also had to eat where they slept. This was most unsatisfactory, and the day after we left Sydney this situation was partly relieved by finding a separate eating area.'

According to notes made by Jack Ranken, 'Boat pulled away from wharf at 1205 hours ... troops covering all vantage points on the boat, cheering and singing on way down the harbour ... within an hour we were in the open sea. Some being sick.'

As Lex Fraser recalled, 'When we went through the Heads there was a large swell, and it coincided with the evening meal. In the confined space and situated near the toilets, a great number of troops were ill, and those detailed to mess duty were unable to serve the meal.'

Zealandia was escorted by the armed merchant cruiser, HMAS *Manoora*. Early on the morning of 15 July the two ships arrived in Brisbane, where the troops aboard *Zealandia* were granted a 24-hour shore leave. The following day *Zealandia* and *Manoora* departed, and were joined for the voyage north by *Montoro*, bound for Port Moresby.

Montoro and *Zealandia* carried 1190 troops between them on this trip, which was designated convoy ZK3. As Lex Fraser wrote, '*Montoro* could do about 8 knots and the *Zealandia* was not much faster, but the *Manoora*, much to our delight, occasionally clapped on a burst of speed and circled the convoy with a great show of style. Our ship being a coal-burner, stoking of the boilers was necessary and to relieve the monotony of the trip, a few of us would go down to the boiler room and feed the fires while the crew looked on.'

On 17 July the 1st Independent Company was advised that their orders had been changed and their destination was now Kavieng, on the island of New Ireland. The ships arrived off Port Moresby on 18 July, but while *Montoro* berthed there as planned, *Zealandia* and *Manoora* turned east and voyaged on to Rabaul, anchoring off the town on the morning of 23 July. *Zealandia* stayed there just three hours, then continued unescorted to Kavieng, where she arrived at midday on 24 July. Here the 1st Independent Company left the ship, while the CCC workers on board were allowed a brief shore leave. Early on 24 July, *Zealandia* was on her way again, heading back to Australia, berthing at Bowen in Queensland on 29 July, still with the CCC workers on board.

Over the next two days the CCC workers were again granted shore leave, while an additional 150 troops joined the ship, then before dawn on 1 August *Zealandia* left Bowen, once again headed north. Rounding Cape York, on 3 August she arrived at Thursday Island, where the troops embarked at Bowen went ashore. At midday on 4 August, *Zealandia* left Thursday Island and continued west to Darwin, where she arrived on 6 August, to find that *Montoro* and *Manoora* were already there, having come directly from Port Moresby. As the two ships were docked, *Zealandia* had to anchor out in the harbour until the next day, when she was also able to go alongside, and disembark the CCC workers, who had been on board for three weeks.

The first three ZK convoys dispatched carried 4112 troops and civilian workers, of whom 525 landed at Thursday Island, 916 went to Darwin, 1078 to Port Moresby and 1593 to Rabaul and Kavieng. *Zealandia* and *Montoro*, again escorted by *Manoora*, also constituted convoy ZK4, carrying 1190 troops to Port Moresby and Rabaul. *Zealandia* arrived back in Sydney on 13 October 1941 and was then prepared for a trooping voyage to Singapore.

The defence of all the Pacific Islands from possible enemy incursion was impossible, but steps were taken during this period to send reinforcements to Fiji by the New Zealand government. In May 1941, the inter-island ferry *Rangatira*, which had made two trips to Suva late in 1940, was dispatched on two more voyages to Fiji. These were followed by two more trips in August. In November 1941, another New Zealand inter-island ferry owned by the Union Steam Ship Company, *Wahine*, was also dispatched on a voyage to Fiji with troops.

During July 1941 the Shipping Control Board began requisitioning Australian-flag ships. Though many remained on their regular commercial trades, their accommodation was controlled by the SCB, and was often utilised to transport troops around the coast. At that time two liners, *Duntroon* and *Katoomba*, were operating on the main route from Sydney and Melbourne to Fremantle, while *Canberra* and *Ormiston* ran up the east coast from Melbourne and Sydney to Queensland ports as far as Cairns.

On 15 November, *Katoomba* departed Fremantle on a regular voyage to Sydney, carrying among her passengers 150 military personnel. *Katoomba* was then taken over by the Department of the Navy in Sydney on 27 November and allocated to transport 699 troops north, of whom 135 would be disembarked at Port Moresby while the remainder went to Rabaul. As before, the ship was not altered, so the troops not accommodated in cabins had to use hammocks or mattresses laid on the floor in public rooms. *Katoomba* was in Port Moresby when, on 8 December 1941, reports came in of the Japanese attack on Pearl Harbor. *Katoomba* was detained at Port Moresby, then on 13 December the troops originally destined for Rabaul were also disembarked. Compulsory evacuation of non-combatants had been declared for Papua and New Guinea, and at 4 pm on the afternoon of 20 December, *Katoomba* departed Port Moresby, having on board 34 men, 367 women and 230 children, a total of 631 persons, who were transported to Brisbane and Sydney, where they arrived on 29 December. *Katoomba* was then released from requisition and returned to the coastal trade again.

When the feared entry of Japan into the war had become reality, Australia braced itself for the anticipated onslaught. At 5 pm on 8 December 1941, Australia officially declared war on Japan. The disposition of the cruisers of the Royal Australian Navy on that day saw *Adelaide* in Port Moresby, *Australia* in the Indian Ocean en route to Fremantle, *Canberra* and *Perth* in the Tasman Sea, and *Hobart* in the Mediterranean. The armed merchant cruisers *Kanimbla* and *Manoora* were in Singapore, while *Westralia* was in Darwin, preparing to escort *Zealandia* on a special mission to Koepang.

After disembarking her troops in Singapore at the end of November 1941, *Zealandia* had proceeded straight to Darwin, and was there when Japan entered the war. The Dutch East Indies were now also under threat from the Japanese, and at the request of the Dutch government, a contingent of 1402 Australian troops was organised to be sent to Timor, most of the troops coming from the 2/40 Battalion.

The 2/40 Battalion was the only such unit recruited almost exclusively in Tasmania, joining with the 2/21 and 2/22 Battalion, recruited in Victoria, to form the 23rd Brigade of the Eighth Division. After initial training in Tasmania, on 7 January 1941, 33 officers and 817 men of the 2/40 Battalion had embarked on *Zealandia* at Launceston for the short voyage to Melbourne, where they went into camp. In February 1941, the 22nd Brigade of the Eighth Division was sent to Singapore, being joined there in August that year by the 27th Brigade, but the 23rd Brigade was retained in Australia. In May 1941 the 2/40 Battalion had been sent overland to Darwin, where they would be based for the foreseeable future.

It had been arranged that the men of the 2/40 Battalion would be sent back to Tasmania for leave during November and December 1941, and several groups had left under this arrangement. *Zealandia* arrived in Darwin early in December and was due to take a large number of troops due for leave on her trip to Sydney and Melbourne, but the entry of Japan into the war changed that quite dramatically. Instead, the troops were prepared for a move to Timor, even though over 150 men were away on leave.

Known as Sparrow Force, 766 men of 2/40 Battalion were embarked in *Zealandia* on 8 December, and 268 men of the 2/2 Independent

Company joined the ship two days later. Meanwhile, *Westralia* took on board 445 soldiers, from various units, including 126 members of the 2/1 Heavy Battery, and 52 from the 2/1 Fortress Engineers,

However, the loading of supplies on *Zealandia* was proceeding at a very slow pace because the Darwin wharf labourers were on a go-slow campaign. One of the soldiers on board, Ray Higgins, later wrote, 'We stood on the decks looking at the wharf labourers fiddling around loading our gear. They'd break off for morning teas, there'd be no work at night, and they wouldn't let us touch it ourselves because we weren't union members. But when it came to ammunition being loaded they wouldn't do it. We loaded it ourselves.' The war diary later noted the supplies were loaded 'in a very careless manner and were not stacked properly ... Many valuable stores including wireless sets had been lost or damaged.'

In his history of the 2/2 Independent Company, Bernard Callinan states that, when they arrived on the wharf on 10 December to embark on *Zealandia*:

> The 2/40 Australian Infantry Battalion had embarked before us and they had already taxed the accommodation, and when our two hundred and seventy were added there were bodies everywhere. We stayed on the ship for two days while the wharf labourers made a travesty of the loading, but eventually, on the evening of the twelfth, we moved slowly down the harbour and left behind the lights of Darwin, which even the tropical night air could not make romantic.
>
> In the morning we could see the *Westralia*, and armed merchantman, and a small naval vessel moving with us on a perfectly calm sea. Hudson planes from Darwin came over and escorted us through the day until darkness fell ... Later that day the battalion band played for us and we appreciated their efforts very much, but the heat prevented them playing for long. Our troops were scattered throughout the ship, and it was difficult to exercise control, but they were well disciplined and the voyage passed off pleasantly without any bother ... The old ship plodded along doing her eight knots by day, and at night when there was no risk of the smoke being seen the speed went up to ten or even twelve knots.
>
> The sun sank as a fiery ball into the sea, and I watched it, hoping to see the phenomenon of the green shaft of light which is sometimes seen in the tropics to shoot into the sky just as the sun finally disappears. I was disappointed; but the phosphorescence of the water as it eddied along the side of the ship was fascinating ... There was a little beer available in the lounge, which had been taken over as an officers' ante-room cum orderly-room; we went down and head a few beers, but the heat was stifling,

The armed merchant cruiser *Westralia* was used to carry troops from Darwin to Koepang.

so I collected my bedding from the cabin and moved up to the deck below the bridge.

In the morning there was land ahead. I went below, shaved and packed my gear, and the orderly officer went around to check up on our troops. By the time we had completed breakfast we were entering the Roti Strait, and we sailed in between Roti and Timor, and eventually turned into the actual harbour of Koepang ... Also in the harbour was the *Westralia* which, with its greater speed, had come in the previous evening and discharged a battery of the 2/1 Australian Heavy Regiment. There was considerable delay in sending a launch out to the ship, and when it did arrive it hardly touched the ship before it pulled away and I, who had been ordered to go with the first party, was left behind. Shortly after, a launch towing some barges came alongside, and the Company Sergeant-Major and I got into it and eventually set off for the shore ... The tide was out and when we arrived near the shore we were still about a hundred and fifty yards from the causeway which jutted out into the mud. We dropped over the side and waded through water and mud to the shore ... The movement of the barges was delayed due to the inability of the natives in charge to prevent other natives from diving over to recover articles thrown from the ship. The articles varied from empty beer bottles to long woollen underpants.

Eventually all the men on board *Zealandia* were landed, along with their equipment and supplies, and the vessel arrived back in Darwin on 16 December.

Meanwhile, additional troops were still being transported to Darwin, with the Western Australian coastal vessel *Koolama*, escorted by HMAS *Warrego*, arriving from Fremantle on 19 January with 100 reinforcements on board. Prime Minister John Curtin had declared it was imperative that Darwin and Papua New Guinea should be made

The Western Australia coastal vessel *Koolama* also carried troops to Darwin.

as strong as possible, so that they could not be invested by enemy forces and used as a springboard for an invasion of the rest of Australia. As a result, it was arranged that some troops would be sent to Port Moresby, while the 2/22 Battalion should be sent to Rabaul, being known as Lark Force. The 2/21 and 2/40 Battalions of the 23rd Brigade would be located in the Darwin region, ready to be moved to the islands further north, mainly Timor and Ambon, should it become necessary. Within days, the 2/21 and ancillary units had been formed into Gull Force, numbering about 1150 men, and were prepared for immediate departure for Ambon. Three small Dutch-flag vessels, *Both*, *Valentijn* and *Patras*, that had been operating commercial services in the Dutch East Indies were ordered to divert to Darwin, where they arrived complete with civilian passengers and numerous livestock. Once they had been offloaded, the troops went on board, and the three vessels, escorted by HMAS *Adelaide* and the corvette HMAS *Ballarat*, left Darwin on 14 December 1941.

One of those on board was Don Findlay, a member of the 2/21st band, who recalled, 'Just on dusk you'd see the old *Adelaide*. She'd blow off a lot of black smoke … and suddenly off she'd go. She'd disappear and we used to think, "Gawd, where's she gone … we've got no protection." But what she was doing, she was going in a big sweep all night right around us and the next morning she'd be out there bang in front of us again.' The small convoy and escorts arrived at Ambon on 17 December. The troops of Gull Force linked up with the 2600 Dutch troops already on the island, but in the end they would be no match for the overwhelming numbers of Japanese troops who arrived on the island and the whole force went into captivity in February 1942.

Within days of Japan entering the war, their soldiers were landing in widely spread areas of the islands to the north of Australia, with Borneo and the Celebes soon overrun. The threat to Papua New Guinea was obvious, and there was an urgent need to strengthen the forces already there. The transfer of Australian troops to the Middle East had been stopped by the Japanese entry into the war, but *Queen Elizabeth* was in Sydney, having returned from convoy US13, along with *Aquitania*, which had carried troops to Singapore in convoy US12A, and arrived back in Sydney on 29 November. It was decided that *Aquitania* would be utilised to transport troops to New Guinea, along with two smaller ships, *Sarpedon* of Blue Funnel Line, and *Herstein*, a 6000 ton Norwegian freighter.

These three vessels constituted convoy ZK5, which departed Sydney on 28 December, *Aquitania* carrying 4250 troops of the 39th and 53rd Militia Battalions, while the other two vessels had loaded 10,000 tons of equipment and supplies destined for Port Moresby. The increased danger of travelling in Australian waters was emphasised by the size of the escort, which consisted of four cruisers, *Australia*, *Canberra*, *Perth* and *Achilles*. The troops aboard *Aquitania* were all militiamen, or conscripts, who were not allowed to fight outside Australia. When they had boarded the troopship in Sydney, none was aware of their destination, though the general consensus of opinion was Darwin. The convoy reached Port Moresby safely on 3 January 1942, much to the shock of the troops. Some of the men, thinking their excursion to Darwin would not be of a serious nature, had managed to bring tennis rackets and even golf clubs with them. Many men considered they had been tricked, and been sent overseas, but Papua and New Guinea were Australian Territories, and as such the government was within its rights to send militiamen there.

The harbour facilities in Port Moresby were stretched to the limit to cope with the sudden arrival of the three ships. *Aquitania* was much too big to go alongside, so had to anchor well out in the harbour, her troops being ferried ashore on naval ships. *Herstein* and *Sarpedon* were able to dock, but the single wharf could only handle about 600 tons of freight a day, which meant delays in unloading the cargo ships. Once the troops had disembarked, *Aquitania* returned alone to Sydney, arriving on 8 January. However, it was soon discovered that faulty loading in Sydney, described in a later judicial inquiry as 'gross carelessness and incompetence,' had resulted in all the camping equipment needed by the recently landed troops being stowed at the

Sarpedon of Blue Funnel Line was included in convoy ZK5.

bottom of the cargo ship's holds. Thus, when the troops landed they had no tents to sleep in, or other basic facilities. Following hurried discussions on the wharf, temporary arrangements were made.

Some two thousand of the troops were marched eleven kilometres out of the town to Seven Mile aerodrome and ordered to establish a camp, as were the rest of the men who were dispatched to two other locations nearer to Port Moresby. Without tents, beds, mosquito nets, sanitary and cooking facilities, the men were in a very poor state, and even when the equipment was unloaded it was discovered that there were insufficient sanitary pans and mosquito nets. Many men came down with fevers, and there was general discontent, leading to an outbreak of lawlessness and a complete breakdown in discipline.

The situation became so bad that a Special Commission was set up by the Australian government to investigate the matter. Although much of the blame was placed on the unit commander, Major General Morris, he was strongly defended by General Blamey, who stated, 'General Morris had an impossible task. The responsibility for what happened lies less with the commander on the spot than with those responsible for providing him with inadequate and incompetent forces ... The state of defences and of the Army in Australia were poor and these general conditions were present in a most aggravated form at Port Moresby early in 1942. Even after the arrival of 5,000 additional troops on 3 January, making 6,200 in all, the commander and his senior officers were aware that the troops available were grossly inadequate ... The lamentably poor quality and discipline of the troops in Moresby reflected the general condition of the AMF in Australia. The 53rd Battalion sent to Moresby were of an average of 18½ years, many of them in the army for a period of weeks only, and all unfamiliar with arms or discipline.' Yet, despite this stinging criticism, these were the men who in the following months would fight bravely against the Japanese as they tried to take New Guinea.

It was not only the situation in Port Moresby that caused concern in New Guinea. After unloading her cargo, *Herstein* went on to Rabaul, arriving there on 19 January to load a cargo of copra to be taken back to Australia. Rabaul was being subjected to constant Japanese air attacks, and the local deputy administrator, H.H. Page, had sent an urgent request to Canberra on 15 January that 300 civilians in the town be evacuated as soon as possible. With the arrival of the *Herstein*, Page sent another request that the ship be used to remove civilians immediately. To his amazement, he was told that no personnel were to be evacuated, and the ship loaded as planned with copra, which was considered to be an essential cargo. As a result, instead of boarding 300 or more civilians and leaving the danger area immediately, *Herstein* remained at Rabaul overnight loading copra, and was still there next morning, 20 January, when Japanese bombers again raided the town. A sitting target, *Herstein* was hit repeatedly by the dive bombers and set on fire, drifting across the harbour and running aground, where she burned all night. On 23 January the Japanese captured Rabaul, and on 3 February Port Moresby suffered its first air raid.

The entry of Japan into the war, and their rapid advances in the Pacific, brought forth more fears about the security of Fiji. On 31 December 1941, the inter-island ferry *Rangatira* departed Wellington on another voyage there with troops. Needing more ships urgently, on 5 January 1942 the New Zealand government requisitioned the Bass Strait ferry *Taroona*, which was owned by the Union Steam Ship Company of New Zealand, but operated for Tasmanian Steamers Pty Ltd on the overnight service between Melbourne and Launceston. *Taroona* was undergoing an engine overhaul in Melbourne when the message from New Zealand was received. As a result of herculean efforts by those involved, the engines were put back together, and *Taroona*, painted grey all over, left Melbourne on 7 January for Auckland.

On 12 January, a contingent of New Zealand troops, comprising 36 officers and 644 other ranks, was embarked. Escorted by the former trans-Tasman liner *Monowai*, another unit of the Union Line, which had been converted into an armed merchant cruiser, and was also carrying troops, *Taroona* left Auckland on 13 January, reaching Suva three days later. As the two ships neared Suva on 16 January, they were

Taroona was used to carry New Zealand troops to Fiji in January 1942
(*C.T. Reddings collection*)

attacked by gunfire from a surfaced Japanese submarine, but neither was damaged and they docked in Suva the same day. Arriving back in Auckland on 19 January, *Taroona* boarded a number of New Zealand military personnel, who were carried back to Melbourne, after which *Taroona* returned to her regular Bass Strait service.

Meanwhile, *Rangatira* made another trip to Fiji in January 1942, this time in a convoy, being accompanied by *Wahine* and the cargo ship *Port Montreal*. The three ships departed Wellington on 9 January 1942, escorted by HMS *Leander*. Early on the afternoon of 11 January the escort was greatly strengthened by the arrival of three more cruisers, *Australia*, *Perth* and *Achilles*, which scouted some twenty miles ahead of the three merchant ships until they neared Fiji. On the evening of 13 January, *Rangatira*, escorted by *Achilles* and *Perth*, split from the convoy and proceeded to the port of Lautoka, while *Wahine* and *Port Melbourne*, escorted by *Australia* and *Leander*, continued on to Suva. *Rangatira* made her final trooping voyage to Fiji in March 1942.

Evacuation of civilians from Darwin became of prime importance, and on 16 December 1941 the War Cabinet approved a recommendation that all children and women other than nurses and missionaries be compulsorily withdrawn. The first group, numbering 225, departed on 19 December on the Western Australian coastal vessel *Koolinda*, which took them to Fremantle, then on 20 December, 207 women and 357 children departed on *Zealandia*, bound for Sydney, where they arrived on 2 January 1942. Three days later the American ship *President Grant* left Darwin for Brisbane with 225 aboard, followed by *Montoro* on 9 January with another 203 bound for Sydney. On 25 January, the Western Australian coastal vessel *Koolama* left with 173 more women and children to be taken to Fremantle, while the final

The New Zealand inter-island ferry *Wahine* also carried troops to Fiji.

such voyage was taken by *Koolinda*, departing Darwin on 14 February for Fremantle, carrying 77 evacuees. This left some 2500 civilians in Darwin. On its way south, *Koolinda* called at Broome on 21 February, when a further 136 women and children came on board.

It was even more imperative that additional troops and materials be rushed north, with *Zealandia* designated to carry them. Among those ordered to board the ship were eight officers and 150 other ranks of the 41 Anti-Tank Battery from 11 Anti-Tank Company, which had been based at Ingleburn Camp, where they were inspected by the Governor-General on 19 January 1942. Two days later stores and equipment began being loaded on *Zealandia*, which was berthed at 12 Pyrmont, and on 24 January the troops arrived by train, and went straight onto the ship. Also on board was the interestingly named 116 Mobile Bath Unit, comprising a sergeant and five other ranks, as well as reinforcements for units already in Darwin, along with their equipment, a total of 332 troops in all. In addition, civilian workers were also taken to Darwin with their supplies to erect protection for the oil tanks there.

At 6.30 pm on 24 January 1942, *Zealandia* left her Pyrmont wharf, escorted by *Westralia* along the east coast. It was a slow trip, and *Zealandia* did not arrive in Darwin until 10 am on 6 February. The wharves were all fully utilised, so *Zealandia* had to anchor out in the harbour, with disembarkation for the troops a slow process into barges. *Zealandia* was still at anchor, having unloaded only half her cargo, when Japanese aircraft appeared over the town on 19 February. Soon *Zealandia* was under attack, and a bomb exploded in no. 3 hatch, just behind the engine room, setting the ship on fire. The blaze spread rapidly, and soon was out of control. *Zealandia* later sank, leaving her two tall masts showing above the water. Amazingly, of the 145 men on board at the time of the attack, only three were killed.

Zealandia on fire in Darwin Harbour, 19 February 1942. The hospital ship *Manunda* is in the background.

15
The Singapore Convoys

When war broke out in 1939, the Royal Navy presence in the Far East was insignificant, comprising the aircraft carrier HMS *Eagle*, four old cruisers, nine destroyers and a few submarines, but within months most of these vessels had been ordered back to Europe. It was not until after the Battle of Britain in 1940, when the threat of a German invasion of Britain had been contained, that the three armed services were asked for their assessment of the minimum military strength that would be required, in the event of a Japanese invasion, to defend Singapore until the arrival of Royal Navy capital ships from Britain, which had been estimated would take between 70 and 90 days. At a conference in October 1940, it was deemed prudent to station 582 modern aircraft in Singapore, as at that time there were only 88 aircraft on the Malay Peninsula. Unfortunately, the majority of these planes were never sent, and by the end of 1941 the total had increased to only 158, none being of the most modern types.

In May 1941, the Admiralty decided to establish a fleet to be based on Singapore, comprising six battleships, one battle cruiser, an aircraft carrier and suitable support ships, but the earliest date given for the assembly of this fleet in the Far East was March 1942. However, once again, most of the ships that would comprise this fleet would be elderly, four of the battleships, *Ramillies, Resolution, Revenge* and *Royal Sovereign*, and the battle cruiser *Renown* having served in World War I. By August 1941, Winston Churchill, was pressing the Admiralty to consider the use of at least one King George V-class battleship, the newest in the

HMS *Repulse* was sent to Singapore in late 1941.

Royal Navy, of which three had been completed, *King George V*, *Prince of Wales*, and *Duke of York*. In a message to the First Sea Lord, Churchill wrote, 'It should become possible in the near future to place a deterrent squadron in the Indian Ocean. Such a force should consist of the smallest number of the best ships. The most economical disposition would be to send *Duke of York* ... She could be joined by *Repulse* or *Renown* and one aircraft carrier of high speed. This powerful force might show itself in the triangle Aden–Singapore–Simonstown. It would exert a paralysing effect upon Japanese Naval action.' This was a gross overestimate by Churchill on the effect such a force would have on the Japanese, but at least it was a move in the right direction of establishing a major fleet in Far Eastern waters.

Three days later the Admiralty responded, giving reasons why all three active King George V-class battleships should remain in British waters, primarily to contain the huge German battleship, *Tirpitz*. The Admiralty repeated their intention of basing older warships in the Far East, but Churchill would not accept this. Aware that the Australian government was in favour of the establishment of a Far Eastern fleet of any sort, in a fiery reply dated 28 August 1941, Churchill stated: 'It is surely a faulty disposition to create in the Indian Ocean a fleet considerable in numbers, costly in maintenance and manpower, but consisting entirely of slow, obsolescent or unmodernised ships which can neither fight a fleet action with the main Japanese force nor act as a deterrent upon his modern fast heavy ships ... The R's in their present state would be floating coffins ... No doubt the Australian government would be pleased to count the numbers of old battleships in their neighbourhood, but we must not play down to uninstructed thought.

On the contrary, we should inculcate the true principles of naval strategy, one of which is certainly to use a small number of the best ships to cope with a superior force.'

Even at this late stage, Churchill, along with many others in leading positions in the British government, considered the Japanese entry into the war was not a real threat. In the same message to the Admiralty, Churchill wrote, 'I cannot feel that Japan will face the combination against her of the United States, Great Britain and Russia ... Nothing would increase her hesitation more than the appearance of the force mentioned ... and above all a KGV. This might indeed be a decisive deterrent.'

On Monday, 20 October 1941, at a meeting of the War Cabinet's Defence Committee held at 10 Downing Street, Churchill again pressed the Admiralty on the matter of sending a strong force to the Far East. It was decided that HMS *Prince of Wales* would be dispatched as soon as possible, along with the battle cruiser *Repulse* and an aircraft carrier, HMS *Indomitable*, the fleet to be known as Force G. In fact, *Repulse* was already in the Indian Ocean, having escorted convoy WS11 from Britain to Suez via the Cape of Good Hope.

Prince of Wales had only been commissioned on 19 January 1941, and within four months had been in action, accompanying HMS *Hood* to attack the German battleship *Bismarck* when it tried to break into the Atlantic. In a short, tragic encounter, *Hood* had blown up and sunk with the loss of all but three of her 1419 man crew. *Prince of Wales* had also sustained damage, but not before inflicting one major hit on the German ship that caused it to change course, and be destroyed a matter of days later. *Prince of Wales* had returned to Scapa Flow, the major naval base in the far north of Scotland, and on 25 October 1941 departed on the long voyage to the Far East, having to travel around Africa, escorted by the destroyers HMS *Electra* and HMS *Express*.

Indomitable was brand new, and had been sent to the West Indies to work up prior to entering active service. However, on 3 November the vessel ran aground on a reef off Kingston, suffering such extensive damage it had to be sent to an American yard for major repairs. While the work was completed in just twelve days, the delay would prove fatal, as by the time *Indomitable* had returned to Jamaica to collect her aircraft, then set off for the Cape of Good Hope and Singapore, she would be too late arriving to influence future events.

Meanwhile, *Prince of Wales* continued on her way east, arriving in Colombo on 28 November, where she was joined by *Repulse* and two more destroyers, HMS *Encounter* and HMS *Jupiter*. The two large warships, and their accompanying destroyers, departed Colombo on 29 November. Three days later, on the afternoon of 2 December, the vessels arrived at the Singapore Naval Base. This was reported in the *Singapore Free Press* as 'bad news for Japan which may begin to see the shattering of her hopes for an unopposed naval advance to the south.' Yet it was just two days later that, unbeknownst to the British, the main Japanese invasion convoy of nineteen transports left Hainan for the four-day voyage to the Malay Peninsula. In fact, so confident were the British of the deterrent value of their two mighty warships it was decided to send *Repulse* on a visit to Darwin, and possibly on to Sydney. The battle cruiser duly left Singapore on 5 December, accompanied by two destroyers, one of them Australian, HMAS *Vampire*.

On 6 December, a British reconnaissance aircraft sighted the Japanese convoy making for the Malay Peninsula, which resulted in *Repulse* being ordered to return to Singapore, where she arrived early on 7 December. No-one could obtain a clear picture of the Japanese intentions, but at 0045 on 8 December the first landings took place at Kota Baharu. This was just over an hour before the infamous Japanese attack on Pearl Harbor, which occurred on the morning of 7 December there, as Hawaii was on the other side of the International Date Line.

Also on 8 December 1941 the Japanese also began a series of landings at Singora and Patani in Thailand. These forces and those landed at Kota Baharu would sweep down the peninsula towards Singapore, which suffered its first air raid the same day that Japan entered the war. The two British capital ships, HMS *Prince of Wales* and HMS *Repulse*, departed Singapore on the evening of 8 December, their plan of action being to attack the Japanese ships supporting the landings. Instead, the two mighty warships came under intense attacks by waves of Japanese bombers, and both were sunk on 10 December.

Desperate attempts by Allied forces to slow the Japanese advance down the Malay peninsula proved futile. On 31 December 1941 the Japanese entered Kampar, south of Ipoh, while on 11 January 1942, Kuala Lumpur fell to them. Meanwhile, a new command structure for the Malay Peninsula and surrounding areas, under the command of General Wavell, was established on 3 January. Known as ABDA (American–British–Dutch–Australian) Command, it was formed to combine the Allied effort against the Japanese under a single command. The first British reinforcements reached Singapore on 2 January 1942, with more arriving on 12 January. However, there was a

Gorgon was one of eleven ships in convoy MS1.

desperate need for more troops, and reinforcements were organised in Australia to strengthen the 8th Division, it being decided to send a series of convoys, which were given the designator MS.

Convoy MS1 departed Melbourne on 10 January, initially comprising seven ships, but they carried only equipment and motor transport. Escorted by the armed merchant cruiser *Kanimbla*, a converted coastal liner, the convoy called first at Fremantle, where three more ships joined, while the cruiser HMAS *Hobart* was added to the escort. The convoy departed Fremantle on 16 January and the next day another ship, *Gorgon*, joined from Geraldton, bringing the convoy strength up to eleven ships. *Gorgon*, operated by Blue Funnel Line, was well known in Western Australia, having been built in 1933 for a service from Fremantle to Singapore, with cabins for 84 first-class passengers, and temporary quarters for an additional 60 passengers when required. It could also carry a large amount of cargo, including livestock.

Convoy MS1 arrived at the entrance to Sunda Strait on 28 January, where *Kanimbla* turned back to Australia, being relieved by two destroyers, HMS *Tenedos* and HMS *Stronghold*. Once the convoy was through Sunda Strait, it split into two sections. Six of the ships, *Enggano*, *Java*, *Tjikandi*, *Tjikarang*, all under the Dutch flag, as well as *Peisander* and *War Sidar*, went to various ports in the Dutch East Indies, while *City of Manchester*, *Derrymore*, *Gorgon*, *Pan Europe* and *Phrontis* continued towards Singapore, still escorted by *Hobart*. On 29 January, as the five merchant ships and their escort were passing through Banka Strait, they were attacked by five high-flying Japanese bombers, but their bombs all missed and the convoy continued on its way unharmed, arriving off Singapore at dawn on 1 February.

The ships all went to berths and commenced unloading, though this was constantly interrupted by air raids. As the local wharf labourers had all fled, the crew had to work the cargo, but even when it was landed on the wharf there was no-one there to collect or distribute it. Even desperately needed war materials, including Bren-gun carriers and other vehicles offloaded from *City of Manchester* and *Derrymore*, and fighter aircraft in crates, remained on the wharves, and often were destroyed there during air raids.

Convoy MS2 comprised only one ship, *Aquitania*, which had returned to Sydney on 8 January from Port Moresby. Objections were raised to sending such a large ship to Singapore, which was being subjected to daily air raids, but *Aquitania* was the only ship then in Australian waters that was suitable for the task of transporting a large number of troops, as using *Queen Elizabeth* was out of the question. Eventually it was agreed that sending *Aquitania* to Singapore was too risky, so it was arranged that she would go only as far as Ratai Bay, in the Sunda Strait, where her troops would be transferred to smaller ships, provided by the Dutch, for the final leg of their journey. *Aquitania* departed Sydney on 10 January 1942, carrying 3456 military personnel, including 78 from the RAN and 105 RAAF, as well as 76 civilians, being escorted by HMAS *Canberra*. Among the troops on board *Aquitania* was the 2/4 Machine Gun Battalion, which had been raised in Western Australia in October 1940. In June 1941, Fred Airey, a veteran of World War I, was appointed regimental sergeant major in the battalion. Writing later, he recalled that, in July 1941, the battalion was moved from Northam in Western Australia to Woodside Camp in South Australia, then in October 1941 they moved again, through Alice Springs to Winellie Camp, near Darwin. When Japan entered the war the battalion was ordered to move to New Guinea, and on 31 December they left Darwin on two small vessels, which Airey neglected to identify. As he recalled, 'We had a most pleasant few days voyage, the sea was like glass all the way.'

The 2/4 Machine Gun Battalion arrived in Port Moresby on 3 January 1942, the same day *Aquitania* arrived from Sydney in convoy ZK5. Fred Airey later wrote, 'After berthing at a jetty, the adjutant and

I went ashore to find a campsite, but we were almost immediately recalled. A large ship, the *Aquitania*, was standing by, and our troops were collecting their gear and running across a long plank from the smaller ships. We were told they were expecting a Japanese air attack at any moment.' Apparently a change of orders had been received, and the battalion were to board the *Aquitania*. But, as Fred Airey wrote, 'We were still bringing the baggage over, and about half of it was still on the smaller boat, when the *Aquitania* shot off like a rocket, doing a fair clip for such an old vessel. We got to Sydney very quickly, and were given two days shore leave. Many more soldiers were taken on board here, though we still weren't told where we were going. Everyone hoped we would call in at Fremantle.'

After a fast voyage across the Great Australian Bight, *Aquitania* arrived off Fremantle on 15 January, anchoring in Gage Roads. This was particularly good news for the men of the 2/4 Machine Gun Battalion, who were all from Western Australia, and, as Fred Airey recalled, 'As soon as we found we were going there, leave applications started flooding into orderly rooms. Men who had been away nearly six months were really looking forward to seeing their loved ones again. You can imagine then how upset they were when on arriving in Fremantle the order was issued, "Command refuses leave to all troops." There were some very annoyed and despondent men aboard that ship as we sat out in Gage Roads, in full view of the shore.'

Fred Airey asked why there was no shore leave, and was told it was for security reasons, though he could not understand this, nor could any of the other men on board the ship. As Airey wrote:

> Many of the Western Australians on board would gladly have foregone leave in Sydney if they could have come ashore in Fremantle instead. It was really bad for morale, and there was mutiny in the air as the soldiers of the 2/4th stood at the railing gazing shorewards, some no doubt wondering how easy it would be to swim.
>
> Then someone spied a barge coming out from the shore, and some men decided they would commandeer it if it came to our ship. Sure enough the barge tied up alongside the ship and started pumping water into the ship's tanks. As it did so, rope ladders were dropped down the side of the ship and men began swarming onto the barge. It cast off again, loaded with soldiers taking unofficial shore leave.
>
> Other barges came alongside with fuel and water, and each of them was commandeered by the troops. The CO came along and ordered me to have the ladders pulled up — there were three of them down by now

— and for once in my life I became a popular RSM. I went to the first ladder and said, 'Look, fellows, I'm ordered to pull up this ladder, so please go and use one of the other ones.' I got two men and rolled up the ladder and tied it into place, and then I was ordered to get the other ladder up. I went along and said I had been ordered to pull up that ladder and that they should go and lower the other one again. Away they went and did so. The CO said, 'Any warrant officer or NCO who goes ashore loses his rank.' He meant it too, but I think that a lot of the fellows just didn't care any more ... Later I went on deck and found all the ladders under strict guard.

Fred Airey would have liked a trip ashore too, but decided he had to set an example, so stayed aboard *Aquitania*. As he recalled, 'I had important work to do. The new submachine gun had been put aboard, and no-one knew how to use it, so I had to learn it from the book and teach it to all officers and NCOs before we disembarked.'

After an overnight stay at anchor in Gage Roads, *Aquitania* raised her

Both was one of seven small Dutch flag vessels to transfer troops brought by *Aquitania* from Ratai Bay to Singapore. (*C.T. Reddings collection*)

anchor next morning, and at 11 am steamed away. As Fred Airey wrote, for some of the troops it was time to 'meet their punishment. When routine orders came out, all NCOs that had gone ashore and returned lost rank, some all of their rank, others just a stripe or two. Worst of all, we left ninety-six well trained soldiers on the shore waving us goodbye, as they had been unable to get anything to convey them back to the ship.' However, as events would develop, those left behind would be spared the long period of captivity under Japanese control that befell most of the men who did return to the ship and went on to Singapore.

Escorted by HMAS *Canberra*, *Aquitania* steamed north at top speed, entering the Sunda Strait and arriving on 20 January in Ratai Bay, where her troops were transferred to seven small Dutch ships, *Both*, *Reael*, *Reijnst*, *Sloet van de Beele*, *Van der Lijn*, *Van Swoll* and *Taishan*. The men of the 2/4 Machine Gun Battalion were loaded into two of these ships, but, as Fred Airey wrote, 'The operation was held up for twelve hours, because there was supposed to be a Jap submarine lurking somewhere nearby. Finally the sub was sunk by a British destroyer, and we proceeded to move, under cover of darkness, with an ever-present fear of air attack. We knew by this time that we were going to Singapore.' Designated convoy MS2A, the seven small ships arrived safely in Singapore on 24 January. Three weeks later, all the troops carried by *Aquitania* were either dead or prisoners of war, with the exception of a few who managed to escape.

As soon as the last soldier left the ship, *Aquitania* raised her anchor and left, again escorted by HMAS *Canberra*, making a fast passage back to Sydney, arriving on 31 January. On 10 February *Aquitania* left Sydney, this time carrying no troops, bound for Honolulu, then made her way to New York.

At the same time, further MS convoys were being organised in Australia, as the situation in Malaya worsened. Convoy MS3 was composed of eleven vessels, of which seven were tankers, *Erling Brovig*, *Elsa*, *Herborg*, *Manvantara*, *Marpessa*, *Merula* and *Seirstad*, all destined for Palembang. The other four ships in convoy MS3, *Antilochus*, *Charon*, *Mangola* and *Marella*, were carrying troops and supplies destined for Tanjong Priok in Batavia.

Antilochus and *Charon* were owned by Blue Funnel Line, the former quite a veteran, having been completed in 1906 as a cargo liner, with accommodation for twelve passengers. *Charon* was a sister to *Gorgon*, which had been included in convoy MS1. *Mangola* and *Marella* were both owned by an Australian firm, Burns Philp. Prior to the war, *Mangola* had operated services from Sydney to the Pacific Islands, carrying a small number of passengers. At 7474 gross tons, *Marella* was the largest of the four vessels, with accommodation for 150 passengers, and had previously been on a service from Sydney to Singapore.

Convoy MS3 departed Fremantle on 30 January, escorted by HMAS *Canberra* until 6 February, when the ships were near Christmas Island. Here *Canberra* turned back for Fremantle, handing over escort duty to the cruisers HMS *Dragon* and HMS *Durban* and two destroyers. Once through Sunda Strait, the convoy split into two sections and headed for

Marella was the largest vessel included in convoy MS3. (*C.T. Reddings collection*)

their destinations, those going to Tanjong Priok arriving on 10 February.

The relentless Japanese advance on Singapore had continued, and on the morning of 31 January the last Allied force, comprising British, Australian and Indian troops, retreated across the causeway linking Singapore to Johore, which was then blown up. A large convoy, BM12, bringing British troops from Bombay, escorted by the sloop HMAS *Yarra*, arrived in Singapore on 5 February, but was subjected to a concerted attack by 27 Japanese aircraft, during which two ships, *Felix Roussel* and *Empress of Asia*, were set on fire. The fires on *Felix Roussel* were brought under control, but those on *Empress of Asia* could not be extinguished and the vessel subsequently sank. In a daring manoeuvre, Lieutenant Commander Harrington in command of *Yarra* took his ship alongside the burning troopship and took off 1304 of her troops, while smaller numbers were rescued by HMAS *Bendigo* and HMAS *Wollongong*. Harrington was so concerned with his ship's stability he ordered all on board to sit on the deck and not move around. A further convoy of eight ships carrying supplies, which had left Colombo on 3 February, arrived in Singapore four days later. Before they could unload they were ordered to leave, as Japanese forces had crossed the strait between Johore and Singapore in small boats on the night of 7/8 February, and bitter close-quarter fighting ensued on Singapore Island.

As convoy MS3 was en route, convoy MS4, composed of four tankers bound for Palembang, and two cargo ships, departed Melbourne, initially escorted by HMAS *Adelaide*. After calling at Fremantle, the convoy continued its journey, and on 15 February *Adelaide* handed over escort duty to HMAS *Perth*. However, on that same day the Allied forces in Singapore surrendered to the Japanese, and it would clearly

The Dutch cargo ship *s'Jacob* was one of six vessels in convoy MS4. (*C.T. Reddings collection*)

not be too much longer before the Japanese were in control of the Dutch East Indies too. There was no point in continuing with convoy MS4, so five of the ships were ordered to return to Fremantle. However, one small cargo ship, the Dutch flag *s'Jacob*, was ordered to continue its passage north, escorted by *Perth*, and later they were joined by two more Dutch flag ships, *Swartenhondt* and *Karsik*. However, on the evening of 21 February, when 600 miles south of Sunda Strait, the convoy was ordered to return to Fremantle. *Perth* escorted the ships back to a point 700 miles from Fremantle, where the *Yarra* took over the escort. Then the cruiser reversed her course, heading north again to join the battle against Japanese naval forces. Two weeks later, on 1 March 1942, HMAS *Perth* was sunk in the Battle of the Java Sea. *Yarra* escorted the convoy to a position 200 miles south of Christmas Island, then handed them over to HMAS *Vendetta*. *Yarra* returned north, and on 4 March was sunk by a Japanese naval force, with the loss of 138 of her 151 crew members.

Instead of a regular flow of ships towards Singapore and the Dutch East Indies, the waters north of Australia were now filled with ships of all sizes, types and descriptions fleeing south, away from the Japanese onslaught. Among this armada were the ships that had been involved in the first three MS convoys. Six of the tankers sent to Palembang in MS3 were amongst a convoy of 28 ships which was attacked off Sumatra by Japanese aircraft. *Merula* and *Manvantara* received direct hits which set them on fire, and despite heroic efforts to save them, both were lost. Another casualty was *Derrymore*, from MS1, still loaded with ammunition, torpedoed by a Japanese submarine and sunk.

The American troop transport *Williard A. Holbrook* joined convoy MS5. (*C.T. Reddings collection*)

There was one further MS convoy to depart Australia, but this carried American troops, though using Australian ships. The American troop transports *Mariposa* and *President Coolidge*, carrying American troops bound for Singapore, and escorted by the cruiser USS *Phoenix*, arrived in Melbourne on 1 February 1942, berthing at Station Pier. It had been intended that *Mariposa* and another American transport, *Williard A. Holbrook*, would carry these men on to Colombo, but *Mariposa* was withdrawn, and transport for her troops was needed at very short notice. In the meantime, the troops from *Mariposa* and *President Coolidge* were disembarked and taken to camps at Bacchus Marsh and Royal Park. At that time there were still several liners operating on the Australian coast, and two of these, *Katoomba* and *Duntroon*, were ordered to be made available in Melbourne, free of passengers and cargo, on 3 February, when they would be requisitioned by the Department of the Navy.

Duntroon arrived in Melbourne from Fremantle on 1 February and discharged all passengers and cargo, but her machinery was in need of an overhaul, while the cooling system had to be adjusted for operation in tropical waters, which meant the vessel would not be ready until 8 February. *Katoomba* arrived in Melbourne from Sydney on 2 February. Both the Australian ships berthed in the Yarra River, though they had to move to Station Pier to load ammunition and equipment, then returned to their berths in the river.

Williard A. Holbrook, having embarked 700 American troops in Brisbane, arrived in Melbourne to take on some of the troops from the other ships. It had been planned that *Duntroon* would carry 750 troops, while *Katoomba* would transport 650, but she actually had 664 on board when the three ships departed Melbourne on 12 February, as convoy MS5, escorted by *Phoenix*. By the time the ships reached Fremantle, Singapore had fallen to the Japanese, so on 21 February the destination of the convoy was changed to Bombay, with a stop at Colombo en route. While in Fremantle *Katoomba* took on more troops, increasing her complement to 774. This was made possible by installing hammocks in addition to the temporary bunks already being used by many of the troops on board.

The American freighter *Sea Witch*, carrying 27 crated aircraft, and the aircraft tender USS *Langley*, carrying 32 aircraft, joined the convoy at Fremantle, these two ships being destined for Java. Convoy MS5 left Fremantle on 22 February, but the next day *Langley* and *Sea Witch* were ordered to detach and proceed unescorted at best speed to Tjilatjap. *Langley* was faster than *Sea Witch*, so went on ahead, and on 26 February was joined by two destroyers sent out from Tjilatjap to escort her into port. However, on the morning of 27 February the three ships were attacked by Japanese aircraft, leaving *Langley* ablaze and crippled. Her surviving crew members abandoned ship, then *Langley* was sunk by one of the destroyers. *Sea Witch* reached Tjilatjap safely on 28 February and unloaded her crated aircraft, but they were too late, and all were destroyed in their crates when Tjilatjap was abandoned by the Allies on 3 March.

The remaining ships of convoy MS5 continued their journey, and on 28 February *Phoenix* handed over escort duty to HMS *Enterprise*. The ships arrived safely in Colombo on 5 March, but by then their destination had been changed again, to Karachi, where the ships arrived safely on 13 March. This convoy ended the large scale movement of troops from Australia to overseas destinations, as attention had now turned to bringing as many Australian troops as possible back home, so they could be sent to Papua New Guinea.

16 Operation Stepsister and the Fall of Singapore

The decision taken by the Australian government in 1939 to send troops to the Middle East had been contingent on the attitude of Japan. As long as Japan remained on the sidelines of the war, there was no immediate threat to Australia. The events of 8 December 1941, and the days immediately following, changed that situation entirely. Japanese forces were suddenly marauding far and wide through the Pacific region and Asia, and Australia, felt extremely vulnerable. Initially the British tended to treat the Japanese onslaught as something that could be contained, expressing the opinion that Singapore would hold fast and Australia would not be endangered. Prime Minister John Curtin, on the other hand, was greatly concerned about the threat posed to Australia by the seemingly unstoppable Japanese forces, especially in Malaya, where they were advancing steadily down the peninsula towards Singapore.

Within days of the Japanese entering the war, British Prime Minister Winston Churchill had completed arrangements for a trip to the United States to hold face-to-face talks with President Roosevelt and the senior members of his government. Churchill went north from London to Glasgow, where he boarded the battleship *Duke of York*, which conveyed him and his party, including all the senior British military leaders, to Baltimore. During the voyage, Churchill remained in constant touch with all aspects of the war, and sent a telegram to the Australian government regarding the transfer of some Australian troops from the Middle East to either India or Singapore. When the battleship arrived in Baltimore, Churchill and his party travelled by train to Washington, arriving a couple of days before Christmas.

With the Japanese advancing rapidly on all fronts, the British had been forced to change their opinion of Japanese military ability very quickly. Just a week after Japan entered the war, Churchill raised with his Chiefs of Staff the proposition that elements of the 1st Australian Corps, which comprised the 6th, 7th and 9th Divisions, be transferred post-haste from the Middle East to bolster the garrison in Singapore.

On Christmas Day, Churchill, then staying at the White House, sent a cable to Curtin which began by noting the movements already under way of British and Indian troops to the Malay Peninsula to counter the Japanese advances. He then went on: 'A week ago I wirelessed from the ship to London to suggest that you recall one Australian division from Palestine either into India to replace other troops sent forward or to go direct, if it can be arranged, to Singapore. I have impressed upon the military authorities the importance of not using up forces needed for the defence of Singapore and Johore approaches in attempting to defend the northern part of the Malay Peninsula. They will fall back slowly, fighting delaying actions and destroying communications.'

Churchill went on to stress that both he and President Roosevelt did not agree with Curtin's previous cable, 'that there is the danger of early reduction of Singapore fortress, which we are determined to defend with the utmost tenacity.' Churchill then noted that President Roosevelt was anxious to move United States troops through Australia to the Philippines, or if they fell to the Japanese, to Singapore. The President had also expressed a willingness to send American troops to Australia, Churchill added. He concluded the message, 'You may count on my doing everything possible to strengthen the whole front from Rangoon to Port Darwin.'

On 3 January 1942, Churchill sent a further message to Curtin, asking him to agree to the transfer of two Australian divisions from the Middle East to the Dutch East Indies. The Australian War Cabinet, on the advice of the Chiefs of Staff, sent a reply agreeing to the transfer of the 6th and 7th Divisions. At that stage it was thought likely that one division would go to Java, the other to Sumatra. The Australian 8th Division was already in Malaya, involved in bloody battles with the advancing Japanese, while the 9th Division was to remain in Lebanon and Syria. The result of this interchange of communications was an agreement to transfer 64,000 troops, plus all their equipment and maintenance facilities, a huge undertaking. Arrangements were hurriedly made to transport the troops in several convoys, this movement being codenamed Operation Stepsister.

The Dutch East Indies, the Malay Peninsula and Burma had been designated the ABDA (Australian–British–Dutch–American) theatre of the war, and on 29 December 1941 General Wavell had been appointed Supreme Commander of the region. In preparation for the transfer of the Australian divisions from the Middle East, an advance party, including the commander of the 1st Australian Corps, General John Lavarack, was dispatched by air, reaching Java on 26 January 1942. Lavarack reported to Wavell the day after he arrived, but in a report sent ten days later expressed his doubts that Java and Sumatra could be defended, also referring to the fact that another Australian division was 'cooped up in Singapore, and relies largely on our efforts for its eventual relief.'

Meanwhile, the first elements of the 1st Australian Corps had left their bases, and were en route to Port Tewfik in Egypt, to begin the journey to the Dutch East Indies in convoy JS1. This initial movement included men from the 2/3 Machine Gun Battalion, the 2/2 Pioneer Battalion, 2/2 AA Regiment, 2/6 Field Company, 105 General Transport Company, 2/2 Casualty Clearing Station, and several smaller units.

The first party of men and materials to be dispatched was allocated to eight small ships, *Adrastus, Prominent, Filleigh, Modasa, Yoma, Lulworth Hill, Hai Lee* and *Hermion*. In contrast to the converted liners used to transport these troops to the Middle East the previous year, the ships of JS1 were mostly freighters, with little or no proper accommodation. Compared to the 80,000 gross tons of the two Queens, *Prominent* was just 2232 gross tons. Convoy JS1 departed Port Tewfik in mid-January.

Probably the best description of conditions endured by those on board these ships can be found in comments made by Sergeant H.J. Hale. 'Ours was not a luxury liner,' he wrote. 'It was a glorified sort of tramp, and we were the aft gun crew. Bang went our visions of hot and cold water, gadgets for producing stewards, and spring beds. Weeks went by, and each day seemed longer and more monotonous than the previous one. Bully 'n' biscuits comprised the main diet. Rats gnawed the tongues of our boots. Cockroaches pranced, route-marched, and did the polka in every corner and crevice. The only water on the ship was highly chlorinated. Gradually we explored, hunting in holds for tucker boxes that had been stored in vehicles. One of our chaps was something of a cracksman in an amateurish way, and there was not a padlock that did not yield to his knife and piece of wire. At last every crib had been cracked and everything edible eaten.'

Convoy JS1 arrived in Colombo at the end of January, to refuel and take on stores. After a week in port, JS1 departed Colombo on 3 February, escorted by the cruiser HMS *Cornwall*, with two Australian corvettes, HMAS *Bathurst* and HMAS *Lismore*, providing anti-submarine protection. On 5 February the corvettes left the convoy, which continued eastward at a slow, steady pace. Nearing the southern approaches to Sunda Strait on 10 February, JS1 was met by HMAS *Hobart*, which took over escort duty from *Cornwall*. Soon after, the escort was strengthened by the arrival of the cruisers HMS *Exeter* and *Java*, the destroyer HMS *Electra*, and the Indian sloop *Jumna*. Nearing Sumatra, the convoy split into two sections. *Filleigh, Yoma, Lulworth Hill, Hai Lee* and *Hermion* went to Oosthaven, on the southern tip of Sumatra, where they arrived on 13 February, while the other three ships reached Tanjong Priok, in Batavia, the following day.

Back in the Middle East, more ships were being collected in Egypt to transport the rest of the troops to the Dutch East Indies, but as had been the case with JS1, most of the available tonnage was small and slow. The 2/3 Machine Gun Battalion had been stationed at Fih, in Syria, when the order came to move, going first to Palestine on 14 January, then boarding at train on 31 January which took them to Kantara. Having crossed the Suez Canal in boats, the battalion again entrained, and finally arrived at Port Tewfik early on 1 February.

The harbour was filled with a variety of vessels, mostly small cargo ships, and numerous wrecks from enemy bombing raids, but standing out amongst all this was the troopship *Orcades*, the only large vessel available, having just arrived in a convoy from Britain. *Orcades* embarked 3400 Australian troops, who were to be the advance guard for the 7th Division, and it was planned they would be landed at Tanjong Priok. Also joining *Orcades* was a medical unit, the 2/2 Casualty Clearing Station.

During the morning on 1 February 33 officers and 603 other ranks from the 2/3 Machine Gun Battalion had boarded *Orcades*, only to find the ship already full of men. Most of the battalion ended up sleeping on B deck aft with a groundsheet and blanket. However, they were soon treated to an excellent three-course lunch, including roast lamb, which proved so popular many men went back for seconds, until the purser said, 'That's enough! We have served 5000 meals.' On the afternoon of 1 February, *Orcades* was dispatched alone as convoy JS2,

Orcades was the sole ship in convoy JS2. (*National Library of Australia*)

travelling at twice the speed of the ships that had comprised JS1, but the soldiers on board were unaware of their ultimate destination.

As the history of the 2/3 Machine Gun Battalion stated: 'At the end of the first week in February 1942 the bulk of the battalion less kitbags was therefore on board the *Orcades* steaming fast and unescorted to Colombo, while all the vehicles, Vickers guns, ammunition and other stores were preparing to leave Tewfik on a number of other ships, mostly small slow freighters ... In spite of the overcrowding, the *Orcades* was a vast improvement on the *Ile de France* as a troop ship. The food was excellent and the weather bearable. Physical training kept all ranks fit and Lieutenant Harry Fraser made his No. 8 platoon practise unarmed combat.'

Meanwhile, more troops were arriving in a steady stream at Port Tewfik, but not all could be found a place on *Orcades*. Among these was the whole of B echelon and the Quartermaster's staff of the 2/3 Machine Gun Battalion, along with various small units from other outfits on the move. Over several days, these men and many others plus vehicles, guns, ammunition and other stores, would be loaded aboard a variety of ships. Eventually, a convoy was gathered at Suez, made up of over a dozen ships, among them *Eastern Prince, City of Paris, City of London, Esperance Bay, Egra, Salween, Silverwillow, Penrith Castle, Mathura, Madras City, Empire Glade, Lavington Court* and the Polish *Kosciusko*. They were a motley collection, mostly cargo ships, only a few having proper accommodation, one of these being *Esperance Bay*, the largest vessel in the convoy, which had been built in 1922 for the Australian government to carry migrants from Britain to Australia with four sister ships, but was now owned by the Aberdeen & Commonwealth Line. In all, 10,090 troops of the 7th Division were taken on board these vessels, along with their equipment.

Among those to board these ships on 29 January were some troops

Esperance Bay was the largest vessel included in convoy JS3.

of the 2/14 Battalion, who found themselves spread among various vessels. Their vehicles were transported aboard *Empire Glade* and *Empire Glen*, along with their drivers, while others found themselves on the *Kosciusko*, *Lavington Court* and *Madras City*. The convoy, designated JS3, departed Suez on 30 January 1942. Its speed reduced to about 10 knots by the slowest vessel, convoy JS3 crawled across the Indian Ocean, going first to Bombay.

Whenever further ships were available in Suez to transport the Australians, another 17,800 troops were boarded at various times to be carried to Bombay, where they disembarked to await the arrival of smaller ships for the onward passage to the Dutch East Indies. Troops from the 2/14 Battalion who had not been able to join their comrades in convoy JS3 were ordered to Port Tewfik, leaving Suez by road between 30 January and 1 February. In Port Tewfik they boarded the giant troopship *Ile de France*, which had previously carried Australian troops to the Middle East. Also on board were most of the troops of the 21st Infantry Brigade.

On the voyage down the Red Sea and across the Indian Ocean, the Signals Platoon stood submarine watches on the bridge. Unlike the ships in convoy JS3, *Ile de France* made the passage at high speed, but there was considerable discomfort for the troops. Crossing the Indian Ocean there was a heavy sea running, while the food they were served was only fair, consisting primarily of bully beef and beans. The ship was also heavily overcrowded, and the amenities provided for the troops could not cope adequately. During the voyage most of the men amused themselves by playing swy or two-up, and dice games. There were also lectures, mostly concerning the coming fight against the Japanese,

City of Paris took on more Australian troops in Bombay. (*C.T. Reddings collection*)

including ship and aircraft recognition. The troops all disembarked when *Ile de France* arrived in Bombay on 6 February, and spent the next three days at Colaba Barracks.

On 9 February the troops from *Ile de France* went aboard some of the ships that were included in convoy JS3, which were still in Bombay. Some of the men of the 2/14 Battalion found themselves crowded onto the *City of Paris*, while 21 Brigade boarded the Polish *Kosciusko*. However, the ships remained at anchor in the harbour another four days before departing Bombay on Friday, 13 February, along with the rest of convoy JS3. The ships stopped briefly to refuel at Colombo before continuing their slow passage towards the Dutch East Indies, where the situation was worsening every day.

Medical units were also being moved, with the 2/5 and 2/11 Australian General Hospital units joining troops on board the liner *Mauretania* at Suez for a swift passage to Bombay, where they all disembarked. Some members of these medical units had also been placed on board *City of Paris* as well as *Esperance Bay*, but it was then discovered that all the equipment and personal baggage of the members of the 2/5 AGH had been placed on board *Orcades*.

Meanwhile, on *Orcades*, as one soldier wrote later, the big question was, 'what was their destination? That was the subject that puzzled everyone. Australia was probably the most favoured and Burma had its backers, but everyone was given food for thought when a lecture was given one day on the Netherlands East Indies.' On 8 February, *Orcades* arrived in Colombo, but no shore leave was granted and the next morning the liner departed, escorted by the cruiser HMS *Devonshire*. On 14 February, nearing Sunda Strait, the escort was taken over by the cruiser HMS *Dragon* and destroyer HMS *Encounter*. On that same day, Japanese forces began landing in southern Sumatra. *Orcades* was rerouted to Oosthaven, arriving there on 15 February, the day Singapore surrendered. A total of 133,814 Allied troops were marched into captivity by the victorious Japanese, including 15,384 Australians, two brigades of the AIF.

Some of the troops on board *Orcades*, mostly drawn from the 2/3 Machine Gun Battalion and the 2/2 Pioneers, were supplied with guns, then offloaded into a small Dutch coastal cargo vessel, the *Van Spilbergen*, and taken to Telok Betong, a short distance up the river from Oosthaven. Here the troops were intended to make a stand against the advancing Japanese, but only a few landed. Instead, they were told that the Japanese were advancing rapidly, being only eleven miles away, and the party was ordered to return to *Orcades*. The *Van Spilbergen* made its way back out to the anchorage, but it was a very dark night, with heavy rain falling. It seemed impossible to locate the blacked-out liner until a single bright flash of lightning illuminated the vessel, and the captain of the *Van Spilbergen* was able to bring his vessel back alongside. All the troops were reboarded in pouring rain, and an issue of hot cocoa and sandwiches was most welcome.

At the same time, the troops who had disembarked from the five ships of convoy JS1 that had gone to Oosthaven were ordered to destroy their equipment already landed, and reboard their ships, which were still in the port. On 16 February, *Orcades, Filleigh, Yoma, Lulworth Hill, Hai Lee* and *Hermion* departed Oosthaven in two sections, both bound for Tanjong Priok. *Orcades* and *Yoma* were escorted by the destroyers HMS *Tenedos* and HMS *Encounter*, while the other ships were escorted by HMAS *Yarra*. All these ships arrived on 17 February in the harbour of Tanjong Priok, which was filled with ships, many having escaped Singapore in the final days before it surrendered.

Among the ships in Tanjong Priok was the former Blue Star cargo liner *Empire Star*, which was one of the last to leave Singapore. The events surrounding the departure of *Empire Star* were mirrored by many other vessels that escaped at the last minute, but in the case of this vessel stories would later surface describing some of those she carried to safety as both deserters and murderers. *Empire Star* had carried supplies to Singapore, arriving on 28 January, having survived several air attacks already. On the day she arrived, Singapore was subjected to ten air raids, and more continued over succeeding days. The docks were the main target, so the master of *Empire Star* decided to move his ship to an anchorage, but eventually the ship returned to the wharf, where the crew worked desperately to unload the cargo of military supplies, even though there was no-one to take them away from the wharf. By the afternoon of 11 February, *Empire Star* was one of the few ships still left in the port. Reports spread that she would be the last ship able to leave the island, so it was rushed by civilians and Allied military personnel desperate to get away before the Japanese crossed the causeway and captured the island.

Soon there were over a thousand people crowded on board the ship, some shinning up mooring lines to avoid the chaos at the single gangplank, while others climbed cargo nets hung over the side. Among those on board were a number of RAAF officers and some Australian Army nursing staff. Suddenly, a group of about twenty armed Australian soldiers appeared at the foot of the gangway and demanded to be taken on board. The men trying to control the situation on the dock attempted to stop them, but the Australians pushed them to one side and climbed onto the deck of the ship. The master, Captain Selwyn Capon, ordered them to leave, but the men refused, so military police were called. They threatened to use their weapons on the soldiers, who remained defiant, and the police, unwilling to create further mayhem, returned ashore. However, to prevent further trouble, Captain Capon ordered the gangplank be raised.

In subsequent years, this incident was sensationalised to the point where it was claimed that a group of 200 armed Australian troops had deserted their posts and descended on the ship. When refused permission to board, the story claimed, they had shot dead the harbour master, Captain Atkinson, and pushed aside women and children to get aboard the *Empire Star*. It is in fact doubtful that Captain Atkinson was involved in the incident at all. He was able to get away from Singapore on the day before the surrender on board a small local tug, which was attacked by a Japanese cruiser in Banka Strait, and sunk with the loss of almost all on board, including Atkinson.

Once on board, the twenty Australians actually were quite helpful, draining petrol from the tanks of military transport vehicles still sitting on the deck to reduce the fire risk if the ship were to be hit during the regular air raids. Late in the afternoon of 11 February, *Empire Star* pulled away from the dock, but had to anchor out in the roads, as the tide was unfavourable. While it was lying at anchor, several more troops were able to join the ship. These men had been part of the 22 Brigade, fighting on the Malayan peninsula, which was overrun by the Japanese on 9 February. They had walked towards Singapore, until reaching the coast and joining three sailors in a sampan they found. As it did not have a sail, the men were forced to paddle the boat, and eventually came close to Singapore, where they were sighted from *Empire Star*. A net was dropped over the side, and the men climbed on board.

Soon after, the overcrowded vessel departed, but next day they came under attack from Japanese aircraft, during which several people on *Empire Star* were killed, including six men handling the improvised gun emplacements around the decks. Eventually, *Empire Star* reached Tanjong Priok, but as they approached the port Captain Capon had sent a message stating he had 'unwelcome passengers' on board. As a result, when the ship docked at Tanjong Priok the wharf was filled with about 200 armed men, including 40 marines from HMS *Durban*, which was also in port. The twenty Australians agreed to hand over their weapons and went ashore quietly, but were then driven to the local prison. Several days later, all were released, after the matter had been questioned by Brigadier Lloyd, in private life a leading barrister.

The same night that *Empire Star* left Singapore, a convoy of about a dozen smaller merchant ships also slipped away from the port, among them *Gorgon* and *Derrymore*, which had been in convoy MS1 that arrived on 1 February. *Gorgon* headed directly back to Fremantle, with 358 passengers on board, far in excess of her available accommodation, and made the journey successfully.

Derrymore was not so fortunate. Unable to unload her cargo, which had been loaded in Britain five months previously, and included Spitfire aircraft in packing cases along with 2000 tons of explosives, she had now been ordered to make for the Middle East, departing with several other ships on 12 February. All through 13 February the convoy managed to escape detection by Japanese air or naval forces, as they steamed towards Tanjong Priok, but on that night, about 9 o'clock, when the ships were almost into Sunda Strait, the *Derrymore* was hit by a torpedo and took a heavy list to starboard. Only one lifeboat was left undamaged, but the crew was able to manufacture makeshift liferafts out of hatch covers and empty oil drums before the ship sank. Among those on board were about 200 Royal Australian Air Force personnel, including fighter pilots wounded in action, who had been recovering in the Singapore hospital until it was evacuated and they were able to get on board *Derrymore*. Nine of these RAAF personnel lost their lives when the ship was sunk, but among the survivors picked up next day by the corvette HMAS *Ballarat* was one fighter pilot who had been recuperating in the hospital, John Gorton, later to become

Prime Minister of Australia. The survivors were taken to Tanjong Priok, where Gorton was again hospitalised. He was later fortunate to escape being captured there by securing a place on a small ship that managed to reach Fremantle safely on 3 March.

Already in Tanjong Priok was *City of Manchester*, which had also been included in convoy MS1. Despite the daily air raids, the crew had worked tirelessly to unload as much of the cargo as possible, but on the afternoon of 3 February the ship was forced to leave its wharf, where fires were raging. At that time the ship's master had gone ashore to try and obtain orders for his ship, but he was eventually able to return to his command, anchored in Keppel Harbour. With air raids increasing in intensity, *City of Manchester* slipped out of Singapore on 4 February, and two days later arrived in Oosthaven. *City of Manchester* was again on the move on 9 February, arriving the following day in Tanjong Priok, where she was able to berth and unload some more ammunition and military vehicles, including a staff car. *City of Manchester* and *Empire Star* joined the rapidly growing group of vessels jamming into the docks and harbour of Tanjong Priok. Most were busy loading refugees, and convoys were being dispatched several times a day.

In view of the rapidly deteriorating situation in the Dutch East Indies, the Australian government expressed grave doubts about the possibility of Australian troops that had arrived from the Middle East aboard *Orcades* and the other ships being employed to any advantage in the area. Prime Minister Curtin was still pressing Churchill that all the Australian troops then on the move should return home, and General Lavarack strongly supported him. In spite of this, on 19 February, the same day Darwin was bombed for the first time, 2400 troops from *Orcades* were disembarked and joined others from convoy JS1 being dispersed through Java to protect Allied airfields. Among those to go ashore was the 2/2 Casualty Clearing Station, under the command of Lieutenant Colonel E.E. Dunlop, better known as 'Weary' Dunlop, who set up his unit in the high school at Bandung.

By this time, Japanese forces were closing on Tanjong Priok, and many of the ships that had taken refuge there were forced to flee once again. On 16 February, *Empire Star*, accompanied by a Dutch vessel, *Plancius*, left the port, crammed to overflowing with some 3000 refugees between them. Once away from the immediate danger, the two ships separated, *Plancius* making for Colombo, while *Empire Star* succeeded in reaching Fremantle after some frightening days at sea.

The ships that had made up convoy JS1 departed Tanjong Priok on 20 February as part of a large convoy heading for Colombo, carrying thousands of refugees. *Orcades*, which had gone to anchorage outside the port, was ordered to return on 21 February, to collect as many refugees and soldiers as possible. The liner left for Colombo at midnight, carrying about 10,000 persons, again travelling alone and unescorted, being the last large vessel to leave the Dutch East Indies.

Also departing Tanjong Priok on 21 February was the *Marella*, which had arrived from Australia in convoy MS3. *Marella* had on board Australian and New Zealand Air Force ground crews whose airfields had been evacuated, some army personnel, a number of British seamen who had survived the sinking of *Empress of Asia* off Singapore a few weeks previously, and hundreds of civilians, including women and children. The vessel joined up with a convoy of eleven ships, being escorted by HMAS *Yarra* and HMS *Exeter*, which stayed with them until they reached Sunda Strait. A few days later, both warships were sunk. *Marella* reached Fremantle safely on 27 February, departing again on 3 March for Melbourne, where she arrived six days later. Meanwhile, the Australian troops left behind fought valiantly against overwhelming odds in Java, but over 2700 became prisoners of war when they were forced to surrender on 8 March.

City of Manchester remained in Tanjong Priok for ten days, her crew unloading as much cargo as possible, but this was never used against the Japanese, and most ended up being destroyed on the wharf. On 20 February, the vessel departed, escorted by the cruiser HMS *Exeter*, bound for Tjilatjap, where they arrived on 23 February, and moored to a buoy in the river off the port. Eventually a signal was received, advising that all Allied shipping should leave the area immediately and proceed independently to Australia. Just before midnight on 27 February, *City of Manchester* slipped out of Tjilatjap. However, just before dawn the next day the ship was struck by a torpedo and burst into flames. The Japanese submarine then surfaced, and fired on the ship with its gun, and within a few minutes *City of Manchester* had sunk. The survivors were rescued from lifeboats by an American naval vessel which took them back to Tjilatjap, where they were taken to a Dutch Army camp just outside the town, where they remained there until 1 March.

Another vessel to Tjilatjap on 27 February was the *Kota Gede*, a Dutch cargo ship of 4500 gross tons. Among the hundreds on board was Jack Woodward, along with a number of his RAAF colleagues, who had only arrived in Singapore on 24 October 1941. Woodward was posted as a navigator on a Blenheim bomber based at Palembang, on

Sumatra, which was ordered to fly to Java on 15 February. The plane crash-landed near Batavia, but the crew all escaped and spent the next twelve days near Batavia before being ordered to evacuate. At Tjilatjap they boarded the *Kota Gede*, alongside which was a much larger vessel, the *Abbekirk*.

Jack Woodward later wrote, 'By about 2 pm the ship was very crowded — almost chock a block — yet still more men were coming aboard. It was quite evident that the ship would be very much overcrowded and congested, and that it would be a most uncomfortable journey.' During the afternoon the *Abbekirk* and *Kota Gede* pulled away from the wharf, only to drop anchor in the harbour, and as night fell there were fifteen ships ready to leave. The convoy began leaving the harbour about 6 pm, and the men on board *Kota Gede* heard a rumour that their destination was Fremantle.'

During the first night at sea, *Kota Gede* separated from the rest of the convoy and set off alone on a westerly course. *Abbekirk* and the other thirteen ships continued on a course to Fremantle, but were subjected to numerous attacks by Japanese bombers. Eventually *Abbekirk* lost contact with the other ships, and managed to reach Fremantle safely on 6 March. One other ship from the convoy limped into port two days later, but the other eleven were all sunk. However, the men aboard *Kota Gede* did not learn this until much later.

On *Kota Gede*, Jack Woodward estimated, 'The number on board was about 2,500 plus! All of the complement were Air Force personnel, and it was roughly estimated that forty percent of those on board were aircrew. The commissioned officers were in the deck quarters, whilst all other ranks were in the holds or on the decks.' Each of the holds had several levels, and access from level to level, and the deck, was by ladder. Once under way, Jack Woodward went to check out the hold in which he was to travel.

> We then went down into the rear hold, and estimated the total number in there would have been well over a thousand people. Naturally, being just below the equator, it was very hot and humid, the air was most stifling, and it was to prove that way for the rest of the journey ... If we were to be attacked and the ship sunk, there were only five lifeboats, each probably catering for no more than forty or fifty men. Also there were two rafts, probably holding twenty men each. There were no lifejackets that we noticed, and certainly none in our section.
>
> For such a crowd, there was insufficient sanitation available in the

ship itself ... Full credit had to be given to the Captain and crew for the construction of toilet facilities over the side of the ship, with salt water showers running on the side of the deck at the rear for washing oneself after toilets and also for showering. Fortunately the seas were relatively calm for the whole nine days at sea, otherwise it would have been very awkward to climb the steps on to the improvised toilet seats over the ship's side.

Eating created a problem for such a large crowd, with few suitable facilities available. There were three meals a day — tinned bacon with two army biscuits for breakfast, biscuits (again two only) with margarine and jam for a snack lunch (if you felt like it) and maconachie stew (made and canned in England) and two army biscuits for dinner at night. All were served cold, though a mug of hot to warm tea was always available. It was not a very sustaining diet, but it sufficed, and we were grateful to have that much ... Breakfast commenced at about 6.30 am finishing at about 10.30, with the dinner starting at about 3.30 pm and continuing until all were served. The eating procedure meant large queues, stretching from the front of the ship into each of the holds and through to the point at the rear of the ship where the food was served. At all times of the day, meal queues were in evidence.

It was impossible to freely move round the ship, and the only movement was joining the queues for meals. With such a number, it was impossible to provide for any type of amusement or recreation. After finishing a meal, the general rule for everybody was to return to one's place of bedding and rest.

Despite the calm seas, some on board succumbed to seasickness. There were also some men on board with other medical problems, but no drugs were available, and few instruments, so several men died and were buried at sea.

Instead of heading towards Fremantle as they hoped, *Kota Gede* turned west, and after eight days at sea dropped anchor outside Colombo harbour on the morning of 6 March. Tenders were sent out from shore to take the sick ashore, which numbered about a hundred men, but the rest remained on board. 'As soon as the sick were taken off,' wrote Jack Woodward, 'orders came for the *Kota Gede* to proceed to Bombay.' The captain was quite concerned with this order, and suddenly the men were told they could have a fresh-water shower. When these were finished, the captain sent a message that he had insufficient fresh water on board for a voyage to Bombay, so the *Kota Gede* was allowed to enter the port, and anchor. The men remained on board overnight, and it was not until late the following afternoon that they disembarked into ferries for the trip to the wharf, from where they went by truck to the railway station, and were taken to the town of Galle.

On Friday 13 March, most of the Australians from *Kota Gede* were back in Colombo, looking forward to the final stage of their trip back to Australia. They found themselves on board a much larger vessel, the 25,554 gross ton Union Castle liner *Stirling Castle*. They left Colombo the next afternoon, being escorted by the battleship HMS *Malaya*, two cruisers and several destroyers until night fell, then they were on their own. In contrast to the 2500 who had packed aboard the *Kota Gede*, there were only 800 on *Stirling Castle*, which voyaged non-stop to Melbourne, berthing there on 28 March.

Back in Batavia, on 1 March, the survivors from *City of Manchester* were able to get aboard one of the last ships to escape Tjilatjap, the Dutch flag *Zaandam*. The experiences of *Zaandam* in the desperate situation in the Dutch East Indies were typical of these confusing times. *Zaandam*, completed as recently as December 1938 for Holland America Line, was a 10,909 gross ton Dutch liner with accommodation for only 125 passengers, and a large cargo capacity, being one of a class of four built in the late 1930s for a secondary service across the Atlantic from Rotterdam to New York. Soon after war broke out in Europe, *Zaandam* was transferred to the Pacific, and operated a service from American west coast ports to the Dutch East Indies and Singapore. The vessel had been scheduled to depart San Francisco on 7 December 1941, but this was cancelled following the attack on Pearl Harbor the same day. Instead, *Zaandam* left on 26 December, carrying a full cargo of military materials, bound for Batavia. Voyaging by way of New Zealand and around the southern coast of Australia, the ship was to have berthed in Oosthaven, but instead was directed to Lampong Bay, arriving there on 3 February.

On 8 February, *Zaandam* left Lampong Bay, and two days later arrived in Tjilatjap, only to find the port crowded with shipping. The ship remained there two weeks, hoping to unload the precious cargo it carried, but this proved impossible as no berth was available. On 27 February, all the ships in Tjilatjap were ordered to proceed to sea, but soon after leaving, *Zaandam* received a message to return to the port, as the ship had been designated to carry evacuees. After spending the night circling off the coast, *Zaandam* began closing on Tjilatjap, but was attacked by three Japanese planes. The ship's gunners managed to keep the planes at a distance while the captain turned his ship in circles. In a final attack the three planes came in from the sun and dropped four or five bombs, but all missed, though the decks and funnel were peppered by splinters. In their next attack, the planes went for the bridge, firing their machine-guns as they approached, then dropping another four or five bombs, but the planes were too high for this attack to be effective. Eventually the planes departed, but *Zaandam* remained at sea that night, then berthed in Tjilatjap on the morning of 1 March.

During the day evacuees scrambled on board *Zaandam*, these including Australian and British troops as well as some Dutch airmen and their families, the staff of the United States consulate and some civilians. In the reigning confusion no check was made of the number of people boarding the ship, and when it finally departed Tjilatjap that night, under a clear full moon, there were 892 passengers on board. The hard-pressed crew had to make hasty arrangements for carrying such a large number, as the ship was still in its regular configuration and had not been converted for war service in any way. The 60 staterooms were allocated to women and children as well as the injured, while officers were assigned to the lounge and smoking room, the lucky ones managing to secure a sofa or chair while others were forced to sleep on the floor. The rest of those on board had to make do with any available space on the deck.

Also leaving Tjilatjap at the same time were six small vessels owned by another Dutch company, KPM, all filled with desperate refugees. However, Japanese air and sea forces were out in strength and only one of these KPM ships was ever seen again, though the radio room aboard *Zaandam* picked up many calls for help from ships under attack. Another vessel to escape Tjilatjap at that time was *Sloterdyk*, a cargo ship also owned by Holland America Line, which rescued 330 Dutch naval personnel and succeeded in carrying them to Fremantle. The day after leaving Tjilatjap, *Zaandam* came upon a small sloop, crammed with 29 people, including survivors from two ships sunk the previous night, and they were taken on board, increasing the number of passengers to over 900. The huge number of persons on the ship created a major problem when it came to meals, but this was solved by providing coffee and sandwiches for breakfast each day, a good stew at lunch, and more coffee and sandwiches in the evening. Women and children took their meals in the dining room, while all others were served on deck.

Having escaped detection in the dangerous waters around the Dutch East Indies, *Zaandam* set course for Fremantle, where it arrived safely on 6 March. Here the military personnel disembarked, but the civilians had to be kept on board, as all the schools, church halls, movie theatres and other venues made available for evacuees were already full. On 10 March, *Zaandam* departed Fremantle, still carrying 309 passengers, and proceeded to Melbourne, berthing there on 15 March. At last the remaining passengers were able to disembark and the cargo was also unloaded. *Zaandam* then loaded a cargo of wool, and on 27 April departed Melbourne to again cross the Pacific. The vessel subsequently returned to the Atlantic, serving as a transport. However, having survived the Japanese onslaught on 2 November 1942, *Zaandam* was torpedoed by a German submarine in the North Atlantic and sank with the loss of 135 lives. In one of the most amazing survival stories of the war, three survivors were found in a lifeboat 82 days after the sinking.

Back in the Middle East, troops were still being gathered at Port Tewfik and Suez to be transported to the Dutch East Indies. Medical units also continued to be moved, including the 2/2 and 2/9 Australian General Hospital and the 2/1 Casualty Clearing Station. The staging camp at Suez was known as 'The Aviary,' because it was surrounded by a high barbed-wire fence and had only one entry and exit gate. Among the ships gathered at Suez for the initial stage of the move was the former P & O liner *Strathallan*, whose captain refused to take women on board when he was advised his complement would include nurses. Eventually the situation

Strathallan eventually carried troops all the way back to Australia.

was resolved and the nurses of the 2/9 AGH joined the ship, which departed Suez on 17 February, two days after the fall of Singapore.

The official war history of the 2/9 AGH described the voyage to Colombo thus: 'The conditions at sea were cramped and uncomfortable, cabin space was limited, and the men slept on the decks. Kit bags and gear had to be kept on the bunks, even when sleeping, deck space was limited — most of it being "out of bounds" for women — and the blacked out cabins were hot and humid. Boat drill was carried out frequently and attendance was compulsory. Allotted to one of the lifeboats was a medical officer with a nice sense of humour, twenty sisters and one old experienced sailor. Captain Ellis Finney remembers the medical officer explaining to the sailor that none of the nurses could row, but the sailor replied in very emphatic terms, "They'll bloody soon learn!" ... On 1 March the *Strathallan* arrived in Colombo ... All plans for the 2/9 AGH to set up in Java were cancelled.' Instead, *Strathallan* joined a convoy bound for Australia.

Also in this convoy was the *Andes*, which had previously carried New Zealand troops to Britain in convoy US3. *Andes* had boarded Australian troops in Egypt, including the 2/3 Light Anti-Aircraft Regiment, who found the food good and the ship clean. *Andes* departed on 20 February, and arrived in Colombo on 27 February. As with the other ships, it had originally been planned that the troops on *Andes* would be sent to the Dutch East Indies, but that had been changed by the time the ship arrived in Colombo. The Commanding General of the 6th Division, Major General Herring, and members of his staff, were in Colombo, and had been destined to fly back to Australia, but instead they joined *Andes* on 28 February. It was not until 2 March that *Andes* left Colombo, in a convoy that also included *Orcades*, *Strathallan* and *Durban Castle*, escorted by the cruiser HMS *Glasgow*.

Several days after leaving Colombo, with little danger of Japanese attack, the convoy was able to disperse, and the troopships proceeded alone at their top speeds. On 11 March, *Strathallan* and *Andes* arrived in Fremantle, where the 2/11 Battalion disembarked, then the liners continued their voyage. The crossing of the Bight was quite rough, with many men being seasick. Meanwhile, *Orcades*, the fastest of the liners, had proceeded directly to Port Adelaide, arriving there on 14 March, though her troops did not disembark until the following day. The same day, 15 March, *Andes* also arrived in Port Adelaide during the afternoon, General Herring and the remaining troops disembarking the following day. *Andes* then went on to Melbourne, and across the Pacific. *Strathallan* arrived in Adelaide on 16 March, her passengers disembarking the following morning.

The futility of sending more Australian troops from the Middle East to the Dutch East Indies had become transparently apparent to Prime Minister Curtin. With the Japanese moving ever closer to Australia, and the bombing of Darwin on 19 February, the Australian government decided it was imperative that the remaining elements of the 1st Australian Corps still in the Middle East, or en route to the Dutch East Indies on ships, including convoy JS3, must be diverted to Australia. This was to cause a major dispute between Curtin and Churchill.

It all began with a message from General Wavell to Churchill and President Roosevelt, sent on 14 February, the day before Singapore surrendered. Wavell stated that the 'unexpected rapid advance of the enemy on Singapore and approach of escorted enemy convoy towards South Sumatra necessitates review of our plan for defence of Netherlands East Indies … .If Singapore falls, enemy air and land forces will be available not only to attack Burma, but also to reinforce southerly action,' this latter remark referring to a possible landing on Australia's north or west coast. Regarding the Australian troops then en route from the Middle East, Wavell stated that 'from the purely strategic aspect there are advantages in diverting one or both divisions to Burma or Australia.'

The next day, General Sturdee, Chief of the Australian General Staff, prepared a paper on the best use of the troops presently in transit. At that time, there were the 10,000 troops on the way to Java in convoy JS3, plus another 17,800 troops in Bombay awaiting transfer to smaller ships for the voyage to the Dutch East Indies. General Sturdee expressed the opinion that these troops could not arrive in Sumatra in time to be of any help. He concluded by recommending that the troops in Bombay, and those in convoy JS3, be diverted to Australia, and that the 9th Australian Division also be recalled from the Middle East to Australia at an early date.

Curtin found himself in full agreement with his Chief of General Staff and sent a message to Churchill embodying Sturdee's recommendations, but couching them more in the form of a suggestion than a demand. However, at almost the same time, Churchill received another message from General Wavell suggesting that the Australian troops in convoy JS3 should be diverted to Burma, which was being seriously threatened by the advancing Japanese and in danger of collapse.

The proposal to send the Australian force to Burma rapidly gained acceptance with the War Cabinet in Britain, where even the Australian representatives supported the idea. High Commissioner Stanley Bruce cabled Curtin that, 'in my view it is essential we should agree to the 7th Australian Division going to Burma,' and in this he was supported by Sir Earle Page, special envoy to the War Cabinet. In exchange for the Australians going to Burma, it was proposed that two American divisions would be sent to Australia. Curtin, however, remained firm in his conviction that the Australian troops had to come back to Australia. He sent a long message to that effect on 19 February, which ended with the statement that, since the Dutch East Indies had been ruled out as a destination, the troopships now in the Indian Ocean 'should come to Australia with the greatest possible expedition.' This view was strengthened within the government when, also on 19 February, Japanese aircraft raided Darwin for the first time. There were also Japanese landings in Java and in Timor, where the invaders were met by Australian troops. The war was now right on Australia's doorstep.

The Curtin message crossed with one sent by Churchill on 20 February, which began: 'I suppose you realise that your leading division, the head of which is sailing south of Colombo to NEI at this moment … .is the only force that can reach Rangoon in time to prevent its loss. It can begin to disembark at Rangoon about 26th or 27th. There is nothing else in the world that can fill the gap … We are entirely in favour of all Australian troops returning home to defend their native soil, and we shall help their transportation in every way. But a vital war emergency cannot be ignored, and troops en route to other destinations must be ready to turn aside and take part in a battle. Every effort would be made to relieve this division at the earliest moment and send them on to Australia.'

Churchill then went on to stress the importance of the troops being sent to Burma, stating 'your greatest support in this hour of peril must be drawn from the United States. They alone can bring into Australia the necessary troops and air forces, and they appear ready to do so.' The message from Churchill concluded, 'we must have an answer immediately as the leading ships of the convoy will soon be steaming in the opposite direction from Rangoon, and every day is a day lost. I trust therefore that for the sake of all interests and above all your own interests you will give the most careful consideration to the case I have set before you.' Sir Earle Page, strongly recommended that Australia agree to Churchill's request.

Despite his request for an immediate reply, Churchill decided he could wait no longer to alter the course of the convoy, and had already sent orders that the ships turn towards Rangoon prior to sending his message to Curtin. Churchill also requested President Roosevelt to send a message to Curtin, which he did the same day. Unaware of the change of course of the convoy, the Australian War Cabinet met on 21 February to consider the appeals from Churchill and Roosevelt. The Cabinet decided they could not accede to Churchill's request and decided that the convoy should be diverted to Australia immediately.

A message to this effect was dispatched to Churchill, which he received on 22 February. Curtin referred to Churchill's 'rather strongly worded request at this late stage,' then went on to point out that 'Malaya, Singapore and Timor have been lost and the whole Netherlands East Indies will apparently be occupied shortly by the Japanese.' He also pointed out that the enemy had 'commenced raiding our territory in the north-west and also in the north-east from Rabaul.' Curtin then gave a brief appraisal of the situation as he saw it, expressing his fear that should the Australian troops go to Rangoon there could be a recurrence of 'the experiences of the Greek and Malayan campaigns.' Curtin concluded by stating that, in view of the services rendered by the Australian Imperial Force in the Middle East, 'we have every right to expect them to be returned to Australia as soon as possible with adequate escorts to ensure their safe arrival.'

President Roosevelt accepted the Australian decision, but Churchill responded quite differently, stating in a note to Curtin, 'we could not contemplate that you would refuse our request ... for the diversion of the leading division to save the situation in Burma.' He then went on to tell Curtin that he had already ordered the convoy to change course for Rangoon and that the convoy 'is now too far north for some of the ships in it to reach Australia without refuelling. These physical conditions give a few days for the situation to develop and for you to review the position should you wish to do so. Otherwise the leading Australian Division will be returned to Australia as quickly as possible in accordance with your wishes.'

Curtin was shocked to receive this message, and on 23 February sent a stern reply, stating that Churchill had treated his 'approval of this vital diversion as merely a matter of form.' He went on to say, 'now you contemplate using the AIF to save Burma. All this has been done as in Greece without adequate air support.' Restating his obligation to protect Australia from the advancing Japanese, Curtin concluded that 'in the circumstances it is quite impossible to reverse a decision which we made with the utmost care and which we have affirmed and reaffirmed.' On receiving this message from Curtin, Churchill admitted defeat. On 23 February, having issued the necessary orders, he replied to Curtin, 'your convoy is now proceeding to refuel at Colombo. It will then proceed to Australia in accordance with your wishes.'

Dr H.D. Steward was Medical Officer with 21 Infantry Brigade on board *Kosciusko*, and wrote in his diary on 21 February, 'After a whistle signal from the leading ship, the convoy turned around and set a course which we thought would take us to Rangoon.' This course was maintained for two days before the convoy again turned around, this time heading back to Colombo. For the troops on board the ships, the previous few days had been quite bewildering, with reports of their destination constantly changing, but their hearts were lifted when word spread that they were now to go home. There is no doubt the stand taken by Curtin saved many thousands of Australian troops from being killed or taken prisoner. Even if this convoy had arrived in Rangoon on 26 or 27 February, the troops would not have been fully operational for at least ten days. There was also the fact that several of the ships involved in convoy JS3 had suffered mechanical defects and put into the port of Cochin for repairs. Among these were *Empire Glade* and *Empire Glen*, which were carrying the bulk of the vehicles, mortars, other weapons and ammunition required by the troops in the convoy. The Japanese occupied Rangoon on 8 March.

Although John Curtin had succeeded in convincing Winston Churchill that the Australian troops sent overseas should be returned home as soon as possible, there was still a desire within the British War Cabinet that some of these troops should remain overseas. On 24 February, the day after Churchill agreed to divert the troopships of convoy JS3 away from Burma to Australia, Sir Earle Page sent Curtin a message regarding a meeting of the War Cabinet held on the previous evening at which the question of the defence of Ceylon had been raised.

Page pointed out that the Japanese could now mount an attack on Ceylon from Singapore, which would cause major disruption to Allied shipping in the Indian Ocean and could adversely affect Australia. With reference to the troops in convoy JS3, Page continued that as 'the convoy carrying the Australian 7th Division is to refuel at Colombo, which will take several days, I would submit for your serious consideration whether the Australian government should offer to allow these Australian troops to remain in Ceylon until at least the 70th

British Division could arrive and get into battle order, which would be a month or six weeks at the latest.' Page indicated that this matter had not actually been raised in the War Cabinet, but rather was being proffered as a suggestion.

Unfortunately, Curtin was ill at this time and confined to his bed, so the reply to Page, drafted by the Minister for External Affairs, Dr Evatt, was less than sympathetic, rejecting outright the idea of providing troops for Ceylon. In contrast, when the Australian Chiefs of Staff considered the implications of Page's message they reached the opposite conclusion. In a report to Curtin on 26 February they stated that the 'objections held to diverting an AIF Division to Burma do not apply to Ceylon.' Two days later, in a further report to Curtin, the Chiefs of Staff further amplified their agreement, stating, 'should the British government make a request for temporary retention of an AIF Division in Ceylon, we recommend that the equivalent of one Division should be retained under the following conditions:– (a) Dispatch to Australia of remaining two Brigade Groups of 6th Australian Division now awaiting embarkation (in Suez). (b) The return to Australia of the 9th Australian Division now in Syria at the earliest date. (c) Provision of maximum possible fighter cover and bomber force in Ceylon and Southern India.' However, no definite decision to provide troops for Ceylon was made at that time and the Australian government continued in their insistence that the troops in convoy JS3 return to Australia as quickly as possible.

At the same time the argument between Curtin and Churchill over the destination of convoy JS3 had been raging, the American transport *Mount Vernon*, formerly the North Atlantic liner *Washington*, had boarded 4668 Australian troops in Bombay and set off alone for the

The troops on board the American transport *Mount Vernon* were the first to arrive back in Australia. (*C.T. Reddings collection*)

Dutch East Indies. When Churchill gave the order for convoy JS3 to turn north to Rangoon, *Mount Vernon* had also been ordered to comply and duly changed course. Once Churchill had acquiesced to Curtin's demand, *Mount Vernon* was ordered to proceed directly to Australia, as she had sufficient fuel supplies to complete the journey. Her troops were the first to return home in Operation Stepsister, disembarking in Adelaide on 9 March.

Having turned south, convoy JS3 headed back towards Colombo, where it arrived on 25 February and the ships were refuelled. Now that the destination had been changed to Australia, it was also decided that the designator code of the convoy should be changed. Instead of JS3, the convoy became SU1, the first to operate in the reverse direction to the US convoys that had carried troops to the Middle East for the previous two years. Convoy SU1 departed Colombo on 1 March, escorted by four units from the Royal Navy, the battleship HMS *Royal Sovereign*, cruiser HMS *Cornwall*, destroyer HMS *Express* and corvette HMS *Hollyhock*, and three Australian ships, the armed merchant cruiser *Manoora*, and the destroyers HMAS *Nizam* and HMAS *Vampire*.

The atmosphere on board the ships was now very different, as troops looked forward to returning to Australia. Dr Steward on board *Kosciusko*

The battleship HMS *Royal Sovereign* was the major escort vessel for convoy SU1.

recorded that the days were very hot and the men spent their time sunbathing or playing deck sports. At night, with the ships blacked out, it was too hot to sleep in the cabins, where those who tried were soon a lather of sweat, so most men slept on the open decks.

Convoy SU1 arrived safely in Fremantle on 15 March 1942 and the troops enjoyed a few days of leave. However, as Dr Steward recorded, arriving in Fremantle 'meant home to most men of our Battalion, the only West Australian unit in the convoy. Necks were strained to detect familiar landmarks as thoughts turned to happy family reunions, but hopeless Army bungling made sure nothing went right. We had to wait in the stream for more than a day, envious as troops from other states disembarked for local leave. Worse followed. Leave was granted for 24 hours, after which most of the troops were back on board, only to be told that because of refuelling difficulties, the ship's departure would be delayed, but nobody knew for how long. At sailing time about 350 men, or one-third of the Battalion, were missing, and had to travel to Adelaide by train.'

The ships continued to their final destination, Port Adelaide, though this was not done in convoy. *Empire Glade* was among the ships that arrived on 22 March, followed the next day by others, including *City of Paris*, *Kosciusko* and *Madras City*. Most of the convoy had arrived in Port Adelaide by 24 March, as on that day the list of ships berthed in the outer harbour included *City of Paris*, *Salween*, *Egra* and *Esperance Bay*, while berthed in the river were *Eastern Prince*, *Masula*, *Empire Glade*, *Cape Wrath*, *Empire Oriole*, *Silverwillow*, *Silvermaple*, *Mathura*, *Kosciusko*, *Madras City*, *Penrith Castle*, *Empire Pintail* and *Sophocles*. *Empire Glen*, still suffering machinery problems, finally limped into port on 29 March. In all, the men had been at sea for up to seven weeks.

The cargo ship *Madras City*, which carried troops and equipment in convoy SU1. (*C.T. Reddings collection*)

The troops were all glad to be home again, even though they realised theirs would be but a brief respite before being sent north to face the Japanese. However, many were shocked at some of the carefree attitudes they found in Australia towards the war. As Dr Steward wrote, 'We saw this attitude on the Fremantle docks where wharf labourers lounged about with hands in their pockets when there was work to do. Adelaide's wharfies refused to unload a ship carrying artillery guns and twenty-five pounder shells unless they got "danger money." "Bloody lovely," said one of the

Battalion's famous Goldfields Mob from Kalgoorlie; "they're not worth two bob, the bludgers." "Two bob?" said another miner, "a zack the lot!"'

Not all the troops had to suffer slow trips aboard small ships, as had been the case with convoy JS3. The 2/5 Regiment, which had been operating in Lebanon and Syria, reached Transit Camp 157 on the outskirts of Suez on 8 February 1942, and a few days later embarked on *Nieuw Amsterdam*, then usually employed on a shuttle service between Cape Town and Suez. After a four-day voyage to Bombay, the troops disembarked, and four days later boarded the much smaller *Nevasa*, which had taken part in convoy US2. The vessel left Bombay in a convoy destined for the Dutch East Indies, but by the time they reached Colombo the Japanese invasion of Java and Timor was well under way, and Darwin was being bombed by Japanese aircraft. As a result, *Nevasa* was redirected to Australia, arriving in Adelaide in early March.

Throughout this period, the strain of leading a nation in wartime was taking a heavy toll on John Curtin. During the days he was trying to secure the return to Australia of the troop convoys originally destined for the Netherlands East Indies, he endured many sleepless nights. The strain on Curtin at this time was said to have been so intense that his hair turned grey and his health almost broke down completely as he waited for coded messages reporting the progress of the convoy. He was confined to bed, but unable to rest.

For Curtin, these were some of the worst days of the war, and the strain only intensified as the convoy neared Australian waters. Late one night, the Clerk of the House of Representatives, Mr Frank Green, came across Curtin walking in the grounds of the Lodge, his official residence in Canberra. When asked why he was not asleep, Curtin replied, 'I have taken the responsibility of bringing one of our divisions back to defend our north. How can I sleep when their transports are in the Indian Ocean in danger from enemy submarines. Don't you know they are a few days from the west — and no air coverage. Suppose they were attacked. They'd all drown.' Green replied, 'I know, I know, Jack, but you can't do anything about it. Can't you get to bed.'

By the beginning of March, Curtin was well enough to once again attend meetings of the Australian War Cabinet, where the matter of providing Australian troops for the temporary defence of Ceylon was again the major topic. Curtin was made aware that two brigades, the 16th and 17th, of the 6th Division, were about to embark on troopships in Suez for their return trip to Australia. On 2 March Curtin sent a message to Churchill which began, 'We are most anxious to assist you in your anxieties over the strengthening of the garrison at Ceylon.' Curtin went on that 'for the purpose of temporarily adding to the garrison for Ceylon we make available to you two brigade groups of the 6th Division … .embarking from Suez … and that if you divert the two brigade groups they will be escorted to Australia as soon as possible after their relief. We are also relying on the understanding that the 9th Division will return to Australia under proper escort as soon as possible.' This offer of two brigades to help in the defence of Ceylon was duly accepted by Churchill.

One of the contingents to be sent to Ceylon was the 16th Brigade, including the 2/1 Australian Infantry Battalion. They had been involved in the ill-fated landings in Greece, and after that debacle, and their subsequent rescue, had returned to Egypt, where they had originally landed. Subsequently the 16th Brigade had been stationed in Syria, and then Palestine, being at Beit Jirja when orders were received for their transfer to Ceylon. On 7 March 1942, the brigade boarded a fleet of civilian buses which took them as far as El Majdal, where they transferred to cattle trucks for the rail journey to El Kantara. From there most of the troops were taken to Port Tewfik and embarked on a former Orient Line vessel, *Orontes*, on which they had journeyed to the Middle East in the first convoy in January 1940. However, their vehicles and heavy weapons were loaded on board a Dutch ship, *Aalsum*, along with the truck drivers, and some field engineers and elements of the 2/1 Field Regiment.

The 17th Brigade had also been stationed in Palestine, after returning from Greece, and had originally been ordered to prepare for a move to Malaya, but on 23 February came an order cancelling the move indefinitely. For the next ten days, the troops awaited further orders, meanwhile undergoing further training, and taking part in a brigade sports meeting on 3 March. As Bill Dexter recorded in his diary that day, 'Brigade sports meeting, less the 2/5 Battalion as they left yesterday … Beer was free so had a fair bit. Arrived back in lines to find all tents down and stacked up. Leaving in the morning, thank goodness.' Next day the troops boarded a train, which took them to Suez, where they arrived on 5 March. Over the next four days embarkation checks were completed, then on 10 March the battalion boarded another Orient Line vessel *Otranto*.

Also boarding *Otranto* were men of the 2/2 Field Regiment, including Sidney Raggett, who later wrote, 'On Tuesday 10 March 1942 … we left camp at 7 am with full pack and gear for the five mile march

Orontes and her sister, *Otranto*, carried Australian troops from Egypt to Ceylon.

to Shell wharf, where we marched past the *Orontes* and the *Viceroy of India* and climbed aboard the *Otranto*. A nice big ship. The rations and supplies were still being loaded during the afternoon, including bottled beer in cases of four dozen bottles. The cases were falling out of the slings into the waters of the harbour because of the way the Wog labourers were loading them, so we managed to guide six of the Wog carriers with their cases as they trundled along the passageways and distributed the goods around our mess deck.'

Also on 10 March the 2/5 Infantry Battalion embarked on *Otranto*, which eventually had 3500 troops aboard. *Orontes* and *Otranto* departed Port Tewfik on the evening of 10 March. As the 16th Brigade history records of *Orontes*, 'In contrast to the luxury accommodation of 1940 and 1941, nearly 4,000 troops were packed in our 20,000 ton liner. As an instance of the crowding, A Company, of 140 men, had hammocks in what had been the second-class saloon.' Colonel Wood, Commanding Officer of the 2/6 Battalion noted, 'Conditions on *Otranto* fair. Food Good. Water severely rationed. Trip down Red Sea comparatively cool. Discipline very good.'

Sid Raggett recorded that the ship called into Port Sudan on 12 March, departing the next day at 7 am into 'very rough seas and water breaking over C Deck.' During the stop at Port Sudan Lieutenant Colonel Starr of 2/5 Battalion went ashore, returning to the ship with a roll of papers that looked like maps, along with instructions that they were not to be opened until the ship was 24 hours clear of Aden.

Sid Raggett noted that *Otranto* arrived off Aden at 7 am on Sunday 15 March, where the ship took on water, then departed at 5.30 pm. Exactly 24 hours later the maps were opened, displaying the units ultimate destination, Java. However, by that time Java was in Japanese hands.

On board *Orontes*, 'Sporting competitions were arranged:– boxing, tug-of-war, debating, also bridge tournaments and band recitals. As the whole brigade was on the ship it gave a "togetherness" which we had seldom experienced before, and the men got to know one another a lot better. There was a ship's choir, a male quartet, soloists and a ship's orchestra plus the three regimental bands of the brigade — all the ingredients for a really first-class concert. On the fourth day out of Tewfik we dropped anchor and for four days the silhouette of the "Barren Rock of Aden" was our only scenery. On 16 March the 17th Brigade Group sailed past leaving us sitting outside Aden. The following morning we moved into the harbour to an oiling berth where we took on fuel and next morning were on our way. The shipboard life during the next week was made as interesting as possible while we travelled across the glassy Arabian Sea.'

As the two ships crossed the Indian Ocean towards Ceylon, the troops were still not sure of their final destination. 'What are they going to do with us,' Bill Dexter wrote in his diary on 20 March, 'whether we are to make another gesture.' On 21 March *Otranto* arrived in Colombo Harbour, and Bob Fox noted, 'We are here in Ceylon, don't know what for. All hoping we shove off for Aussie.' Instead of disembarking straight away, the troops remained on board the transport for three days. Once they did get ashore, 2/1 Battalion was loaded onto trains and transported south to Koggala, a hot, humid place surrounded by jungle where they took over responsibility for protecting a large seaplane base. The 2/5 Battalion went by train to Galle, where they were based in an old Dutch fort.

Orontes was several days behind, as 'on the morning of 26 March, we passed inside a breakwater where the sign stood high over the skyline reading "Ceylon for Good Tea." We were back in Colombo and were informed this time we were to remain there for some time. Preparations were made to disembark the next day.'

Meanwhile, the troops of 16 Brigade who had been embarked on the *Aalsum* were still on their way to Colombo. Their ship, which had not left Port Tewfik until 14 March, was described as 'a rusty iron cargo boat rigged up to accommodate men to drive the vehicles which were on board or to take over other vehicles quickly on coming to port.

Galleys were built along the limited decks and one hold was given over to hammocks. Our officers were crammed in with the ship's officers in their quarters and partnered them in watches as, without escort, she zig-zagged along a roundabout course.'

Aalsum finally arrived in Colombo on 4 April, but 'before unloading commenced, "Air Alert" was sounded. Warships and submarines pulled out southwards, followed by *Aalsum*, which then sailed up the west coast of India. It anchored in Cochin for a few days and the troops were granted shore leave in this city ... There were no defence forces there, but there was an unmanned aerodrome where Hurricane planes had been dumped in a hurry, still in crates, waiting to be assembled. The local Boy Scout troop was guarding them. When *Aalsum* reached Colombo on 11 April, one sign of damage caused by the raid was numbers of cigarette cartons floating in the water.'

Further troops destined for Ceylon departed Port Tewfik on 12 March on various ships, including *Westernland*, which also carried the 2/4 Australian General Hospital. They arrived in Colombo on 25 March. The Transport and Carrier Platoons of the 2/6 Battalion had not travelled with the main body of men, but found themselves embarking on a cargo ship, the *Clan McTavish*, which, according to Philip Burbury, one of those on board, 'left a trail of smoke from Port Tewfik to Colombo.' They arrived early in April, just in time to see the harbour cleared of naval shipping on 5 April, sent out to meet a Japanese force reported to be closing on Ceylon. Two of the ships the men watched depart were the heavy cruisers HMS *Dorsetshire* and HMS *Cornwall*, both of which were sunk by the Japanese a few hours later.

Another large transport used to bring troops back to Australia was the American liner *West Point*, formerly the *America* of United States Line, which had only been completed in 1940. *West Point* was one of a number of transports delegated to rush British reinforcements to Singapore, where she arrived on 29 January 1942. The next morning Japanese aircraft attacked the port, during which *West Point* was straddled by bombs and showered with shrapnel. Having disembarked her 5272 troops and boarded 1946 evacuees, *West Point* left Singapore for Batavia, where more evacuees were embarked, then the vessel left for Colombo, arriving on 6 February. Two days later, *West Point* left for Bombay, from where it departed on 16 February for Port Tewfik. Here 5333 men from the 7th Division were embarked. Departing on 17 March, *West Point* travelled at high speed alone across the Indian Ocean, stopping first at Fremantle, then arriving on 31 March in Adelaide, where all the troops disembarked.

Although not directly involved with Operation Stepsister, the hospital ship *Oranje* arrived at Port Tewfik on 17 February to collect wounded soldiers to be returned to Australia and New Zealand. This former Dutch liner, now staffed by Australian medical personnel, was on its third voyage since being converted at Sydney in the middle of 1941. The liner had to anchor out, with patients being transported from land on lighters, a tedious and slow process, but eventually a total of 403 Australian soldiers and 199 from New Zealand were boarded, and *Oranje* set off on her return trip.

With the Indian Ocean being deemed a major danger zone, it was decided that, instead of the hospital ship steaming at night with all lights on, as allowed by the Hague Convention, it would only show red and green navigation lights, otherwise being blacked out to avoid unwanted attention from Japanese naval forces known to be in the area. Extra lookouts also were posted to immediately extinguish the red and green lights should the ship be sighted or attacked. As a further safety precaution, *Oranje* followed a course that took her much further south than previously, running into very heavy seas before reaching Australia safely.

For the troops not fortunate enough to be transported directly from Suez to Australia, it was a case of first being taken to Colombo, to await further transportation. Suitable ships were in very short supply, and for some men it was quite a long wait in Ceylon. In late March 1942, the situation was further complicated by Japanese naval incursions into the Indian Ocean and the growing fear that Ceylon could be invaded.

Just how dangerous the overall situation had become can be illustrated by convoy SU4, which was to have comprised two ships, the American transport *Williard A. Holbrook* and the former Australian coastal liner *Duntroon*. This pair, along with the *Katoomba*, had arrived in Karachi on 13 March as Convoy MS5, carrying American troops. *Williard A. Holbrook* and *Duntroon* had then gone on to Bombay, where they were to board more Australian troops to be returned home. On 25 March the former Cunard liner *Laconia* arrived in Bombay from Egypt. The Australian troops on board were disembarked and immediately taken on board the waiting *Willard A. Holbrook* and *Duntroon*, which first carried them to Colombo, where more troops were to be taken on board.

By the end of March, *Williard A. Holbrook* and *Duntroon* were ready to depart, only waiting for a suitable escort. On 2 April, the cruiser *Cornwall* was detached from fleet operations in the Indian Ocean to proceed to Colombo for escort duty. However, on 4 April a reconnaissance aircraft sighted a large Japanese naval formation southeast of Ceylon and headed for the island. Immediately all warships in the area were ordered to sea, including *Cornwall*, which departed Colombo in company with another cruiser, HMS *Dorsetshire*, to meet up with major units of the Royal Navy already at sea. Next day, Colombo Harbour was attacked by Japanese carrier-borne aircraft, sinking the armed merchant cruiser *Hector* and the destroyer *Tenedos*, but doing little other damage.

Meanwhile, *Cornwall* and *Dorsetshire* were heading south to link up with the Eastern Fleet, but at 1 pm on 5 April they were spotted by Japanese aircraft. In the ensuing attack by dive-bombers from a Japanese aircraft carrier, both British warships were sunk. On 9 April, Trincomalee was subjected to several air attacks, while out to sea further disasters befell the Royal Navy. Carrier-borne Japanese aircraft located the aircraft carrier HMS *Hermes*, which came under intense attack and was sunk, along with one of its escorts, the Australian destroyer HMAS *Vampire*. Other attacks were made by Japanese aircraft on various unescorted merchant ships found in the waters around Ceylon. Japanese naval forces now virtually controlled the Bay of Bengal and it seemed inevitable that Ceylon would be invaded within a short time.

With the Japanese relentlessly advancing on several fronts, it also appeared to be only a matter of time before they also invaded Australia. There were still insufficient forces available in the country to put up even a reasonable resistance, and Prime Minister Curtin continued to insist that all Australian troops overseas be brought home.

Meanwhile, *Katoomba* left Colombo on 12 April, bound for Mauritius, carrying civilian evacuees and some military personnel. In Mauritius, *Katoomba* took on board more civilians and 101 Australian military personnel, including thirteen under detention, who managed to break out during the passage across the Indian Ocean en route to Adelaide.

Williard A. Holbrook and *Duntroon* remained in Colombo, ready to depart but still lacking an escort, following the loss of HMS *Cornwall*. Eventually *Duntroon* was sent off on her own. Among those on board was Bob 'Hooker' Holt, who later wrote:

> At Port Tewfik, early in March, we embarked on the decrepit English tramp steamer, *Laconia*. We called into Aden but there was no shore leave and we sailed on to Colombo ... The *Laconia* had stores to unload and

The Australian coastal liner *Duntroon* made a voyage to Ceylon with American troops, returning with Australians. (*R.J. Tompkins collection*)

the troops aboard were transferred to the Australian ship, *Duntroon* ... We sailed for Fremantle the following night. Shortly after leaving port the ship was hit with something that made her shudder from stem to stern. It was strong enough to throw fellows off their feet. We never did find out what happened, but next morning we were informed that instead of sailing to Fremantle our next port of call was Bombay.

'The *Duntroon* was a far different ship from the overcrowded and dirty *Laconia*. It was clean and the food was first class. Bluey and I wrangled a job in the galley and we shared a cabin. The work was easy and we did not have to attend any parades. We got on well with the crew and in general lived 'The Life of Riley.' On arrival in Bombay we were given leave for the day. About half the troops had gone ashore when a message was relayed over the loudspeaker that all leave was cancelled. Provosts were posted on the gangway to see that the order was enforced.

The French liner *Felix Roussel* was added to convoy SU4, and between them the ships carried 4415 troops. Unable to release a warship to escort the convoy, the job was delegated to an armed merchant cruiser, *Chitral*, a former P & O liner that was familiar in Australian waters in pre-war years. On 6 May, Convoy SU4 finally departed Colombo. The danger posed by Japanese warships and aircraft to the convoy was known, but there was another, unknown threat to the safety of the ships. On the afternoon of 10 May, the radio officer aboard *Felix Roussel* picked up an emergency signal from the British merchantman *Nankin*, which stated it was being attacked by aircraft and a German raider. Sixteen minutes later came another message from *Nankin* saying they were abandoning ship, followed by silence. Much later it transpired

The armed merchant cruiser *Chitral* was delegated to escort convoy SU4. (*C.T. Reddings collection*)

that *Nankin*, which was owned by the E & A Line, and prior to the war had operated between Hong Kong and Australia, had become the first victim of the German surface raider *Thor* in the Indian Ocean, a situation that was to cause even more concern to the Allies over the next few months.

Unable to risk disclosing their position by making a radio report, the ships of convoy SU4 could not pass on information of the raider attack until they arrived safely in Fremantle on 14 May. The next day, a Swedish ship arrived in Fremantle having survived an attack by the *Thor*. Meanwhile, the ships of convoy SU4 refuelled, then continued their journey, arriving in Sydney on 30 May.

On leaving Bombay alone, *Duntroon* had headed west, across the Indian Ocean towards East Africa, stopping in Mombasa, then continuing down the coast of East Africa to Durban. As Bob Holt

The French liner *Felix Roussell* arriving in Fremantle on 14 May 1942. (*National Library of Australia*)

recalled their arrival in Durban, 'There was a lady on the breakwater signalling a welcome to us with flags. It was the famous "Durban Signaller," who had made a name for herself during the 1914–18 war, welcoming Anzac troops passing through South Africa. She was a wealthy woman in her own right and a poet of renown.' During the several days *Duntroon* remained in port, the Durban Signaller invited some of the men to stay at her home. As Bob Holt wrote, 'She arranged leave and accommodated the men in beautifully appointed rooms in a manicured garden. It was luxury living with a vengeance, with the finest food and drink laid on, with servants at everyone's beck and call. I have wondered since if this open-hearted generous woman ever received any reward from the Australian and New Zealand governments for her mighty efforts on behalf of Anzac troops in two world wars.'

All too soon the days in Durban came to an end, and *Duntroon* departed, once again bound for Fremantle. Bob Holt recalled, 'We must have pretty near gone to the Antarctic for the weather was as cold as charity and the seas were really rough until we made land at Fremantle,' berthing on 15 May. From there *Duntroon* continued to Melbourne, where the Victorians on board disembarked, but no leave was granted to the New South Welshmen. After the short trip up the east coast, *Duntroon* arrived off Sydney Heads on the afternoon of Sunday, 31 May.

The entrance to Sydney Harbour was protected by a boom net stretching between Chowder Bay and Neilson Park. There was one section that could be opened whenever a ship arrived or departed, which presented a major security problem. *Duntroon* had to wait off the port until the boom was due to open again, which happened at about 4.30 pm, when the hospital ship *Oranje* departed, en route to Wellington with New Zealand casualties from the Middle East. *Duntroon* then entered, accompanied by an American warship. What no-one on any of these ships, or on shore, knew was that at that moment lying off-shore was a flotilla of five Japanese submarines, three having midget submarines attached to their hulls. These submarines must have had *Duntroon* and *Oranje* in their sights, but they did not attack, instead launching the three midget submarines, one of which managed to penetrate Sydney Harbour and launch an attack, though with minimal success.

Over a period of three months, more than 70 ships became involved in Operation Stepsister, some carrying equipment and motor vehicles as well as troops. Despite the many dangers faced by the ships involved in Operation Stepsister, none was lost. Most of the ships terminated their voyages in Adelaide, where 54,813 troops, 6950 vehicles, 156 guns and 25,065 tons of stores were landed. For many of the troops the respite from war would be very brief, as within a matter of weeks they were regrouped, and sent north to Papua New Guinea to fight the Japanese.

However, the 16th and 17th Brigades of the 6th Division had not returned home as planned in Operation Stepsister, having been diverted to the defence of Ceylon. John Curtin had only offered these troops on the understanding they would be required for a matter of a few weeks, then sent on to Australia, but the retention of the force in Ceylon went on much longer than had been anticipated.

As the period of their stay in Ceylon extended, Curtin began asking Churchill when he could expect the Australians to be relieved by British troops, and on 6 May cabled Churchill that he was 'gratified to learn that the Australian troops in Ceylon will be relieved about the end of May.' However, this did not happen, and in response to further queries Curtin was told on 19 June that the two brigades would be leaving Ceylon 'as soon as possible after the 25th June.' Again, this did not happen, and going into July, with no indication of a departure date, Curtin again started sending urgent messages to the British War Cabinet, stating that the two brigades were now 'urgently required in Australia in connection with the reorganisation and re-disposition of the Australian land forces.' At last, Curtin was able to secure a definite release date for the troops, and ships were procured for the convoy to bring them home.

This convoy was given the code name Schooner, eleven ships being assembled in Colombo to board the 12,120 troops of the 16th and 17th Brigades, and all their vehicles and equipment. In addition, 1043 other AIF troops, 178 Royal Australian Air Force and 57 Royal Australian Navy personnel, plus 76 nursing sisters of the 2/4 Australian General Hospital, were also embarked. The ships that comprised Schooner convoy were diverse in size and capacity, the largest being the 25,564 gross ton former Union Castle liner *Athlone Castle*, while the smallest was a British India Line vessel, *Aronda*, of just 4062 gross tons. This pair plus three other passenger vessels, *Westernland*, *Rajula* and *Devonshire*, carried the bulk of the troops and other personnel, while their equipment and supplies were carried on the cargo ships *Ekma*, *Clan Macdonald*, *City of Canterbury*, *Dunedin Star*, *Martand* and *City of Lille*, though some of these ships also carried a couple of hundred troops as well.

Many of the men had bought souvenirs of their stay in Ceylon, as the 2/1 Battalion history states a 'valued Ceylon product was that of black elephants carved from ebony. Many bought them, large and small ... On the great day, 7 July, the companies snaked in, single file, from their defensive positions and set off down the road to Katakurunda, a long procession of happy souls, all their worldly goods on their backs, including overloaded packs, many with elephants tied on the straps ... The train took us straight to the dockside at Colombo Harbour. A shuttle service quickly ferried us to our ship.'

The ship they boarded was the *Devonshire*. 'Including reinforcements, the battalion boarded with 38 officers and 910 Ors. Getting aboard entailed disembarking from the ferry boat on to a pontoon and then climbing the gangway up the ship's side. It was noon on a very hot tropical day with a clear sky and all personal gear and weapons with 1st line ammunition was being carried ... After finding our quarters on the ship, which was designed to carry one British peacetime battalion and their families, we set about exploring the lovely vessel. There were some very interesting places sign-posted such as Governesses' Quarters, The Nursery, Officers' Gun Lockers, Troops' Helmet lockers and others. On board with us were approximately 500 all ranks of 2/1 Anti-Tank Regiment and a detachment of 2/4 Aust General Hospital. The AGH staffed the excellent little ship's hospital. Altogether the AIF complement on the ship was 1,800 and we were by far the best accommodated troops in the convoy. All mixed agreeably and it was a very happy voyage ... It was six days before the whole convoy was loaded and in the meantime the usual routine prevailed — boat drill, issue of life belts and training. *Devonshire* having been built as a troop ship, there was plenty of deck space for work and play.'

Meanwhile the 2/2 Field Regiment had left their camp on 8 July, as Sid Raggett noted in his diary, 'Up at 0300 and ready to move at 0500 ... After a good train trip we went aboard the *Aronda* at 11 am. A good new clean ship and though there must be some mistake ... Everyone who can walk is going aboard these ships. No-one wants to be left behind now that we are going home.'

'Among those on board *Athlone Castle* were the 2/5 Infantry Battalion, and the 2/6 Infantry Battalion, which comprised 36 officers and 889 other ranks. One of the last to embark, on the morning of 13 July, was Bob Fox, who had been in hospital for three weeks with dengue fever and yellow jaundice. As his diary recorded, on 13 July he 'left hospital early. Made way to wharf. Taken out to *Athlone Castle* — about 4,800 chaps. Pulled out at 8.15 pm.'

Schooner convoy departed Colombo on 13 July, *Devonshire* slipping her moorings at 1530 and leading the ships out of the harbour. Due to the losses sustained by Allied forces in recent weeks, they could only be escorted by the cruiser HMS *Gambia* and the armed merchant cruiser *Worcestershire*.

According to the 2/1 Battalion history, *Devonshire* 'headed the convoy out of the breakwater past the lighthouse into the teeth of a south west monsoon which soon made its presence felt. By 1800 Ceylon was out of sight.' Soon most of the troops were succumbing to seasickness. The bad weather, with blinding rainstorms, kept up for about a week, and the War Diary for 14 July recorded, 'Sea very rough. Has reduced ranks considerably. Breakfast particularly unpalatable.'

Sid Raggett also made notes about the departure, writing that *Aronda* 'left 13 July 1942 in convoy of 14 ships, two escorts.' The convoy sailed west for two hours, then south. It was raining, blowing a gale, the sea was rough and getting rougher, and most of the men on board were seasick. 'Next morning it was still raining and rough as hell as we crossed the Equator with the speed held down to about 10 knots by the slowest ship.'

The speed of the convoy was actually set at 11.5 knots, but *City of Lille* had great difficulty in maintaining even this speed, and the other ships were frequently forced to slow down so that *City of Lille* could catch up. On 16 July, *City of Lille* was detached from the convoy, and ordered to proceed independently.

Sid Raggett noted in his diary that early on the morning of 16 July 'the sun was actually shining and the sea not so rough, but by 11 am it was rough and raining again ... Some of the smaller ships looked more like submarines in the rough seas.' It was still rough the next day, but, 'although the weather was rougher than we had had it before one could not be below decks all the time as it was stifling down there ... The sea was so rough that many of the chaps didn't come in for meals at all.' On 18 July, Bob Fox recorded in his diary, 'Woke up amidst spray and heavy winds. Had a go at two-up and won a few bob. Turned in on deck. Feeling goodo now. It's hard to realise that at last we are going home.'

Gambia was relieved on 19 July by the cruiser USS *Phoenix*, while the next day the Australian armed merchant cruiser *Kanimbla* arrived to relieve *Worcestershire*. It was also on 19 July that Sid Raggett noted, 'at 1.30 pm three more old ships pulled into the convoy ... everyone was hoping that the convoy would be split now and the speed increased but no such luck ... We were always very relieved when darkness set in, as we were advertising our presence by long trails of black smoke billowing back along the convoy from the funnels of the coal-burners ... During this period I managed to catch my share of influenza which was rapidly doing its rounds right through the ship.'

On Sunday, 26 July, the convoy came to a halt, in a flat calm ocean, while a Catalina flying boat landed nearby and the Force Commander, Major General Boase, was rowed over and flown to Perth. Approaching the Australian coast next day, Sid Raggett recorded, 'at 8 am we were joined by two corvettes and at 3 pm the convoy split. *Athlone Castle* and three others set off south for Melbourne and Sydney taking the Yank cruiser and another escort with them.'

Athlone Castle, *City of Canterbury*, *Dunedin Star*, and *Martand* did not need to refuel at Fremantle, so continued on their way to Melbourne, escorted by *Phoenix* and *Kanimbla*. The ships arrived off Port Phillip Heads on the morning of 3 August, and at 12.45 pm *Athlone Castle* passed through the heads into Port Phillip Bay, along with the other transports. However,

Dunedin Star carried supplies and equipment in Schooner convoy. (*C.T. Reddings collection*)

instead of proceeding directly to a wharf, the four ships dropped anchor overnight and did not berth until the following morning. For the 2/5 and 2/6 Battalions, following disembarkation they boarded trains at Port Melbourne and were taken to a camp near Seymour. It was not until 7 August that the troops were sent on two weeks home leave.

The other six ships, *Rajula*, *Aronda*, *Ekma*, *Westernland*, *Devonshire* and *Clan Macdonald*, headed for Fremantle. They arrived in Gage Roads on 27 July, dropping anchor overnight, then berthing in Fremantle the following day. Sid Raggett noted, 'Tuesday 28 July, arrived

Fremantle, docked noon. Leave from 6 pm to midnight, next day leave 11 am to midnight, also 30th. Left 31 July in convoy of six ships.'

The ships that had stopped at Fremantle left the port on 31 July, their escort having been strengthened by the addition of the armed merchant cruisers *Manoora* and *Westralia*. The 2/1 Battalion history noted, 'As our voyage continued, the first surprise was that the food on *Devonshire* had vastly improved. This does not imply that we had been badly fed before this but as *Devonshire* had previously revictualled in wartime Bombay the difference in quality was appreciated. The trip across the Bight was glassy smooth and training continued on the individual level.'

As dawn broke on 7 August, the ships entered a foggy Port Phillip Bay and proceeded slowly up to Port Melbourne, where they berthed, an army band playing on the wharf to welcome the troops home. 'By midday we had disembarked, entrained and after stopping for a time at Flinders Street Station, were taken to Mangalore. It was bitterly cold that night and four blankets were not enough as we had come directly from the tropics to a Victorian winter. Arrangements were at once made for most to go on 14 days leave … Thus the 2/1 Aust Infantry Battalion came home from the Middle East. It had with it less than 100 men of those who had sailed away on 10 January 1940.'

For some of the troops, the arrival in Melbourne did not mean a quick disembarkation. Sid Raggett recorded that on Tuesday 6 August the *Aronda* berthed at Station Pier, with *Westernland* on the other side. The troops did not disembark from *Aronda* until the next day, then were taken by train to Seymour camp, from where they were sent on fourteen days leave.

The safe arrival of the ships of Schooner convoy heralded the end of the initial phase of the return of Australian troops sent overseas in the first years of the war. For John Curtin the return of these two brigades was a great relief, and enhanced the defence of the country. For the troops, though, there was to be but a brief respite from the war, as the 16th Brigade was dispatched to New Guinea in September 1942, and by 20 October were in action against the Japanese. The 17th Brigade remained in Australia until January 1943, then was flown to Wau to counter moves by the Japanese to capture the village and its airfield.

17 Operation Pamphlet

Prime Minister John Curtin had succeeded in securing the return to Australia from the Middle East of both the 6th and 7th Divisions, but the 8th Division had been lost with the fall of Singapore. This left just the 9th Division overseas, and Curtin now turned his attention to securing their return to Australia as well.

The nucleus of the 9th Division comprised troops sent from Australia in convoy US3, which had been destined to join the 6th Division then undergoing training in the Middle East. Instead, US3 had been diverted to Britain, where it arrived in June 1940. Subsequently these 8000 Australian troops were dispersed through southern England, as part of the garrison force in case the Germans invaded. Eventually these troops were sent to the Middle East, and the 9th Division was formed.

The 9th Division was sent to support the garrison holding the port of Tobruk in North Africa and gained eternal fame as the 'Rats of Tobruk' by holding out against superior German forces from April to December 1941. When the 6th and 7th Divisions returned to Australia, the 9th Division remained and was incorporated into the British Eighth Army.

As early as February 1942, the Australian Chiefs of Staff had included in a report on the security of Australia a comment that the 9th Division should be returned home as soon as possible. Curtin had amplified this in a message to Winston Churchill on 2 March 1942, stating he was 'relying on the understanding that the 9th Division will return to Australia under proper escort as soon as possible,' but no definite arrangements had been organised. As Japanese conquest and expansion in the Pacific continued to threaten Australia, in September 1942 the Australian government sent a request to President Roosevelt for additional land and air forces to help defend Australia, but in his reply Roosevelt had been less than accommodating. The Australian government then decided that the matter of the return of the 9th Division to Australia must be raised again with the British government.

On 1 November, President Roosevelt sent a message to Curtin offering to send as American division then in Hawaii to Australia. Roosevelt continued he could not 'too strongly stress that leaving the 9th AIF Division in the Middle East will best serve our common cause.' At that time, the 9th Division was involved with the rest of the British Eighth Army in an all out assault on the German forces under Field Marshall Rommel in North Africa, which began on 23 October with the Battle of El Alamein. Once again the 9th Division covered itself in glory, and increased its growing reputation as a force to be reckoned with. However, with the position of Australia looking increasingly precarious, Prime Minister Curtin became insistent that it must return to Australia as soon as possible. With the battle in North Africa going well, and the Germans routed, Churchill finally agreed to release the 9th Division from duty in Africa at the end of 1942, and arrangements were made to bring the troops home.

In late November, the various units began preparing for a move east to Egypt, and by early December the Australian forces had been removed from the front line, and most were back near Cairo. Troops were given periods of leave, and kept active in camps with sport and some training. There were also preparations for a divisional parade, which was held at Gaza on 22 December, reviewed by General Alexander, General Officer Commanding Middle East. As Barton Maughan described it in *Tobruk and El Alamein*, 'The pride that the Ninth Division had developed in itself and in its reputation was exemplified on that field in Palestine on the 22nd December by the smartness of the turnout of every man and the exemplary marching and arms drill of every unit at the parade.' However, the troops were still unaware of the fact that they would soon be departing the Middle East for Australia.

The transfer home of the Australian troops was given the code name Operation Pamphlet. Fortunately, four of the liners involved in the 'monster' convoys that had carried so many troops from Australia, *Queen Mary, Aquitania, Ile de France* and *Nieuw Amsterdam*, were available

Queen Mary had been operating across the Atlantic when called upon to transport Australian troops again.

to carry the 9th Division home. These liners were ordered to make their way to Suez to board the Australian troops. However, there was a shortage of warships to provide an escort, so the armed merchant cruiser *Queen of Bermuda* was allocated for this task, and also to carry about 1700 troops.

One problem with utilising these huge liners was the inability of Port Tewfik to handle more than one or two of these vessels at a time. This meant that embarkation of the troops would have to be staggered over several days, with *Queen Mary* boarding her troops first. Since completing her service transporting Australian troops overseas, the liner had undergone an extensive refit and could now carry over 10,000 troops at a time. She had been used primarily on the North Atlantic, bringing American troops to Britain, and on her second voyage, which departed New York on 2 August 1942, had transported an entire United States Army Division, comprising 15,125 troops, from New York to Gourock.

On 27 September 1942, *Queen Mary* departed New York on her fourth voyage to Britain with American troops. For most of the trip the liner travelled alone at full speed, which she relied on to avoid attacks by enemy submarines. As the liner approached the west coast of Ireland, she came within range of German Condor long-range bombers based in France. To provide protection, *Queen Mary* was joined by a small escort, comprising the anti-aircraft cruiser HMS *Curacoa* and three destroyers. *Curacoa* was quite old, having been built in 1917, and could not keep pace with *Queen Mary*, even though the liner followed an irregular zigzag course, while the cruiser followed a straight line.

During the morning of 2 October, *Curacoa* took up station several miles ahead of *Queen Mary*, but over several hours the liner gradually closed the gap. At midday the *Queen Mary* swung to starboard, following her prearranged zigzag pattern, while *Curacoa* remained on a straight course. As the two ships converged, each captain thought the other would take avoiding action, but neither did, and the bow of *Queen Mary* sliced into the much smaller cruiser near its stern. The huge liner sliced right through the warship, the two sections sweeping down either side of her hull as *Queen Mary* continued at top speed. Most of the 324 men on the cruiser were lost as it sank within minutes, but *Queen Mary* was under orders not to stop for any reason. Nearby destroyers rushed in to look for survivors as *Queen Mary* steamed on, and next day arrived safely off Gourock.

News of the disaster was suppressed until near the end of the war. *Queen Mary* suffered some minor bow damage, but many on board had been unaware of the collision, which was felt as merely a slight bump on the liner. Temporary repairs were completed in Scotland, then *Queen Mary* steamed back across the Atlantic, going into drydock in Boston for permanent repairs. On 8 December, *Queen Mary* left New York again with 10,389 American troops on board, who were transported to Gourock. The liner was then prepared for another long voyage, which would take her to Australia once again.

On 23 December, *Queen Mary* departed Gourock carrying 10,669 British troops, voyaging by way of Freetown, Cape Town and Aden to Suez, where she arrived on 18 January 1943. Once the British troops had disembarked, 9995 troops of the 9th Australian Division embarked, then the liner left Port Tewfik at 8 pm on 25 January 1943 and proceeded slowly down the Red Sea to Massawa, in Eritrea, which had been captured from the Italians the previous year. The approaches to the port were difficult to negotiate for a ship of such size, there being a 70 mile channel surrounded by islands and shoals. *Queen Mary* proceeded down the channel at slow speed, reaching Massawa at dawn on 28 January, then anchored off the entrance to the inner basin to await the arrival of the other ships. The huge liner was to spend a week in the sweltering heat of the Red Sea port, causing much discomfort to the troops on board.

One of the units included in the convoy was the 2/13th Battalion, which had been stationed in the Middle East for two and a half years, most recently at Julis in Palestine, from where they had departed by train on 20 January, arriving at Port Tewfik three days later. In his diary, Les Clothier recorded on 24 January, 'we spent the first night out of Julis at Bir Asluz, a patrol point in the desert, the second night at Ishmailia and the third night at Quassassin. The train left at 2 am arriving in Tewfik at 6.15 am. At present we're in a staging camp at Tewfik awaiting orders to embark. The *Queen Mary* is in harbour but she is being loaded so we won't be on her. Rumour has it that the *Aquitania* will be our transport.'

Since leaving Australian waters in February 1942, the veteran *Aquitania* had been employed carrying both American and British troops, her first two voyages being from California ports to Hawaii. However, in August 1942 the liner departed Boston on a long voyage that would bring her back to Australia one more time. On the first leg of the trip, *Aquitania* carried American soldiers and airmen to Egypt, arriving there on 31 October. Once the Americans had disembarked, *Aquitania* took on board Australian and New Zealand troops being returned home on leave, as well as some Italian prisoners of war, who were carried to Sydney, where *Aquitania* arrived in mid-November. On 24 November *Aquitania* departed for New Zealand, arriving in Wellington on 27 November. Several days later a contingent of Royal New Zealand Air Force personnel boarded *Aquitania* and were transported to the Middle East, the liner calling at Fremantle en route to Suez, where she arrived on 5 January 1943 and remained at anchor for almost three weeks.

Immediately *Queen Mary* was clear of Suez, *Aquitania* went in to embark her troops, a full infantry brigade, which included the 2/13 Battalion. There were also numerous other smaller detachments, including some from the Jerusalem Detention Barracks, complete with prisoners, a total of 7000 men, who would all have to board in a single file. Before embarkation, nominal rolls were completed in triplicate, identification and paybooks checked.

On 26 January it came time for the 2/13 Battalion to depart, and next day Les Clothier wrote, 'we came on board the *Aquitania* yesterday. There was the usual Emu bob and Bn parade, right dress and all that sort of silly thing before we started. We marched one and a quarter hours, full marching order, without a spell and were taken out to the *Aquitania* on ferries.' However, the final stage of embarkation did not go quite according to plan. One trooper was posted at the top of the liner's gangway, with instructions to hand each man as he boarded a card showing the location and number of his bunk, and the times and place he would have his meals. The troops began embarking in single file, but after a few hundred had entered the ship, the file ground to a halt. Then came an order, 'Tell the men to sit on their gear,' followed some time later by an order to about turn, and the long column of men slowly retreated from the ship to the tender. It turned out the cards were being handed out in the wrong order, so the boarding soldiers were filling the ship from the top deck down, instead of from the bottom deck up. Eventually the situation was sorted out, the soldiers boarded, and prepared for the journey back to Australia. 'We've got fairly good bunks,' Les Clothier wrote, 'in pairs, and four high. There are supposed to be 7,000 troops on board, which is twice as many as this ship carried between Aussie and the ME.'

For two more days *Aquitania* remained at anchor off Port Tewfik before heading off down the Red Sea to join *Queen Mary* at anchor off Massawa. 'We sailed out of Tewfik at 4 pm,' Les Clothier recorded in his diary on 30 January, 'and are expected to arrive at Massawa any time now. The trip so far has been okay.' Later the same day he wrote, 'we have pulled into Massawa, in Italian Eritrea, and will be there three or four days, probably awaiting the convoy to assemble.'

The men of the 2/13 Battalion had hoped they would be travelling on the *Queen Mary* again. At first they were inclined to be rather suspicious about the ancient engines of the *Aquitania*, and were rather scared by the way the old ship vibrated as it tore down the Red Sea at 20 knots. However, they settled into shipboard routine with efficient ease, considering the tiers of bunks on stretched canvas over iron frames to be the acme of comfort. They also loudly applauded the officer commanding on his decision that, because of the great number of troops on board, no parades other than those absolutely essential would be held. It was probably the only time in their army careers that the troops were able to attend 'A' parade in bed.

With the departure of *Aquitania* from Port Tewfik, *Ile de France* was the next to embark troops, leaving the Egyptian port on 28 January and joining the other two off Massawa three days later. *Nieuw Amsterdam* and *Queen of Bermuda* then went in to embark their troops. The smallest vessel to be included in the convoy, *Queen of Bermuda*, had been converted into an armed merchant cruiser, but was still capable of carrying a large number of troops. Built in 1931 for the luxury service

Ile de France was one of the large transports to take part in Operation Pamphlet. (*C.T. Reddings collection*)

between New York and Bermuda, during the 1930's *Queen of Bermuda* and her sister, *Monarch of Bermuda*, had been known as the 'millionaire's ships,' due to the wealthy clientele they carried. Within days of war being declared, *Queen of Bermuda* had been requisitioned for military service, being rushed across the Atlantic for conversion into an armed merchant cruiser. *Queen of Bermuda* was sent to the South Atlantic, patrolling off the coast of South America, and later went deep into the Antarctic to protect the Norwegian whaling fleet from German surface raiders, a far cry from the warm waters for which she had been built. In 1943, *Queen of Bermuda* was refitted to carry up to 4500 troops, but retained her armaments, and began operating in the Indian Ocean, carrying troops between the Middle East and India, and later to Burma.

Nieuw Amsterdam had been operating a shuttle service along the coast of east Africa between South African ports and Suez. Having

Queen of Bermuda was the major escort for the convoy as well as carrying troops. (*Stephen Card collection*)

Nieuw Amsterdam was taken of the shuttle service from Durban to take part in Operation Pamphlet.

departed Durban on 19 January carrying 6420 British troops, the Dutch liner arrived in Suez on Sunday, 31 January, immediately disembarking her troops. As soon as the last British soldier was ashore an advance party of 312 Australians came on board to finalise arrangements for boarding the rest of the troops, who began embarking early the next morning.

Also boarding *Nieuw Amsterdam* was Australian war correspondent Kenneth Slessor, who had already travelled with the troops to Britain in convoy US3, and then from Britain to Egypt early in 1941 in another convoy. Now that the last Australian troops were leaving the Middle East, he too was in Suez, preparing to return home. Although he held no military rank, either official or honorary, he was generally treated with the same deference as an officer. In his diary on 30 January, Slessor wrote, 'Meeting in afternoon at which details for move tomorrow were disclosed. We leave by train at 9.00, and embark at 10.00. Baggage to be dumped at 6.45, and breakfast at 6.00, which means reveille at 5.30. A freezing cold night again.' Next day he noted, 'Up at 5.30, saw baggage away, hurried breakfast, and marched to Tessah Station, about one and a half miles distant ... A cold grey day, with showers of rain and fits of pale sunlight. Rained heavily as we left the train and climbed aboard lighters at Port Tewfik. Passed the *Queen of Bermuda*, another transport, in bay — she is heavily armed with at least eight guns. Went aboard *Nieuw Amsterdam* at about 11.00 and found myself allotted tiny cabin with six berths, and so far three other officers. Lunch from rations of biscuits and bully beef. To bed early in evening.'

Awaking the next morning, Monday 1 February, Slessor noted 'Orders this morning that no-one is to leave quarters or cabin all today, while embarkation of sisters and 24th and 48th Battalions takes place.' Slessor was less than impressed by his cabin, which he was to share with three other officers. 'My cabin is about the size of a hat-cupboard, and holds six berths, in two tiers of three. What would happen if the other two berths were filled, I can't imagine. Almost impossible as it is to find room to stand to dress, or to pack baggage or hang clothes. No cupboards available. Cabin is evidently a normal two berth one, converted to hold six.'

Departing at midday on 1 February, *Nieuw Amsterdam* and *Queen of Bermuda* proceeded into the Red Sea, Slessor noting, 'Ship moved off from Port Tewfik at 12.30 ... Said that our first call is to be Aden, where the convoy is to meet.' He then went on to state that *Nieuw Amsterdam* was 'fairly fast, though soon after leaving she developed a great vibration from the engines, very noticeable in the upper parts, which shake and tremble violently.' As far as the others on board, including over 6000 troops, were concerned, 'OC troops in ship is my old acquaintance, Lieutenant Colonel Sparkes, who was in both *Mauretania* and *Franconia*. The GOC, Morshead, boarded *Nieuw Amsterdam* at 12.15, about a quarter of an hour before we sailed. The ship is full of brass hats and red tabs, also about 250 sisters and VADs ... Lounge was opened in evening, and played bridge. To bed before 11.00. Night noticeably warmer. Some say we'll reach Melbourne in under a month.'

The following day found *Nieuw Amsterdam* and *Queen of Bermuda* steaming at their top speed south through the Red Sea. As had happened on the other troopships, boat and emergency evacuation drill was held, but that on board *Nieuw Amsterdam* was described by Slessor as 'A scene of complete chaos — men struggling through confused swarms on decks. I found myself at Station 16, at the back of 22 ranks — no boat available for us, but just a rope at the side of a raft, to cling to while in water. Fact is that the ship is so crammed that boat drill is almost impossible — what will happen if there is an attack or disaster I don't like to picture ... Not enough boats to go round, and such crowds quartered on the decks that movement is congested to impossibility. If the ship takes an hour and a quarter to sink, all will be well. Otherwise — !' Describing the day, 'Orders today that shorts are to be worn — a sign of the approach of tropical heat again. A fine, windy, sunny day, the sea tranquil and no sign of any other shipping near us. Hot, close night in cabin, due to blackout, and ship rolled heavily, making it hard to sleep.'

As if the heat and rolling weren't bad enough, Slessor also noted in his diary the next day, 3 February, 'Another officer arrived in cabin yesterday afternoon, thus making five in it — a hat-cupboard, meant for one, with barely room to edge round the two tiers of bunks ... My meal-session ticket changed to No. 1 — breakfast at 7.00, lunch 11.30, dinner 5.30! Which means I probably shan't have breakfast (or need it). This just another example of the systematic contempt with which correspondents are treated by the AIF. I now mess with the subalterns, junior lieutenants etc., though paid as a full colonel.' During the morning there was 'Another chaotic and futile action-station drill at 9.30 on promenade deck — a jostling mass of troops, without order ... The ship is a coffin-ship under present conditions.'

Meanwhile, on the same day *Queen Mary*, *Aquitania* and *Ile de France* were finally able to raise their anchors, and head back to sea along the tortuous channel. As *Nieuw Amsterdam* and *Queen of Bermuda* passed Perim they were joined by the three larger liners, and the five ship convoy steamed down the Red Sea together, passing Aden on 4 February.

The previous day, Les Clothier on *Aquitania* noted, 'have spent 3½ days here at Massawa and have just pulled out (7.45 am). The *Queen Mary* was here when we arrived and the *Ile de France* came in on Monday.' Next day he wrote, 'we moved out of the Red Sea this morning and have been joined by two or more transports, six destroyers and a cruiser.' Also on 4 February, after a 'Hot sticky choking night in crowded, blacked-out cabin,' Slessor 'woke feeling exhausted. At daylight, we were passing land on both sides, evidently the Straits near Aden, and shortly after 9.00 kept our rendezvous with the rest of the convoy.'

The Operation Pamphlet convoy was indicative of the changing conditions under which troops were being carried as the war progressed. When the first convoy left Australia and New Zealand in January 1940, it comprised eleven liners carrying 13,500 troops in reasonable conditions. In Operation Pamphlet, the entire 9th Division, 31,451 men, was divided among five ships as follows:

	Tonnage	Troops	Crew	Total
Queen Mary	81,237	9,995	877	10,872
Aquitania	45,646	6,953	606	7,559
Ile de France	43,450	6,531	675	7,206
Nieuw Amsterdam	36,667	6,241	465	6,706
Queen of Bermuda	22,575	1,731	253	1,984

For the first part of the voyage, two destroyers provided additional escort, but off Cape Gardafui they departed, and the cruisers HMS *Gambia* and HMS *Devonshire* joined the convoy. Soon the troops were again becoming accustomed to the monotony of day after day at sea, with no clear idea of when they would reach the next port, though this time they did know their destination. Unlike the raw, partially trained soldiers they had been on the voyage from Australia, when the atmosphere had been light-hearted, with considerable skylarking, they were now seasoned veterans of war, and maintained a more dignified, almost solemn demeanour.

Once the convoy was in open water, the four 'monsters' formed up in line abreast, with *Aquitania* on the starboard wing, *Ile de France* next to her, then *Queen Mary*, with *Nieuw Amsterdam* on the port wing. By day the ships travelled at a distance of three cables apart, extending to four cables at night. *Queen of Bermuda* varied her position, depending on the time of day and circumstances. The speed of the convoy was fixed at 17 knots, this being the best *Queen of Bermuda* could maintain over a lengthy period. Slessor noted on 5 February, 'Escort closed in this morning, and now seems to consist of the cruiser *Devonshire* and four destroyers, plus, of course, the armoured merchantman *Queen of Bermuda*.'

The convoy commodore was Captain James Bisset, in command of *Queen Mary*, who later wrote of how frustrated he felt throughout this entire operation. Having fumed at the week-long delay in Massawa, Bisset was also angered by having to travel in convoy, and at a speed of only 17 knots. Had *Queen Mary* been allowed to travel independently, as she usually did, and at top speed, her troops could have been disembarked in Australia in about eighteen days from Suez, but instead the entire trip would last 33 days.

Apart from the armament carried by *Queen of Bermuda*, each of the transports was fitted with a pair of 6-inch guns, and also some anti-aircraft weapons. The *Queen Mary* had 66 anti-aircraft guns in all, which required the inclusion of over 100 gunners on her permanent crew. However, the greatest fear for Captain Bisset as the ships crossed the vast expanse of the Indian Ocean was submarine attack. With over 10,000 persons on board, a successful torpedo attack on *Queen Mary* would have been a total disaster, with heavy loss of life.

For the bridge officers aboard *Ile de France*, the strain of the voyage was also intense. *Queen Mary*, on their port side, was Commodore ship, and thus could not be out of station at any time, as all the other liners had to conform to her movements. On the starboard side of *Ile de*

France was *Aquitania*, with plenty of room to manoeuvre on her starboard side. The watchkeepers on *Ile de France* had to be alert at all times, as the convoy maintained a zigzag course across the Indian Ocean, as any delay in following a change of direction could bring them into contact with one of the two liners on either side. The navigating officer of *Ile de France*, Captain G.A. Wild, remembered this voyage as the worst he had in the entire war, with watchkeeping officers ending their four-hour shifts completely exhausted.

The troops on board *Aquitania* were pleased to find the old ship did not roll like the *Queen Mary* had, though this was probably because they had a very smooth passage across the Indian Ocean. They spent their days sunbaking, playing games such as bridge and five hundred, yarning or doing some exercises. To relieve the monotony there were concerts, boxing tournaments, two-up at night, and for some, watches on the ack-ack guns. There had been no shortage of volunteers for this duty when the voyage started, as ack-ack watch was considered a good lurk, but those selected found themselves sharply reminded of that old army adage, 'never volunteer for anything,' doing two four hour shifts a day while their mates were able to loaf and bludge throughout the voyage.

The weather was not the best, as on 6 February Slessor noted it was an 'Overcast, windy day, and pelting showers of rain in morning,' which was followed by 'Another grey, oppressive day, with a swell of sea that made the ship toss violently, and many people now seasick.' This being a Sunday, 'Ship full of church parades in morning.' The weather was also getting warmer, as 'After a couple of days of comparative coolness tonight sticky and hot and I expect we are in region of Equator.' Sleep was hard to come by. 'Stifling hot below deck, and woke feeling that I was being choked at 5.00 am,' he wrote on 8 February, 'so dressed and went up to the sun-deck, where I watched the dawn ... Course is now south of southeast by the compass in the ceiling of bar-room.'

Instead of heading towards Ceylon, as the troops had expected, the ships had set course for the middle of the Indian Ocean. Rumours about a place where they would be stopping to refuel had begun spreading through the ship, and Slessor noted on 8 February, 'Padre Hohenhouse says that we are to call at an island in the Chagos Archipelago tomorrow for water and oil.' So after 'Another choking and oppressive night in calm,' Slessor was again up before dawn, as the 'sweating, dripping tropical heat continued all day.' Then, 'Between 5.00 and 6.00 in evening, we came within sight of land — a low, flat flange of scrub and sand, which later separated itself into three or four small islands, said to be the Chagos Group. Convoy dispersed, and we followed in a wide sweep behind the *Aquitania* and the three other troopships as they entered a harbour between two of the islands ... We followed to anchor behind four other ships, *Queen Mary* in lead — escorted by seven or eight destroyers and sloops, circling to watch for submarines, and three reconnaissance planes (naval).'

The place was Addu Atoll, otherwise known during the war years as 'Port T,' which was actually the southernmost of the Maldive Islands, almost on the equator, and usually uninhabited, being far off the shipping routes in peacetime. With the Japanese advancing rapidly towards Ceylon, the Allies had transformed the tiny atoll into a secret major naval base, and a safe anchorage for the British Eastern Fleet. The atoll consisted of a ring of coral reefs and islands which enclosed a lagoon three miles across, with a sandy bottom and a depth of between five and ten fathoms, or 30 to 60 feet. The location provided excellent shelter for ships inside the lagoon, and was kept top secret throughout the war, the Japanese never being aware of its existence. The ships of Operation Pamphlet arrived off Addu Atoll on the evening of 9 February. They formed up into a single column to enter the lagoon along the deep channel through a gap in the reef.

For the troops on board, the sight was astounding, as the lagoon was filled with warships of all types and sizes, plus maintenance and service vessels, a hospital ship, and flying boats. Ashore there was an airstrip, workshops and a radio station. The four 'monsters' along with *Queen of Bermuda* and the escorting cruisers, were all able to enter the lagoon and anchor in a setting of incredible beauty. The waters of the lagoon were an unbelievable blue, and so clear that it was possible to see the anchors resting on the bottom. The surrounding shores were fringed with white sand beaches and palm trees. After the hardships of the desert, and the days spent at anchor off Massawa, Addu Atoll was a welcome respite.

As Kenneth Slessor described the place, the islands surrounding the lagoon were 'crowded with tents on the beaches, and evidently there is a large military or naval garrison. Submarine-booms and nets between the islands, and many naval vessels here ... The place has evidently been turned into a large and secret naval base. Today more human beings concentrated on the spot than for the last hundred thousand years, I suppose. Oil and water lighters came alongside each ship as she anchored. An overpowering hot night, made worse by the ship's stillness and the blackout shutters. Yet the harbour twinkling and flaring with lights, so evidently the navy doesn't have any qualms about attack. (Now appears that this secret base is in Maldive Group, and not Chagos).'

Overnight all the ships took on fuel and supplies, but no troops were allowed ashore, and the convoy was ready to depart the next day. The troops on board were not told the name of the place, so on 10 February Les Clothier wrote in his diary, 'we pulled into an anchorage in a group of islands somewhere in the Indian Ocean yesterday afternoon. We're taking on oil and water and will be leaving this afternoon.'

Also on 10 February, Kenneth Slessor noted in his diary that, after 'A fearful night in cabin, like being slowly asphyxiated in a bath of hot glue,' he arose at 4.30 and 'went up to sports-deck, where I sat gasping in the dark until sun rose. But light brought little relief, and the day just as hot. Sat in lounge, in stew of sweat.'

At 2 pm on 10 February, the convoy began raising their anchors, and, much to the relief of all on board, steamed out of the Addu Atoll lagoon in single file. Once in the open sea again, the four liners formed up in the same positions as before, still escorted by *Queen of Bermuda*, *Gambia* and *Devonshire*, and still restricted to 17 knots. There now began the most dangerous leg of the voyage, which would bring the ships within range of any Japanese warships that might be marauding from Singapore.

Shortly after the ships left Addu Atoll, units from the British Eastern Fleet hove into sight from the north, led by the battleships HMS *Resolution*, HMS *Revenge* and HMS *Warspite*, accompanied by the cruiser HMS *Mauritius* and six destroyers. The warships closed in on the convoy, and performed several manoeuvres, remaining with the ships until dark, then slipping away to the north again, where they patrolled out of sight of the convoy. No doubt the sight of such an impressive display of naval might gladdened the hearts of the troops aboard the transports, and lessened the fears of the days that lay ahead, Slessor describing it as 'a splendid and reassuring sight.' That night he 'took two blankets and pillow and slept on top deck under the stars — delightfully cool and invigorating after the heat and bad air below.'

As the convoy moved further south, Slessor noted on 11 February that 'Escort now two cruisers, no sign of destroyers, but a reconnaissance plane circling now and again (evidently from a cruiser). *Queen of Bermuda* far to rear of other ships; owing to her slower speed, she is going on straight course, while the rest zigzag.' Next day he noted that '*Queen of Bermuda* now lagging miles behind rest of convoy. Heat less intense but still clammy. At night tried to sleep on top deck again, but driven down to foetid cabin again by violent wind and gusts of soaking rain.'

The anticipation of arriving home kept the troops in good spirits throughout the trip. With the prospect of a month's leave on arrival in Australia, they maintained good behaviour and trouble was minimal. On each ship, a continual range of activities was organised throughout each day to relieve boredom, while those on *Queen Mary* were further entertained by a regimental brass band. Although gambling was officially prohibited, games of two-up thrived in discreet corners of the ships. Aboard *Nieuw Amsterdam* on 13 February there was a concert put on by the VADs, sisters and troops, which was greatly enjoyed by the audience.

By 14 February the weather was getting much cooler, making the interiors of the ships more bearable, although Slessor noted 'heavy seas running all day,' which would have caused some discomfort. The rough seas continued through the following day, and on 16 February, when the convoy was 800 miles out from Fremantle, *Gambia* and *Devonshire* were relieved as escorts by four Dutch vessels, the cruisers *Van Tromp* and *Jacob van Heemskerk* and the destroyers *Van Galen* and *Tjerk Hiddes*. Since the loss of the Netherlands East Indies to the Japanese, these Dutch warships had been based on Fremantle, working with Allied forces.

As dawn broke on 18 February, every vantage point on all the transports was packed with troops eagerly anticipating a first sight of the Australian coast, and a great cheer arose just before noon as land at last became visible along the horizon. As the four 'monsters' approached Fremantle, *Queen Mary* went to her familiar anchorage in Gage Roads, where she was joined by *Aquitania* and *Ile de France*, while *Nieuw Amsterdam* and *Queen of Bermuda*, together with the escorting warships, entered Fremantle Harbour and berthed. The Western Australia troops disembarked here, but the rest were not given shore leave, as the stop was to be brief. Les Clothier on board *Aquitania* noted, 'we pulled into Fremantle on Thursday morning, in warm weather. Quite a few have disembarked here. There is quite a bit of mail in.'

Although the main destination for the convoy was Sydney, one ship, *Nieuw Amsterdam*, would be going to Melbourne. While in Fremantle, 517 men from *Queen of Bermuda* who were also going to Melbourne transferred to the Dutch liner for the final dash across the Bight. Their arrival on board caused considerable overcrowding, the ship now having a total of 6758 troops on board, but it would only be for a few days. This was the end of the voyage for *Queen of Bermuda*.

Travelling across the Indian Ocean, the convoy had been restricted to the speed of *Queen of Bermuda*. However, her engineers had valiantly tried to keep the ships going as fast as possible, and in recognition of this the other ships gave *Queen of Bermuda* a silk ensign. *Queen of Bermuda* remained in Fremantle for ten days, leaving on 3 March. Travelling alone at her top speed, the liner crossed the lonely expanse of the Southern Ocean to Durban, arriving on 16 March. Continuing her lonely voyage, *Queen of Bermuda* rounded the Cape of Good Hope and steamed into the South Atlantic once again. Dodging two U-boats on the way, the liner reached Freetown on 3 April, and after refuelling, continued her northerly voyage, to enter the River Clyde on 13 April.

There was only one complaint about the voyage so far from the troops aboard *Aquitania*, the food was poor. The ship had been provisioned for the voyage in Britain, where severe rationing was in force, and there was not enough food available to fill the stomachs of hungry soldiers. During the stop in Fremantle, the ship was to receive new provisions, these being taken out to *Aquitania* in barges. The Signal Platoon of the 2/17 Battalion was designated to assist in transferring the foodstuffs from the barges onto the ship, and they set to the task with a will. The first barge contained canned fruit, sugar, tea, sausages and canned milk, which had to be carried aboard the ship and down a corridor to a lift, which descended into the hold. Although twenty men boarded the barge, only four were seen to be working, the rest getting stuck into the delicious food, filling their hungry stomachs. Soon they were joined by volunteers, and the foodstuffs were carried up the gangway and into the corridor, but most did not make it to the lift. When a steward appeared on the scene and realised what was happening, the Signal Platoon and their helpers were dismissed, but the extra food was enjoyed by all the troops on their way around the coast to Sydney.

The safe arrival in Australia of the ships in Operation Pamphlet did not herald the end of the voyage, or of the danger. In fact, the waters around Australia were quite dangerous, and there had been strong expressions of concern about the ships continuing their voyage as planned. At one time it was suggested that the troops should be disembarked in Fremantle and brought to the east coast by train. However, as General Northcott, the Chief of the General Staff, pointed

HMAS *Australia* was one of the warships to escort the transports around the coast of Australia.

out, such a move would overburden the railway system, and the troops would be immobilised for several months. In order to provide adequate cover for the transports between Fremantle and the east coast, Task Group 44.3 was sent to meet the convoy.

Task Group 44.3 comprised the cruiser HMAS *Australia* and the American destroyers USS *Henley*, USS *Helm* and USS *Bagley*. They had been exercising in Moreton Bay, then proceeded to Sydney, from where they departed on 17 February. Meanwhile, in Fremantle the transports were refuelled, then left port on 20 February, escorted by the cruisers HMAS *Adelaide* and *Jacob van Heemskerk*, and the destroyer *Tjerk Hiddes*. Kenneth Slessor noted, 'The ship cast off and moved out to sea at 7.00 this morning, leaving *Queen of Bermuda* behind and joining *Queen Mary*, *Aquitania* and *Ile de France* which had been waiting off shore … Ship anchored near the other three, just off the shore … Remained off Fremantle all afternoon, while other ships took in water, oil and supplies, and eventually moved off again at 6.00 in evening.' Next day Les Clothier wrote, 'we left Fremantle yesterday evening at 6.30 pm and are on the last leg. Rumours are rife (as usual) as to what will happen when we reach Sydney, but one thing is certain — we won't have to wait long before we're proceeding on leave.' The same day, Slessor observed 'Convoy now consists of *Queen Mary*, *Aquitania*, *Ile de France* and our ship, with a couple of destroyers and a very light cruiser as escort.'

For safety reasons, the convoy was routed well south of the Australian coastline, and on 23 February, Slessor wrote, 'Weather now unexpectedly cold, with a gusty bleak wind on deck and the sea a metal grey — evidently we have gone far south, before striking up to Melbourne.' Next day the convoy met up with Task Group 44.3, and soon after the convoy split into two sections. Slessor wrote that, 'At

5.00 pm *Nieuw Amsterdam* swung away from the rest of the convoy (which is going to Sydney direct) and headed north for Melbourne — escort one light cruiser, three destroyers, rather significantly large for Australian waters.' The cruiser escorting *Nieuw Amsterdam* was HMAS *Adelaide,* and at ten on the morning of Thursday, 25 February, the ships passed through the Rip at the entrance to Port Phillip Bay.

By 1 pm the ships were 'gliding towards the city, in a ghostly silence — a truly decorous Melbourne welcome, unlike Sydney cockadoodles, day grey, but rather heavy with slight heat. At 1.30 we had arrived at the Port Melbourne wharf, where a crowd of people, including a galaxy of red tabs and brass hats, waiting, and two military bands. Troops began to disembark immediately ... Our arrival was sooner than we'd expected but trains were waiting for troops for all states — to go to various staging camps first and the movement, which had been expected to take until Saturday, was put ahead unexpectedly — all troops to be off the ship by this evening (much to their delight).'

Meanwhile, *Queen Mary, Aquitania* and *Ile de France,* escorted by the ships of Task Group 44.3, had remained on a course that took them below Tasmania, whose coastline was sighted briefly on 25 February, then they were able to turn north and proceed up the east coast to Sydney. As the convoy passed the eastern end of Bass Strait the escort was strengthened by the return of *Jacob van Heemskerk,* accompanied by the French destroyer *Le Triomphant.* In the early afternoon of Saturday, 27 February 1943, the convoy arrived off Sydney Heads and formed up into a single line in preparation for entering the harbour.

It was a glorious sunny summer day, and despite the supposed secrecy covering the movements of the convoy, word had spread throughout Sydney of the pending arrival of the troops. Every vantage point around the harbour was filled as the three huge troopships passed between the Sydney Heads, and then proceeded slowly down the harbour. *Aquitania* and *Ile de France* berthed at Woolloomooloo, while *Queen Mary,* the last to enter, returned to her familiar anchorage off Bradleys Head.

Aquitania berthed at 7 Woolloomooloo wharf, and next day Les Clothier wrote, 'came off ship at 5.45 pm and embussed in double-deck buses on the wharf, which took us straight to Walgrove. How different Sydney looks after the ME and what a great sight it looks! On arrival in Sydney there were thousands of people lining the foreshores and streets overlooking the harbour, waving and cooeeing to us. They all seemed to know we were coming.'

After the war, the history of the 2/13 Battalion recorded, 'Of all the ships we sailed in, we loved the "Aqua" best. Perhaps it was the antiquity of her sharp, clean lines. Perhaps it was because it was she who brought us back to Australia, but most probably it was because she possessed that intangible "something" which makes every sailor love a good ship, and was capable of transmitting it even to landlubbers, that we grew to speak of her with an affection we did not ever develop for any other troopship ... Four tall funnels superimposed over a frame of greyhound sleekness, the erstwhile "Queen of the Atlantic" was the answer to our prayers. We were going home ... Whatever her faults, and they were all due to old age, she will ever remain for us "The good old Aqua!" ... When we entered Sydney Heads, steamed majestically down the Harbour and tied up at number 7 Woolloomooloo, we repulsed the grand old ship that had treated us so well by giving her not a backward glance as we rushed down the wharf and back onto good old Australian soil again.'

In *Commodore*, the third volume of his autobiography, Sir James Bissett recounted a story that became popular concerning the arrival of *Queen Mary* on that February afternoon and one of the coal-fired tugs sent out to assist the liner to her anchorage. This particular tug took up station directly beneath the towering bridge of *Queen Mary*, when suddenly great clouds of dense black smoke belched forth from the funnel of the tug, filling the wheelhouse of the liner with acrid

Queen Mary arriving in Sydney, with black smoke pouring from the funnels of the attendant tugs. (*Vic Scrivens collection*)

fumes. According to the story, Captain Bissett tolerated this situation for a short while, then walked to the bridge wing, megaphone in hand, and shouted down to the tug's captain, 'Hey, skipper, if you don't stop making black smoke, I'll spit down your funnel and put your bloody fires out.' In his book, Sir James stated, 'Now, would I have said a thing like that?'

This voyage marked the last appearance in Australian waters of *Queen Mary*. She remained at anchor in Sydney Harbour until 22 March, when, having embarked 8326 American troops, she left for Britain. Travelling alone, at a speed of 28 knots, the liner reached Fremantle in just over four days, then proceeded to Cape Town, and Freetown for refuelling, before arriving safely in Gourock on 22 April.

In Melbourne, *Nieuw Amsterdam* embarked 2189 men, including representatives from the Royal Australian Navy, Royal Australian Air Force, Royal Air Force, and both the British and American armies. The liner departed Melbourne on 6 March for the short trip to Wellington, being escorted by the American destroyers USS *Helm* and USS *Grayson*. Arriving in Wellington on 10 March, 426 of those on board left the ship, which then departed on 11 March, escorted only by the *Grayson*, for the long trip to San Francisco, berthing there on 22 March.

18 New Guinea and the Islands

Within weeks of Japan entering the war, their forces were launching assaults on numerous fronts. Their immediate objectives were the capture of Hong Kong, which fell to them on Christmas Day 1941, and the Malay Peninsula, the major prize being Singapore, which was forced to surrender on 15 February 1942. The Japanese then turned the full weight of their considerable military forces to securing the Netherlands East Indies, and further to the east Papua and New Guinea. The threat these moves posed to the safety of Australia was clear, and the movement of troops to the new battlegrounds began in earnest.

On 23 January 1942 the Japanese captured Rabaul, and on 3 February Port Moresby suffered its first air raid. Since the distance to New Guinea was relatively short, aircraft could be used to transport troops quickly, but there remained the necessity to use ships as well. One of the first to be taken over for this role, on 12 March 1942, was the Bass Strait ferry *Taroona*, which had already seen a brief period of military service for the New Zealand government. Requisitioned by the Royal Australian Navy for duty as a fast troop transport, *Taroona* was quickly converted in Melbourne to provide quarters for 678 officers and men. The vessel was painted naval grey, and the top section of the aft funnel was removed. Under the command of Captain R. Huntley, who had been in charge of the ship since 1936, *Taroona* was immediately pressed into service, on her first voyage carrying 480 military personnel to Port Moresby, where she arrived on 25 March.

The Bass Strait ferry *Taroona* after conversion into a troop transport.

The next day, *Taroona* was leaving Port Moresby to return to Australia when she ran aground on Nateara Reef. Held fast from the bow to below the bridge on the port side, *Taroona* remained there for the next three days. Initial refloating efforts by the corvettes HMAS *Cessnock* and HMAS *Colac* were unsuccessful, with *Colac* also running aground for a brief period. During this time, Port Moresby was being subjected to daily air raids by Japanese bombers, but they failed to notice the vessel stranded at the entrance to the harbour. At 8.30 am on 29 March, *Taroona* was finally refloated and steamed back into the harbour for a brief inspection, then left on a fast trip to Townsville, where repairs were quickly carried out.

While the final repairs were being completed on *Taroona*, 434 officers and men of the 2/5 Independent Company left Spencer Street Station in Melbourne on 9 April 1942 on the long rail journey to Townsville, where they arrived on the afternoon of 12 April. The soldiers were immediately transported to the wharf and boarded *Taroona*. After their long and tiring journey, the men were hoping to be granted shore leave prior to departure, but this was refused. Despite this, some men managed to slip ashore, avoiding the military police guarding the gangway by sliding down ropes to the wharf. Fearing a mass exodus of troops, the officer in charge ordered that *Taroona* be moved about 20 feet from the wharf and held in position there by a tug, but some men then jumped overboard and swam ashore. Most of the equipment and supplies needed by the soldiers was still waiting to be loaded and so, surrendering to the inevitable, it was then decided that all the men would be allowed shore leave until midnight, and

Taroona was moved back alongside the wharf. At midnight every soldier was back on board.

At 0600 on 13 April, *Taroona* left Townsville for Port Moresby, escorted by two corvettes. The ship was very crowded, and conditions on board were not the best. As John Boxall later recalled, 'The mess was situated in the hold, with tables erected on trestles. Meals were obtained from the ship's galley on the deck above the hold floor … We were told that *Taroona* had struck a reef on one voyage, and some water was still trapped in the bilges. Despite the calm seas, this water would cause the ship to give a sudden lurch to either port or starboard, and the Mess orderlies then had the job of cleaning, and resetting the tables. Sandshoes had been issued for shipboard use, to avoid damage to the decks by hob-nailed boots. On most decks this was an advantage. However, for the men detailed to Mess duties, the orderlies had to traverse the narrow steel stairway between the galley and hold, and the sandshoes were a hazard. The galley steel floor plates were very hot, resulting in the sandshoes becoming quite slippery. Apart from being Mess orderlies, the only activity on board was Boat Drill and Anti-Aircraft Drill, with the Bren mounted on a tripod.'

Also on board for that trip was Andy Pirie, who later wrote, 'The chief drawback was the shortage of fresh water. Fortunately we were only on board for four days. The weather was very pleasant and it was a pretty trip, through an area most of us had never seen before.' On the voyage north *Taroona* passed through the Whitsunday Passage and along the Great Barrier Reef. On 17 April *Taroona* arrived at the entrance to the harbour at Port Moresby, to find the town being attacked by the twenty-fifth air raid mounted by Japanese bombers since they entered the war. Fortunately none of the aircraft paid any attention to *Taroona*, which tied up to the wharf as the final bombers were departing.

Over the next four years, *Taroona* played an important role in the Australian war effort. In all *Taroona* completed 94 voyages, during which she made 183 visits to ports around the South West Pacific. Most of her visits, 74, were to Milne Bay, along with 46 to Port Moresby and nineteen to Lae. There were also eight calls at Langemak Bay, seven to Wewak, five to Jacquinot Bay in New Britain, four to Torokina, three to Thursday Island, two each to Buna, Madang and Oro Bay, and single visits to Aitape, Rabaul and Merauke, in Dutch New Guinea.

During her war career *Taroona* carried 93,482 troops while logging 204,535 sea miles, but the strain of maintaining a hectic and tight schedule imposed an enormous burden on Captain Huntley. Eventually the strain of command in wartime took its toll, and on one voyage, as the ship was returning to Townsville, he collapsed on the bridge, and died shortly after. For the remainder of the war command of *Taroona* was shared between Captain D.M. Keith and Captain C.W. Ostenfeld.

Convoys were still being dispatched from various ports in eastern Australia to New Guinea under ZK code names, but most now carried only supplies, and few troops. One exception was convoy ZK8, composed of four small Dutch transports, which left Sydney on 18 May for Port Moresby carrying 4735 troops of 14 Brigade. The convoy was escorted by HMAS *Arunta* and the Dutch light cruiser *Van Tromp*.

May and June 1942 were probably the most momentous months for Australia in Word War II. The Japanese strategy was to capture Papua and New Guinea, dominate the Coral Sea, then expand into other Pacific islands, cutting off Australia from her main source of supply, the United States. The key element of this strategy was the capture of Port Moresby. Japanese forces had established a major base in Rabaul, and on 3 May they occupied the Solomon Islands. The next day a major Japanese invasion force, escorted by three aircraft carriers and other major units, departed Rabaul, bound for Port Moresby. The Allies had Task Force 17 operating in the area, composed of two American aircraft carriers and other large warships, assisted by two Australian cruisers, *Australia* and *Hobart*.

When the Japanese forces was spotted by reconnaissance aircraft, the American carriers launched their planes, while the Japanese did the same. Although referred to as a naval engagement, the Battle of the Coral Sea was fought entirely by aircraft, with two of the Japanese carriers and one American carrier being sunk. HMAS *Australia* was also damaged in numerous severe attacks, but the Allies came out victors, as the Japanese force turned round and retreated to Rabaul.

Just a month later, Japanese and American aircraft carriers were again involved in a major engagement, but this time the result was more decisive. The Japanese had planned to finish the job they started at Pearl Harbor and destroy the remnants of the American Pacific Fleet, but the Battle of Midway ended with all four Japanese aircraft carriers being sunk, while the Americans lost one. Once again the two naval forces never actually sighted each other, but the heavy losses sustained by the Japanese caused them to abandon further invasion plans in the Pacific, becoming the turning point of the Pacific war.

Among the units to be sent to New Guinea was the 2/3 Light Anti-

The Burns Philp vessel *Macdhui* was still in commercial service when required to carry troops to Port Moresby. (*R.J. Tompkins collection*)

Aircraft Regiment, which had returned from Egypt and regrouped in Queensland. On 3 June 1942, their equipment was loaded onto the small Dutch vessel *Karsik*, along with a small contingent of men, and the ship left for Port Moresby a few days later. The majority of the regiment embarked on the Burns Philp liner *Macdhui* at Townsville on 12 June for their trip to New Guinea. The ship was still in civilian service, and as one diary noted, 'men were in cabins which had bunks with sheets and pillow slips. There was a wet bar, use of the dining salon, crisp white tablecloths and silver, and a menu to delight any tourist, even stewards to wait on tables.' *Macdhui* arrived in Port Moresby on 15 June. A small number of men travelled north in less comfort aboard another Dutch vessel, the *Swartenhundt*.

The Japanese may have lost the sea battle, but they still held much

The small Dutch freighter *Karsik* carried troops to New Guinea. (*C.T. Reddings collection*)

The Burns Philp vessel *Malaita* was lucky to survive after being torpedoed. (*C.T. Reddings collection*)

conquered territory, from which land-based planes could launch raids. Darwin was attacked fifteen times between 19 February and 27 April, then came a lull until 13 June, when the attacks resumed. A favourite target for planes from Rabaul was Port Moresby, which suffered its sixty-first raid on 17 June.

Among the ships in port that day was the *Macdhui*, which had disembarked her troops, but still had a cargo of aviation fuel in drums in the holds being unloaded. When the attack commenced, *Macdhui* quickly unberthed and steamed around the harbour, being struck by one bomb which exploded three decks down, causing a fire. Once the raid ended, *Macdhui* returned to the berth and the fire was extinguished. Next day the Japanese bombers returned, and again *Macdhui* left its berth for the open waters of the harbour. This time four bombs found their mark, killing the captain and ten crew, leaving the ship ablaze and listing. *Macdhui* drifted across the harbour until running onto the reef off Tatana Island, where the vessel rolled over and sank.

Another vessel owned by Burns Philp was lucky to avoid a similar fate several months later. *Malaita* had been operating from Sydney to the Pacific Islands since entering service in 1933. The vessel had remained in commercial service until 11 March 1942, then was requisitioned for war duty, but continued to operate from east coast ports to Port Moresby, carrying supplies and some troops. *Malaita* left Sydney on her fourth wartime trip on 12 August 1942, going to Port Moresby.

On 29 August *Malaita* departed Port Moresby escorted by HMAS *Arunta*, but the pair had hardly left the harbour when *Malaita* was struck on the starboard side, just forward of the bridge, by a torpedo fired from the Japanese submarine RO33. *Malaita* immediately began to list to starboard as the bow sank low in the water, and the crew abandoned ship, only to return shortly after when it became apparent *Malaita* was not about to sink. While *Arunta* sought out and eventually sank to submarine, *Malaita* was taken in tow by the store ship HMAS *Potrero*, assisted by the Burns Philp small island vessel *Matafele*, and brought back into the Port Moresby harbour.

The ship was made as seaworthy as possible, and left Port Moresby on 9 September for Cairns, where logs were loaded in the centre holds to increase buoyancy. *Malaita* then continued down the Queensland coast towards Brisbane, but by the time she arrived there the bow was in danger of breaking off where it had split at the point of impact by the torpedo. In Brisbane several lengths of railway line were bolted across the split deck, and then the vessel continued its voyage south, arriving in Sydney on 13 November. Despite this incredible voyage, *Malaita* was anchored in Sydney Harbour, with no. 2 hold open to the sea, for the next three years, and played no further part in the war. However, in October 1945 repair work commenced, and in April 1947 *Malaita* returned to service.

The Allies had decided to establish a forward airbase at Milne Bay, and on 24 June the Dutch flag transports *Bontekoe* and *Karsik*, escorted by HMAS *Warrego* and HMAS *Ballarat*, left Port Moresby carrying an advance party of 800 troops from 55 Battalion to defend the new airstrip. They reached their destination next day and quickly offloaded their troops and supplies, though the ships were disguised and camouflaged with tree branches while alongside. On 11 July another Dutch transport, *Tasman*, escorted by *Warrego*, arrived in Milne Bay, carrying advance elements of 7 Brigade and the newly appointed commanding officer of Milne Force, Brigadier J. Field.

The Japanese had invaded Timor on 25 January 1942, and on 23 February had assumed control of Dutch Timor. However, in Portuguese Timor, 350 Australian commandos continued to harass the Japanese for several more months. By early September the Australians fighting in Timor were in desperate need of relief, and a rescue operation was organised. The veteran destroyer HMAS *Voyager* was sent from Fremantle to Darwin, where relief troops were boarded, and on 22 September the warship departed for Timor.

Next evening *Voyager* closed on Betano Bay, where the troops on board would be put ashore and the tired group on land taken off. The anchorage was surrounded by reefs, and in an attempt to move the ship to deeper water, *Voyager* ran aground at the stern on a reef. Soon after the wind and seas began to rise, driving the ship more firmly aground, and on 24 September it had to be abandoned, but not before it was totally disabled by the crew.

It took a while to organise another rescue effort, but on 29 November two corvettes, HMAS *Castlemain* and HMAS *Armidale*, left Darwin. They met up with the small vessel *Kuru*, which had rescued civilians the previous night from Timor, and they were transferred to *Castlemain*, which returned to Darwin, while *Armidale* and *Kuru* headed for Timor. Early in the afternoon of 1 December, *Kuru* and *Armidale* came under heavy air attack, with *Armidale* being sunk within minutes. The survivors were flung into the sea, being supported by two rafts and a motorboat. The motorboat left the rafts and went for help, but did not meet any other vessels until 5 December. Meanwhile the men on the rafts had found the whaler, which was baled out, and 28 men piled on board, leaving 49 men on the two rafts. The whaler also set off to find help, but on 7 December search aircraft sighted the two rafts, and the next day they were seen again by a Catalina flying boat, which was unable to land due to the rough sea. While returning to Darwin, the Catalina also sighted the whaler, whose men were rescued next day, but the two rafts were never seen again.

The coastal liner *Duntroon* after conversion for war service. (*C.T. Reddings collection*)

The coastal liner *Duntroon*, owned by the Melbourne Steamship Company, had been selected for conversion into an armed merchant cruiser in October 1939, but as the liner had a history of engine problems, this plan was changed and *Duntroon* returned to commercial service on the Australian coast. On 20 November 1940, *Duntroon* was involved in the first loss suffered in the war by the Royal Australian Navy, when the liner collided with the small trawler HMAS *Goorangi*, which had been converted into a minesweeper. The smaller vessel sank immediately, with the loss of 24 lives.

In February 1942 *Duntroon* was requisitioned for service as a troop transport, being given a very basic conversion before being sent to Melbourne, from where she carried Australian troops to Ceylon in convoy MS5, returning to Australia alone, as described elsewhere, arriving back in Sydney on 30 May. It had been planned that the liner would make a commercial voyage to Western Australia, but instead work began converting *Duntroon* into a full-time troopship.

As a passenger liner, *Duntroon* could carry 381 passengers, but after conversion she had a trooping capacity of 1178. In addition to the cabin berths, there were 388 bunks installed in the holds and a further 219 in cabins, while 190 hammocks were hung along the promenade deck. A mechanical ventilation system was installed, and extra ablution blocks, while escape ladders also had to be fitted. The vessel was armed with one 4-inch gun, a 12-pounder, two Bofors and six Oerlikons, and two pillarbox rocket launchers.

On 4 July 1942, *Duntroon* left Sydney for Fremantle carrying Australian military personnel, 45 officers and 1033 other ranks. On the return trip the vessel carried 1108 United States Army nurses, while in the holds were the trucks belonging to the recently formed Signals WA Field Troops, who were being posted to New Guinea, though the men themselves were not told this. They were to be transported to the east coast on *Westralia*, which was also in Fremantle. Among them was James Henderson, who in *Onward Boy Soldiers* wrote, 'In the miserable grey morning of 27 July 1942 a fleet of trucks delivered us at Fremantle wharf. Our unit trucks were by now aboard the merchant cruiser *Duntroon*, and we were shuffling in stages of about one mile in a long line toward our troopship, HMAS *Westralia*, when sea kitbags, a small extra burden, were distributed.'

On leaving Fremantle, *Westralia* linked up in a convoy with *Duntroon* and *Kanimbla* and headed south, where, James Henderson wrote, 'the outlines of more ships came up on the bow, one a great ocean liner bringing some of the AIF troops home from the Middle East to help defend Australia. We joined in with it and a couple of slower moving and smoky merchant ships. A sleek low cruiser painted in brown and green camouflage, identified as the Dutch *Tromp* ... was soon racing continually round the entire convoy with surprising agility. Another cruiser, the American USS *Phoenix*, was overtaking us from astern.'

On board *Westralia*, most of the men were playing cards, 'which appeared the most popular pastime for those not writing letters home, or the unlucky ones already on the list for shipboard duties. These, I was to find, included washing mountains of dishes, peeling potatoes and other chores to assist the crew in the greasy steam filled galley on a lower deck where the seawater occasionally gushed through an open porthole.'

Because the convoy included several cargo ships, which could not maintain a high speed, it took ten days to reach Sydney, but finally, on 5 August, *Westralia*, *Kanimbla* and *Duntroon* steamed into Sydney Harbour and their passengers thankfully disembarked. The men of the Signals WA Field Troops were loaded into buses and taken to a staging camp at Liverpool, where they learned they had been given a new name, Signals C Force. On 8 August, *Duntroon* was freed from government control, and made two commercial trips to Fremantle, but on returning to Sydney on 19 October 1942 the liner was again taken over for military duty, which would keep her occupied for the remainder of the war.

One of the older coastal liners, *Katoomba*, had also been taken over previously for brief periods of military duty, but then returned to regular commercial service. On the evening of 4 August 1942, as *Katoomba* was crossing the Great Australian Bight from Fremantle to Adelaide blacked out, shells began falling around the ship, apparently fired by a Japanese submarine. Speed was increased to nearly 17 knots as *Katoomba* outpaced her attacker, reaching Adelaide on 7 August, then continuing to Sydney, arriving on 13 August. *Katoomba* was then taken over once again for war service, being extensively refitted to carry 1200 personnel. *Duntroon* and *Katoomba* were used to transport troops from various ports along the east coast of Australia to New Guinea.

Due to the shorter distance involved, transporting troops to New Guinea did not require the extensive forward planning and concentration of ships into convoys as had applied to movements to the Middle East, Britain and Singapore. As a result, troops tended to move in smaller

The Dutch vessel *Cremer* carried troops to Milne Bay. (*C.T. Reddings collection*)

groups, and on a wide variety of vessels, some of which were not originally designed to carry large numbers of passengers at all.

A few days after their arrival in Sydney from Fremantle, the men of the newly renamed Signals C Force found themselves on the move again, this time by train to Brisbane, where they were accommodated in tents set up on Ascot Racecourse. Several days later they were on the move again, this time to the Brisbane docks where they boarded an old Dutch ship, *Cremer*, for the trip to New Guinea. They linked up with a convoy heading north, and after several days some vessels split off, going to Port Moresby. Meanwhile, the men aboard *Cremer* were then told, 'Our destination is Milne Bay at the eastern end of Papua, and from now on we are to be known as Signals Milne Force.'

As the ship approached its destination, James Henderson later wrote, 'Out of the tropical mist ahead could be heard the hum of distant aircraft engines. As it grew louder an order was called for helmets to be worn, and the destroyer escort HMAS *Stuart* sped into the lead ... I, in a group standing at the rail near the bow, saw four dark shapes appear out of the mist, their wings taking shape as they raced almost at sea level towards the convoy. The low-wing silhouettes looked dangerous. "Zeros?" a couple of voices speculated. "No, Kittyhawks," I declared confidently ... The four planes climbed and banked steeply above our ship to display their RAAF markings on wings and fuselage as they thundered past, the pilots waving a cheerful welcome from opened cockpits ... The *Cremer* berthed at 5 pm on Friday, 21 August 1942. The tropical night seemed to close in on us suddenly.'

Conditions ashore were terrible. After working for several hours to unload cargo, 'we staggered into the waiting tents, three or four men to each, spread our rubber groundsheets on the damp ground, then a blanket, and flopped down to a sleep of utter exhaustion, ignoring the whine of mosquitoes and the rain drumming on the canvas ... I awakened in the morning with my feet under water, my clothes and blanket soaked in the floodwater running past and through the tent.'

In August 1942, the 2/2 Battalion was once again on the move, also to New Guinea. Although, since their return to Australia in Schooner Convoy, the men were always aware that such a move was more than likely, it still came as something of a shock to them. As one of them, Roy Waters, recalled, 'News came through that we were leaving for the battle front again. Feelings were mixed as we stood on parade and the CO told us what was doing. There was feverish activity as we prepared to leave our land again. The move to Brisbane went without a hitch as we were now past masters in moving.'

For the men of the 16th Brigade, the departure for New Guinea was a marked contrast to the excitement of their leaving for the Middle East. In Brisbane there were no cheering crowds to see them leave, just wharf labourers who had gone on strike in protest at not receiving overtime payments for loading ships after midnight. Instead of a large liner, the men found themselves boarding an American cargo ship, *John Steele*, which provided them with few comforts, sleeping arrangements being mattresses laid on the floors of the holds.

After a low-key departure from Brisbane, the ship went north to Townsville, then continued on a northerly course through the islands of the Great Barrier Reef, though they were shrouded from the troops by heavy rain. As Roy Waters wrote, 'From here on we were on the alert and all available weapons were mounted against air attack.' The *John Steele* arrived safely in Port Moresby, passing the semi-submerged wreck of the *Macdhui* as it nosed its way towards the one remaining wharf. Roy Waters wrote of their arrival, 'the boys crowded the rail to see this frontline of Aussie. The Tobruk of the Pacific ... what a sight greeted us, here was Port Moresby ... What a God-forsaken hole it looked.' Soon the troops were streaming ashore and being loaded into trucks to be transported inland to the Owen Stanley Range, to confront the Japanese.

When the 2/14 Battalion, which had also returned to Australia in Schooner Convoy, was ordered to New Guinea, the men were transported on a number of American Liberty ships from various ports to Port Moresby. On 5 August 1942, one contingent was informed they would be leaving their camp near Glen Innes in northern New South Wales at 0400 the following day, being transported to the coast.

Although not advised of their ultimate destination, the troops were certain they were headed for New Guinea, and so it turned out. They went aboard the American Liberty ship *James Fenimore Cooper* in Brisbane. There were two other ships with them in the convoy, another Liberty ship, the *James Wilson*, carrying the 2/16 Battalion, and the small Dutch vessel *Both*, which had a contingent from the 18th Brigade on board.

As the 2/16 Battalion company history recorded regarding the Liberty ships, 'shipboard life was very congested — steel decks and confined quarters and poor messing facilities. Improvised kitchens were built on the deck. Petrol burners were used for cooking meals. Most experienced a mild form of dysentery. A small amount of training was carried out and quite a lot of time was given to lectures on the Japanese Army.' Among the troops on board were the Signals Platoon, who worked with the US signallers on the bridge and semaphore instruction was given to rifle companies.

On their fifth day at sea, the *Both* left the convoy, and headed off alone for Milne Bay. The other two vessels arrived in Port Moresby on 12 August, where something of a shock awaited the troops on board. 'The men's expectation of New Guinea was nothing like the sight that met their eyes. It was far below their expectations. A hive of army industry unfolded where they were expecting clean white beaches, coral reefs, waving palm trees and cool green jungle. They disembarked and moved through Moresby to Itiki by transport, a never to be forgotten journey.' Unable to berth alongside the wharf, the two vessels had to anchor out, their troops being ferried ashore by the corvette HMAS *Lithgow*.

Also travelling to New Guinea in September 1942 was Lloyd Tann, who was with the 2/5 Field Ambulance. Having returned from the Middle East, where he spent some time in Tobruk, he recalled, 'When they said we were going to New Guinea, it was more a relief than anything else. You don't want to sit on your bum. You want to fight the Japanese. I went up to Milne Bay on the *Anshun*. It was a commandeered Chinese tramp steamer.' Actually *Anshun* was owned by a Hong Kong-based British company, Swire Shipping, who operated China Navigation Company. *Anshun* and the Dutch *s'Jacob* formed convoy S2, which left Townsville on 2 September. The same day another convoy, P2, consisting of two ships, *Taroona* and *Sea Witch*, also left Townsville, all four vessels being escorted north by the sloop HMAS *Swan* and the corvette HMAS *Castlemain*. Convoy P2 was bound for Port Moresby, while the other two ships were headed towards Milne Bay.

Conditions on board the *Anshun* were not very comfortable, Lloyd Tan soon discovered. 'Two thousand troops aboard, and not one toilet. You had to hang over the side on a scaffold, holding on to the rail. Sometimes the sea was rough, and one minute you'd be sixty feet in the air, the next your backside would be almost in the water.'

On 6 September *Anshun* arrived at her destination. 'We were just coming into Milne Bay when the destroyer *Arunta* came up to us and the commander said — I can remember it word for word: "There is a Japanese cruiser in the vicinity, and we are going off to look for it. Under no circumstances should you enter Gili Gili port tonight" — that's the harbour at Milne Bay. "Remain here off Samurai Island." The *Arunta* went off to look for the cruiser, and the *Anshun* just went on, straight into Gili Gili harbour. We all disembarked. Then, about an hour, hour and a half later, the cruiser came into the harbour and fired a broadside and sank the *Anshun* at the wharf. Then it turned its searchlights onto the *Manunda*, a hospital ship. It was all lit up and showing the red cross, and we thought, oh no! They're going to sink the hospital ship! But the cruiser swung its searchlights up and sailed away. That was the only time I saw the Japs respect the red cross.'

Fortunately the captain of *s'Jacob* had heeded the warning, and kept his ship at sea overnight. On 7 September *Arunta* arrived at Milne Bay, collected the survivors from *Anshun*, and took them directly to Townsville. *S'Jacob* and HMAS *Swan* headed off to Port Moresby, where they arrived on 8 September. Despite the attack, on 9 September HMAS *Arunta* again left Townsville, escorting two more transports, *van Heemskerk* and *Japara*, also bound for Milne Bay, where they arrived on 12 September.

Back in Queensland, the 16th Brigade, part of the 2/1 Australian Infantry Battalion, which had returned to Australia in Schooner Convoy from Ceylon, were preparing to leave for New Guinea. As the battalion history states, 'On 9 September the warning order was received for the battalion to move to New Guinea and to entrain on 11 September. For security purposes, troops were told that they were going to a point in Northern Australia but as the equipment being taken was "Jungle Order," nobody had any illusions as to the ultimate destination ... We left Greta by train on the night 11/12 September, arrived at South Brisbane the following night, then changed trains and rattled through the suburbs of Brisbane to the wharf ... Awaiting us was the *Anhui*, a China Navigation Co. cargo ship of 3,494 tons. Some men went aboard at once, but most remained standing amid stacks of piled up crates and gear for what seemed like hours ... The hold-up, it was learned, was because the wharf labourers were refusing to load stores after midnight unless paid at time-and-a-half. Army orders were for us to sail at 0300, with or without stores. Amid rumblings that the whole waterfront would be called out, the CO took charge of proceedings ... 14 Platoon loaded the stores while the wharfies walked off.'

This caused a delay in departure, but *Anhui* did leave, 'with the battalion and its stores. Accommodation and conditions were poor. Including attached troops, we numbered 1,003 all ranks and most slept wherever they could on the decks on account of the heat below. September 14 saw the convoy proceeding up the coast of Queensland and all were thankful that the weather was good. The daily routine included having every Bren gun mounted for anti-aircraft defence.' One corporal was suffering severe stomach pains, and the medical officer removed his appendix during an operation 'carried out on the bridge in hot and humid conditions during "brown-out" in the early hours one morning. The CO had to hold Joe down, as he was wriggling due to the limitations of the anaesthetic.'

There were also problems with the crew of the *Anhui*, when 'rumours were heard that the crew were in revolt and wanted to be placed ashore because they had heard that the ship was en route to New Guinea and might be attacked.' When the ship arrived off Townsville, it dropped anchor for several hours, then was able to berth. 'Sure enough, deckhands, stewards and ship's cook walked off, leaving the battalion the only alternative, "man the bloody ship ourselves." Volunteers for firemen were called for and there was a ready response. The cooks and stewards were easily replaced and so the convoy moved on. The ship's owners offered to pay wages at the current rates to those who manned the ship ... Our volunteer stokers varied in their performance. By night our ship would fall behind the convoy and by day the stokers would pile it on and we would lead the way. Next morning we would be behind again.'

From time to time there were deaths on ships, from illness or accidents. On this voyage there was a particularly sad tragedy. 'On Saturday 19 September at about 0900 ... those aboard were shocked to hear the staccato cracks of five Bren shots going off. Incredibly, a Bren gun, taken off its mounting to be cleaned in a hurry, had its loaded magazine replaced before the barrel was pushed into place.' Two privates were killed, including one who had escaped after being captured by the Germans in Crete, while a corporal was wounded.

'Both men were buried that afternoon in the turquoise waters of the Grafton Passage. It was a very moving ceremony and a firing party was supplied.'

It was also in September 1942 that a most unusual accident occurred, though fortunately without fatal consequences. A convoy of five ships carrying American troops, and escorted by the corvettes HMAS *Armidale* and HMAS *Ballarat*, was battling its way north through a severe storm, when during the night a huge sea swept across the Liberty ship *Henry D. Thoreau*. Stores and ammunition stacked on deck were swept overboard, as was a small launch, called *Windsong*, belonging to an Australian unit, the 30th Dock Company of Pioneers. Unfortunately the five Australian troops accompanying the launch had decided to sleep aboard it rather than below decks, and the men found themselves in the water, with the launch capsized. Eventually the launch righted itself, and the five men managed to struggle up on deck, only to find the boat sinking fast beneath them. They managed to get into the launch's dinghy, only to find it had also been holed, but it was all they had to cling on to.

Meanwhile, the captain of the Liberty ship had advised *Ballarat* of the mishap, and the warship made a search for the missing men, using its searchlight, but could not locate them. Just as *Ballarat* was about to abandon the search and rejoin the convoy, cries for help were heard, and at last the dinghy was sighted, quite close to the warship. Four of the soldiers were recovered quite quickly, but the fifth was unconscious. A sailor from *Ballarat*, Leading Seaman Philip Emms, dived overboard with a line tied around him, and succeeded in dragging the soldier back to safety. For his brave act, Emms was later awarded the George Medal.

In October 1942 it was the turn of the 2/5 Infantry Battalion, which had been part of the 17th Brigade left in Ceylon as a garrison, to be moved to New Guinea. Having had just two weeks special training at Singleton, the battalion was moved by train to Brisbane, where they arrived on 4 October. Four days later 860 troops of the battalion boarded the small Dutch vessel *Maetsuycker*, along with five trucks and a large amount of ammunition. The ship already had several anti-aircraft guns in place, but 50 Bren guns and eight anti-tank rifles were also positioned around the decks by the troops. The voyage north was slow and tedious, and *Maetsuycker* did not arrive in Milne Bay until 17 October.

The same month 2/6 Infantry Battalion, which had also been part

Maetsuycker was converted to carry some 700 troops. (*C.T. Reddings collection*)

of the 17th Brigade left in Ceylon, moved to New Guinea. After returning to Australia in early August on the transport *Arundel Castle*, the battalion had been allowed just 21 days leave before regrouping, and then being transported by train to Brisbane where, on 13 October, they boarded the 5000 gross ton Dutch vessel *Bontekoe*. Colonel Wood was still in command, and he recorded in his diary that 'conditions on the *Bontekoe* were crowded but the food good and plentiful and the ship's staff helpful. Discipline throughout the voyage was very good.' During the days at sea, the troops were given lectures on Japanese tactics, and also on health problems they may encounter in New Guinea, particularly malaria. After an uneventful voyage, the battalion disembarked on 20 October at Milne Bay, where they moved into a tent camp and began jungle training.

The 2/5 and 2/6 Infantry Battalions, along with the other units of the 17th Brigade, was being held in reserve at Milne Bay. Fred Quinn wrote on 20 October, 'We disembarked and went out to camp by motor transport ... Our camp was just one big pool of water, but we made the best of it.' Ken Brougham wrote in a letter home, 'Conditions here are very similar to what we encountered in Ceylon, although the rainfall is considerably heavier, so one is never dry by day or by night ... After a week of sleeping on the mud with only a groundsheet under us, we have at last rigged up beds of bamboo. Although uncomfortable they keep us off the ground.' Despite the regular issue of anti-mosquito cream, cases of malaria began to occur in increasing numbers. In November alone, 113 men of the 2/6 Battalion had to be evacuated from the camp with the disease, some going to local hospitals, while the more serious cases were sent back to Australia by ship.

On 3 January 1943 orders were received for the 17th Brigade to move to Port Moresby, from where they would be flown to Wau. The

2/6 Battalion was to be the first unit to leave Milne Bay, so on 10 January they were transported to the wharf to embark on the *Pulginbar*. Unlike the huge liners that had transported them to and from the Middle East, or even the smaller *Bontekoe*, *Pulginbar* was tiny, a 350 ton cargo vessel with limited passenger accommodation, which before the war had operated from Sydney to ports along the north coast of New South Wales.

Colonel Wood inspected the ship, decided it was much too small to transport the entire battalion, numbering 776 men, and reported this to divisional headquarters, but they told him to go ahead as ordered. Colonel Wood then went to the naval officer in charge, who also inspected the vessel, and instructed that only 280 men would be permitted to board. Even then it was a tight fit, Frank Casey recalling, 'The trip was so cramped that we had to sit around with our backs to the top structure and our feet pointing to the deck railings — and it rained all night.' Mercifully, the trip was quite short, and the men disembarked in Port Moresby the next day. The rest of the battalion followed in other small ships, and eventually the unit was together on 12 January at Port Moresby.

In January 1943, the Mortar Platoon of 2/14 Battalion was due to be relieved and sent home for some leave. On 7 January they were relieved near Gona by 14 Brigade, and began the trip home with a march to Soputa, where they were due to board planes to take them to Port Moresby. Unfortunately bad weather prevented the planes taking off, so the unit marched to Popendetta, only to meet the same problem again. As the battalion history records, 'Orders were then received to march to Dobadura 7 hours march away. Full marching order and extremely hot weather made the march particularly difficult. Next day the unit emplaned for Moresby. After two hours flying Moresby was reached, and they embussed for Donedabu, where all troops were completely outfitted with new clothes. Part of the Platoon was already on the way to Australia, including personnel who had been evacuated sick and reinforcements, who had been stationed at Bootless Inlet before leaving.'

On 10 January 1943, most of the troops from the Mortar Platoon embarked in the American Liberty ship *Isaac Coles*, while the remainder were taken on board another Liberty ship with an American crew, both ships being routed to ports in northern Queensland. The unit gathered together again at Ravenshoe on 26 January, where they spent the next nine days, during which short route marches and working

Canberra was another coastal liner used to transport troops to New Guinea. (*C.T. Reddings collection*)

parties were organised to fill in the time. Then it was time for home leave, but only for fourteen days.

Following their return from leave, the Mortar Platoon engaged in further training and other exercises for several months, then as July came to close, rumours began flying about an impending move. As the battalion history records, 'The unit started to pack up, and a few days later, early in August, the first lift departed for an unknown destination. The second lift embarked on 6 August 1943 in *Taroona*. Ship life was uneventful, and on 9 August the troops disembarked at Port Moresby once again and were transported to Bootless Inlet in pouring rain. A route march was ordered even before the camp was reached. There was much mud.'

It was also in early July 1943 that the 25th Brigade was advised to prepare for a move to New Guinea. Most of the troops were transported north on three Australian ships, *Duntroon*, *Taroona* and *Canberra*, with the final unit arriving in Port Moresby on 26 July on board *Katoomba*. In early August the 21st Brigade was also transported to New Guinea, while the 18th Brigade had also arrived in Port Moresby by 12 August.

The 2/12 Field Regiment, having returned home with Operation Pamphlet, had a brief period of leave, then reassembled in Victoria, only to be sent by train to Python Hill, in north Queensland, near Cairns. On 1 August 1943, Regimental Headquarters, the Signals Section and Light Aid Detachment personnel were transported to Cairns, where they boarded *Manoora*, which departed the next day.

After a quick trip north, they arrived at Milne Bay on the evening of 3 August. *Manoora* anchored out, and even though the rain was pouring down, immediately all the troops on board began to disembark, having to clamber over the side of the top deck and down scramble nets into landing craft. This had to be done overnight, as *Manoora* had to depart the area by dawn. Other elements of the 2/12 Field Regiment made the trip north on several ships, including the small Dutch vessels *Van Heutz* and *Van der Lijn*, of which one gunner later wrote, 'I was seasick all the way and the only tucker was bully beef and cold mashed spuds.'

Included in another group, Ted Cassidy wrote, 'We moved to Trinity Beach on 3 August 1943 and embarked on *Henry T. Allen* at 1600 — a dry boat unfortunately. A lecture on ship routine by an American on the 4th and damn-all to do all day. Under way at 0400 on 5th, and reached Milne Bay on Friday, August 6th. Americans made a mess of disembarking and after frigging around all day we disembarked via nets at 1700. Unloaded stores from LCU's until relieved about 2100. No sooner in bed than up again to unload ration trucks until 0600. When it rains here it certainly rains. The mud is very sticky.'

The *Manoora* returned to Cairns, and at 1000 hours on 8 August the men of 2/43 Battalion began to embark. Since returning from Africa in Operation Pamphlet, the battalion had regrouped at the Springwood Camp near Adelaide, then been transferred by train to the Atherton Tableland in north Queensland, where they commenced jungle training at Kairi. By 1500 on 8 August all the men were on board *Manoora*, which pulled away from the Cairns wharf and headed north once again. *Manoora* arrived in Milne Bay early in the afternoon of 10 August. Disembarkation commenced at 1630 hours and continued through the night.

The men of the 2/13 Battalion enjoyed a brief spell of home leave after returning to Sydney aboard *Aquitania* in Operation Pamphlet, but all too soon it was time to return to their unit and prepare for their move to New Guinea. In mid-April 1943 the battalion arrived at a camp in the hinterland behind Cairns, where they spent the next three months in training. Les Clothier was still with the battalion, and continued to maintain his diary, including the fact that 25 April 1943 happened to be both Anzac Day and Easter Sunday, a coincidence that would not happen again for 94 years. He also recorded the extensive jungle training the troops were put through, including bivouacs during which 'most of the boys were covered in little red ticks and had a good dose of scrub itch.' Les Clothier also became ill and was transferred to hospital, his diary on 3 July recording, 'Am writing this from the 2nd AGH, having been evacuated on Thursday afternoon with a temperature of 104. There is a chap from A Coy in here with scrub typhus — he's been here for 50 days.'

On 19 July Les Clothier rejoined his battalion, which was packing up at the camp in preparation for the trip to New Guinea. Five days later he noted, 'At present we're packed up ready to board a boat — and it looks like a trip to New Guinea. This week we've done little else but swim and muck about. We pulled our tents down on Thursday and the 2/23rd moved in on the site. We've slept in the open the last few nights, with two blankets, and it wasn't too warm. The precautions here against malaria are fairly stringent. We sleep under nets, take atabrin tablets daily and have to roll our sleeves down after 5 pm. Some of the companies have moved out already. Looks like the trip being in a small boat as the Battalion is only allowed 700 men and has to leave some behind to travel with another unit. According to the Yanks we're going to have a go at Lae.'

At last the time to board ship came. On 26 July, Les Clothier wrote, 'Am writing this from on board a Dutch boat of about 9,000 tons, in Cairns Harbour. We left camp by MT [Motor Transport] last night, and waited five hours just outside the wharf before boarding. We had a sloppy stew for breakfast and sat on a dirty floor to eat it. As usual, the officers are in cabins and eat like civilised beings.'

The Dutch boat the troops were on board was named *Maetsuycker*, and far from being 'about 9,000 tons' as Les Clothier thought, was only 4272 gross tons, and a mere 376 feet long, a far cry from the huge *Queen Mary* and *Aquitania* on which the same men had been transported to and from the Middle East. *Maetsuycker* had been built in Holland in 1937, with accommodation for just 55 passengers, for the Dutch KPM company, which operated numerous services in the Dutch East Indies, and also to Australia and New Zealand. *Maetsuycker* had been a regular visitor to Sydney and Brisbane before the war. When Holland was invaded in 1940 the ship was handed over to the Allies, and based in Australia, though retaining her original crew of Dutch officers and Javanese seamen. Despite her limited passenger spaces, *Maetsuycker* was converted into a troop transport, capable of carrying about 700 men, with officers being accommodated in cabins, while other ranks were spread though the various holds and 'tween decks. Fortunately the trooping voyages made by *Maetsuycker* were usually quite short.

The trip from Cairns to New Guinea was anything but pleasant for the troops. On 28 July, Les Clothier recorded, 'We left Cairns at 6 am yesterday and are going fairly slowly N and NE alternatively. There has been a swell since leaving coastal waters and quite a few of the mob are sick.' In the official history of the 2/13 Battalion, *We Had Some Bother*, the discomfort of the trip to New Guinea was covered in some detail.

'The displacement of the *Maetsuycker* we were never to learn, but we do know that her dead weight in pounds per passenger was rapidly reduced as the journey lengthened. Perhaps it was the weather, which was anything but calm for most of the trip, but we are inclined to think it was a combination of the stench of sun-drying fish, the crew's quarters, and a fiendish heaving of the ship itself. These factors, combined with a diet of bully beef stew and canned peaches, made our sojourn on the *Maetsuycker* anything but pleasant. A larger number than ever succumbed to a desire to feed the fish. We remember one young officer who made the mistake of standing at the taffrail, either to soliloquise or merely to watch the churned-up wake of the ship fold in and open out as she lifted to the swell. It was foolish to go there in the first place and much worse to remain. Within a space of ten minutes he had changed colour three times and heaved his dignity and his dinner into Neptune's lap.'

As was usual on trooping voyages, the unit on board supplied men for ack-ack duty. On *Maetsuycker*, this consisted of a solitary rocket bracket on the poop deck. It was a job nobody wanted, as close by the rocket platform was a crate of stinking fish, 'seasoned enough to turn the stomach of the most hardened mariner.'

The sanitary arrangements on the ship were also less than had been experienced on previous ships, as the battalion history recorded. 'We were very impressed by what we came to refer to as "the house of the rushing waters." "The House" consisted of a galvanised shed erected at the stern of the ship, and boasted an ingeniously built-in seawater supply. A raging torrent of water hurtled down a tin trough over the top of which we teetered precariously on a piece of steel whenever Nature's demands became excessively urgent. Most of us preferred the agony of constipation to the ever present risk of drowning, but those hardy souls who braved the dangers assured us that it was quite a novel idea — in fact the only place they had ever been in where a bath could be obtained with intestinal relief — and all for nothing, too!'

The crew of the *Maetsuycker* also were recorded for posterity.

We will never forget the captain of that ship. Dressed in a spotless white uniform, he would inspect the boat-drill parades and invariably address each station thus: 'ze hooter vill hoot ... ze clew vill lower ze boat ... ze clew vill get in ze boat ... ze hooter vill hoot — ounce — dwice — zen you vill get into ze boat.' We often wondered what would happen if 'ze hooter' was unable to hoot.

On all previous ships, our main relaxation at night was to visit the Swy. On the *Maetsuycker*, however, we were reduced to watching the crew — Javanese all — play Pontoon. They would bet up to 100 pounds on a five-cards-under-hand and when they lost they did so without turning a hair.

Few of the men on board were sorry when the ship finally steamed past Samarai, 'with its pretty red bungalows and green palms,' and entered the long sweep of Milne Bay. On 29 July, Les Clothier wrote in his diary: 'We rounded the E tip of New Guinea and headed W and at present are anchored off some place which is full of ships, large (10,000 tons) and small (corvettes and shore craft). One of our Javanese crew told us the place is Gilli Gilli. There is not a strict blackout on shore as lights can be seen in plenty. Parts of the shore are picturesque, but as we can guess what's ahead of us, we don't appreciate it so much. There is cloud on the hills all round and we have had some sharp showers.'

On 1 August, Les Clothier wrote: 'We came off the ship and were put straight into MT on Friday morning and taken to a "camp." There were tents up and that's all. Most of them leaked. Militia troops fostered us in and as usual they fought the battle all over for our benefit. They had us ducking from shells and diseases everywhere. We've spent about 40% of our time in the Army, so far, on active operations against the enemy. On Friday night I slept in a puddle, due to the tent leaking. There are plenty of scrub typhus and malaria in this district, according to our MO.'

Also sent to New Guinea on a small Dutch vessel were B Company of the 2/3 Machine Gun Battalion. This unit had been one of the first to become involved in Stepsister Convoy in early 1942, and many of their men had ended up in the Netherlands East Indies, to be captured by the Japanese within days of landing there. Other elements of the unit were more fortunate, their ships being diverted to Australia, but over the subsequent months the battalion was heavily reinforced to bring it back up to full strength again. Once this had been done, the battalion moved to Cowra, in New South Wales, to begin training, and prepared to return to the war, this time in Papua New Guinea.

B Company of the 2/3 Machine Gun Battalion was the first to be sent away, moving north to the Kalinga staging camp near Brisbane in early June 1943, waiting there for transport to their planned destination, Merauke. While at Kalinga, the men of the company were kept busy, at one time working on the nearby docks to load ships, but, as the battalion history records, 'Sergeant S.J. Woods, who was acting CSM ... suffered a broken leg while supervising work on the wharves. The wharf labourers resented the speed and efficiency of our men's work, and one day a fracas developed and Woods was the victim. An additional cause of friction was that the machine gunners were making pilfering more difficult.'

On 18 June 1943, B Company, less 9 Platoon, departed Kalinga for Brisbane, where they entrained for Cairns, going into camp on arrival at Redlynch. The men of 9 platoon remained in Brisbane to load the company's motor vehicles, which included two jeeps, three 15-hundredweight trucks, two 3-ton trucks and a watercart onto an American vessel which carried them and the men to New Guinea. The rest of the battalion remained behind in Brisbane until August 1943, when they moved north as well, to the Atherton Tableland.

On 28 June, four officers and 98 other ranks from B Company were transported to the docks at Cairns and boarded the small Dutch vessel *Janssens*. The ship was already full of soldiers, and eventually carried 380 personnel altogether. The battalion history stated, 'there were no cooking facilities. Improvised heating for hot water was organised but all meals on the voyage consisted of hard rations served cold. A second blanket was issued and the troops slept between decks.' From Cairns the *Janssens* steamed to Thursday Island, one day's sailing from Merauke, and dropped anchor there. On 1 July the voyage continued, and next day the *Janssens* arrived off Merauke, a small town on the southern coast of what was Dutch New Guinea, now known as Irian Jaya. The men of B Company became part of Merauke Force, whose job was to deny the enemy a base close to the north of Cape York.

There was also a steady movement of troops from New Guinea back home for leave and regrouping. On 13 September 1943 the 2/5 Infantry Battalion, which had arrived in Milne Bay in October 1942, returned there, and eight days later boarded the Dutch vessel *Bos Fontaine* to be taken back home, arriving in Cairns on 23 September.

The Australian coastal liner *Canberra* was making regular trips from Townsville to Port Moresby with troops, and in September 1943 also carried a detachment of nurses from the Australian Army Medical

Janssens was another of the small Dutch ships used to carry troops north. (*C.T. Reddings collection*)

Women's Service. Most of these nurses had come from Western Australia, making a 5000-mile journey which required seven changes of train, and a lengthy stay in Sydney en route to Townsville. The history of the AAMWS, *Our Kind of War*, recorded what happened next:

> Townsville, the port of exodus to the Islands, was crowded to suffocation point. There was no staging for the AAMWS who were to go on board immediately. They stumbled down the wharf in the blackout, with only the silhouettes of the tallest women against the lighter sky to give a point of reference to the shorter ones. Trying to keep balance with the clumsy gear was quite exhausting.

Another view of *Canberra* during the war years. (*R.J. Tompkins collection*)

After boarding the troopship *Canberra*, the nightmarish feeling persisted. There was a stunned silence, then a voice was heard remarking that the ship seemed to lack the appointments of a luxury liner! In the brown-out below decks, it was apparent that the *Canberra* lacked many things, including sheets to cover hideously stained mattresses.

At last some vexation of spirit was apparent and a senior officer of the 2/1 AGH staff ordered an issue of one new grey woollen blanket to be spread over each bunk — cosy in that climate — but clean. The women scrubbed their cabins, NCO's were sent on picket duty to 'deter fraternising with the male troops on board' and all spent the daylight hours in a restricted deck space.

From our sailing position on the outside of the convoy we saw only the solitary patrol boat skimming over the Coral Sea. When it came within hailing distance the crew advised those lining the rails to 'pull your heads in, you look like a cattle truck.' On the morning of September 16th 1943, the *Canberra* arrived in Port Moresby. After landing at the jetty, the AAMWS climbed into the waiting jeeps and took the scenic drive through Moresby along dry, dusty gravel roads. The friendly drivers pointed out the cottages built over the water; the *Macdhui* sunk by enemy action; the paddock where a fuel dump had been blasted during one of the many air raids ... The troops along the road welcomed the women with cheers, jeers and warnings.

Another group of AAMWS nurses left Townsville on 22 November aboard *Taroona*, bound for Buna. *Taroona* stopped first at Milne Bay, staying there overnight, then continued on to Oro Bay, where the AAMWS disembarked and were taken by buses to Buna, where they joined the 2/11 AGH.

As the Australian soldiers began to force the Japanese into retreat, the war front moved slowly further away from Australia. By the middle of 1943 New Guinea and Papua were almost entirely back in Australian hands, and plans were being formulated for attacks on the last Japanese strongholds at Salamaua, Lae and Finschhafen in September. In October 1943 *Duntroon* carried troops to Milne Bay, then in November went to Buna for the first time. Late in November 1943 *Duntroon* took on board 1450 troops at Buna, who were to be carried to Milne Bay in a convoy, escorted by several destroyers.

Among the escort was the USS *Perkins*, and on the night of 23 November the commander of the naval vessel decided to practise manoeuvring exercises. Both *Perkins* and *Duntroon* were fully blacked out making exact positioning difficult, but the *Perkins* attempted to cross the bow of *Duntroon*. Misjudging the speed of the liner, the destroyer could not complete the manoeuvre and the bow of *Duntroon* sliced into the warship between its two funnels, cutting it in two. The two sections sank quickly, but only five men lost their lives, the rest of the destroyer's crew being rescued by *Duntroon*, which received serious bow damage. However, the troopship was able to limp into Milne Bay and disembark its troops, then headed back to Australia. Repairs were not completed until the middle of March 1944, when *Duntroon* again made a trooping trip to the islands, only to have to return to Sydney again, this time for engine repairs, which were not completed until September 1944

Katoomba had been mainly operating out of Townsville, transporting troops and equipment to Port Moresby. On 4 October 1943, *Katoomba* had been berthed in Port Moresby discharging ammunition when a case of projectiles fell onto cordite charges, resulting in an explosion that killed one man and injured seven others, and a fire in no. 1 hold which was soon brought under control. The vessel was able to continue in service, and began carrying troops to Milne Bay, then in December 1943 went to Buna for the first time. So fast was the Japanese retreat that in January 1944 *Katoomba* was able to go to Lae for the first time, then in March she went to Finschhafen. Following this, *Katoomba* returned to the Australian coast for a while, going to Fremantle in June 1944 and Darwin in September, but then it was back to the islands, with a voyage to Lae, returning to Townsville on 4 October 1944. On the night of 8 October a fire broke out in no. 1 hold, which had to be flooded to douse the flames. *Katoomba* was able to depart Townsville on 17 October, bound for Milne Bay, then went on to Morotai before returning to Sydney by the end of the year for overhaul.

The Mortar Platoon of the 2/14 Battalion remained in New Guinea until January 1944. The battalion history states, 'On 6 January the Platoon flew back to Port Moresby … Late in January the advance party left for Australia … The unit packed up and embarked on the good ship, *Both* on 8 March.' The *Both* was one of the many Dutch flag ships handed over to the Allies when Holland was invaded in 1940. Owned by the KPM company, *Both* was quite small and had traded in the Dutch East Indies prior to the war. It was also a coal-burner, and it was noted that 'twenty men from the Mortars helped coal the vessel in Bowen. They arrived in Brisbane on 15 March, and were transported to Kallangur, entraining for respective home states on 18 March.'

At the end of 1944 it was the turn of the 2/13 Battalion to return to

Australia for some well-deserved leave, after eighteen months fighting against the Japanese. The vessel that carried most of the men back home was named *Cape Perpetua*, which had an American crew. This was a standard C-1 class vessel, built by the Consolidated Steel Corporation at Wilmington, California, and completed in May 1943. Several months later the vessel was converted into a troop transport, with an extended superstructure, and able to carry up to 2006 troops, though in very cramped quarters.

The battalion history stated, 'We found her rough in her finish but comfortable withal — who were we to care, headed for home? ... We admired her plumbing, especially with the comparison of the *Maetsuycker* to fall back onto. We developed an intense dislike for hominy, which was served for breakfast every morning, and envied the crew their thick steaks and fresh vegetables. It was, we are sure, a bad tactical blunder to march the mess line past the portholes which opened out from the crew's mess. We liked the ship, her speed, and her newness, but we did not really come to know her; the close proximity of home and leave were too constantly with us to spare much thought to our mechanical beast of burden.'

The bulk of the 2/3 Machine Gun Battalion had remained in Australia training for over a year, but as 1944 drew to a close they also prepared to move to New Guinea. The advance party of the battalion left Cairns for New Guinea on 11 November 1944, travelling on a ship named *Mexico*. Orders were received for the battalion to move in mid-November, but as happened on many occasions, these orders were cancelled on 23 November. Two days later came new orders to prepare for embarkation on the Australian coastal liner *Katoomba* at Cairns, but these were also cancelled. On 30 November further orders were received, and this time the battalion entrained at Wondecla and moved to the Redlynch camp, near Cairns. On 4 December the battalion was transported to Cairns, where they boarded the *Evangeline* for the trip north.

Evangeline was an American vessel, and a vast improvement on the Dutch ships others had travelled on. Built in 1927, *Evangeline* was a passenger vessel, having operated along the east coast of America, mainly between New York and Boston, for the Eastern Steamship Company. Although there were over one thousand troops on board, the facilities for troops were quite good and the trip to Aitape went smoothly. *Evangeline* anchored in the bay off Aitape on 8 December, but it was not until 10 December that the men of the 2/3 Machine Gun Battalion went ashore. As Shorty Foster of C Company described it: 'We had to climb down landing nets into a huge barge which carried the whole Battalion. Very hairy going over the side complete with all gear. However the manoeuvre was carried out without any real injury. To say Aitape is the plughole of the world would be an understatement. Beach–coconut grove–swamp–mountain. Where was the tropical paradise we had heard so much about?'

Other units to depart for Aitape at this time were the 2/5 and 2/6 Infantry Battalions, which had already served one tour of duty in New Guinea, from October 1942 to October 1943. After leave and a time of rebuilding the unit in the Atherton Tablelands, the 2/5 was the first to go, embarking on *Duntroon* at Cairns on 24 November, arriving at Aitape five days later.

On 1 December 1944 the 2/6 Battalion, comprising 38 officers and 792 other ranks, embarked on the American Victory ship *Thomas Corwin* at Cairns. As Cliff Hirst remembered the voyage, 'The Victory ship was good for transporting troops on a short voyage ... having the whole Battalion on board did not allow for much movement on deck or anywhere else ... Quite a few of the troops were seasick. I remember Theo French played cards for nearly 48 hours continuously to ease his seasickness as he could not eat or lie down on his bunk.'

On 6 December the *Thomas Corwin* arrived off Aitape, where a heavy swell was running, making disembarking more difficult than usual, the men having to climb down scramble-nets on the side of the ship into American landing barges which took them to the beach, where they waded ashore. They were then transported to a tent camp, erected by a small advance party, which was located near the beach and airstrip. Kevin Harrington recalled, 'As we landed from barges to take over from an American division the Yanks backloaded their supplies. Here the scrounging ability of the Australian soldier was demonstrated. The Yanks had checked their stores before we arrived. As we pitched our tents others dug holes in the floor area whilst others organised scrounging teams. Dozens of cans of tinned food were quickly souvenired and buried ... We ate well for weeks.'

Also leaving Australia for New Guinea was the 2/2 Battalion, the third time they had been sent away since the war started. On 19 December 1944, 35 officers and 1099 other ranks boarded the American transport *Jane Addams*, aware they were going to New Guinea, but not advised of their actual destination until the third day at sea. This trip was a more pleasant experience for the men on board, as the meals provided were varied and of a high standard. Christmas Day was spent at sea, with a church service, carol singing, and a reading of the King's Christmas message to the men by Major Green. The next day, 26 December, the *Jane Addams* anchored off Aitape, the coastline being described by one soldier as, 'bleak, sandy, coconut-lined.'

However, it would be another four days before the men were able to disembark, due to heavy congestion in the area, with too many ships and too few docking facilities. These four days were uncomfortable for the troops, as the ship moved uneasily in swelling seas, caused by the north-western monsoons, and men who had survived the trip north without problem succumbed to motion sickness. At last it was time to go ashore, with landing barges coming alongside, and the men, heavily weighed down with their gear, scrambling down nets on the side of the ship. The barges took them to the beach, where they had to wade ashore through two or three feet of water to reach dry land. After the comforts of the ship, their first camp was very unpleasant, being located next to a graveyard from which bodies were being exhumed by American soldiers, to be returned to the United States.

By early February 1945, the 2/13 Battalion was again in camp, once more preparing for a trip overseas. Les Clothier had recorded in his diary on 12 February, 'Have been promoted to sergeant and am now living in the sergeant's tent and eating is a lot better.' Over the next few weeks, Les noted the monotony of camp life, stating on 3 March, 'everyone knows there's a move on, but the destination is a big worry,' while on 9 April he wrote, 'there is still no sign of our Brigade moving yet, but it is rumoured that one of the other Brigades is on the water. We're beginning to think that the Philippines is our next stop.'

Five days later came the diary entry, 'Things are coming to a head now. We've been issued with sea kitbags, mosquito repellent and First Aid kits and all the impediment for a move. The Orderly Room staff have been making out nominal rolls, embarkation rolls, etc., by the dozen. Our tents have been struck and we're busy cleaning up the camp.' On 18 April the battalion was finally on the move, Les recording on 20 April, 'We arrived at Redlynch staging camp yesterday in the wee small hours by train. Present pointers are that we'll be here for a few days before embarkation. We're going in either a Victory or a Liberty ship — Morotai looks a moral.' As usual, the men were kept in the dark about their future movements, and still did not know their ultimate destination when, on 29 April, Les Clothier wrote, 'Left Redlynch yesterday afternoon at 5 pm in large troop carriers and proceeded to embark immediately. The SS *Charles Lummis* is our transport — a Victory ship manned by Yanks. We're in tiered bunks in holds and on two meals a day. Left Cairns this morning and soon were out of sight of land.'

Between 25 and 29 April 1945, the 2/13 Battalion embarked in Cairns on three ships, *Frederick Lykes*, *David C. Shanks* and *Charles Lummis*, for what was to be their final trip as a unit, although the ships did not travel together as a convoy. As the battalion history noted, 'Compared to the *Maetsuycker* these were luxury cruisers, though not in the same class as the old *Aquitania*. For a change, we had no duties to perform and, with the exception of a few perfunctory boat drills, our time was mostly taken up with playing cards or Swy or trying to guess where we were headed.'

The three ships transporting the 2/13 Battalion were quite different in design and fittings. Despite Les Clothier describing the *Charles Lummis* as a Victory ship, it was in fact a Liberty ship, which had only been completed in May 1943 by the California Shipbuilding Corporation at Terminal Island, Los Angeles. This was one of several shipyards established in 1942 specifically to construct Liberty ships, their target being set at twelve ships a month, though by 1943 they were exceeding this.

The *David C. Shanks* was one of a series of standard C-3 class cargo ships intended for the United States Lines North Atlantic services, this one to have been named *American Farmer*. Shortly after construction began, all these ships were taken over by the United States government, and the ship was redesigned to carry passengers, being launched in April 1943 as *Gulfport*. It was then completely redesigned as a transport for the United States Army, with a capacity of 1935 troops, being renamed *David C. Shanks*, and measuring 12,097 gross tons. Compared to the Liberty and Victory ships, the facilities provided for troops on the *David C. Shanks* were far superior, though still crowded.

The *Frederick Lykes* was the second of a pair of 7800 gross ton cargo ships built in 1941 for Lykes Line, a major American shipping firm. As with the other ships, it had been converted to carry troops, though in very cramped quarters.

As the 2/13 Battalion headed north once again, on 1 May 1945 Les Clothier made an interesting entry in his diary, indicative of the varied life in the army during the war; 'Today is the Battalion's 5th birthday. The 1st was spent at Tobruk, the 2nd in Syria, the 3rd in Kairi, the 4th at Ravenshoe and the 5th at sea.' Reverting to his current situation, Les wrote, 'Yesterday was a bit rough and most of the boys were sick. Today we sighted land at 6.15 am, which was the south-east corner of

New Guinea. Went through the China Strait, turned west past Milne Bay and are now beating up the coast towards Buna, Lae, etc.'

On 2 May, 'Today the weather has been fine and the seas very smooth. We're keeping a fair way out from shore and it's hard to recognise any landmarks. Went past Finschhafen last night at 7.30 and it's like a miniature city, with thousands of lights everywhere. Much different from when we last saw it.' The voyage continued, proving to be monotonous and uninteresting for the troops. On 5 May Les Clothier was writing, 'The Yanks told us yesterday that we passed Hollandia. Word has come through that Aussies have landed in Borneo. If it's the 26th Brigade, which we think it is, then it won't be long before we're into it ourselves.'

That evening, the ships finally came to a stop, but it was not the final destination for the troops. The battalion history stated, 'we anchored overnight off what we were afterwards told was Biak, about the smelliest place in the Pacific at that time.' Les Clothier's diary note on 6 May was somewhat kinder: 'We arrived at Biak Island last night at 6 pm. It seems to be a fairly large base. There's another troop transport anchored nearby and it looks as if we'll be proceeding from here in convoy.'

On the afternoon of 6 May, the *Charles Lummis* left Biak, as Les Clothier noted, 'in convoy with 10 LST's and a Liberty, escorted by three small warships. We'll get to Moort sometime Wednesday and from there, who knows?' After two days at sea, on 9 May, 'sighted land at 6 am this morning and should be in before long. We'll be disembarking today sometime and are being given a stretcher each.' So it was that the men of the 2/13 battalion arrived for their final term of active service in the war.

Also being transported north, first to Moort then on to Borneo, during March and April 1945 were the 9th Division Engineers. These units had been camped near Cairns for some months, training and waiting for orders to move, which finally came in March 1945. The first unit to depart was Headquarters RAE, who left Ravenshoe in mid-March, being deluged by the wet cyclonic weather as they joined ships in Cairns Harbour. Over the next six weeks the remaining units were all moved north and, as recorded in *The Sappers' War*:

> The voyages north from Cairns or Townsville brought troops across the Coral Sea in the cyclone season and most had rough passages under crowded conditions on American Victory ships. These ships were equipped to provide cooking and messing facilities when used for troop transport, and generally were superior to the Liberty ships of earlier experiences.

One transport, the *Sea Barb*, sighted a floating mine 100 yards distant in choppy seas inside the reef north of Cairns. The ship hove to and ship's gunner's turned their Oerlikon and Bofors guns on it, but failed to explode it. Then some infantry joined in with rifles, but the bobbing mine and pitching ship made conditions difficult. As dusk fell the ship again got under way. Some hours later the engines stopped and the anchor was dropped. The noise of this in the forward hold full of troops caused a scare as men rushed for the stairs, thinking we had struck trouble. When we eventually passed out into the Coral Sea it was very rough, and there was little need for the cooks to prepare meals that day.

As before, the days at sea passed slowly for the troops, with little space to exercise or move around. There was also an element of inconvenience as 'These troopships usually required a "stand to" on deck, with life jackets worn from 0500 to 0700 hours, as this was considered the greatest danger time for submarine attack.' So the voyage continued, 'Through China Straits at the south east of Milne Bay, and Vitiaz Straits between Finschhafen and New Britain ... First landfall beyond New Guinea was at an island base, Biak ... Lights and films were allowed on deck, but air raid alerts interfered with such luxuries at times ... From Biak the ship headed west ... The voyage from Cairns took up to twelve days for some ships.'

On arrival at Moort, the Field Park Company diarist recorded, 'ships everywhere from LCM's to cruisers; hospital ships to tenders: It was a moving sight.' The island of Moort was described as 'quite beautiful with coconut palm fringed beaches, level coastal areas, and heavily wooded hills further inland. Roads, stores dumps, camp sites and activity abounded. Units were fairly quickly moved to areas where they had to establish a temporary camp.' From here, the Engineers went on to take part in the landings on Tarakan in April 1945, although, as Ken Ward-Harvey later wrote, 'The voyage from Moort took seven days and was more monotonous than eventful.' From Tarakan the Engineers moved on to Labuan Island, and were there when the war ended.

The Japanese were not only being beaten back in Papua New Guinea and the Dutch East Indies, the Pacific Islands and the Philippines, but were also losing their hold on the Malay Peninsula. As the Allies relentlessly pressed onwards, drawing ever closer to the islands of Japan, plans were being prepared for the invasion of Japan. It was realised that this could be very costly in lives, so President Truman approved the dropping of two atomic bombs, the first on Hiroshima on 6 August 1945, followed three days later by a similar attack on Nagasaki. The huge amount of destruction caused by these two bombs horrified the Japanese, who on 15 August 1945 announced their surrender, bringing World War II to an end.

However, some pre-planned movements overseas continued, despite the cessation of hostilities. On 18 August, 118 Australian General Hospital, which had been preparing to depart for New Britain at a staging base at Punchbowl, in Sydney, were advised that their move was to go ahead as planned.

The members of 118 AGH, and a contingent of troops, boarded the *Taroona* at Darling Harbour on the morning of 25 August, and that afternoon the vessel undocked and headed off down Sydney Harbour. However, as the ship neared the boom at Middle Head, engine problems arose, so *Taroona* turned around and began returning to her berth. However, she was given a warm welcome by tooting ferries and waving passengers, who thought she was troopship returning with her decks crowded with service men and women.

On 28 August *Taroona* pulled away from Darling Harbour again, and this time made it out to sea. During a stopover in Brisbane, 300 more troops embarked, making conditions very crowded. As recorded in *Our Kind of War*, 'For the next ten days those first on the crowded deck after meals could sit on their life jackets, while others stood around waiting to pounce on any vacated spot.'

It took five days for *Taroona* to reach Milne Bay, then it was on to Wewak, 'whilst preparations for disembarking included rubbing antimite powder into socks, gaiters and trouserlegs, as a precaution against these carriers of Scrub Typhus.' Wewak was the original destination for 118 AGH, but events had changed this and their new destination was Jaquinot Bay in New Britain. *Taroona* carried on along the coast to Finschhafen, then went on to Jaquinot Bay where, eighteen days after leaving Sydney, 118 AGH disembarked.

The end of the war did not mean the end of active service for many Australian troops, as they were to remain in various parts of the Pacific theatre of the war for several more months. For those unfortunate enough to have been captured and imprisoned by the Japanese, often in the most horrendous conditions, the end of the war did signal an end to their suffering and the chance to return home at last.

19 Going Home

As the war in Europe came towards a conclusion, there were still many Australians actively involved, mostly flying with the Royal Air Force. Of the tens of thousands of men who had volunteered for flying duty, many had paid the ultimate price, but some were lucky, survived to complete their schedule of missions, and could then think about going home. On Wednesday, 6 December 1944, David Scholes, who arrived in Britain in July 1943, flew his last mission with Bomber Command, in a Lancaster on a raid over Giessen, a railway junction. On his return to England he could at last relax, knowing he will not have to undertake any more missions and could look forward to a return to Australia.

It was not until 8 March 1945 that David Scholes and other fliers returning home could board their ship, *Empress of Scotland*, at Liverpool. This liner had taken part in several convoys transporting Australian troops to the Middle East under her previous name, *Empress of Japan*, which was changed in 1942. The ship did not depart until 0800 the next morning. As Scholes recorded in his diary that day, 'Just before lunch we pick up several more quite large troopships and two destroyers. It appears therefore that we are to proceed in convoy. It is a cold cloudy day and I get my last glimpse of England through a mist-like smoke haze. After lunch we are six ships strong, plus the two warships ... Evidently we are to pick up more ships en route from the Clyde and Solway before nipping off round the north tip of Ireland and down south. First stop I believe is Gibraltar.'

Next morning, 'I get up to find we have quite a roll on ... Later on in the morning we join up with some more ships and an escort

Empress of Scotland berthed at Woolloomooloo in Sydney. (*National Library of Australia*)

carrier. Altogether we are 15 ships strong now plus an escort of five destroyers and the carrier. The sea becomes quite choppy after lunch and several WRENS go for the big spit! However I have not yet made a glorious rush for the taffrail or bucket or any other receptacle … I can see, however, that I am going to become very bored indeed with four weeks of this business. Never shall I want to see water in such abundance again in my life … Towards evening we become increasingly enveloped in mist and one by one the other ships become invisible … At this stage a queer affair is let out and trailed behind which produces a fountain of foaming water. On sight of this any ship overtaking us knows of our position and takes the necessary avoiding action.'

Despite the fact that the Allied armies were sweeping across Europe towards Germany from both east and west, the situation at sea was still dangerous, with German submarines engaged in a last-ditch stand against Allied shipping, so safety precautions on the troopships were as strict as ever. David Scholes noted, 'As was the custom on other troop ships I have been on, we carry at all times our life preservers. Never are you allowed to be without it. It is even present when having a bath, at meals and when visiting the little place. On this ship we have also been issued with a small floating torch and a tin of emergency rations which we must carry at all times. The temptation to open any issue of this nature immediately is great, but OC troops forewarns us regarding this lot. We have to hand them in again at the end of our journey or pay for them and apart from this, his dog rejected the contents once he declares so it can't be anything too tasty inside.'

As always on troopships, the next port of call, and even the destination of the ship, was a closely guarded secret, and rumours abounded. On 13 March, David Scholes was writing, 'The rumour has spread about that today some time we are to leave the convoy and proceed on our own to and through the Panama Canal ... I very much would prefer to go through the Mediterranean and thereby complete a voyage around the world ... Lo and behold, at 1815 we alter course, increase speed and leave the convoy. This is indeed a blow, Panama it is most certainly, and so, no round the world cruise. This is a trifle now as a new and yet more severe blow has hit me. We shall be disembarked at Sydney and not Melbourne. I am not, even at this early stage, looking forward to the train trip between. I believe it takes 16 days to go from Panama to Sydney. I'll go nuts, that's all about it.'

A week later, Scholes was feeling a bit happier about things, as on 21 March he wrote: 'The last few days have certainly warmed the cockles of my heart. We have all been attired in shorts and shirts, and for a while revelling in the joy of seeing and feeling the real sun again after so long a time. I have paid dearly for grabbing too much sun for I'm almost frizzled up and a fiery colour ... Below deck is like a furnace and I sleep, or try to in my birthday suit. The sweat trickles away all night until in the morning the bunk is quite wet. We are on A deck — I hate to think what it would be like on D deck! It is more a coma than a sleep you fall into.'

Next day, 22 March, the ship arrived in Cristobal, at the entrance to the Panama Canal. 'Last night was terribly hot,' wrote Scholes, 'and I get up at 6 am this morning to get out for some fresh air and enjoy the cool breeze before the sun rises ... We pick up a pilot and enter through a gap in the stone breakwater into a tidy little harbour ... by 0930 we are safe and sound docked and tied up at No. 8 wharf.' Although the troops on board were not supposed to go ashore further than the dock gates, many managed to evade the police and spend some time enjoying the town.

Next day *Empress of Scotland* went through the Panama Canal. David Scholes found himself a good spot on the sundeck, 'and still very much amazed by the scenery already viewed, begin to be further amazed ... We have begun to pass through the canal. Soon we reach the first series of locks ... We glide into the lock, stop, large gates close behind us — in comes the water and up we go, open the gates at the other end and on to the next ... We are towed along by electrically driven caterpillar tractors using the elastic steel cable idea. The whole procedure is intensely interesting although slow. On through the three lifting locks and we pass, with much whistle-blowing, into the fresh water lake — Lake Gaton. It is announced that fresh water baths will be available now for at least three hours ... Lunchtime comes before we know it so we slip down to gobble our meal so as not to miss too much ... On to the next lock. We are surprised to find ourselves let down instead of up. Out we sail into a small lake ... At the other end of the lake we enter another series of two locks, again letting us down. On we go through a larger waterway ... and so we glide down to Gamboa, the town which marks the Pacific side of the canal ... It has taken us about 10 hours to go from the dock in Cristobal to the pilot barge out from Gamboa ... It has been a most interesting day there is no doubt, and an experience that I shall for ever remember ... As the sun sets we are well into the Pacific ... You can smell the saltiness of the Pacific in the air, quite strongly at times. This is a characteristic not found with the Atlantic.'

Now the ship was on the long final leg of the voyage to Australia. On 25 March they crossed the equator, but 'unfortunately, the Master will not allow any form of ceremony of the Ancient Rights of the Deep to be conducted ... Was it ever hot trying to sleep last night? I woke up this morning feeling like a washed out rag. Tonight the Southern Cross is just visible and I can't help feeling a sort of thrill at the sight of it.' The heat remained with them for another five days, then, on 30 March, 'the hot weather seems to have broken. Today there is a cold wind blowing and quite a roll on.'

As the days passed, rumours continued to fly. Scholes wrote on 6 April, 'Latest rumours suggest that we are due on Monday morning. Whether we are to disembark on Monday too or not I don't know. I certainly hope so. I am becoming very restless. Today I put on my battle dress to begin with. After breakfast I go up on the sun deck in the sun. It's too hot up there so I come down and change into shorts and up again. This time it's too cold so I go to the lounge. It's still too cold there, so I go down to my cabin again and get my battle dress jacket and return to the lounge. Then I can't find anything to do. I smoke, drink lemonade and try to sleep. Finally I get a brainwave. I'll write a story about trout fishing. This has proved very successful so far for I have been at it continuously not even noticing the time slip by. People think I'm mad. I wonder who'll go mad first — me with writing or them with boredom?'

Empress of Scotland arrived in Sydney on the morning of Monday, 9 April 1945, and the troops on board disembarked and headed for home. David Scholes was too excited to record anything in his diary that day, but the following day he wrote, 'What a magnificent day it is today. If it was teeming with rain it still would be. I have not had time to write these last few days for I have been too excited I think and therefore too restless. I'm home and still alive!'

When the war in Europe ended in May 1945 with the surrender of Germany, plans were soon formulated to send home those Australian and New Zealand troops who had been captured in the desert campaign, and spent several years as prisoners of war. In May 1945, *Dominion Monarch* took on board 710 Australians recently released from prisoner-of-war camps in Germany and brought them home, arriving in Sydney on 17 June. Another liner to repatriate Australians from Europe, mostly Air Force personnel, was *Andes*, which arrived in Sydney on 28 July 1945.

Early in July 1945, *Mauretania*, which had carried so many troops to the Middle East, took on board about 1500 Australians and New Zealanders who had been released from prisoner-of-war camps, and were anxious to return home. The liner crossed the Atlantic, and passed through the Caribbean en route to the Panama Canal. Captain Howard L. Wentworth was one of the two pilots assigned to the liner, and some years later he recalled *Mauretania*

> in her dull grey war colours ... with Australian and New Zealand troops who had been prisoners of General Rommel in Africa. There were 1,500 of them. Arriving in Cristobal on 12 July 1945, she tied up at Dock No. 8, and about one half were given shore leave. These men had not had any recreation in years and in about four hours they owned the city of Colon, Republic of Panama. It took all the MP's on the ship and many US Army MP's to get them back on board. Many of the Republic Police were in the hospital. It was a wild night.
>
> I was assigned one of the Pilots ... We sailed from Dock No. 8 at 0700 July 14. This being my first big passenger ship, I wondered if she would be in one piece upon arrival on the Pacific side of the Canal. I am happy to say she was, and with very little paint scraped off her sides. Upon clearing Miraflores Locks at 1515 and stopping in Balboa Basin to disembark Canal seamen and pick up an agent, who brings out ship's clearance, I looked over port side to see if all boats were clear. I noticed a young woman in the agent's boat who seemed to be in tears. I thought she may have come out to the ship to say goodbye to some friends. On mentioning this to an officer on the bridge he said that she had been brought on board at the last port before Cristobal by one of the New Zealand soldiers in his duffle

bag. She had been undetected until three days prior to arrival at Cristobal. The young woman was sent ashore at Balboa to be repatriated to her home country, unknown by me. About two months later, I saw in the local paper where the soldier who had smuggled her aboard was returning to marry her. We proceeded to sea buoy and I disembarked. A very interesting transit from the point of view of a pilot.

Mauretania then continued her voyage across the Pacific, and after disembarking her New Zealand troops, carried on to Australia, berthing in Sydney Cove on 8 August 1945, when the rest of the troops came ashore.

Early in August 1945, Sergeant John Blythe, a New Zealander who had voyaged to the Middle East aboard *Aquitania*, found himself one of the lucky ones being sent home from Egypt. After several days in Cairo, he arrived at Port Tewfik, where 'the *Strathaird* was waiting and we went aboard. It was completely unreal, just like a dream. I examined the ship, 28,000 tons and plenty of room. It had required a 47,000 tonner, the men packed in like sardines, to bring our single reinforcement and now two drafts were returning in a ship almost half the size. About a quarter of us were coming home; the lucky ones.'

Even though the war in Europe was over, the Japanese were still holding out, so wartime restrictions, including nightly blackouts, prevailed. It was extremely hot inside the ship so

> we slept anywhere, on the decks where the fire hoses woke us at dawn, or on a table in the sergeant's mess. The ship must have rolled heavily one night because, flat on my back on the hard table, the bulky lifejacket under my head, next morning I couldn't raise my chin.
>
> We sailed for Ceylon escorted by a cruiser but two nights out from Colombo all lights on the blacked-out ship came on and radio blared that Japan had capitulated. The war was finally over. I suppose we cheered. But did it matter? We were more concerned about the many Japanese submarines we knew were in the Indian Ocean and we felt that they were taking a lot for granted lighting us up like a Christmas tree. If we had had anything to do with it we would have continued blacked-out. Just because Japan had capitulated was no guarantee that one would not have a crack at such a juicy target ... We went to bed feeling horribly vulnerable.
>
> Next morning the escorting cruiser came alongside with her crew dressing the decks. They cheered, we cheered, and as the cruiser fell astern to bear away I knew this was the final act, the beginning of a great wind-down, the reversion to civilian status ... We were not allowed ashore

Strathaird berthing at Station Pier, Melbourne, her first visit to the port since July 1939.

at Ceylon but sat out in the stream. They said there was a famine there and perhaps there was ... It was wonderful weather for cruising and for weeks we sailed south-west ... In the late afternoon, following the sun, my favourite spot was on a metal canopy housing one of the winch motors, with our backs against the foot of the bridge ... We sailed with a permanent lean to starboard day after day, suspended in balmy blue space. But the weather had to change, and as we sailed slowly up Port Philip Bay to Melbourne it was cold and blustery.

When *Strathaird* berthed at Station Pier, her first visit to Melbourne since July 1939, all the troops, Australian and New Zealand, disembarked.

More released prisoners of war were put on board other liners well known in Australia before the war. *Orion* departed Liverpool on 8 August 1945 carrying 600 released prisoners and 106 members of the Royal Australian Air Force. The ship arrived in Sydney on 9 September. The following day the former P & O liner *Maloja*, also carrying released prisoners of war, berthed in Sydney Cove. Another Orient Line vessel, *Otranto*, also carrying released prisoners, arrived in Sydney on 29 September. The P & O liner *Stratheden* brought RAAF men from Egypt, having embarked at Port Tewfik on 26 September. The liner called at Melbourne on 17 October, arriving in Sydney three days later, berthing

Maloja berthing in Sydney Cove on 10 September 1945.

at Woolloomooloo. Another liner to carry Australian troops home from Britain late in 1945 was *Arundel Castle*, on her final wartime voyage.

With the end of the war in the Pacific in sight, plans for the eventual demobilisation of the Army were being put together. It was later announced that a points system would be established which gave priority to men with five years of war service, married men with families, and also those with certain vocational skills.

When the Japanese announced their surrender on 15 August 1945, the war officially came to an end, but it would be some time before all the areas captured by Japanese forces during the conflict were handed back. In some cases, Japanese soldiers refused to believe that their Emperor had surrendered and continued to wage war against Allied forces, with the result that troops continued to die and be injured. Over a period of weeks, most of the islands held by the Japanese were surrendered to the Allies, along with Hong Kong.

Among the first Allied vessels to enter Hong Kong was the hospital ship *Oxfordshire*, a real veteran, having been built in 1912 for the Bibby Line and now serving in her second war. *Oxfordshire* had arrived in Sydney on 25 December 1944 and remained there two months acting as the base hospital unit, then was sent north to the Pacific Islands. She had returned to Brisbane with casualties on 7 June 1945, then was sent to Subic Bay, from where, on 28 August, she was ordered to proceed to Hong Kong. Linking up with the Royal Navy Task Force

The hospital ship *Oxfordshire* berthed in Sydney. (*National Library of Australia*)

assigned to occupy Hong Kong, which included the battleship HMS *Anson* and aircraft carrier HMS *Indomitable*, *Oxfordshire* entered Hong Kong harbour, mooring alongside No. 1 wharf at Kowloon.

The first concern for the medical staff was the prisoner-of-war camps at Whanshui-Po and Stanley Bay, from where those in most urgent need of treatment were taken on board the ship, which departed Hong Kong on 3 September. The patients were brought back to Brisbane and Sydney. *Oxfordshire* then returned to Hong Kong, from where she made a voyage to Britain with further released prisoners of war.

Despite the Japanese government agreeing to terms of surrender, this message did not get through to some of their field commanders for some time, in several cases it being a matter of weeks before the local commanders agreed to surrender. On 6 September the Japanese forces in the Rabaul area surrendered, the ceremony taking place on the flight deck of HMS *Glory*. The Japanese forces in New Guinea did not officially surrender until 13 September, in a ceremony held at the Wewak airstrip.

With the news of the Japanese surrender, it was realised that Singapore would be regained in the near future, but the only Allied troops in the area were in prisoner-of-war camps and would not be able to return to active service. As a result, *Duntroon* embarked troops in Sydney to be sent to Singapore as a garrison, along with the 2/14 AGH. Accompanied by a British vessel, *Arawa*, owned by Shaw Savill Line, and escorted by HMAS *Hawkesbury*, *Duntroon* departed Sydney on 27 August, their first stop being Darwin. From there they continued their journey north, while on 6 September British troops liberated the island city.

On 10 September the Australian hospital ship *Manunda* had been

Duntroon arriving in Sydney carrying men of the ill-fated 8th Division who had been Japanese prisoners of war in Singapore.

guided through the Japanese minefields outside Singapore Harbour by British naval ships and tied up at the docks. Medical staff on board immediately had been taken to the prison camp at Changi, where they were horrified by the conditions and appearance of the Australians who had been held there for over three years. Some were little more than human skeletons, and sadly a few were too far gone to be saved. As gently as possible, the former prisoners were transferred to the comfort and care of *Manunda*, to be nursed back to health.

To provide as much care as possible, *Manunda* remained alongside in Singapore, being joined on 11 September by another hospital ship, *Oranje*. This vessel had left Avonmouth in Britain on 10 July carrying 856 wounded New Zealand troops home, arriving in Wellington on 14 August, the day before the Japanese surrendered. Departing Wellington six days later, *Oranje* had steamed across the Tasman Sea to Sydney, where she took on board 210 wounded and sick from the British Pacific Fleet, to be returned to Britain. On 7 September, *Oranje* arrived in Colombo, where it was scheduled that more British casualties would be embarked, but instead all the men already on board were taken ashore and the ship left immediately for Singapore.

For five days the medical staff and crew of the *Oranje* were kept busy giving treatment and sustenance to the starving survivors of the prison camps. Then 840 of the most serious cases were taken on board, and *Oranje* left for Australia. The first port of call was Darwin, then on to Brisbane, Sydney and finally Melbourne, where the ship arrived on 1 October.

On 12 September 1945, the Japanese commander in Singapore officially surrendered to Lord Louis Mountbatten, and the next day *Duntroon* and *Arawa* arrived in the port. When the troops they had brought went ashore, they were met by the survivors of the Australian 8th Division, who had just been released from three years of hell at the hands of the Japanese.

Stan Arneil was one of the troops who had endured years of cruel imprisonment in Singapore, and was now enjoying his first days of freedom. He kept a diary, and on 13 September 1945 wrote, 'Doug, Bernie, Fred and I went into town … and had the luck to be on the wharf when the *Duntroon* loaded with Aussies pulled in. I cannot describe the welcome they gave us, we ate our first scones, ice cream and other delicacies for years. They threw everything at us that we wanted and we came away loaded with tinned fruits, biscuits, chocolates and cigarettes. The excitement was almost too much for us but it was all worth it.' The men were given a generous supply of rations to take back to their camp and as his diary entry for the next day recorded: 'We all took things very easily today and from our private larder we had for lunch fried sweetbucks, salmon, sardines, green peas and buttered biscuits. It was a triumph for us and we are putting on weight like steam. For breakfast we prepared our own fruit salad from papaya, bananas, scrounged tinned fruits and evaporated milk. Tonight the boys we met on the boat yesterday came out and we entertained them as best we could with our modest resources.' On 20 September, *Duntroon* and *Arawa* also left Singapore carrying former prisoners of war, bound first for Darwin, then on to Sydney for an emotional homecoming.

Among those on board *Duntroon* was Neil Collinson, who had voyaged to Singapore on the *Zealandia* in June 1941 with the 4th Anti-Tank Regiment. He had endured the agony of forced labour on the Burma railway, and was at a prisoner-of-war camp in Thailand when the war ended. Along with some of his colleagues, he was flown to Singapore, from where it was intended they would fly on to Melbourne to give evidence to a war crimes commission, but there was no plane waiting for them in Singapore. After waiting several hours at the airport, they found a truck, hot-wired it and drove into Singapore City, where they abandoned the truck and walked around to try and find help.

As Neil Collinson later recalled, 'We came upon a long queue of Australian soldiers outside the Cathay Theatre. We joined in the queue, and when we got inside were each handed £50 and a ticket to board a ship back to Australia ... We all took off and made our way to the dock area where the troop ship *Duntroon* was the greatest sight we had beheld in a long time ... We still had to line up and wait another couple of hours until we went on board. Each man was issued a bunk ticket and, after searching up and down, I eventually found my allocated hammock. There was someone in the next hammock apparently asleep, and so, for a joke, I began to swing the hammock and heard this voice begin to swear. I could not believe my ears as the voice and the face that appeared from the blanket was that of my old mate, Hock Case. We had sailed from Australia in adjoining bunks and after not seeing each other for over two years, I was amazed at the coincidence.'

On their arrival in Brisbane on the *Duntroon*, Neil Collinson noted, 'We did not go directly home but were held on the *Duntroon* in Queensland for about six weeks to recuperate. I was six stone when released and quickly progressed to nine stone in those few weeks.' *Duntroon* then continued down the coast to Sydney. Once they were released, Collinson and his mates journeyed by train to Melbourne. From the station they were taken to Royal Park, where they were reunited with their families.

In the meantime, two more ships had arrived in Singapore, the sisters *Largs Bay* and *Esperance Bay*, which would be loading released prisoners of war and then returning them to Australia, sailing together. For Stan Arneil, there were a few more days of waiting before his turn came to start the voyage home, boarding the *Esperance Bay* on 22 September. He wrote in his diary, 'We are on board. It is hard to realise but here we are with our feet actually planted on the deck of the ship which is to take us home.' However, the joy of the moment did not last the day, as he noted in his diary:

10 pm. Well here I am again with what may surprise you, more growls than a grizzly bear. First of all we have been promised since the war ended a million privileges. They blared at us over the air what we were to receive and every day in orders we were told what to expect in the way of good things and here we are, thankful to God of course, for even being alive, but full of complaints for which there are no excuses. Food so meagre that tonight Doug and I opened a couple of tins of stew which we had brought as a precautionary measure (old POW's are hard to catch). Bernie, as an old campaigner went to the kitchen and brought back a pocket full of delicious little buns, Doug found a tin of butter and we enjoyed a feast ... Canteen is not yet open. We have no wet canteen, instead we are to be issued as a special concession with a bottle or two on the voyage.

Esperance Bay was also sent to Singapore to repatriate released prisoners of war.

Accommodation for the troops, after what was said about comfort for POW's is a bloody disgrace and the only reason that it is bearable at all is because the troops, as ex-prisoners, have little or no gear. Doug and I with four Sgts have a cabin and for ourselves we are not complaining, the bunks with mattresses are quite luxurious to us. The two reception units which came to Malaya to look after us are evidently stopping there for a holiday. Their job was to take over all duties and we were told that our shipboard duties would be negligible. Well I suppose growling is of no avail but the duties here are terrific and the troops have even been used in the cook-house in this ship.

Next day things were looking up a bit, as Stan wrote in his diary, 'Well I feel a lot better tonight after what I admit in fairness was a nice tea (poultry). I raised my spirits at least 100 per cent by having a terrific argument with one of the Sgts over the issue of cigarettes. The authorities have had the gross impertinence to issue us with or rather tell us that the total issue of cigarettes for the voyage will be twenty per man. Doug, Bernie and I conspire together on most things, and tonight, a glorious night of stars, we are sitting on deck chairs on the boat deck (out of bounds) with the sea breeze against our cheeks. The ship is pushing through the calm waters ... Singapore is behind us and our life as prisoners is finished. We are free men again on the last stage of the road which began at Sydney Showground five and a half years ago. God is good to us.'

As the voyage proceeded, things continued to improve. On 24 September, Stan was writing, 'A good day in all, meals were good, a couple of enjoyable arguments and an issue of one bottle of beer.' On 27 September he enthused, 'The seas are of mill-pond smoothness and the old *Esperance Bay* is churning along like a steady old grand-dame. I am enjoying myself so much that I do not care how long the trip takes but I really think that if we meet a head-on storm she will go backwards ... If things were any better I could not stand it.' On 30 September *Esperance Bay* berthed in Darwin, where, as Stan recorded, 'We were promised mail and beer and we received none.' It was not the homecoming the troops had expected, and on 1 October Stan wrote, 'We are on our way again, thank God; our stop at Darwin was a disgrace to the Australian government. We think now that the only welcome we are likely to receive in Australia will be from our own homes.'

Esperance Bay and *Largs Bay* passed Thursday Island on 3 October, then rounded Cape York and turned south again, on the final leg of the voyage. As excitement increased, Stan noted, 'We are getting closer to home and the ship is seething with unrest, the troops cannot sit still and for myself, I find I must be running from place to place all the time.'

On Sunday, 7 October, the two ships separated for the first time. Stan recorded, 'The *Largs Bay* left us this morning and turned into Brisbane; we heard over the wireless that a great welcome was given to them, so great indeed that it took two hours to clear the wharf ... The ship has dropped to quarter speed and all day we have been barely making way down the coast. The weather has been exceptionally calm and fine and the Captain took the boat in close to land and we have been drifting from headland to headland.'

The next day the voyage was all but over, and Stan wrote: '7.30 pm. Lights of Sydney are on the starboard side and we are all very excited ... 10.30 pm. We are in Sydney Harbour at anchor after the funniest couple of hours we have had for years. The pilot came aboard from a rowing boat ... we entered the harbour and saw not one boat; except a Manly ferry which passed by within a few yards and its six people on board the ferry waved at us.' The ship remained at anchor overnight, then, on the morning of Tuesday, 9 October, *Esperance Bay* proceeded up the harbour and berthed. '9.30 am. On deck by the rails and we should leave the ship within half an hour. We are receiving a nice little welcome from half a dozen launches and everybody on the ship is laughing all the time. It is great fun but we are starting to get a little tired now and will be glad when we disembark ... Everyone is excited and all are terribly happy. In half an hour we will have our feet on Australia.'

As with so many returning troops, Stan Arneil found the following hours of reunions with family and going home almost unbearable. That evening he wrote: '11.45 pm. Today has been tumultuous and too much to place on paper. I am home, united with my family. It is very still and very quiet in the house and as I sit here my thoughts are of all my friends who will never come back as I have done. Thank you dear God for watching over me and bringing me home. It is all over now. This diary is finished.'

Meanwhile, back in Singapore the medical staff on board *Manunda* continued to treat and care for as many of the released prisoners as possible, until they could be put aboard other ships for the trip home. On 5 October a group of nurses rescued from Sumatra were received on board, a most emotional experience for the staff of the hospital ship. Several days later, *Manunda* left Singapore, arriving in Fremantle on 18 October, then continuing to Melbourne, and finally Sydney, where she berthed on 27 October, enabling the last of her patients to disembark and return to their families.

Another Australian hospital ship, *Wanganella*, was also involved in repatriating prisoners of war from the Pacific Islands. *Wanganella* had arrived back in Sydney on 8 August from Morotai with 456 casualties on board. Within days of the Japanese surrender, *Wanganella* was heading north again, this time in search of prisoners of war. Going first to Morotai, arriving on 6 September, the vessel went on to Labuan, then headed for Borneo, going to Kuching in Sarawak, arriving there on 12 September, were they located Australians just released from shocking conditions in a local camp.

As Sister Wreford later described it: 'The following day our shockingly emaciated patients arrived in small boats. Their faded remnants of uniforms literally hanging on them, they made a brave attempt to mount the gangway unaided ... a demonstration of the indomitable spirit that had kept them alive for 3½ years and a moving experience for the whole ship's company. At first they protested at being treated as patients. Soon they fingered the white sheets on the bunks, giggled as they donned pyjamas, drained their china cups and

The hospital ship *Wanganella* brought home many sick former prisoners.

looked at them in wonder. Then they asked questions. The hideous ulcers, sores and swellings seemed to fade as we talked.'

From Kuching, *Wanganella* proceeded to Labuan, where more former prisoners were taken on board, then it was back to Morotai, arriving on 19 September, when those in need of urgent medical care were taken ashore to the local hospital. Then it was the long trip back to Sydney, where *Wanganella* arrived on 20 October. A week later, *Wanganella* left on what was to be her final trip as a hospital ship. More former prisoners were taken on board, as well as medical personnel at Labuan, also returning home. Departing Labuan on 10 November, *Wanganella* was back in Sydney again on 23 November.

Meanwhile, many former prisoners of war had been released from camps in parts of China that had been occupied by the Japanese. Most of these men were transported to Hong Kong, to be cared for until they could return home. On 18 September 1945, the aircraft carrier HMS *Vindex* took on board a large contingent of these released prisoners, and, with a call at Manus Island on the way, brought them to Sydney, where they arrived on 3 October.

Highland Brigade carried troops home from Singapore and Thailand.

There were also a large number of prisoners of war in Thailand, most of whom had been used as slave labour to build the Burma railway. Among them was Fred Airey, who was in the Kanchanburi camp for the last year of the war. He was among 600 of the least healthy prisoners in the camp who were ordered to be moved to another camp by train, but on the day they departed news came that the war had ended. They still went on the train, by during the trip their Japanese guards vanished, and when they arrived at Bampong they were given a warm welcome and food by the local populace. The next day they were flown in groups to Rangoon, where they spent the next six weeks.

As Fred Airey recalled later, 'News came through the grapevine that ex-prisoners in Singapore were being sent home ahead of us, and that we would not be processed until they had gone. This caused quite a bit of discontent, and some officers even hitched rides on planes to Singapore so that they could shortcut the process. Finally we embarked on the *Highland Brigade*. This is it, we all thought, Australia, here we come! Imagine our horror, then, when the ship hove into Singapore harbour and we were disembarked. Word went round that we were to be put ashore so that other returning prisoners could take our place. There was near mutiny, but fortunately most of the men were only delayed a couple of days.' Most of the men were able to return aboard

Highland Brigade, which carried them first to Fremantle, then on to the eastern states. Fred Airey was not one of them, and had to stay in Singapore for several weeks before he finally returned to Fremantle on board the *Moreton Bay*.

Any available form of vessel was used to transport released prisoners of war and serving troops back to Australia from Asia and the Pacific Islands as soon as possible after the war ended. However, Australia could only supply sufficient ships to carry 6500 troops a month back home, in addition to aircraft to transport a further 6000. The Australian government sent a request to the British government to provide enough shipping to transport 23,500 men a month, which meant that over 100,000 men could have been returned to Australia between October and December 1945. However, London replied that they could only supply sufficient ships to carry 12,000 troops a month between October and December, dropping to 10,000 a month after then. Among the British ships placed at the disposal of Australian forces were three aircraft carriers, HMS *Implacable*, HMS *Formidable* and HMS *Glory*, along with other craft of various types and sizes.

With the surrender of Japan, Allied teams were quickly sent into the Japanese countryside to locate prisoners of war, and arrange for their repatriation. Not unnaturally, the survivors were keen to get home as quickly as possible, but it was a major logistic operation to move the large numbers of men, and some parties of nurses, found scattered in camps throughout Japan. The 2/15 Field Regiment had gone into captivity on 15 February 1942, when Singapore surrendered, but over the next three years the men were transported several times by their captors and many ended the war working under atrocious conditions in Japan. During the period of their captivity, 294 men died.

Bob Rowsell, who had arrived in Singapore from Australia to join the 2/15 Field Regiment in January 1942, and became a prisoner within four weeks, was one of those who survived a nightmare voyage to Japan on the *Byoki Maru* and his subsequent harsh treatment. After some weeks wait, he and his fellow prisoners were taken to a Japanese port, and placed on board an American hospital ship which took them to Manila. Here the men all left the ship and were taken to an American base where they were placed in huge tents, each holding 28 men.

Despite being granted generous rations of food, beer and cigarettes, the men were desperate to return home, but it was several weeks before a vessel became available, this being the aircraft carrier HMS *Formidable*. While not the most ideal form of transport, it was all that was available, but there was a problem. As Bob Rowsell recalled, the ship could not accommodate all of the released POWs who were quartered at the American base, and it was announced that one man from each tent would have to stay behind. Just how the selection was made is not known, but Bob Rowsell was advised that he was one of those to miss out on the voyage home. With heavy heart he watched the other 27 men in his tent pack their meagre belongings and leave for the port, and home.

Fortunately, the situation was not all bad for Bob and the others left behind. Each remained alone in his tent, but the rations allocated for each tent remained the same. Thus each day Bob and the others were able to go to the NAAFI and draw cigarette and beer rations for 28 men. Bob recalled that during this period he drank a lot of beer and, even though it was not as strong as the Australian brew, it helped him put on quite a lot of weight. HMS *Formidable* berthed in Sydney in October 1945, and two weeks after his mates had left, Bob Rowsell found himself on a plane which took him as far as Darwin. From there it was another flight to Brisbane, then on to a train for the final leg to Sydney.

Many others, both soldiers and sailors, including survivors from HMAS *Perth*, had been transported to Japan to labour in a coal mine at Ohama, at the southern end of the island of Honshu. As word of the Japanese surrender spread among the prisoners, scepticism gave way to belief. They were not sent down the mine any more, and the next day each man received an issue of milk supplied by the Red Cross, plus a parcel of food to be shared between every four men. It was some time before a message arrived from the Red Cross Protective Powers advising the men at Ohama that they would be leaving as soon as possible. However, a further two weeks passed before some of them were taken to Osaka and embarked on an American hospital ship, *Consolation*, which took them to Okinawa, where they were taken ashore and cared for by the Americans. Other *Perth* survivors were taken to Tokyo, where they boarded another American hospital ship, *Benevolence*, which looked after them until they could be transferred to an aircraft carrier, HMS *Speaker*, which carried them to Manila, from where they were flown home. Meanwhile, the men taken to Okinawa were moved on to Manila, where they boarded HMS *Speaker* for the voyage back to Australia, arriving in Sydney on 14 October.

The 2/13 Battalion ended the war in Borneo. As the battalion history states:

> After Borneo, with the war over, all manner of craft brought us home, and at varying times, depending on the 'points' system of priority for discharge then operating. Included amongst them were the USS *Lloyd*,

The former coastal liner *Kanimbla* brought many troops back home from the Pacific islands. (*C.T. Reddings collection*)

the USS *Liddle* and the *Kanimbla*. The Unit Cadre — consisting of four officers and twenty other ranks — left Labuan on the *Pachaug Victory*.

Those fortunate enough to get a passage on the *Kanimbla* will never forget the first breakfast they had on board her — large fresh pork chops headed an appetising menu of items that we had almost forgotten existed. More significant than anything else, however, was the fact that these troopships, with their cargoes of exuberant and victorious soldiers, were the first ones in which we sailed that went across the ocean with every light ablaze.

Another unit to enjoy a trip on the *Kanimbla* was the 2/14 Battalion, who were based in the Celebes at Pare Pare when the war ended, their final duty being to guard Japanese prisoners. On 22 January 1946 the entire unit boarded *Kanimbla* for the journey home, arriving in Brisbane on 4 February. *Kanimbla* continued to return Australian troops home throughout 1946 and 1947, remaining under government control until the middle of 1949.

Another former coastal liner to be heavily involved in repatriating Australian troops was *Manoora*, which made 24 voyages between September 1945 and December 1947 from Singapore, the Dutch East Indies, India and Japan. Among the troops to return aboard *Manoora* was Ken Ward-Harvey, of the 9th Division Engineers, whose unit was based at Labuan when the war ended. In *The Sappers' War* he recorded his memories of his return to Australia in October 1945, recalling, 'Once marched out from their unit, troops usually had several days wait in transit camps, before being allocated to a ship for movement. Many ships carried large groups of returning prisoners from Singapore. Some of their stories of mistreatment were frightful, but mainly they talked of the humour, and the methods used to retaliate against their captors. They also wanted to hear an outline history of the war, since they had been denied direct news for over three years. Their main concerns however were for their families and their future.'

Ken Ward-Harvey and others from his unit were taken from Labuan to Morotai, from where, on 3 October 1945, he 'was fortunate to return on the *Manoora*, manned by the Royal Australian Navy. At our first meal on board the sailors were complaining because it was pork chops again. For soldiers it was wonderful to have such luxury. Food had been sufficient throughout the campaign but limited in variety. Only the major Army food depots had refrigeration, so pork was not on army menus.'

Compared to previous journeys during war, 'Conditions on board were wonderfully relaxed, without blackouts or stand to at dawn. Malaria restrictions did not apply at sea, so shorts only was the common dress. We had been on board in such attire for several days before reaching Torres Strait, but while travelling south along the Cape York coast, almost everyone got sunburnt. We knew Australia had a special feel about it, and this was it.'

The ship remained close to the North Queensland coast. 'We passed Cairns with its magnificent mountain background, and traversed the wonderful Whitsunday Passage in bright sunny weather, then saw a school of whales cavorting as if welcoming the ship home, and eventually reached Moreton Bay after twelve days at sea. As the ship moved up the Brisbane River residents were waving and shouting. Boats and vehicles tooted a welcome as we gradually pulled into Newfarm Wharf,' this taking place on 15 October.

The 2/12 Field Regiment finished the war on Labuan Island, where over 50 members of the regiment were included in a guard of honour which was inspected by Lord Mountbatten on 9 December 1945. By Christmas most of the regiment had departed for Australia on a variety of vessels, including *Westralia*, *Manoora*, *Duntroon* and *Kanimbla*, the freighter *River Clarence*, and the Liberty ship *Robert T. Hill*. The final group, comprising seven officers and 53 other ranks, departed shortly after New Year's Day 1946 on the *Reynella*. This vessel was a former Italian liner, *Remo*, which had been seized in Fremantle in May 1940 when Italy came into the war and used by the Allies as a troop transport.

The trip back to Australia aboard *Reynella* was quite different to their previous voyages, Hugh Melville recording in his diary, 'We take turns for the various shipboard duties, otherwise I read or sunbake. Messing facilities are woeful. Occasionally the gunners sneak showers in the officers' showers, otherwise on deck in the rain, if the weather is right. On 6 January great chunks of the Halmaheras slide past including an active volcano. We continue playing cards, reading, sunbaking.'

On 7 January there was great excitement on board when a man was rescued after he fell overboard. The event was recorded in the ship's newspaper:

> At 1330 hours, January 7,1946, the cry of MAN OVERBOARD! reigned throughout the ship. Gunner Hughes was adjusting his washing which was trailing alongside the ship attached to a piece of rope. In endeavouring to untangle the washing he held on to the ship's lifeline which, at the identical moment, dipped and dragged the gunner overboard. Hughes said he felt himself hit the side of the ship under water and his immediate reaction was to kick away from the ship's propellers. The suction of the props was so strong, the shorts he was wearing were dragged off during his struggle.
>
> His concern was not whether the ship would stop but to obtain one of the many lifebelts which had been thrown overboard. This he succeeded in doing in a few minutes. He did not hear the ship's siren but was relieved when he saw the ship turned and a life-boat put out for his rescue.
>
> After being rescued and attended by the ship's medico he was allowed to go to his quarters after drinking a bottle of Nelson's Blood. THIS should not be an inducement as we are now out of rum. A report to the effect that Major Carter had to be restrained from diving overboard to put the victim on a charge sheet, is not confirmed.

The slow voyage home continued, and Hugh Melville wrote, 'On January 11 we stopped at Thursday Island to pick up a pilot and we can now see Australia. Continued the journey on one engine (third breakdown).' Passing slowly down the coast of Queensland, the *Reynella* finally arrived in Brisbane early in the morning of 17 January. Their arrival was unannounced, so there was no-one on the wharf to greet them. They were taken out to the camp at Chermside, then ten days later finally arrived back in Victoria, at Puckapunyal, where they were demobbed.

There was also a large number of personnel from all three services stationed in the United Kingdom when the war ended, and arrangements had to be made to bring them back to Australia. A variety of vessels were used for this, all still in their rather austere wartime condition, but the voyage home was certainly more pleasant than the trip overseas had been. Late in 1945, *Aquitania* made a trip to Australia in this capacity.

The only large liner to serve in both World Wars, *Aquitania* had become well known in various Australia ports during the first three years of the war, carrying troops overseas. In 1945 *Aquitania*, the last four-funnelled liner afloat, was the fourth largest passenger ship in the world and had carried over one million passengers in her long career, travelling over 3 million miles. Although still fitted out as a troop transport, with her hull painted grey, the liner once again proudly wore the famous Cunard red and black funnel colours.

At the end of October 1945, *Aquitania* departed Liverpool bound for Australia, carrying 4639 passengers, comprising 2366 men from the Royal Australian Navy, 2155 Royal Australian Air Force, and 38 Australian Army, along with 80 dependants. The first stop on the voyage was Sierra Leone, then Cape Town, from where *Aquitania* departed on 13 November, arriving off Fremantle on 22 November, dropping anchor in Gage Roads, where she remained for two days. Disembarking here were 213 Western Australian members of the RAAF, and four AIF former prisoners of war, along with 229 South Australian members of the RAAF, who then travelled by train from Perth to Adelaide. Continuing her voyage, *Aquitania* arrived in Sydney on 29 November, where the remaining passengers went ashore.

Departing Sydney on 9 December, *Aquitania* was carrying 4750 passengers, most of them service personnel again, but also a number of civilian passengers and children. Arriving back in Gage Roads on 14 December, 1046 service personnel disembarked, these being 315 Royal Australian Navy, 65 Royal Australian Air Force and 666 Australian Army, their places on board being taken by civilian passengers going to Britain. This was the last time this great liner visited Australia.

By the end of 1945 some 76,000 Australian troops had been repatriated home, so that in January 1946 there were only 20,000 men left to be returned home from the Pacific theatre of the war. However, an additional 45,000 troops were allocated to remain in the Asian region, including Japan, in a garrison capacity.

Aquitania departing Sydney on 9 December 1945. (*National Library of Australia*)

20 The Korean War

With the end of World War II, it was hoped that universal peace would return, but such was not to be the case. With eastern Europe falling under Russian control, the spread of communism would ensure many more years of unrest, and wars. Communist forces began waging wars in several countries, including Malaya, which eventually brought Australian troops into action again. Civil war in China resulted in a communist victory, while turmoil in the Dutch East Indies eventually saw the end of Dutch control. A similar situation also happened in Vietnam, where the French were defeated and the country divided into two, one part being under communist control.

Another country to be divided in this way was Korea, which had suffered under Japanese occupation from 1910. In 1945, the Korean peninsula was still occupied by the Japanese, but after their surrender it was up to the Americans and Soviet Union to restore the country. Eventually it was agreed that Korea should be divided into two, with the Soviets controlling the area north of the 38th Parallel, while the United States controlled the southern end of the peninsula. The Soviets quickly installed a communist puppet government in their sector, while the Americans allowed the Koreans to develop their own democratic government in the south. Attempts to reunify the country were rejected by the communists, and a hostile situation developed between the two Korean governments.

Despite the fact that 21 million Koreans lived in the south, and only 9 million in the north, on the morning of Sunday, 25 June 1950, the North Korean Army suddenly launched an attack across the 38th

Parallel. The North Koreans quickly overwhelmed the weak South Korean military forces stationed along the border and began marching south. On the night of 27 June the southern capital, Seoul, was abandoned by the government and most of the population, being captured by the North Korean Army the next day. Refugees streamed south across the Han River.

On 27 June, President Truman offered to commit American forces to support the South Korean Army, and the same day the United Nations Security Council voted in favour of member nations supporting the Americans in Korea. Among the 21 nations to answer the call for help from South Korea were Australia, New Zealand, Canada, South Africa and Great Britain, who would form a Commonwealth Force, joining with forces from several European countries, as well as Ethiopia, Colombia, Thailand and Turkey. By 30 June, when the final decision was made in Washington to send in American troops, the North Korean Army had captured almost the entire Korean peninsula, apart from a small area around the port of Pusan, in the extreme south.

In 1950 there were still Australian military forces stationed in Japan, including a single RAAF fighter squadron, No. 77, based at Iwakuni, in the south. It had been due to begin withdrawing from Japan on 26 June, but instead they found themselves preparing for war, and on 2 July began flying their first missions against the North Koreans. Two Australian warships based in the area, HMAS *Shoalhaven* and HMAS *Bataan*, were placed at the disposal of the United Nations force, which would be commanded by General Douglas MacArthur.

Large numbers of American ground forces were soon pouring into the Pusan area, and managed to blunt the North Korean advance temporarily, but then the communists resumed their attacks and the United Nations force was compelled to fall back. MacArthur wanted more troops to enable him to stop the communist forces. He knew that the 3rd Battalion, Royal Australian Regiment, was based in Japan, though not up to full strength, and the Australian government initially was reluctant to commit them to Korea. However, following a direct request from General MacArthur, it was decided on 26 July that 3 RAR would be sent to Korea.

Prime Minister Menzies was keen to see all British Commonwealth troops operating together as a single Commonwealth Division in Korea, and this was agreed to by the Americans. In Australia, reinforcements for 3 RAR were hurriedly gathered during August and early September, and flown in Qantas aircraft to Japan to join the battalion, which eventually had a strength of 39 officers and 971 troops. In Japan they underwent extensive training prior to being sent to the war zone. In the meantime, the first British troops arrived in Korea on 28 August and were soon heavily engaged in battles.

As September drew to a close, 960 officers and men of 3 RAR was transported to Kure, along with attached units, including a field ambulance, 17-pounder anti-tank guns and vehicles. On 27 September, in pouring rain, they boarded the American transport *Aiken Victory*. This vessel was one of hundreds of standard design Victory ships built during World War Two, designed as cargo ships, though some were fitted with very basic troop quarters. *Aiken Victory* had been built by the Bethlehem-Fairfield Shipyard at Baltimore, being placed in service in December 1944 as a transport for the United States War Shipping Administration. In 1950 the vessel was briefly handed over to the United States Navy, but later the same year had been transferred to the Military Sea Transportation Service.

When the men had been selected for the movement to Korea, there was a group who would be remaining in Japan, to be sent over later when reinforcements were required. One of these men, Roderick Gray, did not want to be left behind. He made his way to Kure, and persuaded some Japanese wharf labourers to hoist him on board the *Aiken Victory* by crane. His presence on the ship went undetected until the ship was at sea, and Gray began asking some of the troops if they had a spare rifle that he could have. When he was found out, it was decided he could remain with the contingent.

The facilities provided for the troops on the ship were extremely basic, but it was not a matter of great importance, as the voyage to Korea would only last a few hours. On arrival in Pusan on the morning of 28 September, the Australian troops were welcomed by military bands from both the United States and South Korean armies, and a large number of Korean women wearing national dress and waving small Korean and United Nations flags. The troops were transported by train to Taegu, where they joined British troops in the 27th British Commonwealth Infantry Brigade.

The same day the Australians landed at Pusan, the United Nations forces drove the North Koreans out of Seoul. Over the next few days the United Nations forces succeeded in pushing the North Korean Army north of the 38th Parallel, but instead of stopping there as originally planned, MacArthur pushed on into North Korea, determined to capture the whole peninsula. To thwart this, China began sending troops into North Korea to assist their allies, and the expected easy victory by the United Nations became a serious conflict. By the end of November, in the face of overwhelming numbers of Chinese troops, the UN forces were retreating. Soon they were back south of the 38th Parallel, and on 4 January 1951 Seoul was again in enemy hands. However, the UN forces rallied and began a counter-offensive, and it was at this time that it was decided more troops were needed to combat the huge Chinese Army.

In February 1951 a request was made to Australia to send further ground forces to Korea, but the Australian Army was so understrength it was not possible to send any reinforcements at that time. However, the recently delivered aircraft carrier HMAS *Sydney*, carrying three naval air squadrons, was sent to join the naval task force. It was not until early in 1952 that a second battalion could be raised in Australia, which became 1 Battalion RAR. After completing their training in Australia, the battalion was moved to Ingleburn Army Base, near Sydney, to prepare for their move overseas. At Ingleburn they were joined by 145 New Zealand soldiers. The departure of these troops would be the first such happening in Sydney since 1942, and it was arranged to be a major event.

On the morning of 3 March the troops were transported from Ingleburn by train to Sydney Central Station. Here they got off and prepared for a march through the city to No. 2 Wharf, Circular Quay, where they boarded the British troop transport *Devonshire* for a voyage to Japan, from where they continued on to Korea after further training. 1 Battalion RAR comprised 1,250 officers and men. Along with the 145 New Zealanders, they began their march at 12.40 pm, being cheered by thousands all the way to Circular Quay, which was reached at 1.25 pm. The soldiers then went straight on board the *Devonshire*. Once they were all embarked, the barriers surrounding the wharf were lifted, allowing an estimated 7000 family, friends and onlookers to stream onto the wharf to farewell the troops, whose departure was scheduled for 4 pm.

As departure time drew near, the wife of one of the soldiers on board *Devonshire*, with her two small children in tow, broke through the cordon near the gangway. She was carrying a box, and when stopped by a military policeman, explained that inside the box were clothes she had washed for her husband, so he would have clean things to put on. The policeman took the box from her, carried it up the

Troopship *Devonshire* berthed at No 2 wharf Circular Quay in March 1952. (*C.T. Reddings collection*)

gangway, and handed it over to an officer on board the ship, and it eventually reached the soldier. At 4.18 pm, *Devonshire* drew slowly away from the wharf, and after backing out into the harbour, turned east and headed off towards the sea.

Devonshire was the last of four sisters built in the mid-1930s in Britain as troop transports. The other three, *Dunera*, *Dilwara* and *Ettrick*, all carried Australian troops to the Middle East during World War II, in which *Ettrick* was later sunk. The 11,275 gross ton *Devonshire*, which was owned by the Bibby Line, only entered service three weeks before World War II started, and had a busy time during hostilities, which continued after the war, mostly transporting British troops to and from the Far East. The ship could carry up to 1150 troops in dormitory style quarters, while officers had the use of cabins.

On their arrival in Kure on 18 March, the troops of 1 Battalion went into camp, where they underwent further intensive training. They were subsequently transported by the British vessel *Empire Longford* the short distance to Korea, where they arrived on 1 June 1952, being attached to the 28th British Commonwealth Infantry Brigade.

As the war dragged into 1953, it was time for 1RAR to return home. They were to be replaced in Korea by 2 RAR, which had been brought up to full strength during the previous year. The majority of the men making up 2 Battalion were from Victoria, with reinforcements from New South Wales and other states. Most of the men in 2 Battalion had

The migrant ship *New Australia* carried troops from Australia to Korea.

no previous combat experience, but there was a nucleus of veterans in their ranks, including men preparing for their second trip to Korea. On 4 March 1953, 2 RAR paraded through the streets of Melbourne, then were transported by train to Sydney, where they arrived at 9 am at the Pyrmont wharves, and immediately boarded the migrant carrier *New Australia*, which would be carrying them to Korea. As the ship pulled away at 1 pm, family and friends of the troops on the wharf threw streamers to the ship.

New Australia had been built in 1931 as *Monarch of Bermuda* for Furness Bermuda Line, and at that time carried 830 first-class passengers only on the luxury route between New York and Bermuda. Converted into a troop transport in November 1939, the vessel survived the war without mishap, but in March 1947 it was gutted by fire when being renovated for a return to civilian life at Newcastle, England. The hull and engines were still intact, so it was rebuilt for the Australian migrant trade, entering service as *New Australia* in August 1950. In this role the vessel could carry 1600 passengers in one class, occupying a mixture of cabins and dormitories. In 1952, *New Australia* was taken over by the British government to carry British troops to Korea. The vessel had left Southampton on 28 January 1953 on a regular migrant voyage to Australia, arriving in Sydney on 1 March, berthing at No. 13 Pyrmont Wharf.

New Australia provided much better facilities for the troops than the average troop transport. Officers each had a cabin to themselves, while the men were allocated two in a three-berth cabin, or three in a five-berth cabin. Included in the Ship's Routine Orders posted on the notice board on sailing day was the advice that stewards and stewardesses would make their beds and clean their cabins. The troops were only asked to keep their gear tidy. There would also be table stewards serving them in the dining room, and the food would be the same as served when the ship was carrying migrants. The menu for lunch on departure day was published in the newspapers. It consisted of crême andalouse, poached codling with parsley sauce, roast beef ribs and Yorkshire pudding served with marrow au beurre and roast or steamed potatoes, college pudding, cheese and coffee. For officers there was also a savoury course, and apple tart with cream for dessert. A reporter asked some of the crew if they minded making such a voyage when they could not expect to earn any tips. They replied that even on migrant voyages they were seldom given tips, but were grateful to have secure jobs on the ship.

After a pleasant voyage, *New Australia* arrived in Pusan on 21 March. The men of 2 RAR disembarked the same day and were transported to their base camp. With the arrival in Korea of 2 RAR, it was the first time all three Australian battalions of the Royal Australian Regiment were together at one location. The opportunity was taken to hold a parade, with the men from all three battalions forming up in a hollow square on the parade ground of the US 1 Corps, Camp Casey, on 21 March 1953. After the parade, 2 RAR joined the 28th British Commonwealth Infantry Brigade, while the departing members of 1 RAR were transported to Pusan, where they boarded *New Australia* for their journey back to Australia, arriving in Sydney on 6 April.

At various times the warring parties had held armistice talks, but these had ceased in September 1952. However, they were resumed at Panmunjom, on the 38th Parallel, on 6 April 1953. A major sticking point between the United Nations and the communist negotiators concerned repatriation of prisoners of war. Many of the 100,000 Chinese and North Korean soldiers held by the UN forces did not want to return to their home countries, but the communist negotiators were insistent that all prisoners of war be returned. The UN negotiators said that they could not force this on those who did not want to return home.

On 6 June 1953 the communists suddenly withdrew their demand, but the government of South Korea were totally opposed to communists staying in their country. As a result, on 10 June the Chinese mounted a series of major attacks, but within weeks the war came to an end. On 27 July 1953 an armistice was signed at Panmunjom, bringing an end to the conflict.

The end of the war did not mean an immediate return home for the Australian forces. In April 1954, 2 RAR returned to Australia, being relieved by 1 RAR. 3 RAR was withdrawn from Korea in November 1954, while 1 RAR remained in Korea until March 1956. A Commonwealth Contingent, which included 80 Australian signals personnel, remained active in Korea until 26 August 1957, when it was disbanded, and the troops returned to their home countries. A total of 17,808 Australians saw service in Korea during the conflict, of whom 10,844 were in the army, 5771 with the Royal Australian Navy and 1193 in the Royal Australian Air Force. Of these, 341 lost their lives, while 1216 were wounded.

21 The Vietnam War

The Vietnam War arose out of similar conflicts to those that caused the Korean War. In both cases, a country was divided into two sections along an artificial imposed border, with the northern section being under communist control, while the southern region tried to develop a democratic government. With the spread of communism throughout the Asian region being supported financially and materially by the Chinese, it was inevitable that a country such as Vietnam would become a flashpoint.

Vietnam had been a French colony for many years, part of an area known as Indo-China, which comprised Laos, Cambodia and Vietnam. During World War I a resistance movement developed in Vietnam, but it was not until after the war that the communists, led by Ho Chi Minh, declared Vietnam independent of the French and set up their capital in Hanoi, in the north of the country. The French poured large numbers of troops into the country, but they were forced to retreat into small enclaves, and eventually surrendered their control of the country in 1954. At a subsequent conference, Vietnam was partitioned into two sections, while both Cambodia and Laos also won their independence, but as single entities.

From the start there were some anti-government guerilla forces in the south, but in 1960 communist forces from the north began a civil war against the government of South Vietnam. The South Vietnamese Army had American advisers, and in 1961 their numbers were greatly increased in the face of the communist threat. In May 1962 the Australian government agreed to send 30 Army advisers to South

The troop transport HMAS *Sydney* berthed at Garden Island in Sydney. (*Fred Roderick photograph*)

Vietnam, though in non-combat roles. In January 1964 the government of President Diem was overthrown by a South Vietnam military junta, which only encouraged the communists to increase their efforts. As a result, American troops began to arrive in South Vietnam to take on combat roles, and their numbers soon began to escalate. Australia also contributed more advisers, as well as medical staff and six RAAF Caribou aircraft.

On 29 April 1965, Prime Minister Menzies announced that Australia would be sending 1 Battalion, Royal Australian Regiment, consisting of 778 infantrymen, to Vietnam. During May an advance party flew to Vietnam in Qantas aircraft, while the bulk of the troops, along with their equipment, prepared to embark on the troop transport HMAS *Sydney* at Garden Island in Sydney.

HMAS *Sydney* had been laid down in Britain as a Majestic-class light aircraft carrier, and was to have been named HMS *Terrible*. With the end of the war, the Royal Navy decided they did not need any further aircraft carriers, so the incomplete vessel was bought by the Royal Australian Navy, along with a sister vessel, which became HMAS *Melbourne*. Commissioned as HMAS *Sydney* in Britain on 16 December 1948, the vessel saw active service during the Korean War, from August 1951 to January 1952. In subsequent years the vessel also served in Malayan waters, but in 1960 was relegated to the Reserve Fleet, being laid up in Athol Bight, Sydney Harbour. In March 1962 *Sydney* returned to active service as a training ship, and in early 1964 completed a refit which would enable her to also operate as a fast troop transport. Her first voyage in this role was in May 1964, carrying troops and their supplies from Australia to Malaysia, which at that time was involved in confrontation with Indonesia. The vessel was very lightly armed, only having four single 40/60 Bofors guns and some machine-guns. As a transport, the crew comprised 40 officers and 567 sailors.

HMAS *Sydney* was far from being an ideal troop transport. She had been designed in Britain for use by the Royal Navy in the North Atlantic and other cool regions, so had a limited ventilation system. During service in tropical waters, the areas below the flight deck were always very hot and muggy, causing discomfort to both crew and troops. Although classified as a troop transport, the quarters provided for the enlisted men were quite spartan. The men were allocated hammocks slung in the former aircraft hangar spaces, where little or no natural light penetrated, and the heat was often overwhelming. As the former flight deck was usually filled to capacity with vehicles and stores, there was not very much open deck space available for the men to escape the claustrophobic conditions below deck, though many tried to find alternate places to sleep.

On the voyage from Australia to Vietnam, which lasted up to ten days at sea, a full schedule of programs was drawn up to keep the troops occupied. These included training sessions with various weapons, physical exercise classes, lectures on the war and the Vietnamese people, and sometimes shooting at targets. Meals were all eaten in the mess rooms below deck, though sometimes the temperature was so high men would rather forgo their meal than have to sit in the heat. Because the ship had only a limited capacity of fresh water, showers were kept to a minimum, though soldiers often resorted to washing themselves in sea water, then rinsing off in fresh water.

There was a daily allocation of one can of beer a day, and in the evenings films were shown. One of the few breaks in the monotony of the daily routine on board came when the ship crossed the equator, and a full crossing-the-line ceremony would be held, complete with King Neptune and his retinue. Usually it was only the more senior officers of the units who were forced to go through the full induction routine, being liberally doused in mysterious concoctions devised by the ship's cooks.

Prior to the departure of the first voyage, there was some uncertainty as to just where the Australian troops should be disembarked. At first it was considered that the ship should proceed up the Mekong River as far as Saigon. This was possible, as the river was wide and deep enough to allow such a passage, but there was always the possibility that the enemy could lay mines in the river, especially after the ship had made the passage up to Saigon, where it could be trapped indefinitely. In the end it was decided that the vessel would anchor off the port of Vung Tau.

Even here, though, there was always the threat of an enemy attack, and suitable precautions were put into effect. In the official instructions issued to the commander of the ship, it was stated that 'Vung Tau anchorage is an open anchorage in the Mekong Delta which provides access to Saigon. Much of the Mekong Delta is infiltrated by Viet Cong who are in a position to mount underwater or clandestine surface attacks. The anchorage may also be within range of shore mortars. *Sydney* is considered to be the prime RAN target due to her size and role but the possibility remains that the escorts may be selected as alternate targets.' Whenever *Sydney* was in Vung Tau, a patrol of small boats constantly circled the ship, with sailors throwing occasional hand grenades into the water, especially at night, to deter attempts by enemy swimmers to attach mines to the hull.

To enable the troops and their equipment to be transported ashore at Vung Tau, *Sydney* was equipped with six landing craft. These vessels had been specially designed for the task and were constructed during 1965. They were 56 feet long, powered by a pair of 450hp GM diesels, and could carry a load of 120 troops or 34 tons of equipment.

To prevent the possibility of interference or attacks on the ship from Indonesia, a route was drawn up that took the vessel through the southern Philippines. Usually this involved passing through Basilan and Balabac Straits, south of the large island of Mindanao. For security, the passage through both these waterways would be made at night, and hopefully unobserved. This was made more difficult in the Basilan Strait, as the large port of Zamboanga City was on the northern shore of the strait. The city was a blaze of lights, while *Sydney* and her escorts slipped through blacked-out. It was always a relief when the lights of Zamboanga disappeared below the horizon. It would then be a day's run across the Sulu Sea before the ships passed through Balabac Strait the following night, again totally blacked out. This time there were no large population areas to worry about, and the ships would be in the South China Sea before daybreak, when the course was set slightly south of due west to avoid extensive shoal areas off the island of Palawan that extended far into the South China Sea. The final two days of the voyage were done at top speed in the open ocean, followed by a pre-dawn arrival at Vung Tau.

When the announcement was made of the first trip to Vietnam, *Sydney* was in the Captain Cook drydock at Garden Island for a refit. This almost proved a major problem, as protests against the involvement of Australia in the Vietnam conflict began to spread through the country. The union movement was strongly opposed to the sending of troops and, in an attempt to stop *Sydney* being used as a transport, started a strike that could have trapped the ship in the drydock. Despite these problems, the refit was terminated and 153 sailors were recalled from leave. While the ship was still in drydock most of the military supplies were loaded. It was only a couple of days before departure that *Sydney* was moved out of the drydock, completed trials, and then was prepared for the first troops to come on board.

On the evening of 27 May 1965, 450 soldiers of B Company of the 1st Battalion, Royal Australian Regiment trooped on board HMAS *Sydney*, along with some supporting units. These comprised elements of the Support and Administration Companies, the First Australian Logistic Supply Company, the First APC Troop and their vehicles. There were also five press correspondents from various Australian news media.

The troops had been brought by buses from the Holsworthy Army Base near Liverpool to Garden Island. The men had inevitably been apprehensive about the voyage and what awaited them when they arrived in Vietnam. To help ease them through the adjustment to life at sea, the soldiers were divided into groups, each of which was allocated a sailor, or 'sea daddy,' to show them around the ship and familiarise them with routines and duties on board a naval ship at sea. Due to the continuing protests, it had been decided that *Sydney* should depart Garden Island at 1 am, but despite the late hour, there were many people waiting to see her go.

Bruce Davies was a 21-year-old regimental signaller with 1 RAR when he boarded HMAS *Sydney* for that first voyage to Vietnam. He later recalled:

> I always remember HMAS *Sydney* as we sneaked out of Sydney Harbour in the middle of the night, and I don't think it had anything at all to do with the tides! At that time they were trying to keep our deployment as confidential as they could.
>
> There was the usual confusion about getting soldiers and support people sorted out aboard ship; obeying the rules of the Navy; sleeping in hammocks; overcoming seasickness and things like that. There was some training on board the ship and a small amount of physical fitness training. There were also lectures on the country we were going to and the type of people. When we were sailing through the Philippines, and going through a central channel, there was a guy in a boat with an outboard motor that was in front of the *Sydney* and he was trying to start the motor and it wouldn't start. I won't forget the look on his face as he sort of surf-skied off the bow waves with everyone cheering his exploits.

There was nothing startling about the trip up. We were probably feeling trepidation about where we were going. No-one really knew where South Vietnam was and we really didn't understand what it was all about. We only knew what we did from some fairly intensive briefings about being called on to support the regime of South Vietnam against communists from the North; the domino theory; that it was a protectorate of the South-East Asia Treaty Organisation; it was a protected state; and that we had been called upon by our ally the United States to assist. I think we accepted that.

For this first voyage, the destroyer HMAS *Duchess* was to escort *Sydney* all the way from Sydney to Vietnam and back. The only break in the daily routine of the passage was a refuelling stop at Manus Island, during which troops were not allowed ashore. Such was the secrecy surrounding the voyage that it was not until *Sydney* had left Manus Island that the commander of B Company, Major I.D. McFarlane, was allowed to open his sealed orders, and discover their ultimate destination in Vietnam was Bien Hoa. From Manus Island the ships proceeded towards the Philippines, passing through the Basilan Strait on the night of 5 June. As the two ships passed through the Sulu Sea, the escort was strengthened when HMAS *Parramatta* joined, along with HMAS *Melbourne* and HMAS *Vampire*.

Melbourne and *Vampire*, accompanied by the oiler HMAS *Supply*, had left Subic Bay, in the Philippines, to rendezvous with *Sydney* and her escorts. On the morning of 3 June, *Melbourne* refuelled from *Supply*, which then detached, while *Melbourne* and *Vampire* met up with *Sydney* at 0100 on 4 June. That afternoon, *Supply* joined the group, and refuelled *Sydney* as well as her two escorts and *Vampire*, then *Melbourne*

HMAS *Parramatta* joins the escort of HMAS *Sydney*, with HMAS *Melbourne* in the background.. (*Allan Batt*)

HMAS *Supply* refuelling HMAS *Sydney* and HMAS *Vampire* on 4 June 1965. (*RAN photo – Rodney T. Nott collection*)

topped up her tanks before *Supply* again detached and returned to Subic Bay.

For the first two days a Wessex helicopter from *Melbourne* maintained a constant aerial patrol around the ships, which passed through Balabac Strait on the night of 6 June. From then on two Wessex helicopters were constantly deployed, while a Gannet aircraft was also kept aloft during daylight hours on anti-submarine patrols. In addition, Sea Venoms were flown off *Melbourne* at dawn and dusk on probe missions. As the official report from the Captain of HMAS *Melbourne* stated, 'The ship remained at Defence Stations during the passage. Long periods of inactivity gave sailors a real appreciation of the monotony of escort duties. No incidents occurred.'

At 5.30 am, just before dawn on 8 June, *Sydney* slipped into her allotted anchoring site off Vung Tau. As soon as it was daylight, locally based barges began ferrying the troops ashore, and once all had disembarked, their equipment followed. According to Bruce Davies, 'We moored out from shore in Vung Tau harbour. First impression was hot and sweaty and there were a few helicopters around and a lot of activity in the area. There were the usual rumours of divers who were going to blow the ship up, mines, and all that sort of stuff. The activity of getting off the ship was typically a balancing act of taking everything off with you in kitbags and going down the side of the ship and stepping into watercraft that took you to shore. I am not too sure that some bits of equipment weren't lost over the side before we even got to the shore.'

The troops were greeted by the senior American officers stationed in Vietnam, including General Westmoreland, the overall commander.

HMAS *Sydney* at sea en route to Vietnam. (*RAN photo – Rodney T. Nott collection*)

As Bruce Davies said, 'When we disembarked, Westmoreland and a typical bevy of staff officers associated with a four-star general met us. I think there were some girls there with what could be called leis to be placed on the appropriate "senior" neck that came ashore. I think some of the men thought we were going to charge into battle immediately … We were transported by bus to the airfield, where we were flown to Bien Hoa, which was an airbase north of Saigon. We were to be part of the 173rd Airborne Brigade. There was the usual logistics nightmare of getting all the people from the *Sydney* and their bits and pieces to Bien Hoa.'

Neil McInnes was an Able Seaman Gunner on board HMAS *Sydney* on the first voyage to Vietnam. 'Going into Vung Tau harbour,' he recalled,

> I remember the terrain was mountainous on the actual headland, which was Cap St Jacques. We were apprehensive and didn't know what to expect. We had been told that ships had been sunk in the harbour, which they had. We were told to be on the alert all the time except when you were off duty and asleep, except there was so much noise in and around the ship it was impossible to sleep. There was a continuous sequence of helicopters even on the way in.

Immediately we dropped anchor there were ammunition barges alongside with American and Vietnamese stevedores. The Americans told us that even though the Vietnamese had been screened they did not know how loyal they were so we had to keep one eye on the job and one eye on them. The discharge of cargo was by all sorts of helicopters — Sky Cranes, Chinooks, Iroquois and heavy-lift choppers. At one stage General Westmoreland came out in an Iroquois to have a look at the operations on the ship.

One of our jobs during the loading and discharging was flight deck sentry. We would be armed with a weapon, and also one box of scare charges to throw over the side if you thought you saw anything diving or anyone trying to attach a mine to the ship. This went on for the two or three days we were in the harbour. We would hear bangs on the side of the ship at all hours of the night. When you found out it was a scare charge you would try and go back to sleep.

The commanding officer of HMAS *Sydney*, Captain Crabb wrote that, after anchoring off Vung Tau, 'We unloaded soldiers and equipment as quickly and as best we could but there were many hold-ups due to inexperience in cargo handling and the slow turnaround by the barges taking equipment and stores ashore.'

Sydney remained at anchor off Vung Tau for four days, eventually departing on 11 June, again escorted by *Duchess* and *Parramatta*. The voyage back to Australia was more relaxed for the crew, with the ship carrying no troops or equipment. Instead of heading back to Sydney, the vessels swung west. *Parramatta* detached and proceed to Singapore, while *Sydney* and *Duchess* arrived at Fremantle on 26 June. The other vessels that had escorted *Sydney*, *Melbourne* and *Vampire*, both returned to Sydney on 22 June.

HMAS *Sydney* made only one further voyage to Vietnam during 1965, following a request from the Americans for more troops. The Australian government agreed to send an additional 350 troops, in a movement codenamed Tanton. *Sydney* departed Sydney on 11 September, then called at Brisbane on 14 September to complete embarkation of the troops and their equipment. This time there was no escort provided until the troop transport left Manus Island after refuelling on 20 September, at which time the destroyers HMAS *Duchess* and HMAS *Vendetta* joined *Sydney*. Arriving at Vung Tau at 6.30 am on 28 September, one hour earlier than scheduled, the troop transport again spent two days offloading the men and their stores. *Sydney* departed Vung Tau on the evening of 30 September, arriving back in Sydney on 20 October.

Able Seaman Neil McInnes recalled:

As we got progressively closer to Vietnam, in the mornings we would go to action stations called 'class three,' in preparation for any defensive movements that would have to be made by the ship. As we got closer the intensity of the action stations would start to step up. Action station red was the imminent one in preparation for an enemy attack. The guns were 40/60mm anti-aircraft Bofors. These guns were on sponsons on the side of the ship. The ship was so old that if they fired one all the decking around it fell into the sea because it was so rusty. We had a lot of small weapons on board; plus we had choppers armed with depth charges. When we got closer we would usually pick up an escort of American fighters, which would escort us right into Vung Tau.

The *Sydney* never came under attack but we did exercises all the way up in preparation. However, the degree of danger for the *Sydney* was far more than the government admitted. The Veteran's Association acquired documentation — government papers marked 'top secret' — on the actual risk that the enemy posed to us. They related to a signal from the Department of National Intelligence reporting about an enemy platoon setting up a medium mortar and a 122mm rocket in an endeavour to shell the harbour of Vung Tau. If that were the case it would have put the *Sydney* in danger, especially if the ship was loaded.

On the way up one night we went to full action stations and the ship did a 90-degree turn to port at full speed. There was a Yank submarine escorting us and they thought there was another submarine in the vicinity. Apparently they did a search and we continued on our way. We wouldn't have lasted long with all the ammunition we were carrying.

The mess decks were pretty crowded on the way up and it was like a sauna. When we got closer to Vietnam, we were on action stations and all the watertight doors were shut all around the upper deck. The ventilation, which forced air into the mess decks, was turned off because of the possibility of smoke and fire coming through the ventilation. We used to go down for meals, and when you have three times the complement on the ship that you should have it was pretty uncomfortable. The rules were that you had to wear a shirt and on one occasion there was a bit of a shindig when a Digger and a sailor refused to put shirts on. They were told that if they didn't put their shirts on they wouldn't eat.

When not required as a transport, *Sydney* operated as a training ship. Following the second trip to Vietnam, said Neil McInnes, 'It was a couple of months before I did the next trip. We did a bit of a trip around Australia in the meantime, then we loaded up again to take more soldiers, reconnaissance aircraft, choppers, APCs, trucks and a heap of ammunition.' In fact it was six months before *Sydney* was called upon to make another trooping trip to Vietnam, the first of two during 1966. Departing Sydney on 24 April, the vessel was unescorted until joined by HMAS *Vampire* at Manus Island, where *Sydney* refuelled on 27 April.

'On the third trip,' recalled Neil McInnes, 'we took the Centurion tanks. On the trips up every day the Diggers would go down into the hangars and start up the APCs and trucks and run them for a couple of hours. They would open the hangar lift wells to let the fumes out and the noise was deafening. We used to have to go in with the Diggers for fire control and we would have to be in there for four hours ... We also had to do helicopter sentry. You can imagine what it was like on the flight deck with four hours of constant helicopter engines and being right next to them, followed by four hours with the APCs.' It was as a result of these duties that Neil McInnes and others suffered partial hearing loss.

As *Sydney* approached Vietnam, HMAS *Melbourne* and HMAS *Yarra* also took up escort duty, having come from Singapore. According to the report filed by the captain of *Melbourne*, two Wessex helicopters were maintained at Condition One with depth charges available for loading, dawn and dusk searches were carried out by Gannet aircraft and a midday search was made by a Sea Venom aircraft. On one patrol, a Sea Venom aircraft crashed into the sea. The pilot survived, but the observer was lost, his body not being recovered, despite an extensive search being carried out. *Melbourne* and *Yarra* detached from their escort duties at 0200 on 4 May. *Sydney* dropped anchor off Vung Tau in the pre-dawn darkness of 4 May. Two days later the anchor was raised, and the return trip commenced, ending in Sydney on 18 May.

After only a week in port, *Sydney* was again off to Vietnam. Having embarked army troops and equipment as usual, there was also the 9th Squadron RAAF on board. Departing Sydney on 25 May, *Sydney* was escorted all the way to Vietnam by HMAS *Vendetta*. At 1415 on Thursday, 2 June, *Sydney* and *Vendetta* linked up with HMAS *Melbourne* escorted by HMAS *Yarra*, which were accompanied by HMAS *Supply*. All four ships refuelled from the oiler, then *Supply* detached while the other four ships continued towards Vietnam at 17.5 knots. HMAS *Derwent* joined the escort for the final few days. *Sydney* arrived off Vung Tau in darkness on the morning of 6 June, again staying two days. On departure from Vung Tau on 8 June, the transport headed north instead of south, arriving in Hong Kong on 11 June.

From time to time there would be an unusual activity on board *Sydney* to divert the attention of the troops for a while. During the voyage north, one of the ship's divers would be positioned on the quarter deck, in case anyone fell overboard. Two or three times on each voyage, there would be a practice rescue, when one of the diving team jumped overboard. The standby diver would then go over the side, find the person in the water and keep them afloat until a rubber Zodiac was lowered and rescued them both. During this the ship's speed was reduced, but it would not stop, and once the Zodiac had been recovered, full speed would be resumed.

It was also inevitable that the Australians would devise a nickname for the ship they were travelling on, and before long HMAS *Sydney* was known far and wide as 'The Steak and Kidney.' As her trips to Vietnam settled into a regular pattern, the operation also became known as 'The Vung Tau Ferry.' On her first four trips to Vietnam, *Sydney* wore the same White Ensign as that on ships of the Royal Navy, but on 1 March 1967 the Australian White Ensign was introduced, to be worn by all units of the Royal Australian Navy from that time on. As a result, *Sydney* became the only ship to be involved in the Vietnam war under two ensigns.

It would be another ten months before HMAS *Sydney* was again needed to transport troops to Vietnam, but she then made three trips in six weeks. With elements of 7 Battalion RAR on board, *Sydney* departed Sydney on 8 April 1967 on her fifth trip to the war zone. Also on board were four Westland Wessex helicopters, which were to be used for anti-submarine duty when the ship was near the Vietnamese coast. This was the first of seven voyages on which the helicopters would be carried, coming from either 725 or 817 squadrons of the Fleet Air Arm.

Conditions for the crew of HMAS *Sydney* were far from ideal. This was the first voyage on the transport for Acting Sub Lieutenant Dennis Jones, who recalled:

> I joined the 'Vung Tau Ferry' in March 1967 ... All who sailed in HMAS *Sydney* will remember how hot and uncomfortable living conditions were in the ship particularly when she was in the tropics. I shared a cabin in 2 Sierra section ... Conditions in the cabin, which was immediately below the flight deck and adjacent to a large bathroom, were so bad it was impossible to sleep without the application of copious quantities of calamine lotion to ease the discomfort of severe skin rashes caused by the temperatures which never dipped below 40 degrees Celsius.

Despite recording temperatures in excess of this temperature over a prolonged period and requesting the cabin be deemed uninhabitable, the Surgeon Commander did agree that the cabin was indeed too hot for human occupancy, but it was okay for sub lieutenants! Such was our lot, however, eventually we managed to have a section of the quarterdeck set aside for bridge and engineer watchkeepers to sleep on stretchers.

Joined at Manus Island by HMAS *Vampire*, *Sydney* arrived off Vung Tau in the early hours of 20 April. This time, instead of staying two days, the vessel was able to offload troops and equipment in one day, and before midnight she had raised anchor and was steaming south, still escorted by *Vampire*. Their destination was Singapore, which was reached on 22 April. Over the next few days, 5 Battalion RAR, which had been based in Malaya, was loaded onto *Sydney*, which left Singapore on 28 April. Again escorted by *Vampire*, they arrived off Vung Tau on 30 April, leaving the same day. While *Vampire* headed back to Singapore, *Sydney* steamed straight to Sydney, arriving on 12 May.

After only a couple of days respite, *Sydney* was on her way again, to Brisbane to embark 2 Battalion RAR for the next trip to Vietnam. Departing Brisbane on 19 May, *Sydney* was escorted by HMAS *Stuart* all the way to Vung Tau, where they arrived on 30 May. Gordon Hirford was an Infantry Platoon Commander with 2 RAR, who recalled:

> In my platoon, 11 Platoon, Delta Company, 2 RAR, we had about one-third regulars and the rest were nashos ... On the trip over, our days were spent training to a fairly ambitious program along the lines of up at six, breakfast at seven, PT at eight, rifle shooting at nine, Vietnamese language at ten and so on. The whole day was totally structured, but as the boat trip wore on each day got progressively slower until about day four it seemed that no-one even bothered to get up and things became very relaxed. We then started into boxing competitions, tug-o'-war and all that sort of thing. About every third day there was refuelling of our escort ships.
>
> After ten days we arrived in Vung Tau and went ashore by Chinook. It was the first time we had seen these huge helicopters. We were all lined up on the flight deck in our chalks with our packs and sea bags and a Chinook came in to land. About three guys nearly got blown over the side by the downdraft and in fact one bag got blown overboard. We flew to the helicopter pad at Eagle Farm in Nui Dat and took over from 6 RAR. They were extracting as we came in.

For the first time *Sydney* would be carrying troops on the southbound voyage too. As the men of 2 Battalion were taken off the ship in helicopters, on the return trip from the shore they brought men of 6 Battalion RAR, who had completed their tour of duty and were returning to Australia. 6 Battalion had lost eighteen of its men in the Battle of Long Tan, while many others had been wounded. One of the men returning home on *Sydney* was Bob Buick, who later wrote, 'Flying out to *Sydney* in Chinook helicopters was a beaut feeling, dressed in smart greens and not going on operations, we were finally going home.'

The amount the battalion had suffered over the year they were on duty in Vietnam was quite evident. As Buick wrote: 'Of the Officers and senior NCO's to arrive in Vietnam with D Company, a total of 11, five saw the time out with the Company. Of 11 Platoon ... seven only from the original platoon remained with the platoon. About 62 soldiers passed through the platoon during the tour. Thirty-three were killed and wounded, a platoon, I believe with the most casualties of any platoon to go to Vietnam.'

Departing on the evening of 30 May, *Sydney* headed south, escorted for several days by *Stuart*. Bob Buick remembered:

> For us going home we got under way about an hour before sundown. I

HMAS *Stuart* first escorted *Sydney* in May 1967. (*RAN photo – Rodney T. Nott collection*)

> for one leaning on the railing looking back to the slowly fading Long Hai Hills as we steamed south towards home. I didn't know if I would be back, would the war still be going on in a couple of years, for the moment I didn't care.

The food on *Sydney* was great and the accommodation luxurious when comparing it to what we had had for twelve months. Just being able to hang around, doing nothing and looking towards the distant blue horizon was a change to green scrub 10 to 15 metres away. That was a total experience in itself.

Corporals and below settled in the sailors messes. Sergeants and above slept in what was the air crew quarters just forward of the Officer's quarters near the stern. Our meals were taken in the Petty Officer's Mess which was near the forecastle adjacent to the forward sponson on the port side. The tucker could not be faulted and the friendliness and assistance shown and given by the sailors was beaut. We must have been a pain in the arse to them, getting in the way and wandering around for a couple of days before we found our way through the passages and hatches when moving through the ship. We soon discovered that when the man overboard drill was on you hugged the wall, to avoid being knocked down by the Zodiac crew as they raced to launch the 'rubber duckie' to recover a diver who had jumped over the side.

For the returning troops, there were no organised programs to keep them busy, as on the northbound trips. They were left much to their own devices, with space on the empty flight deck for walking, or sports. Otherwise, they could watch the daily routines of the sailors and ships. '*Sydney*'s escort was *Stuart*, a frigate,' wrote Bob Buick, 'and daily I would watch the escort move off to a side, come back, move ahead or astern of *Sydney* as we steamed on. It was like the Vung Tau Ferry and all aboard were a mob of sheep and *Stuart* a lone sheep dog keeping her safe. Close to Singapore, *Duchess*, a destroyer, joined us for the return to Australia ... There was a resupply at sea every few days for the escorts and they would come along the starboard side of *Sydney* and when in the right place, a fuel pipeline passed over and the escorts refuelled from *Sydney*. I would watch, admiring the skills of all those involved. The ships steaming along, waves and rough water between the two as the skippers kept the ships in perfect station for up to half an hour.'

Stuart remained as escort until it diverted to Darwin, while *Sydney* continued south. As the ship closed on the coast of north Queensland, 'cruising south through the Barrier Reef was something to see and remember,' recalled Bob Buick, 'the water being calm and with little wind I could see the reef each side of the ship as we picked our way down the shipping channel. Because *Sydney* was berthing starboard side to the wharf on arrival at Brisbane, that side had to be patch painted, covering the rust patches and streaks with grey paint. We stopped in the lagoon at Lizard Island for a day while the paint pots were issued to the sailors. Lizard Island is famous today for being the place the rich go for a holiday and catch marlin and sailfish, back in 1967 I think there was only a shack or two that could be seen on the shore. How things have changed over 30 years.'

With the painting completed, *Sydney* headed off south again, and a couple of days later was preparing for arrival in Brisbane. 'The trip home took about two weeks,' Buick recalled, 'and on the last night I stayed awake looking at the coast of Queensland, the town lights along the Sunshine Coast and the friendly winking eyes of the lighthouses guiding us towards Brisbane.' *Sydney* arrived in Brisbane on 14 June, when the troops disembarked.

It would six months before *Sydney* again headed for Vietnam. Having embarked 3 Battalion RAR at Adelaide in mid-December 1967, *Sydney* steamed across the Great Australian Bight to Fremantle. After refuelling there, the vessel departed on 20 December, heading north. Nearing Vietnam, *Sydney* was joined by HMAS *Yarra*, which had come from Singapore, as escort. The two ships spent Christmas Day at sea, arriving off Vung Tau in the early hours of 27 December. The troops disembarked during the day, and shortly after nightfall *Sydney* and *Yarra* were heading out to sea. The destroyer stayed as escort for only one day, then diverted to Singapore, while *Sydney* retraced her northbound course, arriving back in Fremantle on 3 January 1968, then proceeding around the southern coast of Australia to Sydney.

Within a few days, troops and equipment had again been taken on board, and on 17 January *Sydney* was on her way north again. On 27 January HMAS *Stuart* arrived from Singapore to act as escort, but instead of heading straight to Vietnam the pair diverted to Sattahip, in southern Thailand, where they arrived on 31 January. Leaving the same day, they continued their voyage to Vietnam, but it was also on 31 January that the Viet Cong launched what became known as the Tet Offensive, with attacks on all seven major cities in South Vietnam as well as numerous provincial towns.

Despite the increased danger, *Sydney* and *Stuart* continued their voyage, and reached Vung Tau on 3 February. As Dennis Jones later recalled, 'the amount of air and ground military activity was immense with seemingly endless bomb, rocket, cannon and napalm strikes taking place in close proximity to *Sydney*'s anchorage. A decision to sail from Vung Tau as soon as possible was made and increased pressure applied to complete moving troops and equipment as quickly as possible. Adding another dimension to the frenetic departure activity was the report that a merchant ship had anchored in the main channel believing there was a mine attached to its hull. This news required that the normal departure sailing plan from Vung Tau, via the main shipping channel, had to be hurriedly changed so both ships could sail via the alternate western channel ... Command approval of the departure plan saw both *Sydney* and *Stuart* leave harbour, and the Tet Offensive, with considerable alacrity.' *Sydney* returned to Sydney on 16 February.

Trip ten for HMAS *Sydney* to Vietnam departed Sydney on 27 March 1968, carrying 1 Battalion RAR on their second deployment. Since their return to Australia in June 1966, the battalion had undergone an extensive change in personnel, though a solid core of experienced NCOs and Warrant Officers remained. As with other battalions, the strength was made up with a combination of national servicemen and regulars. The advance party was flown to Vietnam, leaving Sydney on 17 March, while the bulk of the battalion boarded HMAS *Sydney*. A lone piper, brother of one of the departing soldiers, played as the ship pulled slowly away from Garden Island.

Soldiers reacted to the voyage in different ways. To Reg Yates it was 'almost boring; just enough to keep us amused. Hours just sitting. I don't think it was good for us. I was more homesick on the *Sydney* going over than I was when I got there.' He found the ship was 'like a small city, and caters for most needs. We even have a film every night, and it's usually a pretty recent one. We still have our training though — shooting, drill, PT, lectures.' As the regimental history notes: 'A variety of training and recreational activities flourished in various parts of the ship. The cavernous aircraft storage deck became a firing range, where air-rifles were used to introduce and practise the then-new "shoot to kill" aiming and firing technique — convenient and cheap training.'

As usual, a refuelling stop was made at Manus Island, then the voyage continued north, with *Sydney* being escorted in the final stages by HMAS *Parramatta*. On 5 April the troops formed the number and initials 1 RAR on the flight deck, while a helicopter flew overhead carrying a naval photographer. Following standard procedure, *Sydney* approached Vung Tau in darkness, dropping anchor just after dawn on 9 April. The battalion had been advised they would be going ashore in helicopters during the morning, so all troops were roused from their hammocks at 0300, with breakfast being served at 0400. They were to be on deck by 0500, with the first helicopter due to lift off at 0600. However, the helicopters did not arrive, and at 0800 it was announced that they had been sent elsewhere and the trip ashore would be in barges. As the disembarking troops walked ashore from the landing barges, they were met by 7 Battalion RAR, who had completed their time in Vietnam, and were going out to join *Sydney* for the trip home. By 1400, all 1 RAR was all ashore, and 7 RAR had taken their places on board the transport. As darkness fell, *Sydney* raised anchor and headed south, arriving back in Sydney on 26 April.

On 21 May, *Sydney* departed Brisbane with 4 Battalion RAR on board, being escorted all the way to Vietnam by HMAS *Anzac*. Staying in Vung Tau for only one day, 1 June, *Sydney* brought home 2 Battalion RAR, who disembarked in Brisbane on 13 June.

Five months later, on 9 November 1968, *Sydney* departed Adelaide, where 9 Battalion RAR had boarded. Among those who joined the ship that day was Barrie Crowley, a regular soldier attached to the Intelligence Section. Later he wrote about his experiences in the Vietnam war, starting with the trip from his camp outside Adelaide to the ship.

> At camp we milled around, we queued, we queried, we waited. Then we were all eventually summoned, bundled on to open trucks, and driven off down the road. With freshly hungry eyes I had one last glimpse of all the beauty around us ... and absorbed one last time the placid, fertile rural scenes. Then our descent into Adelaide began ... Now we were in the bustling city streets. In the back of the open truck you had to adapt to being ogled like hogs off to the abattoir. I didn't blame the people, it's a normal human reaction, but a few waves and a smile would have been appreciated.
>
> By the time I hit the wharf most of the battalion were on board, except for a few with wives or lovers still hanging off them ... I got straight on board with no waiting ... The military police prised the last of the women clear and we shoved off.

Once *Sydney* was at sea, there was time to have a look around what would be home for the next few weeks. Barrie Crowley decided it was

> not a bad sort of a boat if you're an off-duty officer. Officers had a beautiful messroom just below the flight deck at the stern. Huge windows right across, their own balcony to view where they'd just been ... The accommodation for the rest of us wasn't much, though I wasn't too badly off. Intelligence Section, which is a designation not a compliment, were at least up on deck. For peasants that was well placed. We had air, we had

our own outdoor railed section, we had views. We had our upstairs neighbour's arse pointed at us as we slept, but there was about a foot of freeboard and a thickness of canvas hammock between your nose and a nasty surprise from the tenant above.

I'm not complaining but the other poor bastards should have been suing. For most of them, the accommodation meant being down in the bowels of the ship or sleeping on the steel flight-lifts lowered into the holds. Flight-lifts were probably the worst because they were used during the day for PT and weapon handling, that sort of frolic. Not only did you have to pack your gear up each morning but you were a known face, and known faces get most of the shit jobs. We worked our passage, doing crappy cleaning jobs and training.

On any sea voyage, be it a world cruise on a luxury liner or a short passage on the meanest cargo ship, food becomes a major topic of interest and conversation. With several hundred men to be fed three meals a day from galleys designed to cater for less than a quarter that number, the cooks were hard pressed to please everyone, and it seems they seldom did. Barrie Crowley wrote:

> The cooks were at their spiteful best throughout the trip. They all liked to think they were comedians. Served pork chops the first night. They assumed that it made soldiers crook, but it was the best meal we had all trip. Just a pity they hadn't kept the pig alive to eat the rest of the slop they served up.
>
> Our messroom was right in the guts of the ship. Ventilation and insulation had obviously been rubbed off at the drawing-board stage when this tub was slapped together. You could smell every dish cooked for the last month as you sweated, rolled and tried to eat a meal no better than the last thirty. We had to be there perhaps twenty minutes a day, if you were fit enough and hungry enough, and then only in three short bursts. The cooking staff were a lot longer and it showed in the end product. They generally tend to be cranky bastards and not good at personal public relations, but they have my respect, if not my affection. Beer was rationed to one large can a night and there were few fights over the spares. We were staying alert.
>
> The trip offered a few views for those who had access to them and the time and inclination to see them. Crossing the Bight there were views of moody skies, a dark blue sea and one night a well-lit cargo ship passing close by. Then a view of Fremantle harbour, where we docked briefly. A number of wives and lovers had flown in from all over the country just for that.

Sydney spent 13 November in Fremantle, and among the relatives there were Barrie Crowley's father, mother, elder sister with her two children, and his younger brother, then aged just four. However, visitors were not allowed on board the ship, and those with relatives ashore could not go far. Crowley wrote, 'there was only the dock to roam, no kiosk or anything open, which had Mum browned off — she needed tea like I need a smoke. It was a welcome interlude but no great wrench when we steamed off again.'

So the voyage continued. 'We lumbered up the west coast, a few dolphins said hello now and again, then the call went out: "Last chance to glimpse Australia." I didn't figure on it being my last, but I went to have a look anyway. I was on the port side, and followed my mob through the short cut — which was all steel ladders, bulkheads, dead-ends and no-go areas — so by the time we surfaced back where we started from we were probably passing Timor!. Missed the glimpse at any rate.'

So the soldiers settled down to the daily routine of life at sea, and preparing for war, though there was the occasional diversion. 'A friendly sailor offered a few of us a look at the engine rooms. I had to see that. It had been my Dad's lot in the Second World War, only he was mainly on submarines. Here it was a strange environment: huge engines and massive spinning shafts and counterweights, gauges, conduits, all colour coded. Dim puddles of light, a constant throb, oil smells, and silent, attentive watchers in overalls. Better than being a cook but not my scene. The *Sydney* was an aircraft carrier from which they had removed the planes, and they were probably wearing out its last refit using it as a troop carrier. It may have boasted a meritorious past for all I know but it didn't reveal it in comfort.'

There were the occasional changes in weather and scenery to break the monotony:

> The *Sydney* passed through the Doldrums. We entered the area from an emerald sea under a brilliant blue sky. The Doldrums was a golden, glowing wonderland enticing you to step off the boat and walk away into it. As we travelled through the stillness it changed: the sky dimmed to copper, the sea paled to a milky beige. At dusk flying fish broke the surface in flocks of thousands and flew, silver wings driving them on endless mirrored flight a metre above the flat, still sea.
>
> Saw Krakatoa real close; half the mountain missing on our side, very eerie to see. It was big, but the devastation which it once caused I couldn't imagine coming from this tiny islet. We moved through a fleet of junks

gliding between shimmering flights of fish. Large, hand-hewn, wood-planked craft straight out of the seventeenth century. Dun-coloured sails fanned out by bamboo battens waiting in hope of a breeze, kerosene lanterns glowing softly over castle sterns and up above on the rigging. Dark figures manning long heavy wooden tillers, burbling motors inching them away from our course. Night fell and the lights from the lanterns slowly winked from view.

Our RAN escort now arrived — a destroyer, a supply ship, and a frigate, I was told. We refuelled at sea. Some thought that interesting. The sailor's rigged a bosun's chair between *Sydney* and one of the escorts, and swung a few people back and forth ... Most days the rifle companies just blew shit out of large weighted weather balloons bobbing in our wake ... My little band were supposedly there for our ability to observe and interpret, not our ability to kill, so we didn't get a look in. Suited me. There was also piped music on board. I don't know what source it came from — bland unmemorable crud for the most part except for one song, a minor classic from the Sergeant Pepper's album, transformed by Joe Cocker. Still kicks me in the guts whenever I hear it.

On 20 November the long journey at last was about to come to a conclusion, as HMAS *Sydney* approached Vung Tau in the rapidly brightening daylight. The arrival brought a buzz of excitement to the soldiers aboard, as they now were about to come face to face with their uncertain futures. As Barrie Crowley wrote: 'Vung Tau dead ahead! A wide blue sunlit bay, skirted by a ribbon of silver sandy beach with a dark unnatural patch notched into its centre. I'd climbed onto the flight deck to watch the port emerge. It was a scrap heap. Native junks similar to those I'd seen earlier were bullying aside small open-decked fishing boats of similar age, even a few ancient wicker coracles. That was lovely to see. The water tobacco-brown and glinting, the air full of strange smells and the raucous voices of the native crews as they recognised or bollocked one another. But the main harbour was a real shock. None of the sleek fighting vessels I'd expected, just a clutch of narrow-gutted old US destroyers, real ugly bastards, chained together. The rest was a very dreary scene. Every type of work vessel — dredgers, sweepers, cablelayers, coastal supply ships — all naked guts, rust and neglect, like a million tonnes of floating scrap-processing depots.'

As the carrier moved slowly towards its anchoring spot, the soldiers on board were being organised for disembarkation, which began almost the moment the ship glided to a stop. According to Barrie Crowley:

We disembarked in landing barges, just like D-Day. Great views — grey steel deck underfoot, high grey steel walls, high grey steel drawbridge forward. Crane your neck to snapping point and you could see the landing barge crowd controller up on the bridge with the skipper. We could look up at the sky, but brilliant blue is just blue after a while and the sun's glare made me sneeze. A dull thump and scrape, engines throttled back from reverse roar to idle. We're there. Get the ramp down! Let's have a look!

Expecting something else? What we see is a shale and stone beach like much of England's coast, only sunny. Treacherous underfoot weighed down as we are — have to keep our eyes directly in front. Only when solid sand is underfoot can we look up and see Vietnam for what it is. Vung Tau is like a huge open warehouse. We're awaited on the red gravel road by identical trucks and personnel to those who started us off on our journey. We clamber on and start to weave our way through countless rows of tarpaulined, crated and containered equipment blanketed with red dust.

So 9 Battalion arrived in Vietnam for their tour of duty. The same day 3 Battalion boarded *Sydney* for the return trip, along with an unusual item of cargo, an RAAF Caribou aircraft that had been damaged in Vietnam and could not be repaired on location. It was brought out to *Sydney* slung under a huge Chinook helicopter, and deposited on the flight deck, the largest aircraft ever carried by the vessel. The troops aboard *Sydney* disembarked at Port Adelaide on 2 December, while the aircraft was offloaded by crane when the vessel reached Sydney.

Sydney made three trips to Vietnam during 1969, the first in February. Departing Sydney with elements of 5 Battalion RAR on board, the vessel went around the south coast of Australia to Fremantle to refuel. Leaving there on 8 February, *Sydney* was joined on 15 May by HMAS *Derwent* as escort, the pair arriving off Vung Tau on 15 February. The disembarking troops were ferried ashore in barges, which brought back to the ship members of B Company of 3 Battalion RAR, which had completed its year in Vietnam.

Leaving Vietnam brought mixed emotions to some of the men. Tim Foster said, 'It was a day filled with sadness, because we were leaving a country filled with many sad memories. At the same time, we were elated to have been lucky enough to survive the year and be going home.' As the ship departed, Tim recalled standing at the rail looking at Vietnam 'for the very last time and the country was almost covered in a blue haze, and was slowly disappearing over the stern. I took one last look at that country and turned away with mixed emotions, walked away, and never looked back.'

John Eaton remembered the voyage back as 'some of the most relaxing days of my life. That quiet adjusting period of 10 or 11 days. The officers never bothered us, there were no pressures, we just had a few minor duties to perform. The flight deck was empty, there was tons of room for exercise if you wanted it, there was a can of beer per man, a large one, and your best friend was someone who didn't drink.'

The voyage back was interrupted by a stopover at Townsville on 25 February, where some men who lived in Queensland were offloaded. Then it was on to Sydney, where the vessel arrived on 28 February. John Eaton recalled, 'one thing I'll never forget is sailing through Sydney Heads on the morning we arrived. That's a remarkable feeling, coming home from war, in that environment. I guess a lot of guys have experienced it over the years Australia has been involved in wars. It was drizzling rain, and that old coathanger never looked better as we came down through the harbour to berth at Garden Island.'

The second voyage for the year to Vietnam by HMAS *Sydney* commenced in Sydney on 4 May, but the vessel did not have any troops on board until 6 Battalion RAR boarded in Townsville on 8 May, along with further equipment and stores. Being too large to go alongside the wharf in Townsville, *Sydney* anchored some distance out, beyond Magnetic Island.

Among those soldiers who joined the ship was Gary Blinco, who had been part of the tenth intake of the national service program, being enlisted on 4 October 1967. He went through the intensive training schedule before being posted to 6 Battalion, which was based in Townsville. As with all other soldiers preparing to depart for Vietnam, he was allowed a brief home leave, then returned to the base a few days before their scheduled departure date. As Gary Blinco later wrote:

> The waiting, the training and the posturing were all suddenly over as the battalion marched majestically through the main street of Townsville, to the delight of a large crowd of well wishers, and the dismay of a small group of anti-war protesters. Families, friends, relatives and curious observers thronged the streets, as we marched behind our leaders, and the battalion pipes and drum band. Like conquering heroes we stamped noisily along the hot tarred streets, somewhat naïve young men full of pride and hope, many off to war as their fathers had done.
>
> At the Strand on the waterfront, we were allowed to break ranks for a short period, to bid farewell to loved ones. Then we were to embark on

the Magnetic Island ferries, which would take us out to HMAS *Sydney* that wallowed in the sea beyond Magnetic Island ... None of my family or civilian friends were at the Strand to see me off ... I did not want any more sad goodbyes, I was happy to be alone with my thoughts on this weirdly solemn occasion. I wandered around the Strand, looking at the farewell scenes. Some were pretty painful, when small children and young wives were involved. I wondered how many of these men, including myself, would come home alive. The scenes, I thought, were probably much the same as they had been during those other wars, the Boer War, Great War, the Second World War, and Korea. The world did not seem to learn a great deal from the past I concluded ... I was glad when the waiting was over, and we were assembled again as a fighting unit. I checked that my section was complete, and we were herded onto the ferries for the short ride out to the ship.

The HMAS *Sydney* was too large to dock at the Townsville wharf, it drew too much water for the shallow harbour, or so we were told, but I suspect the real reason had more to do with security. Hence the need to use the ferries to embark the troops. On arrival at the ship, we embarked by climbing up cargo nets that were draped over the side of the vessel, to secure boarding access. This was rather frightening as we were carrying quite a lot of kit, and the ship and the ferry tossed alarmingly in the swell. At last the whole battalion, and some support units, were aboard without major mishap or loss of equipment and we were able to relax.

Our battalion equipment, such as trucks and vehicles, had been loaded earlier ... and these were now secured on what had once been the flight deck of the ex-aircraft carrier. The remainder of our gear was stored in the huge hold below the deck.

Once on board, the troops could settle in for the voyage, and had time to explore their home for the next ten days. To Gary Blinco, 'The ship seemed huge to me, and one could wander around it for days, and still not explore every nook and cranny. While we all had our designated areas, we pretty much had the run of the ship. There appeared to be bathrooms, and messing areas scattered all over the ship. We simply wandered around until we found one we liked and used it. This may have contravened the official intentions, but we were never challenged.'

From the start, a routine was established to keep the soldiers occupied during the long daylight hours. Gary Blinco recalled:

> Every day we paraded on the huge flight deck, an area on the top of the ship that looked like a couple of football fields. The equipment, stored in

the middle of the deck, took up a lot of room, but there was still ample space to conduct a parade. After roll call and first orders of the day, we broke into various training details, or work parties, to help run the day to day admin of the huge ship. We took turns at working in kitchens, and the other support areas of the ship. While the Navy owned the boat, we were basically required to look after ourselves.

At night we set up hammocks, or crawled into a cargo cage and made a temporary bunk for the night. Some of the nights were very hot, and many soldiers slept on the quarter decks. These were small openings along the side of the ship, on different levels. They looked very much like patios or verandahs. Our training program was not neglected, nor was our physical fitness, and we took daily work outs and long runs around the flight deck. I was keen on long distance running, and had taken long runs, in addition to the training programme, throughout my service to date. I think the running helped me deliberate, and to keep a clear head.

Some days, we had rifle shooting practice from the rear deck of the boat. We section commanders gave fire instructions, as the troops shot at coloured balloons, partly filled with water for weight, that had been released from the stern of the ship. Not to be outdone, the Navy gave impressive fire demonstrations, with the ship's collection of 40 millimetre 'Bofors' machine-guns, pumping away at the collection of balloons that receded along the foaming wake of the ship.

The ship was full of narrow gangways, staircases and a labyrinth of small rooms. One had to be careful when barging about in these confined spaces. Sailors hurrying around would call 'Watch your back.' This became a catch cry for the landlubbers, who took the mickey out of the Navy. 'Watch your back' often became 'Watch your bum,' but the sailors took it in good spirit. I suppose they had been carting infantry soldiers to and from the war for years, so they were used to it. 'We are just friggin' bus drivers to you blokes,' a sailor complained one day. 'You pricks get all the glory.'

At the end of the day there was time for the soldiers to relax, and socialise with the men with whom they would be spending the next year. 'Each night,' wrote Gary Blinco, 'we were allowed one can of beer per man, albeit a big one. The beer came in 26 ounce cans, and, as some of the soldiers did not drink beer, we who did could usually scrounge an extra can or so. At twenty cents a can, it was not going to send anyone broke. The nightly beer fuelled some lively discussions, and helped the various section members bond together. With the dress rehearsals over, we would soon be depending on one another to survive. Few men are prepared to trust their back to someone they do not know and trust pretty well, so the sea passage had some hidden benefits.'

There was also the odd occasion when something different occurred to break up the monotony of endless days at sea. Gary Blinco wrote later, 'As the ship crossed the equator, we had the obligatory "Crossing the Line Ceremony." The senior NCOs and officers embarrassed themselves by dressing up in King Neptune outfits, and dunking each other in a tub of water. That night we had a variety concert in the main hall, and I was amazed at the depth, and the variety of talent, that existed in an infantry battalion. Acts of such diversity and quality emerged that I felt the concert could have drawn crowds to the Sydney Opera House. Many were humorous, many took the mickey out of our naval comrades, but most showed a hint of uncertain emotions facing these men as they were about to face the real war. The songs and poems came from other wars, or times of crisis in the past. I smiled as a makeshift band closed with a medley of songs from World War Two, as well as some current hit tunes. The final number, delivered beautifully by a young NCO from one of the support units was "I'm Leaving on a Jet Plane." No-one appeared to notice the fact that we sat in the hold of a troop ship, as we listened quietly to the suddenly haunting song ... "I wish this was a movie," I thought, so it can all end soon and I can go home.'

HMAS *Sydney* was escorted on the final stages of this voyage by HMAS *Vampire*, and the two ships arrived at Vung Tau on 19 May. Although the arrival of the ship meant the soldiers on board were now about to go to war, Gary Blinco wrote:

By the time the *Sydney* arrived at the South Vietnamese port of Vung Tau, I was sick of the ship and its confined spaces. I could not wait to get my men onto dry land, and get started on the tour of duty. Our tour was for twelve months, or 365 days, as we preferred to measure it. When we sighted the Vietnamese coast some wag yelled, 'You beauty, only 364 and a wakey to go,' the countdown had begun, and would continue. Few days passed without someone calling the time. I spared a thought for our temporary enemy whose tour would endure to the end of the war, whenever that may be.

To disembark from the ship, we were loaded into Landing Barges for the short journey to the shore. These were open, box like vessels, from which it was impossible to see where we were, or where we were heading. I had heard stories of old diggers on their second tour of duty, ordering the green young soldiers to fix bayonets, and be ready to storm out of the barges on landing. Fully prepared to charge up a bullet swept beach, and secure the beach head, they would rush from the barge as the landing door was lowered. To their embarrassment and surprise, they would be on a sedate white beach, occupied by bathing soldiers, on rest leave at the Vung Tau support base and amenity's centre.

Fortunately, our leaders had briefed us properly on the landing conditions, and we expected to arrive on a secure and calm beach, followed by a short walk to a helipad. We trudged up the beach, laden with our packs and other equipment, and found the busy helipad. When our turn came, we boarded large troop carrying helicopters called Chinooks.

These helicopters flew the soldiers to their new home base at Nui Dat, from where 4 Battalion RAR were brought by the same helicopters, to board the same landing barges for the trip out to the *Sydney*, and were brought back to Brisbane, arriving on 30 May.

It was almost six months before *Sydney* was required to make her next journey with troops. 8 Battalion RAR boarded in Brisbane on 17 November 1969 for the trip to Vung Tau, where *Sydney* arrived on 28 November, escorted by HMAS *Duchess* for the entire journey. By now the turnaround procedure in Vung Tau had been refined to such a level that the ships would only need to be at anchor, when they were at their most vulnerable, for a matter of hours.

The gunnery officer on board *Duchess*, R.T. Nott, later wrote, 'On Friday 28 November 1969 at approximately 0400 HMAS *Duchess* in company with HMAS *Sydney* entered Vung Tau Harbour. After *Sydney* anchored *Duchess* anchored about 1.5 cables ahead of *Sydney* to act as anchor screen whilst *Sydney*, via barge and helicopter, disembarked 8 RAR and then embarked 9 RAR and their equipment for the return voyage to Adelaide. This unloading and loading operation was quickly and efficiently completed in about seven hours ... HMAS *Duchess* weighed anchor shortly before midday, prior to HMAS *Sydney* getting under way, and took up station ahead to lead her out of harbour. Both ships cleared Cap St Jacques by about 1330.' After a stop at Fremantle on 5 December, the men of 9 Battalion RAR were home for Christmas, disembarking at Adelaide on 9 December.

Sydney made only two trips to Vietnam during 1970, the first departing Sydney on 16 February, with 7 Battalion RAR on board, and escorted for the final few days of the trip by HMAS *Yarra*. The arriving troops disembarked at Vung Tau on 27 February, when 5 Battalion RAR came aboard for the trip home, leaving the ship at Fremantle on 5 March. It was not until October 1970 that *Sydney* again headed north to Vung Tau, passing through Fremantle on 21 October and anchoring off Vung Tau on 1 November, escorted by HMAS *Vendetta*. On the return trip, *Sydney* embarked 8 Battalion RAR, who left the ship at Brisbane on 12 November.

1971 would be the busiest year for HMAS *Sydney* in her role as a troop transport, making six return trips to Vietnam during the year. On 15 February 3 Battalion RAR boarded the ship at Port Adelaide. 3 Battalion was the only major regular unit of the Army to be based in South Australia, and had already completed one deployment to Vietnam, in 1968. The unit had undergone almost a total change of personnel when it began to build its strength, including national servicemen, for a second deployment. After several months of intensive training, the advance party, numbering 150 personnel, was flown out of the RAAF Edinburgh Airfield on 11 February 1971. The rest of the battalion, some 500 men, were transported to the outer harbour at Port Adelaide, where they boarded HMAS *Sydney* early on the morning of 15 February.

The ship departed at 11 am, with the troops lining the flight deck to farewell family and friends lining the wharf. *Sydney* voyaged non-stop to Vietnam, being escorted part of the way by HMAS *Yarra* and refuelling at sea. On arrival at Vung Tau on 25 February, elements of 7 Battalion RAR came aboard for the trip home. *Sydney* stopped at Fremantle on 4 March, then continued on to Sydney, where the troops disembarked on 11 March.

Less than two weeks later *Sydney* was on her way from Sydney again, stopping in Port Adelaide on 26 March to load further troops and equipment. Escorted by HMAS *Duchess*, *Sydney* arrived in Vung Tau Harbour on 5 April, but no troops embarked, as the ship went north to Hong Kong, arriving on 8 April.

On returning to Australia, *Sydney* went to Townsville to embark 4 Battalion RAR on 13 May. As with other troops who were sent to Vietnam, 4 Battalion underwent extensive training prior to departure, starting at Canungra, and finishing at High Range and Mount Spec north of Townsville. When the battalion was ready to deploy to Vietnam, 118 men were sent on Qantas 707 aircraft direct to Saigon as the advance party. The rest were transported to Townsville to board *Sydney*. Among them was Gary McKay, who had been called up in the second intake of national servicemen in 1968 and was now an officer and platoon commander. His record of the voyage to Vietnam is included in his book, *In Good Company*, probably the best book written on the experiences of Australian soldiers in the war.

The battalion was stationed at Lavarack Barracks, but McKay spent his last night before departure at home with his wife, who drove him to the barracks about 5.30 am. After a hurried goodbye,

> there was very little left to do but call the platoon roll, load our worldly possessions onto the trucks and head off for Townsville.
>
> We were dressed in our best starched greens with all the trimmings as we marched through Townsville down Flinders Street and took the salute from the Task Force commander. We had been briefed by our company commander on what action to take if demonstrators gave us a hard time. I don't believe any of us expected trouble from the locals; the students at James Cook University would have taken on a situation too big to handle, as there were over 3,000 soldiers in Townsville. So our march was uneventful save for some good-natured barracking from the mates who had come to see us off.
>
> The scene at the wharf was a real anti-climax. We waited in our company lots for six Navy landing craft to ferry us 12 km out to the HMAS *Sydney* which was anchored out in the channel of Cleveland Bay behind Magnetic Island. Whilst we were waiting we were issued white cards with numbers which we had to stick in our hats. These were our 'boarding passes.' They allowed us to be directed to where we had to go on the ship and kept our hands free to carry our gear. We were wearing our webbing and large packs, and carrying our personal weapon, a kit bag and echelon bag. Getting onto the landing craft was easy, but getting the landing craft off the wharf was a different matter. We were crammed on with our several hundred pounds of kit and as we stood waiting for the dramatic departure we were offloaded back onto the wharf because the ramp wouldn't shut properly. Loaded back on we finally said goodbye to firm land for the next ten days.
>
> The trip out to the *Sydney* was not the greatest even though the sea was dead calm. The landing craft is flat-bottomed and not swift and we wallowed around in these boats, packed in like sardines for about an hour before we could scramble aboard. Our helmsman, a midshipman under training, was not a great driver. He had three attempts at parking, all the time being berated by an officer on board the troopship who had a loudhailer. The young midshipman must have found this somewhat unnerving (we certainly did) as he practised parking using the Braille method; I was sure he was trying to sink the *Sydney* with the naval officer yelling abuse at him from above.

Once the landing craft had secured itself to the Sydney, the soldiers were able to clamber on board the troopship, where they were directed to their quarters by sailors. The other ranks were surprised to find that they would have to sleep in hammocks in cramped quarters below decks, while officers were allocated cabins. As Gary McKay later wrote:

The officers were quartered in the aft section of the ship and the subalterns had cabins above the quarterdeck next to what felt like were the boilers. The cabin was the size of an average bathroom and incredibly crowded. It had no portholes; and ventilation — the ship being designed for the North Atlantic — was non-existent.

After everyone was on board we got underway — around 1315 hours. I went off in search of my platoon and eventually found them packed into a mess deck somewhere down in the bowels of the ship. They all seemed pretty happy and were looking forward to dinner when they would get their beer ration. It was only one can but it was a big one. It was in fact a 26 ounce Fosters and the lads were already scouring the unit looking for non-drinkers to buy their beer ration. I visited them during their evening meal and found the food was good. The beer cost 20 cents for the big can but I heard that the black market had already pushed the price of a spare ration ticket up to five dollars.

Also on board *Sydney* on this trip was Private Garry Heskett, who later recalled, 'Apart from anything else on the ship, I remember the first night was the quietest I ever spent on that ship. It was absolutely deathly silent. You could have dropped a pin as far as I was concerned; we all just lay there and I remember laying there, on the bunk and waiting for the Captain to come through and do his inspection or whatever it was at that time, and just looking around and it was deathly silent. People must have been thinking. My mind was going back and thinking, well here it is, I am actually going to war. So, what's it going to be like? All the things that could face you; the terrors; the fears.'

Once the *Sydney* was under way, a daily routine was organised to keep the men active during the voyage. As Gary McKay wrote:

> The working day was from 0900 hours to 1600 hours, which we considered almost a holiday compared to the 18 to 20 hour days we had had in the bush on exercises. I was to run the battalion weapon training which consisted of 'snap-shooting' from the rear of the ship up on the flight deck. This turned out to be a great job as the diggers were doing something active and didn't have to listen to lectures in the stifling heat of the day or do weapons drill and safety checks.
>
> The shooting was run in rifle section lots. The soldiers would stand at the very rear of the ship, on what was called 'the captain's walk.' This was a perforated steel grating which was suspended some 80 feet above the boiling wake. Two coloured balloons, with a small amount of water inside for ballast, were tied together and dropped over the side of the ship; they would then drift out into the wake about 100 feet aft. The firers were numbered off and I would call a number at random and the soldier would

engage the balloons with two quick shots ... It was a lot of fun but hot work standing on the flight deck for six hours a day and with no shade from the tropical sun. Once night fell we finished for the day and we could sit down and relax.

Compared with the frenetic activity on board the ship during daylight, night time was relatively quiet. Gary McKay writes that:

> We had to change into our polyester dress at night, and this was an art in itself. The showers were salt or fresh water and because of the tropical heat even the cold water was hot. It was too hot to towel off in the showers so I used to stand out on the sponson deck outside and let the breeze of the moving ship cool and dry me and then carefully climb into my polyester dress and move quickly down to the air conditioned comfort of the wardroom.
>
> The wardroom was the focal point for the evening's entertainment and a favourite game to play was liar dice. The ship's chaplain, Lieutenant Commander Ed Rolf, was a great player at that game — perhaps it was the fact that he was a padre that misled us into believing his outrageous calls but he hardly ever lost a game.
>
> It was usually too hot to sleep in our crowded cabin, so most of us took our bedding and slept down on the quarterdeck where a beautiful breeze blew all night and one could get a decent night's sleep. On one particular evening everyone traipsed down to the quarterdeck with their stretchers and bedding under their arms — only to find one of our fellow platoon commanders sound asleep ... We went up to the sick bay and talked the medic into giving us a pile of bandages, and, while Dan slept peacefully, we wrapped him into his stretcher so he resembled a large cocoon. This in itself was bad enough, but every morning the matelots would come down to the quarterdeck at 6 am and shout 'Clear the decks, swabbing in five minutes, sirs!' If you weren't up and off the deck the sailors would hose on regardless. So, the next morning the sailors came down and we all leapt to our feet except poor Dan who was unceremoniously hosed down by grinning seamen as he tried to wriggle out of his stretcher.

So the long voyage north continued. On Wednesday, 19 May, *Sydney* passed between Timor and Java and came close to the coast of Bali. During this part of the journey the troopship was often surrounded by native fishing boats, some of which came so close the shooting exercises from the stern had to be stopped. At 1430 on 21 May the troopship crossed the equator, and, Gary McKay noted, 'To celebrate, the notables in the unit put on a ceremony where King Neptune and some of his mermaids initiated some who hadn't crossed the equator before. Some of our corporals grabbed unsuspecting souls and dunked them in a custard type of mess that looked awful ... We then had a tug-of-war against the navy boys and later that evening a party with our Pipes and Drums, putting on a performance that everyone enjoyed.'

This was the twentieth trip to Vietnam by HMAS *Sydney*, and as the troopship was about a thousand kilometres from Vietnam, it was time for an escort, which appeared quite suddenly one morning and impressed all on board *Sydney*. 'From nowhere two destroyer escorts, the HMAS *Duchess* and the HMAS *Parramatta* appeared. They looked rather spectacular as they steamed towards us and then heeled over some 20 or 30 degrees with a white plume of spray behind the fantail. A Royal Fleet Auxiliary tanker appeared and for about three hours we took on fuel and water.'

Sydney arrived off Vung Tau on the evening of 22 May and remained at anchor overnight, the first time this had happened in several years. However, it was not a peaceful night for those on board because, as Gary McKay wrote, 'all through the night a water-borne patrol in a rubber dinghy circled the ship dropping "scare charges" to dissuade any would-be Viet Cong from mining the ship.'

The soldiers were told they would be taken ashore in huge Chinook helicopters the next morning, which was 'a typical muggy, steamy day in South Vietnam,' wrote Gary McKay. 'We had been up since first light and had been given briefings on where we had to muster in order to get out onto the flight deck in correct order. There wasn't much room as most of the flight deck had 114 trucks parked on it ... We were finally moved in a seemingly endless queue from the mess deck muster areas toward the hangar deck and then lifted up onto the flight deck.' The soldiers then boarded the Chinook for the short trip ashore. The same day, 23 May, 2 Battalion RAR came aboard *Sydney* for their trip home, arriving in Townsville on 1 June.

After a break of over three months, *Sydney* departed Sydney on 20 September 1971 on its next voyage to Vietnam, carrying a full complement of troops from various units and their equipment. This time the escort over the final stages was HMAS *Swan* and the two ships arrived off Vung Tau on 6 October. Again the ships remained overnight, with 3 Battalion RAR joining *Sydney* for the trip home. They had been transported from Nui Dat by RAAF Iroquois helicopters, which deposited them on the flight deck of *Sydney*. The next day *Sydney* and *Swan* slipped out of Vung Tau, with the transport anchoring off Fremantle on 13 October. The West Australian members of the battalion went ashore while the majority of the troops remained on

HMAS *Swan* escorted *Sydney* in October 1971. (*RAN photo – Rodney T. Nott collection*)

board as the ship proceeded to Port Adelaide, arriving on 16 October. As *Sydney* came alongside its berth in the outer harbour, the wharf was lined with family and friends welcoming the troops home.

Sydney continued from Port Adelaide to Sydney, where after only a few days break, the crew were busy preparing for another trip to Vietnam. By this time the war was slowly heading towards a conclusion, and no more Australian troops would be sent north. When *Sydney* departed Garden Island on 26 October 1971, it was carrying only Defence Aid stores, but still rated an escort for the final days of the trip, this being provided by HMAS *Derwent*. On arrival at Vung Tau on 6 November, the stores were sent ashore from *Sydney* and men from a variety of army units came on board for the trip home. Departing Vung Tau on 7 November, *Sydney* docked at Garden Island on 18 November.

A mere six days later, on 24 November, *Sydney* was heading north again, picking up HMAS *Swan* as escort before arriving off Vung Tau on 8 December. Elements of 4 Battalion RAR came on board, along with the 104 Battery, Royal Australian Artillery, and 9 Squadron RAAF with its sixteen Iroquois helicopters. When all the soldiers were on board, President Nguyen Van Thieu of Vietnam arrived on the flight deck in a helicopter, having come to thank the Australian troops for their assistance and the sacrifices they had made since 1962. After inspecting sailors, troops and airmen lined up on the flight deck, the President had lunch on board as the guest of Captain R.J. Scrivenor.

Departing Vung Tau on 9 December, *Sydney* and *Swan* headed south.

Sydney arrived in Townsville on 17 December, when 4 RAR disembarked, then the transport continued its voyage south to Sydney. When off the Queensland coast near Caloundra, the RAAF helicopters flew off the flight deck to their home base, and *Sydney* was virtually an empty ship when it berthed at Garden Island on 21 December.

On 14 February 1972, *Sydney* again left Garden Island bound for Vietnam, though carrying no troops, but still escorted into Vung Tau, by HMAS *Torrens*. Arriving on 28 February, the transport stayed overnight, embarking 457 troops from various Australian Army units, as well as seventy vehicles and 102 containers of equipment. Departing on 29 February, *Sydney* disembarked the troops at Townsville on 9 March. Apart from a small team of advisers, these were the last Australian troops to be withdrawn from Vietnam.

Able Seaman George Brew was a crew member on board HMAS *Sydney* on the final voyages the vessel made to Vietnam. He recalled:

> The *Sydney* was really a ship that was made for the North Atlantic and it was awfully hot aboard. It was very cramped and it depended on how senior you were as to the comfort of your living arrangements. I met several of the soldiers as they returned from South Vietnam. They all had good stories to tell but all we were doing was keeping them out of trouble and occupied. They were always getting lost on the ship and hated the showers. You had to be pretty quick in the shower as we didn't carry much water. I also remember distinctly the smell of the greens the soldiers had worn in the jungle.
>
> When the ship was actually anchored in Vung Tau harbour I remember on the first night the clearance divers circled the ship all night dropping 'scare-charges.' They were grenades. They also used to drag barbed wire along behind the boats to snag VC sappers.

George Brew also told a story about 'one Digger who threw his washing over the side of the *Sydney* in a laundry bag to give it a good rinse, and three days later when he decided to pull it back in, all that was left were the wooden handles of the laundry bag.'

On 1 November 1972, HMAS *Sydney* left Sydney on what was to be her final trip to Vietnam, though no troops would be carried in either direction. Going north, the ship carried only Defence Aid equipment, and was escorted by HMAS *Vampire*. The two ships arrived off Vung Tau on 23 November. The aid stores were discharged, and miscellaneous equipment taken on board to be returned to Australia. Departing Vung Tau for the last time on 24 November, *Sydney* went first to Hong Kong before returning to Australia, and terminating her involvement in the Vietnam War. During the Vietnam conflict, HMAS

Sydney transported some 15,600 Army and RAAF personnel, along with their equipment.

HMAS *Sydney* spent some time over the next year or so in her alternate role of training ship, but eventually was laid up at Athol Bight in Sydney Harbour. In October 1975, the vessel was sold to shipbreakers, and towed away later the same month.

HMAS *Sydney* at anchor off Vung Tau. (*RAN photo – Rodney T. Nott collection*)

Appendix
Major Convoys in World War II

Convoys to the Middle East, Britain and Singapore, January 1940 to November 1941

US1	Jan. 40	*Dunera, Empress of Canada, Empress of Japan, Orcades, Orford, Orion, Otranto, Rangitata, Sobieski, Strathaird, Strathnaver*
US2	Apr. 40	*Dunera, Ettrick, Neuralia, Nevasa, Strathaird.*
US3	May 40	*Andes, Aquitania, Empress of Britain, Empress of Canada, Empress of Japan, Mauretania, Queen Mary*
US4	Aug. 40	*Aquitania, Empress of Japan, Mauretania, Orcades*
US5A	Sep. 40	*Christiaan Huygens, Indrapoera, Nieuw Holland, Slamat*
US5B	Oct. 40	*Johan de Witt, Nieuw Zeeland*
US6	Oct. 40	*Aquitania, Mauretania, Queen Mary*
US7	Nov. 40	*Batory, Orion, Strathmore, Stratheden*
US8	Dec. 40	*Awatea, Aquitania, Dominion Monarch, Mauretania, Queen Mary*
US9	Feb. 41	*Aquitania, Mauretania, Nieuw Amsterdam, Queen Mary*
US10	Apr. 41	*Ile de France, Mauretania, Nieuw Amsterdam, Queen Elizabeth, Queen Mary*
US11A	Jul. 41	*Aquitania, Queen Elizabeth, Queen Mary*
US11B	Jul. 41	*Johan van Oldenbarnevelt, Marnix van Sint Aldegonde, Sibajak*
US12A	Sep. 41	*Queen Elizabeth, Queen Mary*
US12B	Sep. 41	*Aquitania, Johan van Oldenbarnevelt,*

| US13 | Nov. 41 | Marnix van Sint Aldegonde, Sibajak, Queen Elizabeth, Queen Mary |

Convoys to New Guinea and the Islands, March to December 1941

ZK1	Mar. 41	Katoomba, Zealandia
ZK2	Apr. 41	Katoomba, Zealandia
ZK3	Jul. 41	Montoro, Zealandia
ZK4	Aug. 41	Montoro, Zealandia
ZK5	Dec. 41	Aquitania, Herstein, Sarpedon.

The following ships carried troops to New Guinea 1942 to 1945 on individual voyages:

Anhui, Anshun, Bontekoe, Both, Canberra, Charles Lummis, Cremer, David C Shanks, Duntroon, Evangeline, Fenimore Cooper, Frederick Lykes, Henry T Allen, Isaac Coles, James Wilson, Jane Addams, Janssens, John Steele, Karsik, Katoomba, Macdhui, Maetsuycker, Manoora, Mexico, Pulginbar, Swartenhundt, Taroona, Thomas Corwin, Van der Lijn, Van Heutz

Convoys to Singapore, January and February 1942

MS1	Jan. 42	Seven cargo ships, no troops
MS2	Jan. 42	*Aquitania*
MS3	Jan. 42	*Antilochus, Charon, Mangola, Marella*, and seven tankers
MS4	Feb. 42	Four tankers, two cargo ships, no troops
MS5	Feb. 42	*Duntroon, Willard A. Holbrook, Katoomba* (all US troops)

Troopships and transports involved in Operation Stepsister from Egypt to India and Australia, January to March 1942

| JS1 | Jan. 42 | *Adrastus, Filleigh, Hai Lee, Hermion, Lulworth Hill, Modasa, Prominent, Yoma* |

JS2   Feb. 42   *Orcades*
JS3/SU1 Feb. 42   *City of London, City of Paris, Eastern Prince, Egra, Empire Glade, Empire Glen, Esperance Bay, Kosciusko, Lavington Court, Madras City, Mathura, Penrith Castle, Salween, Silverwillow*

The following ships made independent voyages with Australian troops from Egypt to India or Australia, or from Colombo to Australia, as part of Operation Stepsister:

Andes, Clan McTavish, Duntroon, Felix Roussel, Ile de France, Mauretania, Mount Vernon, Nieuw Amsterdam, Orontes, Otranto, Strathallan, Westernland, Willard A. Holbrook, West Point

Troopships and transports involved in Schooner convoy from Colombo to Australia, July 1942

Aronda, Athlone Castle, City of Canterbury, City of Lille, Clan Macdonald, Devonshire, Dunedin Star, Ekma, Martand, Rajula, Westernland

Troopships involved in Operation Pamphlet from Egypt to Australia, February 1943

Aquitania, Ile de France, Nieuw Amsterdam, Queen Mary, Queen of Bermuda

Bibliography

Books

Aplin, Douglas, *Rabaul 1942* (Lark Force Assoc., Melbourne, 1980)
Barker, Anthony J., & Jackson, Lisa, *Fleeting Attraction* (University of Western Australia Press, Perth, 1996)
Barter, Margaret, *Far Above Battle* (Allen & Unwin, Sydney, 1994)
Bean, C.E.W., *The Story of Anzac* (University of Queensland Press, Brisbane, 1981)
Beaumont, Joan, *Gull Force* (Allen & Unwin, Sydney, 1988)
Bellair, John, *From Snow to Jungle* (Allen & Unwin, Sydney, 1987)
Besley, Harvey, *Pilot – Prisoner – Survivor* (Darling Downs Institute Press, Toowoomba, 1986)
Bissett, Sir James, *Commodore* (Angus & Robertson, Sydney, 1961)
Blinco, Gary, *Down a Country Lane to War* (Boolarong Press, Brisbane, 1997)
Blythe, John, *Soldiering On* (Century Hutchinson NZ, Auckland, 1989)
Braga, Stuart, *Anzac Doctor* (Hale & Iremonger, Sydney 2000)
Breen, Bob, *First to Fight* (Allen & Unwin, Sydney, 1988)
Broadbent, Harvey, *The Boys who Came Home* (ABC Books, Sydney 1990)
Buckley, Martin J., *Sword and Lance* (self-published, Lismore, 1988)
Callinan, Bernard, *Independent Company* (William Heinemann Australia, Melbourne, 1953)
Cassells, Vic, *For Those in Peril* (Kangaroo Press, Sydney, 1995)
Charles, Roland W., *Troopships of World War II* (Army Transportation Association, Washington DC, 1982)
Clarke, Michael, *My War* (Michael Clarke Press, Melbourne, 1990)
Colville, John, *The Fringes of Power* (Hodder & Stoughton, London, 1985)
Combe, G., F. Ligterwood & T. Gilchrist, *Second 43rd* (Second 43rd Battalion, Adelaide, 1972)
Critch, Mary, *Our Kind of War* (Artlook Books Trust, Perth, 1981)
Crowley, Barrie, *View From a Low Bough* (Allen & Unwin, Sydney, 1997)
De Haas, Dr C., *De Grote Drie* (Unieboek BV, Bussum, 1976)

Dickens, Barry, *Ordinary Heroes* (Hardie Grant Publishing, Melbourne, 1999)
Doman, Peter, *The Silent Men* (Allen & Unwin, Sydney, 1999)
Dunlop, E.E. (ed.), *The War Diaries of Weary Dunlop* (Nelson Publishers, Melbourne, 1986)
English, Michael C, *The Riflemen* (Australian Military History Publications, Sydney, 1999)
Field, Laurie, *The Forgotten War* (Melbourne University Press, Melbourne, 1979)
Fry, Eric, *An Airman far Away* (Kangaroo Press, Sydney, 1993)
Gill, G. Hermon, *Royal Australian Navy: 1939–1942* (Australian War Memorial, Canberra, 1988)
Gill, G. Hermon, *Royal Australian Navy: 1942– 1945* (Australian War Memorial, Canberra, 1988)
Gillan, Hugh (ed.), *We Had Some Bother* (Hale & Iremonger, Sydney, 1985)
Goodman, Rupert - Our War Nurses (Boolarong Publications, Brisbane, 1988)
Gordon, Malcolm R., *From Chusan to Sea Princess* (Allen & Unwin, Sydney, 1985)
Hall, Timothy, *New Guinea 1942–44* (Methuen Australia, Sydney, 1981)
Harding, Steve, *Gray Ghost* (Pictorial Histories, Montana, 1982)
Hay, David, *Nothing Over Us* (Australian War Memorial, Canberra, 1984)
Henderson, James, *Onward Boy Soldiers* (University of Western Australia Press, Nedlands, 1992)
Holt, Bob, *From Ingleburn to Aitape* (R. Holt, Sydney, 1981)
Horner, D.M., *High Command* (Allen & Unwin, Sydney, 1982)
Horner, David (ed.), *Duty First* (Allen & Unwin, Sydney, 1990)
Jeremy, John, *Cockatoo Island* (NSW Press, Sydney, 1999)
Jones, Ian , *Australians at War: The Australian Light Horse* (Time-Life Books, North Sydney, 1987)
Kludas, Arnold, *Great Passenger Ships of the World* (Patrick Stephens, Cambridge, 1972)
Konings, Chris., *De Nieuw Amsterdam* (Den Boer Uitgevers, Middelburg, 1988)
Konings, Chris, *Queen Elizabeth at War* (Patrick Stephens, Wellingborough, 1985)
Luidinga, Frans, & Nico Guns, *Indrapoera* (Van Soeren & Co., Amsterdam, 2001)
Marcus, Alex., *DEMS? What's DEMS* (Boolarong Publications, Brisbane, 1986)
McAulay, Lex, *The Fighting First* (Allen & Unwin, Sydney, 1991)
McKay, Gary, *In Good Company* (Allen & Unwin, Sydney, 1987)
McKay, Gary, *Delta Four* (Allen & Unwin, Sydney, 1996)

McKay, Gary, *Bullets, Beans and Bandages* (Allen & Unwin, Sydney, 1999)
McKernan, Michael, *Padre* (Allen & Unwin, Sydney, 1986)
McNab, Alexander, *We Were the First* (Australian Military History Publications, Loftus, 1998)
McNeill, Ian, *To Long Tan* (Allen & Unwin, Sydney, 1993)
Middlebrook, Martin, & Patrick Mahoney, *Battleship*, (Allen Lane, London, 1977)
Miller, William H., & David F. Hutchings, *Transatlantic Liners at War* (David & Charles, London, 1985)
Mulholland, Jack - Darwin Bombed (Australian Military History Publications, Loftus, 1999)
Nelson, Hank, *Prisoners of War: Australians Under Nippon* (ABC Books, Sydney, 1985)
Nott, Rodney, & Noel, Payne, *The Vung Tau Ferry* (General Aviation Maintenance, Melbourne, 1998)
Odgers, George, *Remembering Korea* (Lansdowne Publishing, Sydney, 2000)
Parsons, Max, *Gunfire* (2/12 Australian Field Regiment Association, Victoria, 1991)
Payne, M.A., *HMAS Australia* (Naval Historical Society of Australia, Sydney 1984)
Pearson, Ross A., *Australians at War in the Air, 1939–1945* (Kangaroo Press, Sydney, 1995)
Pirie, A.A., *Commando Double Black* (Australian Military History Publications, Loftus, 1994)
Plowman, Peter, *Emigrant Ships to Luxury Liners* (University of NSW Press, Sydney, 1992)
Plowman, Peter, *Passenger Ships of Australia and New Zealand* (Doubleday, Sydney, 1981)
Potter, Neil, & Jack Frost, *The Elizabeth* (Harrap, London, 1965)
Potter, Neil, & Jack Frost, *The Queen Mary* (Harrap, London, 1961)
Raynor, Robert J., *The Army and the Defence of Darwin Fortress* (Rudder Press, Sydney, 1995)
Rimmer, Gordon, *In Time for War* (Mulavon Publishing, Sydney, 1991)
Robertson, John, & John McCarthy, *Australian War Strategy* (University of Queensland Press, St Lucia, 1985)
Scholes, David, *Air War Diary* (Kangaroo Press, Sydney, 1997)
Seabrook, William C., *In the War at Sea* (Holland America Line, New York?, 1946?)
Slader, John, *The Fourth Service* (Robert Hale, London, 1994)
Slader, John, *The Red Duster at War* (William Kimber, London, 1988)
Slessor, Kenneth, *The War Diaries of Kenneth Slessor*, Clement Semmler, ed. (University of Queensland Press, Brisbane, 1985)
Speed F.W., *Esprit de Corps* (Allen & Unwin, Sydney, 1988)

Stanford, Don, *Ile de France* (Cassell, London, 1960)
Steward, H.D., *Recollections of a Regimental Medical Officer* (Melbourne University Press, Melbourne, 1983)
Stokes, Edward, *Innocents Abroad* (Allen & Unwin, Sydney, 1994)
Stuart, Lurline, & Josie Arnold, *Letters Home, 1939–1945* (William Collins, Sydney, 1987)
Swain, Bruce T., *A Chronology of Australian Armed Forces at War, 1939–45* (Allen & Unwin, Sydney, 2001)
Turner, Robert D., *The Pacific Empresses* (Sono Nis Press, Victoria, 1981)
Various authors, *Soldiering On*, (Australian War Memorial, Canberra, 1942)
Ward-Harvey, Ken, *The Sappers' War* (Sakoga, Sydney, 1992)
Whitelocke, Cliff, *Gunners in the Jungle* (2/15 Field Regiment Association, Sydney, 1983)
Whiting, Brendan, *Ship of Courage* (Allen & Unwin, Sydney, 1994)
Williams, Keith (ed.), *Letters to Mother From a WWII RAAF Pilot* (K. Williams, Sydney, 1990)
Woodward, Jack, *Three Times Lucky* (Boolarong Publications, Brisbane, 1991)
Wrench, C.M., *Campaigning With the Fighting 9th* (Boolarong Publications, Brisbane, 1985)

Periodicals and Magazines
Australian Sea Heritage
Marine News
Sea Breezes
Steamboat Bill

Merchant Ships Index

Aalsum 351, 353,354
Abbekirk 337
Aberdeen 20
Adrastus 327
Afric 40, 49, 68
Aiken Victory 444
Ajana 61, 63
America 354
American Farmer 415
Andes 114,121-123,126,128-132,137139,143,161,183,342, 423
Anglo-Egyptian 40, 49, 57
Anhui 398, 399
Anshun 397, 398
Antenor 176
Antillian 31
Antilochus 320
Antonia 117
Aorangi 38
Aquitania 114, 120-123, 126,128,129,132,135,137-139,143,145-147,151, 153-155,160,170, 171, 173, 175, 179,200, 201, 203-209, 211, 220, 222-227,239,244-248,252-254, 264,285, 306, `317-320
Arab 16, 17

Arawa (1) 44, 49, 55
Arawa (2) 427, 429
Argyllshire 40, 49, 52
Armadale 40, 49
Armenian 24, 27
Aronda 360-364
Arundel Castle 187, 190, 401, 426
Ascanius 40, 48, 49, 52, 57, 68, 72
Athenia 89
Athenic 49
Athlone Castle 196, 360-363
Athos II 99, 100
Atlantian 24
Aurania 30
Ausonia 270
Australasian 11-16, 22
Awatea 84, 170, 171, 173, 175, 179, 269-273
Ayrshire 61, 63, 64

Bakara 61, 63, 64
Ballarat 72
Barambah 61, 63
Barunga 61, 63
Batory 161-164
Benalla 40, 46, 48, 49, 52, 72
Benevolence 437
Berrima 37, 38, 60, 63, 64, 66, 70
Bontekoe 391, 401,402

492

Merchant Ships Index

Boonah 61, 73
Boorara 61, 63, 72
Borda 60, 63, 64
Bos Fontaine 408
Both 305, 320, 397, 411
Britannic 29, 34
British Princess 31
Byoki Maru 436

Calchas 259
Cameronia 187, 193
Canberra 301, 403, 409, 410
Cannstatt 60
Cap St Jacques 209
Cape Perpetua 412
Cape Wrath 349
Ceramic 60, 63, 64, 260, 261
Charles Lummis 415, 416
Charon 320
Chitral 357
Christiaan Huygens 148-151, 158, 160, 176
City of Canterbury 360, 363
City of Lille 360, 361
City of London 329
City of Manchester 316, 317, 335, 336, 339
City of Paris 329, 331, 349
Clan Buchanan 221
Clan MacCorquodale 40, 49
Clan Macdonald 360, 364
Clan MacEwan 68
Clan McGillivray 68, 72
Clan McTavish 354
Columbian 31
Consolation 437
Cornwall 20
Cremer 395
Custodian 31-33

David C Shanks 415
Demosthenes 69
Denbighshire 278
Derrymore 316, 317, 322, 334

Devonshire 176, 178, 360-364, 445, 446
Dilwara 159, 160, 175, 176, 178, 258, 264, 265, 446
Diomed 261-263
Dominion Monarch 170, 171, 173, 175-177, 423
Drayton Grange 34
Duchess of Bedford 114, 190, 192
Dunedin Star 360, 363
Dunera 86, 90, 93, 95, 96, 101-104, 109, 110, 159, 258, 446
Duntroon 81, 301, 323, 355-359, 393, 394, 403, 410, 411, 413, 427, 429, 430, 439
Durban Castle 342

Eastern Prince 329, 349
Egra 329, 349
Ekma 360, 363
Elsa 320
Empire Glade 329, 330, 346, 349
Empire Glen 330, 346, 349
Empire Longford 446
Empire Oriole 349
Empire Pintail 349
Empire Star 296, 332-335
Empress of Asia 56, 321, 336
Empress of Australia 114, 187, 192, 195
Empress of Britain 114, 121-123, 126, 127, 129, 132, 136, 137, 139, 143, 161, 183
Empress of Canada 86, 88, 90, 93, 96, 101, 114, 121-123, 127, 129, 135-138, 143, 144, 161, 182-186, 296
Empress of Japan 86, 88, 94-96, 100, 101, 114, 121-123, 126, 127, 129, 130, 136, 137, 146, 147, 187, 189, 192, 195, 419
Empress of Scotland 419-422
Enggano 316
Erling Brovig 320

Esperance Bay 329, 331, 349, 430, 432
Ettrick 103, 104, 106, 107, 109, 111, 159, 446
Euripides 40-42, 48, 51, 52
Euryalus 24
Evangeline 412, 413

Felix Roussel 321, 357
Filleigh 327, 328, 332
Fortunas 30
Franconia 186-198
Frederick Lykes 415

Ganges 16
Geelong 40, 43, 46, 49, 50, 52
Georgic 248
Golden State 276
Goorangi 393
Gorgon 316, 320, 334
Gulfport 415

Hai Lee 327, 328, 334
Harlech Castle 29
Hawkes Bay 49
Hector 356
Henry D Thoreau 400
Henry T Allen 404
Herborg 320
Hermion 327, 328, 332
Herstein 306, 308
Highland Brigade 435, 436
Hobart 60
Hororata 40, 41, 46, 49
Hymettus 40, 49
Iberia 11-16
Ile de France 200, 213, 214, 216-220, 222-224, 253, 329-331, 366, 370, 374-376, 379-382
Indrapoera 148-151, 175, 176, 211, 229
Isaac Coles 402

James Fenimore Cooper 397

James Wilson 397
Jane Addams 413, 414
Janssens 408
Japara 398
Java 316
Johan de Witt 148-151
Johan van Oldenbarnevelt 224, 227, 229-237, 239, 244-248
John Steele 396

Kanimbla 81, 302, 316, 363, 393, 394, 438, 439
Kanowna 36, 38, 69
Karoola 69
Karroo 49
Karsik 322, 389, 391
Karumba 155
Katoomba 227, 228, 231, 232, 234, 297, 298, 301, 302, 323, 324, 355, 356, 394, 403, 411, 412
Katuna 49
Kent 19, 20
Khedive Ismail 209
Knight of the Garter 61, 63
Koolama 304, 310
Koolinda 309, 310
Kormoran 252
Kosciusko 329-331, 346, 348, 349
Kota Gede 336-339
Kuru 392

Laconia 355-357
Lancashire 158, 160, 176, 178
Langton Grange 20
Largs Bay 259, 430, 432
Lavington Court 329, 330
Leinster 279, 280
Leopoldville 271
Limerick 44, 49
Lulworth Hill 327, 328, 332
Lusitania 16

Macdhui 389, 390, 396, 410
Madras City 329, 330, 349

Merchant Ships Index

Maetsuycker 400, 405-407, 412,415
Maimoa 166
Malaita 390, 391
Maloja 425
Manchester Merchant 31
Mangola 320
Manhattan 27, 31
Manoora 81, 297, 298, 300-302, 348, 364, 403, 404, 438, 439
Mantua 73
Manunda 81, 398, 427, 428, 433
Manvantana 320, 322
Maori King 23
Maplemore 31
Marathon 72
Marella 265-267, 288, 320, 336
Marere 40, 49
Mariposa 255, 258, 268, 269, 275, 323
Marnix van Sint Aldegonde 224, 227, 229, 230, 232, 234, 235, 237, 239, 245-248
Marpessa 320
Martand 360, 363
Masula 349
Matafele 391
Mataroa 275
Mathura 329, 349
Maunganui 44, 46, 49, 59, 69, 296
Mauretania 103, 114-116, 118-120, 122-143, 145-147, 151, 153-155, 157, 159, 170-176, 179, 181, 186, 189,201-203, 205-207, 209, 211, 213, 214, 216, 217, 220, 222-224, 247, 248, 264, 331, 373, 423, 424
Medic 20, 40, 48-51, 68
Melbourne 60
Merula 320, 322
Mexico 412
Militades 40, 49
Modasa 327
Moeraki 39

Monarch of Bermuda 114, 161, 187, 192, 371, 447
Monowai (1) 20, 23, 24, 39, 40
Monowai (2) 81, 270, 308
Monterey 258
Montoro 288, 299-301, 309
Moravian 22
Morayshire 29
Moreton Bay 436
Mount Vernon 274, 284, 347, 348

Nankin 357
Nea Hellas 282, 283
Nemesis 13, 14
Nestor 259
Neuralia 103-107, 109-111, 113
Nevasa 103, 104, 109, 176-179, 209, 350
New Australia 447, 448
New York 283
Niagara 170
Nieuw Amsterdam 200-297, 209, 211, 213, 214, 216, 217, 220, 224, 227, 350, 366, 370-375, 379, 381, 382,384
Nieuw Holland 150
Nieuw Zeeland 150, 151, 176
Nineveh 19
Normandie 114, 117, 200, 213
Notou 147

Omrah 40, 46, 49, 52
Orama 73
Oranje 355, 359, 428
Orara 94
Orari 44, 49
Orcades 86, 87, 91-93, 96, 98, 100, 101, 146, 147, 162, 183, 328, 329, 331, 332, 335, 342
Orford 86, 87, 91-94, 96, 98, 101
Orient 29,34

Orion (British) 86-88, 90, 93, 95-97, 100, 101, 161, 163, 164, 169, 186, 199, 425
Orion (German) 147, 148
Ormiston 301
Ormonde 187, 195
Oronsay 281, 282
Orontes 258, 351-353
Orsova 66, 68
Orungal 289-291
Orvieto 40, 46, 49, 50, 56, 58, 59
Osterley 51
Otranto 86, 87, 91-93, 96-98, 101, 181, 183, 198, 351-353, 425
Oxfordshire 426, 427

Pachaug Victory 438
Pakeha 72
Palermo 69
Pan Europe 316
Pasteur 279, 280
Patras 305
Peisander 316
Pennland 188
Penrith Castle 329, 349
Pera 49
Persic 60, 63-66, 70, 71
Pfalz 60
Phrontis 316
Pilsudski 86, 161
Pinguin 166, 221
Plancius 335
Port Brisbane 166
Port Chalmers 296
Port Lincoln 49
Port Macquarie 61, 63
Port Montreal 309
Port Sydney 72
President Cleveland 276
President Coolidge 255, 323
President Grant 309
Prince Rupert 270
Prominent 327
Pulginbar 402

Queen Elizabeth 115-117, 200, 201, 208, 211-215, 217, 219-222, 224-227, 239-241, 243, 247, 249-251, 253-256, 264, 265, 279, 281, 285, 306, 317
Queen Mary 103, 114, 116-118, 120, 122-143, 145, 151-158, 160, 161, 170, 171, 173, 175, 176, 179, 182, 200, 201, 203-209, 211-215, 217, 219-222, 224-227, 239-244, 249-251, 253-255, 264, 278, 285, 291, 366-370, 374-379, 381-384, 405
Queen Mary II 144
Queen of Bermuda 367, 370-375, 377-381

Rajula 367, 370-375, 377
Ranee 31
Rangatira (1) 46, 49
Rangatira (2) 293, 294, 301, 308, 309
Rangitata 86, 88, 90, 93, 96, 98, 100, 101, 103
Reael 320
Reijnst 320
Reina del Pacifico 181, 183
Remo 439
Reynella 439, 440
Rhona 158-160, 176
River Clarence 439
Robert T Hill 439
Romolo 81
Ruapehu 44, 49

Salamis 24, 28
Saldanha 49
Salween 329, 349
Sarpedon 264, 306
Sea Barb 417
Sea Witch 324, 397
Seirstad 320

Shropshire 40, 49, 52, 57, 72
Sibajak 148, 224, 227, 229, 230, 232-235, 239, 244-246
Silvermaple 349
Silverwillow 329, 349
'sJacob 322, 397, 398
Slamat 148-151, 209, 229
Sloet van de Beele 320
Sloterdyk 340
Sobieski 86, 90, 93, 96, 101
Sophocles 349
Southern 49
Southern Cross 22
Star of England 40, 49
Star of India 49
Star of Victoria 49
Stirling Castle 267, 339
Strathaird 86, 88, 90, 93, 96, 101, 103, 104, 109, 110, 424, 425
Strathallan 84, 85, 341, 342
Stratheden 161-169, 186, 425
Strathmore 161, 163, 164, 168, 183
Strathnaver 86-88, 91, 93, 95, 96, 100, 101, 183
Suevic 60, 63, 64
Suffolk 40, 41, 49, 72
Sumatra 60
Surrey 22
Swartenhondt 322, 389

Tahiti 44, 49, 69
Taishan 320
Talma 209
Taroona 308, 309, 385-388, 397, 403, 410, 418
Tasker H Bliss 276
Tasman 391
Themistocles 60, 63, 64
Thomas Corwin 413
Thor 358
Tjikandi 316
Tjikarang 316
Tofua 72

Turakina 72, 147
Tuscania 282

Uganda 68
Ulysses 60, 62, 63, 70, 72, 259

Valentijn 305
Van der Lijn 320, 404
Van Heemskerk 398
Van Heutz 404
Van Spillsbergen 332
Van Swoll 320
Verdala 61, 63
Vestalia 61, 63
Viceroy of India 183, 351
Victorian 25, 27
Volendam 270

Wahehe 266
Wahine 301, 309
Waimana 49
Wandilla 69
Wanganella 81, 237, 238, 433, 434
War Sidar 316
Washington 274
West Point 354
Westernland 209-211, 354, 360, 363, 364
Westralia 81, 162, 294-296, 302-304, 310, 364, 393, 394, 439
Williard A Holbrook 323, 355-356
Willochra 61, 63
Wiltshire 40, 49, 53, 54
Windsor Castle 187, 195
Worcestershire 270, 271, 362, 363
Wyreema 73, 74

Yoma 327, 328, 332

Zaandam 339-341
Zealandia 227, 228, 251, 252, 289-304, 309-311, 429
Zephyr 250

Naval Ships Index

Achilles 80, 147, 214, 294, 296, 306, 309
Adelaide 78, 84, 95, 106, 108, 230, 245, 251, 291, 293, 297, 298, 302, 305, 321, 381, 382
AE1 38
AE2 38, 60, 63, 64
Albatross 139
Alden 255
Amphion 79
Anson 78, 427
Anzac 467
Apollo 79
Archimede 281
Argus 141
Armidale 392, 400
Arunta 388, 391, 398
Australia (1) 36, 40, 78
Australia (2) 78, 90, 94-96, 123, 126, 130, 135, 188, 190, 192-195, 214, 217, 219, 225, 302, 306, 309, 381, 388

Bagley 381
Ballarat 305, 334, 391, 400
Bataan 443
Bathurst 328
Bendigo 321

Bismarck 77, 78, 314
Brilliant 282
Brisbane 36, 78

Canberra 78, 81, 90, 94-96, 123, 126, 130, 131, 133, 147, 148, 151, 156, 165-167, 171, 173, 206, 209, 219-221, 232, 234, 241, 242, 249, 250, 302, 306, 317, 320
Capetown 177
Carlisle 159, 178
Castlemain 392, 397
Cessnock 386
Chatham 80
Chester 255
Colac 386
Cornwall 161, 250, 328, 348, 354, 356
Coventry 178
Cumberland 137
Curacoa 368

Danae 228, 246
Decoy 113
Defender 113
Derwent 460, 471, 482
Devonshire 141, 331, 375, 378, 379

498

Diomede 80
Doris 72
Dorsetshire 141, 354, 356
Dragon 320, 331
Duchess 455, 458, 464, 476, 477, 481
Duke of York 78, 313, 325
Dunedin 80
Durban 207, 208, 211, 220, 251, 252, 320, 334

Eagle 99, 100, 312
Electra 324, 328
Emden 44, 47, 48, 54-57
Emerald 190, 192, 194, 195
Encounter (1) 38, 72
Encounter (2) 315, 331, 332
Enterprise 324
Exeter 328, 336
Express 314, 348

Formidable 436, 437

Gambia 362, 275, 378, 379
Glasgow 245-247, 342
Glory 427, 437
Gneisenau 39, 44
Graf Zeppelin 78
Grayson 384

Hampshire 56, 57
Hawkesbury 427
Hawkins 195
Helm 381, 384
Henley 381
Hermes 139, 140, 356
Hermione 280
Hobart 79, 81, 99-101, 165, 166, 202, 203, 205, 206, 214, 270, 302, 316, 317, 328, 388
Hollyhock 348
Hood 77, 141, 314
Howe 78

Ibuki 45, 48, 55-57
Illustrious 286
Implacable 436
Indomitable 313, 427

Jacob van Heemskerk 379, 381, 382
Java 328
Jumna 328
Jupiter 315

Kashmir 177
Kelly 177
Kent 96, 99, 113
Kimberly 177
King George V 78, 313
Konigsberg 44, 54, 56, 57

Langley 324
Le Triomphant 382
Leander 80, 90, 123, 126, 130, 131, 209, 309
Liddle 438
Lismore 328
Lithgow 397
Liverpool 113
Lloyd 437

Malaya 339
Mauritius 378
Melbourne (1) 36, 45, 47, 48, 55-57, 78
Melbourne (2) 451, 455, 456, 458, 460
Minotaur 45, 48, 50, 55
Montcalm 40
Musashi 78

Naiad 188
Nelson (1) 77
Nelson (2) 280
Newcastle 56
Nizam 348

Norfolk 76

Parramatta (1) 159, 196, 210
Parramatta (2) 455, 458, 466, 481
Partridge 27
Perkins 410, 411
Perth 79, 139, 147, 151, 154-156,
    163, 166, 168, 169, 233, 302,
    306, 309, 321, 322, 437
Phaeton 79
Philomel 39, 45
Phoebe 188
Phoenix (HMS) 72
Phoenix (USS) 323, 324, 362, 363,
    394
Potrero 391
Prince of Wales 78, 313-315
Protector 27
Psyche 39, 45, 72
Pyramus 39

Ramilles 89, 90, 93-100, 103, 106,
    108, 109, 112, 113, 188, 312
Renown 195, 312-315
Resolution 312, 378
Revenge 312, 378
RO33 391
Rodney 77
Royal Sovereign 312, 348

Scharnhorst 39, 44
Shoalhaven 443
Shoreham 113
Shropshire 131, 133, 137, 159, 161
Speaker 437
Stronghold 316
Stuart (1) 395
Stuart (2) 462-466
Suffren 96, 99, 111, 113
Supply 455, 456, 460

Sussex 99, 100
Swan (1) 94, 397, 398
Swan (2) 481-483
Sydney (1) 36, 38, 40, 45, 48, 55-
    57, 78
Sydney (2) 78, 81, 94, 108-112,
    169, 215, 219, 228, 231, 232,
    241, 246, 249, 251, 252, 269,
    271, 272
Sydney (3) 445, 451, 453-484

Tenedos 316, 332, 356
Tirpitz 77, 78, 313
Tjerk Hiddes 379, 381
Torrens 483

Vampire (1) 81, 266, 315, 348, 356
Vampire (2) 455, 456, 458, 460,
    462, 475, 484
Van Galen 379
Van Tromp 280, 379, 388, 394
Vendetta (1) 322
Vendetta (2) 458, 477
Vindex 434
Voyager 391, 392

Wakakura 80
Warrego (1) 38
Warrego (2) 304
Warspite 378
Westcott 100, 101
Wollongong 321

Yamato 78
Yarra (1) 38
Yarra (2) 94, 321, 322, 332, 336
Yarra (3) 460, 465, 476, 477

Military Units Index

Boer War

Army Nursing Service 22
Australian Army Medical Corps 34
Australian Commonwealth Horse
    31, 32
First Australian Horse 19
Imperial NSW Mounted Rifles 31
NSW Army Medical Corps 20, 22,
    31
NSW Imperial Bushmen 24, 29
NSW Lancer Squadron 19, 22
NSW Mounted Rifles 19
NSW Naval Brigade Volunteers 28
Queensland Imperial Bushmen
    29, 31
Royal Australian Artillery 25
South Australian Imperial
    Bushmen 31
South Australian Mounted Rifles
    23
Victorian Imperial Bushmen 31
Victorian Naval Brigade Volunteers
    28
Western Australia Imperial
    Bushmen 31

World War One

1st Brigade 53
3rd Division 65
5th Battalion 46
9th Battalion 46
12th Battalion 43
13th Australian Light Horse
    Regiment 65
13th Battalion 62
22nd Battalion 70
24th Company, Army Services
    Corps 70
Australian Imperial Force 74
Australia & New Zealand Army
    Corps 65
First Australian Naval & Military
    Expeditionary Force 36, 37
First Australian Expeditionary
    Force 46, 52
Kennedy Regiment 36
New Zealand Expeditionary Force
    46

World War Two

1 Anti-Aircraft Regiment 289, 293
1 Anti-Aircraft Search Light Cadre 291
1st Australian Corps 327
4th New Zealand Brigade 90
11 Anti-Tank Company 310
14 Heavy Anti-Aircraft Battery 291
41 Anti-Tank Battery 310
54 Anti-Aircraft Search Light Company 289
105 General Transport Company 327
116 Mobile Bath Unit 310
2/2 Anti-Aircraft Regiment 327
2/1 Anti-tank Regiment 124, 361
2/4 Anti-Tank Regiment 429
2/1 Australian General Hospital 93, 94
2/2 Australian General Hospital 106, 341
2/4 Australian General Hospital 354, 360, 361
2/5 Australian General Hospital 152, 155, 331
2/9 Australian General Hospital 206, 210, 211, 341, 342
2/11 Australian General Hospital 331
2/13 Australian General Hospital 237
2/14 Australian General Hospital 427
119 Australian General Hospital 297
2/3 Australian Light Anti-Aircraft Regiment 172, 176
2/3 Australian Machine Gun Battalion 216-220, 222, 223
2/1 Casualty Clearing Station 106, 341
2/2 Casualty Clearing Station 152, 327, 328, 335
2/6 Division Cavalry Regiment 217
2/2 Field Ambulance 106
2/3 Field Ambulance 124
2/5 Field Ambulance 154, 155
2/10 Field Ambulance 234
2/1 Field Artillery 93
2/2 Field Company RAE 106
2/3 Field Company RAE 124, 181
2/6 Firled Company 327
2/7 Field Company RAE 163
2/12 Field Company 234
2/13 Field Company 181
2/1 Field Regiment 351
2/2 Field Regiment 351, 361
2/11 Field Regiment 217
2/12 Field Regiment RAE 163, 164, 166, 167, 169, 439
2/15 Field Regiment 231, 232, 234, 436
2/1 Field Park Company 124, 181
2/4 Field Park Company 171, 175
2/6 Field Park Company 234
2/3 Field Regiment 124, 143, 181
2/1 Fortress Engineers 303
2/1 Heavy Battery Regiment 303, 304
2/1 Independent Company 299, 300
2/2 Independent Company 303
2/3 Light Anti-Aircraft Regiment 342
2/1 Machine Gun Regiment 124
2/3 Machine Gun Battalion 327-329, 332
2/4 Machine Gun Battalion 317
2/2 Pioneer Battalion 327, 332
Australforce Engineers 181
Australian Tropical Force 291
Civil Construction Corps 299-301
Darwin Infantry Battalion 294-296
Darwin Mobile Force 289
Elbow Force 203
Gull Force 305

Infantry Battalions

2/1 83, 84, 92, 351, 353, 361, 362, 364
2/2 83, 92
2/3 83
2/4 83
2/5 104, 105, 351, 352, 353, 361, 363
2/6 104, 352, 354, 361, 363
2/7 104, 166,
2/8 104,
2/9 123, 134, 164
2/10 123,
2/11 129, 342
2/12 123,
2/13 152, 156, 369, 370, 382, 437
2/14 151, 152, 153, 330, 331, 438
2/15 171, 290, 291
2/17 152, 380
2/18 203
2/19 203
2/20 203
2/21 302, 305, 330, 331
2/22 302, 305
2/23 163, 164
2/24 372
2/25 296
2/26 234
2/27 152, 154,
2/28 171
2/29 234
2/30 234
2/39 306
2/40 293, 302, 303, 305
2/43 171-179
2/48 372
2/53 306, 308

Brigades

2/16 83, 92, 94, 351, 353, 360, 364
2/17 83, 104, 105, 353, 360, 364
2/18 83, 124, 180, 181
2/20 152,
2/21 154, 158, 346
2/22 203, 204, 227, 302
2/23 302, 305
2/24 171,
2/25 180,
2/27 229, 234, 302

Divisions

2/6 83, 84, 94, 104, 105, 123, 326, 360, 365
2/7 83, 152, 326, 328, 329, 346, 354, 365
2/8 203, 227, 228, 302, 316
2/9 163, 180, 326, 365-367, 374, 438

Lark Force 297, 305
'M' Battery Special Force 299
Sparrow Force 302
7 MD Survey Company 299

Korean War

1 RAR 445, 446, 448, 449
2 RAR 446-449
3 RAR 443, 444, 449
27th British Commonwealth Infantry Brigade 444
28th British Commonwealth Infantry Brigade 446, 448
No 77 Fighter Squadron, RAAF 443

Vietnam War

1 RAR 451, 454, 466, 467
2 RAR 462, 467, 481
3 RAR 465, 471, 477, 482
4 RAR 467, 476, 477, 482, 483
5 RAR 462, 471, 477
6 RAR 463, 472
7 RAR 461, 467, 476, 477
8 RAR 476, 477
9 RAR 467, 471, 476
1st Australian Logistic Supply Company 454
1st APC Troop 454
9th Squadron RAAF 460, 482
104 Battery, RAA 482
755 Squadron Fleet Air Arm 461
817 Squadron Fleet Air Arm 461